BLUEJACKET

BLUEJACKET

In Harm's Way From Guadalcanal to Tokyo
or
"The Golden Gate . . . Or Pearly Gate . . . By '48"

By
John A. Hutchinson
Former Radioman First Class
United States Navy

VANTAGE PRESS
New York

Published by Vantage Press, Inc.
516 West 34th Street, New York, New York 10001

Manufactured in the United States of America
ISBN: 0-533-11182-X

Library of Congress Catalog Card No.: 94-90316

0 9 8 7 6 5 4 3 2 1

THE BLUEJACKET

This Book Is Dedicated To

THE UNITED STATES NAVY ENLISTED MAN

In Peace and In War

© Stanley Bleifeld

"THE LONE SAILOR"—courtesy United States Navy Memorial

SUBTITLE

"THE GOLDEN GATE ... OR PEARLY GATE ... BY '48"

In the first five weeks of the Guadalcanal Campaign, the United States Navy lost three heavy cruisers in one furious night battle; an aircraft carrier, two destroyers, and an attack transport were sunk in other actions; and two more carriers, plus the lone battleship in our dwindling Fleet, were put out of action. We had but one carrier left operational in the entire Pacific Fleet, and our air power was severely reduced.

Ashore, an undermanned, undersupplied First Marine Division, against almost impossible odds, was clinging by its fingernails to a tiny perimeter around strategic Henderson Field, where the "Cactus Air Force" begged for "more baling wire" just to hold its battered fighters together.

Our beleaguered forces, dubbed "The Thin Red Line", were getting thinner and bloodier each passing day, with little help seen from any quarter, while superior Japanese air, naval, and land units were steadily being reinforced. Our future was not only uncertain but desperate and foreboding. Both Vice Admiral Robert Ghormley and General Douglas MacArthur, deeming the operation hopeless, recommended withdrawal. But here in these tropical islands the course of the War had to reach a turning point. There could be no retreat.

It was during those darkest, most crucial days of August and September, 1942, that a grim little rhyme circulated among us—the battle-weary sailors and Marines of the South Pacific Command. If first we did not end up in a watery or jungle-lined grave, the road home would be a long, bitter, sanguinary struggle against an implacable foe. Thus we could only look forward to

The Golden Gate ...
Or Pearly Gate ...
By '48!

TABLE OF CONTENTS

AUTHOR

ONLY THE NAME HAS BEEN CHANGED . . .

I was christened *John Anthony Hutchinson*—the *John* after my father, the *Anthony* for both my mother's father and her brother. Although I was not a "Junior" (my dad's middle name was *Reardon*, pronounced and sometimes misspelled *Raredon*), the family called me that until my mother, Marguerite, rebelled against it. I didn't like "Junior" either, and was pleased when she insisted that, henceforth, I was to be called *"Jack"*.

When I got to high school, I got another moniker. With other Jacks around, some of my schoolmates called me *"Hutch"*, a name which other members of my family were sometimes called. In the Navy, where nearly everyone is addressed by his last name, it was inevitable that my rather long surname be abbreviated *Hutch* there, too. Only a small handful of my close shipmates ever called me *"Jack"*.

When I got into radio broadcasting as a civilian, I first used *Jack Hutchinson* on the air, but it was unwieldy and listeners were always mispronouncing it. Then, in 1950, I was hired at WCOG, Greensboro, North Carolina. The station manager, Hank Sullivan, suggested I change my air-name. An announcer at a competing station was also named *Hutchinson,* and Hank felt listeners would confuse us.

Between Program Director Bill Jackson and me, we came up with *Holiday*. By that time, I'd come to feel *"Jack"* was more fitting for a young boy than a serious broadcaster or newscaster. I reverted to *John;* and to distinguish it further, dropped the *h* to become *Jon.* A few months later, to avoid the problem of having two names, I had my name legally changed to *Jon A. Holiday.*

To my family and schoolmates, I'm still *Jack;* to my old shipmates, it's *Hutch;* and to all others, I'm *Jon.* I'll answer to *Hutch, John, Jack,* or *Jon,* but not to "Junior"!

John A. Hutchinson
(Jon A. Holiday)

JOHN A. HUTCHINSON, S1c USN, NOVEMBER 1941

FOREWORD BY COL. MITCHELL PAIGE C.M.H. USMC (RET)

In reading *BLUEJACKET,* my very first impression was that author John Hutchinson, besides being a superb storyteller of World War II, has certainly done his homework in extensive research for this book. When I read about places I had been to, certain incidents that I am familiar with, ships that I had sailed on, and battles that I had participated in—my interest expanded with each page.

This memoir's combination of a bluejacket's personal experience, plus painstaking research, gives the reader not only a seductive story, but also something to hang his or her hat on, an appealing and engaging history of the Pacific War to sink one's teeth into. The story is punctuated with enough pithy detail to cut through the fog of elapsed time, placing in focus those stirringly vivid images that only someone who was there can share with his readers.

The author's eyewitness accounts are supported and supplemented by striking passages from eyewitnesses' letters, ships' war diaries, and commanders' action reports. They describe some of the most exciting episodes of World War II. Those hard-won victories in the Pacific War against the Empire of Japan on the part of the Navy and Marine Corps, constituted an acid and final test of our nation's will to win the War and defeat the Japanese.

John Hutchinson believes his memoir to be unique in that it constitutes the only book, of which he is aware, which covers the prewar, wartime, and postwar Navy career of a bluejacket from the perspective of the enlisted man. As a "Mustang Marine", coming up through the ranks from private in the U.S. Marine Corps, I can appreciate in every respect the writer's resoluteness to "tell it like it was."

The Navy and Marine Corps have worked as a team since the birth of our nation. Nowhere has this been more manifest than in the War in the Pacific against the Japs. This cooperation is unmistakably reflected in these chapters where we find accounts of Marine Corps amphibious operations—such as at Guadalcanal, Tulagi, New Georgia, Tarawa, Saipan, Tinian, Guam, Peliliu, Iwo Jima, and Okinawa.

xiii

This chronicle refers to hundreds of ship's participating in the Pacific War—for instance, the U.S.S. McCAWLEY, on which I served prior to World War II in amphibious maneuvers. We went over the side every day for weeks, down rope ladders and into Higgins Boats, to assault the beaches—Onslow Beach in North Carolina and several islands in the Caribbean—then climbing back up the rope ladders, hand over hand with our heavy equipment and weapons.

Also, I was familiar with the U.S.S. FOMALHAUT, a liberty ship on which my machinegun platoon sailed out of Norfolk, Virginia, on 10 April 1942, through the Caribbean and Panama Canal, across the South Pacific to Polynesia, arriving in Apia, British Samoa, on 10 May 1942. I was also familiar with the PRESIDENT HAYES, which I boarded in early 1943 at Guadalcanal bound for Australia.

The writer recounts certain "firsts": such as the first use at Tinian of napalm, which was so effective against enemy troops in caves; also the first mass kamikaze attacks when Japanese pilots guided their planes as human bombs into American warships, which led to the loss of so many ships and sailors, so much agony and suffering, in our American Fleet around Okinawa.

Hutchinson's stirring accounts tell of rescuing fellow Americans whose ships had been sunk—in the Solomons, in the Philippine Sea, and at Okinawa. His first-hand account of the destroyer sailors—who usually took the brunt of naval engagements while screening larger ships, endeavoring to protect convoys, seeking out enemy submarines, being the first to meet the enemy on the seas—is especially noteworthy.

Every reader will find this book both fascinating and instructive reading. Here we see human nature revealed in both humorous and heart-rending incidents. We see how sailors had to conquer the fear that hides in every man. The historian writes of many dramatic sea battles, giving a succinct overview of the Pacific War. The storyteller who was there brings out the fact that U.S. Navy ships were manned by men born of smoke and the danger of death.

BLUEJACKET is a book in which we see the War in the Pacific as the author himself saw it. Any member of our Armed Forces who served in the Pacific will find accurately recounted many situations analogous to his own experiences: the fear, the anger, the frustrations, the uncertainties, the loss of close friends, the devastation from the skies, the awesome power of naval gunfire, the ubiquitous enemy submarines, and all the horrors of war that only an eyewitness can really perceive.

The author makes no bones about his opinions and convictions on the Pacific War. For example, that Admiral Frank Jack Fletcher lacked aggressiveness; that General Douglas MacArthur was a publicity hound. He has no love for American PT-boats, especially John F. Kennedy and his PT-109. That the U.S.S. McCAWLEY was sunk by a U.S. Navy Lieutenant Commander, commanding a PT-boat squadron, who was later given command of a destroyer, promoted and decorated, demonstrates why so many military decorations and combat awards were not fair.

John Hutchinson writes about the social and sexual ethics of the day. He tells of his poignant love for the girl of his dreams. He shares his struggles with marriage as a bluejacket apart from his bride for months on end. He expresses his love for the Naval service and his dedication and loyalty to the U.S. Navy and certain of his Commanding Officers.

At the same time, the chronicler candidly and courageously pulls no punches when taking to task officers for their conduct and incompetence in the performance of duty. Without a doubt, his scorn and disgust are in some cases justified; as for instance in the much misunderstood incident, whitewashed for the American public by the powerful and the press, of John F. Kennedy and the PT-109, which whitewashing baffles many of us who fought in the South Pacific to this day.

BLUEJACKET is not only an arresting history but an action-packed story written for easy reading. It could be inspirational reading for Navy recruits. The book would also constitute an ideal part of the personal library of all U.S. service personnel past and present. It would be especially valuable to those servicemen who participated in the Pacific War—on land, at sea, or in the air—and their families, especially their wives, children, and grandchildren.

If anyone wants to begin to understand the generation of men that fought in World War II, and what they went through, I suggest he or she read *BLUEJACKET.* It is a book which I enthusiastically recommend.

> Colonel Mitchell Paige, C.M.H.
> United State Marine Corps Retired
> Palm Desert, California
> October 26, 1992, 50th Anniversary
> Third Sendai Division Attack at Guadalcanal
> Battle of the Santa Cruz Islands
> A Turning Point of the Pacific War

PROLOGUE

LOGGING A BLUEJACKET'S CRUISE

For nearly forty years, I "buried" the War. I joined no veterans' organizations, kept no contact with my former shipmates, and after a few frustrating attempts shortly after returning home discussed my experiences with no one. Most of my closest acquaintances were unaware of my military service.

As a combat sailor returning to the States, the War was still very fresh in my mind, and the automatic responses to certain stimuli to which I responded in the "forward areas" were still intact. Such ordinary sounds as a child's balloon popping, a car backfiring, a low-flying airplane, or a police siren so like those that signaled "air raid", would cause me to break out in cold sweats and near panic. Nightmares, flashbacks, and "the shakes" plagued me.

I tried to talk with members of my family, but they could not relate to my problems. There was no empathy from family or friends; they simply could not understand the effects of long years in combat. There was some "pop" psychology at the time, advising that conversations about combat with veterans should be avoided because "it might distress them." The bad dreams and all the rest I kept to myself, pushing them deeper and deeper inside.

I had no civilian clothes when my ship was in Bremerton, Washington, upon coming back from occupation duty in Japan, so I wore my uniform. The War had been over only a couple of months, but civilians were already reverting to their old attitudes about sailors. Nicer restaurants and bars, which would have given me a warm welcome while the fighting was still going on, now shunted me back out of sight or made a point of serving civilians first. It was as if I were *persona non grata*.

On the street, people either wouldn't look me in the eye, or gave me looks that said: "What are you doing in uniform? The War's over." I could almost see in their eyes the old signs that dotted lawns in pre-War Norfolk: "Sailors and Dogs—Keep Off!" I was completely unprepared for this attitude and quickly concluded from both the behavior of strangers and the reactions of my family that nobody gave a damn.

From then on, I just kept silent about the War altogether, and wore "civvies" as soon as I could get them.

But I still had to live with the recollections of the War that continued to trigger emotional upset. These I "buried" deeper and deeper within until the nightmares and flashbacks became only a sometime thing. The only way to do that was to avoid any situation or conversation which would bring them to the surface. Time, however, has a way of ameliorating, if not healing, old troubles and ills, allowing them to be resurrected and dealt with. Sometimes, though, a catalyst is needed. For me, it came in 1981.

My daughter, Toni, brought home her high school American history text. It treated World War II in but five pages. The Pacific Campaigns got only three mentions: Pearl Harbor, the Iwo Jima flag raising photo, and the A-bombing of Hiroshima. I decided, then and there, to leave a record for my children and grandchildren so they would know there was more than *that* to the Pacific War.

For eight years, I assembled material for what originally was intended to be an "in family" chronicle. The more I collected, it seemed, the more I needed. I ended up with boxes of personnel records, deck logs, war diaries, action reports, letters from old shipmates, magazine articles, and numerous books. But the project was therapeutic. In bringing me back in contact with "my Navy" and its people, the process slowly but surely began to crack the shell I'd kept around me. I began to attend reunions of the NORTH CAROLINA crew, Guadalcanal Campaign Veterans, and Tin Can Sailors. Still I could not bring myself to begin the actual writing.

The process of unravelling the threads of the cocoon I'd woven around remembrances of the War was both protracted and erratic. The first fruitful experience was a 1982 meeting with my old Executive Officer on the IRWIN, Commander J.D.P. Hodapp, Jr. Later came attendance at a NORTH CAROLINA crew's reunion, meeting old IRWIN shipmates Bob Martin and Fred Stafford at a Tin Can Sailors reunion, a visit to the Guadalcanal Campaign Veterans Memorial in Michigan, being a guest at a PRINCETON reunion, and contacting a shipmate from the McCAWLEY.

At a Guadalcanal Campaign Veteran's West Coast mini-reunion, I met and talked with Mitch Paige. As a sergeant in the 1st Marine Division, it was he who led his machinegun platoon, all killed or wounded, to hold off the Japs' Sendai Division attacking Hanneken's Ridge, 26 October, 1942. The loss of this battle, which turned the tide at Guadalcanal, might have changed the course of the Pacific War. For this he received the Congressional Medal of Honor and is now a retired "bird" Colonel. Mitch has graciously consented to write the Foreword to this chronicle.

When I finally began to try to write, curious phenomena occurred. As I read the unadorned, unemotional, crisp lines written decades ago in war diaries and action reports, my mind would, as in a time machine, transport me back to the time and place of the event. I would actually "see", in detail, the action taking place, as if it were projected on a movie screen. But with this "viewing" came the flood of emotions I'd felt at the time. I was reliving it all, and it was difficult to handle. Thus, it took several years to cope with the complex feelings brought on by reliving the War, and to begin to put events and experiences down on paper. Even then, I would cease writing for days after recounting incidents that were particularly traumatic. So, if there are a few pages marked with tear stains, you'll understand.

I never intended to write a book for publication until Ted Mason, who was working on his second book *We Will Stand By You,* telling of his service on the fleet tug PAWNEE, contacted me through Ted Blahnik of the Guadalcanal Campaign Veterans. Ted was looking for firsthand accounts of the sinking of the McCAWLEY. During our conversation, I mentioned I was writing down my war experiences. Ted asked that I send him a couple of chapters and responded to them by urging me to consider publication. "This", he said, "is a story that *must* be told." Others whom I respected concurred, encouraging me to write for public consumption, rather than simply recounting the experiences for my family.

Now, the project took on a different focus. Certainly it would accomplish the original purpose of leaving a personal memoir for the family. It would also, I began to hope, make a significant contribution to the history of World War II in the Pacific from a perspective not found in any book of which I am aware. Most books on the subject are written by officers, many of whom have a personal axe to grind, or by historians who simply follow the paper trail. This would be an eyewitness, first person story of an *ENLISTED MAN!* Largely ignored in most of the other accounts, the ordinary sailors of the Fleet—the combat veterans—might now have their contributions to victory recognized. Their experiences would finally find a place, in some small but perhaps representative way, in the history of the Pacific War.

This book is dedicated to the enlisted man of the United States Navy. More specifically it is inscribed to those of the Regular Navy, the professional volunteers who man the Fleet in peace and in war, forming the nation's First Line of Defense. These are the career sailors, dedicating their lives to keeping America from harm. Civilians generally make no distinction among Regulars, ready Reserves, and the "duration of the War" servicemen. Consequently, there is little understanding of the role and contributions of professional bluejackets.

Isolationism and President Roosevelt's promise in 1940 never to send "our boys" into a foreign conflict kept our armed forces at a pitifully small level. There were only some 215,200 men on active duty in the Navy when I entered the service. Of these, some 192,200 were enlisted men, of whom roughly 173,900 were Regulars (USN) and only 18,300 were Reserves (USNR), mostly men of prior service or experience. Many of our ships were old, some dating from World War I; most were undermanned, and had not been modernized to fight the kind of conflict we would be called upon to wage. As events would prove, it would be the Regulars of the Navy who would pay for America's unpreparedness and lack of modernization with their blood.

They were Regulars, the men of the PANAY, who took the first casualties of World War II, when Japanese planes sank the gunboat on the Yangtze River in 1937. Regulars died when U.S. destroyers were attacked by German U-boats, when the KEARNY was damaged and the REUBEN JAMES was sunk in October, 1941. They were mostly Regular Navy, the 2,008 who died in the treachery of Pearl Harbor; as were the 1,252 lost in the Battles of the Coral Sea and Midway, and the 4,910 who stopped the Japanese in the Solomons. Add to these the men who went down in the Java Sea actions, in the First Battle of the Philippines, in early North Atlantic convoy duty, and in actions elsewhere around the world.

It was what was left of this small Regular cadre who intensively trained the raw-assed recruits from cities, towns, and farms into fighting units—while, at the same time, still holding our enemies at bay, until full mobilization was realized and ships were built for the recruits to man. It was the Regulars who led these men into combat, and the "old salt" petty officers who ran the shipboard divisions because the "90-Day Wonders", those college kids who'd had three months training and were commissioned as officers, were so inexperienced they couldn't find their way to the head.

At its 1945 wartime peak, the U.S. Navy had some 3,405,500 people in uniform. Of these roughly 2,932,600 were enlisted men, of whom only some 327,100 were Regulars. Of the roughly 173,900 Regular Navy bluejackets on active duty when I enlisted, I've often wondered how many survived the three years and eight months of the War.

Thus the title *BLUEJACKET* and the dedication to THE UNITED STATES NAVY ENLISTED MAN in Peace and in War—to *"THE LONE SAILOR"!*

Forthwith this frame of mine was wrenched
With a woeful agony,
Which forced me to begin my tale;
And then it left me free.

Since then, at an uncertain hour,
That agony returns:
And till my ghastly tale is told,
This heart within me burns....

I have strange power of speech;
That moment that his face I see,
I know the man that must hear me:
To him my tale I teach....

O Wedding-Guest! this soul hath been
Alone on a wide, wide sea;
So *lonely* 'twas, that God himself
Scarce seemed there to be....
                    Samuel Taylor Coleridge
                    The Rime of the Ancient Mariner

                        John A. Hutchinson
                        Former Radioman 1st Class
                        United States Navy
                        Coos Bay, Oregon
                        August 24, 1992
                        Fiftieth Anniversary
                        Battle of Eastern Solomons

P.S. The author welcomes communcations from readers, which may be sent to him via VANTAGE PRESS (address on page iv); especially from people mentioned in *BLUEJACKET,* or Pacific War veterans and historians, who may be able to provide information of interest, which perhaps could improve the quality and accuracy of a second edition of this book.

EPIGRAPH

THE NAVY, THE SAILOR, AND THE SEA

I intend to go *in harm's way* (1778).
I have not yet begun to fight (1779)!

John Paul Jones

The sailor's life is bold and free,
His home is on the rolling sea.
And never heart more true or brave
Than his who launches on the wave.
Afar he speeds in distant climes to roam,
With jocund song he rides the sparkling foam.
Then here's to the sailor, and here's to the hearts so true,
Who will think of him upon the waters blue!
Sailing, sailing, over the bounding main;
For many a stormy wind shall blow, ere Jack comes home again!
Sailing, sailing, over the bounding main;
For many a stormy wind shall blow, ere Jack comes home again!

Old Sailing Song

The LORD reigneth. . . . Thy throne is established of old: thou art from
everlasting . . . .*The LORD on high is mightier than the noise of many
waters, yea, than the mighty waves of the sea* . . . .For the LORD is a great
God . . . .*The sea is his, and he made it.* . . . Thou rulest the raging of the
sea: when the waves thereof arise, Thou stillest them . . . .And they feared
exceedingly, and said one to another, *What manner of man is this, that
even the wind and the sea obey him?* . . . In journeyings often, . . . perils of
waters, . . . perils in the city, . . . *perils in the sea* . . . .

And I saw another angel . . . having the *everlasting gospel* to preach to
them that dwell on the earth, and *to every nation and kindred, and tongue,
and people,* Saying with a loud voice: *Fear God, and give glory to him;* for
the hour of his judgment is come: and *worship him that made heaven, and
earth, and the sea, and the fountains of waters* . . . .And I saw the dead,

small and great, stand before God; and the books were opened: and another book was opened, which is the book of life: and the dead were judged out of those things which were written in the books . . . .

And the sea gave up the dead which were in it; and death and hell delivered up the dead which were in them: and they were judged every man according to their works . . . *And whosoever was not found written in the book of life was cast in the lake of fire*. And I saw a new heaven and a new earth: for the first heaven and the first earth were passed away; *and there was no more sea* . . . . And God shall wipe away all tears from their eyes; and there shall be no more death, neither sorrow, nor crying, neither shall there be any more pain: for *the former things are passed away.*

Holy Bible (Authorized Version)
Ps. 93:1, 4; 95:3, 5; 89:9.
Mark 4:41. 1 Cor. 11:26.
Rev. 14:6, 7; 20:12, 13, 15; 21:1, 4.

BLUEJACKET

1

BOOTS

Jimmy O'Neill shouted: "Hey Jughead, come here."

Chief Gunner's Mate James A. O'Neill called all the recruits in his company "Jughead". But we always seemed to know *which* "Jughead" he was addressing. This time it was I.

The Chief put his left hand on my shoulder, his arm below the elbow blazing red with the six "hash marks" signifying his more than 24 years of service in the United States Navy.

"You look like you have a little more smarts than some of these other Jugheads", he said. "Are you plannin' to make the Navy a career?"

"Yes, Chief", I replied.

"Then go get your *Bluejacket's Manual.*"

When I returned, Jimmy instructed me to turn to Chapters 4 and 5, dealing with "Rules and Regulations". I scanned the subtitles: discipline, respect for authority, good behavior, nature of duty in the Navy, articles for the government of the Navy, rules regarding salutes and other subjects dealing with the principal dictates of military life.

"I'm gonna tell you how to make life easier for you and keep you out of trouble. You *memorize* these regulations. They tell you what you can do and what you can't do. Follow 'em and your cruise will be smooth sailing. Break 'em and the Navy'll break you."

He paused, then smiled: "Remember, though, if you run into any situation *not* covered in that book, you're on your own. Use your own best judgement."

Jimmy taught those two chapters to the other recruits, of course, but not with the same intensity as he did with me. It was the best advice I ever received in the service. And Jimmy made sure I did my homework, testing me on the "Regs" each time there was a break in our recruit training.

It was fate perhaps, destiny doubtless, that got me into Jimmy O'Neill's company at the Naval Training Station in Newport, Rhode Island.

I had committed to enlisting for six years in December, 1940, but

1

my family had wanted me home for Christmas. The Navy recruiter had agreed, and I'd been summoned to report to the Naval Recruiting Station in Philadelphia on 29 January, 1941. Following the physical exam, I was sworn in with about 25 other recruits and assigned my Service Number: 243-86-51. My starting pay would be $21 a month. We went by bus to Newport where I was assigned to a company for the three month "boot camp" instruction period.

Just a few days after arriving, I ended up in Sick Bay with aches, pains, and a 103° fever. The attack was severe enough to warrant transfer to the nearby U.S. Naval Hospital with a diagnosis of "acute cat fever"—medical shorthand for catarrhal fever. It was like a bad case of flu, and it kept me hospitalized for the better part of two weeks.

The worst part was not so much the fever as the spinal tap. There had been a couple of cases of spinal meningitis at the Norfolk Naval Training Station, and when I complained of severe back pains, the duty nurse decided to take no chances. She called in the Medical Officer (M.D.) who made the decision to take a sample of my spinal fluid to determine if I had contracted the dread disease.

During the preparation for the tap, I got a quick lesson in protocol in the Navy Medical Corps. I asked the doctor a question, using the term "Doc". I was brusquely informed that Medical Officers *must* be called "Doctor". Enlisted pharmacist's mates and hospital corpsmen may be called "Doc", but not Navy doctors.

Unfortunately, the Medical Officer had been spending that Saturday evening at a party. He was near three sheets to the wind and listing a bit to starboard. In the operating room, a corpsman doubled me around so my chin was on my knees. The "Doctor" waved around the *biggest* needle I'd ever seen and stabbed it in my back. He did it, not once, but four times, with me screaming at the top of my voice and calling him every name in my profanity vocabulary. The pain was excruciating.

The next day the corpsman told me those stabs had been three too many; that the Medical Officer had been "partying it up pretty good" when he was called in. That's why, said the corpsman, it took him four tries to find the range. Although my back was still exceedingly painful, from the fever and the needles, I never complained again. No more spinal taps for me, thank you. The test of the spinal fluid was, thank goodness, negative.

Upon release from the hospital, I returned to the training station and was told I'd be assigned to a new company. I'd been away too long and my original company was far into its training. That's how I ended up under Company Commander Jimmy O'Neill—that tough, wiry little Irishman who'd spent most of his Naval career on Asiatic Station.

"Asiatics", men with long periods of duty in the Asiatic Fleet, were looked upon as everything from super heroes to out-and-out crazies. They *were* a different breed. Time spent among Orientals and away from Western civilization seems to have afflicted them with strange ideas and mannerisms that sometimes awed, sometimes puzzled, and sometimes flabbergasted ordinary sailors.

All "Asiatics" had reputations for being well able to take care of themselves in any kind of brawl, for they were reputed to have fought in every bar, "happy house", and back alley from Chefoo to Singapore. Whether Jimmy had indulged in such activity was never stated, but his prowess at the manly art of self-defense was soon to become a part of the legendary lore at Newport, known in the Fleet as "the Navy's toughest boot camp".

There were times when it became necessary to circumvent the regulations, using, of course, some subterfuge. Jimmy demonstrated one of these instances when, to maintain discipline, he had to take matters into his own hands.

We had a big Texan in the company. He'd competed in the rodeo at New York's Madison Square Garden, but won no prize money. Finding himself broke with no way to get back to the "wilds and woolies" of the West, he enlisted in the Navy. The trouble with this "Texican" was his inability to adapt to Navy discipline, proper wearing of the uniform, and standards of cleanliness in the service. In other words, he was a slob, forever (to cleanse an all too common phrase) "fouling up".

Chief O'Neill finally took the six-foot-two, 220-pound cowboy to task during a morning mess formation, pointing out the Texan's deficiencies, among them looking as if his uniform were "applied with a pitchfork", lack of military bearing, and incapacity even to keep in step when marching. The cowboy took exception to Jimmy's remarks and told the Chief that, if he didn't have that uniform on, he (the Texan) would clean Jimmy's clock. It is, of course, against regulations for a petty officer to fight with a seaman, but (theoretically) with the Chief's insignia off, there's no way to tell he's a petty officer. Jimmy calmly shed his jacket, handing it to me, reminded the company it was still in formation, and invited the cowboy to step behind the barracks with him.

Most of the company really liked the Chief, despite his ironhanded way of training us. And we didn't particularly care for the loudmouthed Texican whose lack of cooperation kept us from being a 4.0 (perfect score) outfit. As the two disappeared behind the barracks, the consensus in the ranks ran towards Jimmy getting the equivalent of a keel-hauling (a gruesome punishment in the old Navy). He was giving away 100 pounds and over 20 years, and even though he was pretty wiry and had earlier demonstrated to us some knowledge of jujitsu, the odds appeared against him. We really feared for his safety.

In a matter of seconds there came sounds from the back of the building resembling those during a "Pier 6 donnybrook". There were three loud crashes and some of us swore the barracks shook. Then, there was silence. We waited, expecting to see a battered Chief Gunner's Mate come stumbling out. To our surprise and delight, here came Jimmy without a scratch, a bead of sweat, even a smudge on his white shirt, or a wrinkle in his black tie. Staggering behind him was a thoroughly thrashed and vanquished Texican, stained from stem to stern with mud and blood. It seems those crashes we heard were from 220 pounds of Texas beef smacking the side of the barracks, head down and feet up. Jimmy had made one big believer out of the cowboy and believers of the rest of us as well.

There was another time the rules got "bent like a bowline on a bight" (Navy lingo for bent out of shape). Also in the company was a Middle Easterner. We were never quite sure of his ancestry, but his name and appearance led us to call him "the A-rab". Whatever his motivation, the A-rab refused to bathe, and the barracks began to take on the odor of a camel corral. The Chief never gave us any instructions on how to handle the situation, but he did relate how some of his former shipmates had taken action in a similar case. We waited until Jimmy was conveniently off the station on liberty before launching "Operation Sandblast".

The A-rab knew we had something in mind and would sit up in his bunk, armed with a bayonet, until he thought the rest of the company was asleep. But he couldn't keep his vigil forever. One night, several of us grabbed him, took away the bayonet, stripped him and tossed him in the showers. Thrown in with him was his entire seabag of smelly clothes. As the Chief had described in his story, we had equipped ourselves with several pairs of leather gloves and two buckets of sand. The A-rab was sand-scrubbed until, it seemed, the whole outer layer of his skin was gone. Anyhow, he sure shone a bright pink. He was then forced to scrub all his belongings from his seabag, the seabag itself, his hammock, and his bedding.

A couple of days later, the A-rab was gone from the company. We heard he'd been discharged as unsuitable for Naval service. The incident served a secondary purpose, though; it got a strong message across to a couple of others who were somewhat slovenly in their appearance and personal habits.

There were, of course, disciplinary measures meted out for various infractions and unbecoming conduct. Improperly wearing and/or caring for the uniform could result in an hour or more of marching on the "grinder" (parade ground) "in a military manner". Being late for formations, dropping a rifle or not properly cleaning it, failing to be cleanly shaven, or not knowing the General Orders could all result in punishment.

The "gigs" (demerits) resulted in push-ups, extra duty, head (toilet) cleaning detail, and perhaps the worst: lashing and relashing your hammock and seabag 50 to 100 times. The line used in lashing was rough hemp. After pulling on the rope a few times to make it sufficiently tight, with the marlin hitches exactly seven inches apart, the skin on your fingers and hands would get raw, then get torn and bloody before the punishment was over. Pity the poor boot who was sentenced to do 100 lashings! Because we were all fallible, no one in the company escaped some kind of disciplinary action; and most of it was, to say the least, unpleasant and physically exhausting.

Not all was fun and games. The training Chief O'Neill put us through was intense. There was what seemed to be interminable drilling on the parade ground. It was, as Rudyard Kipling had written, a pure case of "Boots, boots, marching up and down again, boots, boots . . . ."

When we weren't marching, we were executing, over and over, the "Manual of Arms" drill while standing stiffly at attention—right shoulder arms, left shoulder arms, port arms, order arms, inspection arms, trail arms—until the nine-pound 30.06-caliber Springfield rifle weighed nine *tons*. After we got all of that drilled into us, the Chief would order the company to march and execute the arms drills simultaneously. That is, we'd step off in formation, doing all 48 different positions in the "48 count marching manual" in cadence. It was a grueling exercise, practiced every day during the 90-day recruit training. We would march to the flank, march to the oblique, march in column, march to the left, march to the right, march in columns of three and columns of four, open ranks, close ranks, *ad infinitum*. Hell, it seemed all we did was MARCH.

But there was other training, too. Because Rhode Island's inclement winter weather precluded small-boat-handling out of doors, we used a giant indoor pool with a mock-up of a boat under oars. Sitting on half-thwarts (seats), we would respond to orders to "stand by our oars, shove off, out oars, give way together", and practice all the other commands indigenous to rowing a boat in concert.

Qualification was mandatory in two categories, swimming and rifle-firing. I'd been swimming since before I could remember. My sister says my dad threw me in the ocean when we lived in Fort Lauderdale and let me go it alone. I was in a minority as an experienced swimmer. Most of the company, particularly the city kids, had to attend regular classes to meet the minimum requirement.

The test for Class "A" Qualification included: (1) Swimming—175 yards in 4 1/2 minutes, 25 yards breast stroke, 25 yards right side, 25 yards left side, 25 yards back stroke, and 75 yards free style. (2) Lifesaving— 20 yards to a drowning person, breaking hold encountered, 20 yards to safety with victim, with ability to break all holds. (3) Resuscitation—ability to apply the technique to a person who has nearly drowned. I passed the first time through in all phases, swimming the 175 yards in less than four minutes. In my service record is a description of the test and a notation that I qualified as a Class "A" swimmer. These skills would pay off handsomely in the then unknown future.

On 5 April, 1941, the company bivouacked at the Coddington Point Rifle Range to qualify with the then standard U.S. Military rifle, the 1903 or 1909 bolt-action 30.06 caliber Springfield. The weapon is clip-fed, with five rounds per clip. One round may be in the chamber. It had (and still has) a reputation of being extremely accurate in the hands of experts. It also packed one helluva kick when fired. Bruised shoulders, skinned thumbs, and even bloody noses were not uncommon when neophytes first fired the piece. Some of our company had never seen nor handled a real rifle. Having been raised in the city, they had real difficulty qualifying. Not a few were actually afraid of the weapon.

Living alternately in South Jersey and South Florida as a lad, I'd hunted small game (including quail, pheasant, ducks, squirrels, and rabbits) in the fields and woods of Salem County, New Jersey; and in Broward County, Florida, I'd gone after deer and other game in the Everglades with the Seminoles. My dad had taught Sunday school at the Indian Reservation, and I spent a great deal of time there living with the tribe for weeks on end. So I had grown up around rifles, shotguns, and handguns. We had a whole closet full of weapons at home in Jersey.

But I faced one problem in firing for qualification. I'm a southpaw; however, on the range I was required to fire according to the regulations, using a sling and firing righthanded. The sling on the Springfield is a belt-like adjustable strap, anchored to the front of the wooden foregrip and, at the rear, to the stock. When firing, it is wrapped around the left forearm to steady the piece. I'd never used one before and it was extremely awkward for me to put that sling around my left arm. At the same time, I was squeezing the trigger with my "wrong" finger, sighting with the "wrong" eye, and working the bolt-action with the "wrong" hand.

Final qualifying called for firing five clips of five rounds from each of the five different positions—standing, squatting, kneeling, sitting, and prone—at a target 100 yards down the range. There was a time limit, too, requiring rapid fire to complete the exercise. Despite the awkwardness with the sling and firing from my starboard side rather than port, an entry in my service record reads:

"Qualified as MARKSMAN on the Coddington Point Rifle Range during the week ending 4/5/41."

While waiting for others to finish, I scrounged around and collected two clips of ammo. I asked the chief Range Officer if I could fire them after qualifying was completed.

"Sure", he said, "if we have time." Transportation back to the barracks was late, so the Range Officer told me to go ahead and use up the ten rounds, adding I could fire any way I wished.

I pulled the sling tight to get it out of the way, made a slight correction in windage, snuggled the stock up to my *left* shoulder and began firing as rapidly as I could, changing position after each round. Even though I had to eject each empty case by reaching over the piece to throw the bolt with the "wrong" hand, I finished the clips in a matter of seconds.

"Pretty fast", commented the Range Officer. "Let's see if you hit anything."

When the target was raised up out of the butts after the crew had marked the hits, each and every marker was clustered in a small pattern in the center of the bull. My great-uncle Bert, who'd taught me to shoot, would have been proud. The Range Officer was impressed and my company shipmates began to treat me with a little more deference afterward.

Our training progressed. Implicit in all the exercises was "Pride In Service", a strong sense of duty to the Country and to the Navy, respect for authority, cheerful and immediate obedience to orders, and the teamwork necessary to the survival of all.

Part II of the *Bluejacket's Manual,* "Subjects All Enlisted Men Should Know", covers everything from "Discipline and Duty" to "Painting and the Preparation of Surfaces Therefore". The 14 chapters are familiarly referred to as "A to N", and among the subjects we studied were: "What the Service Offers", "Pay and Accounts", "Navy Customs, Naval Organization", "General Characteristics of Ships", as well as other phases of Navy life that would affect us.

There are ten pages alone on "Regulations in Regard to Uniform and Clothing". The Navy issued one full set of the "Prescribed Outfit" to each enlisted man, including the equivalent of three sets of blues and four sets of white uniforms; plus underwear, shoes, peacoat, dungarees, and other items. Unlike the Army and Marine Corps, it was the only free clothing we would get. After that, we had to buy all our personal gear.

In boot camp we hand-washed all of our laundry. In the Fleet ships had laundries aboard, but many of us chose to continue to hand wash our dress uniforms. We were taught how to stow properly all of the items in a seabag. Uniforms were *rolled,* inside out, and secured with white clothes stops (cords). The inside-out storage accounts for the creases in trousers and jumpers being inverted when worn. All clothing had the man's name stenciled on each item. Having another's personal effects in a sailor's possession, could result in severe disciplinary action.

Other instruction centered around shipboard terminology, ship nomenclature, marlinespike seamanship ("lines and tackle", pronounced with a long *a*); visual communications, including signal flag identifications; rudimentary navigation, e.g. boxing a compass; gunnery, including weapons systems; and history, customs, and traditions of the United States Navy.

We learned the differences among all the channel buoys we'd see upon entering and leaving ports, and knew that red buoys were always to starboard when entering port. "Red Right Returning" was the phrase we memorized to keep a vessel in the channel.

Also, we memorized the code words for all of the signal flags and pennants: *A*ffirm, *B*aker, *C*ast, *D*og, *E*asy, *F*ox, *G*eorge, *H*ypo, *I*nterrogatory, *J*ig, *K*ing, *L*ove, *M*ike, *N*egative, *O*ption, *P*reparatory (or "Prep"), *Q*ueen, *R*oger, *S*ail, *T*are, *U*nit, *V*ictor, *W*illiam, *X*ray, *Y*oke, and *Z*ed—plus the corresponding signal flags. All these have changed. At last count, only *M*IKE, *V*ICTOR, and *X*RAY remain. The changes began shortly after the War started, ostensibly to conform to the British phonetic alphabet. All that did was cause mass confusion. All the old-timers used the original, while new recruits were taught the new. Only some desk jockey in Washington could have come up with this change for sake of change; it sure didn't originate in the Fleet. We never understood why the U.S Navy had to change to something *British*.

Today, we have another example of making changes for no apparent reason. From early days, the Navy named battleships for states, cruisers for cities, destroyers for Navy heroes, fleet tugs for Indian tribes, submarines for fish and sea creatures, and aircraft carriers for famous American battles or illustrious U.S. sailing vessels. All that has been abandoned, and now there's no way to identify instantly a ship's type by its name. They've got subs named for states, cruisers for men, etc. Whoever sanctioned that mess should've been "deep-sixed to Davy Jones' Locker"!

There were watches to be stood in boot camp, of course. One of the watch stations was on the "berthing deck" (barracks room) from taps 'til reveille. The newest recruits at Newport were berthed in the "Old Quarters" —brick buildings that, legend had it, were the first structures built by the Rhode Island Colony when old Roger Williams got kicked out of Massachusetts back in 1636. Or maybe they were left over from 1847 when the Naval Academy was on Narragansett Bay before moving to its permanent site on the banks of the Severn River at Annapolis. Maybe not quite that old, but the quarters did lack some of the more modern conveniences, primarily a good heating system.

It was so cold that February and March, 1941, that we took to sleeping fully clothed: socks, longjohns, turtleneck sweaters, undress blue uniforms, peacoats, and watch caps. We further buttressed ourselves against the chilling temperatures by properly slinging our hammocks. Landlubbers know little of the technique of rigging a hammock. First, it must be stretched as taut as possible to eliminate sagging in the middle. The clews (lines by which a hammock is slung) are separated by wooden spreaders, and the mattress is centered in the hammock. To ward off cold, however, we dispensed with the spreaders so the hammock, mattress and all, would completely encompass us. The berthing deck at taps took on the appearance of embryo butterflies sacked out in their cocoons.

The watchstander (sentry) had no such protection. While there was an ancient steam radiator (one to a deck), it emitted only enough heat to keep itself from freezing solid. Since leaving a post was a court martial offense, those of us who drew these watches simply had to bear the discomfort. And there was always at least one visitation from the "Quarterdeck" (duty office) by a "square knot admiral" who'd invariably make us recite one, some, or all of the General Orders for a sentry walking his post.

A "square knot admiral" was a recruit who had been elevated to a sort of petty officer status, and who wore a rating badge complete with eagle and the single chevron of a 3rd class petty officer. In the space where the specialty insignia is displayed, there was a white square knot. Often the "admirals" were the butts of derision, since not a few got their positions by the age-old practice (indigenous to all Navy rates and ranks) of toadying up to (currying the favor of) the Company Commander. Once in the Fleet, however, the temporary rating meant nothing and the badge was discarded. I never heard anyone brag about once having been a "square knot admiral" when boot camp was over.

The one watch post universally hated by every one was "The Point", a strip of beach near a big boulder we called "Plymouth Rock" because it resembled the one up on Cape Cod. Surely that sentry post was about the most miserable one in the Navy. There was no shelter from the cold, wintry blasts of arctic air and snow flurries blowing across the white caps of Narragansett Bay. It's a wonder none of us became frostbitten out there.

As graduation approached after nearly three months of tough training, we began to speculate on what our ship assignments would be. Although I have always been somewhat of a loner, I had made some pretty good buddies, the closest of whom was Jimmy MacPherson, a brash Scotsman from Tampa, Florida. "Mac" was kind of a nut who was always plotting some sort of prank. He was among the leaders in "Operation Sandblast" against the "A-rab" and indulged in such activities as knotting guys' shoelaces together. We'd end up on the same ship together. Mac had one problem: his nickname. Everybody in the Navy and Marine Corps in those days was called "Mac", a sort of generic appellation. Whenever someone called out "Hey, Mac!", Jimmy would respond. It caused him no little trouble.

The last bit of business prior to graduation was submitting our requests for training at one of the various Navy trade schools. I applied for aviation ordnance school, hoping it would lead to flying as a gunner's mate and aircraft carrier duty. I never heard anything more of it. Apparently the request ended up in someone's File 13.

As we prepared for the standard seven days' "boot leave", we rejoiced in finally getting rid of those dreaded leggings, the "boots" continuously worn by recruits. The canvas contraptions were perhaps the most frustrating and useless bit of attire since the invention of the chastity belt. For one thing, they had to be scrubbed daily with a hard-bristle brush and soap. In donning them, a strap was buckled in place under the instep. On the outside were laces, held in place by metal hooks. They were a pain in the neck to get just right. If laced too tightly, they cut off circulation; too loose, and they'd come undone. Not a few new recruits put them on the wrong legs so that the hooks and the lacings were on the inside of the leg. Then, when they walked, the hooks on one leg would catch the lacings on the other; and they would, as my granddaddy used to say, go "ass over tin cups", much to the amusement of bystanders.

We'd also be shedding the undress blues we'd worn throughout training for the snappy dress blues. While the trousers were the same, the dress jumper had three white stripes around the collar and a white star on each corner. Both jumpers, in those days, had a white stripe sewn around the right shoulder, showing the wearer to be a seaman. The undress jumper didn't indicate the seaman's class or rate; but the dress jumper had cuffs on the sleeves, buttoning at the wrist, on which cuffs were stripes: one for Apprentice Seaman, two for Seaman 2nd Class, and three for Seaman 1st Class.

To correct a couple of misconceptions about the bluejacket's uniform: First, the collar stripes have been said to commemorate British Admiral Horatio Nelson's biggest victories. But that's not true. The United States Navy was not about to honor any English Admiral. There's no significance to the stripes. They're just decorative.

Second, regulation Navy trousers are not true "bell bottoms". They are "stove pipe", i.e. straight-legged. The inverted creases and the width of the pants do give them a flared appearance. They are so cut in order to make it easy to roll them up when swabbing decks. Nonregulation uniforms ("tailor-mades"), however, invariably are styled with bells.

Another feature of the uniform trousers are the thirteen buttons on the front flap that serves as a fly. We took a little ribbing about those buttons, but they were just another detail that made the Navy uniform different. As sailors, we wanted to be as distinctive as possible in our dress. We did not want to be mistaken for Marines, those "seagoing bellhops", nor for the Army's soldiers with their "bus driver" uniforms.

While all the other Armed Services refer to a man's position in the military hierarchy as "rank", the U.S. Navy is different. Only officers hold "rank". Enlisted men hold "rates". After Seaman 1st Class, the rates progress to Petty Officer 3rd Class, to P.O. 2nd Class, to P.O. 1st Class, and then to Chief Petty Officer. A new rating, Master Chief, has since been added. But Chief was the highest non-commissioned rate during my years of service.

When I first went in the Navy, ratings were divided between the "right arm" and the "left arm" rates. But sometime during the War (I don't recall precisely when it was) another one of those stupid change for change's sake dictums came down, making all rates "left arm". And another well-established tradition went down the slop chute.

The right arm rates were those specialties that existed prior to the advent of steam and modern technology. The "deck rates"—boatswain's mate, quartermaster, gunner's mate, signalman, carpenter's mate—were among those who wore their rating badges on the right arm.

With the coming of the "modern" Navy, new rates were introduced for the "black gang": e.g. machinist's mates, water tenders, electricians, and other engineering specialists. Later added to these were radiomen, sonarmen, radarmen, etc. All these were left arm ratings.

A petty officer with a right arm rate was senior to a left arm P.O. of the same rank. But all this changed when someone buried deep in the Navy's bureaucracy got a wild hair and decided differently, and tradition was blown out the tubes.

In my brand-new dress blues, single cuff stripe and all, I headed for home. We were less than eight months away from the "date which will live in infamy"—the sneak attack on Pearl Harbor by the Japanese.

The seven-day leave would be my last for two and a half years.

2

HOME . . . AND BACK TO NEWPORT

I was born February 4th, 1922, on Georgetown Road, Upper Penns Neck (now Carney's Point) Township, Salem County, New Jersey, to Marguerite de Valois Sieverdin and John Reardon Hutchinson. The family farm was on the outskirts of Carney's Point village, adjacent to the Borough of Penns Grove (the post office address).

The house (now gone) and the bedroom in which I was brought into this world, was (in nautical terms) at 74° 28′ 01″ West longitude, 39° 43′ 26.3″ North latitude. Historically significant, this latitude, for by extending it westward across the Delaware River, it becomes the Mason-Dixon Line, the boundary between Pennsylvania and Maryland and the unseen divider between the North and the South. It went right through the bedroom. With details lacking, I'll never know whether I was born a Yankee or a Southerner, at least technically speaking.

On the south side of Georgetown Road (so named, so I was told, because three men named "George", including my grandfather, owned farms along it) stood our main house, the barn, and the outbuildings. It was to this place I was returning. As I took the train out of Providence for Wilmington, directly across the Delaware River from home, I mused about my childhood, the strong morals and ethics under which I was raised, and the heritage and traditions of my ancestors.

Unlike many Americans, my father's family were not immigrants to the United States. Today, it is fashionable to say that all non-Indians are immigrants, thus implying that descendants of colonial settlers do not belong here. I am a native American by virtue of the fact that my ancestors settled in this land and participated in founding a new nation.

My first American ancestor of record, Nels (Nelson) Matsson (and his son known as Anthony Nelson), arrived from Sweden and settled along the Delaware River in 1654, roughly a century and a quarter before we became a free and independent country. He fought against the Dutch in 1655, during the fur trade war; and his descendants took up arms to protect their colonies, to fight for liberty and independence, and to establish the United States of America.

My paternal grandmother, née Margaret Harker Nelson, was a direct descendent of Anthony. He had moved across the Delaware to what was then called West Jersey in 1684, and the Nelsons had settled in Gloucester and Salem Counties. The genealogy of the Nelson family, from the 17th to the 20th centuries, is given in Elmer Garfield Van Name, *Anthony Nelson . . . and Some of His Descendants* (1962), a booklet my father stumbled upon in the records of the Salem County Historical Society.

My grandfather, George Tomlinson Hutchinson, was the great-grandson of Aquilla Hutchinson, possibly descended from Scots from the Isle of Skye and probably from Hutchinsons in Talbot County, Maryland, going back to the 17th century. At any rate, cousin Bill (William Huber Hutchinson), who researched this subject, established that Aquilla was a farmer in Salem County, New Jersey, before the American Revolution. There in 1798 he married my great-great-great grandmother Ann Dunham (or Anna Dunnam) the ceremony being performed by Presbyterian minister Nathaniel Harris.

From the beginning, both the Nelsons and the Hutchinsons were involved in military service, howbeit as citizen soldiers. Each of the earlier generations served in the militias of their day. For instance, several Nelsons fought in the Revolutionary War. Indeed, at the onset of the Revolution, my great-great-great grandfather, Daniel Nelson (and his three brothers) enlisted in Captain Nieukirk's Salem County (Pittsgrove) Foot Militia, 2nd Battalion, to serve the American cause against British tyranny.

During the Civil War, great-grandfathers Daniel Nelson and James Hutchinson enlisted in Company K, 24th Regiment, New Jersey Volunteers. According to Hutchinson family tradition, James was captured by the Confederates during the Battle of Fredericksburg in 1862, and later returned to the Army of the Potomac by way of a prisoner exchange. According to his service records, he was wounded at Chancellorsville in 1863. His older brother William, who died in 1864, also served in the Union Army.

According to Nelson family tradition, Daniel Nelson enlisted as an underage drummer boy in 1861, and served until 1865. According to his service records, he rose in the ranks to become a regimental headquarters sergeant in the Army of the Potomac. He was captured at Gaines Mill in 1862 and again at Spotsylvania Court House in 1864, returning to the Union Army twice via prisoner exchange, the second time after incarceration in the infamous Confederate prison at Andersonville.

I can still hear my grandmother talking about how much her father "loved his Flag." She often recounted his great devotion to the Grand

Army of the Republic, which continued unabated 'til his death in the early 20th century.

When I joined the Navy, I was following in the footsteps of my forebears who had literally laid down their plows, taken up their muskets, and volunteered when our country needed them. They had left in my care our native land to protect and preserve. I took the only natural course.

In contrast to my father's deep American roots, my mother was a newcomer to this country. Born in East Grange, Scotland, near St. Andrews, she was the daughter of Antoine Henri Sieverdin and Rose Caldwell. After the death of her father, she left Scotland as a young girl with her mother, moving to Canada and later to the United States. During World War I, she took a job at the Dupont Powder Plant #1 in Carney's Point, New Jersey. It was here she met my dad and, after a whirlwind courtship, they were married.

Mom's dad was from Lille, France, but apparently fled to the British Isles when the Prussians overran the city in the 1870 Franco-Prussian War. According to my mother, he was a well-educated man, speaking several languages. He taught Romance languages at Clytha College in Glasgow, Scotland, and later in St. Andrews. At one time, he was headmaster of his own boys' academy.

Antoine Sieverdin's mother, my great-grandmother, was Marie de Valois from a distinguished French family. According to family tradition, right or wrong, the family went back to the House of Valois which ruled France from the 14th to the 16th centuries, eventually succeeded by the House of Bourbon.

Despite her very Gallic name—Marguerite de Valois Sieverdin—my mother was exceedingly proud of her Scottish birthright. And there was Scottish (MacKevett) blood on her mother's side, even though her mother, Rose Caldwell, was born on the Isle of Wight. Thus, I am a native American of Swedish-Scottish-French heritage—and who knows what else!

I caught the old ferry from Wilmington across the Delaware and was met at the Penns Grove slip by Uncle Bert (Gilbert C. Hutchinson, my grandfather's bachelor brother). Here was the man who'd had more of a hand in raising me than had my father. A big, strong, quiet man, he believed hard work was a virtue. He made even shoveling dirt or ploughing a straight furrow an art form.

While the aim of many today is to find happiness, it was Uncle Bert's credo that the ambition of a man should be to become useful. It was he who taught me how to hunt, to handle and break horses, to drive first a

Author Home on "Boot" Leave, With Brother George April, 1941.

tractor and then a car, to plant and nurture crops, and to do all the tasks involved in the operation of a farm.

Uncle Bert didn't teach honesty verbally, but set an example by being both honest and honorable. To him, a lie was an abomination. He only went to church when there was a death in the family; but he had a deep and abiding faith in God, the principles of the Ten Commandments, the Golden Rule, and the American way of life. He never told me whether he was proud that I was in the service. But he sized me up with a practiced eye when he picked me up at the ferry:

"I see they're makin' a *man* out o' you, Jack." To be a *man* by Uncle Bert's standards was the ultimate compliment.

My grandmother had been cooking and baking for two days, readying an old-fashioned farm supper. Now, Gran wasn't a great cook, compared to my mother, but nobody ever went away from her house hungry. That night, the table sagged under the weight of roast chickens, vegetables (both fresh and home-canned), fresh strawberries, and several varieties of pies and cakes. As usual, there were mounds of mashed potatoes and a huge bowl of gravy. Gran always claimed she'd made enough gravy in her lifetime to float a battleship! We had a glorious time, and I waddled when I got up from the table.

Later, I headed for a couple of places where the old "gang" usually could be found. I rounded up a few of the guys and gals, and we spent most of the night reminiscing about the "good old days"—which had, for me, ended but three and a half months before.

Wasn't it Thomas Wolfe who said, "You can't go home again"? Up to a point that's probably true. I no longer felt a part of the "inner circle" of my friends. A great deal had changed in the short time I'd been away. There were different pairings among those dating; and a few of the old bunch were now gone, either enlisting in one of the Armed Services or being called up in the National Guard.

During my leave, I had no trouble getting dates with some of the girls I'd gone out with while a civilian. But it was not the same. We all knew nothing permanent, or even semi-permanent, could come of our friendships. At parting, two of the girls succumbed to tears, probably because they knew our world was changed forever and only God knew the future. Now we were just old friends going different ways—"parting is such sweet sorrow" as Shakespeare had put it.

The only negative incident during that boot leave came when a couple of my shirt-tail relatives avoided me by crossing to the other side of the street when I approached. I was in uniform and apparently they didn't wish to be seen with a sailor. Didn't Lord Byron once write: "Sailors are in fact a different kind"?

The old prejudices surrounding military men, particularly those of us of the seagoing sort, were still alive. We were stereotyped somewhere below the Untouchables in the caste system; characterized as ne'er-do-wells, persons of low morals, and drunks. I'd see more evidence of this bias against sailors on liberty in Norfolk. It was not uncommon in that Virginia city to see signs on lawns warning: SAILORS AND DOGS—KEEP OFF! This attitude tended to change on December 7th, 1941, and those who entered the service after hostilities began experienced less humiliation.

Historian Richard Kolb, writing of *FDR's Undeclared War in the North Atlantic* in the eleven months of 1941 prior to the Pearl Harbor attack, refers to one of President Franklin D. Roosevelt's advisors speaking concerning the American public's apathy toward career military personnel: It seems Americans always have considered the men in their regular armed forces (Army, Navy, and most of all, Marine Corps) as rugged mercenaries who signed up voluntarily, like policemen and firemen, for hazardous duty. Of course, it was tough luck when any of them were killed in the line of duty—it was all in a day's work. The average American simply did not identify with the professional sailor or soldier.

In the case of draftees, however, the attitude was entirely different. They were "our boys" who must be kept from harm at all costs. Since there were no draftees in the Navy, there was no great popular indignation for the attacks on the U.S.S. KEARNEY, torpedoed 17 October, 1941, with the loss of 11 killed and 24 wounded. Nor was there any outcry when the U.S.S. REUBEN JAMES was sunk on 30 October with the loss of 115 men. Both ships were victims of German submarine attacks.

The Regulars—the professional sailors, soldiers, airmen, and Marines—have always been *"The First to Fight"*, and rightfully so. But Americans have almost always turned their backs on us Regulars in "peacetime". Our countrymen have not known nor appreciated the risks Regulars routinely take.

As for us bluejackets, we had to combat a long history of prejudice and discrimination on the part of the proprietors of public places—as portrayed in one of the classics of American naval literature, namely Fred J. Buenzle's autobiographical *Bluejacket*. According to the author who served in the U.S. Navy at the turn of the century: "we were not wanted, for we wore jackets of navy blue."

In the early part of the century, professional bluejacket Fred Buenzle, a Chief Yeoman deaf from the booming guns in the Battle of Santiago in 1898, with the support and encouragement of President Theodore

Roosevelt embarked on a successful legal crusade to outlaw public discrimination against those in uniform on the principle: "Self-respecting men . . . should be made to feel proud of the official garb they were required to wear in their country's defense forces."

In 1939 old bluejacket Buenzle summed up his crusade as follows: "I had made up my mind that something drastic must be done to end the abuse. In order to bring the evil to the attention of the people of the United States, with the approval of my naval superiors at Newport, Rhode Island, I made a legal stand against the old prejudice represented by the sign 'No Uniforms Allowed'. I instituted a test case against a local amusement place where seamen in uniform were refused admittance for no other reason than that they did not wear civilian clothing—a thing that Navy regulations did not permit. Painful remembrances of the many indignities heaped upon my comrades in the sea service had urged me to initiate and prosecute the case at my own expense; but for long it seemed that the law was unquestionably on the side of those who turned away the decent Jack from their doors."

"After two years of court reversals, we succeeded in having laws passed that made any discrimination against the uniform of our Army or Navy a misdemeanor in every state and territory. I knew that the greatest struggle of my life was won, and well won. No longer would grave injustices against the lads who spent the best years of life in naval service be legally condoned. The sign 'No Uniforms Allowed' was taken down and shelved with other anachronisms. . . . No longer may the American uniform be considered a pretext for ejecting decent seamen from restaurants and theaters and public buildings, and forcing them into the arms of shore sharks in dives and water-front hangouts. The garb of the bluejacket has, in T.R.'s phrase, truly become a badge of honor."

Commenting on Buenzle's crusade and the problem of discrimination against bluejackets in the decades before Pearl Harbor, his editor Neville T. Kirk writes: "With the entry of the United States in World War I, the surge of patriotic support for the armed services submerged traditional hostility to their uniforms, though some wearers then resented the imposition of the accompanying ban on serving them alcoholic drinks. The coming of peace in 1919 brought about some revival of the old discrimination against the uniform; it remained a very minor problem, however, until the impact of Pearl Harbor effected its complete and permanent elimination."

On the basis of my personal experience both before and after the War, this pronouncement overstates the case and understates the problem, especially when one takes into consideration private as well as public discrimination.

Incidentally, for personal accounts of the life of the enlisted man of the United States Navy in the 19th century, see Herman Melville's classic *White-Jacket* (1850) for the first half of the century; and Fred Buenzle's *Bluejacket* (1939) for the end of the 19th century and beginning of the 20th. For the bluejacket's life in the U.S. Navy in the forty years prior to my service, see Frederick S. Harrod, *Manning the New Navy: The Development of a Modern Naval Enlisted Force, 1899–1940* (1978, Greenwood Press, Westport, CT, pp. ixff, 166ff).

According to Harrod, the ability and character of enlisted men are crucial to the efficiency of the United States Navy. Yet they are disregarded by naval historians. "*Enlisted personnel are the forgotten men of naval history.* Historians write of tactics and technology but ignore the people who compose the service. This omission leads to accounts that are not so much incorrect as incomplete."

On the issue of discrimination against bluejackets, Harrod summarizes the first forty years of the 20th century as follows: "Recruits began to share a primary identity as Americans, not as seamen, and the Navy, with a recruiting network spread across the country, became a national institution. Furthermore, as sailors came to represent diverse areas of the United States, bluejackets gradually shed their former status as social outcasts."

Again, from my experience, such an assertion is, to put it mildly, an overstatement. Other enlisted men serving in my day would witness to bluejackets' being mistreated and exploited by civilians ashore. This is the testimony of *Battleship Sailor* Theodore C. Mason, who reflects on his experience in 1941: "The occupation of *bluejacket* had not yet become respectable . . . , and one quickly learned that he had few friends away from the ship."

Harrod makes the point that the early 20th century witnessed the modern Navy's recruiting thousands of young men unfamiliar with the sea, which necessitated the Navy's becoming a great educational institution.

"Because the young men who flocked to the new Navy were not familiar with their duties aboard ship, the [Navy] department had to develop a new, large-scale training system. In place of the small apprentice program, which had been the old Navy's only significant educational activity, the service in the twentieth century began instructing all recruits in elementary seamanship. This training provided a sufficient number of men for the expanding fleet but did not secure individuals in the skilled ratings required aboard a modern warship. To satisfy this need, the [Navy] department developed shore schools and correspondence courses. Taken together, these efforts mark the emergence of the service as a major educational establishment."

The following observations of Harrod describe the character of education in the Navy in relation to American society in the years prior to the time of my service and beyond.

"In the area of education, formal instruction at recruit training facilities and in advanced courses helped the department provide a uniform learning experience for its men. The development of correspondence-type Navy training courses helped insure that even the education the men undertook on their own time met service needs. Supervision of instruction was enhanced by central preparation of such training aids as drill books, movies, and slide films, and the issuance of a common manual to all recruits. . . . During the formation of the modern force, the department acted in self-imposed isolation. New ideas arose only as conditions in the service itself demanded, seldom as the result of learning from the experiences of others."

"The formation of extensive educational facilities within the Navy meant that the service no longer had to recruit men familiar with a trade. The very creation of an independent source of supply, however, seems to indicate that in the end the Navy was not able to compete effectively against the lures of private employment for skilled manpower. The department therefore strove to build its own closed world. In developing this separate system, the Navy demonstrated its ability to isolate itself from much of society . . . . By the late twenties the service possessed an enlisted force characterized by high morale and good performance. Secure, almost complacent, the Navy could watch the 'upheaval in American institutions' from the sidelines."

"The personnel system that the department developed in the first part of the twentieth century formed the basic structure under which the Navy has subsequently operated. After World War II erupted, the strength of the enlisted force swelled to thirty times its prewar level. The influx of thousands of men and women diluted the career force, but *the bluejackets of the thirties provided the experienced petty officers that the enlarged Navy required.* By 1940 such developments as inland recruiting, training stations, trade schools, and recreational offerings were taken for granted. With the advent of war, they provided the framework that permitted the service to attract, train, and utilize thousands of new men and women, and the Navy had only to concern itself with extending and refining the programs it already possessed. So satisfactory was this personnel system in fulfilling the needs of the modern Navy that it has remained at the core of the Navy's manpower policies to the present day."

The seven-day boot leave was over all too quickly. I said my goodbyes and returned to Newport to report aboard one of the most illustrious ships in the history of the United States Navy.

The United States Frigate CONSTELLATION—the 36-gun sailing vessel built in 1797 and sister ship to "Old Ironsides" (the CONSTITUTION)—was berthed at the Newport Training Station. At the time, she was being utilized as a Receiving Ship, where sailors were billeted while awaiting assignment or reassignment. Together with other recruits returning from leave, I took up residence in that marvelous old vessel, so steeped in the history and traditions of the United States Navy.

The CONSTELLATION was, even then, a showpiece. Her rigging was intact, the main weather deck holy-stoned daily, her brass was kept mirror-polished, and her berthing and gun decks were waxed so slick they looked like ice to skate upon. It was the daily duty of those aboard to keep her shipshape. The least desirable assignment was holy-stoning her teakwood weatherdeck, until it was as white as new-fallen snow, and I was one of the detail assigned to that task. Barefooted, with pants rolled up to the knee, we scrubbed that deck "to a fare-thee-well".

A holy-stone is a brick of pumice-like rock with an indentation in the top. Into this depression is fitted a swab handle; the maximum amount of elbow grease is then applied by the deck hand so that all dirt, brine, rubber heel marks, and other soiling agents are removed. Often it was necessary to discard the swab handle, get down on hands and knees and scrub with the stone in hand, all the while dodging streams of water from the hoses used to wash 'er down. On the coolest mornings, it was not the most pleasant way to start the day.

All the Navy's shipboard rituals and ceremonies were scrupulously observed, including quarterdeck routines, striking of the ship's bell to mark the time, and piping to call shipboard activities. The boatswain's pipe indicated impending duties to be performed.

From an old Chief Boatswain's Mate, I was introduced into one bit of the "Olde Nyvy" which I follow to this day. It was a ritual among sailors of the old windjammers (sailing ships) upon seeing the Flag each morning, to salute the Colors and say *"Good morning, Uncle!"* How the practice began, or why it has passed out of Naval lore, I have no idea, but it will remain alive as long as I do.

Sleeping aboard the old windjammer was not the most comfortable experience. My berthing space was on the port side of the gun deck. Of course, we slung hammocks instead of sleeping in bunks. The hammock hooks were imbedded in the huge crossbeams of the old vessel, beams that had been set by architects when sailors averaged several inches less in stature than those that now peopled the CONSTELLATION. Consequently, there was no way for a six foot bluejacket like me to get the hammock taut enough to keep it from sagging. To add injury to insult, my space was just above the breech of one of those 24 pounders, and every time I moved, my posterior would thump against that solid old gun. Not infrequently, I arose in the morning with several bruises.

About the third day aboard, I was summoned by the bos'n (boatswain) to get into dress blues, traditional flat hat and leggings, and then report to the Shore Patrol Officer. "Damn", I thought, "will I never get rid of these boots?" But they were uniform for Shore Patrol (SP) duty.

At the SP office on the beach, two of us were briefed by a lieutenant (jg), i.e. junior grade, on our duties for the evening. We were to patrol the area out on a pier near a bar known as the Blue Moon Cafe. The officer emphasized we were not to act as "cops", but to lend assistance to any sailors who might get into trouble, or be unable to navigate after taking on too much of old John Barleycorn's potent nectar.

Outfitted with the ubiquitous military duty belts, SP brassards (armbands) and night sticks, two very green teen-age sailors gingerly approached the Blue Moon's pier. We were apprehensive for good reason. That gin mill had the reputation for being one of the toughest rendezvous for men of the Fleet, it was said, "from Frisco to Port Said."

At the time, there were several ships at anchor off Newport, including the old battleships TEXAS (BB-35) and NEW YORK (BB-34), as well as destroyers, cruisers, and other vessels. Adding to the mixture were submarine sailors from the Narragansett Bay Torpedo Base. With these diverse elements converging on the Blue Moon, there was a good possibility for a seagoing version of the Battle of the Little Big Horn.

We watched, with misgivings, the liberty boats discharging their parties at the fleet landings, wondering just how two "wet behind the ears" recruits with inflammatory Shore Patrol badges on their arms would fare *this* night. But things remained relatively calm during the early hours of the evening. The club's own bouncer ejected a couple of the more obstreperous patrons, who then weaved their way on a zig-zag course back toward the landing, each with a notable list to starboard and with much shouting and snatches of bawdy song. We let them alone, since they caused no trouble.

We made a couple of sorties inside, but spent most of our patrol out on the pier until about 2130 or 2200 (9:30 or 10:00 PM). The noise level in the bar steadily increased as the hour grew later and finally was climaxed with a loud crash. The inevitable had come to pass. It seems some battlewagon sailors had made derogatory remarks about the fighting capabilities of submarine sailors and added the crowning insult by calling subs "pig boats"!

We ran into the Blue Moon, not quite sure what we'd do, just two young'uns among a few dozen seasoned salts. By the time we got inside the door, the altercation already involved ten or twelve John Gobs (enlisted sailors) who had progressed from just passing nasty judgments about each others' heredity to swinging fists. Hanging back and enjoying the show were several destroyer sailors, awaiting the outcome of this battleship versus submarine affray.

As Shore Patrolmen, we were supposed to intercede in any such activities. My partner shouted out a "belay that!" It was a naive attempt to restore order. But the sound of his voice was swallowed up in the racket. The brouhaha had reached a fever pitch and some of those with lesser pugilistic expertise began to use chairs, tables, or any other object that came to hand. It was when the bottles started flying that my sidekick and I took positive, if evasive, action. He dove behind the bar and I took refuge in the telephone booth. You can see how brave we were!

Curiosity got the better of my good sense and I raised up from my crouch to peek through the glass in order to watch the melee. It sure was hot and heavy. The Blue Moon's cheap breakaway furniture had all but been reduced to kindling, and the fight would have made a John Wayne movie brawl look like a tea party. Hollywood should have been there to see how it's *really* done.

Even after an airborne bottle broke the phone booth's glass above my head, I continued to watch. As the casualties began to diminish the number of battleship and sub sailors in the gang and one-on-one matches, the destroyermen could stand it no longer. They joined in the party. Admittedly their foes were weakened by losses, but it took only minutes for the tin can sailors to clean house and emerge as the victors. It was a GREAT fight—one of the best I ever saw during my career in the Navy.

When the dust had settled, my partner and I hesitantly emerged from our safe havens. With most of the participants both wearied by the exertion, and still feeling the effects of their drinking bouts, it was fairly easy to round up the combatants and escort them outside. Besides, we were now joined by a half-dozen Shore Patrolmen from the ships, led by the Shore Patrol Officer.

The fates of those involved were never known to us, but the next night the Blue Moon was back in business with all new furniture and a fresh supply of firewater. However, the scene was a bit more tranquil. The only bluejackets present were the destroyer sailors who, by virtue of having the most men standing at the end of the brawl, asserted their bragging rights and held full sway in the bar.

Three days later—5 May, 1941—I received my orders to join the Fleet. With several others of our recruit company, I was to report to Brooklyn Navy Yard for assignment to ship's company, U.S.S. NORTH CAROLINA (BB-55).

Our transportation was unique. We boarded the civilian Providence Night Boat for New York City, scheduled to arrive the next morning. Jimmy MacPherson and I shared one of the staterooms, but hit the sack only after cruising the vessel, unsuccessfully, in a search for unattached girls.

It took a while for us to get to sleep. We were speculating about our assignment to sea duty; and we were both excited, anticipating our first posting to a U.S. Navy ship o' the line!

3

THE SHOWBOAT

The U.S.S. NORTH CAROLINA (BB-55), dubbed "the Showboat" by the media, was the first battleship to be built by America in 17 years. There were limitations on her size and armament, imposed by the Washington Naval Treaty of 1922, limitations which kept her standard displacement at 35,000 tons.

Other factors controlling her width and the height of her super-structure, were practical considerations. She could not be so wide as to prevent her passage through the Panama Canal, nor could any mast be so high as to keep her from passing under the Brooklyn Bridge. Nearly as long as two and a half football fields, the NORTH CAROLINA measured just over 728 feet from stem to stern. Her beam was over 108 feet wide and she drew 35 feet of water. That is, that much of her hull was below the water line.

The main deck amidships was 20 feet above the water line, the Bridge 50 feet; and it was roughly 130 feet to the top of Sky Control. Heavy steel plate protected her vital parts: belt armor below the water-line was 12 inches thick; gun turret armor was up to 16 inches, as was the conning tower protection.

Her nine 16-inch/.45-caliber main battery rifles ("the big guns") could fire a 2,700-pound projectile over 36,900 yards (in excess of 21 miles). The twenty 5-inch/.38-caliber secondary dual purpose battery (for air and surface targets) could fire its 55-pound shells skyward 37,200 feet. Originally equipped with sixteen 1.1-inch AA (anti-aircraft) machinegun mounts, she would later replace these with sixty 40-milli-meters; and for close-in AA protection, she mounted forty 20-millimeter (mm) machineguns. For reconnaissance and target spotting, she had two OS2U "Kingfisher" single-float seaplanes which were launched from two catapults on her fantail.

Even with all this and a projected wartime complement of 2,339 men (144 officers and 2,195 enlisted men) she had a rated maximum speed of 28 knots (in excess of 33 miles per hour). The huge power plant that drove her four screws (propellers) could supply enough electricity for a fairly large city. For all practical purposes, the ship was a small town, with a post office, "gedunk stand" (soda fountain), restaurants (messes for officers, chiefs, and crew), a barber shop, and even a jail (the brig).

As our detail of recruits was marched from the Brooklyn Navy Yard's Sand Street Gate toward the piers, I looked up at the bow of the biggest ship I'd ever seen. On that graceful prow were the numerals "55." It was the NORTH CAROLINA, brand-spanking new, commissioned just three weeks before, and my new home. She had not yet had her sea trials, and "yard birds" (Navy Yard civilian workmen) were still putting the finishing touches on her. She was the newest, most powerful, and deadliest dreadnought in America's arsenal.

Passing the imposing bow, we proceeded toward the stern of the ship and the enlisted man's brow or gangway. We were almost dumbstruck by the overwhelming size of this 35,000-ton man o' war, with her guns bristling from every deck and superstructure level. Those 16-inch rifles, mounted three to a turret, were massive; and the twenty 5-inch .38s in twin mounts, five to a side, gave the ship the appearance of a porcupine in rage. The sixteen 1.1-inch mounts added more substance to that analogy. To use the word "impressive" to describe the NORTH CAROLINA, would be severely understating the awesome impression she made on us.

Ascending the brow, the bridge-like walk-way extending from the dock to the ship's main deck, we smartly saluted the Colors wafting in the East River breeze, saluted the Junior Officer of the Deck (J.O.D.) and stood in formation as the Quartermaster signed us in on the deck log. The J.O.D. then turned us over to a master-at-arms (shipboard equivalent of a police officer) who led us down a ladder to the starboard of Turret Three, through the mess deck where the midday mess was being prepared in highly polished, stainless steel cauldrons and on the galley ranges.

After navigating our way through several berthing spaces, we were temporarily assigned bunks near the 7th Division—the Marine detachment aboard. We stowed our gear in the aluminum lockers which left little room for extras. In a space about two and a half feet square by two and a half feet deep went all uniforms, underwear, shoes, toilet articles, and other personal items. Peacoats were put in separate lockers, and our seabags and hammocks were taken further below to storage.

The bunks were aluminum frames with heavy wire squares suspended by small springs to accommodate the mattress. Unlike the Army and the Marine Corps, we didn't have cots that had to be made up like a regular bed. Our bedding consisted of a mattress, mattress cover (just

U.S.S. NORTH CAROLINA (BB-55)
Still being fitted out as she looked when author reported aboard, 6 May, 1941.
(New York Herald Tribune - 1941 - Courtesy Albert Phillips)

a big, long pillow cover into which the mattress was slid), and a blanket. Two elastic belts with aluminum hooks held the bedding in place when the bunks were pushed up and secured against the bulkhead during working hours. Few, if any, enlisted men used pillows and there were no top sheets. We slept in our "skivvies", i.e. boxer-type shorts and T-shirts. While we usually referred to hammocks as "sacks", bunks became "racks" in our lexicon, although the terms were interchangeable.

Traditional aboard ship was the practice of familiarizing new crew members with the home in which they'd be living. For the next three days, groups of new crewmen were escorted on tours all the way from the shaft alleys near the keel to Sky Control atop the foremast. We explored engine and boiler rooms, gun mounts and turrets, ammo handling rooms, Combat Information Center, repair party stations, carpenter and machine shops, boat decks, the Bridge, the chain locker—every place aboard except "Officers' Country".

In the process we learned that ships have traffic patterns. When going forward, you travel on the starboard side; when going aft, you use the port passageways. We were taught how the transverse frames and the compartments are numbered and how the watertight integrity system works. We also learned what happened to those who committed very grave infractions of Navy Regulations. We saw the brig. It later would be called "Stryker's Hotel" after one of the Executive Officers we had.

Commander Stryker sent serious offenders to the brig—although he thought it was unjust for prisoners to sit around in cells, reading comic books, while their shipmates were doing all the work. Visiting the brig made a point that was well-taken. No one wanted to be incarcerated down there deep in the bowels of the ship.

Within a week, all new recruits were summoned to the mess decks where junior officers, seated behind mess tables, reviewed each sailor's records and assigned the duty station each would have aboard. There is no underestimating the importance and impact of these assignments. They determined the course of a man's career throughout his service in the United States Navy. Those assigned to deck divisions would be on track to become boatswain's mates; to ordnance divisions, gunner's mates or fire controlmen; to engineering divisions, machinist mates or watertenders, etc.

When it came my turn, the interviewing lieutenant scanned my record, noted I was a high school graduate with good grades, and then looked over the list of divisions needing seamen.

"Well, lad", he said, "I'm assigning you to the CR Division. Report to Chief Radioman Baldock in Radio Central."

The lieutenant's decision would have momentous consequences, determining my whole military and subsequent civilian career. "CR", I'd discover, stood for "Communications/Radio"; but I didn't even know where Radio Central was, and had no idea what a radioman did. Being enamored of guns, I was disappointed in not being posted to a gunnery division. But, being a lowly apprentice seaman, I was not about to argue with a full lieutenant.

The only possible reply was: "Aye, aye, Sir."

I scanned a cut-away diagram of the ship on the bulkhead and located Radio Central next to the Combat Information Center (CIC) four decks below the main deck, far down in her innards. Wending my way through compartments and down ladders, I had somewhat the same sensation that a miner has going down a shaft.

When I opened the watertight hatch with a small brass plate reading RADIO CENTRAL, I stepped into a whole new world, a new profession, and began training that would govern my entire service in the Navy. Chief Baldock looked at the piece of paper the lieutenant had given me on which he'd written my name and division assignment.

"You just became a radio striker, Hutch", he said. "I'll start you out on Lister's watch."

The Chief stepped to a bulletin board and wrote my name at the bottom of a list headed "Lister's Watch". I noted I was due on duty at 1200 (noon) and on the advice of another striker hurried up to the mess deck to get into the watchstanders' early chow line.

A "striker," in Navy parlance, is a non-rated enlisted man in shipboard training for a specific rating. This differentiates him from a "school graduate", a man who has attended one of the Navy's specialty schools and comes aboard with some of the skills needed in his rating. School grads had a tendency to lord it over strikers to whom they were senior, considering themselves superior. But this usually passed once a striker began moving up in rate and experience. It was not uncommon for men who'd begun as strikers to outdistance school grads in getting promotions.

Lister, my Radioman 3rd Class watch petty officer, asked if I knew how to type. Since I didn't, he sat me down at one of the radio positions where a typewriter was in a well. To the right of the well was a telegraph key for sending messages. Above the position was mounted a huge high powered receiver.

"This", he explained, "is a *mill,* and the first thing you've got to learn, Hutch, is how to type on it."

"Mill" is slang for a telegraphic typewriter. All its letters are in capitals. Most of the ones I used in the Navy were Royals or Underwoods.

Lister showed me the "home keys", gave me a Navy instruction booklet on *How to Type* and left me to my own devices. Aside from that bit of instruction, I am a self-taught touch-typist, but I never did learn to touch-type numerals. It was strictly hunt and-peck on those keys.

Until I learned to type and to send and receive Morse code, my watch duties would be confined to messenger duty, making coffee, and keeping the Radio Shack shipshape. So far, I thought to myself, so good. This looked like pretty good duty.

Much of the time the NORTH CAROLINA was in Brooklyn Navy Yard, the ship assumed the duties of SOPA (Senior Officer Present Afloat) which made us the communications guard for all ships in the Yard. Maintaining a watch on NSS FOX schedules (one-way transmissions from Washington) and on a Western Union telegraph land line, we had the responsibility not only to cover all incoming and outgoing messages for our own ship, but also for all others in the Yard, including foreign naval vessels.

As communications messenger, I delivered all official incoming messages to the addressees aboard ship. The uniform of the day was required, plus the duty belt—that webbed belt used throughout all the Armed Services, from which were hung canteens, side arms, first aid kits, etc. A white hat was mandatory on the weather decks. Unlike the other Services, in the Navy saluting is dispensed with when "uncovered" (i.e. when bareheaded). Hats are removed in enclosed spaces, so there is no saluting indoors or below decks. This is Navy custom because of the confined spaces.

The message forms all had routing spaces at the bottom, and each addressee was required to initial the *original* upon receipt of his copy. All official communications were routed first to the Captain. Other officers frequently were designated in the routing, requiring the messenger to have full knowledge of the various locations on board where any and all department heads might be found at any given time. Trips into "Officers' Country" were frequent. I garnered wide experience in dealing face to face with senior officers, and in learning every nook and cranny of the giant battlewagon.

Occasionally I would deliver dispatches to other ships in the Navy Yard, and got my first close-up look at a foreign warship when a message came in for a British cruiser being repaired after suffering torpedo damage. She was moored across the Yard from us, and we watched with some amazement as the crew executed the lowering of her colors one evening. It was all pomp and ceremony, somewhat like our own, except for one thing.

In the U.S. Navy, we Americans treat the Flag with respect and even reverence, never letting it touch the deck, and folding it in the tri-cornered manner for storage until the next morning. We were flabbergasted at the Limeys who lowered their colors from the staff and just let it lie on a pile of cordage on the deck until the next day. The detail carrying out the ceremony just stepped over the Union Jack as it lay, all sooty and dirty, and went on their way.

The next day, as I walked up to the Quarterdeck of the cruiser with the message board in my hand, I could not believe how filthy she was. After the spotless, well-scrubbed NORTH CAROLINA, this ship looked like one of New York's garbage scows. Gear was all over the place, the paintwork appeared not to have been washed down since the Battle of Jutland in World War I, and both officers and enlisted men were about as military looking as the crew of a South Seas tramp steamer.

The senior officer aboard was in the wardroom, and as I delivered the dispatch, he offered me a cup of tea. The cup he held in his hand originally had been white china, but was so black on the inside with stain and dregs, I politely declined. I was not about to drink from anything that vile!

When I brought up the subject of cleanliness to one of the enlisted men as I was ready to leave the cruiser, he just sniffed condescendingly and excused all the dirt, grime, and slovenliness with: "We've been fightin' a war, myte."

The cruiser had come in escorted by a corvette, a ship about the size of one of our old World War I destroyers, and which was moored to a pier opposite the starboard side of the NORTH CAROLINA, so we got a good look at her and her crew. The men would line up for liberty call in absolutely the dirtiest uniforms imaginable. They were in New York for months, yet I never saw any of them in really clean clothes. No American bluejacket would ever wear such uniforms even to the cleaning of the slop shute!

I got more insight into all this slovenliness when I had occasion to deliver dispatches to a barracks on Columbia Avenue where the British cruiser's crew was billeted while repairs proceeded on the ship. There was a U.S. Navy master-at-arms there to watch over the place. After I'd gotten signatures on the messages, he stopped me as I was leaving.

"Hey, Sparks, you wanta see something nutty?"

When I nodded, he took me into the officer's head. Posted on the bulkhead was a sign: "ALL OFFICERS WILL TAKE A BATH AT LEAST ONCE A WEEK TO SET A GOOD EXAMPLE FOR THE ENLISTED MEN"!

For lack of any other comparison I concluded from all this that the British had the filthiest navy in the world. After we got into the War, I never saw *any* U.S. Navy vessel that wasn't spic and span, even after long periods of combat steaming and battle action.

In between running messages, I practiced typing and spent innumerable hours learning International Morse code—sending and receiving on the practice oscillator, simulating a radio circuit—with boot camp buddy MacPherson, along with Campbell, Phillips, and other strikers. The very first set of letters we learned was NIBK, the NORTH CAROLINA'S international call sign.

Ability to send and copy code has nothing to do with a person's intelligence. Some very smart people could never get beyond a few words per minute while others, for no apparent reason, seemed to learn code and reach acceptable speed in a short time. Increasing speed doesn't come in regular increments. The first goal, after learning the meanings of the various combinations of the dots and dashes (which radiomen call "dits" and "dahs"), was to reach sending and receiving speeds of five words per minute (wpm); then, with constant drill, build up to ten words, and keep increasing until the operator could copy the FOX schedules at 18 wpm and become a qualified radio watchstander. It was mandatory for all U.S. Navy ships and stations to maintain a continuous watch on the FOX "skeds", the one-way communications from the theater command center.

It's strange that once an operator gets up to around ten or twelve wpm, it's common to run into a "block", where getting by that pace seems impossible. Then all at once, he may make a sudden jump to 15, 18, or 20 words. I never understood why it happened that way. Luckily, I was one of those to whom code came easily and I qualified early. It just seemed to come naturally.

All ships and stations have call letters assigned in accordance with international telecommunications treaties. The first letter of all U.S. Navy call signs is "N". Shore stations are identified by three letters: NSS, Washington; NPG, San Francisco; NPM, Pearl Harbor (Wahiawa); etc. Ships have four letters in their calls, as in the NORTH CAROLINA's NIBK. That translates in Morse code to "dah-dit/dit-dit/dah-dit-dit-dit/dah-dit-dah." However, when sent faster, with a rhythmic feel it sounds like "dah-dit/did-it/dah-di-di-dit/dah-di-dah."

Each CW (continuous wave) code operator has a different "fist", that is, a different way of combining the letters and rhythm as they are transmitted. This "fist" is as identifiable as a fingerprint. Good operators can immediately tell who is on the other end of a circuit just by the way a sender forms his letters and the cadence by which he sends, assuming they've worked together before. Identifying a fist is easier among "speed key" operators because they seem to be more individualistic.

There are two kinds of telegraph keys. Most familiar to civilians is the one with the knob on which each dot and dash is sent individually. We called it a "hand key". The speed key has a vertical paddle and a long arm which makes contact in such a way dots can be sent automatically and continuously. It's difficult to explain without demonstration, but suffice it to say a good speed key operator can transmit up to 70 words a minute. With a hand key, even the best operators can't do much better than half that.

Once I'd become proficient with a hand key at about 25 wpm, I ached to get a speed key, but wondered how well I could use one. Being lefthanded, I had learned to use the right-handed positions and surprised myself by being able to send equally well with either hand. Speed keys, as far as I could find out, were made only for righthand operation. But I was so determined to have one that I went ahead and got a shiny Vibroplex (trade name of a particular speed key) that became my pride and joy, learning to operate it with my right hand. I intended to become good enough to qualify for a "speed key ticket" (permit) to use it on U.S. Navy circuits.

One of the phenomena in learning Morse code is "hearing" code in one's head when there are no transmissions around. Somehow, the constant receiving sets up a mechanism in the brain, and I've had the experience of lying in my bunk and having the sounds of dots and dashes going through my head. Other sailors, aware of this, called us "dit happy", claiming all radiomen were a "little strange".

Eventually, I became a better than average radio operator. In retrospect, I view my proficiency with some mixed emotions. It got me into some pretty unusual and dangerous situations. But, overall, I still take pride in my reputation as one of the top operators in the Pacific Fleet when I was on Admiral Richmond Kelly Turner's Staff during the War.

One of the first designations a Navy radio operator gets when he becomes qualified is his "sine". The sine is two initials which a radioman puts on every message he copies. Mine was "JA" and, after over fifty years, I still use it today when I'm asked to initial any papers. Written, to make it distinctive, it's ringed with a circle: (JA•)

By far the *most* important duty of the messenger of the watch was the brewing of coffee—the life-blood of the Navy—known variously as "mud", "java", "joe", "jamoke", "diesel fuel" and doubtless several other names. In my Navy, coffee brewing and the drinking thereof was raised almost to a religious rite.

The United States Navy, at least during my years of service, was the world's largest consumer of coffee. As such, we got the pick of the very finest coffee beans from the South American plantations. Provided to ships in 100-pound bags, the beans were freshly ground and the coffee was usually made, particularly at sea, with water about as pure as you could get, evaporated from sea water.

When I was rotated from Lister's watch to Jackson's, I was challenged to make only *perfect* coffee. That "Radioman 3rd" was a connoisseur of the nectar of the brown bean. He had founded what he called "The Society of the Silver Certificate of the Golden Joe Pot", awarded only to those who brewed mud to his exacting standards. Upon passing his taste test, the sandy-haired Alabaman would award the deserving striker his typewritten document, embossed with the coffee cup ring from the bottom of his cup. It was a singular honor I really treasured. In the absence of any other known claimants, I believe I am the sole survivor of the Society.

On 29 May, 1941, I got another boost when I was promoted to Seaman 2nd Class. My pay went from 21 dollars a month to the princely sum of THIRTY-SIX BUCKS! What a day!

As time went by, we settled into the "peacetime Navy" routine. After I was assigned to the Radio Gang, I moved to the CR Division living compartment (A331-L) on the third deck for berthing. Below decks, a Navy combat vessel is divided into comparatively small spaces, each completely watertight. In the event of collision or combat damage, flooding is thereby kept isolated so the ship can remain afloat. The system, with sealed bulkheads and sealable hatches, is known as "watertight integrity".

Our particular compartment could house 33 men, and was not completely full when I joined the division. So I got "dibs" on a top bunk next to a fresh-air blower. Since there was no air-conditioning in the ship's berthing spaces, proximity to the blower supplied some relief in the summer and in the tropics. It also pumped warmed air in the winter.

The United States Navy has the cleanest ships of all the world's navies. Even though the NORTH CAROLINA was brand new, she was constantly kept spit-and-polish clean and shipshape. Bulkheads were scrubbed weekly (at least), decks swabbed and polished daily, and every bit of shiny metal was polished to dazzling brilliance. The hatch coamings, spit kits (ash trays), and aluminum lockers (my locker number was 552) could all be used as substitute mirrors.

Compartment cleaning was supervised by one of the 3rd class petty officers, assisted by the strikers, and the duty was rotated among all the junior men in the division. Each work day began at 0800 with the shrill of a boatswain's pipe over the speaker system and the order:

"Sweepers, man your brooms. Clean sweep down, fore and aft. Sweep all decks and ladders. Turn to! Turn to!"

Friday was designated "field day" when all spaces aboard were super cleaned in advance of Saturday's Captain's Inspection. Not only was the ship inspected, but the crew mustered at quarters for review by the Commanding Officer. Depending on the weather, the uniform was either dress blues or dress whites. We didn't have to change for liberty call which usually sounded immediately following inspection and "secure from quarters!"

The Navy's organization of a ship's crew insures that every man has a place to be and a job to do. Each division is divided into port and starboard watches. The watches are subdivided into first, second, third, and fourth sections. Each watch has a senior petty officer in charge, and each section has a leading petty officer. Watch assignments (duty stations) are usually assigned by the P.O.'s. To "have the watch", means a man is on duty at a work station or other assigned post.

In port in peacetime, only the minimum watches are stood, and the granting of liberty is generous. The Navy uses terminology different from the other Armed Services in defining time off. "Liberty" is time away from ship or station, usually from the end of the work day (1600) until a specified time the following morning (0730 in most instances). Three days off is a "72-hour liberty".

Despite Hollywood's versions of Navy life, there is no such term as "shore leave". It's redundant. Obviously, if a sailor is "on leave" he is ashore. The Navy grants 30 days paid leave a year, and it may be taken in less than 30-day increments. Leave-granting, particularly in wartime, is conditioned by the demands and necessities of the ship and its duties and missions in the Fleet.

The Navy uses the same terminology whether the assignment is aboard ship or on a shore station. Thus, the term "on the beach" is often misinterpreted by landlubbers. A sailor is "on the beach" any time he is not aboard a ship or station. He can, for instance, be in Times Square or in the Rocky Mountains, and he is still "on the beach". When he's on liberty from a shore installation, he is, in Navy parlance, "ashore" or "on the beach".

When a Navy man is late returning from liberty or leave, he is "over-leave". After more than 24 hours without reporting, he is "absent without leave" (AWOL). One of the most serious violations of Navy regulations is "missing ship", the failure to be aboard when the ship puts to sea. *Every man* in ship's company—regardless of rate, rank, or duty station—is considered vital to the ship's ability to fight and carry out her mission. The loss of any *one* man is tantamount to putting the ship, her crew, and her *raison d'être* in jeopardy; and, by extension, could be "the nail lost" that would contribute to the defeat of the Fleet in battle. "Missing ship" is cause for a General Court-Martial with extreme penal consequences. In the Navy, only desertion is a worse crime.

In port, all U.S. Navy vessels have good food, although it's routine to complain about it and characterize the ship's cooks and storekeepers as "belly robbers". Since crew members come from a wide assortment of backgrounds, the food is not like *any* Mom's; but overall, during my service, peacetime mess was pretty good. The food was not highly seasoned; the menus were good, solid basic chow with few or no frills. There were plentiful amounts of *fresh* fruits, vegetables, milk, meats, and baked goods. For most ships, particularly smaller vessels, this would change dramatically when the Fleet was deployed for long periods of time overseas, when a wartime supply line was as long as 8,000 miles.

The menu on the NORTH CAROLINA, as on all Navy ships, was highly predictable. Sunday dinner was always chicken; Saturday breakfast was baked beans and corn bread; Saturday dinner was baked ham. The chow we got for Tuesday was exactly the same menu every Tuesday. Food items got tagged with some interesting descriptive names: Catsup was called "red lead" (i.e. red paint). "Sea gull" was chicken; "moo" was milk. It was "worms" for spaghetti, "sand" for salt. "Spuds" (stored in the "spud locker") were potatoes; "cackleberries" were eggs; and "collision mats" were pancakes. There were some other Navy terms for certain foods that are unprintable.

This brings me to correct a longstanding misuse of the term for the ubiquitous "SOS" ("shit on a shingle"). The *real* SOS was NOT—repeat NOT—creamed chipped beef on toast. That had one of those unprintable names. Originally and properly, SOS is a mixture of ground beef and tomato sauce (somewhat like a Sloppy Joe). Also served on toast, it more aptly fits the description of "shit on a shingle" than creamed chipped beef. Both concoctions were regularly served in the Navy (and may still be). Creamed chipped beef, despite the unprintable and disgustingly descriptive name sailors gave it, is still one of my favorite dishes to this day.

Most civilians bristle at the thought of beans for breakfast, but we had 'em every Saturday morning for a good, practical reason. The galley always came in for an intensive "white glove" check during Captain's Inspection at 1000 on Saturday. The easiest meal to serve, requiring little clean-up effort, was baked beans, since only the big pans needed to be scoured. That, and a quick wipe of the ovens, and the galley was ready, all other cleaning having been done during the preceding night watch.

In port, with most of the crew on liberty, Saturday evening mess most often was lunchmeat sandwiches. Lunchmeat was another of those foods with an unprintable name. Along with fresh-baked bread, these cold cuts were also the staple of "night rations", food supplied the midwatch on duty from midnight 'til dawn.

The pre-commissioning crew, and those reporting aboard in the first couple of months after commissioning, were hand-picked to form a cadre of the most qualified men in the Navy, responsible for putting ship's company through rigorous training to make the NORTH CAROLINA a fighting unit. As the first of a new class of dreadnoughts, she was highly visible in the public eye and the Navy wanted no smudges on her escutcheon.

The CR Division was headed by Lieutenant Commander S.A. Shepherd. He and Chief Radio Electrician Byron Phillips were the top two electronics experts in the Navy at the time. They were backed up by two men of long experience, Chief Radiomen Baldock and Suggs. The Radio Gang was not yet at full complement when I was assigned. There were four of us strikers who formed sort of a "fearsome foursome", going on liberties and hanging out together aboard ship. Jimmy MacPherson, Al "Red" Campbell, Al "Phil" Phillips, and I (they all called me "Hutch") were almost inseparable.

In the Division were others I remember well and with whom I stood many watches. In addition to the "unholy four", among my shipmates were: the Ferrell brothers, Con and Virgil; Harry Haines, P.K. Hellis, Julius Hope, Shelby Mays, Bob McCollough, and Chuck Paty. Then there were: Lew Metz, Bob Yolen, Ed Cohen, the Warner brothers, and Paulus (some given names, after all these years, escape me). Among the rated radiomen with whom I stood watches were: Jackson, Bolter, Lister, Ochoa, Baker, Barone; along with "Armie" Armstrong, "Johnny" Johnston, Denzil Myers, and C.T.E. Meyers. Some of the Gang were assigned to the Transmitter Room (Radio Two), and I saw little of them, but did know "Ski" Koslowski pretty well. There were others, among them Mario Sivilli, Satrape, and Cooper, who came into the Gang later. All in all, the first Radio Gang of the Showboat was a good bunch of guys and good radiomen—the "Sparks" of the NORTH CAROLINA.

Perhaps more than any other ship in U.S. Naval history, the NORTH CAROLINA had a great deal of activity aboard that was not ordinary peacetime routine. For all practical purposes, the people of the city of New York had adopted this new battleship in their midst. In fact, Walter Winchell, who was both a newspaper columnist and one of the most influential broadcasters of the day, took the ship under his wing. Winchell was also a Lieutenant Commander in the Naval Reserve: "Mr.

and Mrs. America and all the ships at sea . . . ." Due to his interest in the Navy and his clout in the entertainment business, Winchell regularly escorted aboard major stars of stage, screen, and radio. We were treated to some excellent shows performed on the fantail, where some very popular radio broadcasts also originated, including Phil Spitalny and His All Girl Orchestra. When we steamed out of port for initial sea trials, the populace lined the East River banks to watch, and there were front page pictures in all the papers.

I'm not quite sure when the NORTH CAROLINA was first referred to as "the Showboat", but all this attention was not lost on the crew of our sister ship, the U.S.S. WASHINGTON (BB-56), under construction in Philadelphia. The first time our paths crossed, the WASHINGTON was anchored in the stream in Hampton Roads (Norfolk), Virginia. As we came steaming into port, the ship's band on the BB-56 struck up a rousing version of "Here Comes the Showboat" from Jerome Kern's musical production. The name stuck, and to this day our ship is still affectionately known throughout the Navy as "the Showboat".

The attention accorded the ship had a salutary affect on the crew, engendering a great deal of pride and contributing to an *esprit de corps* that bound officers and crew firmly together. The result produced an effective, well-trained, and devoted force of men who would perform admirably in the War to come.

4

LIFE, LIBERTY AND THE PURSUIT OF . . . GIRLS

The Radio Gang was a pretty close-knit group aboard ship, but we often went our separate ways on liberty. Because we were from different backgrounds—some city, some country, some more educated than others, some more urbane—we usually went ashore in twos or threes, according to mutual interests. Some of us often went solo, and I was one of those.

I had grown up in situations that contributed to a "loner" existence. When my family lived in Fort Lauderdale during the Depression, Mom and Dad both worked, and much of the time I saw them only on weekends. My sister Betty did look after me, but she was only a few years older than I. So I was left pretty much on my own in a neighborhood with few other boys, and I was the youngest of the bunch. Consequently, I learned to find my own amusements and became used to solitude. When I'd be shipped north to New Jersey during times when my parents had very little money, I lived on my grandparents' farm, the only child in the family.

All that moving around also put me in different schools so often that I had little opportunity to form long-lasting friendships. Being alone much of the time became a way of life. When my father and mother separated, I was about eleven or twelve years old. My sister was in nurse's training, my dad went back to Florida, my mom moved to Arizona (then California), and I was left at the farm—the only kid I knew whose parents were getting divorced. As a result, I had many acquaintances, but seldom got close enough to others to form real friendships. Being on my own had one salutary result: I also became a survivor, learning very early to take care of myself. I felt I was the only one on whom I could rely, so I asked little of others.

On my first liberties in New York, I went ashore with Jimmy MacPherson, Red Campbell, and Phil Phillips. We had little experience in being on our own in the Big City, and as four teenagers we felt more comfortable in company. We made the mandatory tourist excursions to Times Square, Central Park, and some of the other famous-name places. Most of these, we soon learned, were tourist traps. Jack Dempsey's bar and restaurant was typical. A rumor was started every day that Jack, the famed world champion boxer, the "Manassas Mauler" himself, would be in the joint. People would wait for hours, anxious to see him, meanwhile buying drink after drink. Jack never showed, at least during the times I was there.

Like most lads our age, we looked for girls, but those in the bars and bistros were hardly ideal for us. They fell into several categories, none of which fit the image of "the girl back home". If there was one common thread among them, it was that each had a sad tale to tell and needed one more drink. Some were "B" girls who got a split from the house off the drinks anyone bought for them. Others were "chippies" or "sea gulls" (similar to today's "groupies") who followed the Fleet from port to port. Others made little secret of their profession, the oldest in the world. For seventeen, eighteen, and nineteen year old sailors, most of these gals were a little too old, and certainly far too expensive, considering the tiny stipend the Navy paid us.

To find a real date, for a sailor in pre-War days, was a test of perseverance. Servicemen were not yet the heroes nor the boys from back home they would become in the public's eye once the War started. And "nice" girls were not likely to be pick-ups for the "low-lifes" sailors were portrayed to be. Besides, 36 dollars a month didn't supply much in the way of financial leverage to entice a girl to go out when she knew a "Coke date" was about all a "gob" (slang for an enlisted sailor in the U.S. Navy) could afford.

Some of my shipmates were more successful than others. Shelby Mays, a Seaman 1st striker, was known for an unusual technique. He claimed he propositioned *every* girl he met. When asked about the results, Shelby said, well, he got his face slapped a lot, but he also went to bed with a lot of women, too. Of course, this couldn't be proven. Shelby usually went ashore by himself. But by his own profession at least, he embodied the line in Gilbert and Sullivan's *H. M. S. Pinafore:* "Sailors should never be shy."

There was one incident on liberty for which I was completely unprepared. I must have been sixteen or seventeen before I was aware there was any such word as "homosexual"; and "queer", used in that context, had little meaning to me. The terms just did not enter conversation in the small communities where I grew up. It wasn't until I was aboard the NORTH CAROLINA that the words took on any significance. I learned there actually were men who preferred other men as sexual partners. Older petty officers warned of their presence in New York City, and cautioned that they preyed upon naïve young sailors. I gave little thought to the warning since I couldn't envision myself in a situation where such might happen.

MacPherson, another striker, and I had gone over to Manhattan to see a movie at the Paramount. Afterward we stopped in a small bar near Times Square we'd visited before without incident. We had some drinks and were getting ready to leave when I felt the call of nature and headed for the men's room. Shortly after I entered, a civilian came walking in. He was about 30 to 35 years old, looked like a stockbroker, well-dressed in a Brooks Brothers suit with all the trimmings. Now I wasn't drunk, but I was a little fuzzy around the edges, so I was fumbling a bit to refasten the thirteen buttons on my regulation Navy trousers.

Suddenly the man was beside me, saying "Here, let me help you with those." He reached over and stuck his hand down my pants and grabbed me. In a flash I was consumed with rage, reacting instantly and instinctively. Taking a couple of backward steps to put swinging distance between us, I then stepped forward, putting my full weight behind the hardest left hook I ever threw in my life. *"You queer son of a bitch!"* I yelled. My fist caught him full in the face and he went down like the proverbial felled ox. Two, maybe three, of his front teeth were knocked out, and his nose was decidedly to the port of the center line. Bleeding profusely, his face looked like a plate of spaghetti with extra sauce.

I was furious and considered kicking the hell out of him right there and then. Instead, I ran some cold water on my bruised and bloody knuckles, wrapping my hand in a towel from the wash stand. The guy was writhing and groaning on the deck, so I just stepped over him and headed to the door, all the time launching a stream of invectives at the queer bastard that turned the air blue as I stomped out. I felt *dirty,* violated, and shaken to think this could happen to me. My first acts on returning to the ship were to take a long, hot, shower; and scrub my dress blues, trying to wash away the filth I felt was there. Perhaps the sudden loss of any innocence I might have still harbored had something to do with it.

Certainly I could empathize with any woman who had been the target of attempted rape or unwanted sexual aggression. The degrading experience left an indelible mark. I can't stand homosexuals (I refuse to call them "gays") and loathe their very presence. Everyone I know who's experienced a similar incident harbors the same attitudes. This was certainly the case in the Navy. As Ted Mason recounts in *Battleship Sailor,* antipathy to homosexuals ran deep in all Navy rates and ranks.

"Homosexuality was considered a loathsome disease, a failure of masculinity and morality."

While approaches and attempted seductions by civilian homosexuals of sailors were not epidemic, neither were they uncommon. However, homosexuals among *Navy personnel*, at least in my experience, were rare. It would take exceptionally clever deception, subterfuge, and Oscar-caliber acting, especially in the Fleet, to hide homosexual tendencies, and even more to conceal overt acts. One would have to invent a heterosexual façade and maintain it through the long months of overseas deployment while confined in close quarters with men who knew most of the intimate secrets of their shipmates. Thus, the canard that "hundreds of thousands of homosexuals have served and died for their country", is certainly open to serious question.

I heard of only a few instances of homosexuality during my service—none on the NORTH CAROLINA—but with well over 2,000 men aboard it is possible there were cases. Later in the Solomon Islands, a rumor circulated that a senior petty officer on Admiral Turner's Staff had "turned queer", but I heard nothing to substantiate it. Hearsay had it the commanding officer of a combat ship in the South Pacific had an enlisted man as a lover—also unconfirmed. But late in the War, when I was serving on the destroyer IRWIN, a seaman was swiftly transferred when it became apparent he was homosexual. He was lucky to get off the ship in one piece. Any homosexual walking the weather decks on a dark night, then and now, could be courting disaster. He just might meet the fate sailors call "The Deep Six".

If I just wanted to go have a few drinks and carouse around, I'd go ashore with a group. But I had a fervent passion not shared by many others. One of my prime interests was listening to and dancing to the music of the Big Name Swing Bands. I'd played alto sax and clarinet in all the high school music organizations—marching band, dance band, orchestra—and had played professionally in a few bands before joining the Navy.

Benny Goodman was my hero; and I was an ardent fan of the likes of Artie Shaw, Glenn Miller, Count Basie, Tommy and Jimmy Dorsey, et al. New York was the mecca for the bands and a heaven-sent opportunity for me to see and hear them live and in person. I made all the ballrooms and theaters where they played: the Paramount, Frank Daley's Meadowbrook over in Jersey, the Glen Island Casino on Long Island, the Cafe Rouge, and even went up to some of the night spots in Harlem to hear Count Basie and Duke Ellington.

At first, I'd go without a date and dance with just about any unaccompanied girls who might be present. But good fortune finally smiled down upon me. At one of the shows Walter Winchell brought aboard, I spotted one of the civilian guests, a lovely girl around my age, standing back away from the rest of audience near the barbette (cylindrical base) of Turret Three. Summoning up my courage, I introduced myself and began chatting with her about the show, the ship, and any other subject that came to mind.

Her name was June, and she was as beautiful as the proverbial "Day in . . . ." Light brown hair, blue eyes, and a most ladylike manner that belied her youth. She was a very poised seventeen-year-old. She shared my enthusiasm for the Big Bands, and I asked if she'd like to go see Benny Goodman, then playing the Paramount. A big smile flashed across her face and she accepted.

"Here, Jack", she said, "I'll give you my phone number, just in case. But since I live on the Upper West Side, I'll meet you at the theater." Time and date were set, and I floated back down to Radio One to toast my good luck with a cup o'joe.

It was with June that I went to the Glen Island Casino, the Meadowbrook, and other ballrooms. Often, as a serviceman, I could get "Annie Oakleys" (free passes). There were several show business charities that, by 1941, had taken an interest in helping us enjoy entertainment at little or no cost. June knew, too, that my pay was small, and when I'd offer to buy something for her, she'd usually demur.

Yet, it was a wonderful relationship. Our times together were mostly quiet, except for the dancing. We'd go for walks, sometimes necking, other times just holding hands and talking. She didn't have to tell me there'd be no sleeping together. It was implicit in her manner, and I'd been raised to respect and accede to a lady's wishes. And June *was* a lady. It wasn't all completely platonic, for we cuddled and kissed on every date, but that was as far as it went.

Since a sailor's life ashore puts him into many and diverse situations involving the opposite sex, perhaps it's necessary to comment on the social morals and manners of the young people of my generation compared to the sexual mores and ethics of many of today's young folks.

It's an accepted cliché that the kids of today know more about sex than did their grandparents in *their* teens; that those days of yore were a period of innocence and naïveté. Don't you believe it!

In the first place, much of America was still rural, and no one living on a farm or owning pets could be ignorant of how females became pregnant and offspring were born. We watched foals, calves, and piglets being born. We knew the function of a boar, stallion, and bull in the reproductive process. We knew that human beings were conceived and birthed the same way—something, incidentally, not all today's young-sters know.

We knew how easy it was for a girl to become pregnant, and we also knew the consequences demanded by our society if she weren't married. The rule then was: "Get a girl in the family way (i.e. pregnant) and you marry her." *Period.* In other words, the father of the child had to accept *his* RESPONSIBILITY. There were a lot of guys who got close to "going all the way" but backed off at the thought of facing a girl's irate father with a "white shotgun".

On the girls' part, it's fairly safe to say that a majority felt they should save their virginity for their future husbands. At the same time, they were aware of society's condemnation and the stigma of being an unwed mother, parent to a bastard. Consequently, most girls were closely watched by their parents who wanted to know who the boys were, where they where going, and what time they'd be home. Few mothers would allow a daughter out after midnight, except on special occasions, and the boy was held responsible for getting her home on time.

This was *not* a case of parents mistrusting their children, but a recognition that youngsters in their teens are highly susceptible to temptation and peer pressure, and neither mature enough nor emotion-ally equipped to handle many situations, sex included. Many parents today allow their kids to "grow up too soon." If you think lax parents are correct in condoning the permissiveness in today's society, then look around at the number of unwed teen-age mothers and the overflow at abortion clinics.

Two other factors contributed to controlling "sexual experimenta-tion" among young people in the 1930s and '40s. One factor was the churches. Some 90 percent of Americans then professed to be Christians of some sort, and *every* Christian Church taught that premarital sex was a major SIN. It was brought home to children from early Sunday school, and it was most powerful deterrent to young people taught to respect the teachings of Christianity and the professed morals of their elders.

Another factor was the danger of sexually transmitted diseases. We were fully cognizant of the consequences of contracting venereal dis-eases; and while AIDS was unknown, the rest of them were around. The medical community, back then, did not have penicillin and other miracle drugs to treat these diseases, and thus they were serious afflictions. The Navy's regulations were quite severe in punishing those who came down with any sexually transmitted ailment. For example, some sailors were court-martialed and dismissed from the service for contracting syphilis.

No one is so gullible as to think that the '30s and '40s were so pure that pre-marital, extra-marital, or promiscuous sex were unknown. But our society—through its ethics, parental restrictions, and church teachings—put some very effective brakes on it.

Nor does anyone believe that many young men, freed from parental supervision and away from home where they were unknown, shied away from efforts to seduce girls they dated. Some also patronized houses of prostitution. Most, however, considered these sexual excursions to be "flings", and still looked for "*the* girl" they could take home to Mom. There was the hope, too, that "*the* girl" would be "as pure as driven snow".

Sailors knew where to look for sex if they wanted a one-night stand. It was as near, in most cases, as the closest bar. But faced with a "nice girl", or "the girl I left behind" type, the years of parental and religious training most often would take over.

Nevertheless, morals slipped quite a bit after the War started. The "this is my last night ashore" argument often won out over common sense and moral teaching. This may have signaled the beginning of the decline in moral values for which we are now paying the piper.

Back to Brooklyn in 1941.

Then there was Peg. I met her when a buddy of mine, an airman in a PBY patrol squadron at Brooklyn's Floyd Bennett Field, invited me to go on liberty with him. Peg came with Jim Stoner's girl friend, and the four of us went to a neighborhood spot where young folks hung out. There was a dance floor, a juke box, a soda fountain, and they served hamburgers and sandwiches. Pretty nice place, with booths, dim lights, and the inevitable crystal-mirrored ball spinning over the dance floor.

Peg was a pert, sassy, sometimes irreverent bundle of energy, quick with quips and needing no excuse to laugh at life. Almost-black hair, hazel eyes, and a great figure, she was one of the best dancers I ever knew. There was instant and mutual admiration. She started off needling me about "bell-bottom trousers, coats of Navy blue".

This old sailor song became a popular hit during World War II:

> *Bell-bottom trousers, coats of Navy blue.*
> *She loved a sailor, and he loved her too!*

The popular song cleaned up the lyrics of the seasoned sailor's song sung by old salts:

> Once there was a barmaid, down in Drury Lane,
> Her master was so kind to her, her mistress was the same.
> Along came a sailor, happy as could be,
> And that was the cause of all her misery.
> *Bell-bottom trousers, coats of navy blue,*
> *He'll climb the rigging like his daddy used to do.*

He asked her for a candle to light his way to bed,
He asked her for a pillow to put beneath his head;
And she, like a silly girl, thinking it no harm,
Climbed into the sailor's bed to keep the sailor warm.
Bell-bottom trousers, coats of navy blue,
He'll climb the rigging like his daddy used to do.

If you have a daughter, bounce her on your knee,
But if you have a son send the bastard out to sea.
Singing bell-bottom trousers, coats of navy blue,
He'll climb the rigging like his daddy used to do!

In personality and demeanor, Peg was 180 degrees from June. The only common thread was that both had "Class" with a capital "C". In looking back I've often wondered why I was so evenly attracted to two such widely different girls. It's still a mystery to me.

"Come on, Sailor", Peg urged. "Let's see if you can dance on this deck as easily as you can swab it!"

We spent the entire evening on the dance floor. Since she loved dancing so much, I broached the subject about going to one of the big-name ballrooms. But she scotched the idea.

"Too stuffy, too formal, and too crowded", she said. No amount of cajoling would persuade her differently. So, all of our dates were basically Coke dates, dancing to band music from Wurlitzer juke boxes, munching hamburgers, and exchanging spirited repartee.

Dating Peg was both economical and convenient. Cokes were a nickel, hamburgers a dime, and the juke box was only five cents a play. To see her, I needed only to go out Brooklyn's Flatbush Avenue, not very far from the Navy Yard. But those were not the reasons I dated her. We were physically attracted to each other; and we had compatible interests in music, dancing, and conversation.

At the end of our first date, I walked Peg home and kissed her "goodnight" on her front step. On our second date, she sent me much the same message as had June, only she wasn't quite so subtle about it. I was taking her home after dancing all evening when she stopped in the middle of the sidewalk on the tree-canopied street, threw her arms around my neck and really planted one on me—a kiss that left me gasping for air.

"That", she said firmly, "is as far as we go. We can have fun, dance, laugh, talk, kiss and cuddle in a corner *but no further.* Agreed?"

I nodded affirmatively without hesitation. I wasn't going to spoil this relationship with a girl as wonderful as Peg. I was seeing her more often than I was June principally because Peg was almost always available and nearby. But, if put to the test, I could not have made a choice if compelled to give up one or the other.

June called me one day to ask if I'd escort her to a function at the Waldorf-Astoria Hotel. Of all the elegant hotels in the world, the Waldorf was the ultimate. It was the place where royalty, diplomats, movie stars, and other notables stayed while in New York, and epitomized luxury and class.

"It's a formal occasion", June advised.

"But I don't have any civvies at all, Honey, let alone a tux."

"Your dress blues are formal, Jack", she said. "Besides, others will be there in uniform, too. Just be in the lobby at eight o'clock Saturday evening."

Resplendent in my brand-new tailor-made blues, I met June by the elevators and we soared up to the Starlight Roof. As we walked over to the party, I was dumbfounded! I'd never seen so many Navy brass in one place in my life. And I was the only bluejacket in sight!

June could barely hide her amusement at my consternation. With her hand on my arm, she guided me over to a striking man with the four gold stripes of a Navy Captain on his sleeves. Beside him was a beautiful woman who, there was no doubt, was June's mother.

I'm not sure how I got through the introductions, but the Captain shook my hand firmly and warmly, and June's mother kissed me lightly on the cheek. I felt my ears getting red and about all I could do was mumble something about being so pleased to meet June's parents.

Here was a lowly seaman amid some of the biggest gold braid in the Navy. Fortunately, and thankfully, June and her father and mother made me feel most welcome, and the discomfort I was experiencing began to fade. It was a wonderful evening, thanks to some of the most gracious and understanding people I ever met.

A few days later, I got a call at the ship from June.

"What's the matter, honey?" I asked. "You sound like the world's coming to an end."

"Daddy's been reassigned", she answered tearfully. "He goes tomorrow on a hurry-up trip to Hawaii, and Mother and I are going home to Virginia until he can get us transportation to Honolulu. Jack, we're leaving right away."

"I have the duty today, dear, but I'll see if I can get a standby."

"There's no time, darling. We're packing right now and we'll leave as soon as it's finished. I'll write to let you know where we'll be. I love you."

It was the first time she'd used those "three little words". Before I could reply, she'd hung up the phone. We exchanged letters for several months, but I was spending so much time at sea our correspondence diminished. When the NORTH CAROLINA reached Pearl Harbor the following summer, I learned June and her mother had been evacuated back to the States just after the Japanese attack. With war activity at its height, I lost track of June after that.

Peg and I continued to date as long as the ship was operating out of New York. But when the War broke out, we both knew our times together were coming to an end, at least for a long time. Our last date before I left Brooklyn for the final time was spent just sitting and holding on to each other. We were fully aware that we probably would never meet again. We wrote to each other for a while, then the correspondence ended.

In October, 1943, a few weeks before I left the Solomons, after almost fifteen months in and around those infamous islands, to return to the States, I got a note from Jim Stoner. Peg was engaged to be married.

5

THE BATTLESHIP NAVY

A new sense of anticipation began to spread throughout the NORTH CAROLINA. We were getting closer to the date when we'd take her to sea for the first time, and an undercurrent of excitement was beginning to build among the officers and the crew. We were proud to be part of the "Battleship Navy".

The sea trials were doubly important. Not only would we be testing our ship, but we were aware that any deficiencies found in the NORTH CAROLINA, as the prototype of a whole new class of battleships, would also have to be corrected in our sister ships. We hoped for their sake, as well as our own, that "the Showboat" would come through with flying colors.

With the acceleration of the wars both in Europe and in Asia, we knew we would need to be combat ready, despite President Roosevelt's vow that "no American boys will fight on foreign soil." Some edge had been taken off that promise when the President, in a directive on 8 January, 1941, ordered that all United States warship crews be "gradually" brought up to full strength. Up to that time, most combat vessels were operating below complement, with crews still at peacetime levels.

The NORTH CAROLINA's crew was not yet up to combat strength, but then we were still in the process of fitting out and testing and were not ready to join the Fleet. Even though the 1,600 officers and men who were among the pre-commissioning crew had been hand-picked, and many of those non-rated men who were assigned to the ship later were the cream of the crop from training stations and service schools, not every man was a paragon of *"The Compleat Sailor"*. We had a couple of guys in the Radio Gang for a short while who failed to measure up.

One of the two was a seaman who'd been transferred off a four-piper destroyer on North Atlantic Patrol because he constantly succumbed to seasickness. It was the Navy's profound wisdom that he only needed to be on a larger ship that didn't pitch and roll like a cork. All was well with him as long as the ship was tied up at the fitting-out pier in the Navy Yard. Then, one morning, the engineering department lit off the boilers for dockside tests. We weren't going to get under way, just sit there still as a statue. The poor seaman felt the throb of the power plant and immediately became sick as a dog. Two days later, he was transferred to shore duty, diagnosed as having chronic seasickness.

The other seaman assigned to us as a striker stayed in the Gang a shorter time. He just didn't have the mental capacity to learn code or typing. Someone should have known up front. He was a "hash-mark Seaman 1st". That is, he had over four years in the Navy and had yet to make 3rd class petty officer. We soon discovered he'd come to us from another battleship, the U.S.S. CALIFORNIA (BB-44). This guy had spent his entire four year cruise assigned exclusively to the "spud locker" (peeling potatoes) on the "Prune Barge"! That's about as far down the Navy's totem pole as you can get, short of the garbage detail.

Speaking of the U.S.S. CALIFORNIA, for an excellent introduction to the Battleship Navy and its unique mystique, I recommend "Theodore C. Mason's *Battleship Sailor*" (1982) based on his experiences in 1940 and 1941 aboard the "Prune Barge". With the biggest ships and biggest guns, the Battleship Navy believed it was impervious, unsinkable, the heart and soul of the U.S. Navy. Replete with pride, battlewagon sailors looked down on other branches of the Fleet, for example aircraft carriers that were hardly fighting ships. Battleship sailors were smarter, tougher, and more disciplined than the others, in particular rival carrier sailors known derogatively as the "Brown Shoe Navy".

Mason's memoir of the showy Battleship Navy and its often insufferable officers, of spit-and-polish battleship sailors, "proud and profane professionals" as he calls them—is especially enlightening for the reader of these chronicles since he too was a radioman. Ted points out that in the Battleship Navy the CR Division included the elite of enlisted men. In many respects, radiomen lived apart from the rest of the crew in a world of their own; they had special privileges and were envied by other battlewagon sailors. His book helps re-create "the radioman's world-within-a-world."

As a kid living in Fort Lauderdale, I'd gone to sea on the fishing boats which supplied my dad's markets with sea food, and had been aboard Coast Guard cutters when the "Hooligan Navy" had open house, allowing civilians to take a short cruise on the cutters. I was one of only a few strikers in the Radio Gang who'd ever been out on blue water. The upcoming sea trials would be a brand-new experience for most of the non-rated men.

The first time we put to sea, I was standing back aft on the fantail, as the ship rose and fell gently on the smooth waters, when another striker, Julius Hope, came up to me. We both stood looking out across

U.S.S. NORTH CAROLINA (BB-55)
Identification Photo.
(OUR NAVY Magazine)

the ocean for a moment, then Hope—a lanky Tennessean who'd never seen anything much bigger than a stock pond in his life—took off and walked completely around the ship. When he returned, with eyes a little wide, he turned to me.

"Ya know, Hutch", he said incredulously, "there ain't a gawddam tree out there—NOWHERE!"

Centuries before, the Roman poet Virgil had put it more subtly, or at least more matter-of-factly, in the *Aeneid*: "on all sides nothing but sky and sea."

Perhaps the lines of John Keats, on the unique appeal of the sea, are apropos to the world-weary youth of each generation:

> O ye! who have your eyeballs vexed and tired,
> Feast them upon the wideness of the Sea;
> O ye! whose ears are dinn'd with uproar rude,
> Or fed too much with cloying melody . . . .

When Captain Olaf M. Hustvedt, our Skipper, determined the NORTH CAROLINA was ready for her maiden sea trial, all preparations were made for getting underway. It was an historical moment for all aboard. With the help of yard tugs, the mighty vessel was backed down from alongside her pier and nudged out into "the stream" of New York's East River. Then her bow was pointed southward, the tugs pulled away, and we proceeded out of New York Harbor under our own power.

As we sailed past the tip of Manhattan, Governor's Island, and the Statue of Liberty, we could see hundreds, if not thousands, of New Yorkers lining the shore to view America's newest addition to their Navy. Within a comparatively short time, the bow was slowly rising and falling, signaling that we were riding the ground swells and entering salt water—the Atlantic Ocean. This time there would be no high-speed runs nor any firing of our ordnance. That would come later. This trip was sort of like a ride around the block in a new car.

The first thing we saw when we got back into port was our picture on the front page of nearly every New York newspaper. The city had really taken us to heart, and its now famous Showboat was the center of everyone's attention. We continued to make short sorties to sea to work out any bugs before embarking on the much longer and intensive "shakedown cruise". Then we'd test out *every* facet of the ship's construction—gunnery, engineering, superstructure, navigation, communications, etc.

To Americans of all walks of life, the battleship was a striking symbol. "To the citizens, the battleship was a symbol of the nation's power, bringing them a thrill of patriotism. So long as those great . . .

ships of the line were out there, they knew that the nation's continued freedom was ensured" (Mason).

Around the joe pot in the forward section of Radio Central, the conversation usually centered on girls, liberty, girls, drinking, girls, and what's for chow. But as these subjects were exhausted, the talk became more serious. The topic: War!

From shortly after I came aboard, I was aware that all the older hands *knew* for a fact we would have to fight the Japanese—sooner or later.

Some old salts were probably aware of the testimony before the Senate Naval Affairs Committee a year earlier. On 22 April, 1940, Rear Admiral Joseph Taussig told the Senators war between Japan and the United States was inevitable. The former Assistant Chief of Naval Operations said flatly that Japan would foment a crisis in the Pacific as a prelude to a program of conquest. It would involve the Philippines, Dutch East Indies, French Indochina, and other countries in the region. The Admiral also informed the Committee that Japanese plans for conquest and expansion had been submitted to Emperor Hirohito in July, 1927, less than a year after he had ascended the throne.

According to David Bergamini's mammoth book *Japan's Imperial Conspiracy* (1971), from 1927 on the Emperor knew and approved the Japanese Government's plans to dominate East Asia and the Western Pacific, which the Japs realized would lead eventually and inevitably to war with the United States and probably other Western Powers. Thus Emperor Hirohito and the Sons of Nippon were obviously willing to risk a world war; they apparently had no moral scruples about rapacious wars of conquest, their only reservations being realistic fears that they could or would eventually lose in a war with the West.

In July of 1927, ambitious Japanese plans for expansion in East Asia were presented to the Emperor by his Prime Minister, retired General Gi-ichi Tanaka. Afterward, Chinese intelligence agents tried to reconstruct Tanaka's report to Hirohito; and later in the 1930's published their Chinese version, for anti-Japanese propaganda purposes, as the *Tanaka Memorial*—an imposing forgery with some basis in fact, which was widely circulated in the West and became one of the most infamous documents in Japanese history.

According to the *Tanaka Memorial*, apparently known to Admiral Taussig, the Japs believed that it was their destiny to conquer the world. The first step was to occupy Manchuria. Then, they were to subjugate China. Next, the Japanese were to "crush the United States", then subjugate all of Asia—all this with a view to controlling the economic resources of Asia and North America "in order to conquer the world."

As outlandish as all this may seem today, there were at least some officers in the Japanese military who apparently thought it feasible. In preparation for the execution of the campaign, spies and agents were dispatched from Japan to Hawaii and California to report regularly back to Tokyo on all military and naval installations, troop and ship movements, and to collect other strategic information. Whether the Japanese High Command believed such a scenario was possible, is a moot point. But Japanese expansion in East Asia certainly followed the initial phases outlined in the *Tanaka Memorial*.

Conventional history proclaims that World War II began with Hitler's invasion of Poland in 1939, completely overlooking the *real* beginning: Japan's conquest of Manchuria in 1931, eight years earlier. This was the Japanese Empire's second foothold on the Asian mainland. The Treaty of Portsmouth, following the Russo-Japanese War, gave Japan control over Korea, which it annexed in 1910, literally enslaving the entire population of the peninsular nation.

Then, in 1937, Japan began a systematic war to gain control of the richest parts of China, including all Chinese ports. In the process the Japanese 6th Route Army slaughtered an estimated 300,000 Chinese civilians in the Rape of Nanking, and devastated city after city. One of the most strikingly horrible pictures of that phase of World War II was a widely circulated photograph of a tiny baby, alone between railroad tracks amid the rubble of the Shanghai train station, screaming in terror after a Jap air raid against the defenseless city. Any Chinese who even showed the slightest resistance was shot or beheaded on the spot by Japanese soldiers given license to execute anyone "suspect".

American newspapers and radio carried news of the Japanese expansion in Asia. But among most Americans, at least on the East Coast, it was Germany's conquest of Europe that got the most attention. After all, China was halfway 'round the world. Europe, ancestral home to most Americans, was just a short hop across the (Atlantic) pond. New York, with its concentration of Jews, was particularly sensitive to Hitler's *Blitzkrieg* and his persecution of Jews. Americans generally gave only passing notice, if any, to the signals coming from the other side of the International Date Line.

Besides, weren't the Japs little bandy-legged people, more like monkeys than men, who couldn't see without their coke-bottle-bottom glasses? Why, we'd wipe 'em out in two weeks if they messed with the good ol' U.S.A. The notion that these servile copycats could challenge us was ridiculous. "To say that we underrated the Japanese as potential adversaries would be an understatement" (Mason).

But American sailors who'd witnessed the Nipponese armies from their vantage points aboard ships of our Asiatic Fleet were not convinced the Japs would be a pushover. They knew the evidence pointed to a tough fight in the future. Yet, despite all the evidence and warnings, such as Admiral Taussig's testimony, Washington seemed to take little or no precaution against a possible attack by Japanese forces. Nor, apparently, was there much concern about Japanese spy networks in Hawaii and California.

It was not that America was completely ignoring "the winds of war". The draft had been instituted, Reserve and National Guard units had been mobilized, all in the name of national *defense*. The Navy, which had only some 215,000 men when I joined, would add another 168,000 by 7 December, 1941 (the number would reach over 3,400,000 by War's end). But these men would have to be trained, ships built for them to man, and a logistical system established to supply them.

Any early initiation of hostilities by Japan would see us up against formidable odds. Tokyo had blatantly breached the post-World War I Washington Naval Treaty even before the ink was dry, and had built a navy second to none in the world. Moreover, Japan's highly trained and motivated armies had been fighting, without a defeat, on the Asian mainland for most of ten years.

A short time after our first sea trial, we began guarding an additional frequency in the Radio Shack. Added to the mandatory NSS FOX schedules from Washington was the International Distress Frequency—500 kilocycles. The monitoring of the circuit was purely for informational reasons, since the NORTH CAROLINA was in port a great deal and could not respond to any ships in distress. Yet we kept copying signals from merchant vessels that were calling for assistance.

By international agreement all such requests were to begin with "SOS". But now, the merchant marine radio operators had adopted a new and more menacing-sounding signal—"SSS", i.e. SUBMARINE ATTACK! As the summer of 1941 wore on, the number of these distress calls became more and more frequent. German U-boats were taking a terrible toll on merchant shipping the full length of the Atlantic seaboard. Some ships went down a-flaming within sight of the Jersey shore. We know, now, that at least one German sub penetrated New York harbor and took pictures of the skyline.

Officially we were not at war with the Germans, yet there was some Navy reaction to the submarine menace. I went out to Floyd Bennett Field one Saturday to meet Jim Stoner. We were going on liberty together. As I arrived, Captain's Inspection of the air base and its PBY squadrons was underway by a visiting senior officer. It was not a very well kept secret that the PBYs were dropping bombs on any German submarines they spotted while on patrol. Some of the crews of the flying boats brazenly bragged of their successes by painting Nazi flags on their hulls. When the inspecting officer spotted them, he flew into a rage.

"Paint those gawddam things off of there!" he screamed. "You want to start an international incident? We're not at war!"

Cans of paint and brushes were rushed to the scene and the swastikas were hastily blanked out.

Going to sea began several changes in personal and shipboard routine. Progress toward becoming a qualified watchstander meant different assignments for me, and for the other strikers and school graduates who'd not yet earned their "crows". The term "crow" applies to an enlisted man's rating badge, first awarded when he makes petty officer 3rd class. The colloquial reference in U.S. Navy vernacular is to the eagle at the top of the insignia.

I was now standing regular watches on the FOX skeds, and had started studying a CREI correspondence course in radio materiel. My battle station assignment was changed from Radio Three (Emergency Radio) to Radio Central, and I was intensifying my code practice to build more speed in both sending and receiving. Sending is easier than receiving because the operator knows what he's going to say, but he doesn't know what the guy on the other end of the circuit is going to send.

There were a couple of benefits I gained in operating technique during this period. When I'd spend part of a watch monitoring the distress frequency, I first had difficulty copying the merchant ship operators. They sent code in an unusual rhythm pattern we dubbed "banana boat swing". It was not the precise cadence of Navy "fist" or machine-generated transmissions. Rather it slurred the characters together and accented the "dahs" and "dits" in a different manner. Once I got the "feel" of it, however, I not only became rather adept at copying it, but also got very good at sending it.

At the same time, we had a telegraph link from ship to shore when in port. This circuit used a different code—Continental Morse, sometimes called "landline" Morse—which Western Union and railroad telegraphers used. There was not the electronic sound of radio transmissions but the "clickety-clack" of the "brass pounders" key, and the dot-dash combinations for many letters were different from International Morse code. A year or so later, my proficiency in "banana boat swing" and "landline" Morse would pay some handsome dividends in serving to confuse and frustrate an enemy determined to disrupt our communications.

Another objective I had was to be promoted to Seaman 1st Class

(S1c). For that, I had to pass the same tests as any other aspirant aboard. Although my radio responsibilities did not require deck seamanship as such, I would have to demonstrate proficiency in the rudimentary skills traditionally required of all professional sailors. To prepare, I not only studied the Seaman's requirements but also studied the handbooks for both 3rd Class Quartermaster and Signalman. These skills also would come in handy later.

In early June, 1941, I applied for a 72-hour liberty so I could spend a couple of days back home. In order to get more than just overnight liberty, it was necessary to come up with a believable reason for the extended time. I said my grandmother was ill and I wanted to see her, which was only stretching the truth a little bit. Gran was always complaining about some ailment or other.

As I arrived at the farm, Uncle Bert was standing at the head of the lane, between the two weeping willows on either side, looking very grim.

"Your grandfather died last night", he said, trying to subdue the emotion he felt about the loss of his older brother, with whom he had lived since the age of sixteen.

Grandpop George Hutchinson was one of my most favorite people, and his death of a heart attack at age 70 was a shock. He was the first of my close relatives to die. More would follow. It was my first close encounter with death. Before long, there would be many more.

I immediately applied for a two-day extension to my 72-hour liberty so I could attend the funeral. Before I got approval from the ship, a Red Cross Gray Lady came by, checking to see if I were telling the truth. After all, I had applied because my grand*mother* was ill and now wanted an extension because my grand*father* had died.

Unfortunately, the Gray Lady arrived at the most hectic time and was met at the door by my grandmother. As soon as she found out the Red Cross had been sent to validate the reason for the extension, Gran hopped all over the poor Gray Lady: first, for intruding on the family in its moment of grief; and secondly, for doubting my word. I hadn't told Gran my original request claimed *she* was ill.

The Gray Lady apologized profusely before beating a hasty retreat. But I caught up with her at her car and did some apologizing of my own. Gran, however, never forgot the incident and, despite a later explanation from me, fumed about it for years.

After my grandfather's funeral, I immediately returned to the NORTH CAROLINA. More sea trials and the shakedown cruise were in the offing.

It was good to get back to the ship—I seemed to belong there. More and more the ship seemed home, shipmates and friends seemed family.

Many enlisted men, as true in my case, came from broken homes. For us, the Navy and our *shipmates*, which included all enlisted personnel, gradually became our extended family; our immediate family consisted of close shipmates with whom we experienced a real and remarkable camaraderie.

Before the War the Navy was small and selective, and it was no foregone conclusion that one would make it into or in the service. Many were rejected, initially or somewhere along the line. For poor sons of the Depression, the Navy offered the opportunity for steady employment, to be accepted and gain some respect, to wear nice clothes that matched for a change.

There subsisted among bluejackets a certain ethos according to which the respect of one's shipmates was paramount. This ethical code, however, did not always apply to civilians or to officers. For example, lying to officers, to protect oneself or one's shipmates, could be considered perfectly proper. But lying to, or stealing from, shipmates—this was anathema.

"What the enlisted men had in fact evolved (and many former navy officers may be wholly unaware of it) was a code of conduct, a rough-and-ready approximation of the honor code of the military academies: I will not lie, cheat or steal; and I will not tolerate anyone who does. Though seldom discussed and never, so far as I know, reduced to written form, the code was operative, its existence proved by the remarkably few violations" (Ted Mason).

The bluejackets' unwritten code of honor held sway among us in a powerful way. I'm convinced it was stronger than that existing among officers. Anyone caught stealing from a shipmate, the most mortal of sins, was dead in the water. If the offender didn't get a court-martial, he was ostracized on the ship, and his life wasn't worth much ashore. I could leave my locker unlocked, or money openly lying on my bunk, and never have to worry about it.

Helping a *shipmate* (the word still produces profound emotions after all these years) in any way—this was the highest virtue. We supported and protected each other, aboard and ashore, when hassled by overbearing ("chickenshit") officers or by civilians. Whenever a shipmate got in trouble, or in a fight, we always came to his aid. The bond among bluejackets was very strong—there's no way to put it into words—especially among those serving in the same shipboard division. The longer we were together, the more common our experiences, the tighter the bond became.

As the Showboat became more operational, there was less need to go into the Navy Yard each time we returned to port. We began anchoring out in Gravesend Bay off Brooklyn's Bay Ridge section. The crew wasn't too happy about this. It meant "commuting" from ship to shore via motor launches, and a long subway ride back to familiar haunts. From an almost "free gangway" condition for liberty, we were now standing the standard port and starboard watch schedule, cutting down our time ashore. I was seeing Peg only sporadically now.

With less liberty, the Radio Gang spent more time in the bull sessions; or finding other amusement aboard ship, e.g. movies, card games, acey-deucy (similar to backgammon); or in the case of MacPherson, concocting practical jokes.

Red Campbell was regarded among us as second only to Shelby Mays in successfully pursuing women. Red took great pride in his prowess. One morning, he was sleeping in from the midwatch when Jimmy came into the compartment. Spotting Red flaked out in his bunk with his hand on his crotch, Mac got that impish grin on his face and headed for his locker. Returning with a can of shaving cream, he turned Red's hand over and filled it with a huge glob of cream, then turned the hand back to its original position. He and the rest of us stood around to await Red's awakening. As he slowly opened his eyes, Red sensed something was askew. When he felt the foam, he quickly raised his hand, staring at it in abject horror.

"My Gawd! What have I DONE!" he yowled. The whole compartment rocked with guffaws. It was a sheepish Campbell who suddenly realized he'd been the victim of a prank by one of his best buddies.

Phil Phillips suffered from "spick itch" (athlete's foot) more than the rest of us for some reason or other. Medication from Sick Bay seemed to help little, and Phil sought relief by lying in his bunk, spreading his toes wide, and rubbing them up and down on the chains supporting the bunk. The spick itch bothered him so much he finally included it in his fantasy of a Sailor's Paradise. Phil envisioned a tropic isle, replete with a bevy of beautiful wahines, those sensual Polynesian young ladies, to cater to his slightest whim. The picture included sun to warm his back, plenty of salt water in which to soak his toes, *and* his trusty bunk chains on which to scratch 'em!

As the summer of '41 began to wane, the ship prepared for one of our most important tests. We put to sea on 28 August and headed for a position off the coast of Maine. The exercise would take place at night to thwart observation by any German submarines, and far enough at sea to be out of sight of any alien agents. We were going to test our gunnery and do it in a spectacular way.

The test called for firing all nine 16-inch rifles and ten of our 5-inch .38s SIMULTANEOUSLY! A successful firing, without causing structural damage, would mean all the vessels of this new line of battleships would be able to withstand firing such a broadside if needed in combat. Unsuccessful—it would mean back to the drawing board. The firing was set for the moonless night of 29 August, 1941.

On a battleship "buttoned up" at General Quarters, only a handful of men actually see what's going on. My battle station was now in the Radio Director Finder Shack, topside, and from there I was determined to watch this once in a lifetime event.

The principal communications space aboard every ship is most often referred to as the "Radio Shack". The term goes back to the earliest days when radio was hailed as a tremendous innovation in maritime communications. Ships all over the world rushed to have equipment installed which would give them the ability to communicate with shore stations and other ships. Its lifesaving potential, alone, made it invaluable.

The limited space aboard most ships made installation of the then big, cumbersome radio gear a problem. At the same time, the receivers and transmitters necessarily had to be where antennas, usually rigged between the masts, could easily reach the gear. These two conditions led to the building of small structures near or atop the uppermost decks. The little box-like additions looked like (and actually were in many cases) sheds or shacks.

The term "Radio Shack" came into common usage and has never faded from the mariners' lexicon; even though, today, the central radio space may be quite large, and located nearly anywhere a naval architect decides it best fits the needs of the ship. Aboard the NORTH CAROLINA, "Radio Central", sometimes called "Radio One", was a large installation four decks below the main deck, but everyone aboard still referred to it as the "Radio *Shack*".

The "Direction Finder Shack" on the Showboat actually looked like one of those old-time shacks, although made of steel. It sat on a platform deck, topside, between the Signal Bridge and Number One Stack. It, too, had been added on after the ship was designed. The DF facility necessarily had to be in the superstructure so surrounding steel would not interfere with or distort incoming radio signals received by its rotating doughnut-shaped antenna.

As the countdown continued toward "zero" for the firing of the unprecedented broadside, I stuffed wads of cotton in my ears, slipped out the hatch to stand to the leeward of the DF Shack, away from the direction the gun muzzles were aimed. In the darkness, I could just see the outlines of the 5-inchers trained to port. The main battery barrels were obscured from my vision by the superstructure. Then came the command: "FIRE!!"

SHIP FIRING GUNS
(U.S. Navy)

THREE 16-IN. GUNS OF THE "NORTH CAROLINA'S" FORE TURRET ARE FIRED AHEAD. BECAUSE SHIP CANNOT SLIDE SIDEWAYS, SUCH FIRING IS MORE STRENUOUS THAN BROADSIDES

NEW U.S. BATTLESHIP "NORTH CAROLINA" SHOOTS ITS GUNS IN FIRING TESTS AT SEA

There was darkness over the Atlantic. Under a westerly wind the black water had been churned into choppy, spray-topped waves. Even the moon failed to light up the hulls of U. S. warships as they moved, unlighted, through the night, 350 miles off Nantucket.

Biggest ghost of all was the new U. S. battleship *North Carolina*. For her this was no ordinary night. It was to be her baptism of fire. For two days she had been testing her guns. First they had been fired singly; then by pairs; then by turret salvos. Now on this night all nine 16-inchers, as well as ten 5-inchers, were to be fired at once. When she had survived that broadside—the heaviest ever fired by any ship—without splitting her sides, she would be ready for action.

The minutes before the salvo were tense. Observers plugged cotton in their ears, spread their feet far apart. The loudspeaker counted off seconds. Suddenly, like the opening of a giant furnace, nineteen streaks of red-yellow flame bolted from the sides of the ship. With them came a shattering roar and the ship rocked like an earthquake, as ten tons of projectiles were hurled into the sea. The *North Carolina* was ready for action.

(New York Herald Tribune - 1941 - Courtesy Albert Phillips)

A great *"BARROOOOOM"* echoed and re-echoed across the North Atlantic, with waves and waves of orange flame lighting the white caps for at least a hundred yards away from the ship. Giant smoke clouds boiled in the light. Only Thor, the legendary hammer-wielding thunder-and-lightning god of my Nordic ancestors, could have generated such an earsplitting pyrotechnic display.

My ears were ringing as if they'd been in the middle of a pair of cymbals clanging. My eyes were reacting as if they'd been up close and personal to a giant fireworks display. The battleship, in recoil from the blast, surprisingly had heeled over to starboard very little, but had slid sideways through the water, leaving a wide and glassy slick where her hull had been. Only very minor damage, a few bursting light bulbs and such, resulted from the firing.

The "big guns" of the NORTH CAROLINA, concurrently with half her secondary battery, had hurled over 32,750 pounds of steel out the muzzles of the 19 guns in the greatest broadside in naval history. That's over FOURTEEN TONS of projectiles! Given the decreased significance of the dreadnought in the coming War, this broadside was an event that would doubtless never occur again 'til the end of time. And I had an unforgettable picture in my mind to last forever.

In between wars, "shakedown cruises" for major vessels often took the new ships on long voyages to foreign ports, in order to exhibit our latest men-o'-war and to "show the Flag." But another war was close at hand, so the Showboat's shakedown would be mostly business, smartly putting her through her paces and checking all her various components as well as her crew. We now headed southward to the warm, placid waters of the Caribbean to operate out of our Naval Base at Guantanamo Bay, Cuba (abbreviated to "Gitmo" by us sailors).

With two destroyers, the WILKES (DD-441) and WOOLSEY (DD-437) as escorts, Captain Hustvedt began putting the crew through the procedures which would reveal any deficiencies in operations or organization. A heavy training schedule was in effect and every bit of equipment aboard was checked and double-checked. The only serious problem to show up in the ship's construction came during high speed runs and maneuvers. The design engineers had theorized that three-bladed screws (propellers) would produce more speed than four-bladed ones. But when pushed to the limit, there was heavy vibration of the fantail. We would go into drydock at a later date to check out the situation.

Mainly, though, the rest of the sea trials turned out beautifully, and the crew was performing well. By this time, my at-sea watch station had been changed from Radio Central to Bridge Radio. Originally, no

U.S.S NORTH CAROLINA FIRING 19 GUN
SALVO - GREATEST IN NAVAL HISTORY .
AUGUST 29,1941.

(U.S. Navy)

radio position had been planned for the Bridge—the station evolved gradually. First, it was just a monitoring position, but later became fully operational with typewriter and sending key. (Later, when voice radio, via TBS, i.e. ultra-high-frequency transceiver, became the primary method of communication between ships, the CW sending key would become obsolete. This would occur after I left the ship.) To give me more mobility, I scrounged around and came up with a set of long leads for the headset, which meant I not only had almost full range throughout the Chart House where the radio position was situated, but I could also go out the port hatch to the wing of the Bridge.

All work and no play . . . ! So the Skipper took us to Kingston, Jamaica, for some of the latter. We arrived at the Port Royal anchorage on 20 September, 1941, to begin two days of liberty. The hook had hardly hit the bottom when liberty call sounded for half the crew. What happened after that produced some laughable moments.

Having lived in the South, I was unprepared for Negroes speaking with a British accent: "Wud ye like a tyxi, Sah?" But there was no language barrier when it came to ordering Jamaica's national drink (part Caribbean, part good ol' U. S. of A.) rum and Coca-Cola. So MacPherson, I, and others ensconced ourselves in a cabana where trade winds whispered through the palm fronds of the roof and availed ourselves of tall, tinkling glasses.

What we didn't realize was the ratio of rum to Coke in the drinks. Jamaican rum is very smooth, and it was also much cheaper than Coke. What we got was about 85 percent rum and 15 percent Coke. Rum is sneaky. It doesn't catch up with you right away. So we put away about three or four glasses each, then decided to go for a hike around the island. No sooner did we step out into the blazing sun when the rum hit with all the subtlety of a broadside. Down we went, right to our knees. Managing to navigate our way into the shade again, we determined our best course was to forego any further imbibing for about an hour before we started sight-seeing.

The Jamaican who'd been serving us said the one attraction we should not miss was the Botanical Gardens. Now, that may not sound like an appropriate venture for a bunch of hard-drinking seagoing men. But with nothing else on the agenda, we thought we'd try it. Besides, where there were flowers there might be girls!

Still a little unsteady, we took a "tyxi" out to the Gardens. The Jamaican was right. It was a spectacular sight—an amazing riot of color. There were flowers everywhere, and a profusion of orchids of every size, shape, and hue. Nowhere on earth could there be any more orchids, nor greater variety of these parasitic plants. The Botanical

Gardens of Kingston and their quiet beauty contrasted sharply with the horrors of war now sweeping nearly half the world. Acres and acres of blossoms—but, disappointingly, no girls.

After returning to the ship, I hung around the fantail where there was at least a little breeze blowing to help keep cool. The CR Division compartment was sweltering in the tropic heat. Late returnees from liberty were coming aboard and among them were sailors who'd consumed too much of old Demon Rum. Not a few were in various stages of undress and were whooping it up like the prospectors in one of Robert Service's poems of the Alaskan Gold Rush saloons. As Ted Mason well observes, the Battleship Navy, "so meticulous about the appearance of its men when they went ashore, took a most tolerant view of their return from the perils of the port."

Most, as they reached the Quarterdeck, managed to compose themselves into some semblance of military demeanor. One seaman, however, who'd lost not only his trousers but his neckerchief and a shoe as well, staggered to the top of the gangway with a huge bunch of green bananas on his shoulder. He gave what might, in the Mongolian Navy, pass for a salute to the Colors and to the Junior Officer of the Deck. The J.O.D. returned the salute and moved to greet the next arrival when the sailor, with a rousing "WAH-HOO", swung around without looking, bashing the J.O.D. full in the face with that bunch of bananas. And the officer went down.

It was an act that brought down the house as well. The returning well-oiled sailors just howled! But, the J.O.D. (a pretty nice guy, normally, who'd overlooked most of the didoes up 'til then) was hardly amused. He had to salvage his dignity and restore order. The "banana sailor" was placed on report, and tolerance of any non-military behavior around the Quarterdeck was severely curtailed from then on.

Our weekend in Jamaica permitted just about everyone in the crew to visit this tropical paradise. Some made the local bawdy houses, some got blasted on rum-and-Coke, some just went sight-seeing, and some got tattoos. Speaking of tattoos, the Navy frowned on them but did not absolutely ban this centuries-old custom of decorating the epidermis. I would have had to be falling down drunk to have gotten one. To me, they weren't very attractive; and besides, I hate needles.

There was another deterrent. In days when some tattoo "artists" were less than sanitary in care of their equipment, infection was not uncommon. The Navy let it be known that any tattooed sailor who became ill as a result of a tattoo would be severely dealt with. No medical assistance would be provided (he'd have to treat himself or go to a civilian doctor) and any loss of time away from duties was subject to disciplinary action. Some sailors were discharged from the service after suffering incapacitating infections.

Leaving Kingston on 22 September, we returned to Guantanamo Bay, where we resumed shakedown exercises, continuing until 2 October. Then we headed northward, following the Gulf Stream, on a course to New York.

After being away at sea for what seemed a long time, we were glad to see the Statue of Liberty. As we passed by her on the way into New York Harbor, the old lady looked mighty good.

6
STILL AT PEACE IN A WORLD AT WAR

As mentioned before, there were two structures in the world, at that time, which governed the height and width of a U.S. Naval vessel: the Brooklyn Bridge and the Panama Canal. No ship could have a beam (widest part of a ship's hull) too broad to prohibit it from traversing the Canal. And no mast or vertical part (e.g. antennas) could be so high it could not pass under the Bridge at high tide. The NORTH CAROLINA's naval architects pushed these two dimensions to the limit.

A silhouette of the battleship will show she has two masts. The forward one, although taller and of more bulk, is not the "mainmast". Following sailing ship designations of masts, the one most forward is the foremast. The second mast astern is the mainmast (on ships with three masts, the third is the mizzenmast) even though it may be shorter and smaller. The mainmast of the NORTH CAROLINA is a "stick" mast; i.e., it is a single pole, with the yardarm rigged athwartships.

Our foremast was sometimes referred to as a "pagoda" because of its resemblance to Chinese temple construction. It served a multitude of purposes. Perched at the very peak is Sky Control, the main battery fire control director for Turrets One and Two. Immediately below, circling the tower-like mast, is a catwalk protected by a splinter shield and used as a lookout station—the modern equivalent of a crow's nest. Just inside an aft-facing hatch is a radio position, with a voice circuit for communication with our own aircraft, either the ship's OS2Us or aircraft carrier planes with which we might operate.

Just below the catwalk, the yardarm protrudes to port and starboard, upon which are rigged the signal halyards. These are another facet of the ship's communications systems—the flag hoists, by which messages are visually sent to other ships. At the tip of the yardarm were anemometers to measure wind direction and velocity, various lights for navigational and signaling purposes, and radio "whip" antennas. The "yard" was also the forward anchor of our radio transmitting antennas which stretched horizontally aft to the mainmast yardarm. We called these "flat-top" antennas. The mainmast, like the foremast, had other whip antennas and navigational lights, and a single jig mast supporting the halyard from which the Flag of the United States of America flew when the ship was underway.

Radar was just being introduced to ships in the Fleet, although there had been experimental use as early as 1939. Originally developed by the British, it was all very hush-hush and not even its name was mentioned. None of the NORTH CAROLINA's radar was installed until after the cruise to Jamaica, and the first unit presented an unusual problem. The huge radar antenna, because of its appearance, was nicknamed "the Bed Spring" (although its official designation was "CXAM"). To get maximum height for longer distance detection of enemy ships and planes, it was rigged on a jig mast just abaft the foremast catwalk. But the installation would make the antenna too high to pass under the Brooklyn Bridge, so it was ingeniously mounted on an electrically powered cantilever, allowing it to be lowered to lie flat straight aft below the critical height of the foremast.

At first only Commander Shepherd, our Communications Officer, Chief Radio Electrician Byron Phillips, and our two chief radiomen, Baldock and Suggs, were allowed anywhere near the radar installations. In an unusual security precaution, strikers stood armed watches outside the small, temporary radar room just abaft the Chart House—even at sea.

I was standing such a watch one evening while we were in port at Norfolk. Mr. Phillips was testing the gear, and had left the hatch partly open. I peeked in but saw nothing startling about the equipment, except for a screen that was somewhat larger than the ones on the regular oscilloscopes we used.

During his work with the equipment, Mr. Phillips let out a muted yell. I stuck my head through the hatch to see what the matter was.

"Hot damn!" he exclaimed. "I just picked up a flight of Army aircraft SEVENTY-FIVE miles out!"

Putting together what data I'd been able to glean from observation and overheard conversations between Commander Shepherd and Mr. Phillips, I figured out what this radar stuff basically was all about. The acronym RADAR stands for "Radio Detection and Ranging". This is an oversimplification, but it works by sending out a radio signal. When the signal hits an object, it bounces back to be picked up on the receiving antenna and is translated into an image on the screen of the scope. Radar operators were trained to interpret these "blips" and were able to convert the data into information about the objects or targets de-tected—including speed, distance, and course.

Radar was *the* electronic miracle of World War II and its contribu-tion to ultimate victory was immeasurable. As more ships were equipped with it, and newer and more sophisticated gear was developed, the secrecy curtain was lifted aboard ship, after which radar operation and maintenance were handled almost exclusively by enlisted men.

It was during that same call in the port of Norfolk that two NORTH CAROLINA legends were born. The Virginia city and environs exist because of the huge Navy installations there, but the local citizenry wasn't very hospitable to sailors. It was considered the *worst* liberty port in the whole world, so much so the men of the Fleet unceremoniously dubbed Norfolk "Shit City". It was here that signs reading "SAILORS AND DOGS—KEEP OFF!" were planted on lawns, and recreational facilities for Naval personnel were mostly confined to the bars in the Skid Row part of town, principally along Main Street. This was where the first Norfolk legend was born.

Ochoa was a pudgy, round-faced Radioman 3rd with whom I was sharing watches. He'd come to the Showboat from the heavy cruiser AUGUSTA (CA-31) after she'd returned from duty as Flagship of the Asiatic Fleet. We'd become friends and were making a liberty together when he challenged me to drink "eggs in your beer", a practice I assumed he'd picked up on Asiatic Station. We repaired to Norfolk's most famous (or infamous) gin mill—The American Bar—where I was to be indoctri-nated into this strange practice. I dutifully broke a raw egg into a stein of beer and took a swig. It wasn't all that bad; but it wasn't all that good, either.

About that time, several Limeys from a British cruiser in port made an appearance. Now, we were not yet in the War, and these "Jack-tars" resented the fact the U.S. Navy was not out there helping them against the Germans. They made little effort to disguise their disgust with us.

Painted on the wall behind the bar was a huge American Flag, which gave the joint its name. As the Limeys bellied up to order their drinks, one of 'em called the barkeep over.

"There's a stripe missing from that flag, myte", he said.

The bartender turned and counted.

"They're all there—all thirteen of 'em", he replied.

"Better look again, myte. The *yellow* stripe's not there."

He no sooner got the word *"yellow"* out of his mouth when he caught a set of knuckles right in the chops and the granddaddy of all donny-brooks broke out. American and British sailors flew at each other with a vengeance. Our Marines quickly pulled off their leather Sam Brown belts, wrapped them around their fists with brass buckles protruding and joined in the fray.

At first, Ochoa and I were just interested observers until I saw a beer stein flying toward us.

"Ochoa! By Gawd, stand from under! Incoming!" And I shoved him behind the bar. The glass shattered above our heads, sprinkling us with its shards. We joined the bartender among the beer kegs, peeking out to watch what was one doozy of a brawl. Our guys were swiftly gaining the upper hand, needing no help, when police whistles sounded outside. The barkeep pointed to a rear exit and Ochoa and I executed a strategic retreat. End of legend one.

Now to legend two. Coming back from that same liberty the next morning, we were standing on the dock of the liberty landing where motor launches from the ships in the stream came in to pick up returning crewmen. From the dock a long brow (a gangplank-like walkway with siderails) extended down to a float that rose and fell with the tides. In a few minutes, we heard someone calling cadence in a loud voice. It was one of the corporals of the NORTH CAROLINA's Marine detachment.

Marching in perfect precision, despite obviously being under the influence, were six other Marines, resplendent in their seagoing dress blues. As they reached the top of the brow, the corporal commanded: "Detail, column left!" The six headed down toward the float. At that moment, the corporal turned to chat with a nearby sailor while his colleagues continued to march.

The corporal kept talking, the Marines kept marching. Down the brow, out on the float they went, straight toward the oily waters of Hampton Roads. Everyone around the landing watched with suspended fascination, expecting the corporal to order "Halt!" He never did, and the Marines, all six of them, dutifully marched over the end of the float right into the murky water!

As the gyrenes surfaced, scrambling to recover their white-covered caps, and blubbering from the shock of chilly waters, the attendant sailors exploded with laughter. The corporal turned to see what was going on, and his face went pearly white. I can't write a postscript. I only know the Marines survived the ordeal, and what they did to their corporal in the aftermath must be left to the imagination. But the story is just one of the legends of the NORTH CAROLINA that's recalled at every reunion of the old crew.

Transportation from ship to shore when the Showboat was anchored out in the stream was by 50-foot motor launches stored in cradles in the superstructure until hoisted over the side by a huge boat crane. We had four of them, plus smaller whaleboats and the Captain's gig. The launches were open with no decking or protection from the weather. Passengers sat on thwarts (bench-like planks at right angles to the bow). Each launch had a crew of four and a capacity of about 100 men. The man in charge was the coxswain (pronounced "cox'n") who steered the launch with a tiller. An engineer, usually a Fireman 1st Class, ran the Gray Marine engine. Two seamen, the bow hook and a deck hand, handled the bow and stern lines.

The most joyous order any John Gob could hear was that from the Officer of the Deck shouting down from the Quarterdeck to the boat:

"Shove off, Cox'n, and make the liberty landing!"

The complement of any U.S. Naval vessel is always in a state of transition. There are men being transferred off to other ships and stations, and new ones coming aboard as replacements. In October, 1941, we were about to get a new Commanding Officer. Captain O.M. Hustvedt was being promoted to Rear Admiral. In his honor a ship's ball was held in the ballroom of Brooklyn's St. George Hotel. I took Peg, the one time I got her to go to a formal affair.

Not only was the Old Man being relieved, but six good buddies from the Radio Gang were being transferred to a new anti-aircraft cruiser under construction—the U.S.S. JUNEAU (CL-52). Lister, Jackson, Ochoa, Pearson, Stiles, and Armstrong left for their new duty on 12 November. It would prove to be a fatal assignment.

The day before the ship's ball, the War was brought into sharp focus by news that one of our destroyers, the U.S.S. KEARNEY (DD-432), had been torpedoed by a German U-boat on the Iceland run when she went to the aid of a convoy under attack by a submarine wolfpack. Eleven crewmen were killed, 24 wounded, but the ship survived. Two weeks later, the old "four-piper" tin can, U.S.S. REUBEN JAMES (DD-245), was sunk on North Atlantic Patrol by another German sub—115 men lost, only 45 survivors.

News reports labeled the sinking of "the RUBE" the first U.S. Naval vessel lost in World War II. Apparently none recalled the unprovoked and unwarranted sinking of the U.S.S PANAY, one of our river gunboats bringing Christian missionaries and U.S. civilians out of Nanking, China, 12 December, 1937, *four years earlier.*

The PANAY was well-marked with a huge American Flag atop her deck house when Japanese aircraft deliberately bombed, strafed, and sank her on the middle reaches of the Yangtze River. They had hoped to provoke America into war, but the U.S. accepted a phony apology instead. Three good American sailors were killed and four wounded. The survivors were forced to walk all the way to the China coast, all the while dodging hostile patrols and army units along the way.

(Courtesy USS NORTH CAROLINA Reunion Association)

It was Ochoa who told me of the day he was on the AUGUSTA (CA-31), anchored off the Bund at Shanghai, when the Jap fleet trained all its guns on the U.S. Flagship in an apparent harassing tactic. The heavy cruiser's Captain ordered all her guns and those of two accompanying destroyers to train on the Bridge of the Nip flagship; then the three vessels got the hell out of there, thus averting an international incident that could have started the War right then and there. So we had plenty of warning of Jap intentions.

Our new Skipper was the most popular officer ever to set foot on the teakwood decks of the Showboat. He was Captain Oscar C. Badger. There's no way to describe the overwhelming affection the crew felt for him. At no time while I served aboard was morale any higher than it was under Captain Badger. Many years later, his daughter, Mrs. John (Isabelle) Schroeder, wrote me about his entry into the service. After attending St. John's College, he entered the Naval Academy when only sixteen. Too short, she wrote, to pass the physical, he had hung from door frames and stretched himself with weights, just eking by, but eventually growing up to reach the height of five feet eleven inches.

Oscar Badger was fifth generation Navy. His father, grandfather,

CAPTAIN OSCAR C. BADGER
(Courtesy Shipmate Charles "Chuck" Pavlic, USMC, Ret.)

and great-grandfather all reached the rank of Admiral. His great-great-grandfather was a Commodore before the rank of Admiral was inaugurated. At the time the young Badger became a plebe, his dad was Superintendent at Annapolis, which did not make his days as a midshipman easy. He took a lot of hazing about being the Superintendent's son, and he had to be extra careful about not putting his dad in an awkward position. He was known as the "Sup's son", and for many years his classmates called him "Soup".

What endeared Captain Badger to his NORTH CAROLINA crew was his empathy and compassion for enlisted men. As the inheritor of a great Navy-family tradition, he knew well the value of engendering an *esprit de corps* among his bluejackets. And he was sincerely concerned about our welfare, confidence in his command, dedication to the ship and our duties—and, above all, serving on a cheerful and "happy ship".

The "Battleship Navy" was renowned for its strict adherence to Navy regulations—the ceremonies, rituals, and tight discipline expected aboard a ship of the line. But too often those regs were enforced, and authority was abused, in ways which alienated enlisted men from their officers. For this the Battleship Navy was notorious.

While enlisted men took great pride in the uniform, the "regulation" blues, worn as proscribed, were without much flair. The "stove pipe" legs of the trousers looked like just that. The jumpers were baggy. The neckerchief, worn with the knot at the jumper "V", and the white hat, perched high and squared on the head, made us look like "sailor *boys*"—a term we enlisted *men* detested.

We suspected officers who enforced that "regulation look" were doing so because they didn't want ordinary John Gobs looking as good or better than they did. When some enforced the wearing of the uniform down to the minutest detail, the enlisted men had a word for it —"horseshit".

It was into this sphere of Navy regulations that Captain Badger blew a blast of fresh air. With a ship's company almost entirely Regular Navy, we took great care to look professional. We headed for the uniform tailor shops along Sand Street to have the original-issue, all-wool, oversized, baggy and ill-fitting dress blues altered. But we had to be careful not to go to extremes for fear the uniform would not stand inspection. That still left them without a great deal of flair.

So some of us not only had our "regs" tailored, but also bought "tailor-mades"—snappy looking outfits of serge with definite bell-bottoms instead of the "stove pipe" look, often lined with satin or silk in parts of the jumper, and with a hip pocket added. The collar was designed to wear the neckerchief tighter at the throat. But we had either to keep them in lockers ashore, or carry them off the ship in a ditty bag, changing later.

In November, 1941, I was promoted to Seaman 1st Class, with my pay going from a measly $36 to $54 a month, and I got the third stripe on my jumper cuffs. I immediately took the cash I'd been saving, headed for Sand Street and bought a great set of tailor-mades for $21—top o' the line!

Now, back to Captain Badger.

Not knowing what to expect from this new Skipper, we were all at our most strictly regulation look for the first of his Saturday Captain's Inspections. Standing near me in formation as we mustered at quarters was a new recruit dressed in baggy, ill-fitting, unaltered blues.

The Skipper was moving briskly along the formation, but stopped in front of the new hand.

"Sailor", he barked, "do you have 21 dollars?"

The boot gulped a couple of times before replying with a quivering "Yes, Sir".

"Then", advised the Captain, "when you're secured from inspection, go buy a decent uniform. I'll not have my enlisted men going around in sloppy-looking clothes."

When the word spread, we took this to mean the Old Man would not object to tailor-mades or regulation blues well-tailored. While the majority on board still stayed with their regs, many of us, particularly younger sailors, began wearing tailor-mades or well-tailored issued blues.

As far as I could ever learn, the NORTH CAROLINA under Captain Badger was the only battleship in U.S. Navy history to allow enlisted men to wear non-regulation uniforms. The Captain immediately became our hero. We intended to make our Skipper proud of us by being the snappiest-looking bluejackets in the Fleet, and we went to great lengths to spruce up our appearance.

The black silk neckerchief was tied closer to the throat, rather than loosely below the "V" of the jumper. Regulation peacoats were tailored to be more form-fitting around the waist. When I had mine done, I also had a satin lining put in, with my name embroidered on it. We began wearing strictly non-regulation white scarves with the peacoats, too.

We wore flat hats as part of the winter dress uniform. Out of use today and almost forgotten, this cap without a bill had a band around the brow, which in pre-War years was embossed with the name of the ship in gold. But by 1941 all ribbons simply read "U S NAVY". To make them look like something more than a Navy blue pancake on our heads, we would press them flat with a steam iron, then insert a wire around the inside so the front would stand up and we could shape the sides to fold down, somewhat like an Air Corps 50-mission cap.

Flat hats were worn only in the Atlantic Fleet. West Coast boot camps didn't even issue them. But the most identifiable naval headgear in the world is our Navy's white hat, and we took inordinate steps to make them the crowning symbol of the professional sailors we strove to be. The first prerequisite in the care and feeding of the white hat is to get it as brilliantly white as possible. After washing (by hand, of course) salt is pounded into the brim, not only to make the hat glisten but to give it more stiffness. Secondly, it is properly formed, with the "wings" molded just so and the symmetry perfectly even. Dried in the sun, that hat will just sparkle!

Hollywood notwithstanding, white hats are *not* supposed to be worn on the back of the head. Regulations require sailors to wear them squared forward, with a two finger space between the headband of the hat and the brow. But real "salts", particularly those who served in the South Pacific during the War, wore their white hats right down on the eyebrows, almost on the bridge of the nose. The hats came in for some ignominious treatment when the War started. At sea, they were too highly visible, and we had to dye any we wore "blue", which made them look an ugly purple. But on liberty in Hawaii and the States, we could proudly wear again our beloved white headgear.

Speaking of Hollywood, I've never seen an actor in a film about the Navy with a properly shaped white hat, nor wearing one properly. This may be because the Navy's technical advisors on movies are all officers, and they don't realize the importance of the enlisted man's pride in his crowning glory.

A final word about uniforms: we washed our dress blues by hand, scrubbing the stripes, rating badges, and stars with a tooth brush. To bleach the white insignia, we rinsed them in salt water, then in fresh water, since salt left in made the wool itch.

While Captain Badger was not uncivil to his officers, he abhorred pomposity and the age-old tradition of "brown-nosing", or as we said "ear-banging", by which not a few junior officers hoped to get better fitness reports upon which rested promotions. Moreover, he particularly didn't care for Reserve officers—feeling, I assumed, that if you were going to be Navy, you should be Navy all the way.

Parenthetically, Regular enlisted men generally didn't have much respect for most Reserves, especially Reserve officers. Among ourselves we'd call them "Reverses" and occasionally "Reverse ossifers". They also fell into a category we called "Feather Merchants"—i.e. goof-offs or non-military types in the service, some of whom we considered bona fide flakes.

While at sea, the Skipper sometimes relaxed on a large leather sofa in the Chart House. During those very rare moments, he pursued his passion for crossword puzzles. He was so occupied one day when a newly assigned Reserve lieutenant, apparently trying to make points, came in through the after hatch and walked by the Old Man, greeting him with a "Good morning, Captain!"

Not raising his head, Badger continued with the puzzle.

The lieutenant went out the forward hatch, around the wing of the Bridge, back through the after hatch, and tried again with a little louder "Good morning, Captain!!"

Same result.

The third time around, the officer stopped in front of the Skipper and, even louder, called out his "Good morning, Captain!!!"

Without even looking up, the Captain finally responded.

"I didn't ask for a damn' weather report!" And went right back to work on the puzzle.

Completely deflated the lieutenant bailed out—and, you know, I don't recall ever seeing him again after that. The quartermasters and I had to make valiant efforts to keep from bursting out with laughter.

I was personally on the receiving end of an example of Captain Badger's concern for his men. It was one of the most unusual events in my military career.

It was pretty cold in Brooklyn Navy Yard the winter of 1941-42, and the wind off the East River was biting. The beefed-up security called for armed sentries on the dock at the foot of each brow to stop unauthorized persons from going aboard. Usually the watches were stood by deck or gunnery division men; but for some reason or other, the CR Division got tapped for the duty on occasion. It was my lot to catch it, this day, and with rifle and ammo belt I took up station at the after (enlisted man's) brow.

The Skipper had been away from the ship, reportedly trying to get the powers-that-be in Washington to let him take the Showboat into combat. On returning, he bypassed the Officer's Quarterdeck, as he sometimes did to avoid the usual ceremony accorded him, and came to the after brow where I stood shivering all the way to my toes. I was hoping I wouldn't turn blue in this last half-hour of my four-hour watch. Despite being stiffened by the cold, I managed a military-like rifle salute as the Old Man approached. Returning it, he peered at me closely.

"You look as if you're freezing, Sparks."

He'd recognized me from my Bridge watches, and "Sparks" is the generic title of all radiomen.

"Yes, Sir, Captain. I sure am."

"Then come with me."

"Aye, aye, Sir."

I followed him up the brow where he instructed me to hand the rifle and ammo belt to the Quartermaster and told the J.O.D. to assign a relief for me. With me in tow, he headed up to his cabin, invited me in, and proceeded to pour a small amount of brandy into a snifter. I almost fell over when he handed it to me.

"This will warm you up, Sparks", he said with a grin.

That was the Skipper his crew knew and loved.

As soon as I finished the brandy, I thanked him and departed as soon as was proper. It was, for me, a most unforgettable moment.

The NORTH CAROLINA continued training exercises and was joined in the Atlantic Fleet by other new warships, including the WASHINGTON and the aircraft carrier WASP (CV-7) along with cruisers and destroyers. The build-up of the Navy was now in full swing.

We were in Brooklyn in 1941 with Thanksgiving coming up. Civilians were beginning to warm to sailors a bit more, now, and we were offered the opportunity to be guests of people who volunteered to have servicemen in their homes for the traditional American feast. Paulus (another striker) and I accepted invitations and made our way over to Manhattan to a street lined with old brownstone houses.

The outward appearance of these homes made us wonder if we'd come to the wrong place. They were dirty, sooty, and sort of seedy-looking. But, having no alternative except to go back to the ship, we went to the address we had and knocked on the door, where we were greeted by a pleasant middle-aged (to us) lady. She bade us a warm welcome and we stepped inside.

The contrast between exterior and interior was surprising, a 180-degree difference. The carpeting was lush and plush, with pile almost ankle deep. Rich tapestries were on the walls; the furniture was of dark, obviously expensive woods; the whole place reeked of elegance. Now, we *really* did feel out of place. But the lady and her husband made us feel comfortable and the dinner was delicious.

The heavy china was hand-painted, the glassware was genuine crystal, the silver service was heavy and ornate. This quiet couple obviously were very well-off, financially, and I was at a loss to understand why the outside of the brownstone was allowed to look so run-down. My curiosity got the best of me, and I questioned our host about it.

"In New York", he explained, "the tax assessors make their estimates only by looking at the exterior of homes. They never come inside. Since they see no opulence from the street, they assume it's a poorer neighborhood, and we save a great deal of tax money each year. Everyone here does it."

Now I knew why they could afford such posh furnishings inside. You learn something new every day.

7

PEARL HARBOR—THIS IS NO DRILL

I was leaning back in my chair, earphones around my neck, nursing a fresh cup of joe while NSS Washington was sending lazy "dits" every few seconds to let operators know the FOX sked had no traffic.

It'd been a light watch so far, with only a handful of routine messages transmitted. I had copied but one dispatch that hour, a lengthy one addressed to ComServLant (Commander Service Forces Atlantic Fleet).

Typical quiet Sunday afternoon in the Radio Shack, duty I would've caught only once in four months. But this Sunday would turn out to be anything but typical.

Suddenly, NSS came alive, sending its "dits" at a 25-word-per-minute rate. I cut the volume on the headphones and put them back over my ears. This was unusual. Once all traffic cleared after the top of the hour, NSS seldom had anything so important it couldn't wait until the next hour.

The "dits" stopped and the code began to spell out NERK NERK NERK V NSS NSS. "NERK" is the call sign for "All U.S Navy Ships and Stations"; the "V" means "from". Radio Washington was alerting every command.

The heading of the message cleared quickly, and the operational sign startled me—it was "O" for "Urgent". Then came the text:

"AIR RAID PEARL HARBOR X THIS IS NO DRILL"!!!

It took a moment for the words to sink in, then I yelled for the petty officer of the watch. I think it was Johnny Johnston. At the same time, I pulled the FOX log out of my mill, zipped a message blank in, and retyped the dispatch on it. Yanking it out of the typewriter, I handed it to Johnston and, in disbelief, stared back at the words I'd copied.

From then on, everything happened so quickly it's difficult to recall the details. Further messages began to come in; all had the ominous "O" at the beginning. Some were plain language, others were encoded. I copied each on separate message blanks so they could easily be routed by the messenger. Following that first dispatch, others identified the attackers of Pearl Harbor—they were Japanese carrier-based aircraft.

Nearly half the NORTH CAROLINA's crew, and at least half the officers, were ashore. The Officer of the Deck immediately took steps to recall all hands, and we began getting Western Union wires out to men on leave. Security was tightened and men with rifles were posted topside and on the pier.

The Communications Officer of the Watch was hastily decoding all the non-plain-language messages, and some other officers came into the Shack, trying to glean more information about the bombing raid on our Pacific Fleet. But details were sketchy and we got little information on how fared our people in Hawaii. All we knew was the God-damned Japs had hit us with a sneak attack and we had suffered heavy losses in both men and ships. It would be several days before we learned the full extent of the devastation along Battleship Row, at Hickham Field, Schofield Barracks, and the other targets of the Jap carrier planes.

We would hear later that Admiral Nagumo's Pearl Harbor Striking Force of six aircraft carriers, carrying well over 400 planes, escorted by battleships, cruisers, and destroyers, had traversed the North Pacific and hit Oahu from the north. Sunday morning's peace was shattered, and all hell broke loose at 0755. At the outset Jap planes swooped so low sailors could see their pilots' haughty and toothy grins, throwing monkey wrenches at them in their extreme frustration. Still, within minutes, bluejackets were valiantly fighting back and trying to save their ships.

But when the Jap planes (29 lost, 70 some shot up) departed at 0945, they left behind 2,008 sailors dead and 710 wounded, some 3,580 casualties counting civilians and all military personnel. Half of our approximately 400 planes on Oahu were destroyed on the ground and most of the others damaged. As for ships, Battleship Row was devastated, seven battlewagons sunk or severely damaged: ARIZONA (BB-39), OKLAHOMA (BB-37), CALIFORNIA (BB-44), WEST VIRGINIA (BB-48), NEVADA (BB-46), TENNESSEE (BB-43), MARYLAND (BB-46). Only Pacific Fleet Flagship PENNSYLVANIA (BB-38) escaped with minor damage. In all, 18 ships of the United States Navy were destroyed or badly damaged.

As I pounded away on the mill, almost attacking it as if it were the enemy, tears of rage, shock, and frustration poured down my cheeks. Those slant-eyed, yellow-bellied sons o' bitches! Those bandy-legged, buck-toothed bastards! Only the long periods of training kept me at my post. I was copying on "automatic pilot", the code signals coming into my ears and out through my fingertips without passing through my

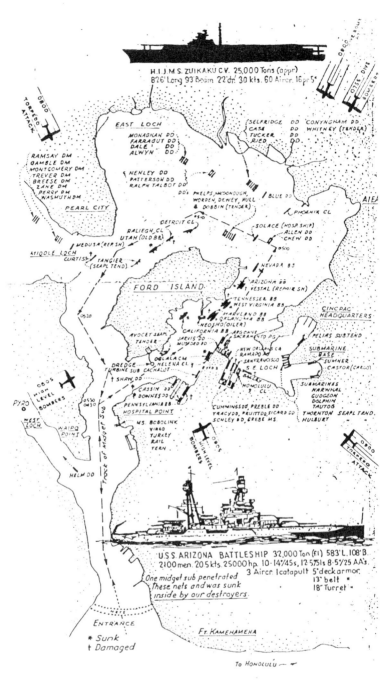

PEARL HARBOR, T.H., DECEMBER 7, 1941
Location of all U.S. Navy vessels at the time of Japanese sneak attack.
(Courtesy Sgt/Maj. Lester Bamford, USMC, Ret.)

brain. Unrealistically, I wanted to get up and DO SOMETHING! ANY-THING! to get back at the dastardly bastards who were attacking MY Navy!

There are many eyewitness accounts of the Pearl Harbor attack. One of the most interesting is Ted Mason's, whose battle station was atop the mainmast of the CALIFORNIA. The last man to leave the ship, Ted abandoned ship three times in one day, while witnessing the improbable death of the Battleship Navy. The impossible was happening. The Japanese were simply incapable of this. We were victims of our own propaganda. Even on the midwatch before that surprising Sunday morning, the consensus was the Japs were only bluffing.

"The Pacific Fleet was under attack by more planes than I had ever seen in the air at one time. . . . I cursed the fate that had made me a radioman instead of a gunner's mate. . . . The pilots' aim was very good. . . . I knew that every hit, and many of the near misses, were bringing death to numbers of my countrymen. . . . "

"This couldn't be happening! The entire scene had the flickering, two-dimensional quality of a B-grade war film. . . . At any moment, the screen would go blank. Then this would again be a typical Sunday morning at Pearl Harbor. . . . But as I stared in disbelief, the nightmare film continued to unreel. . . . Hundreds of men must be trapped below decks, doomed to the horrid end all sailors dread so much that none dares mention it. . . . "

"How could it have happened? American battleships didn't capsize. That, I had been told, was next to impossible. But it wasn't impossible; how could I dispute the evidence of my eyes? . . . At this point my belief in my sanity was taxed. Such things simply couldn't happen. American battleships didn't blow up. . . . I knew that the unthinkable was happening. Why and how, I did not know—and I would be very lucky to survive long enough to find out. . . . Could this be the end of a short and inglorious life? . . . "

"By some miracle, the NEVADA had got up steam. . . . As she approached . . . , I could see that she was down by the head from a torpedo hit well forward. She showed bomb damage on her foremast and quarterdeck. Undaunted, she stood down the channel against a stygian backdrop of billowing black smoke. . . . All her antiaircraft guns were firing, some in the very midst of fire and smoke. At her stern, the Stars and Stripes flew proudly from the flagstaff. . . . "

"I choked with emotion as she came bravely on. . . . In the maintop, we gave the crew of the NEVADA our shouted encouragement and our prayerful curses and our great vows of vengeance. Some of us were crying unashamed tears. In that moment, which would live in history,

I understood why men of a special kind were willing to die for abstractions named Duty, Honor, Country."

Pearl Harbor aroused the American people out of their lethargy, pacifism, and isolationism. The humiliation also gave the U.S. Navy the grim determination to defeat the Japs at any cost. The bastards had not hit our fuel reserves or repair facilities on Oahu, our aircraft carriers had not been touched, and we could still fight back. The story of Pearl Harbor and the Navy's response is well told in Harvard and Navy historian Samuel Eliot Morison's *History of United States Naval Operations in World War II*, Volume III *The Rising Sun in the Pacific*, and subsequent volumes. As Admiral "Bull" Halsey, upon returning to Pearl on 8 December with his carrier Task Force, put it: "Before we're through with 'em, the Japanese language will be spoken only in hell!"

The Seventh of December in the Year of Our Lord Nineteen Hundred and Forty-One was not only "a date that will live in infamy", as President Roosevelt proclaimed the next day; it was the beginning of a long and arduous War, that would take a great toll amongst us. All that stood, now, between the United States and Japanese aims of conquest was a battered and depleted Fleet, manned by a handful of volunteers who would be called upon, as another wartime President had said of earlier Americans, to "give the last full measure of devotion." In Ted Mason's words: "We might have been defeated, but we were not broken by defeat. Ahead, there was a war to win—and we knew we would win it."

As the afternoon wore on, the racing adrenalin subsided, and we were faced with the stark reality that we were at War, that our job was here on the NORTH CAROLINA, and that we would go where we were ordered, when we were ordered. Once I was relieved of the afternoon watch, I went up to the mess deck for evening chow. As I pushed the food around on the metal tray, contemplating the events of that day, trying to sort it all out, I knew combat was inevitable. I thought of the Hutchinsons and Nelsons who'd gone before me and wondered how they'd reacted to the prospects of battle. They had, I knew, performed well, even with valor. I could only hope I would serve as well.

At the time, we could hardly fathom the unfamiliar and foreboding future. Little did we know, that except for one destroyer, the U.S. Navy would send every ship in the Japs' Pearl Harbor Striking Force to the bottom of the Pacific in far-off future battles yet unheard of and unfamiliar to the ear—Midway, Guadalcanal, the Philippine Sea. In Morison's words: "Never in modern history was a war begun with so smashing a victory by one side, and never in recorded history did the initial victor pay so dearly for his calculated treachery."

The usual low hum of sailors eating chow was at a higher level this

PEARL HARBOR
DEC. 7, 1941

USA   *"AIR RAID: PEARL HARBOR-THIS IS NO DRILL"*   USA.

SHIPS DAMAGED

Only ship lost → ARIZONA BB Sunk
OKLAHOMA BB Sunk
CALIFORNIA BB
WEST VIRGINIA BB
MARYLAND BB
TENNESSEE BB
PENNSYLVANIA BB
UTAH (Target) BB Sunk.
HELENA CL
RALIEGH CL
HONOLULU CL
CASSINS DD
DOWNES DD
SHAW DD
VESTAL Rep. Ship
CURTIS Seapl. Tend

NEVADA BB
OGLALA Minelayer
NEWORLEANS CA
HELM DD
DOBBIN Tender
CURTIS Seapl. Tender

AIRCRAFT LOSSES

FORD ISLAND	19 Pat., 4 Fight., 3 Sc. Bombers.
NAS. KANEOHE	27 Pat. B, 1 Obs. Scout.
MAR. AIR. STA.	9 Fight., 18 Scout, 6 Utility.
HICKHAM (Army)	4 Hvy B., 12 Med B., 2 Lt. Bombers.
WHEELER "	40 Pursuit., 2 Observations.
BELLOWS "	2 " , 1 "

Total 176 Aircraft

Total Casualties

NAVY & MARINE	2117 Dead	960 Missing	876 Wounded
ARMY	226 Dead	396 Wounded

The attack on PEARL HARBOR touched off the bloodiest and most merciless war ever waged in the worlds oceans. On that first day, the U.S. Navy lost more men than in all its previous history.

PEARL HARBOR STRIKE FORCE
Vice Adm. Chuichi Naguma
5 - Carriers - AKAGI, KAGA, HIRYU, ZUIKAKU, SHOKAKU, SORYU.
2-Battleships - HIEI, KIRISHIMA.
2 - Heavy Cruisers - TONE, CHIKUMA.
1 - Light Cruiser - ABUKUMA
16 - Destroyers.
11 - Auxiliary Vessels.

ADVANCE EXPEDITIONARY FORCE
Vice Adm. Shimizu
3 Light Cruisers
20 I-Class Submarines
5 Midget Submarines
6 Auxiliary Vessels.
49 lev. bombers 51 dive bombers } 1st Wave
40 Torp. planes, 43 Zero fighters
54 lev. bombers, 80 dive bombers } 2nd Wave
36 Zero fighters

JAPANESE LOSSES
5 Midget Submarines
15 Dive Bombers
5 Torp. "
9 Fighters.

(Courtesy Sgt/Maj. Lester Bamford, USMC, Ret.)

night. There were constant references to the illegitimate parentage of the Japs who perpetrated this stab in the back on our shipmates at Pearl. The feeling of frustration was so thick you could cut it with a knife. To a man, the crewmen of the NORTH CAROLINA wanted to retaliate immediately, in person, against the Japs, even though we were over 5,000 miles away. And there was endless speculation on just exactly what role we would play.

Other crewman aboard always assumed that radiomen knew a great deal about what was going on because we handled communications. The truth is, we seldom had much more information than anyone else. We were merely in a position, from handling certain data, occasionally to make an educated guess. Yet, we were constantly approached by shipmates, asking for "the straight dope".

When there is a dearth of official pronouncements in the Navy, "scuttlebutt" takes over. In the very early days of sailing vessels, a cask or wooden barrel was known as a "butt". The tap through which water was drawn from a butt was known as a "scuttle", and a tapped cask of water thus came to be called a "scuttled butt". It was around this primitive water fountain that sailors gathered to pass gossip. If one were asked where he'd learned of a certain happening, he'd say "by the scuttle(d) butt". Rumors and gossip hence became known as "scuttlebutt".

In the days that followed 7 December, scuttlebutt ran rampant throughout the ship, most of it wishful thinking or figments of overactive imaginations. Since Germany joined Japan in the War against us, we were supposed to be going to sea to go after the Nazi pocket battleships VON TIRPITZ and SCHARNHORST; we were leaving for Pearl in company with our sister ship the WASHINGTON to take on the Jap Navy; we were going to the Mediterranean. There was hardly a place on the globe that the scuttlebutt didn't have us going. All the while, we were sitting here alongside the pier in Brooklyn Navy Yard.

Shortly after Christmas we put to sea, heading for the Gulf Training Area, in company with the WASHINGTON, carrier HORNET (CV-8), cruiser VINCENNES (CA-44), escorted by destroyers CHARLES F. HUGHES (DD-428), HILLARY P. JONES (DD-427), LANSDALE (DD-426), LUDLOW (DD-438), and MADISON (DD-425). The training area was just west of the Florida Keys off the Dry Tortugas. For the next month, we would engage in intensive gunnery exercises, firing at surface targets towed by the fleet tug ALGORMA, and at target sleeves towed by aircraft from the HORNET. In between these exercises, we conducted speed runs and fleet maneuvers.

There were two incidents during that training cruise that stand out in my mind. The first was a natural phenomenon. The Gulf of Mexico was exceedingly calm most of January, 1942; and for one three-day period, the sea was as flat as a table top and glowed a bright gold! It was a most uncommon condition for which we, at the time, had no rhyme or reason. Later I would come to know it as "the Red Tide"—zillions of microscopic sea creatures, one-celled, plant-like animals. The concentration is often in sufficient numbers to kill fish in waters where it occurs. But to me, it was a very beautiful sight.

The other incident involved humans, specifically our OS2U flyers. During main battery firing exercises, we launched the two Kingfisher float planes off the catapults to act as spotters. They were to tell us how close the 16-inch shells were landing to the targets, and by how much the fire controllers would have to correct their aim.

After conclusion of one of the firing exercises, the pilots reported some difficulty with their aircraft and, with permission, proceeded to the Naval Air Station at Key West where they spent the night. Returning in the morning, they again went out on their spotting mission, following which they again reported "mechanical difficulties" and flew on in to Key West. Of course, during their overnight stays they spent the evenings at the Officers' Club, had enjoyable dinners, and (one may assume) the company of ladies.

The planes returned in the morning and we recovered them in routine fashion, but as they were hoisted aboard by the big crane on the fantail and deposited on the catapults, the pilots were summoned to the Bridge "on the double!" Captain Badger had seen through their little subterfuge. As they stood at stiff attention on the Bridge wing, the Skipper said, quietly but firmly:

"Gentlemen, when two aircraft leave this vessel and do not return as scheduled, I will assume that any aircraft approaching this ship the next morning are enemy aircraft, and I shall take appropriate action!"

The pilots got the message, and there were no more "mechanical difficulties" that required an overnight in Key West. To the enlisted men around the Bridge, this was hilarious. A Seaman 2nd who'd only recently come aboard inquired: "The Captain *really* wouldn't shoot 'em down, would he?" To which one of the quartermasters laughingly replied: "Don't count on it! Badger's likely to do anything!"

The exercises completed, we left the Gulf, rounded the Dry Tortugas, and headed north toward Hampton Roads, again following the Gulf Stream as we had after our shakedown cruise. As we passed abreast Charleston, South Carolina, "the glass began to fall"—the barometer indicating a growing low-pressure area, sure sign of heavy weather on the way.

We would get our first taste of a storm at sea, and we hit the worst of it off Cape Hatteras, North Carolina, one of the most treacherous strips of water in the world. It's a virtual graveyard of ships, with hulls of unfortunate vessels strewn across its bottom. The name "Hatteras" is synonymous with "storm" to every man who's ever followed the sea.

If the Bermudas let you pass,
Oh, then beware of Hatteras!

Now, what we ran into was not a hurricane. It was just a plain old Hatteras blow. Yet, in those comparatively shallow waters off the Outer Banks, any severe wind will whip the ocean into a frenzy. We caught it at its worst. The seas turned a dark, foreboding, grayish purple. Squalls lashed at us; the waters rose and fell like huge liquid mountains. In Edmund Spenser's line in *The Faerie Queen:* "The surging waters like a mountaine rise . . . ."

Normally, any ship the size of the NORTH CAROLINA could ride fairly easy in most heavy weather, but we were now getting huge waves and troughs that caused our screening destroyers and the fleet tug that had joined us sometimes to be completely out of sight. At one point, I caught a look at that tug as she perched high on the cap of a huge comber. Her bow was completely out of the water and her screws were churning in open air. In that situation, she was out of control until she slid downward into another trough between the huge seas.

Aboard the battleship all was secured for foul weather, with lifelines rigged to aid any sailors who had to be on the weather decks. The huge battlewagon was pitching and rolling, and anything not secured properly was thrown to the decks. Some of the new lads began to experience that age-old malady of seafarers—seasickness. It was not what one would expect aboard such a large vessel.

From my sea watch station in the Chart House, I was an interested observer to the shiphandling under storm conditions, and to the Navigator's constant checking of charts and weather reports. The big blow was increasing in intensity. As I felt the ship's bow slant downward, a huge comber catapulted tons of water over her. Looking out the port near my station, I saw nothing but a solid wall of "green water" smashing against the Bridge FIFTY FEET above the water line!

The sea broke over the Bridge splinter shield and cascaded astern. This, I said to myself, is one helluva storm! Yet, it was but a gentle breeze compared to the Pacific typhoons I'd experience in later years. The low pressure system was moving southwest to northeast, and we were heading north-by-northeast. So in time, we ran out of it. For the first time, the green hands aboard had an idea of what it was like to be a true blue water sailor. As Edmund Burke, writing on "the Sublime and the Beautiful", once put it: "The ocean is an object of no small terror."

After a brief stopover at Norfolk, the NORTH CAROLINA left the HORNET and the WASHINGTON behind to go on to Brooklyn for dry dock availability. When the Statue of Liberty hove into view, there was an almost audible sigh of relief throughout the ship—no more steaming through storms, for a while anyway.

The primary purpose for drydocking was to permit the Engineering Officer to inspect the propellers, outboard sections of the main shafting, and the sea valves. At the same time, all hands were ordered over the side to clean the hull of barnacles and other fouling elements, and to repaint the hull below the water line. The number four blade on the upper starboard screw had a large crack and had to be replaced. Minor nicks in the trailing edges on all the other screws were filed and smoothed.

On 1 February, 1942, I was promoted to Radioman 3rd Class. To make the rate I not only had to get a perfect score on the radioman's exam, but had to pass the tests for Quartermaster 3rd and Signalman 3rd. The advancement carried an extra assignment. I would man the Radio Direction Finder whenever the Navigator called for it to be utilized. And my base pay went up to a much appreciated $60 a month!

With the apparent completion of all the training necessities and dry dock inspections, I was convinced we soon would be ordered into action someplace. But that was not to happen. I am still mystified why the NORTH CAROLINA, WASHINGTON, and HORNET were not rushed into offensive action somewhere. It has crossed my mind that the powers-that-be in the Navy Department *didn't know what to do with their brand new battleships!* The WASHINGTON did go on a hurry-up convoy trip to Scapa Flow, Scotland, losing an Admiral at sea—he just vanished from the ship. But other than that, both battleships were inactive.

The attack on Battleship Row at Pearl had apparently given the old proponents of surface action between "battle lines" some pause to consider how battlewagons would now be used in this new air-dominated warfare. To any but the most stubborn advocate, the day of the battleship as the dominant offensive weapon in the Fleet was blown out the tubes with the attack on Oahu. *This* War would be won or lost at sea by aircraft carriers and the Navy Air those old hard-liners had pooh-poohed for so many years. So what the hell could you do with the BBs, now? They were useless in Atlantic convoy duty because they had no anti-submarine capabilities, and it *would* be embarrassing to lose one to a U-boat. Thus, for six months after Pearl our powerful dreadnoughts would be kept in limbo until someone thought they might have some use protecting carriers with their anti-aircraft batteries.

In March, 1942, we were ordered to Portland, Maine, ostensibly as part of North Atlantic Patrol, to be used in case of any threat of German battleships attacking supply convoys. Even then, we'd be backing up the British Home Fleet. The journey northward to Casco Bay proved hazardous. The East Coast from the Virginia Capes to New Brunswick was socked in with a pea soup fog. Visibility was virtually nil, leaving the Navigator but two means to chart our course—dead reckoning and radio direction finding. The former uses a table (DRT) into which is fed ship speed and heading, as well as tidal, current, and wind information. From this, he plots the ship's position.

The Direction Finder (DF), which I now was called to man, had a low-frequency receiver and a circular antenna which looked like a big doughnut. It was rotated to pick up signals from shore-based transmitters at specific locations along the coast, each broadcasting a different identifiable signal. I would tune in one at a time, zeroing in on the signal, then adjusting the antenna until I got a "null" which showed the exact direction from which the signal was coming. By reading the calibration on the antenna wheel and the repeater compass, I would have one leg of a triangle. Repeating the process with at least one of the other transmitting DF stations, I would get a second leg. The direction from one DF station to the other was the third leg. By plotting these on a chart, I could locate the seaward intersection that would give me our precise location.

After each reading, I would relay the latitude and longitude to Lieutenant Commander Stryker, then the Navigator. Each time he'd tell me the position did not agree with the DRT; that there were differences of to two, three, and even five miles. This was not critical while we were well off the coast; but we still had to hit the narrow entrance to Casco Bay right on the nose, or end up on the famous "rock bound coast of Maine". As we approached that entrance, I submitted my last position report.

"How good do you think this is, Sparks?"

"That's as close as I can get it, Mr. Stryker", I answered, but experienced some trepidation when he said: "Let's hope you're right. I'm using your triangulations instead of the DRT to take us into the channel to the Bay."

I went back to the DF Shack, double-checked my readings and decided that *was* as close as I could get. We had executed a turn to port. As I stood outside the Shack, I saw through a lifting of the fog the channel buoys and an opening between huge rocks on either side of the ship, seemingly close enough to touch. Glory be! We were right where I'd figured we should be.

The buzzer on the sound-powered phone sounded. (These telephones were powered by sound vibration, not electricity, so we could still communicate aboard ship in case of power outages.) When I picked it up, it was Mr. Stryker on the other end.

"Well done, Sparks." It's the Navy's highest compliment.

We dropped anchor in Casco Bay on 16 March, 1942. According to the old seamen's motto: "A Passage perillus makyth a Port pleasant."

Of all the ports of call I made while on the NORTH CAROLINA, Portland was the ultimate for liberty. We were the first U.S. Naval vessel to make the port since World War I. At the same time, all the eligible young men of the city had either enlisted or were drafted. And Portland was the port of entry for Canadians coming to the States. The legend persisted that incoming French-Canadian young ladies "threw their panties over the side as their ships entered Casco Bay."

With all these unattached girls, both American and Canadian, and no other men around, it was a situation made in Sailor's Heaven. Saint Elmo, the seafarer's patron saint, was smiling down upon us, though doubtless not approving "the alleged sins of seafaring men"!

As the first liberty boats made the landing, they were greeted by dozens and dozens of girls. For the next three months, it was one big blast. Several of us pitched in to rent a room in the Congress Hotel to use as a headquarters when we were ashore. It often was crammed to the gunwales with sailors and their dates. As one of my shipmates so accurately put it, Portland was like turning the candy store over to the kids.

I dated several girls, one kind of seriously. But she lived out in Falmouth-Foreside, and with wartime restrictions the buses didn't run regularly. If I took her home, it was an expensive taxi ride, and that severely dented my finances. We did write each other a few times after the ship left Casco Bay. Her last letter said she'd joined the WAVES.

The WAVES (acronym for "Women Accepted for Volunteer Emergency Service") came into being in September, 1942, as a Reserve component of the Navy. They were organized to fill non-combat jobs, thus freeing more able-bodied men for sea duty. Primarily they were office workers; but they also served as chauffeurs, radio and switchboard operators, and in numerous other positions. Many gave up lucrative jobs to work for the Navy's low pay, such was their patriotism. They made significant contributions to the war effort.

There was not even a *hint* that WAVES would be assigned to any sea duty, let alone be exposed to combat. Such an idea would have spawned intense opposition, not only from men but from women as well. Women in our society of the 1940s occupied a special place. Mothers, sisters, wives, sweethearts and girl friends were to be protected. They were one of the reasons for which we fought—to keep them safe. To subject a woman to combat—to have her experience the gore, blood, and violence of it—was unthinkable.

The heart and soul of any military unit, be it a ship's crew or a frontline Marine infantry platoon, is *discipline*. In recent contacts with some of today's sailors and Marines, I have been struck by the seeming lack of discipline and a prevailing casual attitude toward duty. I cannot help but believe that the mixing of the sexes aboard ship, or in any combat unit, would only exacerbate the situation.

In the "new Navy" women are serving on auxiliary vessels, and their serving on combat ships is only a matter of time. If anyone could convince me this policy enhances, or even maintains, the requirements of readiness, I might buy into it. But sending qualified and experienced men to non-combat ships or shore duty, to replace them with women, defies all rationality. There are morale-busting double standards here. Women, officers and enlisted, simply do not have to meet the same standards of physical training required of men; and men must go wherever they are ordered, whereas only women who volunteer will serve on auxiliary or combat ships. Women may be transferred off ships by simple request, but men are required to serve wherever assigned.

The mixing of the sexes in close quarters aboard ships, auxiliary or combat, creates other significant problems, not the least of which is surreptitious sexual activity. Most of these people are from 18 to 25 years old. No amount of policy mandates or "sensitivity training" will prevent romantic liaisons—it's just human nature. Despite published reports in recent years, the public is generally unaware that some (perhaps most) auxiliary ships with mixed crews have returned to port with many of the women pregnant. In the Fleet these ships are laughingly labeled "Love Boats".

Since, as far as I know, none of the women in these cases have charged rape or sexual harassment, it appears that consensual sexual activity is the unofficial order of the day. Aside from the moral issues, this is a blatant collapse of discipline. Had war suddenly broken out and the ship come under fire, imagine these dilemmas:

A sailor manning one of the ship's weapons systems sees his "girlfriend", whom he knows to be pregnant with his child, in peril. Does he leave his battle station to help her? In the engine room, another man, responsible for executing speed changes ordered from the Bridge, hears his girlfriend screaming for help after being wounded. What does he do?

In both cases even the momentary hesitation taken to make a decision could be disastrous for the whole ship and her crew. When discipline goes out the porthole, so does safety, effectiveness, combat readiness, and above all—survival.

My primary concerns center on survival, combat readiness, and the ability of a ship to carry out its military missions. As an old combat sailor with twelve battle stars, I can speak with some authority, having experienced just about every emergency that can occur aboard ships during wartime. In later chapters you will read of these; for instance, of the rescue efforts when the JOHN PENN and the PRINCETON were lost. In these instances brute strength was the determining factor in saving the lives of men who had to be pulled from the cruel and recalcitrant sea. Most women could not have accomplished such, simply because they do not have the upper body strength and physical endurance. As you read accounts in these chronicles of combat and rescue operations, imagine an 18 or 19 year old 100-pound girl in these situations, and ask yourself if she could or would have survived, or have been able to help others survive.

There is no doubt that women can perform well, sometimes better than men, in many of the various specialties aboard ship, particularly in positions that do not require a great deal of physical strength. That may be all well and good in a peacetime Navy. But in a shooting war conditions change drastically. Sea duty becomes "a different bowl of grits" when the safety of the ship and the lives of shipmates are at stake. I have nothing but the highest respect and regard for those women who volunteer to put their lives on the line for their Country, but in doing so they seriously affect the combat readiness and eventually the survival of the ship and its crew.

War is no place for social experimentation. For well over 200 years the United States Navy has had a great combat record without women—"if it ain't broke, why fix it?"

Back in the "old Navy", stationing women on U.S. Navy vessels just might bring on a mutiny for another reason as well. There were enough of us old salts around who believed the ancient law of the sea (or superstition, if you will) that females aboard ship were Jonahs. Jinxes. Bad luck. Their presence would surely bring down the anger of all the Furies of Hell, and of the sea, herself, upon the hapless ones who defied this dictum of her domain. The sea is not only a demanding mistress, as Herman Melville wrote; she's a jealous one, too.

Sailors are superstitious. If not when they first go to sea, they soon become so. I grew up with a grandmother who had all sorts of taboos and odd beliefs: It was bad luck to put a hat on a bed; a bird singing at night portends a death in the family; the ill fortune caused by spilling salt can be avoided by throwing a pinch of it over the right shoulder; and a myriad of others. But I never bought into any of these or any other common superstitions—on land. But get me to sea, and I become a firm believer in *all* of the mariner's customs and superstitions.

With a ship, it all begins with the stepping (installation) of the mast. The Navy still may observe the ritual of placing a penny under the butt of the mainmast when it is stepped during construction. For good luck, it is said. On the other hand, it's bad luck to change a ship's name, or to begin a voyage on Friday. Rats observed leaving a ship in port, supposedly means the ship will be lost at sea. Surely it's bad luck to sail with women aboard, or for anyone to whistle aboard ship. The latter would bring violent winds. As for bad weather, there's the little rhyme predicting (with some meteorological justification):

> A rainbow in the morning—a sailor's warning.
> A rainbow at night—a sailor's delight.

The sea is so alien and anomalous, so imposing and prodigious, that a 20th century poetess (Anne Stevenson) once observed: "The sea is as near as we come to another world." And the 17th century poet John Milton penned these lines of a fallen world in *Paradise Lost:*

> The secrets of the hoary deep, a dark
> Illimitable Ocean, without bound,
> Without dimension, where length, breadth, and height,
> And time and place are lost . . . .

So many odd things can happen at sea: ships disappearing, men lost under mysterious circumstances, strange sightings that go unexplained in rational terms, and other events for which there seems to be no rhyme or reason. Small wonder men who follow the sea build up a large residue of omens, taboos, and superstitions. In the words of Norwegian playwright Henrik Ibsen: "The sea possesses a power over men's minds. . . . The sea can hypnotize."

According to 19th century American novelist James Fenimore Cooper: "There is a majesty in the might of the great deep, that has a tendency to keep open the avenues of that dependent credulity which more or less besets the mind of every man. The confusion between things which are explicable and the things which are not, gradually brings the mind of the mariner to a state in which any exciting and unnatural sentiment is welcome."

On the other hand, the sublime majesty of the sea, like life itself so teeming with unfathomable mystery, can lead to trust in a sovereign and supernatural God. This is perhaps nowhere better voiced than in the hymn of William Cowper (friend of John Newton, the old slavetrading sea captain, having become an evangelical hymn-writer himself) found in the Army and Navy *Hymnal*.

> God moves in a mysterious way His wonders to perform;
> He plants His footsteps in the sea, and rides upon the storm.
> Deep in unfathomable mines of never failing skill,
> He treasures up His bright designs, and works His sovereign will.

Back to Portland, Maine, in the spring of 1942. The Portland city fathers proved to be almost as hospitable as the girls. They put on a two-day real old-fashioned New England clambake as only Down Easterners can. Out on Little Chebeague Island in the Bay, they served up mounds of clams, oysters, fish, lobsters, coleslaw, corn on the cob, and assortments of other regional delicacies, not the least of which was Indian pudding. And there was an ample supply of beer. It was one grand picnic, and for the only time in my life I nearly got my fill of lobster.

Early in our stay, I came back from liberty one morning, and was still on the Quarterdeck as more bluejackets came up the gangway from the liberty launches. It was *cold!* So cold there were ice floes on the Bay's surface. Up the ladder came two signalmen, both obviously still celebrating their liberty. As the first, a "2nd Class hash-mark sailor", got to the platform at the top of the ladder, the lieutenant Junior Officer of the Deck stepped forward and patted him down, discovering a pint of whiskey in the signalman's inside peacoat pocket.

Now, it's against regulations to have whiskey aboard a U. S. Navy ship. (Although it was common knowledge most officers had bottles, and even cases, stashed away—*they* weren't searched when *they* came aboard.) The J.O.D., thinking to save the signalman disciplinary action, tossed the pint over the side. The "skivvie-waver", pretty much still in his cups, took one look at the splash and the sinking booze.

"My bottle!" he yelled, and in one motion dove over the gangway railing down into the icy waters 20 feet below!

His companion, another 2nd Class Signalman, looked aghast.

"My buddy!" he shouted, and went right over the side as well!

The J.O.D. shook his head, a look of resignation on his face, then called the duty cox'n to man his motor whaleboat, moored to the after boat boom, and fish the two out of the drink. By now, the signalmen had to be completely sober after hitting the icy waters of Casco Bay.

The wet, shivering, now-turning-blue sailors finally made it back aboard and, really sober, were somewhat contrite as they stood meekly before the lieutenant.

"Sorry, Sailors, but I'll have to put you on report for leaving the ship without permission", he told them, but not without some semblance of a smile at the thought of their going over the side after that bottle.

"Lieutenant", I said, quietly so only he could hear, "you may not have a case on that charge."

"Why?" he asked. "They obviously went over the side."

"Yes, Sir, but they were not officially aboard ship. If you'll recall, they'd only reached the top of the gangway, they did not request permission to come aboard, and you didn't grant such permission. They never set foot on the deck proper, Sir. Technically, they were still on liberty. And you couldn't charge them with bringing liquor aboard, either. You, yourself, threw it over the side."

I think the J.O.D. was trying to find a way out, anyhow. He was known as a pretty nice guy, for an officer. He turned to the dripping signalmen, told them they were not on report and waved them below. Amid much ribbing from shipmates around the Quarterdeck, they disappeared down the hatch.

The lieutenant looked at me, nodded, and flashed a grin.

I gave him my *most* military salute and, grinning myself, followed the signalmen below.

During our stay in Portland, Captain Badger made several trips to Washington. The scuttlebutt around the Bridge said he was pressuring CinCUS (Commander in Chief, U.S. Fleet) i.e. Admiral Ernest J. King to let him take the ship into action somewhere—anywhere. But it would be 28 May before we'd leave Portland.

Next port of call: Hampton Roads. There we would lose our favorite Skipper. On 1 June, Captain Oscar C. Badger was relieved by Captain George H. Fort. The man we had most wanted to lead us into combat, when it came, would not be there when we finally got into the War. Lest I leave the impression that Captain Badger was easy on his crew because he liked his enlisted men, let me dispel that right away. He was a tough taskmaster and had honed us to a sharp edge. It was our love and affection that went with him when he was piped over the side the last time.

Four days later Task Force 37 was formed and we got underway under secret orders in company with the aircraft carrier WASP (CV-7), cruisers QUINCY (CA-39) and SAN JUAN (CL-54), and destroyers STERETT (DD-407), STACK (DD-406), LANG (DD-399), FARENHOLT (DD-491), BUCHANAN (DD-484), and WILSON (DD-408). Once at sea, we learned we were headed for the Panama Canal and on into the Pacific

Ocean. It was 5 June, 1942, and over 5,000 miles away our forces were engaged in the critical Battle of Midway. We'd miss that one, but be there for the next one.

As we neared the northern end of the Canal Zone, Mr. Stryker asked that I man the DF Shack, again. When we sighted Cristobal Mole at the northern end of the Canal, my calculations were right on the dot.

Traversing the Canal proved to be a challenge. The NORTH CAROLINA's beam was so broad there was only minimum clearance between our hull and the concrete walls of "the Big Ditch". There were times when we could've used a shoe horn, but we made it O.K.

About halfway through the Canal Zone is Gatun Lake. It was the only place in the world where a seagoing vessel would wash her decks down with fresh water. The deck divisions manned their hoses, brushes and brooms, giving the ship a good cleaning fore and aft to remove accumulated salt and dirt.

On 11 June, we cleared the southern end of the Canal at Balboa. The NORTH CAROLINA then and there joined the Pacific Fleet. Under secret orders from Admiral Chester W. Nimitz, Commander in Chief, Pacific (CinCPac), we were to proceed northward to California with three of our escorting destroyers. The force was redesignated Task Force 18.

There was disappointment in Crew's Quarters and Officers' Country when we learned we were not heading straight for Hawaii and an early crack at the Japs. Since our entire battleship force had been knocked out at Pearl Harbor, the NORTH CAROLINA was the only battlewagon now operative in the entire Pacific Theater.

There may have been some question in the minds of the CinCPac Staff whether we would be a valuable asset or a detriment to the Fleet. The demolished ships along Battleship Row, visible daily to them, were a mute reminder that perhaps ships of the line had no place in an air-sea war.

The scuttlebutt was saying we'd visit Los Angeles and San Francisco to "show off" the newest addition to the Fleet before we'd head for Hawaii. This time, the scuttlebutt was right. But we still thought we should be getting out there as soon as possible and pass up the morale-building propaganda for the civilians.

It was not always easy to fathom the whys and wherefores of command decisions. Apparently, like the Lord, the Navy works its wonders in mysterious ways.

8

ON TO PEARL

In the five months following the Pearl Harbor attack, all news coming out of the Pacific Theater was of one disastrous defeat after another. Historians of the Pacific War tell the doleful details.

The Japanese, who used America's refusal to sell them oil as an excuse to war against us, urgently needed tin, fuel, rubber, and other strategic supplies. The nearest source, particularly for oil, was the Dutch East Indies. Driving southward in a series of lightning-like strikes, the Imperial Japanese forces gobbled up territory like sharks in a feeding frenzy.

Falling prey to the hostiles in the Far East were British-held Hong Kong, as well as Burma all the way westward to the frontier of India—cutting the Ledo-Burma Roads, the Allies' only supply line to Chungking and Chiang Kai-Shek's Kuomintang Chinese Army. Thailand fell, followed by the Malay Peninsula. The British surrendered Singapore. In the Western Pacific, the Japanese drove us out of the Philippines to add the Philippine Archipelago to the Empire of the Rising Sun.

In the Southwest Pacific, the Japs conquered the Dutch-held East Indies islands of Borneo, Sumatra, Java, Bali, and the Celebes. Crossing over the Banda Sea, the hostiles occupied the northern half of Australian-administered New Guinea, drove on to New Britain where they built a base at Rabaul, and swept eastward to the Eastern Solomons. Taking the Gilbert Islands in the Central Pacific, the Japs built bases on Tarawa and Makin. From their new base at Kwajalein in the Marshall Islands, they launched the successful invasion of Wake Island. Guam had fallen three days after Pearl Harbor. In the North Pacific, the Japanese invaded the Aleutian islands of Attu and Kiska, threatening Alaska. The Rising Sun had risen red-hot.

With their pre-Pearl Harbor conquests, the Empire of Japan was now nearly 6,000 miles wide, stretching from the International Date Line to India, some 5,000 miles long from Attu to the Solomons, and diagonally from Kiska to Sumatra over 7,300 miles across. All of Manchuria and Korea, most of northeastern China, including Peking (now Beijing), Nanking, and the Port of Shanghai; as well as the ports of Amoy, Swatow, and Canton, along with Formosa (now Taiwan) and French Indo-China (Vietnam)—were all subject to the brutal control of the Japanese Empire.

Tokyo's propaganda line of "Asia for Asians" and the creation of the "Greater East Asia Co-Prosperity Sphere" were nothing more than euphemisms for naked aggression and the enslavement of whole populations. As for the Western Powers, the Sons of Nippon believed they had burst the bubble of white supremacy. At this point, *the Japanese Empire was the largest in human history!* Their Empire dwarfed Hitler's conquests. Their military occupations were marked by the rape, pillage, torture, and slaughter of civilians by the millions—and the blood-letting went unchecked. This phase of the Pacific conflict is, unaccountably, barely noted in American history books, today.

A pitifully tiny naval force and a handful of land-based aircraft were charged with the impossible task of slowing down the onslaught of the overpowering Japanese fleets, about to strangle the Dutch East Indies with the tentacles of a giant naval octopus. A hastily assembled multi-national force of American, British, Dutch, and Australian (ABDA) ships was thrown into the maw of the enemy's juggernaut. Originally under Vice Admiral Thomas C. Hart, Commander of the U.S. Asiatic Fleet, the ABDA "Navy" had nine cruisers, three of them American: the HOUS-TON (CA-30), the BOISE (CL-47), and the ancient four-stack MARBLE-HEAD (CL-12). Some 26 destroyers, many of World War I vintage, and 39 submarines rounded out the flotilla. Air support or cover was nearly non-existent.

The ABDA force was to have included two "heavies", Great Britain's battleship H.M.S. PRINCE OF WALES and the battle-cruiser H.M.S. REPULSE. But on 10 December, while trying to thwart the Jap landings on Malaya, the British warships came under aerial attack. First, from Saigon, came flights of high-level bombers that scored hits on the REPULSE. But she remained operational. Then came the torpedo planes, swarming like wasps and loosing their "stingers", spearing the battle-cruiser with four torpedoes. She rolled over and sank. The PRINCE OF WALES, with her rudder jammed over from the initial attack, took three more fish. Before a destroyer could rescue her crew, she too rolled over and vanished beneath the sea. In London, the losses stunned the Admiralty. Never before had dreadnoughts, fighting at sea, been so easily and quickly dispatched by air attack.

On 24 January, 1942, Admiral Hart sent four World War I four-piper destroyers after a Jap convoy in Makassar Strait. They sank four ships and got away scot-free. February 4th (my 20th birthday) was a different story. The three American cruisers, two Dutch cruisers, and seven tin cans returned to the Strait after another enemy convoy. High-level bombers so pounded the MARBLEHEAD she barely made it back to the States after an heroic voyage. The BOISE was damaged after grounding on a reef and had to head home. The HOUSTON took a bomb which knocked out her number three main battery turret. But she stayed on, the only U.S. cruiser left to Admiral Hart.

The end came for the ABDA Navy, now under Dutch Admirals Helfrich and Doorman, a month later. On 27 February, five cruisers and nine destroyers (four of them World War I cans) went after an enemy convoy. In the two day/night Battle of the Java Sea, the Japs lost a cruiser and a destroyer. But the superior enemy force first sank the Dutch cruisers JAVA and DE RUYTER, their Captains and Admiral Doorman going down with them according to the old ritual of the sea. The HOUSTON and the Australian cruiser PERTH took out four Jap transports in Sunda Strait before they were shelled and torpedoed into shambles. Both were lost. The HOUSTON counted only 368 men saved out of a crew of 1,064. The next day, the British cruiser EXETER went down, shelled to death by four Jap cruisers.

With complete control of the Dutch East Indian tin mines, oil fields, rubber plantations, and supply sources, Imperial Japan now had the wherewithal to pursue its goal of world domination, of "bringing the eight corners of the world under one roof", supposedly an expression of Emperor Jimmu over 2,500 years before. "No such vast plan of quick conquest had ever been formulated in modern history. . . . This scheme of conquest was the most enticing, ambitious and far-reaching in modern history, not excepting Hitler's. It almost worked, and might well have succeeded *but for the United States Navy*" (Morison)!

In just six weeks the Japs had wiped out the entire Southeast Asia Allied naval forces. The situation was most dire. Flushed with "Victory Disease" attributable to swift and decisive conquests of territories and destruction of the enemies' fighting capability, Prime Minister General Hideki Tojo and the Tokyo military staffs now believed their Navy and Armies were invincible. With great self-confidence, plans were made to capture Port Moresby on the southern tip of New Guinea, establish a base on Tulagi in the Eastern Solomons, and go on to sever the U.S. to Australia supply line by invading Fiji, the New Hebrides, and New Caledonia—with a view to putting troops on the northern coast of Australia.

At the same time, Admiral Isoroku Yamamoto, Commander in Chief of the Imperial Japanese Navy, wanted to lure the U.S. Pacific Fleet into

MAKASSAR STRAIT
23-24 Jan. 1942

BORNEO

CELEBES

OM 4 pipers, FORD, POPE, PAUL JONES & PARROTT sunk 6 Transports & 1 DD here.

MAKASSAR STRAIT

EXETER ENCOUNTER (Br)
USS. POPE To Sunda Stra.
Dia. not make it.
HOUSTON CA (US)
EVERSTEN CL (Br) PERTH CL (Br)
Last seen headed for Sunda Strait.

Japan Convoy:
30 Transports
2 Cruisers
4 Destroyers
o ARENDS IS.

USS. HOUSTON HEAVY CRUISER 10,000 Tons, 32.7 Kts.
9-8"55's 8-5"AA 2-3pd. 8 MGs. 4 Aircr. 2 Catapults 1000 men.
570' x 66' 13,000 mi at 15 kts.

DE RUYTER CA (GT)
JAVA CL (GT)
KORTENAER DD (T)
JUPITER DD (M)
ELECTRA DD (GT)
Minefield (us)

MADOERA
KANGEAN ISLS.

MARBLEHEAD CL
Damaged here at 1027
Steers by engines.

HADAKAZE DD (T)
SOERABAJA
JAVA
TROMP CA (Dutch)
STEWART DD (us) Captured in drydock used by Japs for duration)
BANCKERT DD (Dutch)
WITTE DE WITH DD
(Destroyed to avoid Capture)

P. LANGLEY Seapl. Tend.
1st Operational US
Carrier. Commissioned in 1922.

PIET HEIN DD (G)
PILLSBURY DD

BALI

LOMBOK
SOEMBAWA

2000

ACTION OF BADOENG STR.
Feb. 19, 1942

o PECOS AO
THE BATTLES OF JAVA SEA
FEBRUARY 19-28 1942 EDSALL DD
ASHEVILLE PG

(Courtesy Sgt/Maj. Lester Bamford, USMC, Ret.)

a decisive battle, destroy it once and for all, and bring the War in the Pacific to a quick and decisive conclusion. Not since tangling with the British Navy in the War of 1812–14, had the United States Navy been up against such a disciplined and powerful force—indeed, Japan's Imperial Navy was built on the model of Britain's Royal Navy.

As all professional Navy men—British, American, or Japanese—Yamamoto knew that World War II would be won or lost at sea. With all his martial peers, he well knew the truth of the ancient adage of the Athenian statesman Themistocles (whose navy defeated the Persian fleet of Xerxes I at Salamis in 480 B.C.) as quoted by Cicero: *"He who commands the sea has command of everything."*

It was Admiral Yamamoto who, though personally against war with the U.S., planned and pushed the successful surprise attack on Pearl Harbor as Japan's only hope for a short war. Having studied at Harvard and served as naval attaché in Washington, the Admiral knew the Japanese would lose any prolonged war with American economic and industrial might. Yamamoto also knew the Pearl Harbor attack was flawed since they had missed our aircraft carriers as well as the opportunity to occupy Oahu, a certain source of American carrier-based offensive action in the Pacific. Thus he planned an offensive through the Central Pacific to annihilate our carriers and eventually invade the Hawaiian Islands. For Jap plans see John J. Stephan's *Hawaii Under the Rising Sun* (1984). As Stephan well remarks, Pearl Harbor was "the prologue to an unpredictable drama."

On the American side, New Pacific Fleet Commander Admiral Chester W. Nimitz followed the instructions from his boss, U.S. Navy Commander in Chief Admiral Ernest J. King, who from Washington set as the Navy's task to "hold what you've got and hit 'em where you can." Nimitz had sent his meager force of carriers out to harass the enemy. Admiral William F. "Bull" Halsey led carrier raids against Kwajalein, Wake, and Marcus Islands with the carrier ENTERPRISE (CV-6). The flat-top LEXINGTON (CV-2) had been sent to ruffle the Jap's feathers with a raid on Rabaul, and on 18 April the HORNET (CV-8) launched Lieutenant Colonel Jimmy Doolittle's B-25 bombers on their surprise raid over Tokyo. All these raids accomplished was to let the Japs know we were still in the War, and convince them of the necessity of offensive action against Hawaii.

On 10 April, some 60,000 survivors of the nearly 75,000 American and Filipino troops defending the Philippines, having been forced to surrender when food and ammunition gave out, had begun a forced march of some 85 miles to prisoner-of-war camps in one of the most infamous events of World War II—the Bataan Death March. Barely

scarecrows from malnutrition, emaciated by disease, the ragged survivors were subjected to the gross inhumanity of their Japanese captors.
Stragglers, the wounded, the ill, were beaten nearly every step of the
way. Over 20,000 would not make it to the end of the six-day ordeal.
Bludgeoned to death with rifle butts, bayonetted, and starved, they
stumbled their way toward O'Donnell Prison Camp on Luzon. In one
incident some 300 men were mowed down by Jap machineguns when,
dying of thirst, they tried to get to water. Some of the dying were buried
alive in shallow graves.

The list of atrocities perpetrated by the Japs is too long to detail
here, but they did not stop upon arrival at the POW camps. Thousands
more died during their long internment. The Bataan Death March was
not an aberration. It was indicative of the inhumanity and extreme
cruelty of the Japanese throughout the War, little of which is known to
Americans today.

The atrocities of the Oriental Holocaust, in which far more died than
in Nazi concentration camps, go forgotten. In historian William Manchester's words: "Time has blurred the jagged contours of the Greater
East Asia Co-Prosperity Sphere, but it should be remembered that the
Nipponese were a savage foe, at least as merciless and sadistic as the
Spaniards [when Spain ruled the Philippines]. In Manila they slew
nearly 100,000 civilians; hospital patients were strapped to their beds
and set afire; babies' eyeballs were gouged out and smeared on the walls
like jelly."

American morale reached its nadir on 6 May, 1942. The last bastion
defending the Philippines fell to the Japanese. Corregidor, the rock
island fortress in Manila Bay, had held out for five bloody months. Its
defenders—wracked by malaria and other tropical diseases, out of
ammunition, fuel, and literally starving—hoisted white flags over "the
Rock".

The folks back home were in need of some good news, and it came
not long after the fall of Corregidor. Unknown to the Japanese High
Command, our cryptologists had broken the enemy's secret naval code.
So when Admiral Nimitz found out what the enemy was planning, he
decided to send a carrier force into the Coral Sea in early May to thwart
the Jap invasion of the southern coast of Papua New Guinea. Alerted by
enemy dispatch intercepts decrypted through breaking the Japs JN-25
naval code, Nimitz sent the carriers YORKTOWN (CV-5) and LEX-
INGTON, with five cruisers and nine destroyers, toward the Solomon
Sea.

Steaming out of Rabaul into the Solomon Sea, a Japanese force of
one light and two fleet carriers, eight cruisers and six destroyers,

escorted transports loaded with troops for an invasion of Port Moresby on New Guinea, just a stone's throw across the Torres Strait from Australia. American Admiral Frank Jack Fletcher launched a strike; but instead of finding the main enemy carrier force, his planes spotted the light carrier SHOHO. Dive bombers attacked, sending her to the bottom, the first Jap carrier sunk in the War. Scratch one flat-top! Japanese Admiral Takagi, now forewarned of the American presence, ordered the invasion force to reverse its course and stay clear until he had taken care of Fletcher's carriers.

Uncertain weather postponed a head-to-head confrontation until the next day. At about 0930, 8 May, air strikes were mounted by both sides. Our dive bombers scored hits on the SHOKAKU, heavily damaging the Nipponese fleet carrier. She'd be forced to return to Japan for repairs. Her companion flat-top, the ZUIKAKU, took refuge in a rain squall and avoided attack. Jap aircraft, however, found Task Force 17, scoring torpedo and bomb hits on the LEXINGTON. The YORKTOWN took a 550-pound bomb, killing 66 men, but good swift damage control kept her operational. It appeared the two carriers had escaped disabling damage, but a spark from a generator ignited gasoline fumes on the LEX. A huge internal explosion rocked her, to be followed by another, and she had to be abandoned. The PHELPS (DD-360) scuttled her with a torpedo spread to keep her out of enemy hands.

In this first naval battle in history in which the surface ships involved never saw each other, in terms of losses, the edge went to the Japs. Strategically, however, it was a victory for the Good Guys. It bloodied the enemy's nose; and, for the first time, the Japanese advance toward domination of the Pacific was blunted. The invasion force, retreating to Rabaul, never again attempted a strike toward Port Moresby. So ended the Battle of the Coral Sea.

As the NORTH CAROLINA and the WASP hurried toward the Pacific, our battered forces were bracing for Admiral Yamamoto's assault on Midway Island in the Central Pacific; where he hoped to destroy our dwindling Pacific Fleet, knocking us out of the War, and to establish a forward base for the planned invasion of Hawaii. Again, the breaking of the enemy's JN-25 code gave Admiral Nimitz advance warning. Intercepted dispatches pointed to a massive build-up of a task force that would include two light carriers, four fleet carriers, nine battleships, sixteen cruisers, and nearly thirty destroyers, not to mention an advance force of some sixteen submarines. Aboard transports were 5,000 men to be landed on Midway. It was the largest and most powerful naval force ever assembled to that time.

Against this armada, we had three flat-tops—the ENTERPRISE,

the HORNET, and the very hastily repaired YORKTOWN—screened by eight cruisers and fifteen destroyers. That's practically *all* we had! Thoroughly outnumbered, outgunned, and outmanned as usual, our guys were going into the shoot-out at the O.K. Corral armed with peashooters. David was going out to meet Goliath.

At that moment, the United States of America was facing its greatest danger from a foreign foe since the War of 1812. But only a handful of people in Honolulu and Washington were aware of the gravity of the situation, and that a loss here would be disastrous. The threat of attacks on Hawaii and the mainland's West Coast could suddenly become a reality. The "Europe First" strategy, at this point, didn't look so good.

Admiral Halsey was hospitalized with a skin rash, and on his recommendation was replaced on the ENTERPRISE by a "cruiser Admiral"—quiet, unassuming Rear Admiral Raymond A. Spruance. He commanded Task Force 16 composed of the "Big E" and the HORNET. Senior Admiral Fletcher, in overall command, was on the YORKTOWN, directly commanding Task Force 17.

PBY patrol planes spotted the approaching Japanese on 3 and 4 June. On the morning of the 4th, some 108 enemy bombers struck at Midway Atoll, defended by Marine pilots in slow, old F2A Buffalo fighters and anti-aircraft batteries. Despite the mismatch against enemy Zeros, then the best carrier-borne fighters in the world, Marine planes and ground gunners knocked down nearly a third of the Nip strike squadrons.

In a brilliant bit of strategy, Admiral Spruance had stationed his carriers to the northeast of Midway instead of arraying his forces directly between the island and the oncoming Japs. The enemy would have one helluva time finding them. Admiral Nagumo, commanding the hostiles' Carrier Strike Force he had unleashed on Pearl Harbor, had held in reserve 93 bombers and torpedo planes to be launched when his search planes found Spruance and Fletcher. But when no word of the U.S. carriers came in, Nagumo made a fatal mistake.

The Japanese pilots returning from the first strike on Midway reported heavy defenses—to neutralize them, and to take out the American airstrip, would require a second raid. Nagumo ordered his 93 reserves rearmed to make such a strike. The planes no sooner had been reloaded with bombs when one of the Jap reconnaissance aircraft reporting sighting the YORKTOWN Task Force. In almost a panic, the flight crews had to rearm their planes again, this time with torpedoes, when the Admiral canceled the second attack on Midway in order to attack the U.S. ships.

Back on the ENTERPRISE, Admiral Spruance made a couple of crucial decisions, on advice from Halsey's brilliant Chief of Staff Captain Miles Browning. Rather than wait until his Task Force 16 was within 100 miles of the enemy, he launched aircraft nearly two hours earlier than planned, hoping to catch the Japs recovering and/or refueling and rearming aircraft. And, he shot his whole wad, sending every plane he had, except for the fighter Combat Air Patrol (CAP) over his carriers. Admiral Fletcher delayed launching from the YORKTOWN until 40 minutes later, sending half his dive bombers and all his dozen torpedo planes, escorted by a half-dozen fighters.

Lieutenant Commander John C. Waldron's TorpRon 8 (Torpedo Squadron 8)—fifteen old TBD Devastator torpedo bombers from the HORNET—were the first to spot the enemy carriers and, without fighter cover, went in on the attack. Zeros pounced on them from above; ship anti-aircraft fire burst among them. Every TBD was shot down, and there was but one survivor, Ensign George Gay, left of TorpRon 8. He watched the rest of the battle from a life raft before being rescued by our own people.

ENTERPRISE and YORKTOWN torpedo planes fared little better. Of the 41 launched from the three carriers, only six got back, and no hits had been scored. When the last torpedo attack failed at 1024, the Japs thought they'd won the Battle of Midway. But within the next 100 seconds the tide of battle turned 180 degrees. The sacrifice of the torpedo squadrons was not for naught.

Now it was up to the ENTERPRISE and YORKTOWN dive bombers, under Lieutenant Commanders C. Wade McClusky and Maxwell F. Leslie, those from the HORNET having missed Nagumo's force. While the Zeros had been lured to low altitudes intercepting the TBDs, the SBD Dauntless dive bombers came in at upper altitudes, circled over the Jap force, then a few seconds before 1026 struck with devastating results. The hostiles' carriers had just turned into the wind to launch aircraft, their flight decks jammed with fully rearmed and refueled planes. Three of the enemy flat-tops—SORYU, AKAGI, and KAGA—were wracked with explosions, planes set ablaze, and within minutes began sinking. Scratch three carriers!

The fourth Nip carrier, HIRYU, launched two strikes against our YORKTOWN Task Force. The YORKTOWN took three bombs and two torpedoes. She was still afloat the next morning when an enemy submarine eluded screening destroyers and fired a spread of fish. One hit the HAMMANN (DD-412) alongside the carrier. She broke in two and, with heavy casualties, sank immediately. Despite two hits by the sub's torpedoes, the YORKTOWN hung on until dawn on 7 June. Then she too finally rolled over and sank.

In a measure of revenge, SBD Dauntless dive bombers from the YORKTOWN's squadrons found the HIRYU, and four direct bomb hits sent her to the bottom. She took down with her Admiral Yamaguchi, the Jap Navy's boldest planner, and his dreams of carrying the Pacific War to California. A younger version of Yamamoto, having studied at Princeton and been naval attaché in Washington, Yamaguchi was his probable successor as Commander in Chief of the Combined Fleet.

Now, with insufficient air cover, after considering pursuing surface action Admiral Yamamoto began his doleful withdrawal. Admiral Spruance wisely avoided further confrontation and the Battle of Midway was over—a thundering victory for the United States Navy. (The story is well-told in the movie *MIDWAY*, starring Charlton Heston.) Midway was the first decisive win for us in the War. With it we had evened the odds a little, but more fierce fighting was ahead. Some experts were predicting a nine- or ten-year struggle to defeat the Japanese.

Midway unnerved Admiral Yamamoto and the Japanese Fleet. "In all its long history, the Japanese Navy had never known defeat. . . . Never has their been a sharper turn in the fortunes of war than on that June day when McClusky's and Leslie's dive-bombers snatched the palm of victory from Nagumo's masthead, where he had nailed it on 7 December. . . . The Fourth of June—day that should live forever glorious in our history . . . ." (Morison)!

But who remembers now?

The first two carrier battles—the Coral Sea and Midway—had now been fought. The NORTH CAROLINA missed 'em, but we'd be there for number three.

18 June brought orders for the NORTH CAROLINA to proceed to our first West Coast port of call, Long Beach, California. Anchoring inside the breakwater on what was known as "Battleship Row", we prepared for liberty. When you're young, you do a lot of dumb things, and that liberty ended up being one on which I tied on the biggest drunk of my life.

A bunch of us, probably twelve or fifteen, had watchstanders' liberty. That meant we could leave the ship at 1300 (1:00 PM) instead of waiting until regular liberty call at 1600 (4:00 PM). We hit the first bar nearest the liberty landing, progressed through San Pedro and Long Beach, making "fueling stops" at every watering hole that looked inviting. Along the way, we kept losing one or two shipmates at a time who either couldn't keep up the pace or found other attractions.

It was about dark when we boarded the old Red Car (trolley) and headed for Los Angeles. Only three or four were now left in our stalwart band, and all of us were pretty well oiled from those earlier stops. The rough ride on the Red Car did little to sober us up; but I really do, honestly, remember getting off at the L.A. terminal and heading for a Main Street gin mill. But that was the *last* thing I recall *until* . . . .

Somewhere in the wee sma' hours of the morning, probably about 0200, I had a moment of lucidity. Johnny Johnston and I were sitting on the curb in front of the famous Brown Derby in Hollywood! How we got there, we were never able to ascertain. I started to stand up and all went dark again.

The next moment of consciousness came some five hours later as a cab driver shook me to say we were at the fleet landing back in Long Beach. When I offered to pay him, he said he'd already gotten the fare and a healthy tip. To this very day, I have no idea how we got to the Brown Derby, or how I got in the cab, or who paid for it. There were also those big blanks between early evening and 0200, and between then and about 0700. Johnny wasn't any help either, although he'd returned to the ship a couple of hours before I did.

Weaving my way to the landing, I found no liberty boats, so I took a water taxi, telling the operator to take me to the NORTH CAROLINA. I then crapped out on the bow. The bumping of the prow against a gangway woke me, and I scrambled up the side of the ship, still unsteady on my pins. At the Quarterdeck I asked the Officer of the Deck: "Is this the NORTH CAROLINA?" I saluted the Colors, saluted the O.D., and walked directly into the 16-inch steel barbette of Turret Three, going down like a felled ox.

I came to in Sick Bay with a bump and bandage on my head, but otherwise unscathed. Fortunately, a compassionate and understanding Officer of the Deck did not put me on report. But the tale of my "exploits" soon made the rounds, and I became somewhat of a shipboard legend in my own time, though not exactly the kind of hero I would liked to have been.

Both military and civilian populations on the West Coast were still very apprehensive about possible enemy attacks, although Midway had eased some of the tension. In the weeks after Pearl Harbor, there was a real threat of both Japanese naval and air attacks. With our Fleet in shambles, there was little between Hawaii and the mainland to stop a Jap task force, and fear bordering on panic prevailed. Thus President Roosevelt eventually issued Executive Order 9066 (19 February, 1942) resulting in the detainment and internment of some 110,000 Japanese living on the West Coast.

The internment of the Japanese in 1942 was not notably controversial when carried out, but became so in the course of time. Of the enemy aliens living in the U.S. (i.e. Japanese, Germans, and Italians who were not American citizens) only Japanese non-citizens (*Issei*) were singled out to be relocated in ten special detention camps. President Roosevelt believed detaining German and Italian aliens (e.g. Joe DiMaggio's mother!) bad for wartime morale.

At the same time, not only Japanese aliens but Japanese who were American citizens (*Nisei*) were also interned—despite the fact that Lieutenant General John L. DeWitt, who eventually came to support and execute internment as a matter of military necessity, originally objected on the ground that: "An American citizen is, after all, an American citizen."

Nevertheless, Japanese internment was executed by the "liberal" Roosevelt Administration, supported with one voice by American public opinion, upheld by the Supreme Court of the United States, and defended by "liberal" justices Hugo Black, Felix Frankfurter, and William O. Douglas. Many factors played a role: including war hysteria, racial prejudice, and resentment resulting from Pearl Harbor. The major factor, however, was the fear that some Sons of Nippon were disloyal to the U.S., that Nipponese ancestral and racial bonds of sympathy would prevail, and that it was impossible to distinguish loyal from disloyal Japanese—as emphasized by California Attorney General Earl Warren.

Were racial sympathies and cultural similarities simply negated by geographical location? Would all white Europeans or Americans born or living in Japan be or become loyal Japanese subjects ready to fight and die for the Emperor? Obviously some Japs in the States were in sympathy with Japan. Thus internment was seen to be a military necessity (though the Japanese in more vulnerable Hawaii were not interned, probably because the Hawaiian economy would have difficulty functioning without them). In General DeWitt's words: "The continued presence of a large, unassimilated, tightly knit racial group, bound to an enemy nation by strong ties of race, culture, custom and religion along a frontier vulnerable to attack constituted a menace which had to be dealt with."

The forced evacuation and relocation of the Japanese was unfortunate, since the overwhelming majority of internees were loyal to their adopted country. For example, there were no known (publicly prosecuted and proven) cases of sabotage or espionage. And the Japanese-American (*Nisei*) 442nd Regimental Combat Team served our country well, in the European Theater one should add, receiving more decorations *for its size* than any other unit in our Armed Services.

At the same time, some of the Japs in the internment camps were overtly disloyal. For example, roughly one of four male Japanese-American citizens (*Nisei*) of draft age refused to serve in the American military. Some 8,700 Jap internees refused to swear unqualified allegiance to the United States, in terms of faithfully defending our country from enemies foreign and domestic; and forswear any form of allegiance or obedience to the Emperor of Japan, some *Issei* refusing for fear of having no nationality since heretofore legally excluded from U.S. citizenship. After the War some 8,000 Japanese, most of them *Nisei* having renounced American citizenship, returned to Japan. Of course, Emperor Hirohito and the Japanese Government proclaimed that all those of Japanese ancestry, no matter where they lived or what citizenship they held, were Japanese nationals obliged to obey the Emperor.

It is claimed that the Japanese internees were forced to move from their homes and live under harsh conditions in "concentration camps". Obviously the camps were not like home, but they protected the Japanese from the very real threat of violence on the part of Americans incensed by the Pearl Harbor attack. From the perspective of those of us in the Armed Services, the Japs had better quarters and more amenities than many servicemen on Army bases and in Navy boot camps, not to mention those in fox holes and in submarines. America's draftees were evacuated from their homes, moved around at the will of the U.S. Government, and forced to live in conditions far worse than those of the Jap internees. At the time, it was complained that the Japs received free public services, in the best New Deal style, that ordinary Americans could not get.

From the nature of the case, there were a few unfortunate incidents of violence in the camps—given human nature, a bloody war on with the brutal Japs, and some defiant anti-American feeling among the internees. But to put the matter into perspective, we need only compare the treatment given foreign civilians interned by the Japs. Of some 150,000 *less than 5,000 survived* beating, torture, and slave labor. None of the American survivors of Jap brutality have received $20,000 from the U.S. Government as have the Japanese internees. Nor, for that matter, have those of us who suffered far worse (living and dying conditions) as a result of Pearl Harbor than did the Jap internees.

Getting underway, once more, the NORTH CAROLINA headed up the California coast to "Frisco", as we sailors called San Francisco, much to the dismay of its citizens. The City by the Bay had the reputation of being a World Class liberty port, and that it was. While the ship was being reprovisioned and made ready for sea again, the crew grabbed every opportunity to make our last stateside liberties memorable.

I found a little neighborhood-type bar up on Powell Street. The

"Melody Lane" was complete with a piano bar, a stand-up comic, a stripper (who never quite went all the way), and a most attractive blonde girl singer. The bartender, named Bill, was friendly and the regulars in the place were most cordial. It was a nice place to hang out and relax. Besides, I got a couple of dates with the singer. But I didn't try to set any imbibing records à la Los Angeles.

On 6 July, new orders came from CinCPac (Admiral Nimitz).

"Single up all lines! Make preparations for getting underway!"

The pipe of the bos'n's mate of the watch shrilled through the loud speakers. The Special Sea Detail hastened to stations. Two tugs snugged up alongside to aid the giant battleship out into San Francisco Bay, edging her away from Pier 35, and turning her bow toward the Golden Gate. Outward bound, we sailed under the famous span. I stood on the fantail for a while and watched the graceful bridge fade in the distance. I didn't know whether I'd ever see her again.

Our escorts, the U.S.S. CUSHING (DD-376) and U.S.S. CRAVEN (DD-382), took their protective positions, one off the port bow, the other to starboard as we were greeted by the Pacific's ground swells and headed westward past the Farallon Islands. Next port of call: Pearl Harbor, Island of Oahu, Territory of Hawaii.

The voyage was without incident, but on-board activity took on a more serious warlike tone. We were at General Quarters for an hour each morning beginning a half hour before dawn, and again each evening 30 minutes before sunset—supposedly the times most likely for enemy attack. Training exercises in all divisions accelerated. The 5-inch guns' loading machine was in daylong use as the anti-aircraft battery crews sought to improve their proficiency. Damage control parties simulated casualty drills. Fire controlmen trained on practice targets. And we drilled at manning our battle stations, setting new ship records for quickly becoming "manned and ready" for action.

Rounding fabled Diamond Head, we slowed speed to wait for the anti-submarine nets at the narrow harbor entrance to be swung aside to allow us passage. As we proceeded up the channel, I could see signal lights flashing messages. I could read light faster than most signalmen, and deciphered the flashes from the main signal tower which was alerting ships in Pearl Harbor that the NORTH CAROLINA was coming in.

I watched fascinated as crewmen of destroyers, cruisers, auxiliaries, climbed atop gun mounts and onto superstructures to get a first-hand look at the great and mighty "Showboat" about which they'd heard so much. Then came the cheers from every ship we passed, from the civilians in the Navy Yard, from Ford Island. I don't know if I've ever felt more proud than at that moment. Here were sailors who'd been fighting the damned War practically with spears and arrows, holding back the surging Jap advance with hardly enough ships to fill a bathtub, and *they* were cheering US? Hell, it should have been the other way around. *They* were the ones who'd been doing all the dirty work.

The moment of pride and exhilaration suddenly gave way to shock and overwhelming sadness. In a somber salute we rendered Honors to the ships and to the men who'd taken the brunt of the sneak attack on Battleship Row. Below the still-oily waters of Pearl Harbor rested the remains of sailors like ourselves, men who had given that last full measure. The devastation was even worse than we had expected.

The capsized OKLAHOMA was still showing her keel. The ARIZONA's superstructure was upright. She'd sunk so quickly she couldn't capsize. But salvage work was well under way to reclaim the old battleships. Except for the ARIZONA and OKLAHOMA, all would steam and fight again. The ARIZONA was destined to be the permanent reminder of 7 December, 1941, and of the perfidy of Imperial Japan. The names of 1,144 men whose bodies were to man the battleship forever are enshrined for all time on the rolls of the United States Navy. We shall never let our memories of these men die.

It wasn't just Battleship Row that had been devastated. There were signs of destruction almost everywhere. But if the Japs made one serious error on 7 December, 1941, it was failing to launch their final strike. Apparently assuming enough damage had been inflicted on our Fleet, and not knowing where our carriers were, they aborted the third of their planned air attacks. The targets were to have been Pearl Harbor's vast repair facilities, including one of the largest cranes in the world, the huge hammerhead at Ten-Ten Dock. As it was, all this was virtually intact, and salvage and repair operations had begun almost before the last bomb fell. The entire base was a 24-hour-a-day, seven-day-a-week beehive of activity as repairs to both ships and shore facilities proceeded full speed ahead.

There was, is, and may always be, controversy over whether the Pearl Harbor tragedy was "allowed to happen". The most popular theory says President Roosevelt, anxious for the U.S. to enter the European War on the side of the British, knew Japan was about to strike. Since sentiment in America was strongly against our involvement in a foreign war, he needed an "incident" to get an isolationist public on his side. Thus, the assumption goes, he did not put the Fleet on full alert even though all signs pointed to a Japanese attack. But, as historian Morison points out, this "conspiracy" theory stretches all credulity; in that it would have had to have included other top civilian and military leaders, and a failed attack would have served the President's presumed purpose as well as the "smashing success" allegedly allowed to happen.

One afternoon, while on "yard liberty" (time off the ship but restricted to the Navy Yard) I was enjoying a cup of java with a radioman off the ENTERPRISE (CV-6). The subject of the sneak attack on Pearl came up. He wondered why the entire Pacific Fleet had not been put on the same alert status Admiral Halsey had ordered for the ENTERPRISE task force that had been at sea when Pearl was hit. He said "Battle Order Number One" had put the force on a war footing on 28 November, *ten days before Pearl Harbor was attacked!*

Like a lot of dope going around at the time, I figured this was just more scuttlebutt and it faded from my mind. Off and on, though, I would hear references to it; but it wasn't until 1985 that I saw a full account of the Battle Order and its exact text. Captain Elias B. Mott (USN Ret), an assistant Gunnery Officer on the "Big E" in 1941, wrote the story for the magazine *Shipmate*. It raises more questions than it answers, and adds fuel to the contentions that the attack on Pearl was allowed to happen.

But, given all the other accounts, I tend to feel that Pearl Harbor occurred due to a series of unfortunate blunders, lack of intra-government communication, and the failure of the civilian and military leadership in Washington to recognize the immediate threat. Thus, neither the Navy command at Pearl nor the Army (the latter charged with the specific responsibility to protect Hawaii) were given sufficient information or orders to be on full alert.

The Island of Oahu was still pretty much buttoned up when we arrived. Security was extremely tight, and liberty was under heavy restriction, limited to daylight hours only. But I lucked out. The first person up the brow when we moored alongside Ten-Ten Dock was a civilian yard bird. He spoke to the Officer of the Deck, and the word was passed for me to lay up to the Quarterdeck to meet a visitor. The yard bird was Wally Dowden, an old acquaintance from back home in Penns Grove, New Jersey.

Wally had a rented house at 123 Lewers Street out near the Royal Hawaiian Hotel and invited me to come over if I could get liberty. I checked with the O.D. and found the only way I could be gone from the ship overnight was to have an address and phone number where I could immediately be located in case of emergency. At Wally's I had both and put in a request that was granted.

On the way to Wally's, we stopped to buy some beer. When I pulled out some money to pay for it, Wally told me to put the bills back in my wallet.

Battle Order Number One

Captain Elias B. Mott USN (Ret.)

A couple of weeks prior to the attack on Pearl Harbor, many of us were aware of the deteriorating diplomatic situation with Japan in spite of the presence of two of her envoys. Our Admiral had just returned from a conference with Adm. Kimmel. On 27 November 1941, the aircraft carrier USS ENTERPRISE was moored to its berth at Ford Island in Pearl Harbor. During that day 12 Marine F4F fighter planes were towed to the dock and hoisted aboard the ship. Their Marine pilots came aboard with hastily packed luggage and very recent orders. The Marine fliers were under the command of Major Paul A. Putnam. On the ship we speculated as to why these fighters had been hoisted aboard the ship. The next morning ENTERPRISE was underway early and proceeded out of Pearl Harbor channel. I was a Lieutenant then and was the Assistant Gunnery Officer as well as Antiaircraft Control Officer. I was at my station in Sky Control, a great platform on a tripod mast partially enclosed for weather and 110 feet above the waterline for better visibility of aircraft. The Gunnery Officer, LCdr. Orlin Livdahl '26 was there with me. We soon received orders from the ship's Captain to prepare to arm all our aircraft with live bombs, live gun ammunition and war-ready torpedoes. We were also told to supply all our guns and antiaircraft batteries with live ammunition. In all, this was a tremenduous task requiring thousands of man hours on the part of many men to belt the ammunition and to ready the torpedoes for war shots. The latter operation required major adjustments of the torpedoes and replacement of the exercise head with a TNT filled warhead. I informed the Gunnery Officer that if we made the torpedoes ready for war shots as ordered, we would not be able to undertake an exercise scheduled shortly after we returned to Pearl Harbor. He so informed the Commanding Officer and was told promptly to prepare the torpedoes for war shots.

As we sortied out from Pearl Harbor, the ship went some distance off Barber's Point, turned into the wind and took aboard our own air group of 72 planes including 18 fighters, 36 dive bombers and 18 torpedo planes. We then headed westward and were joined by three cruisers and nine destroyers. We considered our orders to break out the live ammunition very startling.

The Commander of our Task Force, which was named Task Force Eight, was VAdm. William F. Halsey '04, Commander Aircraft, Battle Force. Admiral Halsey had been our flag officer for the past year and ENTERPRISE was his flagship. It was announced that we were going to proceed to Wake Island and deliver the twelve fighter planes. These planes, incidentally, became the only air defense for Wake Island when it fell less than a month later. The Captain of the ship then conferred with Adm. Halsey. Adm. Halsey wanted to impress on everyone the gravity of the situation.

In order to impress the seriousness of the situation on the officers and crew, and the other ships in the formation, Captain Murray '11 of ENTERPRISE drew up for Admiral Halsey's approval "BATTLE ORDER NUMBER ONE", a remarkable document in that it was dated ten days before Pearl Harbor.

CV6/A16-(10-11t)

U.S.S. ENTERPRISE

At Sea,

28 November, 1941

BATTLE ORDER NUMBER ONE

1. The ENTERPRISE is now operating under war conditions.

2. At any time, day or night, we must be ready for instant action.

3. Hostile submarines may be encountered.

4. The importance of every officer and man being specially alert and vigilant while on watch at his battle station must be fully realized by all hands.

5. The failure of one man to carry out his assigned task promptly, particularly the lookouts, those manning the batteries, and all those on watch on deck might result in great loss of life and even the loss of the ship.

6. The Captain is confident all hands will prove equal to any emergency that may develop.

7. It is part of the tradition of our Navy that, when put to the test, all hands keep cool, keep their heads, and FIGHT.

8. Steady nerves and stout hearts are needed now.

G. D. MURRAY (Signed)

Captain, U.S. Navy,

Commanding.

APPROVED, 28 November 1941:

W. F. HALSEY (Signed)

Vice Admiral, U.S. Navy,

Commander Airacraft, Battle Force.

This Battle Order was mimeographed and promulgated throughout the ship to all hands including the pilots. It was also sent by signal to the ships in the Task Force.

ENTERPRISE and the ships in the Task Force immediately assumed wartime conditions. The watches of the lookouts and on the batteries and by the damage control people were set at Condition II, with two different crews operating four hours on and four hours off day and night. Admiral Halsey also ordered all aircraft to bomb, strafe, or torpedo any strange craft that might endanger the Task Force. Orders were given to the pilots to fire on any Japanese submarine or aircraft sighted. Each day combat air patrol fighters were overhead during daylight hours and an anti-submarine patrol of planes ranged ahead of the Task Force with live depth bombs. In addition, the dive bombers and scouting planes searched out in sectors around the ship for two hundred miles each morning and each afternoon. Thus the Task Force had visual coverage for 200 miles in every direction. The ship's mechanics worked frantically to put the Marine planes in top-notch condition, overhauling their motors and radios and getting their guns ready for wartime firing, as there were no overhaul facilities for them at Wake Island.

The Task Froce arrived off Wake Island in due course and flew off the twelve Marine fighter planes, which were to constitute Wake's sole aircraft defense.

The Task Force then reversed course and started on its journey of over two thousand miles back to Pearl Harbor. We were due to arrive in Pearl Harbor on the afternoon of

19

(SHIPMATE magazine, May, 1985)

6 December 1941. As we steamed back at 24 knots, we encountered a great storm near the international date line. The seas were already rough from the re-inforced trade winds and this storm made them considerably rougher. The Task Force made very heavy weather into the waves. Finally the bows of two destroyers were damaged, one of them with cracked seams. This was too much even for Adm. Halsey and he decided to slow down the Task Force and postpone arrival in Pearl Harbor until the afternoon of 7 December. I can only consider this storm an unmistakeable act of Divine Intervention. If it had not occurred, we would certainly have been totally destroyed in the Pearl Harbor Holocaust.

As we approached Pearl Harbor on the afternoon of 6, December, we sent out our scouting planes to the 200 mile limit as usual. Unbeknownst to us, the Japanese Force was also approaching Oahu and our two courses were converging as they were coming from the northwest and we were coming from the west. When the afternoon searchers came aboard, after their 200-mile run on the afternoon of the 6th, one of the pilots, a young Ensign by the name of D. W. Halsey (no relation to the Admiral) reported that he thought he saw the top of the masts of some ships well over the horizon at the end of his search. When questioned why he didn't investigate further, he said that he was at the limit of his search and if he had gone any further by twenty-five to thirty miles, he wouldn't have had enough gas to get back to the ship. As he was young and rather inexperienced not much credence was placed in his report. It was, in fact, dismissed. I wondered later if what he saw may not have been the outer perimeter ships of the Japanese Force going toward Pearl Harbor. If so, it's just as well they didn't sight him as we would have been no match for six Japanese carriers. I now know the Japanese came from the north.

On the morning of 7 December I had watch in Sky Control from 0400 in the morning until 0800. At first light shortly after 0500 General Quarters was sounded on the bugle. Shortly after that Flight Quarters was sounded. It was the custom then to always send one squadron of aircraft into Ford Island at Pearl Harbor the day we returned so that they could make arrangements for our arrival and also as sort of a reward. On this morning it was to be Scouting Squadron Six, led by the Air Group Commander, LCdr. H. L. (Brighman) Young '23. I asked the Gunnery Officer if the bombs should not be removed from the planes before they left. He queried the Flag staff and the order came back to remove the bombs, which was done. I also asked if we should remove the aircraft

gun ammunition from the planes and after a very long pause of several minutes word came back from the staff to leave the ammunition in the planes. At about 0615 the planes were launched from the flight deck and set course for Pearl Harbor. We generally tuned in on the flight frequency when these planes were in the air, often times to relieve the boredom and pick up the chit-chat between the pilots. We did so this morning and nothing uptoward happened until shortly after 0745 when the planes were approaching Pearl Harbor. Then, closer to 0800, we heard one pilot say "Hey, did you see that Army plane shooting at me? What kind of drill is this? I'm going to shoot back at him." Another pilot said, "That's no Army plane that's a Japanese plane. Look at the red circles on the wings." There was more excited shouting between the pilots as they tangled with the Japanese aircraft which were arriving over Pearl Harbor. I got off watch at this time and went below to the radar console which was between the flag bridge and the ship's bridge. Radar was very hush-hush in those days but I knew the radar officer, Lt. (J.G.) Jack Baumeister '36. The console was hidden by a huge black curtain but I went behind it and told Jack what was happening on the aircraft frequency and I said "Jack, can we get anything on the

radar?" He said "it's very strange — I've got a lot of bogies but I shouldn't be getting any. He said they're coming in toward Pearl Harbor near Barber's Point and that there were many of them. He said we were 288,000 yards away or 144 miles so thay have to be very high for me to get them — at least 20,000 feet. I said "Have you reported this?" He said, "Yes, I have." But, of course, in those days radar was very new and not too much credence was placed in it.

At this time our planes had sent numerous reports back and a message came in from Pearl Harbor that Pearl Harbor was under attack by Japanese aircraft — enemy aircraft — and ended with this statement "This is no drill repeat this is no drill. Pearl Harbor is under attack." At this we went to Battle Stations and Adm. Halsey hoisted the battle flag from the fore peak and the other ships in the formation followed suit. The signal was sent to our ships "Prepare for Battle".

We were at war!!!

"That money's no good here", he told me, and handed me several bills, all with "HAWAII" stamped on them in big black letters.

"What the hell is this, Wally?"

"It's invasion money. If the Japs attack and take over, none of the paper money would be any good to them."

The liberty was uneventful. We sat around, sampling the beer, talking of home and people we knew. Then some of Wally's friends came by, including a couple of girls, and we spent the evening dancing to the record player and yakking it up.

This would be my last liberty before shoving off to who knew where.

9

CACTUS/RINGBOLT—A CRAP SHOOT

It was a riverboat gamble. The enemy had aces up and a full bankroll. We had deuces and a flat wallet.

But we couldn't let the sharpie on the other side of the table walk away with the pot. We'd put a dent in his stakes at Midway, but now we'd have to pull the biggest bluff of the game—the gamble at Guadalcanal.

As pointed out in Richard B. Frank's definitive work *GUADALCANAL*, American offensive strategy in the Pacific War after Pearl Harbor, particularly beginning with amphibious landings in the South Pacific and specifically the Solomon Islands, was spearheaded by U.S. Navy Commander in Chief Admiral Ernest J. King. Initially Admiral King's South Pacific strategy was opposed by the U.S. Army and Army Air Force, as well as by Pacific Fleet Commander Admiral Nimitz and his Staff as leaving the Hawaiian Islands vulnerable to Japanese advances via the Central Pacific.

But Admiral King convinced President Roosevelt that his plan was a political and military necessity. Politically, Japanese advances in the South Pacific demanded American action to protect Australia and New Zealand. Militarily, the new ascendancy of air power in naval operations necessitated an island stepping-stone offensive strategy where land-based aircraft could be employed, since U.S. aircraft carrier forces alone would not be sufficient to support amphibious operations for perhaps two years. Such a strategy was feasible in the South Pacific, with its large islands, island chains and archipelagos; but not in the sparsely-islanded Central Pacific, with its tiny coral atolls and far-flung island archipelagos known as Micronesia.

The U.S. Navy's master plan for the Pacific War was drawn up by Rear Admiral Richmond K. Turner, the Navy's chief planner and top expert in amphibious warfare. Approved by Admiral King in April, 1942, Turner's "Pacific Ocean Campaign Plan" involved securing the Solomon Islands and New Guinea in order to control the Bismarck Archipelago and capture the Admiralty Islands, then an advance through the Central Pacific to secure the Marshall and Caroline Islands in order to recapture the Philippines. Having had Turner formulate the plan, King then told him to go execute it. For Kelly Turner, the Guadalcanal Campaign was "one for Ernie King"!

Originally, Admiral King hoped to begin an offensive in the Solomons in the fall of 1942, but in one of the most daring gambles in military history he got the operation underway in July. So hastily did Admiral Turner put together his amphibious forces, so limited were our resources, so superior were the forces and resources the Japs could throw against us—that General Douglas MacArthur and even the Navy's top commanders commissioned to carry out the operation, namely Admirals Robert L. Ghormley and Frank Jack Fletcher, thought that Turner's scheme had little chance of success.

On 15 July, 1942, Task Force 16, under Rear Admiral Thomas C. Kinkaid, sortied off the entrance to Pearl Harbor, formed in cruising disposition, and headed toward the South Pacific. The carrier group was built around the ENTERPRISE—"the Big E" . . . "the Galloping Ghost of the Oahu Coast". The "heavies" protecting her were my ship, the NORTH CAROLINA, the heavy cruiser PORTLAND (CA-33), and the light anti-aircraft cruiser ATLANTA (CL-51). In the outer screen were six destroyers: the BALCH (DD-363), BENHAM (DD-397), MAURY (DD-401), GRAYSON (DD-435), MONSSEN (DD-436), and ELLET (DD-398).

Since the bombing of Pearl Harbor, on the whole our military operations in the Pacific Theater had been defensive, just trying to keep the Jap from pushing us further back. Now, for the first time, we were taking the fight to him. Zigzagging hopefully to disguise our base course and keep enemy submarines from lying in wait for us, we steamed toward a rendezvous some 3,500 miles south and west of Hawaii.

I bummed a cup of joe from the Signal Bridge watch, went down the ladder, and sat with my back against the Radio Direction Finder Shack. As I watched the ships execute a course change on one of the zigzag tacks, it began to creep into my consciousness—"this is no drill!"

We were going out to meet the enemy and I wondered if all those months of training, practice, and discipline had prepared me well for combat. Would I carry out my duties as I had been trained to do, or would I—Heaven forbid—panic and cut and run when the shooting started?

I'd seen all those old World War I movies of doughboys going over the top, and the Lafayette Escadrille shooting down German Fokkers from their Spads. But this was a different kind of War and I had no reference point. I'd talked with a survivor off the YORKTOWN about his ship's sinking and could hardly imagine what that was like: a burning ship, bodies lying here and there, men jumping over the side to survive. A radioman off the ENTERPRISE told about being under air attack. The only similar experience to that was in watching our own planes make simulated runs on us.

As I fingered the Saint Christopher's medal my sister Betty (an Episcopalian Protestant trained as a nurse in a Roman Catholic hospital) had given me, I just asked the Lord to let me do what was right and wondered if He might have a guardian angel to spare to look over my shoulder when the going got rough. I supposed my shipmates, too, were having these kinds of thoughts. They must pass through the mind of every man faced with the unknown and with the possibility of death. But I recall no conversations about it. We just kept our fears and apprehensions within ourselves.

Doubtless some prayers were said, perhaps like the prayer to be used on warships in my sister's Episcopal Prayer Book; or more likely one modeled on it, namely the Prayer for the Navy in the Army and Navy *Hymnal*:

"Eternal Lord God, Who alone spreadest out the heavens, and rulest the raging of the sea: vouchsafe to take into thy almighty and most gracious protection our country's Navy, and all who serve therein. Preserve them from the dangers of the sea, and from the violence of the enemy, that they may be a safeguard unto the United States of America . . . ."

Steaming ever southward, we were about to become "Shellbacks"—that ancient seagoing title awarded sailors when they crossed the Equator for the first time and were initiated into "The Mysteries of the Deep" by *Neptunus Rex* (King Neptune, King of the Sea). Even though it was wartime, the old rite of passage was held on the Showboat, howbeit somewhat subdued compared to the peacetime versions.

Our zigzagging course had us cross the 0° latitude some ten times in a single day, and the westerly course put us "on the other side" of 180° longitude—the International Date Line. That brought another U.S. Navy seagoing tradition. We all became "Golden Dragons", symbolic of service in the Eastern Hemisphere. I was to spend more years than I cared to west of the 180th.

As Frank points out, the Battle of Midway by no means meant that Japan's losing the Pacific War was inevitable. The Japanese military, both Army and Navy including their air arms, was still far more powerful and experienced than ours, and only a small percentage of our forces and resources was in the Pacific. Despite his losses at Midway, the Jap was still pushing to expand his Greater East Asia Co-Prosperity

Sphere, aiming his spearheads toward Australia where we were estab-
lishing bases. From there, we hoped to mount the campaign to regain
control of the Pacific and drive the Jap all the way back to Tokyo. But
the prospects were daunting.

Two major factors must have caused the midnight oil to burn
constantly in U.S. Pacific Command Headquarters.

Compared to the Japanese land and naval forces, we were woefully
undermanned. Not only had the Japs built a mighty fleet, but their
armies were already battle-conditioned from the campaigns on the
Asian mainland. America had let her Navy fall into an inadequate
fighting force, principally because we believed we'd already fought the
last War to preserve democracy when the German Kaiser was defeated
in 1918. Moreover, the Depression of the 1930s had diluted America's
financial position. Most of our ships were old, many of World War I
vintage, and only a few had been upgraded in armament and technology
to fight a modern war. Radar had been installed on but a handful of
ships. The Marine Corps was hard-pressed to field one full 25,000-man
division, and those men had no real battle experience.

The second concern was logistics, namely the supply problem. With
a projected 8,000 mile supply line from the States, we were stretching
capability to the limit. There was also deep anxiety that President
Roosevelt's commitment to Prime Minister Churchill to throw everything but the kitchen sink against Hitler Germany would leave us at
the short end of the supply stick. The latter fear that we would be
fighting a "forgotten war" proved to be a realistic one. Going into the
very first offensive action of World War II for American forces, we were
operating not on a shoestring but on a very thin and fraying thread.

Nevertheless, while steaming in harm's way to meet the enemy, our
spirit was that of our American forefathers. The spirit of the father of
the United States Navy, Captain John Paul Jones, when he uttered
those immortal words in 1779 from the deck of the BONHOMME
RICHARD locked in mortal combat with the H.M.S. SERAPIS in the
Battle off Flamborough Head: *"I have not yet begun to fight!"*

The spirit of the old American sea song reminiscent of naval heroes
of the Revolution and the War of 1812–14:

> Enroll'd in our annals live Hull and Decatur,
> Jones, Lawrence, and Bainbridge, Columbia's pride;
> The pride of our Navy, which sooner or later,
> Shall on the wide ocean triumphantly ride.

The spirit of the now forgotten third stanza of our national anthem penned by Francis Scott Key during the conflict with the British Navy bombarding Fort McHenry in Baltimore Harbor in 1814:

O thus be it ever when free men shall stand
Between their loved homes and the war's desolation;
Blest with victory and peace, may the Heaven-rescued land
Praise the Power that hath made and preserved us a nation.
Then conquer we must, when our cause it is just,
And this be our motto, "*In God is our trust*";
And the Star-spangled Banner in triumph shall wave
O'er the land of the free and the home of the brave.

I had the evening watch in Bridge Radio when the Navigator pulled out a chart and spread it across the dead reckoning table. The long lead on my headphones (cans) permitted me to move around most of the Chart House, and I maneuvered into a position behind Mr. Stryker. Over his shoulder I could see the legend "British Solomon Islands" on the chart. His attention was focused on one of the larger islands labeled "Guadalcanar". Nearby was another called "Florida" and between them a speck marked "Savo". I would later learn our charts were so inaccurate they were almost useless. This one was so old it spelled "Guadalcana*l*" in a way that apparently had not been in use since it became a British Protectorate in 1899!

The Solomon Islands chain, consisting of seven large tropical volcanic islands and innumerable smaller ones, stretches some 600 miles, diagonally from roughly northwest to southeast, between the Bismarck Archipelago to the northwest and the Santa Cruz and New Hebrides Islands to the east and south respectively. The Eastern Solomons were discovered by Spanish explorers in 1598, apparently looking for a land laden with gold similar to King Solomon's treasure transported via the sea (1 Kings 9:27,28); they thus have Spanish names like Florida and Guadalcanal (birthplace of explorer Alvaro de Mendaña).

The Western and Central Solomons were discovered by the French and British in 1767 and 1788 respectively; the northernmost big island was named Bougainville after a French navigator, New Georgia after King George III. Nobody wanted these rugged and uncivilized jungle islands until the end of the 19th century when the German Empire annexed Bougainville, along with the Bismarcks; and the British acquired the rest of the Solomons, which along with the Santa Cruz Islands formed their Solomon Islands Protectorate administered mostly by Australians. By 1942 the Solomons were still virtually unmapped islands in the midst of uncharted seas.

In view of the fierce fighting and costly campaigns during the coming year and a half in the Solomons, one is reminded of Shakespeare's words in *The Winter's Tale*: "unpath'd waters, undreamed shores, . . . miseries enough . . . ."

At dawn, 26 July, 1942, I looked out on a 63-ship invasion force as we sortied some 400 miles south of Fiji, roughly 1,500 miles east-by-southeast of the Solomons. I had never seen so many vessels in one place at one time and thought: "Boy, we're really going to take it to the Japs!"

The size of the force was misleading. It was, in fact, just about everything we had in the Pacific. Admiral Nimitz had scraped together damn' near every floatable bottom under his Pacific command. The thinness of our strength was emphasized by the fact we were committing 75 percent of our aircraft carriers—all three of the four we had, and the fourth would soon be sent to the Solomons. The NORTH CAROLINA was the only battleship. The transports were mostly old merchant or cruise ships, pressed into service. It was a ragtag fleet that was expected to block the Japanese juggernaut and hold on—while the rest of America could get ships, planes, tanks built, and men trained to man them. We didn't have much time, and the call would be close . . . too close.

Now, as we set our course for the Solomons, code words began to crop up in the talk around the Bridge. The campaign was named Operation WATCHTOWER. The jungle island of Guadalcanal, covered with tropical rain forests, was ironically CACTUS; and Tulagi, a small but fortified island nestled in a bay at Florida Island, was code-named RINGBOLT.

Guadalcanal is only 9° south of the Equator and 20° east of the International Date Line. A big island, it's 90 miles long, 25 miles wide, and covers an area of 2,500 square miles with heavily forested mountains reaching heights of 8,000 feet. The jungle is nearly impenetrable; but along the coast there were, in 1942, a few copra plantations. The dried coconut meat is rendered into oil for use in soap, cosmetics, and cooking. The plantations, owned by such big soap companies as Lever Brothers, were worked by Melanesians, the natives of the Solomons. They're short, black-skinned, with black woolly hair. Yet, they do not have the Negroid features of Africans. Disease was rampant among them. Malaria, dysentery, elephantiasis, dengue fever, syphilis, and some diseases still unclassified by medical science, infected many of the natives. With the heat, humidity, tropical rain storms, and jungled terrain, it was a lousy place to fight a war.

In the early 20th century, popular author Jack London's dream of circumnavigating the world ended with a nightmare in the Solomons. Here malaria, skin ulcers, and a mysterious illness paralyzing his hands terminated his trip. It was so bad that London wrote: "If I were a king,

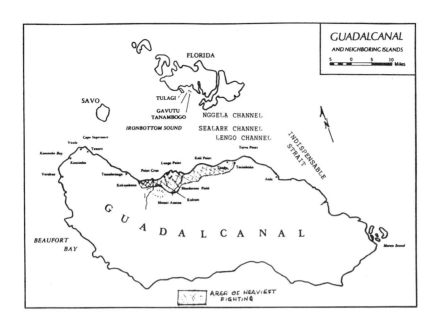

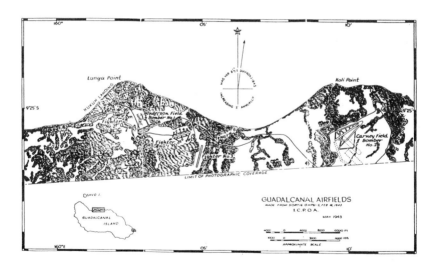

(Courtesy I.C.P.O.A.)

the worst punishment I could inflict on my enemies would be to banish them to the Solomons. . . . On second thought, king or no king, I don't think I'd have the heart to do it."

The fates of all of us were in the hands of our leaders. Commander South Pacific (ComSoPac) was Vice Admiral Robert L. "Goon" Ghormley, headquartered in Noumea, New Caledonia, the French possession some 850 miles south of Guadalcanal. At sea, Rear Admiral Frank Jack Fletcher flew his Flag as Commander Task Force 61, the Naval forces, on the carrier SARATOGA (CV-3). Rear Admiral Richmond Kelly "Terrible" Turner, Commander Amphibious Forces (Task Force 62), made the transport McCAWLEY (P-10) his Flagship. Major General Alexander Archer "Archie" Vandegrift commanded the 1st Marine Division. Commander Air South Pacific, i.e. of all non-carrier-based aircraft (Task Force 63), was Rear Admiral John S. "Slew" McCain. Not all of these would stand the crucible of Cactus, but some would emerge as great heroes of the War.

The Japs had occupied the Eastern Solomons in May and June, initially taking the British seat of government in Tulagi from the Australians on 2 May. The north coast of Guadalcanal, since suitable for an airfield, was picked by Admiral Turner as a possible landing point in early July, 1942, with the suggestion of a September invasion. But when Army Air Force Intelligence (G-2) reports told of Japanese activity on the island, followed by news of airfield construction near Lunga Point, the decision was made to strike sooner.

There had been a helluva lot of politicking and jockeying for position among the higher brass, both in Washington and in the field; and General Douglas MacArthur, although thousands of miles from the Capital, was right in the middle of it. The "Europe First" strategy meant no big Army build-up in the Pacific for MacArthur to command, and he was further relegated to the back burner when the decision was made to split the command in the Pacific. That is, there'd be no single Supreme Commander, a job MacArthur thought he deserved and which he coveted.

But Admiral King wasn't about to put Navy Admirals under the direction of an Army General. King had a point. The Pacific War would primarily be a Navy-Marine Corps show. To head it up, Admiral Nimitz got the job as Commander in Chief, Pacific Ocean Areas (CinCPOA), which included New Zealand, Samoa, Fiji, and all areas east of the 160th meridian. The supercilious MacArthur was appointed Supreme Commander, Southwest Pacific Area. He immediately assumed for himself the title of "Commander in Chief of Allied Land, Sea, and Air Forces in Australia, New Guinea, the Philippines and the Solomon Islands."

When the decision was made to invade Guadalcanal, one of the largest of the Solomons, MacArthur put up a howl, burning up the radio circuits between Australia and Washington. The Solomons, he averred, were part of *his* Southwest Pacific Area. But Admiral King successfully argued that the operation necessarily would have to be an amphibious campaign, with Navy ships and the Navy's Marines. So the boundary between the South Pacific and the Southwest Pacific Areas was shifted westerly to the 159th meridian, putting the Eastern Solomons under ComSoPac, Admiral Ghormley. A Solomonic decision! Old "Dugout Doug" had his wings clipped one more time.

The 1st Marine Division, which was to capture Tulagi and Guadalcanal, was a motley crew comprised of various units hastily pulled together to form a division. Its ranks consisted of young post-Pearl Harbor recruits, mostly under twenty, led by the legendary "Old Breed", seasoned sergeants and perennial privates with long disciplinary records who had no combat experience except as described by one of their Colonels, Samuel B. Griffith, in *The Battle for Guadalcanal*:

"These were the professionals, the *Old Breed* of the United States Marines. Many had fought *Cacos* in Haiti, *bandidos* in Nicaragua, and French, English, Italian, and American soldiers and sailors in every bar in Shanghai, Manila, Tsingtao, Tientsin, and Peking. . . . They knew their weapons and they knew their tactics. They knew they were tough and they knew they were good. There were enough of them to leaven the Division and to impart to the thousands of younger men a share of both the unique spirit which animated them and the skills they possessed."

The spirit of the 1st MarDiv, aboard the Navy's transports headed for Guadalcanal, is indicated by the pep talk, recorded in Richard Tregaskis' *Guadalcanal Diary*, of one of their Colonels: "This is going to be a difficult matter. . . . But it can be done and it must be done and we've got to lead the way. . . . It's the first time in history we've ever had a huge expedition of this kind accompanied by transports. It's of world-wide importance. You'd be surprised if you knew how many people all over the world are following this. You cannot fail them."

The Marines were animated by the spirit of the mimeographed notice of another Colonel to his troops:

"The coming offensive in the Guadalcanal area marks the first offensive of the war against the enemy, involving ground forces of the United States. The Marines have been selected to initiate this action which will prove to be the forerunner of successive offensive actions that will end in ultimate victory for our cause. Our country expects nothing but victory from us and it shall have just that. The word failure shall not even be considered as being in our vocabulary. We have worked hard and trained faithfully for this action and I have every confidence in our ability and desire to force our will upon the enemy. We are meeting a tough and wily opponent but he is not sufficiently tough or wily to overcome us because *We Are Marines*. . . . Good luck and God bless you and to hell with the Japs" (*Guadalcanal Diary*).

Exactly eight months after Pearl Harbor, 7 August, 1942, in the pre-dawn darkness, the bos'n's pipe shrilled through the NORTH CAROLINA's loudspeakers:

"General Quarters! General Quarters! All hands man your battle stations! All hands—MAN your battle stations!"

The staccato quick-tempo'd bugle call for "General Quarters" followed, and immediately after it came the CLANG-CLANG-CLANG of the General Alarm.

My relief at the Bridge station caught the headphones as I flipped them to him, and I sped out the after hatch and up the ladders to my battle station—the catwalk 130 feet above the sea at Sky Control. As my eyes became accustomed to the darkness, I could see only the silhouettes of the ENTERPRISE and the SARATOGA from my vantage point. We had split off from the troop transports during the night and our Task Force was stationed off shore. It wasn't until the sun began to rise that I'd be able to see the shape of an island low on the horizon.

The ENTERPRISE signaled a course change to bring her into the wind, standard procedure for launching aircraft. The only light, except for the stars, were pinpoints of fire from the engines of planes warming up on the Big E's flight deck. The first plane to take off got past the bow and dropped out of sight. I watched for him to come back up again. Not this time. The plane hit the water and crashed. Not an auspicious beginning for Operation WATCHTOWER.

The accident meant only a momentary pause in flight operations as plane after plane shot down the flight deck and became airborne—F4F fighters, SBD dive bombers, and TBF torpedo bombers going to support the amphibious assaults on Guadalcanal and Tulagi. An historic moment, this. For the first time in World War II, American Armed Forces were taking the offensive—the beginning of the long and bloody road to Tokyo.

Throughout the day, the carrier planes swept over "Cactus" and "Ringbolt," supplying air cover and support for the Marines. Some eighteen Jap seaplanes were destroyed at Tulagi, and anti-aircraft and artillery positions were taken out on Guadalcanal. The first reports we got back were encouraging. This time, the Nips were *nipped* (multiple meanings of the term) being taken totally by surprise. There was little or no resistance to the landings on the 'Canal; however, there was heavy fighting continuing on Tulagi, where the Japs had a strong garrison but were subdued by Marine Raiders after fighting with almost unbelievable ferocity.

Later dispatches came in saying the nearly completed airstrip on the bigger island had been captured without enemy resistance, and that the Marines had renamed it "Henderson Field" for a Marine pilot shot down during the Battle of Midway. Why the enemy did not resist our capturing the airfield, is as much a mystery now as it was then. The only explanation seems to be their being caught completely off guard, our people finding breakfast on the table in the Japs' tents. Our forces were harassed off and on by Jap land-based planes, especially Betty bombers and Zero fighters.

Our Task Force was to the south of the islands, and the original operations plan called for us to remain on station for 72 hours to give the Marines all the help they needed. But Admiral Fletcher began to get a little uneasy, worrying about enemy submarines and/or the possibility of attack by land-based bombers from the huge enemy base at Rabaul. He withdrew the carrier groups farther to the southeast in the Coral Sea, out of range for Rabaul-based aircraft. The withdrawal came less than 36 hours after the initial landings and left Admiral Turner's transports and the Marines on the beach without any air cover at all. It put the amphibious vessels in a precarious position, with only a small screen of destroyers and cruisers to protect them.

Admiral Turner was certain the hostiles would hastily storm into the area to repulse our forces, but air reconnaissance failed to locate any Japanese ships. However, he reluctantly decided to pull his transports out the next morning, just in case. Meantime, the screen of cruisers and tin cans was deployed in anticipation of an enemy attack, even though no surface action was expected during the night hours. Rather, our folks anticipated another daylight raid in the morning by bombers out of Rabaul.

Just before midnight of 8 August, I groggily made my way over the darkened decks toward the Chart House to take over the midwatch. Fortified with a cup of quartermaster-brewed mud, I settled back to what I thought would be a routine night.

But 9 August, 1942, was anything but routine for the U.S. Navy. Beginning at 0143 the Marines on Guadalcanal could hear the thunder of naval gunfire off the coast to the northwest.

"We knew then that there was a sea fight going on. Possibly, it was the battle for Guadalcanal. Possibly, if our people out there lost the battle, the Japs would be ashore before morning, and we would have to fight for our lives. We knew the fate of all of us hung on that sea battle.

In that moment I realized *how much we must depend on ships* even in our *land* operation. And in that moment I think most of us who were there watching the gunfire suddenly knew the awful feeling of being pitifully small, knew for a moment that we were only tiny particles caught up in the gigantic whirlpool of war. The terror and power and magnificence of man-made thunder and lightning made that point real. One had the feeling of being at the mercy of great accumulated forces far more powerful than anything human. We were only pawns in a battle of the gods, then, and we knew it" (*Guadalcanal Diary*).

In the early morning hours of the 9th, dispatches began coming in of a surface battle between our cruisers and a Jap force around Savo Island.

"My God!" one of our officers gasped, "we've lost four cruisers!"

The details, continuing to come in for the next several hours, painted a dismal picture. In a brilliantly concealed high-speed run from Rabaul "down the Slot" (the narrow water way between the Northern and Southern, the Western and Eastern Solomons, between Bougainville Strait and Indispensable Strait) an eight-ship enemy force of cruisers and a destroyer under Admiral Mikawa drove into the western screen that was protecting Admiral Turner's transports. Our Allied force of six cruisers and six destroyers—tactically under the command of Royal Australian Navy Admiral Victor A.C. Crutchley, a veteran of the historic Battle of Jutland between the British and German Navies in 1916—was significantly superior to the enemy in firepower. Caught completely by surprise, despite radar and due to a multitude of mistakes by Turner, Crutchley, and others, our ships hardly got a round off in their defense.

The Japs, with superior nighttime operational capability, quickly dispatched the Australian cruiser H.M.A.S. CANBERRA when she was silhouetted in flares dropped by enemy float planes. The CHICAGO (CA-29) was badly damaged by a torpedo but, thanks to a covering rain squall, escaped. Then, in quick succession, the ASTORIA (CA-34), the QUINCY (CA-39), and the VINCENNES (CA-44) came under withering fire from the Jap cruisers and were literally overwhelmed by the attack. All three would be lost. As the enemy withdrew, the RALPH TALBOT (DD-390) got in the way. Badly damaged but still afloat, the destroyer was saved when she took refuge in a rain squall. This time around, Admiral Crutchley did not live up to his name.

It was a devastating defeat, the worst in the history of the United States Navy, and left us stunned and speechless. The loss of the four cruisers severely diminished our strength, cost heavy casualties, and put the lid on any idea this would be an easy fight. "The Battle of Savo

Island initiated a series of night gunfire and torpedo actions that became the hallmark of naval warfare in the Solomons for the next sixteen months" (Frank).

The Battle of Savo Island left another legacy. That strip of water bounded by Guadalcanal, Tulagi, and Savo Island, technically termed a "sound", henceforth would be known, infamously among us, as "Iron Bottom Bay".

The Imperial Japanese Navy had won a thunderous victory in the U.S. Navy's first major surface action since Santiago in the Spanish-American War where (unlike the Java Sea) American Admirals were in overall command. The Japs had sunk four heavy cruisers and a destroyer (the damaged JARVIS was sunk the next day by land-based torpedo planes, going down with all hands and disappearing without a trace) without losing a single ship (though the cruiser KAKO was sunk by an American submarine two days later, the first of many pay-backs for Savo Island).

The U.S. Navy lost 1,270 officers and bluejackets killed and 709 wounded in the battle. But the sacrifice was not in vain; by getting in the Jap's way, they had protected the invasion force. Fortunately, Mikawa and his staff, satisfied with their victory, did not carry out orders to destroy Turner's transports, for fear of being caught in daylight by U.S. carrier planes, not knowing that Fletcher had taken the American carriers out of the area for fear of Jap land-based aircraft. So we would learn later.

Admiral Fletcher's decision to withdraw from Guadalcanal and take us far from the Cactus-Ringbolt area is still a contentious subject, today; and the debacle at Savo Island didn't help put his retreat in very good light, either. Fletcher cited the low carrier strength of our forces with no replacements in sight for another nine months as one reason for pulling out; along with the Japanese superiority in number of carriers, danger from land-based planes, and his interpretation of his orders bearing on risking our carriers. Still many Navy men feel he was overly cautious and left the transports and Marines hanging out there with no air protection.

But there was little Fletcher could have done for the cruisers in the nighttime battle. What he was criticized for was failure to send his planes after the retreating Jap cruisers that sank the QUINCY, VINCENNES, ASTORIA, and CANBERRA in order to extract at least some revenge. Fletcher, however, claimed he knew nothing about the Savo Island battle until 0600 the next morning. Yet, both the NORTH CAROLINA and the other Task Force 61 ships copied Admiral Turner's blind transmissions that night. For some unknown and unexplained reason, the SARATOGA failed to copy. Although Fletcher denied he ever used the excuse of needing to fuel his ships, the impression persists he did withdraw the carriers to refuel, even though it wasn't necessary.

Admiral Fletcher did have reason to be supercautious with our remaining carriers. He was in command in the Coral Sea when the LEXINGTON was lost and at Midway when the YORKTOWN was sunk. But from what we had pieced together on the NORTH CAROLINA, we began to lack confidence in Fletcher's ability as a carrier task force Admiral. In later years, however, some Navy people have concluded that Frank Jack Fletcher was "burned out" from the months of heavy responsibility, commanding the only American force capable of stopping the Japs, and may have lost his nerve.

In the words of U.S. Navy historian Morison: "Savo Island was not a decisive battle, although it might have been if the Japanese had followed it up with energy instead of committing forces piecemeal. Savo was the inaugural engagement of a bloody and desperate campaign and the 9th of August was the first of many terrible days when commanders on either side might well have raised their hands to Heaven like the Psalmist, to cry out, 'For all the day long have I been plagued, and chastened every morning.'"

The loss of the heavy cruiser ASTORIA must have been an especially bitter pill for Admiral Turner to swallow. In 1939 the ship, then under Captain Turner's command, had borne the ashes of former Japanese Ambassador Saito from Annapolis to Yokohama as a gesture of goodwill and friendship. This event inspired a Nipponese poet to write that the people of Japan would never forget their gratitude to the ASTORIA given:

> "The spirit, incarnate of friendship and love
> Deep in the heart of history.
> The record of the human world, full of changes and
>   vicissitudes."

But the Jap military interpreted the gesture as condoning Japan's rape of China, and history's "changes and vicissitudes" overcame the "spirit . . . of friendship and love", sending the ASTORIA to the bottom of Iron Bottom Bay.

From the Battle of Savo Island, Kelly Turner drew a crucial lesson for the U.S. Navy:

"The Navy was still obsessed with a strong feeling of technical and mental superiority over the enemy. In spite of ample evidence as to enemy capabilities, most of our officers and men despised the enemy and felt themselves sure victors in all encounters under any circumstances . . . .The net result of all this was a fatal lethargy of mind which induced a confidence without readiness, and a routine acceptance of outwarn peacetime standards of conduct. I believe that this psychological factor as a cause of our defeat, was even more important than the element of surprise."

The observation of historian Frank is to the point: "This lethargy of mind would not be completely shaken off without some more hard blows to Navy pride around Guadalcanal, but after Savo the United States Navy picked itself up off the deck and prepared for the most savage combat in its history."

In the meantime, the enemy would step up reinforcement of his troops on Guadalcanal; and the Marines were in for a series of bitter, bloody, and hair-raising battles. The first three days of Operation WATCHTOWER had been anything but a rousing success, but no one was ready to give up. In the coming months, the situation wouldn't get a helluva lot better.

There was not a commander in the South Pacific whose primary concern was not AFFAG—Ammunition, Fuel Oil, Food, and Aviation Gasoline. The Cactus-Ringbolt operation had been so hastily mounted that logistical support could not be organized swiftly enough to meet these vital needs. America's merchant marine was almost non-existent. Labor strife in the maritime unions during the Depression had forced U.S. shippers to register their ships under foreign flags, and assembling the requisite cargo vessels and transports would be a herculean and time-consuming task. Meanwhile, critical supplies and spare parts were at a premium.

The United States Navy did not have adequate ships and supplies at Guadalcanal, which was the first American amphibious operation since the Spanish-American War in 1898. As for planes and parts, when President Roosevelt sent a message to the "Cactus Air Force"—the Navy, Marine, and Army Air Corps planes flying off Henderson Field—he asked USMC Captain Joe Foss if there was anything he could send. Foss replied in a masterpiece of understatement: "Just send us more baling wire to hold together what planes we have left."

Even aboard the usually well-provisioned large combat vessels, adequate food supplies were often at a low ebb. On smaller ships and for the poor devils on the beach, the problem was even more pervasive. The Mud Marines were reduced to eating captured Jap rice and fish caught by throwing hand grenades in the rivers. As late as early 1943, Australian mutton, detested by Americans, was about the only fresh meat available on many ships and bases.

Operation WATCHTOWER was dubbed sarcastically "Operation

Shoestring". To many Americans, Guadalcanal became a synonym for privation and misery. The Japanese would call it "Starvation Island" and "the Island of Death"!

7th of August, 1942

The turning point

And when he goes to heaven
To Saint Peter
he will tell:
Another Marine
reporting, sir:
I've served my
time in hell!

PFC Cameron USMC

(Courtesy First Marine Division Association)

10

BAPTISM OF FIRE

Artists' conceptions of sea battles most often depict the ocean as dark and foreboding, as if naval conflict cannot take place in a beautiful setting.

In the summer of 1942, the Coral Sea—that portion of the South Pacific Ocean bounded by the New Hebrides, the Solomons, and Australia—was the stuff of which travel posters are made. Light blue or greenish blue, the waters were more fitting for pleasure cruise ships than for men o' war. More phosphorescent than other seas through which we'd steamed, the Coral turned a brilliant sparkling white as the ships' screws churned up the wakes.

At night, the ship's wake glistened with millions of bluish-white pinpoints of phosphorus light, while overhead billions of stars seemed so close I felt I could reap them from the sky by merely passing my hand above my head. Dominating the constellations of the Southern Hemisphere is the Southern Cross—the five-star formation that was to become the heavenly symbol of the Solomons Campaign.

On this day, 24 August, 1942, the sun was bright and the sky was a pastel blue with towering silvery cumulus clouds on the horizon. But all the vast beauty of this seascape was lost on most of us, more intent on the potential dangers lurking just beyond the horizon. In this serene and picturesque setting, we were anticipating the crucible of combat.

With the Japanese naval victory at Savo Island and Admiral Fletcher's taking his carriers far out to sea, the hostiles had effective control of the sea and air around Guadalcanal. There was nothing to stop them but submarines and Marines. But the Japs did not seize the moment for massive reinforcement of their troops on Guadalcanal with a view to driving the Marines into the sea.

Underestimating the gyrenes' number and will to fight in the jungle, so we later learned, the enemy nonchalantly sent Colonel Ichiki with some 900 men, originally slated to occupy Midway Island, to retake Guadalcanal. The Jap military, especially the Army which had yet to experience defeat, was still suffering from "Victory Disease". After all, the combat-hardened Jap jungle fighter would make short work of the inexperienced gyrenes.

But the Jap was in for a big surprise. His first major encounter with U.S. Marines proved the "jarhead" a better fighting man, even on the enemy's chosen ground. In the night Battle of the Tenaru River (a misnomer since fought along a tidal lagoon known as "Alligator Creek" because it was full of crocodiles!) on 21 August, Ichiki's force was virtually annihilated, some 800 "sons of heaven" being sent to the other place, including the Colonel who apparently dispatched himself to the lower regions in the traditional Jap way i.e. via *hari-kari*. Like Midway, this crucial battle, though relatively small, helped destroy the myth of Jap invincibility in their own minds; the myth of the superior Jap spirit could not overcome our superior firepower.

The conduct of Ichiki's doomed force shocked General Vandegrift, who shortly afterward wrote Marine Corps Commandant Thomas Holcomb in Washington: "General, I have never heard or read of this kind of fighting. These people refuse to surrender. The wounded wait until men come up to examine them . . . and blow themselves and the other fellow to pieces with a hand grenade."

General Vandegrift was a Southern gentleman, a God-fearing Presbyterian, a Virginian from an old Confederate family, who recalled the chivalry of the War Between the States and his grandfather's earnest prayers to the God of Abraham, Isaac, Jacob, R.E. Lee, and Stonewall Jackson. When the general left Guadalcanal, he reflected on Lee's words: "What a cruel thing is war . . . ."

Since the amphibious landings at Guadalcanal and Tulagi, we'd been bracing for a major counter-offensive by the Imperial Japanese Navy, emanating from their huge base at Truk in the Eastern Carolines. Apparently Admiral Nimitz was expecting our commanders, and especially Admiral Fletcher, to be more aggressive in engaging the enemy than heretofore. On 19 August he had sent the following message to the whole Pacific Fleet:

"Suitable targets present themselves only rarely to our guns, bombs and torpedoes. On those rare occasions our tactics must be such that our objective will be gunned, bombed or torpedoed to destruction. Surely we will have losses—but we will also destroy ships and be that much nearer to the successful conclusion of the war. We cannot expect to inflict heavy losses on the enemy without ourselves accepting the risk of punishment. To win this war we must come to grips with the enemy. Courage, determination and action will see us through."

As we steamed in an area due east of the Solomons, the ENTERPRISE (our Task Force 16 under Rear Admiral Kinkaid) and SARA-

TOGA (Task Force 11 under Vice Admiral Fletcher) carried out flight operations, launching and recovering aircraft that were executing search and CAP (Combat Air Patrol fighter cover) missions. The WASP and her escorts (Task Force 18 under Rear Admiral Leigh Noyes) had departed for a fueling rendezvous with an oiler in a rear area after Admiral Fletcher had dismissed the report of a Jap troopship convoy as a bogus sighting.

The sighting by a recon plane said the hostile ships were steaming on course 160° (southeasterly). That heading would put the Nip convoy on a direct route to Guadalcanal. Fletcher ordered an air strike by SARATOGA planes, supplemented with land-based flights from the recently activated Henderson Field. But when our planes couldn't locate the enemy transports, Fletcher concluded their apparent absence meant no Jap attack would be forthcoming for several days. Also, this time around, our intelligence at Pearl Harbor had no clue where the Nip carriers were, no idea they were in the South Pacific. Thus the departure of the WASP, a move that depleted our carrier forces by one third.

As the afternoon of 24 August wore on, we first got reports of a heavy bombing raid over Guadalcanal. This later proved to have been a diversionary tactic to draw our planes in toward the island. Next came the sighting of a Jap carrier force within range of our position; 38 SARATOGA planes were ordered into the air to go after this target, while some 23 ENTERPRISE planes were already in the air on search missions. By now, over sixty of our aircraft were committed aloft. What Admiral Fletcher did not know at the time, was that Admiral Kondo, commanding the Nip naval forces approaching Guadalcanal, had sent out a single light carrier, the RYUJO with cruiser and destroyer escorts, to lure him into thinking it was the main enemy force. Fletcher took the bait, hook, line, and sinker.

The Admiral must have gulped when he received reports that planes from the ENTERPRISE had spotted two enemy fleet carriers, Pearl Harbor veterans SHOKAKU and ZUIKAKU, just 198 miles from us (actually about 230 according to historians of the battle) within easy striking distance and with their planes already airborne. Jap search planes had spotted our carriers about an hour before. With our main aircraft flights out after the decoy carrier RYUJO, and the WASP too far away to lend a hand, we had only fifty some F4F Grumman Wildcat fighter planes to protect our Task Forces against an oncoming Jap attack estimated to be made up of some 85 fighters, dive bombers, and torpedo planes. Admirals Yamamoto and Nagumo probably believed the hour to avenge Midway had come.

The prayer in my sister's Episcopal Prayer Book, to be said before a fight at sea against the enemy, was certainly apropos: "Stir up thy strength, O Lord, and come and help us; for *thou givest not alway the battle to the strong, but canst save by many or by few ....*"

Possibly the familiar lines of the Navy Hymn were going through the minds of some of the officers:

> Eternal Father, strong to save,
> Whose arm doth bind the restless wave ....
> *O hear us when we cry to Thee*
> *For those in peril on the sea ....*

But we ordinary bluejackets were not fully cognizant of the odds stacked against us. We were simply apprehensive, anxious to see action, reacting instinctively to our training, absorbed in the atmosphere of carrying on with our assorted shipboard duties in combat.

The scene set for the swiftly impending struggle was sublime. In Morison's descriptive words:

"Poseidon and Aeolus had arranged a striking setting for this battle. Towering cumulus clouds, constantly rearranged . . . in a series of snowy castles and ramparts, blocked off nearly half the depthless dome. The ocean, two miles deep at this point, was topped with merry whitecaps dancing to a clear horizon, such as navigators love. The scene, with dark shadows turning some ships purple and sun illuminating others in sharp detail . . . was one for a great marine artist to depict . . . .Those handsome clouds could hide a hundred vengeful aircraft; that high equatorial sun could provide a concealed path for pouncing dive-bombers; that reflected glare of blue, white and gold bothered and blinded the lookouts and made aircraft identification doubtful."

No sooner did the incoming strike begin to show up on our radar screens when the bos'n's pipe shrilled, the bugler blew, and the NORTH CAROLINA's General Alarm clanged!

I sprinted up ladders, across the main deck, and up the superstructure, headed for Sky Control and my battle station. Ordinarily my job was to handle radio communications between our Kingfisher spotting planes and the Main Battery Director right above me. But in this situation I had an additional and awesome responsibility: to provide a backup radio station to communicate with our carrier fighters in case the carrier's communications were knocked out. Had this happened, I would have had to provide direction for our carrier planes!

Breathless after the climb, I took a couple of seconds, then put on my headphones. The circuit was a-clutter with all sorts of transmissions from our pilots and fighter control directors. Everyone seemed to be talking at once.

From my position just below the forward Main Battery Director, I had a 180-degree view toward the stern of the ship. By moving farther out on the catwalk, I could increase my vision another 90 degrees or so. Off on the horizon was the SARATOGA, hull down and moving away from us. She would escape the strike as all the Jap planes would end up concentrating on our ENTERPRISE Task Force. The ENTERPRISE was forward of the NORTH CAROLINA, pouring on the coal and making battle speed.

The utter confusion on the radio circuit inhibited the carrier's air controllers from dispatching the Combat Air Patrol (CAP) to counter effectively the incoming Jap flights. It could best be described as the Tower of Babel reincarnate.

Then, above the din and clamor I heard the ENTERPRISE call out: "Bogies [unidentified aircraft] at angels twelve!"

That estimate of 12,000 feet was too low, and our fighter cover vectored below and behind the attacking wave of enemy dive bombers, putting them in a disadvantaged position to counter the strike.

As I watched, the attacking Kate bombers and Val torpedo planes split into two formations and drove toward the ENTERPRISE. Simultaneously, our outnumbered F4Fs tangled with the Jap bombers' Zero escorts. I moved farther out on the catwalk, as far as my headset leads would allow me, to watch dogfights developing all over the sky, and to see how the ENTERPRISE was faring. She now was some 2,500 yards off our port bow.

At 1640 ENTERPRISE's Combat Information Center (CIC) air plot called out: "Enemy planes directly overhead!"

"Gawddam! There's bandits [identified enemy aircraft] EVERYWHERE!" shouted a voice on the circuit.

From my front-row-center seat in the modern equivalent of a crow's nest, I spotted more hostile aircraft. First one, then two, then a whole flight of white-bellied planes, at first barely visible against the high cloud background but approaching with alarming speed.

As the Grumman Wildcats tore into the enemy bombers, they in turn were pounced upon by Zero fighters. The Zekes were trying to keep the F4Fs off the dive bombers' backs so that they could swoop down upon us unmolested by our fighters.

All of this happened in a matter of seconds. As the Jap bombers nosed over and started in on their run at the ENTERPRISE, the NORTH CAROLINA's port 5-inch AA battery of ten rifles, directed from Sky Two, spoke with one deadly voice, blasting away at the planes diving on the carrier. Then, Lieutenant Kirkpatrick in Sky One triggered a blistering barrage from his starboard battery, sending ten rounds every few seconds skyward.

On all sides of me, ships in the screen were laying up a seemingly impenetrable curtain of hot steel. The "Big E" was already firing; and the ATLANTA, PORTLAND, and our doughty tin cans were in the midst of the fray, as well. The pea-green sea was a-boil with "Rinso-white" wakes as Captain Fort maneuvered radically at battle speed to throw off the attackers' aim. The Showboat shuddered and shook under the constant recoil of the AA batteries; and I could hear the 1.1s, 20-millimeters, and .50-caliber machineguns chattering like a tree full of magpies.

Against the silver and blue sky, hundreds of jet-black bursts with brilliant orange centers peppered the air, while white-hot tracers arched outward from the automatic weapons. Great sheets of red flame, followed by broad clouds of black and yellowish smoke, erupted from the muzzles of our twenty 5-inch rifles. The sea was shocked into tall, slender geysers from falling bombs; and it was laced with splashes from our own shrapnel falling back to the waters, looking all the world like a hail storm pelting a mud puddle.

As my eyes took in this multi-dimensional panorama of gray ships spitting fire against the buzzing bees of attacking aircraft streaking across the blue and silver sky, unaccountably I was struck with the stark *beauty* of it all. The myriad of colors from sky, sea, wakes—red flames from blazing guns, the orange and black of bursting shells, the yellow and black of burning aircraft, the black and gray and yellow blowing smoke—formed a tableau that's been retained in my memory in minute detail for a half-century. "My God, how beautiful! How absolutely *beautiful!*"

The thought lasted but a flash as I heard the CIC air controller on the "E" shouting to our fighters: "BREAK OFF! BREAK OFF!" Some of them were following Vals and Kates right into our own flak. I gritted my teeth as two Wildcats stayed too long on the tails of the enemy and, with their quarry, were blown to smithereens.

Then, looking skyward, I spotted overhead about a dozen horizontal bombers, Mitsubishi Bettys, four formations of three each, if I remember right. Historians have disagreed whether land-based bombers were in the area that day, but I was there and I saw 'em. So did others on the ship. As indicated in the Action Reports, a dozen or so (some say eight or ten) high-level bombers—flying at 15,000 feet unopposed, since not sighted sooner due to cloud cover and preoccupation with other attack aircraft—in coordination with the second dive bombing attack let loose a pattern of several heavy bombs, all of which fell harmlessly into the sea between the battleship and the carrier. However, the horizontal bombing attack was not observed from the Big E—doubtless preoccupied with the dive bombers.

In summary, according to the Action Reports, the high-level bombers were part of "a perfectly coordinated attack" of about 60 planes on the two ships: "The attack was initiated by a dive bombing attack on the ENTERPRISE followed by a dive bombing attack on this ship. Horizontal bombers passed overhead before these attacks were concluded and simultaneously low altitude or torpedo bombers attacked from different sectors. During these attacks several planes flew parallel and across the ship passing as close as one hundred yards with the apparent purpose of distracting attention."

As the huge blasts of flame from the muzzles of our batteries, accompanied by vast amounts of smoke billowing up around the NORTH CAROLINA, obscured the ship from the view of other vessels in the Task Force, the ENTERPRISE became concerned that we had been hit and were in trouble. "Are you afire?" came the anxious query from the flat-top twice during the battle. Both times the reply was: "Negative"!

Some half dozen or so Vals decided to take on the Showboat about three minutes into the attack. *That* was a mistake! As I watched them begin their runs on us, I was aware I wasn't breathing; there was an empty feeling just below my rib cage, an ache across the top of my shoulders, and bristling hair on the back of my neck. The assault came from two directions, the starboard bow and the port quarter. Great columns of water blew high above the decks as bombs exploded close aboard in several (some seven) near misses. They were *close!* The blasts deafened some of the topside gunners, and walls of water came cascading back down on the decks.

Despite our valiant but overmatched CAP efforts, the dive bombers were getting through our defenses. They scored three hits on the ENTERPRISE, within less than two minutes, and damn' near got us as their bombs rained down in that two-pronged attack. It was only Captain Fort's emergency maneuvering, at a speed of 27 knots to keep up with the carrier, and the volume of fire from our AA batteries that saved us. All the attackers aiming at the Showboat were either blasted out of the air on the way down or when they finished their bombing runs.

The Big E had a blind spot in her AA defenses. She couldn't bring guns to bear on an attack across her starboard quarter. As I watched, a Jap dive bomber came in from that angle and loosed a bomb that hit in the after starboard gun sponson—an open mount. It was horrifying to see sailors blown over the side into the sea and into Kingdom Come.

THE ENTERPRISE IS HIT!!
Crewman rush to the aid of shipmates after a Japanese dive bomber
drops its bomb on the Group 3 5-inch/38 gun sponson on the after
starboard side. 37 men are killed in this action during the Battle of
Eastern Solomons.
(U.S. Navy Photo - Real War Photos)

As Samuel Taylor Coleridge wrote in *The Rime of the Ancient Mariner*:

> The souls did from their bodies fly—
> They fled to bliss or woe!
> And every soul, it passed me by . . . .

As for their bodies, at least some of them, a Big E pilot later described the scene after the bomb hit:

"Sailors' bodies were still in the gun gallery. Most of the men died from the concussion and then were roasted. The majority of the bodies were in one piece. They were blackened but not burned or withered, and they looked like iron statues of men, their limbs smooth and whole, their heads rounded with no hair. . . . The postures seemed either strangely normal or frankly grotesque. One gun pointer was still in his seat leaning on his sight with one arm. He looked as though a sculptor had created him . . . ."

The casualty list from that one hit, we later learned, would have 37 names on it. Another bomb pierced the wooden flight deck and exploded below in a petty officers' mess, extinguishing the lives of 35 bluejackets. A third bomb detonated on the flight deck, wounding several sailors but causing no fatalities. A photographer's camera lens caught the exact instant of detonation, producing one of the most famous photographs of the War.

Around us the two cruisers, the PORTLAND and ATLANTA, were raising giant wakes as they zigged and zagged, both throwing up AA fire with a vengeance. The outer screen destroyers, generally not targets themselves (the Japs concentrated on the "heavies"), were bravely positioning themselves between the oncoming bombers and torpedo planes and their big charges.

One tin can I couldn't identify in the confusion was in the path of an attacking Val which was flying right "down on the deck" at wave-top height. In an ingenious innovation in countering low-level air attacks, the can's guns were lowered to zero elevation and she fired her 5-inch battery into the sea where the shells exploded, sending geysers of water skyward. The Val tried to dodge the water spouts but its wing caught one and it somersaulted into the unsettled sea.

The enemy bombers and torpedo planes, once they'd loosed their loads, would try to escape by staying very low on the water and zigzagging their way through our formation. This way it was difficult for our gunners to bring their weapons to bear without endangering other ships. At least one of these planes strafed a destroyer. I saw him firing at the GRAYSON and later heard she took some casualties.

THE ENTERPRISE FIGHTS ON
With the NORTH CAROLINA's anti-aircraft fire providing cover over her,
the "Gallopin' Ghost of the Oahu Coast" keeps battling enemy bombers
and torpedo planes despite fires from previous bomb hits. This photo
was taken from the author's battle station in Sky Control at the height of
the Battle of Eastern Solomons.
(U.S. Navy photo - Real War Photos)

There were three bizarre incidents I witnessed from my vantage point:

Coming up from a crouch behind the splinter shield as a bomb exploded near at hand, I caught sight of an F4F chasing a Zero, both going straight up. Now, a Grumann Wildcat wasn't supposed to be a match for a Mitsubishi Zeke. It's much slower and less maneuverable. But this pilot didn't know it. He stuck on that Zero's tailbone. They went so high I lost sight of them until, suddenly, I saw a plane trailing smoke as it went up and over, then straight down. The Zero's smoke left a track in the sky like a big question mark. The F4F headed back down to look for more prey.

Sometime during the battle I glimpsed an all-black plane whose silhouette I could not immediately identify. It had a longer, slimmer fuselage than any Jap aircraft I knew of, and I saw no markings. It was close aboard, pulling out of a dive and disappearing into the smoke. Later I would learn that one of the ENTERPRISE fighter pilots claimed he'd shot down an ME 109—a *black German Messerschmitt!* Whether the craft I'd seen was German, I'll never know, but the possible presence of a non-Jap plane in the fracas is still a mystery.

At the time, I had no inkling others aboard the NORTH CAROLINA might also have spotted the "mystery plane". In 1991, however I received photostats of the Showboat's Action Reports of the battle from Machinist's Mate 1st Leo Neumann, who had acquired most of the pertinent documents from the ship's War Diary. Captain Fort wrote in his Action Report: " . . . several observers reported having seen a MESSERSCHMITT 109."

Another report contained "Observations Made by 20mm Gunners" during the action that day. The gunner on Mount 9, Gunner's Mate 3rd R.A. Jackson, reported: "One *black plane* with a *long fuselage* and wheels came over the ship. My trunnion operator called my attention to it; I trained my gun at it, gave it plenty of lead, and opened fire. The plane went about 200 yards and burst into flames and crashed. CBM [Chief Boatswain's Mate] Dillingham saw this happen."

A signalman striker named Linke manned 20-millimeter Mount 34. His report stated in part: "Finally, a *long black and orange painted plane* came from around the fantail up to the beam, flying low across the water and travelling slowly, about 150 to 180 knots. I opened fire on him and followed him until he was bearing 280° when he turned and went out. I am quite sure I was hitting him in the tail because I had a clear view of my tracers. However I did not see him fall, so I cannot claim to have shot him down. . . . My loader later told me he saw that particular plane fall but I cannot verify this."

THE "SHOWBOAT" CLOBBERS JAP PLANES
Panoramic view of the Battle of Eastern Solomons taken from USS
PORTLAND. The NORTH CAROLINA is just right of center. ENTERPRISE
is far left. White splash to the left of NORTH CAROLINA is an enemy
plane shot down. White streaks in the sky are Japanese aircraft hit by
her AA fire and falling. The intensity of the battle is indicated by the
great amount of anti-aircraft shells bursting in the air.
(U.S. Navy photo - National Archives)

The third incident was far less mysterious. From my elevated position, I spotted a "double-Zero" (a stripped down, unarmed, photo reconnaissance plane) *below* me at an altitude of only about 100 feet. He made a complete circle around the NORTH CAROLINA, taking pictures of us! "The IMPUDENT BASTARD!" I thought. It was only when he came around for a second time that one of our 20mm gunners stitched a seam across his fuselage . . . and down he went. There'd be no snapshots of *this* ship for that Jap's family photo album back in Kyoto!

The eyewitness observations of our gunners give a vivid impression of the action. For example: "When the attack started the crew was calm and worked like a clock works. . . . It wasn't necessary for me to give any orders because the crew seemed to know what to do and they did it. . . . I think every gun that could possibly bear on the plane let loose. One second the plane was there and the next moment it was completely disintegrated. . . . We also saw an attempt of suicide from one of the Jap planes. . . . I saw four planes go down and two bombs were dropped within 50 feet of the ship. . . . My trunnion operator loaded for me, when my loader was killed. . . . "

I'm not sure whether he was the same gunner who got the double-Zero, but it was Aviation Machinist's Mate 3rd Class George Conlon who became the NORTH CAROLINA's only casualty that day. He was cut down when another Jap pilot on a strafing run sprayed the fantail with a hail of bullets. After the battle, Conlon was buried at sea with full military honors.

Suddenly, we went from a conflict in which all the Furies of Hell had been unleashed to almost complete silence. What was left of the attacking enemy aircraft turned to run for home. For perhaps two minutes, all was quiet on the NORTH CAROLINA, broken only by the clank of empty 5-inch shell casings rolling on the deck.

High above, I stood motionless, my hands still gripping the top of the splinter shield until I became conscious of the cramps in the muscles from holding on so tightly. My dungaree shirt was soaked with perspiration and I felt as if I'd been run hard, stopped short, and put away wet. Every nerve in my body was a-quiver.

Yet I stayed aloft for perhaps another fifteen minutes, reliving and replaying in my mind every detail of the battle. There was both a sense of exhilaration (a "high" in latter-day parlance) and a feeling of relief. I had experienced combat, had lived through it, and had been an eyewitness to the third big air-sea battle of the War.

Unknown to me at the time, the second wave of enemy attack aircraft should have arrived not long after the first departed—right at the time when the bomb-damaged ENTERPRISE, beset with steering difficulties, was most vulnerable. But, for some unknown reason, the hostiles changed course and missed our carriers altogether.

Nevertheless I knew we had dodged a bullet. That I had been in great danger, only now was beginning to creep into my consciousness; and I wondered, unaccountably, if I were remaining here at my battle station because I didn't want the intense excitement of battle to end.

As I surveyed the aftermath, the ENTERPRISE was recovering her returning "birds". But others had no place to land on the damaged flight deck. Some of these, with fuel remaining, flew on to Henderson Field. Those low on gasoline tried to make it to the SARATOGA. To make room for them, with no time to spare, some planes on the SARA's flight deck had to be jettisoned in a hurry.

Not a few of our aircraft either ran out of gas or were too shot-up to make a carrier landing. These pilots ditched in the sea; and our destroyers, scuttling back and forth much like water bugs on a pond, crisscrossed the flight paths to rescue the fliers. It was dangerous duty. Once a survivor had been spotted, the tin can had to slow almost to a halt to make the pick-up, putting herself at high risk to submarine attack.

The battle, first named the Battle of Stewarts after a nearby group of small islands, was eventually called the Battle of Eastern Solomons. It put one in the "win" column for the Good Guys, preventing some 1,500 enemy troops from reaching Guadalcanal, but it was not an overwhelming victory. The SARATOGA had escaped attack, but the ENTERPRISE was damaged, and our carrier planes had not been able to attack the two Jap fleet carriers in force. Only two of our attack planes ever found the two big carriers; near misses inflicted only minor damage and casualties, killing six Jap sailors on the SHOKAKU.

On the positive side, the NORTH CAROLINA had proven the new modern battleship was a valuable adjunct to a fast carrier task force. The Showboat's performance in shooting down at least seven Japanese aircraft, plus another seven probables, and in breaking up dive bombing attacks with her withering fire, was testimony to that. And she had, in a sense, wreaked a measure of revenge on the enemy for the dastardly attack on her older sister battlewagons at Pearl, by being the first battlewagon to see action after the December 7th debacle.

Admiral Thomas C. Kinkaid, Commander Task Force 16 on the ENTERPRISE, in forwarding his Action Report to Admiral Nimitz praised our performance:

"The NORTH CAROLINA was handled skillfully and effectively throughout the action on 24 August. This was the first occasion on which a battleship has been present as part of a carrier task force during attack by enemy aircraft. The presence of the NORTH CAROLINA was a distinct asset."

It was the Admiral's assessment that triggered the change in the battleships' combat role forever. Henceforth, the great ships would serve primarily as protectors of fast aircraft carriers, and of invasion forces via shore bombardment—a far cry from the purpose, namely battleline surface action, for which they were originally designed. It marked the end of an era.

The crew of the NORTH CAROLINA received the following commendation in Executive Officer J. A. Crocker's Action Report to Captain Fort: "Throughout the ship the officers and men were calm and eager to engage the enemy, and this spirit prevailed before, during and after the action in every department. There was no exception, no single case of absence of this spirit of determination to destroy the enemy. . . . Every man knew his job and stuck to it."

We had blunted, for the time being, an effort by the Japanese to reinforce substantially their Guadalcanal garrison. But Admiral Frank Jack Fletcher certainly lost the confidence of other commanders due to his decisions before and during the fight. He had dispatched the WASP to refuel at a critical and inopportune time; he had fallen for the hostiles' trick play that left his own precious carriers highly vulnerable to an all-out attack; he had failed to inflict damage on the enemy's main heavy carrier force; and he had only a "possible" sinking of the light carrier RYUJO to put in the positive column.

Later, but not 'til 1943, deciphered Japanese messages did confirm that the enemy carrier actually had been sunk. Another redeeming fact was the loss by the Japs of many of their most experienced and highly skilled pilots, whom they were unable to replace. But Fletcher had missed a great opportunity to damage severely the enemy's offensive capability, and he'd lost the services of the valiant ENTERPRISE until she could be repaired.

On the other hand, Jap losses in men and materiel far exceeded ours. We lost no ships, and only 25 planes, while recovering most of our airmen; whereas the Japs lost three ships and 75 planes including most of their pilots. Besides the light carrier, they lost to land-based air attack the next morning a large transport and a destroyer, and a light cruiser was severely damaged. Still the Nip naval forces were superior to ours, but their heavy ships withdrew to safety rather than continue to fight. Perhaps Midway had weakened their nerve.

Even in the most dire circumstances, humorous events can occur. Captain Elias Mott, a lieutenant on the ENTERPRISE in 1942, wrote: "The ENTERPRISE Strike Force of eleven SBDs and seven

TBFs . . . launched prior to the attack, searched for the Japanese carriers [but couldn't find them]. At dusk, the torpedo planes thought they saw the wakes of ships and went in for the attack. To their embarrassment, they discovered they were attacking the curling white surf of Roncador Reef! The planes low on fuel and 50 miles closer to Guadalcanal than to the ENTERPRISE, landed at Henderson Field to the light of gasoline flares on the runway."

"The Battle of the Eastern Solomons was unquestionably an American victory, but it had little long-term result, apart from a further reduction in the corps of trained Japanese carrier aviators. The reinforcements that could not come by slow transport would soon reach Guadalcanal by other means" (Frank).

As I finally started down the ladders from my battle station, I got "the shakes" and the calves of my legs went weak. It was sinking in that I'd come close to disaster and that only God's little angel on my shoulder had seen me through.

The action was still replaying in my mind with remarkable clarity and it seemed the battle had lasted for hours. Yet, from the first to the last rounds fired by the surface ships, it had been remarkably brief.

The Battle of the Eastern Solomons, for the NORTH CAROLINA, had lasted just *eight minutes!*

11

TORPEDO JUNCTION

The ENTERPRISE got her nickname "the Galloping Ghost of the Oahu Coast" because the Japs had reported her sunk on at least three earlier occasions. Now the NORTH CAROLINA would join her as a "ghost ship", and the announcement would come from none other than that paragon of disinformation—Tokyo Rose. The peerless propagandist of Radio Tokyo jubilantly proclaimed, that very night, that both the Big E and the Showboat had been bombed and sent to Davy Jones' Locker, much to the delight and pride of our crew.

The forward compartment of Radio Central was jammed with the radiomen of CR Division after evening mess. All were talking at once about the ship's performance in her first combat action. Just about all of them had been "buttoned up" below decks and only knew what was happening topside from fragmentary announcements over the loud-speaker system. I tried, a couple of times, to tell of some of the things I'd witnessed; but no one seemed interested, each one having his own version of what happened. Everybody was talking and apparently nobody was listening. So I just sat back and sipped from my mug of java, fascinated by what others were saying.

With the ENTERPRISE returning to Pearl for repairs, the NORTH CAROLINA joined Admiral Fletcher's SARATOGA Task Force. With the newly arrived HORNET plus the WASP, we still had three carriers in the South Pacific, which now were taken farther to the southeast by Admiral Fletcher to a point some 250 miles from Guadalcanal. We were to supply air cover to transports supporting the Marines on the 'Canal. To remain on station, Fletcher had us steaming up, down, and across the Coral Sea in a rough rectangle. Our movements were so predictable they invited disaster.

There was ample evidence we were being stalked by submarines. Sightings of torpedo wakes became almost routine. Then, on the morning of 31 August, 1942, shortly after we'd secured from morning General Quarters, a Japanese Long Lance "fish" ripped into the hull of the SARATOGA, sending a plume of oil and water high into the air. Imme-

152

diately, every ship in the Task Forces began emergency maneuvers as two destroyers, the MacDONOUGH and MONSSEN, raced along the reverse bearing of the torpedo track. But the Jap sub (later identified as the I-26) couldn't be found.

Back on the SARA, damage to her propulsion machinery left her dead in the water until, finally, enough repairs were made for her to get underway again. Fortunately, only twelve men were injured, and they included Admiral Fletcher who had a laceration on his head. The damage to the CV-3, our oldest surviving flat-top, was enough to send her back to the States for at least three months of repair work, and with her Admiral Fletcher. His "wound" apparently was used as an excuse to relieve him as a carrier Admiral. His supercautious vacillations had sorely tested the patience of Admiral Nimitz who had expected more aggressiveness from Fletcher.

Now, we had only two fleet carriers operational, the WASP and the HORNET. And *another* disaster was in the making.

Out there in the area we'd already dubbed "Torpedo Junction"—a grim distortion of the title of one of Glenn Miller's hit records "Tuxedo Junction"—fish were still flying. There were so many torpedo tracks sighted it was said "you could walk to New Guinea on 'em and never get your feet wet!"

On 1 September, the day after the SARATOGA was hit, we joined the HORNET Task Force under the command of Rear Admiral George D. Murray. On the 6th, both the battleship and the carrier narrowly escaped a submarine attack, when a plane off the HORNET dropped a bomb to explode torpedoes whose wakes were sighted in the water heading for the ships.

In the meantime, action around Cactus-Ringbolt was evolving into a strange tactical push-pull situation as both sides attempted to supply and reinforce their positions to gain the upper hand. According to then Lieutenant Len Kenny, the Navigator on Admiral Turner's Flagship McCAWLEY, Turner told him at the beginning of the Solomons Campaign that the key to winning at Guadalcanal was logistics. Whichever side supported and reinforced their ground forces the most, would control the island.

Our efforts to bolster the operations on the 'Canal were severely limited by lack of logistical support. We did, in the main, hold air superiority during the day. But we had neither ships nor supplies in adequate amounts to help the Marines on the beach, who were reduced to eating Jap rice and fish heads. The enemy, on the other hand, controlled the seas at night and were successful in getting reinforcements through. Planes and spare parts were exceptionally hard to come by for the Cactus Air Force, and requests for even a smidgen of help went a-begging.

The upper echelons in Washington were not listening. Army Air Corps Chief, General Henry H. "Hap" Arnold, made an inspection tour of the South Pacific in late September. He acknowledged that we did not have a logistical set-up efficient enough to insure success, and he also admitted that "so far, the Navy has taken one hell of a beating." But, as a single-minded supporter of the Roosevelt-Churchill strategy to win first in the European Theater, Arnold unfeelingly and arrogantly stated: "The Navy [is] hard-pressed at Guadalcanal. They need a 'shot in the arm'—and need it badly; but I [am] not sure the way to give it to them is by sending airplanes that might better be used against the Germans from England." Arnold's Army Air Corps was doubtless getting everything it wanted and needed, and he was leaving the Navy and Marines out there to fight our forgotten war with little more than guts and dogged determination, taking our casualties and begging for help. Meanwhile: "The Thin Red Line" was getting thinner . . . and redder.

Admiral Ernest J. King, Commander in Chief, U.S. Fleet, wasn't too happy with the Navy's situation in the South Pacific. In the summer of 1943, Glenn Perry, assistant chief of the *New York Sun*'s Washington Bureau, quoted the Admiral as saying, in an off-the-record briefing, that "we are six months behind schedule in Pacific." The Admiral further told the gathered reporters that Allied Nations' war strength was being distributed on the basis of *85 percent* against Germany and *only 15 percent against Japan.* So Japan was digging in, he said. The Admiral wanted to see at least 25 percent, or possibly 30 percent, go to the Pacific. He wanted to double the pressure on Japan, but the British were dragging their feet. As we in the South Pacific were crying for supplies—food, fuel, ammo, and aviation gas—Perry quoted King as saying: "The U.S. is putting [munitions and supplies destined for Russia] on the docks of the Pacific coast faster than the Russians can unload it in Siberia" (Naval Historical Foundation Magazine *Pull Together*, Winter, 1991).

Now, fifty years later, I know why good American sailors and Marines were dying, and why we were fighting a war without even the bare essentials. President Roosevelt—the alleged "friend of the Navy"—was helping everybody else but us. *Et tu, Brute?*

By September U.S. forces generally "controlled" the sea around Guadalcanal during daylight. But at night the seas were controlled by Admiral Hashimoto's Tokyo Express, which substantially reinforced the enemy's Guadalcanal garrison now under the command of General Kawaguchi.

The "Tokyo Express"! Fast Jap destroyers that shot "down the Slot" between the Northern and Southern Solomons almost every night with supplies and troops, then hurried out before dawn to be out of range of our planes. The Jap build-up would soon bring one of the most critical land battles of the Pacific War. There were now enough enemy troops on the island for General Kawaguchi to launch a full-scale attack on the Marines' fragile perimeter. Having landed east of Henderson Field, the hostiles' force was nearly invisible in the dense jungle. Thus, scouting reports and air reconnaissance could only hazard guesses as to its strength, and those guesses underestimated the number of enemy troopers.

At sea, the information we got about the ground campaign was fragmentary, but we did learn enough to piece together the basic elements of the fighting.

Marine General "Archie" Vandegrift, cognizant he had too few Marines to protect fully the entire perimeter around the airstrip against an all-out attack, strategically positioned his forces at a number of strong points, each one interlocking with the others. It was a masterpiece of defensive tactics. The keystone of the defense was a ridge overlooking Henderson Field, and to that critical position he assigned Colonel Merritt A. Edson's 1st Marine Raider Battalion, which had fought so valiantly in the invasion of Tulagi. Thus the Marines had the "high ground" manned by one of the best fighting units in the Corps.

But few of the Marine units were at full strength. Certainly casualties from earlier fights had thinned their ranks; but on Guadalcanal disease put twice as many, if not more, men out of action as did the enemy. Malaria, dengue fever, and dysentery were rampant. Medical supplies were short, and hardly a Marine squad did not have one or more men in Sick Bay at any given time.

Around 2230, 13 September, the Nips launched their attack against Edson's Ridge, preceded by star shells and blistering mortar barrages. If the Ridge were to fall, the enemy would overlook Henderson Field and be peering right down the throats of the Marines. At stake was not only the airfield but control of the island itself. Historians may argue what effect the loss of Guadalcanal would have had on the course of the War; but it surely would have been disastrous to our efforts to stem the Japanese advance toward Australia and New Zealand, and certainly would have changed both the course and length of the War.

The first rush up the Ridge was the classic Japanese *"Banzai!"* attack. Into the teeth of the withering fire from the Marines' 105-millimeter howitzers, machineguns, mortars, grenades, and rifle fire—the enemy poured out of the jungle *en masse* through a wall of hot steel, penetrating right into the 1st Marine Division's foxholes. The fighting was nip and tuck. Vicious hand-to-hand combat raged all along the exhausted Marines' front lines. Beaten back time and time again, the Japs just kept coming until the bodies of dead and wounded piled up in windrows, against the barbed wire and on the slopes, like so much new-mown hay.

The battle blazed all through the night. There were times when but a single squad of Raiders was all that stood between victory and defeat! But even as dawn broke over the jungle, the attacks began to diminish, and victory was sealed when every plane of the Cactus Air Force took to the skies to strafe and bomb what was left of General Kawaguchi's force.

The Japs had left a full *fifty percent* of Kawaguchi's command on the Ridge. The brave, fanatical, Japanese soldiers had suffered an overwhelming defeat; beaten by the almost unbelievable courage, resourcefulness, gallantry and individual heroism of the beleaguered Marines and the gutsy determination of the 1st Raiders in holding their positions against all odds. "Red Mike" Edson's Raiders lost a startling *twenty percent* of their strength that night, but their exploits are now a glorious page in Marine Corps history.

The stand on that hill would be known by two names, so take your choice:

"The Battle of Edson's Ridge", or "The Battle of Bloody Ridge"!

Both fit. The morning after the battle, the dead bodies of Japs and Marines were found tangled together where they had fallen locked in mortal combat. For his bravery under fire and inspiring leadership, Colonel Edson received the Congressioanl Medal of Honor.

The day after Bloody Ridge, Admiral Kelly Turner—the gruff, rough commander of the Amphibious Forces—was intent on getting more help to General Vandegrift. On 14 September, he loaded the 7th Marine Regiment aboard six transports at Espiritu Santo in the New Hebrides, and prepared to run the Japanese submarine gauntlet to the 'Canal. Out in front of his convoy would be the HORNET and WASP Task Forces, deployed seven to ten miles apart and some twelve miles ahead of the transports. We had expected to be joined by another of the new, fast battleships, the SOUTH DAKOTA (BB-57); but she had run onto a coral reef at Tongatabu in the Friendly Islands, ripping a hole in her hull, and had to return to Pearl for repairs.

That bit of bad news was followed by word that three enemy battleships, with cruiser and destroyer screens, were headed our way. We started directly for the Jap task force, anticipating a dawn engagement; but at 0330 the Nips unaccountably did a 180° turn, retreating to the northwest. We remained on heightened alert. Our reconnaissance

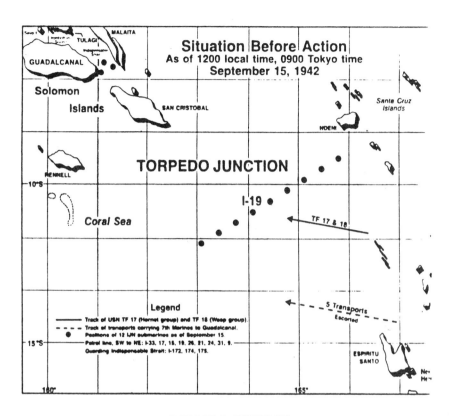

TORPEDO JUNCTION
The deployment of the Japanese submarine force on the "KA Line," and
the courses of U.S. carrier Task Forces 17 and 18, and position of the
convoy of transports, 15 September, 1942.
(U.S. Naval Institute "Proceedings")

told us enemy scouts and snoopers were tracking us. What we didn't know was that nine Japanese submarines were deployed in an arc across our intended course, lying in wait like tigers in the grass. Enemy documents captured after the War called the deployment the "KA Line".

I had come off the Bridge watch at noon, finished chow, and was down in the CR Division compartment with a few other radiomen. As I pulled the cover off my mattress, preparatory to putting it in the laundry bag, the deck canted slightly under my feet, making me aware the ship was changing course. But I paid scant attention as I wrestled with the mattress. It was about 1445, 15 September, 1942.

KAH-RAH-BAH-ROOOOM! The ship lurched sharply to starboard, shaking and shuddering violently from a mighty explosion. Then she staggered back to port. Smoke poured into the compartment through the ventilators and the deck slanted forward as the bow dipped down. I was thrown first into the rack of bunks, then backward to the deck, falling across the Division's record player. The blast had come out of the blue. There'd been absolutely no hint of danger.

"What the Hell was that??" somebody shouted.

"Sounded like a forward magazine", I guessed. Since General Quarters had not sounded, I thought the explosion was probably internally caused. But I wasted no further time on speculation. Automatically reacting to my training, I burst over to the port side and headed aft toward my battle station. As I hit an "up" ladder, the General Alarm began its urgent CLANG-CLANG-CLANG! Other sailors, too, were hurrying to their posts, and I dodged among them as I crossed the main deck and up the foremast ladders to Sky Control.

I no sooner stuck my head outside the hatch below the Main Battery Director when I spotted a great cloud of inky smoke pouring from a carrier. From her relative position and distance from us I knew it was the WASP. At the same time, the JV talker on the sound-powered phone circuit, with whom I shared the battle station, yelled that the Bridge was announcing we'd been hit by a torpedo. Over the loudspeakers came the call for damage control parties to bear a hand and lay forward to combat flooding. The talker then relayed the information that a flash fire in Number One Turret's magazine had been extinguished by flooding—quick and expedient action by the ammo handlers down there. Under my feet, I could feel the ship returning to an even keel from the 5 1/2 degree list caused by the impact of tons of water flooding into the void where the torpedo had hit. Counter-flooding was already underway.

Looking forward on the port side, I could see where the fish had struck. Crewmen were already on the scene, gingerly moving across the oil-and-water-slick main deck. Smoke and steam rose in a cloud, coming

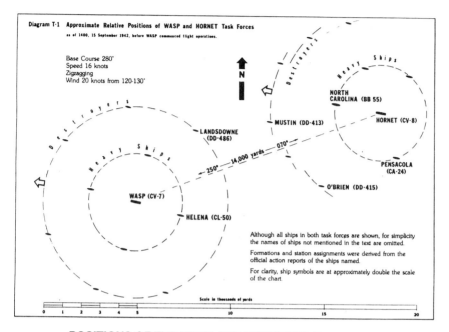

POSITIONS OF THE WASP AND HORNET TASK FORCES
1400, 15 September, 1942,
at the time of Japanese submarine attack.
(Courtesy Battleship NORTH CAROLINA & Capt. Ben Blee, USN [Ret.])

from outboard just abeam of Turret One. As the starboard ballast tanks filled, the ship was already picking up speed. Our fleet guide, the HORNET, was piling on the turns directly ahead of us as evidenced by the high wake she was throwing. And we were keeping pace, now, bending on an unbelievable 25 knots with that huge hole in our skin. We were steaming away from the WASP, although I could see she was still able to make way. Closer aboard, however, the plucky little destroyer O'BRIEN (DD-415) was trailing back in the formation off our port quarter. She was down by the head, a chunk blown out of her bow, leaving a hole like a bite out of a cheese sandwich.

On the NORTH CAROLINA, word now began to filter up to us via the sound-powered phone circuits about the damage done. I listened to the JV talker as I scanned the choppy seas, looking for periscopes and torpedo tracks. We might not yet be out of danger. There had been shipmates in the compartments where the torpedo hit who now were presumed dead. The hole was huge—"big enough to drive a Mack truck through." (Later it would be measured to be 32 feet long and 18 feet high,

THE WASP IS MORTALLY WOUNDED
Great billows of smoke engulf the stricken aircraft carrier, mortally
wounded by a torpedo from a Japanese submarine, 15 September, 1942.
(U.S. Navy Photo - National Archives)

centered some 20 feet below the waterline.) There was some other collateral damage. For example, above my head, the big CXAM "bed spring" radar antenna was askew. The force of the explosion below the waterline had caused a whiplash effect at the top of the foremast and the antenna's supports were sheared off.

Dead ahead, the HORNET was still leading us at maximum speed. Aboard the carrier, the Assistant Navigator Vic Moiteret was astounded as he watched the NORTH CAROLINA maintain her station in the formation. A few years ago, Vic (now a retired Captain) wrote a note to me: "I well remember the day[.] I was sitting in [the] Wardroom drinking a cuppa java when the Gen. Alarm sounded and I pounded my way up to the bridge to get the dope. I was informed [the] WASP and O'BRIEN and NORTH CAROLINA (the 'Showboat') had all taken fish from a sub or subs. I saw the WASP on fire, spotted the O'BRIEN falling away out of formation but I had to ask the QM [Quartermaster] on watch, 'Where's the NORTH CAROLINA?' His reply still sticks: *Right astern of us, Sir, doing 25 knots*"! Vic later told me he just didn't believe a ship could take a hit like that from a Long Lance torpedo and still make that kind of speed. "She should have been dead in the water."

Our damage control parties were working feverishly to shore up the forward bulkheads to limit the flooding and keep adjacent compartments from taking water. They were getting the job done, but called for us to back off to 18 knots to relieve the strain on those weakened crossbeams and bulkheads. The steel watertight bulkheads were actually "breathing in and out" from the pressure.

As I looked toward the WASP, she was still being wracked by one explosion after another. Some 20 minutes after the torpedoes struck her, a huge blast engulfed her Bridge, followed by one from below decks that hurled one of her elevators skyward. The proud ship we'd followed through the Panama Canal was in her death throes. As some of her destroyers were vainly trying to track down her attacker, two others stood by the stricken vessel to lend assistance. But the great ship was doomed. At 1520, Captain Forrest P. Sherman gave the reluctant order to "Abandon Ship!" Then her empty hulk was sunk by torpedoes from the LANSDOWNE (DD-486) to keep her from falling into enemy hands. Her casualty list would be long: 193 dead, 400 wounded.

In the concern over the two heavy ships, the O'BRIEN was almost overlooked. But that gutsy little tin can, that had dodged one torpedo only to turn into another, was still struggling to stay afloat. She would survive for nearly a month, only to break apart and sink while trying to get back to Pearl. In one of the miracles of the War, she took no casualties. The torpedo hit too far forward to endanger her crew.

A JAP TORPEDO STRIKES THE O'BRIEN "IN THE CHIEFS' QUARTERS"
In this remarkable photo, taken at the instant an enemy torpedo
explodes in her forward area, the destroyer is almost obscured by the
violence of the blast. The WASP is shown burning in the background.
(U.S. Navy Photo -National Archives)

As the damage assessments were made and passed on to the Task Force Commander, we got our orders: "Clear the area at best possible speed and return to Pearl Harbor."

Before I climbed down from Sky Control, I took one last look at the silhouette of the HORNET receding in the distance. With her screening cruisers and destroyers, she represented the only carrier task force we had remaining in the entire Pacific. It would be five weeks before she'd get any help from a repaired and returning ENTERPRISE. In the meantime, there were five, perhaps six, Japanese carriers on the other side of the board. It was one of the bleakest, blackest days of the Solomons Campaign. As the HORNET became hull down on the horizon behind us, she looked awfully lonely and vulnerable out there by herself.

However, we would get one bit of good news. Admiral Turner's transports delivered the 7th Marine Regiment to Guadalcanal on 18 September without loss of a single ship or man in his command. But we'd paid an awful price to get them there.

When I took the midwatch at Bridge Radio in the Chart House, the conversation still revolved around the events leading up to the torpedoing. There were then, and continue to be today, differences of opinion on exactly what happened.

Some things were certain. The area into which we steamed was known to be submarine waters, but the gamble had to be taken to get the Marines to the 'Canal. At least two factors contributed to the success of the attack. The torpedoes were launched just as our ships were executing a turn. To keep their proper screening stations, the destroyers in the screen were racing at high speed to reach their positions. There was a deficiency in our sonar (underwater sound detection gear) that made it sometimes unreliable during such maneuvers, thus decreasing the probability of detecting submarines. The second factor was beyond our control. It was perfect "submarine weather". Clear, sunny skies made viewing from a periscope easy; and a 20-knot trade wind was kicking up frothy white caps across the ocean surface, making it virtually impossible to spot either a periscope or a torpedo track.

There is little doubt that the Imperial Japanese Navy submarine I-19 (confirmed in documents after the War) fired a spread of six torpedoes at the WASP in a fan pattern. Three of the Model 95 Long Lance fish scored hits on the ill-fated carrier from the almost point-blank range of 1,000 yards. As the WASP and HORNET completed flight operations, conducted into the prevailing wind, they then executed a right turn to course 280°. All seemed normal and there was no word of alarm. The first indication anyone on the NORTH CAROLINA had that something was amiss came when the Officer of the Deck noted heavy smoke coming from the WASP. At the same time, he spotted several planes apparently jettisoned from the carrier floating in the water. But still there were no communications of any kind, either by radio or by flag hoist. The O.D. assumed a flight deck accident caused the smoke.

It must be noted here that radio communications in the South Pacific were not always reliable. The primary equipment used between ships in the same force was a voice transceiver (talk and listen) called a "TBS". Since it was ultra-high-frequency, its maximum range was line of sight (about fifteen miles) under the best of conditions. But atmospherics and other factors could cause either complete or partial loss of transmissions.

While the ships in our Task Force had no inkling of anything other than a possible accident on the WASP, there came a sudden burst of static out of the TBS speakers and a somewhat garbled transmission: "TORPEDO HEADED FOR FORMATION COURSE ZERO EIGHT ZERO!" The message came from the LANSDOWNE of the WASP's screen. But what formation? Ours or theirs? Then, according to most accounts, another incomplete transmission came from an unidentified source: "TORPEDO JUST PASSED ASTERN OF ME HEADED FOR YOU!" My buddy Red Campbell, who had Bridge Radio as both his watch station and battle station, says no one ever asked him about that day, and that the "unidentified" transmission came from the O'BRIEN. He adds that he entered it on his log as such.

It had been three or four minutes since the fire was first observed on the WASP. Now, inexplicably and without prior signal, the HORNET made a sharp turn to starboard—a highly unusual maneuver. To stay on proper station, Captain Fort ordered the NORTH CAROLINA to follow suit with a "RIGHT FULL RUDDER! EMERGENCY FLANK SPEED!" At that moment, the O'BRIEN, one of our screening destroyers, was struck by the torpedo that took the chunk out of her bow.

Simultaneously, the MUSTIN (DD-413) in our screen urgently hoisted emergency signal flags warning of a torpedo attack. Then, as the compass at the NORTH CAROLINA's helm passed the heading of 295°, the port side of her bow, even with Turret One, erupted with the thunderous blast of the torpedo hitting her. Those forward on the port side, some on watch in the 1.1-inch gun mount, were engulfed in the geyser of oil and water that blew high into the superstructure. When it came cascading down, it surged into the men, one of whom was washed over the side to his death. Hitting just below the armor belt, the fish penetrated deeply inside and a thousand tons of sea water rushed into the forward compartments. That's where four of our shipmates were trapped and lost. Then, from the MUSTIN came word of a sonar contact, and the destroyer launched a depth charge attack on a suspected submarine, but without known result.

The torpedo attack that so seriously crippled our thin forces on that fateful 15th of September, 1942, has long been a subject of speculation and analysis, mostly by people who weren't even there when it happened. One theory holds that the *one* Jap sub I-19 had the incredible luck to have hit all three ships with one spread of six torpedoes. Yet, *two* subs of the Imperial Japanese Navy, the I-19 and the I-15, both reported the sinking of the WASP back to Tokyo. According to the "one sub" theory, three torpedoes hit the carrier. A fourth fish passed her bow, went *under* the LANSDOWNE (in the WASP's screen), passed by the MUSTIN (in our screen), and caught the NORTH CAROLINA. Two other torpedoes passed the WASP's stern, one of them just missing the HELENA; the other went across both formations and struck the O'BRIEN.

But refuting the "one sub" theory are the deck log reports during the attack, from both the MUSTIN and the O'BRIEN, of torpedo tracks coming on courses that rule out the I-19 as the only culprit. Also, the Navy's Bureau of Ships, in a 1949 report based on exhaustive research, says the NORTH CAROLINA was hit, not by a Mark 95 but by the shorter-range Mark 89 torpedo. The latter model had a normal range of 6,000 yards and a maximum of 10,000 yards. It probably could not have traveled the more than 10,000 yards from the I-19's position to the point where our ship was hit.

There are two other accounts from people who were there that day which support the conclusion that there were at least two or possibly three Jap submarines involved in the attack. The Captain of the LANSDOWNE maintained that one torpedo went completely under his destroyer, and it was that one which hit the O'BRIEN. The relative positions of the two tin cans at the time show that such a torpedo had to have come from a sub that was at a different attack angle from that of the I-19. Shipmate Red Campbell wishes he had a copy of the radio log he kept that day. He tells me it would show his entry that it was the O'BRIEN that warned the NORTH CAROLINA of a torpedo heading toward us. The destroyer was not in the same line as the torpedoes which hit the WASP. She was off our port quarter. Red believes there were *three* subs that day.

Neither the I-19 nor the I-15 survived the War, and any Japanese naval records which may have shed further light on the attack were destroyed in the 1945 fire-bombings of Tokyo. But if the BuShips and the destroyers' reports have any validity, the "one sub" theory is pretty well discredited. There is ample evidence to support the "two sub" theory, and there may have been a third submarine in on the attack as well.

The Imperial Japanese Navy (IJN) held a major advantage over the United States Navy in the quality of their torpedoes. American destroyer and submarine sailors were highly critical of our fish throughout the War. We never understood why our supposedly good old American technology couldn't get better ones to us. But then, our little war out in the Pacific was "low priority", and naval battles were not part of the European theater where all the emphasis was being placed.

The Japs had developed their exceedingly deadly Long Lance torpedo sometime around 1933 and refined it extensively in the pre-War years (as they had much of their military weaponry). The Long Lance was oxygen-fueled. Our torpedoes were propelled by alcohol. The IJN Mark 95, with a rated speed of 49 knots, packed 1,036 pounds of high explosives, one third more punch than the contemporary USN 21-inch torpedo. The standard torpedo on our destroyers was the Mark 15, with a range of three miles at 45 knots and 789 pounds of explosive charge. But its reliability was in question; for instance, it was known to run erratically. The superiority of the IJN's Mark 95 over the USN's Mark 15 put us at a distinct disadvantage throughout the War.

When we secured from General Quarters after clearing the area of the torpedo attack, I slowly descended to the CR Division compartment. The bulkhead of the compartment forward of ours was braced with shoring. Had the torpedo hit on the starboard side and a little aft, it could have wiped out the Radio Gang. The Lord's little angel was still on the job.

As I stepped over the hatch coaming, my thoughts were interrupted by MacPherson's voice.

"Hey, Hutch, where were you when the fish hit?"

"Over there by my bunk, Jimmy. Why?"

"Go look at the record player."

The player, itself, was undamaged. But the only copy of Benny Goodman's "*Jersey Bounce*" in the whole damn' South Pacific was smashed to itty bitty bits where I'd landed on it. It was then I noticed a stinging in my derriere. Some slivers of the broken record had penetrated my dungarees.

"You could put in for a Purple Heart, Hutch. Wounded in action!", Mac chuckled.

"And tell people I got shot in the ass by a record player? You gotta be kidding!"

Mac looked at the remains of the record on the deck, shook his head and said, to no one in particular, "War is Hell."

The NORTH CAROLINA, with two protecting destroyers, left the rest of the Task Force behind and settled on a northerly course. We anxiously wished for a quick setting of the sun. From the hole in our bow the ship was trailing an oil slick so long and broad an enemy submarine commander could follow us with his eyes closed. The sooner it got dark the less chance a roving sub or Jap scout plane could cut our track. Blessedly, darkness settled over the Coral Sea with no further evidence of hostiles in the area.

As the stars began to come out, I made my way up to the superstructure with a cup of java and sat looking aft. The phosphorus in our wake was popping like the tiny sparklers of a 4th of July. Any other time, I thought, I'd be entranced by the beauty of the boiling, broad white wake astern, and I'd revel in looking at stars so bright the light cast shadows on ship and sea. But this night I failed to appreciate the loveliness of the Southern Cross and these South Seas. Under that seeming tranquility an enemy submarine could be lurking.

The ship around me was more quiet and subdued than normal. The usual chatter of the gunners on watch in the nearby mounts was reduced to low murmurs; and the lookouts stared mutely at the sea, watching for anything that would reveal the presence of the enemy. It was a complete change from the exhilaration and boisterous self-congratulatory celebration following our performance in the Battle of the Eastern Solomons. For the first time, we realized that even so mighty a ship as the NORTH CAROLINA was vulnerable. And the deaths of our shipmates made us keenly aware of our own mortality.

Until the torpedoing, I had neither consciously nor subconsciously always been completely alert to the "feel" of the ship during course and speed changes. Now, I became acutely aware of every subtle movement of her and on her. When topside, I was constantly conscious, not only of our own movements, but of those of the ships around us, noting any deviation from the normal. Without realizing it I had become a "combat sailor" with that special state of alertness and awareness of dangers, brought on not only from the five ordinary senses but by an intuitive perception of impending peril. The sharpening of these senses would increase intensely every time I headed into the forward area—"west of Honolulu."

These instincts, combined with the training which triggered automatic responses to the stimuli of combat situations, were constant companions for months on end. To live in such a state inevitably takes a toll on mind and body engendering what then was termed "combat fatigue" but what sailors usually called "war nerves". Whatever name this physical and mental condition may be called, it simply was the result of the innate compulsion to self-preservation necessary for survival in war.

The joe in my cup had grown cold, and as I roused myself to head below decks, my thoughts turned to those we were leaving behind in the Solomons. We, in one of the most powerful ships afloat, were abandoning, howbeit involuntarily, a depleted naval force, now down to but a single aircraft carrier and her screen. For the next five weeks the valiant HORNET would be the sole flat-top operational in the Pacific Fleet.

On the beach were those poor damn' Mud Marines, ranks thinned both by enemy fire and debilitating disease, facing nothing less than more of the same. Men like us were on those ships and in those foxholes.

I felt a sense of guilt. We would not be there to help. Lord help 'em.

12

THE DOLDRUMS

"Doldrums" is a nautical term handed down from our sailing ship forebears: "Ocean regions in the 'horse latitudes' (near the Equator) characterized by calms and/or light winds."

In the graphic words of Coleridge's *Ancient Mariner*:

> Day after day, day after day,
> We stuck, nor breath nor motion;
> As idle as a painted ship
> Upon a painted ocean.

The old windjammers sometimes would be becalmed for weeks, even months, awaiting the slightest breeze to fill their sails. Now the term "doldrums" has come to mean a period of inactivity, boredom, or recession. Some perceptive observer of activity and inactivity during armed conflicts rightfully concluded: "War is long periods of insufferable boredom, punctuated by moments of sheer terror."

We on the NORTH CAROLINA were about to get a taste of being in the doldrums and of being bored stiff. We would be out of combat area with little but shipboard routine to occupy our time.

As we wended our way toward Pearl to get the massive hole in our bow repaired, we made a necessary port call at Tongatabu, a coral strip in the Tonga or "Friendly Islands" as they were called by Captain James Cook, inhabited by Polynesians and ruled by a Queen who steadfastly resisted any incursion of her islands by outsiders. But we were there, briefly, to accomplish only a couple of necessary tasks.

Hardly had the anchor chain roared through the hawse pipe and the hook set in the bottom, when hard-hat divers from the repair ship VESTAL were over the side to examine the torpedo damage. With acetylene torches, they cut away protruding slabs of metal plate to trim up the hull for easier movement through the water. I recall how impressed I was with the clarity of the water in that anchorage. You could see straight down over a hundred feet and watch sea creatures moving about on the bottom.

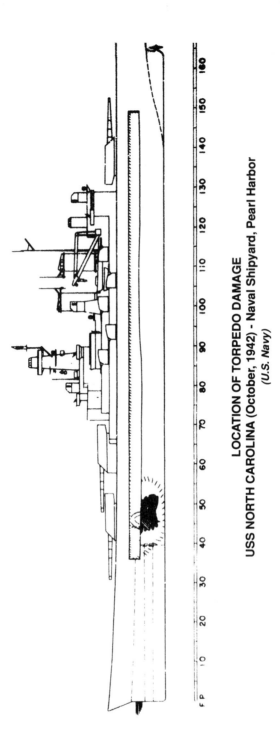

LOCATION OF TORPEDO DAMAGE
USS NORTH CAROLINA (October, 1942) - Naval Shipyard, Pearl Harbor
(U.S. Navy)

I watched with horrified fascination as a damage control working party removed the bloated bodies of our four shipmates from the flooded forward compartments. The experience had a profound effect on me.

There are many divergent ways to get to meet your Maker in wartime; but to me, being trapped below decks with no possibility of escape and no way to fight back, was by far the most horrid and horrific scenario. I suppose I've always been a bit claustrophobic. Even as a child I would fight like a tiger against anyone attempting to hold me down, and would become uncomfortable whenever I was in an enclosed space for any length of time with no view of the outside. Until this moment when those bodies were brought out of the tortured hull, being below decks hadn't bothered me. I'd felt completely safe behind the heavy steel armor belt that girded the ship's sides. Now, that changed dramatically, and I would spend as little time as possible below decks.

We buried our dead at Tongatabu in Captain Cook's "Friendly Islands"—a misnomer during the War since these islanders wanted nothing to do with foreigners. Indeed, the restrictions placed by the Queen allowed only the ship's chaplain and an honor guard to attend the ceremony. Shortly after, we departed the Friendly Islands, arriving in Pearl Harbor on 30 September, 1942.

We didn't get the NORTH CAROLINA into dry dock right away. The only one large enough to accommodate the Showboat was occupied by the SOUTH DAKOTA. She was getting her hull patched, if you remember, after running aground on a reef in Tonga harbor in the same Friendly Islands. The delay, we'd learn later, would keep the Showboat from the upcoming naval battles around Guadalcanal.

When we finally entered dry dock, we got a good look at the extent of the damage as the waters were pumped out of the dock and the area below the water line became visible. The torpedo had struck below the bottom of the side armor at frames 45 and 46, cracking three sections of the armor belt. The second and third decks were buckled, and several bulkheads were ruptured. Number One Turret wasn't damaged, but there was structural damage around it which would need repairs if the guns were to be safely fired. The gaping 18-by-32-foot hole and attendant damage would keep the Showboat in the dry dock for 30 days. Considering the work that had to be done to repair the ship, the yard birds in the Navy Yard get tremendous credit for getting us in and out in that short period.

We'd get some new weaponry, replacements for the obsolete and ineffective 1.1-inch anti-aircraft guns. They were "quad 40s"—the 40-millimeter Swedish-made rapid-fire Bofors, four guns to a mount. They

On photograph: OFFICIAL PHOTOGRAPH
NOT TO BE RELEASED FOR PUBLICATION
CONFIDENTIAL

BB 55   10/11/42   4321-42
LOOKING UP AND AFT AT TORPEDO DAMAGE.

Torpedo Damage
USS NORTH CAROLINA
In drydock, Pearl Harbor, shows 18-by-35 foot hole blasted in the ship's
hull by enemy submarine. Five crewman were killed and 20 wounded.
Photo taken 11 October, 1942.
(U.S. Navy Photo)

were one of the best and most effective AA weapons of the War. The mounting of them, though, caused me some grief.

My field day duty was the maintenance of all antennas calling for any repairs; as well as cleaning them of verdigris, salt, soot, and other soilants. In mounting the new 40s, the operator of the big hammerhead crane got a little careless, swinging one of the heavy mounts across the ship between the foremast and the mainmast. Misjudging distance, he didn't clear the "flat-top" antennas and wiped them out. The woven copper wire whipped around the superstructure like a striking cobra, but luckily didn't hit anyone.

When word reached Radio Central, I got the call and went up to see what had happened. There was no doubt the antennas would have to be replaced, and I spent most of my working hours the next week, up and down the masts and climbing around the superstructure, repairing the damage. There's a difference between splicing ordinary wire rope (cable) and antenna wire. The antennas were of copper, woven around a core, whereas wire rope has no core. The copper breaks much more easily than steel cable; and it was one pain in the neck to splice, not to mention causing cut and stabbed fingers and bloody hands. I began to rue the day I learned how to splice the damned stuff.

In the meantime, the crew was back to in-port routine, a big change from the intensive duty we'd been used to at sea around Cactus-Ringbolt. After a while, the boredom set in.

Off duty one day, I was on the Signal Bridge indulging in one of my favorite pastimes—scanning the harbor through one of the telescopes to see what ships were in port—when I sighted a destroyer with a silhouette I didn't recognize making its way in the channel. Adjusting the scope, I zeroed in on her colors. She was flying the ensign of the Free French, but what she was doing in the Pacific in the first place and why she was coming into Pearl I never discovered.

As I scanned her from stem to stern, I came to a complete halt at the unbelievable sight on her fantail, for there in all their glory was a real live milk cow and about eight crates of chickens! Now, I thought I'd seen everything on foreign vessels at one time or other, and still held the firm belief the British had the dirtiest, but the presence of that black and white cow (it looked like a Holstein) and the pens of leghorns on a COMBAT vessel threw me for a loop. I yelled at the signalmen around the Bridge to come take a look.

"Well, I'll be go-to-hell!" exclaimed the first skivvie-waver to look. "That's a COW! And CHICKENS!" That brought more guys over to the scope while others broke out binoculars.

Soon we were asking each other more questions than we could ever expect to find answers to—all of them with great humor.

"Wonder what rate insignia you get as petty officer in charge of livestock? A bull in a china shop?"

"What's a supply officer to do with a requisition for four bales of alfalfa and two hundred pounds of laying mash?"

"I've heard of mascots, but *this* is ridiculous—*udderly* ridiculous!"

"Boy (groan), did you have to reach for that one!"

"I've seen *crow's* nests on ships . . . but *cow's* nests?"

"You've heard of shovelin' shit against the tide? Now you know where it comes from!"

"*Egg-zackly!*"

"I haven't seen so much chickenshit on a ship since that new smart-ass ensign came aboard, throwing his weight around."

"Does a cow on a destroyer give *canned* milk?"

The next day, one of the signalmen ran across a crewman from the French ship and, with his fractured high school French, learned the Captain of the destroyer liked fresh eggs and milk for breakfast and was determined to have them—war or no war! *C'est la vie! C'est la guerre!*

The granting of liberty was not as restricted as it had been our first time through Pearl, but everything was more expensive. The $72 a month ($60 base, plus 20 percent sea pay) I made as a Radioman 3rd didn't go very far. Oahu really wasn't equipped to handle the large influx of servicemen as the island became the major forward repair and supply base in the Pacific. There was a scarcity of entertainment unless, of course, you counted River and Hotel Streets, Honolulu's Red Light district.

At that time, prostitution was legal in the Territory. All of it in Honolulu was confined to just a few blocks and it was strictly controlled. The girls were subject to weekly medical examinations by Navy doctors, which kept venereal disease at a minimum, the lowest in any State or Territory.

The lines of servicemen, and even a handful of civilians, around the houses were long throughout the day. But the Madams were expert in moving things along in an assembly-line fashion that would have made even Henry Ford proud. All this was to come to a sorry end when Mamas back home learned their "little boys" were frequenting Polynesian houses of ill repute on this far-off tropical island. They were particularly incensed when they discovered it was "condoned" by the Navy, which supplied the doctors. Congressmen got piles of angry letters from all across America, and the lid was clamped down tightly on the "happy houses".

That didn't stop prostitution, of course. The hookers just moved to the nearest bar or street corner. The immediate result was a skyrocketing VD rate, up hundreds of percentage points. Rape, seldom heard of in the Islands previously, increased dramatically.

So much for Moral Mamas.

Adding to the controversy over the whorehouses was an offhand quote from Admiral Halsey. Some reporter wrote that "Bull" proclaimed he didn't want any sailors in his command who didn't smoke, drink, and run around with women. The furor grew louder when it became known that Halsey also sported a tattoo. The Moral Mamas roared their disapproval, and the Admiral was labeled the "Patton of the Pacific" for making unpopular statements. But none of it bothered him. His men loved it and loved Halsey. Besides, he was fighting a War. Did a pretty good job of it too (as did General George S. Patton, Jr.).

The Navy tried its utmost, under trying circumstances, to provide some rest, relaxation, and amusement. We had regular swimming parties out at Barber's Point, where navigating through the concertina barbed wire made getting to the ocean a test of perseverance. We had a couple of luaus near the Kaneohe Air Station. There's where I got my first taste of *okoolyhau* (I *think* that's how it's spelled). It's the Hawaiian equivalent of a moonshiner's white lightning, home-made and as potent as a mule's kick.

Occasionally in the Navy Yard we'd listen to dance bands made up of professional musicians who'd joined the service. There usually were some girls around with whom we could dance, but they were outnumbered by sailors by about twenty-five to one most of the time.

The enforced idleness sometimes caused flare-ups among the sailors who'd been used to the constant vigilance and pressures of being in the forward areas. One of our hangouts was a place called the Wagon Wheel on the way out to Waikiki Beach. A few of us from the Radio Gang were peaceably drinking beer at the joint one afternoon when a fight started over who knows what. Within seconds, nearly everybody in the place was swinging at everyone else. Some of it got nasty, and I still have a faint scar on my left forearm where a sailor with a seaman's knife took a swipe at me. That was enough for MacPherson and me. Jimmy hurled a chair through a plate glass window and we escaped. It wasn't a world-class donnybrook, but it was interesting and it broke the monotony.

One place I'll always remember. It was P.Y. Chong's, a restaurant off Waikiki Boulevard that served the greatest steaks in the Islands. The beef came from the world's largest cattle ranch, the one over on the Big Island. I only went there a couple of times. It was expensive for a

3rd Class Radioman, but it was *classy*. I would sit out on the lanai overlooking the ocean and luxuriate in the surroundings, enjoying the impeccable service. The steaks were prepared to perfection; and it took about three hours, with all the extras that came with it, to enjoy the meal.

I saw Wally Dowden, the acquaintance from back home, only a few times and stayed overnight at his place but twice. He was putting in a lot of overtime at the Navy Yard, and had also gotten involved with a girl. I would be a third wheel.

I eagerly pursued every bit of news and scuttlebutt about the War in the Solomons. Censorship kept a lot of holes plugged, so I took to watching for ships returning to Pearl from Cactus, visiting them and pumping their radiomen for details of the latest events.

In late September and early October, there were several skirmishes and battles along the Matanikau River. For instance, on 8 October there'd been heavy hand-to-hand fighting between Marines and Japs along the Matanikau during a severe tropical rain storm, with the enemy suffering heavy casualties before being repulsed.

On the night of 11/12 October, ships of both sides squared off in what was to be dubbed later the Battle of Cape Esperance. An eight-destroyer enemy convoy, escorted by a three-cruiser force, moved in to bombard our shore installations and to land troop reinforcements. At the same time, Admiral Turner's transports were bringing the U.S. Army's 164th Infantry Regiment of the Americal Division to the beach. Screening them were Admiral Norman Scott's four-cruiser/five-destroyer force, which caught the Jap force by surprise in the darkness.

In the ensuing fight, the light cruiser BOISE and destroyer FARENHOLT were severely damaged; the DUNCAN (DD-485), caught between our ships and a Nip cruiser, got it from both sides and went down, her guns still blazing. On the other side, the hostiles lost force commander Admiral Goto killed in action, one heavy cruiser, and three destroyers. The Good Guys won the sea battle, a great encouragement to the U.S. Navy, but the Japs managed to land fresh troops and artillery on Guadalcanal. Nevertheless Cape Esperance demonstrated that the Japs were not invincible in naval battles at night.

The rest of October and most of November, 1942, would see some of the heaviest fighting of the War on and around Guadalcanal, and the NORTH CAROLINA would not be there to help. A pair of Jap battleships, KONGO and HARUNA, pounded Henderson Field with nearly 1,000 14-inch shells the night of 13/14 October. It was diversionary fire while the Nips landed substantial reinforcements to bring their troop strength up to an estimated 29,000; but to the Marines and Army reinforcements landed by Admiral Turner the previous day, who took the business end of that bombardment, it was pure Hell.

"The Bombardment" (as if there were not many others) by the Jap battlewagons also destroyed some 48 aircraft and virtually all of Henderson Field's supply of aviation fuel. This was doubtless the high point of the Marines' disgust with the Navy, which apparently could not gain control of the sea around Guadalcanal. For the Americans on the island, mid-October was, literally and figuratively, "the pits"!

On 18 October, Admiral "Bull" Halsey relieved Admiral "Goon" Ghormley as Commander South Pacific (ComSoPac). Ghormley had been less than adept at finding solutions to the plethora of problems we faced in the Theater. Apparently he was not able to inspire the SoPac sailor in the crisis. On the binnacle list since before Midway with a skin disorder, Halsey, one of the most dynamic leaders of the War, was charged with getting things moving. In Washington, the Pentagon decided, finally, that it would make victory at Guadalcanal a priority project. In Halsey they had the right man for the job, and his appointment was a huge morale boost to every SoPac enlisted man. The announcement evoked cheers aboard the ships of the South Pacific Fleet.

At the same time, the Japanese High Command was also putting Guadalcanal at the top of their priority list. The second half of October witnessed a ferocious Jap attempt, beginning on 23 October, to retake the airfield and the island. The 17th Army's onslaught under General Hyakutake was spearheaded by the famed Sendai Division. But by the 27th the Marines and Army had held their positions on the Matanikau River, Coffin Corner, and Hanneken's Ridge—the spirited actions making the reputations of such Marine Corps heroes as "Chesty" Puller and Mitch Paige, author of the Foreword to this memoir.

With the mandate, now, to hold Guadalcanal at all costs, our naval forces ended up in a series of sea battles that came in relatively quick succession: 26/27 October, the Battle of Santa Cruz; 13-15 November, the Battle of Guadalcanal; and 30 November/1 December, the Battle of Tassafaronga.

Impatient with the Jap Army's failure to take Henderson Field, Admiral Yamamoto ordered the Nip Navy in the waters north of the Solomons, including five carriers (one carrier, damaged by an accidental fire, had to return to Truk) under Admirals Kondo and Nagumo to find the American carriers and sink them in conjunction with the Sendai Division's attack. They were found on Monday morning, 26 October. The air-sea battle raged all day and into the night. Off the Santa Cruz Islands, the HORNET, which had launched General Jimmy Doolittle's bombers to "30 seconds over Tokyo", was "sunk" by numerous bombs and torpedoes plus two spectacular suicide crashes by crippled Jap attack planes. Even then, though abandoned, she refused to sink and had to be finished off early on October 27th (Navy Day in the U.S.) by Long Lance torpedoes from Jap destroyers, our sorry fish being unable to scuttle her.

The destroyer PORTER (DD-356) was also sunk—scuttled by one of our own destroyers, allegedly after being mortally wounded by a Jap sub while the unfortunate ship was picking up downed American airmen. So we heard—only recently has it become clear that the tin can was hit by one of our own torpedoes loosed from a ditched torpedo bomber. Damaged were the destroyer SMITH (DD-378) and the AA cruiser SAN JUAN. Although hit by a 500-pound bomb atop Number One Turret, the SOUTH DAKOTA escaped unhurt, protected by her 16-inch armor. The big battleship had replaced us to provide AA protection for the ENTERPRISE, which had just returned to the South Pacific in time for the battle. The Big E was damaged by two bomb hits and a near miss; but again, as in the Battle of Eastern Solomons, she survived. However, once again, we were down to only one carrier in the whole damned Pacific, and she was not fully operational.

In the carrier Battle of Santa Cruz, four Jap flat-tops against our two, American aviators did not sink a single enemy ship. But they did severely damage a cruiser (CHIKUMA) and two carriers (ZUIKAKU and ZUIHO), which the Japs could ill afford to lose at the time, knocking them out of the War for many months. Also, our ships' withering anti-aircraft fire, and our fighters, knocked down half of the some 200 Jap attackers. We lost about 80 planes, not the 200 claimed by the Japs, who actually thought they'd destroyed four U.S. carriers. We were buying time. The Japs simply could not repair ships or replace ships, planes, and pilots as quickly as we could. They could not compete with good old American industry and ingenuity, our economy and technology, our will to win and work ethic.

The three day/night Naval Battle of Guadalcanal (13-15 November) shaped up as both sides moved in transports full of troops, each intent on final victory. Apparently Admiral Yamamoto, frustrated not only by the Jap Army's failure to take Henderson Field but also by his own carrier force's failure to knock out the U.S. Navy, was going to depend on surface action to win at Guadalcanal. The Japs were protecting their convoy on 12 November with two battleships, which were going to shell Henderson, a cruiser, and up to fourteen destroyers under Admiral Abe. Senior to Rear Admiral Norman Scott, Rear Admiral Daniel J. Callaghan on the SAN FRANCISCO (CA-38) was designated by Admiral

Turner to lead the cruisers PORTLAND, HELENA, ATLANTA, and JUNEAU, plus eight destroyers, in screening our transports and in a gallant attempt to thwart the overwhelmingly superior Jap force.

In the early morning hours of Friday the 13th, the U.S. and Jap forces met head on. In the ensuing melee Admiral Scott, the hero of Cape Esperance, was killed on the ATLANTA (according to later info, by salvos from the SAN FRANCISCO!) so badly mauled she had to be scuttled. Admiral Callaghan and Captain Cassin Young were also killed, when the SAN FRANCISCO was shelled by a battleship, but the cruiser survived. The PORTLAND took a torpedo in her stern, forcing her to steam in circles, but she also survived. The JUNEAU, torpedoed, limped out of the battle. U.S. destroyers took a terrific beating: four were sunk, the brand-new BARTON lasting but seven minutes in combat, and others were severely damaged—in what one shore observer called an "awesome mêlée of light and sound."

On the other side of the ledger, the Jap battleship HIEI, from which the Emperor had last reviewed the fleet *and* Admiral Abe's flagship, was badly wounded and eventually sunk after daylight by our planes, the first Nip battleship to go down in the War. Two Jap destroyers also went down in the battle, and others were damaged. It was the wildest surface action since the Battle of Jutland in 1916, the two forces becoming intertwined at close range with each other, U.S. destroyers raking the sides of a Jap battleship with machinegun fire—"a barroom brawl after the lights had been shot out."

We took a beating, but we managed to frustrate, howbeit briefly, the enemy's shelling and landing missions. Only the HELENA and two of our destroyers, the FLETCHER (DD-445) and O'BANNON, survived without damage. But it was a post-battle tragedy that not only boosted our casualty total much higher, but brought the battle heartachingly home to me.

At first light that morning, the crippled and depleted U.S. force, with command now in the HELENA, began a slow, painful retreat towards the New Hebrides. The JUNEAU, repaired well enough to get underway, was limited to only 18 knots because of collateral battle damage. Aboard her were two groups of men. One, the five Sullivan brothers, would gain immortality. The other group, my shipmates and buddies who'd left the NORTH CAROLINA Radio Gang for duty on the JUNEAU, would be remembered only by their families and their former shipmates.

An enemy submarine, the infamous I-26, was on station on the course the American force was taking. About 1100, 13 November, the Jap fired a spread of six fish, aimed at the SAN FRANCISCO; but they missed and traveled another 1,500 yards, where at least one of them plowed into the JUNEAU. Lieutenant Commander Bruce McCandless, who'd taken charge of the SAN FRANCISCO when both Admiral Callaghan and Captain Young were killed, wrote in his report:

"The JUNEAU didn't sink—she blew up with all the fury of an erupting volcano. There was a terrific thunderclap and a plume of white water that was blotted out by a huge brown hemisphere a thousand yards across, from within which came the sounds of more explosions. . . . When the dark cloud lifted from the water a minute or so later, we could see nothing of this fine 6,000-ton cruiser or the 700 men she carried."

The next day, I heard at Pearl the JUNEAU had been lost. In giving confirmation of her sinking, another of my sources said she'd "gone down with all hands."

"Oh, Good Lord! Jackson, Lister, Ochoa, and the rest—*all gone!*" My first reaction was one of disbelief. I couldn't accept their loss.

But I finally admitted to myself it must be true. Upon doing so, I went into the head and threw up.

Next, I called Wally Dowden, had him get me a fifth of whiskey, made the first liberty call, and headed for 123 Lewers Street, where I sat on Wally's front step, drinking Seagrams Seven Crown and getting drunk as a skunk. It took the whole damn' bottle and it didn't do any good, either. In the words of the *Ancient Mariner*:

> The many men, so beautiful!
> And they *all dead* did lie:
> And a thousand thousand slimy things
> Lived on; and so did I.

But I hadn't yet heard the worst part. When the NORTH CAROLINA got to Noumea five weeks later, a radioman off the SAN JUAN (sister ship to the JUNEAU) told me more of the ghastly aftermath. There *had* been survivors, he said. About a hundred men either were blown clear or otherwise made it into the water. At that, I began to have hope for my friends. But then, he said: "Only ten of those made it. The sharks got the rest."

"Any radiomen?"

"Not that I know of."

"God *DAMN!*"

For almost half a century, I heard no further details of the loss of the JUNEAU and its radiomen until I read Richard B. Frank's book *GUADALCANAL* published in 1990. All the old emotions came flooding back like a giant sea crashing over a rocky headland. What Frank described was more horrible than I could have imagined.

When the JUNEAU exploded, Captain Gilbert C. Hoover of the HELENA and Commander of the battered U.S. force, deemed it unlikely any crewmen of the AA cruiser could have survived. With that assumption, and fearing lest he endanger his crippled force, he did not order a search, nor even stop to look for any who might have lived through the torpedoing. No search and rescue was mounted early enough to help, and it would be ten days before a more or less full accounting would be made. In the meantime, those who had made it into the water suffered unbelievable hardships and died horrible, horrible deaths.

Weakened by wounds or unable to cope with the minute-to-minute struggle just to stay alive, many just gave up and died. George Sullivan, the only one of the five brothers to survive the sinking, lasted until the fifth night in the water. The little groups of men on rafts or flotsam thinned rapidly as there was no food or fresh water. Some drifted into delirium and disappeared in the water.

Then came the sharks. The most gruesome account of shark attacks is also a story of incredible valor and self-sacrifice. It was told by one of the ten who finally made it to safety, a signalman named Lester Zook. One of the men on Zook's raft was attacked as he tried to shift from the raft to the survival nets. A shark took a huge chunk out of the man's shoulder. His arm, spewing blood, was hanging by only a couple of sinews. In Zook's own words:

"He looked at his shipmates there and realized he was making them nauseated, that he was driving them crazy by just being there, and the sharks were getting around close in the water because of his blood being around there and, knowingly, he pushed himself off the life nets and swam out about five or six feet and let the sharks have him rather than lay there and die like a coward and jeopardize the live[s] of his shipmates . . . ."

"Greater love hath no man than this . . . ."

The JUNEAU's fatality list was 683 names long. At least 1,439 sailors lost their lives in the first phase of the Naval Battle of Guadalcanal.

The second crucial phase of the Battle of Guadalcanal followed swiftly on the heels of the JUNEAU's loss. Despite the fight of the previous night, Jap cruisers got through to bombard Henderson Field in the early morning hours of 14 November. But the next day, planes from both Henderson and the ENTERPRISE, steaming toward Guadalcanal after hasty repairs at Noumea, sank a cruiser and several transports as well as damaging other ships. Our superiority in the air was beginning to tell on the Japs. When Admiral Halsey read the reports, he exclaimed: "We've got the bastards licked!"

Nevertheless, the next night, the hostiles were making another attempt to reinforce their troops, with the remnants of the force that had taken heavy casualties in ships and men during the air attacks on their convoy that day. To support the landings, a Jap bombardment unit under Admiral Kondo sortied, bent on shelling Henderson Field again. The force was composed of the battleship KIRISHIMA, two heavy cruisers, two light cruisers, and a squadron of destroyers.

Racing to meet this latest version of the Tokyo Express, were the WASHINGTON, SOUTH DAKOTA, and four destroyers—the WALKE (DD-416), BENHAM (DD-397), PRESTON (DD-379), and GWIN (DD-433). All these ships were hastily detached from the ENTERPRISE Task Force, under the command of Admiral Kinkaid, to meet the crisis. Admiral Willis Augustus "Ching" Lee, Jr., commanded the force, centered around the two battleships, from the WASHINGTON. They took up defensive positions between Savo Island and Cape Esperance. This infamous portion of Iron Bottom Bay, its bottom littered with sunken ships, was a precarious area in which to operate battlewagons. The waters were shallow, the space restricted, and any miscalculation could see the heavies stranded on some shoal. But Admiral Halsey deemed the risk imperative in view of the grave crisis. The U.S. Navy's not fighting *now* would undermine the Marines' morale on Guadalcanal.

The U.S. and Nip forces collided shortly after 2300, 14 November, the light cruiser SENDAI being picked up by the WASHINGTON's radar and taken under fire, but escaping. Almost simultaneously, our four tin cans became targets of a Nip cruiser and enemy destroyers. In a matter of minutes, all four U.S. destroyers were knocked out of action, two sinking quickly and one eventually scuttled, without getting off a torpedo. Still Admiral Lee, his men throwing life preservers to destroyermen in the water, steamed on without escorts. Then the SOUTH DAKOTA, unaccountably, lost all electrical power. On regaining it, she was silhouetted against the fires of her stricken destroyers. The Japs fired some 34 torpedoes at her, all of which apparently missed! Then about midnight, the enemy targeted her with searchlights and started shelling her. But this let Admiral Lee know the *other* big blip on his radar was the enemy battleship KIRISHIMA, only 8,400 yards away!!

Later reports (perhaps apocryphal) claimed Admiral Lee was heard on the TBS radio circuit shouting: "This is Ching Chong China Lee, and I'm coming through!" Without radar, the Jap battleship had no idea the U.S. battlewagon was there. The WASHINGTON, illuminating the KIRISHIMA with a star shell, poured several rounds from her 16-inch rifles, plus numerous 5-inch shells, into the Jap battlewagon. Flaming and irreparably damaged, she sank to the bottom of Iron Bottom Bay during the night. The Japs also lost a destroyer in the battle.

The SOUTH DAKOTA was heavily damaged. But WASHINGTON and Lee, plus radar, had saved the day, or more accurately the night, for the United States Navy and our forces on Guadalcanal. The victory gave our forces new confidence in final victory, and was a turning point not only at Guadalcanal but in the Pacific War. As a captured Japanese document put it: "It must be said that the success or failure in recapturing Guadalcanal Island, and the vital naval battle related to it, is *the fork in the road* which leads to victory for them or for us."

Admiral Halsey sent a message to all SoPac ships and commands: "You have written your names in golden letters on the pages of history and won the undying gratitude of your countrymen. No honor for you would be too great. . . . ." But who remembers now?

There was one more fight to come—between Lunga Point and Cape Esperance—Tassafaronga.

On 17 November, the NORTH CAROLINA, her repairs made, got underway for the South Pacific. Had CinCPac put us on a priority basis, we could have arrived in time to help out in the upcoming Battle of Tassafaronga, but our trek was almost a leisurely one, for some reason or other. We even stopped over in Fiji on Thanksgiving to have the traditional turkey with all the trimmings dinner. Then we went through a change in command as Captain Wilder R. Baker relieved Captain George H. Fort, who was being promoted to Rear Admiral.

Our air superiority around the 'Canal was making it increasingly difficult for the Japs to send in reinforcements, and it was giving our amphibious units ample cover to bring in more and more of our own troops, who were now beginning to go on the offensive to drive the Japs off Guadalcanal. On 30 November, our coastwatchers reported a force of eight enemy destroyers heading "down the Slot". Admiral Halsey immediately countered by ordering four heavy cruisers—the MINNEAPOLIS (CA-36), NORTHAMPTON (CA-26), NEW ORLEANS (CA-32), and PENSACOLA (CA-24)—along with the light cruiser HONOLULU (CL-48) and six destroyers, to intercept the Japs. The Nip destroyers were loaded with drums of food and supplies, the plan being to dump the drums over the side off their shore positions on Guadalcanal and let the tides float them in to the beach, to be recovered by the Jap land units.

Our cruiser force, Task Force 67, had been hastily formed under Admiral Kinkaid; but, inexplicably at almost the last minute, he was transferred to the Aleutians in the North Pacific by Admiral Nimitz. Kinkaid was replaced by an inexperienced Rear Admiral Carleton H.

Wright. Off Tassafaronga, about 2315 on November 30th, the lead U.S. destroyer FLETCHER picked up a Jap ship on her radar. But for some reason Admiral Wright hesitated and withheld permission to attack, and the element of surprise was gone. Finally, a few torpedoes were launched, all missing. As the enemy tin cans passed abeam of our cruisers, the Admiral then opened fire, with most of the salvos missing or concentrated on only one Jap destroyer, which was quickly put out of action and eventually sank, the only Nip ship to be sunk in the battle.

However, the other enemy ships, steaming in a line under tenacious Admiral Tanaka, fired spread after spread of Long Lance torpedoes at the cruisers. Two struck the U.S. Flagship MINNEAPOLIS, tearing her bow off back to Number One Turret. The NEW ORLEANS, next in line, took a fish in her port bow, blowing off everything back to Number Two Turret. The PENSACOLA, now silhouetted against the blazing NEW ORLEANS, was hit just forward of amidships, lost her power, and sustained ruptured fuel tanks. The HONOLULU, accelerating to 30 knots, evaded the zinging torpedoes. But the NORTHAMPTON, last in line, was blasted by two fish. She eventually rolled over and sank.

Tassafaronga was a humiliating and devastating defeat of a vastly superior force by an inferior one. The Japs posted a big win. The only plus on our side: the fight prevented the enemy from dumping his supply drums; and none of the precious food, fuel, and medical supplies got ashore to the Jap ground forces. Our three severely damaged cruisers made it to safety, but they were out of action for months.

We all wondered what we would face when the NORTH CAROLINA returned to the Solomons.

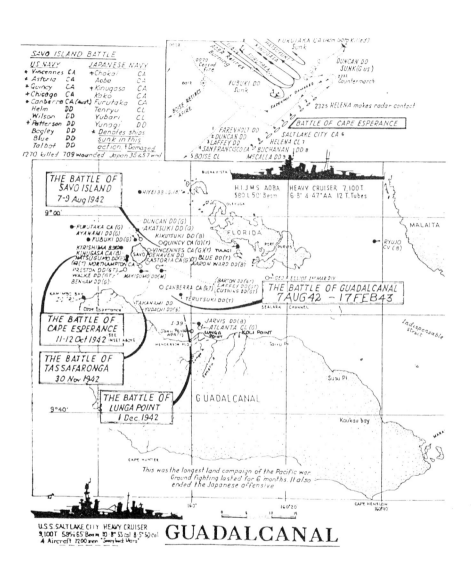

(Courtesy Sgt/Maj. Lester Bamford, USMC, Ret.)

13

THE CROCODILE NAVY

The NORTH CAROLINA was back on station in the Solomons by 9 December, 1942. But the carrier task forces were now playing a different role: back-up to shore-based aircraft and to the fast-moving destroyers and cruisers of the "Cactus Navy". The smaller ships were operating in the relatively confined waters around the islands, and were more effective against the nighttime tactics now adopted almost exclusively by the Japs. The sea war in the Solomons had now taken on a new character and the action had moved farther northward "up the Slot".

Christmas saw us at anchor in the Grand Roads, Noumea, New Caledonia. We had the traditional holiday dinner, church services, and light work routine. A new year was upon us as the Showboat swung around her hook. It was midsummer in the South Pacific, accompanied by oppressive heat and humidity. Topside, the sun-heated steel was hot enough to roast chestnuts, and below decks the muggy high temperatures made staying in the living compartments almost intolerable. Along with several other off-duty radiomen, I took refuge in one of the few air-conditioned areas aboard—Radio Central.

A bull session was at full bore in the forward compartment around the joe pot in the early afternoon of New Year's Eve. There was little talk of the War, and there wasn't even much conversation about the States and "home". Yet, in our minds we were wondering what 1943 would bring. I was listlessly practicing with my speed key on the oscillator while intermittently joining the good-natured joshing going on around me. The guys were engaged in a "cutting session", seeing who could ridicule his shipmates most, but all in good humor.

Without fanfare, a familiar figure stepped over the hatch coaming into the forward section of the Shack. It was Harlan "Harry" Haines, grinning widely. Harry had been one of the radio school grads aboard before the War started; he had made 3rd Class, but was transferred off the ship before we left the States. Harry and I had not been close friends, but he had been the one who had given me my "operator's sine": "JA."

No one aboard had heard from him since the transfer and it was a pleasant surprise to see him again.

Harry had some great sea stories to tell. He was now 1st Class and on the Staff, Commander Amphibious Forces, South Pacific, under Rear Admiral Richmond Kelly "Terrible" Turner, who flew his Flag on the U.S.S. McCAWLEY, a troop transport. Turner's genius in amphibious warfare would earn him another sobriquet from the Japs. They called him "The Alligator". His Flagship had already gotten her nickname; everyone in the Fleet knew her as "The Wacky MAC".

To most of us battlewagon sailors, the Amphibs were a somewhat obscure branch of the service and hardly "real" (combat) Navy. But Harry's tales of the McCAWLEY's exploits during the 7 August invasion of Guadalcanal, and the subsequent air attacks and sea battles, had us realizing he'd seen a great deal more action than we had, and we began to gain some respect for those lumbering old tubs carrying troops.

After a while, most of the guys drifted out of the Radio Shack, and only Harry and I were left.

"I see you're still working on that *bug*", Harry commented, nodding at my Vibroplex speed key. "How're you coming with it?"

"Well", I said, "I'm up around 50 words a minute but, of course, I don't get a chance to use it on a circuit. We don't do much transmitting, just copying, on this ship."

"How'd you like to come over to the Admiral's Staff? I can tell you you'd get your fill of operating with us."

"Oh, I don't know, Harry. That doesn't sound like my kind of duty. I'd just as soon stay on a combat vessel."

"Look, Hutch", Harry replied, getting more serious, "if it's action you want, we'll be going back up to the 'Canal soon, and the Admiral's working on another invasion as soon as Cactus is secured. We are in big need of a good operator, *right now*. If you'll volunteer for this duty, I'll guarantee you'll be 2nd Class by the 1st of February."

We went to chow and chatted some more. It was obvious Harry had been sent out to recruit for the Staff. If push came to shove, he could ask the Admiral to *order* me transferred over. I knew I'd be breaking one of the cardinal rules of military service, namely the commandment: "Never volunteer"—for *anything*. But somewhere inside me was a feeling I had not yet done my part in this War. At the same time, my talent for high-speed sending and receiving was not being fully utilized here on this wagon.

I walked Harry up to the Quarterdeck. As we shook hands, I reached my decision.

"Cut my orders, Haines. But you damned sight better get me that extra stripe or stay off the weather decks at night. I'll deep-six you, myself."

Harry laughed, headed down the gangway, and was off in a Higgins boat.

The Navy bureaucracy can move fast when it wants to. The next day, 1 January, 1943, I was transferred, on paper, to "ComServRonSoPac FFT [for further transfer] to Flag Allowance, ComAmPhibForSoPac", aboard the U.S.S. ARGONNE (AG-3). The McCAWLEY was in New Zealand for yard availability, as well as rest and relaxation. So the ARGONNE was Turner's temporary Flagship.

As I packed my seabag, I looked around Compartment A-331-L. I would miss this place that had been my home for some twenty months, and I'd miss my shipmates a lot more. I said solemn farewells to Red Campbell, Phil Phillips, and the rest of the guys.

Jimmy MacPherson helped me with my gear as I made my way up to the Quarterdeck. We shook hands with more than the usual firmness. Neither of us knew what the future would bring.

"Don't get your feet wet, Hutch", Mac advised, then turned hurriedly away.

The Higgins boat sent over for me by the Flag scooted away from the big battleship toward the ARGONNE. From my place in the stern-sheets, I gazed at the huge gray sides of the Showboat. I had no way of knowing the NORTH CAROLINA would not see any action for the next ten months until she'd support the invasion of the Marshall Islands. And I had no way of knowing those same ten months would see me in some of the wildest, strangest, most hazardous situations of my service in the United States Navy.

It isn't true the U.S.S. ARGONNE was one of John Paul Jones's supply ships, although she seemed that ancient. Now as a utility vessel serving as a Receiving Ship, she was lazily swinging around her hook to the motion of the tides of Noumea Harbor, and she would be my temporary home until the return of the McCAWLEY. The accommodations aboard the old vessel that had seen service in World War I were not the greatest. I was berthed in one of the forward holds, where the bunks had canvas bottoms instead of springs. There were no mattresses. Just spread your blanket or mattress cover and that was it. But the old girl was clean, even though held together by layers of paint applied over some 25 or 30 years. And the chow was passable.

There was no loudspeaker system aboard, so the boatswain's mate of the watch had to go from hold to hold, space to space, sound his pipe and shout out whatever orders or watch changes were pertinent. Talk about being in "the old Nyvy"!

The Radio Shack, in the superstructure, was comfortable and well-equipped. The ARGONNE had, for a time, served as Admiral Ghormley's Flagship. As befits a ship stationary in port, with plenty of time for its crew to forage and make "moonlight requisitions", the ship had some nice amenities, including a pair of fancy joe pots in Radio One, and there was an abundant supply of night rations. Chief Radioman Jim Jett was an "0-1 Reserve" from Oregon, a lanky, easy-going guy and senior enlisted man on the Staff. (The 0-1 Reserves were the Navy's "Ready Reserves", the first to be called up in any mobilization). It was to Jim I reported as soon as I'd squared away my gear.

Routine communications on the ARGONNE were handled by ship's company. As a Flag radioman, I'd be on the Command or Overload circuit. Jim pointed out my watch station, a position slightly aside from the regular bank of receivers. I had my speed key with me and asked if it were all right to use it.

"Sure", Jim replied. "That's why Haines got you on the Staff."

"I don't have a speed key ticket, though, Jim. What if I'm challenged and asked for my ticket number?"

"You're on Admiral Turner's Staff, and no one will ask for your number", Jim answered. "Besides, the ticket thing has pretty much gone by the boards, at least here in the South Pacific."

I pushed the copper contacts of the bug under the manual key and spelled out "NXZ" in code, the call letters of Radio Noumea and Admiral Halsey's headquarters. I no sooner transmitted "K" ("go ahead") when I got an immediate response. I told Halsey's operator I was just testing, no traffic at this time, and signed off with a "VA" (end of transmissions). I felt now I was officially on the Staff, Commander Amphibious Forces, South Pacific. And I was the operator on the direct link between the two most important Admirals in the Theater. Pretty heady stuff for a 3rd Class!

The point must be made that there were *two* Theaters of War below the Equator. The *South* Pacific was under Admiral Halsey's Command and involved all the operations centering around the Solomons. The other Theater was the South*west* Pacific Command under General MacArthur, with most of its activities in and around New Guinea. Those of us who fought in the South Pacific are immensely proud of our service in the Solomons Campaigns; and it rankles us to have people, even many in the military, who mistakenly call other Theaters "South Pacific". Many never distinguished between the South Pacific and the Southwest Pacific, and many called any and all parts of the Ocean "South Pacific"—even areas *north* of the Equator including the Philippines, Iwo Jima, and even Japan!

Americans are notoriously ignorant of geography, that of their own country let alone the rest of the world. It is said that, to this day, most U.S. servicemen in World War II have no idea where they fought. As far as the War in the Pacific is concerned, it could be pointed out in their defense that the geography, or perhaps better oceanography of the Pacific is bewildering to the mind. This is due to the vastness of the Pacific Ocean and the immense expanses of its seemingly endless seas, sparsely speckled with islands of all sizes and shapes—some more or less isolated, others bunched in archipelagos large and small of every configuration. One could probably plop the entire landmass of the earth into the Pacific and still have an enormous ocean left.

The island of New Caledonia (Noumea is its capital) lies due east of Northern Australia, some 400 miles south of Espiritu Santo in the New Hebrides group, and some 850 miles south-by-southeast of Guadalcanal. It's fairly large, with an area of about 6,500 square miles. A French possession (as are some other Pacific islands, notably Tahiti and Bora Bora) the population then was made up of native Melanesians (Kanakas), Siamese and Tonkinese from French Indo-China, and French Colonials.

The United States first landed troops there in April, 1942, when the threat of Japanese invasion became apparent; and it became the SoPac Navy's "home port", so to speak, for well into 1943. As the Solomons Campaign erupted, Noumea's deep-water harbor became crowded with American vessels of every type. But liberty for us was quite restricted. The French authorities were apparently concerned about being overrun by Americans, and they imposed strict limitations on our activities. This may have been due in part to some Frenchmen in the colonial government who were sympathetic to the Vichy authorities in their homeland—the puppet regime installed by the German occupation forces. Only high-ranking American officers had much contact with the Frenchmen.

The mere mention of "Noumea" to any South Pacific sailor still brings a big grin and immediate reference to "The Pink House". It was the only (legal) house of prostitution. And, during liberty hours, long lines of sailors, Marines, and other service personnel awaited their turns. All this was accompanied by a great deal of high-spirited conversation and good-natured friendly insults passed back and forth between the men of the different Services.

There was almost no contact between Americans and the French civilians. On my few brief liberties, I recall seeing only one French woman on the street. We did, however, encounter Kanakas and Indo-Chinese. When taking a hike through the city and out into the countryside, we encountered numbers of Southeast Asians. They were imported by the French as laborers for their cattle ranches and the iron, nickel, chromium, and manganese mines.

It was kind of a shock, when meeting groups of Tonkinese, to get a big smile and a bow from the women. Their teeth were *solid black!* It came from chewing betel nut; and no matter how attractive some of these diminutive women might be otherwise, we were completely turned off by their ebony choppers.

One advantage of being on Admiral Turner's Staff was the privilege to use a tidewater pool normally reserved only for the French. Built out into the harbor, the pool was constructed so that the water level rose and fell with the tides. To have the opportunity to swim there was one of our very few "extras". We were limited to specified hours set aside for Americans only, when no French put in an appearance.

One of the few times I took advantage of the pool brought me face to face with one of the great legendary figures of the War. About four or five Staff radiomen and I took a Higgins boat over, and we were having a grand old time around the pool when a somewhat stocky man wearing bright, multi-colored Hawaiian-style swimming trunks came striding down the side of the pool.

One of the younger radiomen wondered: "Who in the hell is that old guy?"

I took one look, snapped to full-brace attention, and told my shipmates: "That's Admiral Halsey!" They, too, jumped to attention as the famed "Bull" approached. Craggy face and bushy eyebrows made him look somewhat like a bulldog, and we could confirm: "Yes, Bull Halsey sported a tattoo."

The Admiral approached, smiling, and immediately put us at ease with a "Carry on, Sailors." Then he chatted with us for several minutes. Halsey was very gracious and made a point of letting us know we enlisted men were "the backbone of the Fleet". When I mentioned we were from Admiral Turner's Staff, he replied: "Kelly Turner's a good man—my right hand."

After swimming a lap or so around the pool, the Admiral turned, waved to us, said "See you in Tokyo!", and left.

Admiral Halsey's reputation in the South Pacific is epitomized by a true story that circulated among us. It seems two SoPac sailors were walking down a passageway talking about the Admiral when one of them said: "I'd go to hell for that old son of a bitch." Whereupon he felt a heavy hand on his back and heard a gruff voice behind him: "Young man, I'm not that old!"

Because the two Admirals could meet in person in Noumea, there was little radio traffic, at first, on the circuit over which I stood watch. And since NXZ (Halsey's headquarters) and we were the only stations on the frequency, it was like having a private line. In the wee, small hours of the midwatch, I would "chat" back and forth with my counterpart on Halsey's Staff, a 2nd Class Radioman named Frank Condron. Our watches always coincided and we became "friends".

We also showed off some of our operating skills; and to confuse anyone, including the Japs who might be monitoring the frequency, we began using a lot of radio "shorthand" some of which we invented on the spot. It soon became evident both of us knew Continental (landline) Morse, that we could both send and receive at high speeds using "banana boat swing", and that we could clear traffic most efficiently. During these unauthorized and non-regulation CW transmissions, we made arrangements a few times to meet face to face in Noumea. However, other duties prevented it, and Frank Condron is to me still only a distinctive "fist" on a radio circuit. I never met him in person, but our playing around on that circuit would pay off handsomely down the line.

On 10 January, the "Wacky MAC" returned from New Zealand. Sporting a brand new paint job, she also had a new hull number on her bow. The MAC had been redesignated an "Attack Transport"! No longer the "P-10", she was the U.S.S. McCAWLEY (APA-4).

As I stood on the ARGONNE's deck gazing at the MAC across the harbor at Grand Quai, Jim Jett came up to me and said he was looking for a volunteer to fill in temporarily on the MAC's own ship's company Radio Gang.

"Isn't the Staff going back aboard, Jim?" I asked.

"Not yet. The Admiral and the rest of us are staying here until she makes a run up to the 'Canal, and she's short a radioman. Don't worry about the Overload circuit", he grinned. "I'm sure Gizzy Doerr can handle it while you're gone." Louis "Gizzy" Doerr was a Staff 2nd Class, top-notch radioman.

"Well", I replied, "it's better'n sitting here, swinging around a hook."

The next morning, Admiral Turner took his barge over to the McCAWLEY to meet with her Skipper, Captain Robert H. "Speed" Rodgers, and I went in the barge with him to report to the ship's Communications Officer for temporary duty. The ship was already loading troops, trucks, and construction equipment.

When the Navy got the MAC, they must have traded for an 18th round draft choice and two canoes to be named later. She was, and I say this charitably, an old bucket of bolts by the time I went aboard.

The 7,718-ton McCAWLEY was built in England in 1928 and christened the S.S. SANTA BARBARA. From then until 1939, she was

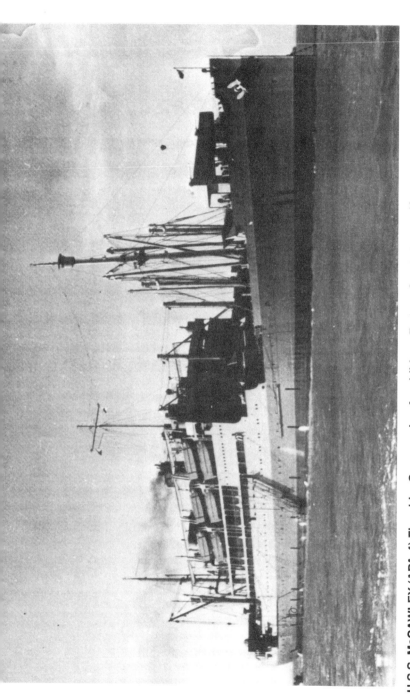

U.S.S. McCAWLEY (APA-4) Flagship, Commander, Amphibious Forces, South Pacific (*Guadalcanal "Echoes" & Ted Blahnik*)

a cruise ship of the Grace Lines plying the Caribbean. Thus she often was derogatively labeled a "banana boat". In July 1940, she was taken over by the U.S. Navy and renamed after a Marine Corps hero of the Civil War—Charles G. McCawley, eighth Commandant of the Corps from 1876 to 1891. All her luxury fixtures and trappings were stripped and she was down to bare bones. Her holds and much of her passenger cabin areas were refitted; and bunks were installed to give her the capability to transport large numbers of troops and their equipment including trucks, artillery, and other cargo.

The ship, of course, had not been designed to carry any armament, and therefore had no kind of space or support in her superstructure on which to install gun mounts properly. The only way she could be armed was to jury-rig gun platforms far forward on her high bow and astern on her fantail. Two 3-inch/.50-caliber AA rifles were mounted on each of the forward and after platforms. The mounts were "open", that is, with no protective covering for the gun crews except for a waist-high splinter shield. Also on the fantail was mounted an old 5-inch/.50-caliber single purpose rifle, good only for firing at surface targets or for shore bombardment, since it could not be elevated enough to fire at aircraft. One wag suggested the weapon was so old it must have been left over from Teddy Roosevelt's Great White Fleet! Then, wherever possible, 20-millimeter and .50-caliber machineguns were mounted to supplement the 3-inch .50s as anti-aircraft defense.

By any standards the MAC was a beat-up old tub. There were no spare parts for her cranky old diesels, so the black gang had to handmake replacement parts for any gear that broke or wore out. Her seaworthiness can best be summed up in the statement made by Admiral Turner when asked *why*(?) he chose the MAC for his Flagship. He could have had almost any ship he wanted, from one of the modern transports like the "President" ships to even a cruiser. But Kelly Turner just said:

"I'll not ask any sailor in my command to ship out in a vessel *worse* than the one I'm on."

That of course endeared him to every man in the Amphibious Forces, and instilled such high morale in the crew of the McCAWLEY that they boasted "no damned Jap will ever sink the Wacky MAC!" After all, she'd survived the original August 7th, 8th, and 9th invasion of Guadalcanal when her gun crews shot down four planes that attacked her. She was in the mid-September convoy, taking in supplies and reinforcements, the one that came under the submarine attack, during which the WASP, NORTH CAROLINA, and O'BRIEN were torpedoed. She was off Lunga Point, leading the transports that were being protected by the cruisers in that fierce November Battle of Guadalcanal. So, she'd seen her share of action, and was still afloat.

The plain fact of the matter is, though, that use of such ships as the McCAWLEY, pressed into service for which they were not designed, too old and decrepit for modern warfare, only emphasizes the lack of preparedness and foresight of our nation. We were no more ready to fight amphibious campaigns in 1942 than the cavalry was to fight an air war. The pitifully small force we were able to assemble for the Solomons almost brought us to defeat and loss to the Japanese of the entire Pacific Rim.

The designation of the MAC as an "APA" did bestow upon her, and the other transports so reclassified, a certain sense of dignity, however. That first "A" stands for "Attack". But the other "A" still means "auxiliary", the term given to "non-combatant vessels". A contradiction in terms? Sure, but it was the APAs which took the troops to the invasions, and their boat crews who got them on the beach, all the while sitting still in the water like so many clay ducks in a shooting gallery. Most of those beachheads meant frontal assaults on a well-dug-in and fierce enemy. That these ships and their crews did their jobs *despite* the obvious limitations placed upon them, can only be attributed to the courage and tenacity of the men who manned them.

The Amphibious Forces are a hybrid service—part sea, part land operations—not unlike the crocodile which became their symbol. It's fitting they were led by a man who gained grudging respect for his amphibious genius from an enemy who called him "The Alligator". Admiral Kelly Turner was that genius who planned and executed most of the landings in the Pacific. It must be remembered, of all military endeavors, amphibious operations are by far the most difficult and dangerous. Indeed British military historian B.H. Liddell Hart, doubtless with the Allied debacle at Gallipoli in 1916 in mind, wrote in 1939 (an observation Turner knew only too well): "A landing on a foreign shore in the face of hostile troops has always been one of the most difficult operations of war. It has now become almost impossible . . . ."

For those who served under Kelly Turner—sailors, Marines, and soldiers—there is a line in the lyrics of the Navy Hymn which is most appropriate when making another beachhead. According to the Amphib version:

> From peril, onslaught, fire and foe
> Protect them where-so-e'er they go.

There was one situation at Noumea which galled the living hell out of the Navy transport sailors. The logistics problem, supplying the

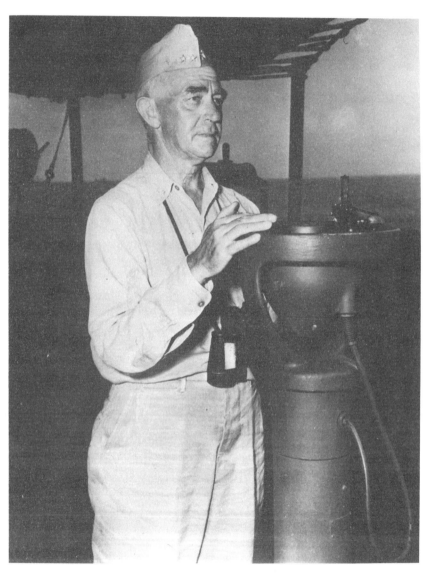

REAR ADMIRAL RICHMOND KELLY TURNER, USN
Commander, Amphibious Forces, South Pacific (1943)

Marines on the 'Canal and the combat ships at sea, was in a mess to begin with; but it was exacerbated by our own Merchant Marine, creating even bigger bottlenecks. Much of our supplies from the States were coming in on merchant vessels, manned by civilians in the maritime unions. Their pay was already exorbitant by the standards of the day; but the unions declared Noumea (850 miles from Guadalcanal) to be "combat area", affording merchant seamen *extra* "hazardous duty" pay. On top of that, they refused to work more than eight hours a day to unload their cargo, and demanded double pay for overtime.

That was irritating to say the least. But then this cargo was tranferred to Navy ships where seamen were making less than $65 a month; and it was those Navy men who had to take it into the War zone to face submarine, aircraft, and surface ship attack. As one of my shipmates put it: "They get the pay. We get the *shit!*" Navy Secretary James Forrestal was aware of the situation and voiced the opinion that if the American people knew of this travesty, "there would be a revolution back home!" Now you know one reason I never joined a union in civilian life.

On 12 January, 1943, Task Unit 62.4.3 was formed, with Captain Rodgers on the McCAWLEY commanding. With us were an attack cargo ship, the JUPITER (AKA-43); and two destroyers, the MAURY (DD-401) and PERKINS (DD-377). At 0530 the following morning, we got underway for Guadalcanal. At 0830, the MAURY picked up an underwater contact—possible enemy submarine. We took evasive action and steamed on. The MAURY subsequently lost the contact. I was back to full combat alert, acutely aware of all that went on around me.

The MAC had loaded fresh supplies in New Zealand; and, for the first evening mess, the ship's cook served mutton. Either the meat wasn't any good, the cooks didn't know how to prepare it, or the Americans hadn't cultivated a taste for it. But not a soul in crew's mess ate any of the damn' stuff. After another try a few days later, the cooks gave up. One dark night, the Supply Officer and a working party opened the sally port and deep-sixed the entire mutton supply.

As we closed Guadalcanal the night of the 15th from about 70 miles out, we witnessed heavy anti-aircraft fire off our starboard bow. Cactus was under air attack. At 0405, we entered Lengo Channel, and by 0615 had dropped anchor off Kukum beach to discharge our troops and equipment. Three times during the day we suspended unloading operations as enemy aircraft approached and "Condition Red" sounded, but our planes intercepted the Japs and we went back to the work at hand as soon as "Condition Green" went into effect. As night approached, we pulled out and moved over to Tulagi where we'd get more protection from shore-based anti-aircraft batteries. But we still went to General Quarters around 2145 when more enemy aircraft were "in the vicinity".

Like many who'd not gotten close-up looks at Guadalcanal, I had assumed the fighting on such a big island was across a broad front. But all of the battles waged over the past five months had been confined to a small area in and around Henderson Field. The actions at Bloody Ridge, Tenaru River, the Matanikau River, as well as other pitched fights and skirmishes, were all within a few miles of each other. This was brought home to me when I asked one of the MAC's officers just how far away the Jap's front lines were. We were off Kukum on the second day, and he pointed northwest to a point of land with a cluster of palm trees on it, then swung around to indicate another point to the southeast.

"That's roughly where the front lines are", he said, "and all of the fighting has been comparatively close to the beach. In most cases distances inland can be measured in hundreds of yards." Actually, it was about 1,500 yards.

I looked up and down the shore line. From point "A" to Point "B", I guessed, was probably not more than ten to twelve miles. There had been one helluva lot of blood shed on those few acres, and it wasn't over yet. On 9 December, Major General Alexander M. Patch, commanding the Army's Americal Division, had taken command of our forces on Cactus, relieving General Vandegrift and the heroic 1st Marine Division. Patch, with the Army's 25th (Tropic Lightning) Division and the 2nd Marine Division in his XIV Corps, began the first phase of the campaign to clear Guadalcanal of the enemy. As we were unloading at Kukum, fighting was taking place all along a front from just northwest of the Matanikau River; the 2nd MarDiv was driving along the coast, while Army units were to battle their way through the heavy jungle to sweep inland, then break to the coast toward Kokumbona.

Casualties from the battle lines were piling up and the MAC's job would be to evacuate as many as we could handle back to Noumea for hospitalization. No sooner had the last of the incoming cargo been transferred to the boat pool craft, when we began to get a steady stream of wounded Marines and soldiers aboard. We would be straining our capabilities to care for the 532 casualties whom we squeezed into the ship. Fortunately, our operations were interruped but once by an air alert. It was only a snooper who was shot down by the Cactus Air Force.

I had just come off watch and was going down a passageway when two Army medics came through, supporting a soldier between them. The GI was obviously in shock, his eyes glazed over in a fifty-fathom stare. Without warning, he wrestled free of the medics, ran down the passageway and threw himself on the deck. Wordlessly, the GI began smashing his forehead into the steel plates so violently he cracked his skull with a sickening sound. Blood squirted from his head and spurted across the deck. The whitish gray matter of his brain seeped out through his hair. As the medics reached him, he became still. They called for a Stokes stretcher and hauled the soldier off towards Sick Bay. One of the medics later told me the private had been on the 'Canal only a couple of weeks, had gone into his first combat, and was the sole survivor of his squad. I don't know if he survived the trip to Noumea.

As the last stretcher cases were being hoisted aboard by the cargo boom, I walked down to the forward well deck. As one case was lowered ever so softly to the number two hatch cover, a Navy corpsman who'd come aboard up a cargo net walked over to the Marine sergeant on the litter. The Marine had lost both legs, severed just below the knees. He had been on the island since the earlier days of the campaign and in most of the bloody battles around Henderson Field. Unscathed, he was finally due to be evacuated as one of the last of the 1st MarDiv to leave. But in the air raid the night of the 15th, he was caught too far away from a foxhole. A Jap bomber loosed a "daisy cutter"—that vicious anti-personnel bomb that scattered shrapnel in a 360-degree pattern about two or three feet off the ground. The shrapnel hit the sergeant in the legs.

"We're finally gettin' outa here, Sarge", remarked the corpsman. He lit the Marine a cigarette. "How're ya doin'?"

The sergeant took a deep drag. Then, in the most heartbreaking and succinct commentary on the Hell that was Guadalcanal during those months, the Marine spoke:

"Thank God, with these", he said quietly, nodding at the bloody bandages on the stumps of his legs, "I'll never have to go back to a place like the 'Canal again."

"Guadalcanal", to those of us who were there, is much more than the name of a tropical island. It is an emotion or whole range of emotions. For Mitch Paige, author of the Foreword to this book, fifteen years would pass before he could talk about it. When Admiral Halsey visited the 'Canal on November, 1942, he noted the Marines' a "gaunt, malaria-ridden bodies"—"their faces lined from what seemed a nightmare of years."

In historian Morison's words: "For us who were there, . . . Guadalcanal is not a name but an emotion, recalling desperate fights in the air, furious night naval battles, frantic work at supply or construction, savage fighting in the sodden jungle, nights broken by screaming bombs and deafening explosions of naval shells. Sometimes I dream of a great battle monument on Guadalcanal; a granite monolith on which the names of all who fell and of all ships that rest in Ironbottom Sound may be carved. At other times I feel that the jagged cone of Savo Island, forever brooding over the blood-thickened waters of the Sound, is the best monument to the men and ships who here rolled back the enemy tide."

Facing almost insurmountable odds, with meager supplies and support, the South Pacific sailors, Marines, soldiers, and fliers were thrown into a six-month-long conflict from which there would be no retreat. The conditions under which both the land and sea battles were fought were abominable. The 1st Marine Division took heavy casualties, fighting in insufferable circumstances. There were times when the outcome hung by a thread flimsy as a spider's web. At sea, the hulks of 24 allied ships (23 American) litter the depths of Iron Bottom Bay in mute testimony to the price that was paid in those six months. Above all, the physical and mental strain took an incalculable toll, affecting the men who were there far into the future.

As historian Frank put it: "No campaign in World War Two saw such sustained violence in all three dimensions—sea, land, and air—where the issue hung in doubt so long."

Perhaps "Guadalcanal" can best be summed up by an anonymous poem that emerged from the campaign, an epitaph on the grave of a Marine private buried on that infamous island. It could be the epitaph of every man who experienced the trauma that was Cactus:

> And when he goes to Heaven
> To Saint Peter he will tell:
> Another Marine reporting, Sir;
> I've served my time in Hell!

On the afternoon of the 17th, the MAC made preparations for getting underway from the 'Canal for "White Poppy" (Noumea).

The next day, we were steaming easily along when one of the plywood Higgins boats broke loose from its davits, tearing a hole in its hull. It fell into the water but didn't sink. To keep from leaving anything that would give an enemy submarine a trail to follow, Captain Rodgers ordered it sunk by gunfire, using the clumsy old 5-inch/.50 on the fantail.

The crew hurriedly fired two rounds, both missing. But from all over the ship came frantic cries of "Cease fire! Cease fire!" The recoil and muzzle blasts from that ancient piece were popping rusted rivets out of the bulkheads of our beloved bucket of bolts! The job was finished off with one round from a 3-inch rifle.

We arrived back in New Caledonia on 21 January, anchoring in Noumea's Great Roads; then we shifted berths to alongside the ARGONNE to facilitate the transfer of Admiral Turner (ComAmphibForSoPac) and Staff to the McCAWLEY.

UNITED STATES PACIFIC FLEET
Flagship of the Commander-in-Chief

Pac-11-Sn
P15

Serial 107   January 11, 1943.

From: Commander in Chief, United States Pacific Fleet.
To: Commander Amphibious Force, South Pacific Area.
Via :   Commander South Pacific Force.

Subject: Transport Divisions, Commendation.

1.   During the entire SOLOMONS campaign I have been
impressed on innumerable occasions by the high quality of the
service performed by the Transport Divisions of your force.

2.   To the best of my knowledge the movement of large
numbers of troops into and out of the Guadalcanal-Tulagi area
has been accomplished by the transports without the loss of a
single soldier from enemy action.

3.   Without the constant movement into Guadalcanal
and Tulagi of ammunition, weapons, fuel, equipment and supplies
of all kinds, our operations in the area could not have been
supported. The cargo ships have accomplished this in a notable
manner in spite of the utmost efforts on the part of the enemy
to prevent it.

4.   While enemy action has been able to inflict
losses on the ships engaged in this movement of men and material,
these losses have never been able to interrupt or even to interfere seriously with this flow.

5.   I take this opportunity to express my commendation of the splendid work which has been accomplished by the
officers and men of the Transport Divisions of the Amphibious
Force, South Pacific Area.

                                /s/ C.W. NIMITZ.

Copy to:
    Cominch.

(Guadalcanal "Echoes")

14
THAT STINKING ISLAND

My first temporary duty (TDY) assignment ended when Admiral Kelly Turner and the rest of the Staff came back aboard the McCAWLEY (21 January, 1943).

First into the Radio Shack was Harry Haines, carrying the kind of news I liked to get. I was sipping a cup of mud and discussing plans with ship's company radiomen for a beer party at Sara-Juan Park when Harry greeted me with:

"Go buy a new crow for your uniform, Hutch. You just made 2nd Class, effective February 1st."

I'd already figured out what my pay would be. The base of $72 supplemented by 20 percent sea pay, added up to $86 a month.

"Just for that, Haines, I'll buy you a beer. We're going over on the beach this afternoon. Wanta come?"

"Got the duty. But I'll take a rain check."

One of the ship's pharmacist's mates, in a time-honored Navy tradition, had been stashing away medical alcohol that hadn't been doctored with a substance to make it undrinkable. It was pure grain stuff. With him and several others, we mustered a liberty party and headed for a small island in the harbor where the crews of the SARATOGA and the SAN JUAN had laid out a baseball diamond and provided a few other amenities. The usual beer ration was two bottles or cans, but with a little bribery and/or coercion, we'd managed to corner the market on nearly a case from guys who didn't drink or thought baseball was more important than suds. We staked out a cool spot under some trees and prepared to get down to some serious drinking. "Icing" the beer down with $CO-2$ from a small fire extinguisher one of the guys had smuggled off the ship, we each took a couple of swigs from the cans, passed them to "Doc" who then poured a goodly "shot of alky" into the beer.

There were a couple of toasts to celebrate my promotion. Then one saluting Rita Hayworth as the most beautiful movie star in the world. Another was raised to the Wacky MAC. And so the afternoon went. As time neared to return to the ship, Doc announced we had to drink up all the alcohol. He didn't want to risk getting caught with it going back aboard. Neither were we about to leave any beer behind. The combination of beer, alky, tropic sun, and the long layoff between drinking anything at all, began to take its toll.

By the time the Higgins boat showed up, we were one motley looking crew, hardly able to make our way to the landing. When the boat nudged the MAC's gangway, a couple of the more sober (or less intoxicated) guys among us tried to navigate the steps, but met with dismal failure, getting only to the lower platform. All of this was accompanied by much shouted advice and boisterous yelling. The Officer of the Deck, peering over the side, eyed it all with an expression of pure resignation. Sizing up the situation, he ordered the "deck apes" to rig out a cargo boom with a net on its hook. The boat crew did yeoman service in getting us all into the net. A couple of guys had already passed out, and the rest of us were feeling no pain.

The O.D. issued the command to "hoist away". I later was told by eyewitnesses that the sight of a cargo net full of drunken sailors—with arms, legs, and other parts of their anatomies hanging out through the cordage—looked all the world like so many eels caught in a "snood" (1940s' version of a hair net). The 2nd Class Bos'n's Mate running the wench was laughing so hard he dropped us on the hatch cover from about four feet up and we were scattered all across the hatch *en masse*. When we'd established a bit of order and staggered off toward our compartments, I noted the O.D. had disappeared. He either had no stomach for witnessing our ignoble landing, or he wanted to avoid bearing witness at any disciplinary masts. But most probable, many of the bunch were Admiral's Staff, and ship's company officers rarely interfered with or had contact with Flag enlisted men, leaving us to our own officers.

In my career I had few confrontations with officers, thanks to Jughead O'Neill's insistence I memorize Navy regulations. I was fortunate to serve mostly under Naval Academy graduates who "went by the book" as well, and their actions were quite predictable. There was also the belief held by us enlisted men that the first lesson an Annapolis plebe learned was: "Chiefs and First Class run the Navy—you're just along for the ride." For the most part, there was mutual respect between Regular Navy bluejackets and Academy officers.

Yet, there was a wide gulf between enlisted men and gold braid. The dictum of R.H.I.P.—"rank has its privileges"—was well established in the hierarchy. It was absolutely *verboten* to mix socially, and this taboo even trickled down to enlisted ranks, where fraternizing was unusual between senior and junior petty officers and lower ratings, particularly in peacetime. Many enlisted men deeply resented the perquisites that went with a commission: the privacy of "Officers' Country", dinner at tables with linen and silver, best seats at ship's movies, free gangway in port (i.e. they could come and go as they pleased if not on duty)—and, at nearly every shore installation, officers' clubs well-stocked with liquor, where they could entertain women, including nurses, who were off limits to bluejackets. It was no secret the officers had liquor aboard ships, strictly forbidden by Navy regulations, but none I ever heard about were caught or disciplined. Nor were they searched when coming aboard as enlisted men often were.

We did not take this lying down. With the ingenuity properly ascribed to American fighting men, we found ways. It is my contention that you could put two U.S. servicemen anywhere in the Universe, and within 24 hours they'd come up with something to drink. With stateside whiskey in the forward areas regularly selling for $50 to $100 (and up) a fifth, stills were to be found in, near, or around every shore base. Some made pretty good stuff. Others produced liquid poison that could, and did, blind or kill imbibers.

Shipboard, sailors found ingenious ways to slip bottles past the Quarterdeck. Hiding them in socks was the most common method, but whiskey also got aboard in bottles labeled as hair tonic or shaving lotion. Such smuggling only was effective for small quantities, so large-scale drinking aboard was a rarity. There were, of course, some alcoholics. They would drink everything and anything from Vitalis to metal polish, the latter filtered through a loaf of bread. Yet I recall only a handful of incidents of drunkenness aboard ships on which I served. On destroyers where there was "torpedo juice", the 190-proof straight alcohol used to fuel the tin fish, there was some imbibing of this elixir. It was so volatile, however, that it had to be mixed with something (usually canned grapefruit juice) so it wouldn't evaporate before it was consumed. It packed one helluva wallop.

While relations with Academy officers were usually business-like, it was different with many Reserve officers, particularly those we labeled "90-Day Wonders" or " . . . Blunders". Most were college kids given three months' training and sent to sea. These "Feather Merchants" were so consumed with their own importance they were obnoxious and a bane to enlisted men serving under them. It was infuriating to watch one of these "wet-behind-the-ears 23-year-olds" chewing out a "four-hash-mark Chief" over some imagined or minor misstep. It was difficult to mask our contempt for such people. Besides, in their ignorance, such idiots could get us killed.

Radio traffic on my watches was picking up considerably, and much of it was "Operational Priority" or "Urgent". Scuttlebutt had it the Japs were tooling up for a major push to retake Guadalcanal. Simultaneously, Admiral Turner's plans were in the works for additional amphibious operations up the Solomon Islands chain. All the messages were, of course, encoded, but there was a lot to be deduced from the call letters of ships and commands to whom these dispatches were addressed. The name Operation CLEANSLATE began to pop up.

Coming off the midwatch, I was just settling down for a few hours in the sack when a striker came down to tell me I was wanted back in the Shack.

Jim Jett greeted me with: "How'd you like some shore duty, Hutch?"

"Make it San Francisco, Jim, and you got a deal", I grinned.

The Chief didn't grin back and a little red flag rose up in my head.

"You know Jack Frost and Rowland are up at Cactus building a Radio Station for us?"

"I heard."

"They urgently need some supplies, radio gear, and another hand up there, and I figured you might like to go."

At that moment, the Flag Communications Officer, Commander George Washington Welker, walked in.

"Have you told him this is a volunteer job, Chief?" he asked.

"I know it now, Commander", I said wryly.

"You'll be preceding the rest of us by only a few weeks", Jett put in. "Besides, you'll get a free airplane ride out of it."

"Yeah, thanks." I was mulling it over as the Chief and the Communications Officer stood looking at me. "It's mighty thought-y of you to arrange all these goodies for me, Jim. To what do I owe all this kindly treatment?"

The pressure was difficult to resist and I didn't feel I really had a lot of choice in the matter.

"Okay, Commander, I'll go", I said. "But one thing. Have I now become the Flag's Designated Temporary Duty Kid?"

"Not unless you volunteer for it, lad", Welker answered, smiling.

"Is he being facetious or is he serious?" I thought to myself. As Jett left the shack, I called after him.

"Hey, Jim, who else did you ask to volunteer?"

"Everybody", he called back over his shoulder. "You were our last hope!"

Jett had given me a list of supplies and radio equipment I'd need to round up, and I went over to the supply dumps on the beach to see how much of it I could scrounge. Some stuff I got with requisitions; but had to commit a little polite thievery at an Army depot to get tubes for receivers, insulators, wire, and something that wasn't on the list, a Signal Corps receiver. It was just there, begging to be lifted.

A messenger woke me before reveille the next morning, and I got saddled up, ready to go. In my pocket was authorization for transportation via SCATS—South Pacific Combat Air Transportation Service—from Tontouta Air Base, Noumea, to Henderson Field, Guadalcanal. As I unloaded the gear from the McCAWLEY Higgins boat into a small truck at the landing, it dawned on me I wasn't exactly heading for a picnic in the park.

"Cactus, here I come", I thought, not without a great deal of trepidation. You bet I was scared. That old "hollow in the stomach weak in the calves" feeling was back. I checked in at the SCATS Operations shack and was told to load my gear on a DC-3 transport sitting on the airstrip's apron.

The word *Combat* from the SCATS acronym didn't do a helluva lot to alleviate my apprehension about all this—my very first airplane ride ever. As I helped the ground crew load my gear, I questioned them about the outfit and the planes they flew. Most of the pilots, I was told, had washed out of fighter or other combat aircraft schools. Due to the shortage of fliers, they'd been pressed into service flying transports; but many still thought they were piloting F4Fs, SBDs, or TBFs. They were as nutty as fruit cakes, the ground crew guys told me, and sometimes would fly right into the middle of Jap formations. I *hoped* those guys were just trying to scare me.

The plane I was boarding, they said, was called a "Gooney Bird" because, like the albatross, it had to flap its wings to get off the ground. But these two-engine Douglas DC-3 transports were (and are) legendary for their ruggedness, dependability, and durability. No other aircraft in aviation history is more famous, even today. Nor is any other more universally loved. As I stepped in the hatch, I looked around to see a Marine Corps bird Colonel trotting out to come aboard. We were the only passengers that day. In a few moments, the engines roared to life and we taxied for take-off. I watched through the port to see if the wings *really* did flap to get us airborne. They wiggled a little and bounced when we went over rough spots in the runway, but no bird-like flapping. Another legend shot to hell.

The Colonel and I settled back for the 850-mile flight, and I was just dozing off to the steady hum of the engines when the plane nosed down into a deep dive. What the Hell!!!??? I pressed my nose against the glass and looked down at the open sea.

"There's a gawddam Jap submarine down there!" I shouted to the Colonel, who was on the other side of the plane.

Our crazy pilot had sighted the sub on the surface, threw that Gooney Bird into a power dive, and was blasting away at the Jap with the only weapon he had aboard—his .45-caliber service pistol! What's more he was leaning halfway out the cockpit window and yelling like a Comanche at a war dance. The sub's skipper, apparently aware only that he was being attacked and not knowing whether we had bombs aboard, immediately crash-dived. Had he stayed on the surface long enough to have manned his deck guns, he'd have had a good shot at knocking down our slow-moving DC-3.

With the sub gone, the pilot circled the area a couple of times, radioed Tontouta about the sighting, then leveled off to resume his course toward Cactus. All the while, the Colonel is muttering under his breath something about "that idiot son of a bitch coulda got us killed!" I was speechless, trying to get the lump I was sure was my heart back down from my throat, all the while "shaking like a drunk with the DTs".

Once back on course, the Captain stepped into the cabin with a big grin on his face.

"Well, they don't call us South Pacific *COMBAT* Air Transportation Service for nothin'!"

The Colonel, by now, had recognized the humor in the strip, and was grinning, too. Today, it is *funny*. But at the time, I wasn't laughing—not one cotton-pickin' bit!

Things really got serious as we approached Henderson. The Captain again came back to the cabin, asking the Colonel if it were absolutely necessary he make it to the 'Canal on this trip.

"I'm carrying urgent operational plans, Captain, and my instructions are to deliver them, today", the Colonel replied.

"All right, Sir, I'll get you to Henderson, but just wanted you to know Cactus Control says they're under a Jap air attack."

The Colonel didn't even pause to consider. "Take us on in, Captain."

I was wishing somebody would've asked me.

"Aye, aye, Sir", was the pilot's crisp answer.

The ports on a DC-3 are small and neither the Colonel nor I would be able to see much of what was going on. I wasn't sure I wanted to watch, anyhow. We continued on course until, suddenly, the plane began to buck and make radical changes in course and altitude. I could hear the unmistakable sounds of automatic weapons. The Colonel, peering out one of the ports, suddenly shouted:

"*HIT THE DECK!*"

I dove horizontally, burrowing my nose in the aluminum decking. I still don't know what hit us. But there was a big noise, a rush of air, a lot of smoke, and a hole in the port fuselage next to the hatch big enough to walk through. The DC-3 reacted violently, then leveled off and began a shallow descent. I didn't know if we were going to crash or land. Thank God, we were landing. But as soon as we hit the strip, the pilot began zigzagging to avoid bomb craters and Marsden mats torn up by the raiding Japs.

As the Gooney Bird slowed, the Colonel called to me. "Come on, Sailor, let's get the hell out of here!"

I followed him out through the hole in the side of the plane, hit the ground running, and belly-slid the last several yards through the mud, like Pepper Martin going in to third base, ending up in a nearby bunker. It was a long time before I rose up to take inventory. Yep, all my component parts were there, and except for some hide scraped off my belly, knees, and elbows, I was all in one piece. Not knowing which to thank, Saint Christopher or the guardian angel, I took no chances. Thanked 'em both—profusely!

"Condition Green", the "all clear", sounded and I gathered myself together, went back over to the plane, and unloaded the equipment and my gear. A driver with a small truck put in an appearance, and within thirty minutes, we were headed down the road to Koli Point. The driver looked at me quizzically when I let out a huge breath. I think it was the first time I'd breathed since the Colonel yelled "Hit the deck!" Some first plane ride!

On a two-rut trail, we drove through the coconut palms of a copra plantation, past various Marine and Army bivouacs and, eight miles later, pulled into a grove of big tropical trees where the SeaBees were hurrying the finishing touches on "The Admiral's Camp".

The Guadalcanal landings in August, 1942, were the first test of our fledgling Amphibious Forces. To say America was not prepared for this type of warfare would be the granddaddy of all understatements. Going into the War, we could muster only a handful of amphibious ships: some sixteen transports (APs), five cargo ships (AKs), and six APDs (old four-stack destroyers converted to high-speed troop transports). To get troops to the beach, the most modern landing craft were plywood Higgins boats, highly vulnerable to enemy shore fire. Metal heavy landing craft, such as LCTs (initially called "tank lighters"), did not make an appearance in the South Pacific until the end of Operation WATCHTOWER.

Thanks to U.S. industrial mobilization, Amphibious Forces, South Pacific, began to get the landing craft and vessels it needed, but not until late January, 1943. By that time, the fragile Higgins boats were being replaced by LCPs (landing craft, personnel), LCVs (landing craft, vehicles), and LCMs (landing craft, mechanized), all carried on transports.

Then came the bigger, self-sufficient craft: LSTs (landing ship, tank), LCIs (landing craft, infantry), and APc's (coastal transports). Other specialized craft would be added as the War progressed. But we must not forget that our initial amphibious operation—Guadalcanal—suffered badly because of our lack of preparedness for offensive amphibious assaults and the logistics to support them.

But we were learning; and this new, innovative arm of the Navy finally found a symbol of its own. The unofficial emblem was that most fearful of all amphibians—the crocodile—first used as far as I know when "The Admiral's Camp" was redubbed "Camp Crocodile".

Guadalcanal is literally a "stinking island"—an appellation used by just about everyone who ever set foot on it. Lying only 9° South latitude and 160° East longitude, its proximity to the Equator keeps it unbearably hot and humid. Along with tropical deluges that regularly drench the place, the temperatures and humidity not only cause rapid growth of the jungle, but also contribute to the rotting of the vegetation. The odor can be smelled for miles away at sea. The rains are not the gentle afternoon showers of Hawaii but full-blown downpours that turn the earth into a sticky goo—mud that adheres to just about everything, making travel, even on foot, extremely difficult. Before the War the Australians, as unwitting prophets, had called Guadalcanal "a bloody, stinking hole".

Yet, there was great beauty to behold. The flora was at times breathtaking. Wild flowers abounded. In the trees lived huge, magnificent parrots in nearly every coloration imaginable. And there were curiosities galore, including bush rats the size of rabbits.

The one thing the Japs were lucky to escape when they pulled out was the myriad of tropical diseases that probably took as many casualties during the fighting as did gunfire. The malaria, dengue fever, dysentery, jungle rot, and many other diseases continued to afflict those of us who still remained on the island.

Warrant Radio Electrician Paul N. "Jack" Frost and Radioman 1st Rowland greeted me when I arrived at the Admiral's Camp. Mr. Frost welcomed me "aboard", then turned me over to Rowland to get settled in my new berth. "Home" would be a khaki tent with four canvas cots, each swathed in mosquito netting.

"Keep that netting tight, Hutch. It's all there is between you and malaria", was Rowland's advice. But there was no way to keep from getting bitten by a malaria-carrying anopheles mosquito sooner or later.

Next in importance to survival was the nearest foxhole with its protective palm log roof; not enough to ward off a direct bomb hit, but it would keep falling shrapnel from hitting its occupants.

The head was nearby, a fortunate consideration for those who came down with the diarrhea that accompanied dengue fever and dysentery. Dysentery or reasonable facsimiles thereof became almost a part of life. That's why Rowland made a point of showing me the head so soon after I arrived. It was put to frequent use.

Our water supply was a 50-gallon Lister bag, that rubberized monster that looked like a black cow's udder with the requisite spigots. Rowland suggested drinking lots of water to replace fluids sweated out in the tropical heat. While it was safe to drink, it tasted of the rubber and usually was a tepid 70° or warmer.

Camp Crocodile faced toward Carney Field, built by SeaBees to accommodate our build-up in air power. Less than 100 yards away was a 90-millimeter anti-aircraft battery, manned by Marines of the 11th Defense Battalion. Behind us, inland, was the almost impenetrable jungle of huge trees, vines, weeds and undergrowth. Our "front yard", between us and Carney, was a growth of kunai (KOON-eye) grass, tall enough to hide a man.

I asked Rowland if he could think of anything good about this stinking island.

He replied: "Yeah, there aren't any snakes."

No snakes, but something even more dangerous, an abundance of those anopheles mosquitos, the lethal little carriers of malaria. There were so many so big it was rumored Carney Field was actually built to provide them with their own landing strip. The female of the species, as Rudyard Kipling had observed, is more deadly than the male. He was speaking of tigers, but the female anopheles mosquito transmits a disease capable of wiping out or disabling more people in a few days than all the big cats in Bengal can in a lifetime. Malaria is so body-wracking that, once afflicted, most victims would rather die than have it recur. I had a comparatively mild case of malaria not long after arriving on the 'Canal, apparently because I was still in pretty good physical shape. Subsequent bouts would be much more severe.

The Solomons are notorious for having "every disease known to medical science and about twelve that ain't." The natives had them all, and we Americans ended up getting at least some of them. At various times, I had malaria, dengue fever, dysentery, and jungle rot. There were other times I turned into Sick Bay only to have the Medical Officer unable to diagnose any known disease from my symptoms. I guess I had "one of the twelve that ain't." These afflictions were no respecters of rank, either. Admiral Turner became so ill with a combination of malaria and dengue fever that at one time he was taken to the hospital ship SOLACE until he recovered.

Neither was the local population immune. Universally called "Malaita boys", these Melanesians not only had the above named diseases but suffered from about every variety of venereal disease, and from one malady I wouldn't wish on my worst enemy—elephantiasis. My medical dictionary describes it as a chronic enlargement of tissue which hardens, and it's caused by an infectious worm. One of its aspects was the subject of the 1980s' movie *ELEPHANT MAN*. Many Solomon Islanders had it in various degrees in different parts of the body. There was one Malaita boy who frequented our Camp whose scrotum was so enlarged from elephantiasis that he wheeled it around in a makeshift wheelbarrow.

The "Malaita boys" were appreciative allies. They hated the Japs for their notorious cruelty, including the rape of their women. Guadalcanal originally had no indigenous population until copra plantations were established in the 1800s, owned and operated by Lever Brothers. Copra, the dried meat of the coconut, is a source of oil used in making soaps and cosmetic products. Hence, Lever Brothers' trademark "Palmolive Soap"! To work the plantations, natives were imported from the populated island of Malaita to the north. Most of the overseers were British, Australian, or men of mixed blood, white and Melanesian. Many of these overseers would become our "eyes", acting as coastwatchers during the Solomons Campaigns.

The Melanesians made a momentous contribution to our victory at Guadalcanal. Under the leadership of the foremost coastwatcher of them all, namely Scottish Cambridge grad Captain Martin Clemens and his illustrious chief scout, retired police Sergeant Major Jacob Vouza of the British Protectorate's Armed Constabulary—whom the Marines all called "Chief"—virtually all Japanese military movements were reported to the American Commanders. Though tortured, interrogated ("I didn't tell them anything") bayonetted and left for dead—Vouza somehow survived to provide vital information on Jap troop movements that enabled the Marines to destroy Colonel Ichiki's crack troops in the August 1942 Battle of the Tenaru—the first and perhaps the most crucial ground battle on the tortuous course from Guadalcanal to Tokyo.

The "Chief" also gathered crucial intelligence that helped the Marines crush the Imperial Japanese Army's crack Sendai Division in their all-out attempt to retake Guadalcanal in late October of 1942. In November and December he served with Colonel E.F. Carlson's renowned Raiders (2nd Raider Battalion) which trained and marched singing America's great patriotic hymns which the Melanesians loved to sing: "The Star-Spangled Banner", "The Battle Hymn of the Republic", "Onward, Christian Soldiers."

Onward, Christian Soldiers, marching as to war,
With the cross of Jesus going on before! . . .
At the name of *Jesus,* Satan's host doth flee;
On then, Christian Soldiers, on to victory! . . .
Hell's foundations quiver at the shout of praise:
Brothers, lift your voices, loud your anthems raise!

A fervent convert from animism to the Christian faith in 1941, Vouza maintained a strong Christian witness. In General Vandegrift's words: "The redoubtable Vouza . . . .There was no one like him." As the Marines confessed: "He prayed with us . . . .He was an inspiration . . . .Here was a man . . . .And he was one of us, though belonging to the Solomon Islands."

Sir Jacob Vouza is the most illustrious Solomon Islander in history. For his exploits in the savage struggle with the Japanese on Guadalcanal in 1942, he received from King George the highest and rarest commendation possible for a British civilian (the civilian counterpart of the Victoria Cross, which couldn't be awarded Vouza since he was not in the British military) namely the George Medal. When asked by some Marines why he served a King so far away he'd never seen, the reply: "King George my King too."

At the same time, the gyrenes kidded the Chief about being an American since most of his blood was American, via blood transfusions! In 1942 the U. S. awarded Vouza the Silver Star for "conspicuous gallantry and outstanding bravery in action." For his contributions to Carlson's Raiders in terms of "extraordinary heroism", Vouza received in 1943 the U. S. Legion of Merit: "His conduct was in keeping with the highest traditions of the Naval service of the United States."

In the 1970s Vouza forged a special friendship with Mitch Paige, gracious author of the Foreward to *BLUEJACKET* on the basis of the old Marine's also being "a God-fearing man." In 1984 the Solomon Islander died in his 90s, receiving an evangelical state funeral with the band playing and the people singing "Amazing Grace" and "Blessed Assurance". The presiding minister made the point that the departed never compromised his Christian convictions and always sought God's kingdom first. Mitch Paige closed the interment with the words: "Farewell, dear friend, farewell . . . .By God's grace we will meet again."

The crucial contribution of Jacob Vouza and the Solomon Islanders to our victory at Guadalcanal, along with his clear Christian testimony, is told by Don Richter, who served with the 1st Marine division in the Solomons and later returned to the islands to serve as a Christian

SGT/MAJ. JACOB VOUZA
British Solomon Islands Constabulary *(Retired)*.
Captured by the Japanese and brutally tortured, Jacob Vouza
escaped to become an invaluable scout and advisor to the First
Marine Division during the Guadalcanal Campaign. He also
extracted a measure of revenge for the treatment he'd received
from the Nipponese, evidence of which is graphically shown in this
photo. That really is the head of a slain Japanese solider in Vouza's
hands, a tribute to his artistry with a bolo (machete).
(Courtesy Tan Blahnik, Editor - Guadalcanal "Echoes")

missionary, in a marvelous book *Where the Sun Stood Still: The Untold Story of Sir Jacob Vouza and the Guadalcanal Campaign* (1992).

The Solomon Islanders historically had a fierce reputation and had been very warlike. Headhunting was a part of their culture until whites outlawed it and Christian missionaries were somewhat successful in converting them to more peaceful pursuits. However, the practice of taking heads was rumored still to be in vogue in the outlying islands. Indeed, there was at least one documented case on Malaita in 1939, only three years before the Americans arrived. Apparently cannibalism had been part of the islanders' way of life. Only gradually, so it seems, did the natives lose their taste for human flesh, which they called "big pig"! Or, since people looked longer than pigs roasting on a rotating spit, more often "long pig"!

I had little time to delve into the mores of these Islanders but I do have some vivid memories of them. They're very short, usually around five feet or so, and I don't recall ever seeing a fat one. They're black but not Negroid in their features. They do have some unusual customs. For instance, I was taken aback when I saw one with bright red hair! "Aha!", I thought. "Some non-Melanesian has been here before us." It was not until later I learned many would color their hair with a red clay mixture. They ofttimes painted their bodies with a whitish substance which I took to be a clay of some sort, and they were quite partial to primitive tattoos. Some were accomplished artisans in wood and mother-of-pearl. Ceremonial war clubs and spear handles were often inlaid with nacre. They wore little clothing, but did fancy American T-shirts so much they'd build an entire thatch-roofed hut for two skivvie shirts or two mattress covers.

The Melanesians are a simple people in their ways and for the most part seemed pretty happy. Yet the Japs' mistreatment of them made them somewhat wary of strangers. This was brought home one day when, down the road in front of the Admiral's Camp, came about a dozen men armed with spears, knives, and war clubs, all looking very sinister. They were escorting one of their women, whom they kept in the center of their ring. They had nothing to fear from us, for the woman they escorted was the ugliest female of just about any species I'd ever seen. She looked a hundred years old, wizened, wrinkled, and bent. Her breasts, completely exposed and hardly bigger 'round than a small hawser (i.e. line, whether rope or cable, for mooring or towing a ship), dangled almost to her knees! As she and her entourage passed, she looked over at the incredulous sailors and flashed a broad toothless smile, waved her hand and continued on her way, secure in the knowledge she was well-protected from any harm.

Then there was the widely circulated story of the Malaita boy who noted the Marine with the most clout was the one with the most stripes on his sleeves. He approached one of the gyrenes, pointed to the insignia, and said in that universal language of the South Seas pidjin English: "Me boy want stripe b'long this boy."

The Marine, seeing a chance to have some fun, explained the stripes were rewards for chopping off Jap heads. The native considered that for a moment and departed. The next morning as the Marines lined up to chow down, here comes the native with a copra sack over his shoulder and a machete in his hand. As the hardened Marines look on horrified, he dumps five Jap heads like so many coconuts out of the sack. As they rolled along the chow line, not a few of those "jarheads" lost their breakfasts right then and there. The boy flashed a big smile, pointed to his arm and said: "Five stripe b'long this boy!" The Marines decked him out in a shirt and the stripes were sewn on. It's said that, eventually, the shirt, from collar to tail, from front to back, became covered with stripes. He got 'em by sneaking behind Jap lines at night and wielding his machete on unsuspecting Nips, then showing up with his trophies as proof of his prowess.

My first night on the island was a sleepless one. Air raids sent us scampering into our bunker, and artillery boomed to the northwest, apparently in the neighborhood of the Matanikau River, some twelve miles away. It sounded like our guys were really pounding the hell out of the hostiles. The next morning, I was to learn some of the details of what was to become known as the Battle of Rennell Island, the last of the seven major naval battles of the Guadalcanal Campaign, and that the hornet's nest we'd flown into the day before was part of the air action of that battle. Admiral Halsey had decided to send in relief for elements of the 2nd Marine Division. The troops were on four transports, protected by five separate task forces. At the same time, enemy movements pointed to another effort to reinforce their units on the 'Canal.

On 29 January, a cruiser force of the WICHITA (CA-45), CHICAGO (CA-29), and LOUISVILLE (CA-28) under Rear Admiral Richard C. Giffen, along with Destroyer Squadron 21 (DesRon 21, "The Cactus Striking Force"), were to sweep "up the Slot" while the transports unloaded at Lunga Point. Japanese submarines reported these movements, and the enemy mounted a twilight air attack against the cruisers. The CHICAGO took a torpedo, went dead in the water, and the U.S. force began its withdrawal. The next day, 30 January, the hostiles launched a two-pronged air attack: a diversionary one at Henderson Field in which the Gooney Bird in which I was flying got hit, and a torpedo attack against the crippled CHICAGO. The cruiser took four more fish, sinking in twenty minutes. The only heavy cruiser to survive the Battle of Savo Island, the first of the seven major naval battles at Guadalcanal, went down in the last. But our transports, meanwhile, successfully landed their troops.

While I was trying to settle in at Koli Point, units of the 2nd Marine Division and the Army's Americal and Tropic Lightning Divisions were sweeping north of the Matanikau, engaging the Japs' 16th and 29th Infantry of their 2nd Division. Our 182nd and 147th Infantry, finding the jungle route to Kokumbona impassable, moved along the beach road, followed by the 6th Marine Regiment. The Americans met heavy resistance from rear guard enemy rifle and machinegun fire. Hard pressed, the Jap made a "last stand" on 1 and 2 February along the Bonegi River, but was crushed by artillery and naval bombardment. On 2 February, the Army's 2nd Battalion, 132nd Infantry, landed at Tambugu, Tuvu, and Vorahu beyond Cape Esperance, in order to drive southward to trap the Jap in a pincers movement.

During that first week in February, I could hear the sounds of heavy bombardment in the distance and, at night, see the flashes of artillery bouncing off the clouds up toward Cape Esperance. Flares were seen off the Cape, and Jap destroyers were sighted, giving rise to scuttlebutt this was a prelude to a major enemy reinforcement effort. At the same time, Jap bombers were hitting us pretty hard in nighttime raids. On the 2nd, there were eight separate attacks, and two more in the early hours of the 3rd. On 4 February, my 21st birthday, I spent the whole damn' night in my foxhole while the Mitsubishi Bettys pounded us in ten separate bombing raids.

The air raids, by high-level bombers and dive bombers escorted by fighters, came in from the northwest, mostly from bases at Rabaul. The primary target was usually Henderson Field and the built-up area around Lunga Point. In pattern bombing, the Japs would just keep "laying their eggs" as they flew southeasterly parallel to the coast. In that path were Carney Field and Koli Point.

The air defense warning system on the 'Canal was divided into four stages, each announced by air raid sirens. "Condition Green" was "all clear"; "Condition Yellow" was "air attack possible"; "Condition Red" was "here they come again"; and "Condition Black", the most feared, was "Jap invasion imminent".

When Condition Red sounded on sirens all throughout our installations, we'd head for foxholes and bunkers. Often, at the Admiral's Camp, we'd stand outside, looking toward Lunga as our searchlight batteries swept the skies for incoming formations. As soon as our AA batteries began pumping shells skyward, we'd edge a little closer to the holes, knowing it would be but minutes before those Jap Mitsubishis would be overhead. It took little time for them to travel the eight miles between Lunga and Koli. Then we'd dive for cover. On the nights of the 4th and 5th, we went from Condition Red to Condition Black, anticipating a Jap landing in force. We didn't know those enemy destroyers off Cape Esperance were not bringing troops *in* but were *evacuating* their forces. The bombing raids were a diversion to mask the withdrawal. There were four more air strikes in the early hours of the 6th.

Apparently the Japanese High Command, seeing their land forces now facing overwhelming odds, had ordered naval task groups to get their troops off Guadalcanal. During the first week of February, Operation "KE" began evacuating Jap units by night. For example, in an almost miraculous operation, 18 high-speed Jap destroyers steamed "down the Slot" under cover of darkness, lay to off the beach on the night of 7/8 February, and loaded Nip survivors of the ground fighting. At the time, however, our Commanders thought the Japs' eminently successful evacuation runs were actually reinforcing their troops.

The destroyers took out some 10,000 Japanese, including headquarters and high ranking officers. But the Japs didn't get all their men out. There would continue to be pockets of resistance in the jungle and mountains, desperate stragglers who didn't get to the beach on time to meet the destroyers. It would take some time to root them out of caves and jungle hideouts in the mountains. Our troops captured some 250 Jap prisoners, the last on 19 April when natives found a solitary Nip soldier near Kokumbona. There's no telling how many tried to survive in the jungle, only to perish subsequently from disease and/or starvation. But one Jap held out in the mountains for *four years*, waiting for rescue by his country. He came walking out to surrender in *1947!*

On 9 February, patrols from two U.S. regiments met at the Tenamba River near Cape Esperance. All organized resistance had ceased. Army General Patch of the XIV Corps announced an end to the fighting on that date. General Patch radioed Admiral Halsey: "TOTAL AND COMPLETE DEFEAT OF JAPANESE FORCES ON GUADALCANAL . . . .TOKYO EXPRESS NO LONGER HAS TERMINUS ON GUADALCANAL."

The island was formally pronounced "secured" on 15 February, 1943. The prophecy of Admiral John S. "Slew" McCain had come true: "The 'Canal will be a sinkhole to the enemy if the Americans remain strong and maintain their stubborn resistance."

There probably will never be an accurate account of Japanese losses on Guadalcanal, which the Japs came to call the "Island of Death". Estimates run up to 35,000 dead. According to Frank's *GUADALCANAL*, roughly 31,400 men of the Imperial Japanese Army were landed on the island, of whom some 10,600 were evacuated, leaving about 20,800 Jap soldiers lost on Guadalcanal, i.e. two thirds of their 17th Army. Almost all the Nip sick and wounded eventually died, and very few Japs surrendered or were taken alive. Unknown numbers died in transports sunk on their way to battle. To the Army dead should be added some 4,800 Navy personnel lost on the island, giving a total of at least 25,600 Jap dead. Given roughly 1,200 airmen lost and at least 3,600 lost at sea, the minimum Nip dead would be 30,400. But there were doubtless many more.

American casualties were comparatively light: roughly 1,700 Marines and Army dead on the ground (out of some 60,000 on the island at one time or another), about 4,910 lost at sea, and some 420 in the air, giving a total of about 7,100 lost in the campaign. U.S. Navy casualties at sea, according to Robert H. Freeman in his book *Requiem For A Fleet* were 7,275. Of those, 4,460 were killed. In any case, while Freeman's figure is less than Frank's, what few Americans know is this: *For every Marine or Army soldier lost on Guadalcanal virtually three U.S. Navy sailors perished at sea!!* While victorious in the end, the United States Navy took one hell of a beating at Guadalcanal, for the forces engaged a much costlier campaign than we experienced later at Okinawa. Some 24 U.S. ships (the 24th sunk in August, 1943!) and one Australian vessel lie in the depths of Iron Bottom Bay, and more than fifty other vessels were damaged and suffered casualties.

Operation WATCHTOWER was over, six long and bloody months after the landings at Cactus and Ringbolt. Not even some of those who were there were aware of how close we came to losing that campaign. As Eric Hammel points out in his book *Guadalcanal: The Carrier Battles*, the Imperial Japanese Army and Navy all but won back at Guadalcanal the initiative they had lost at the Coral Sea and Midway and by allowing American ground forces to seize occupied territory in the Solomons—by virtue of their naval victories and the "Tokyo Express".

Hammel also makes a point with which I and most 'Canal veterans agree when he writes: "The Battle of Midway was not, as historians of the period like to proclaim, the beginning of the end for the hegemonous empire of Japan. She was defeated there, it is true, but America could yet have lost the Pacific War. No, Midway was not the beginning of the end for Japan. . . . The beginning of the end for Japan arrived on August 7, 1942, when nearly 20,000 U.S. Marines assaulted Guadalcanal and neighboring islands at the periphery of the empire of Japan. A war thoroughly defensive became a war haltingly offensive."

The true turning point in the Pacific War, with all due respect to those who fought at Midway, came in the Solomons. This was certainly the persuasion of the enemy's military leaders. As General Kawaguchi put it: "Guadalcanal . . . is the name of the graveyard of the Japanese Army. We lost the campaign and Japan lost the war." Or in Admiral Tanaka's words: "There is no question that Japan's doom was sealed with the closing struggle for Guadalcanal."

For most of the men who survived Guadalcanal there would be other battles, but none that would bring forth such a rush of emotions as the very mention of *THE* Campaign. Those of *The Thin Red Line* speak of Cactus in an almost reverent whisper today. Time further diminishes our numbers, but our epitaphs were written long ago by James Michener, the author of *Tales of the South Pacific*:

"They will live a long time, these men of the South Pacific. They had an American quality. They, like their victories, will be remembered as long as our generation lives. After that, like men of the Confederacy, they will become strangers. Longer and longer shadows will obscure them, until Guadalcanal sounds distant on the ear like Shiloh and Valley Forge."

Lest we forget, lest we forget. . . . "Long may the tale be told in the great Republic" (Winston Churchill).

15

THE WORST SHORE DUTY

There's an old cliché in the Fleet that "the worst shore duty is better than the best sea duty." Anyone who believes that never spent any time on Guadalcanal.

The morning after I arrived at the Admiral's Camp, Jack Frost got me started rigging transmitting antennas. In order to get sufficient height, some of the wire had to be strung between trees, insulated in porcelain rings.

I spent several days shinnying up trunks of trees, trimming limbs out of the way, and anchoring the wire. What I didn't know was the trees were covered with fungi, and within a short time my legs were a mass of open, oozing sores—jungle rot. The pharmacist's mate with the "SeaBees" dusted the lesions with sulfa powder every day, but the sores came and went for most of the time I was in the Solomons.

Building Camp Crocodile was in the able hands of the 14th Construction Battalion—the SeaBees. These guys were unbelievable. They could've built the Empire State Building for you in three days if you asked 'em. They'd already finished Carney Field in record time and were hustling to get the Camp ready for the Admiral's Staff. Central to the plan was the Radio Shack, an already erected Quonset hut to house our communications. Left for us was the installation of all the electronic gear.

In the 1980s, I got a letter from Bob Duey who'd been a lieutenant (jg) and a Company Commander with the 14th SeaBees. He reminisced about their experiences on Cactus:

"Early in October, 1942, when our forces were struggling to hold Henderson Field from attack . . . the Admiral [Turner] felt Guadalcanal needed another field as soon as possible. The first sight [site?] choice at Aola Bay was inadequate because of the terrain. In early November, we moved all our forces and gear to Koli Point where the topography was much flatter and the area adequate for airfield construction. We pitched in and scratched out an emergency strip pronto. Our skipper, Captain James Carney, U.S.N., was a Naval aviator and piloted an SBD [dive bomber] from Lunga Point [Henderson Field] to land on our emergency strip. On the way back to Henderson, the plane developed engine trouble and dumped him and his rear gunner into Sealark Channel. We never saw him again, but we got the field named for him. We also helped build 'The Admiral's Camp' at Koli Point. And I recall how bad the chow was. I made friends with the Admiral's Staff Supply Officer, Lt. Cdr. David Stein, and the two of us would go out to ships in the transport area to bum fresh chow for our outfits."

Duey was right about the chow. Even at this late date, some of the rice was from Jap stores that had been captured. The only meat was the universally despised Spam and something in a canned concoction labeled "hash". All food we managed to get was canned, powdered, or dried. To supplement our rations, we went fishing in the Nalimbiu River nearby with hand grenades. Concussion from the explosions killed the fish and they'd float to the surface of the shallow stream. But we had to knock that off when the Medical Officer said it could be dangerous, that the fish might have been feeding on dead Japs upstream. So, it was back to powdered eggs, powdered milk, canned beans, one slice of Spam per day, occasionally the hash, and captured Jap rice.

The price of a fifth of bonded whiskey rivaled that of the Kohinoor diamond, so stills began to pop up, secluded in the lush flora of the 'Canal. Component parts for stills were hard to come by, especially copper tubing to make the coils. So, when a plane would come into Carney Field all shot-up, the first act was to get the fliers out safely. The next was to salvage the copper fuel lines. The term "jungle jack" came into being to describe the products of these distilleries. But before they became widespread, a simple method of making a potent libation was discovered. Recipe: take one coconut, punch out one of the "eyes", pour in one quarter pound of sugar, put a stopper in the eye, roll out in the hot sun, let ferment for several days. Presto! The *REAL*, the *ORIGINAL* jungle jack!

All the accounts of the Guadalcanal Campaign end with the final departure of the Japanese land forces. To my knowledge no one to date has ever documented or done justice to the ensuing six months during which a great deal of enemy air activity made life on the island perilous. There is some official acknowledgement on the part of the Navy for a portion of that period. A battle star is awarded for: "Consolidation of the Southern Solomons—8 February, 1943 to 20 June, 1943." Yet, air attacks continued on Cactus at least into mid-August, and there was no diminishing of other factors that made it a miserable place to be.

We kept armed guards on our galley and food stores every night, with orders to shoot first and ask questions later. Jap stragglers, starving to death in the hills and jungle, would sneak down to our camps and bivouacs to steal food. In several instances, they'd killed or injured our people whom they surprised or who tried to stop them. Some Japs were killed, too, and others captured.

A few nights after getting to Koli, I was working in the Quonset hut when Condition Red sounded. I took too much time securing the Shack, dousing the lights and cutting the power. Enemy bombers were already overhead and the 90-millimeter battery next door opened fire.

As I darted for cover, almost as an afterthought, I grabbed a foot-long screwdriver off a table. Too far away was a loaded .45-caliber service pistol. Many combat Marines carried such screwdrivers as weapons for use in close-quarter fighting. They had the advantage of not getting stuck in gristle or between bones like a knife blade. I slid the tool into a leather piece with a hole in it fastened to my belt as I scrambled toward safety. Near the Radio Shack was a one-man foxhole left over from earlier fighting and I dove into it.

I was immediately aware I was not alone. In the light of the flares dropped by the attacking bombers, I caught a glimpse of a decidedly Oriental face. My reaction was strictly instinctive. Pulling my only weapon, the screwdriver, I plunged it into the Jap. Then, while my foe was trying to bring his knife into play, I rammed it home again. He went limp. Almost automatically, I grabbed his clothing and dragged him to the edge of the jungle, then hit the foxhole again.

Due to the small holes caused by the slender screwdriver blade, there was little blood. I cleansed the screwdriver by sticking it in and out of the dirt. But I was really shook. Without that weapon, seized only at the last moment, I might not have survived. There was little doubt the desperate Jap soldier was bent on putting me away. Oblivious to a stick of bombs pounding Carney Field, I sat in the dirt, completely numb. My mind wouldn't come to grips with what had happened.

When Condition Green sounded, I crawled out of my hole and walked over to where I'd left my foe. He was gone! Either he had not been mortally wounded and managed to get away, or some of his companions had somehow discovered him, taking him back into the jungle.

I went to my tent and, just in case there were more hostiles around, pulled the '03 Springfield rifle from under my cot, put a clip in and chambered a round. With it, the screwdriver, and my hunting knife, I sat on the edge of the cot, alert to every sound of breezes in the trees, rubbing branches, or crackling in the brush. At dawn, completely exhausted, I finally dozed off. Noise of others around the camp woke me about 0730. I returned to the spot where I'd last seen the Jap in the dark.

There was a small pool of blood, and impressions in the grass where it had been pushed down, but nothing else.

Jack Frost was having a cup of coffee when I went into the Radio Shack. I poured some joe for myself and told him what happened. He went to take a look for himself.

"We'll probably never know what happened to him, lad. But what is important—how are you doing?"

"My insides won't stay still and I feel awfully jumpy."

He looked at me closely. "That's only natural, I guess. Why don't you get some chow and then take it easy the rest of the day?"

I couldn't eat but drank several cups of java and chain-smoked three or four cigarettes. Then I went back to work. It was easier than thinking.

Some of our installations were quite primitive. Lacking the supplies we needed, we had to do some jury-rigging. With no conduits in which to run our leads from transmitter to operating positions, we simply strung insulated wire along planks behind the desks, hooking it on bent nails. Our overhead lighting was installed much the same way.

To get some of the vital equipment we needed, I conducted moonlight requisitioning around many of the supply dumps. We had been promised a 25-kilowatt diesel generator, but it somehow got tied up in red tape and was probably sitting back in Noumea. In one of my forays, I discovered one in an Army depot, and with all the brazenness of a whorehouse hooker, not only stole the generator but used the Army's own crane to load it on an Army flat-bed truck to take it to the Camp. It was quickly hidden in a revetment dug by our Malaita boys under SeaBee supervision.

We were putting the finishing touches on the Shack in preparation for the impending arrival of the Admiral and the rest of the Staff when three natives showed up in the compound. They talked with Mr. Frost and some other people for a while, the conversation ending with a lot of head nodding. After the Melanesians left, Jack came over to me.

"What do you know about TBXs?" he asked. A TBX was a portable transmitter for use by landing parties where no electricity is available. Power is produced by cranking the generator by hand, somewhat like turning bicycle pedals.

"Well", I answered, "I had instruction on them when I was on the NORTH CAROLINA."

"I'm not going to pull any punches, Hutch. One of our coastwatchers had his transmitter crap out on him, and we need his scouting reports badly. You'd have to fly in, instruct him on use of the TBX, and fly out. It's going to be a little risky. Normally, this would be a volunteer mission, but I don't have anyone else to ask."

The coastwatchers were incredibly brave men. Secreting themselves on enemy-held islands they knew like a book, their principal mission was to radio all Jap air, naval, and troop movement information to us. In imminent danger at all times, they knew capture would mean excruciating and prolonged torture before certain death. Their lives depended upon the natives whom they necessarily had to trust implicitly. To the credit of the Melanesians, there's no recorded incident where they betrayed that trust. Constantly on the move to avoid detection by enemy radio direction finders, those coastwatchers lived precariously on the edge. I had met a few when they'd come in from their posts for supplies and/or medical treatment. No swashbucklers, these. They were, for the most part, quiet and unassuming men, just doing their job as they saw it.

Flying by night into enemy territory scared the living hell out of me. Any one of a dozen scenarios could be written for such a mission—all of them, I figured, leading to disaster. The odds of getting in and out in one piece were zero, zilch, zip. No bookie in his right mind would lay odds on this one. Yet, I realized the importance of keeping the coastwatcher network intact. A lot of American lives depended on it. It was their reports that gave us critical early warnings of Jap movements, providing extra reaction time to bombing raids and to the "Tokyo Express"—Nip naval units coming "down the Slot".

Mr. Frost was watching me closely. Surely he could see the apprehension and anxiety in my eyes. I heaved a massive sigh.

"Okay, Mr. Frost, I'll go."

The moment I assented I regretted it. I did not want to go.

That night I loaded the steamer-trunk-size TBX case into the back of a jeep and was driven to Henderson Field. Sitting on the apron were the PBY-5A Catalina flying boats of VP-54, the renowned "Black Cat Squadron". One of their planes made the first landing on formerly enemy-held territory when it touched down on Henderson, 12 August of '42. If I had to fly with anybody, at least I'd be doing so with some of the best in the business. And there was one plus over the DC-3 I'd flown on to the 'Canal. The ebony-painted PBYs mounted guns.

The flight, northwesterly over both sea and islands, was uneventful until we got over our destination. The pilot went in toward a little bay that looked no larger than a bird bath. As I peered out of the plastic "blister" amidships, I saw breakers pounding a reef at the mouth of the lagoon. The pilot almost dead-sticked in with minimum power, and pancaked almost noiselessly on the water. No use waking any Japs.

We were in but could we get out? The size of the cove had me wondering if we had enough take-off room to clear that reef. My thoughts

PBY-5A CATALINA FLYING BOAT
The type in which author flew to deliver transmitter to Coast Watcher.
(U.S. Navy Photos - U.S. Navy Historical Center)

were interrupted by a crewman who spotted a light signal from the jungle at water's edge. With two men, I muscled the trunk into a rubber raft, and we paddled ashore. The coastwatcher, four natives, and I moved the TBX transmitter inland perhaps 50 or 60 yards to full seclusion in the jungle. With a shielded flashlight, I showed the Australian coastwatcher how to operate the gear. In about twenty minutes, he had it down, and a native led me back to the beach.

I looked around for the Black Cat. While I was gone, the pilot had maneuvered the PBY so its tail assembly was virtually in the jungle, its nose pointed toward the reef to get all the running room available we'd need to clear the breakers. Alongside, a crewman stabbed holes in the rubber raft to sink it, and we scrambled aboard. The pilot pushed the throttle wide open while holding the plane almost motionless with down flaps. As soon as the engines reached sufficient power, the flying boat literally leaped forward. Waiting until just the last moment before reaching the reef, the pilot yanked back on the yoke. The P-boat groaned mightily and went into a nearly vertical climb, her two engines screaming in protest.

All this racket woke every damned Jap on the island, and out of the blister I could see streaks of tracers from automatic weapons arching straight at us. The Black Cat just seemed to hang there in mid-air on her props for an eternity while AA fire pierced the dark around us. I was holding on for dear life, too damned petrified even to pray. How so much ammo was expended without knocking us down, I'll never know. Suddenly, the Cat seemed to get her second wind and we were, like Superman, up up and away, hightailing it out of range. Whoever was watching over me that night sure earned his keep.

Jack Frost saw me crawling out of the jeep as I returned to the Admiral's Camp. "How'd it go, lad?"

"I'll tell you, Mr. Frost, I'm rapidly developing an aversion to airplanes", I replied. "Whoever scrapped my request, back in boot camp, for aviation gunner's mate school did me one big favor!"

On 16 February, 1943, the McCAWLEY, along with the transports FULLER (APA-7) and JOHN PENN (APA-23), escorted by three destroyers (the WILSON, LANSDOWNE, and GANSEVOORT), arrived from Dumbea Bay, Noumea. The MAC's deck log notes: "1450—Rear Admiral R.K. Turner, USN, with 25 officers and 43 enlisted men left ship for temporary duty on Guadalcanal."

We began the final stages of preparation for Operation CLEAN-SLATE, the invasion of the Russell Islands, just thirty miles north of the 'Canal's Cape Esperance. D-Day was scheduled for 21 February. Operation CLEANSLATE was an interim move between Operation

WATCHTOWER and the bigger invasion of the New Georgias to come later. The Japs had already abandoned the Russells, and we needed the islands to provide forward air cover and logistical support for future operations. Besides being uncontested, CLEANSLATE was remarkable for another reason. It marked the first use of the new landing craft, the LCTs.

I drew a bye on the Russells. On the binnacle list for five days with my second go-round with malaria, I was in no shape to make the trip. Besides, I didn't miss much. With no resistance to our landings, the operation turned out to be just a good rehearsal for future amphibious invasions.

The malaria attack proved one thing to me. The daily dose of two Atabrine tablets, prescribed as a deterrent against the disease, wasn't worth the trouble. All it did was turn my skin into a horrendous shade of yellow. Where my skin was shielded from the sun, it had taken on a grayish hue, probably from the excessive humidity and the previous bout with the disease. Areas exposed to the tropical sun were burned black. Overlay those colors with the Atabrine's yellow stain, and I had the dam'dest looking hide you could imagine. It was also rumored, falsely no doubt, that Atabrine undermined sexual potency!

In a sense, malaria and related maladies were worse enemies than the Japs. "With malaria came a form of secondary anemia that sapped endurance and resistance. In the South Pacific as a whole, malaria caused five times as many casualties as the Japanese. On Guadalcanal, diseases accounted for nearly two-thirds of all men who became ineffective; wounds disabled only one-quarter" (Frank).

An attack of malaria is more than just debilitating. In the extreme forms I suffered, the first symptom is a rise in body temperature to 104° to 105° or more. My body felt as if it had been immersed in a boiling stew pot. Perspiration poured into my cot in such large amounts I literally was awash in it. Any bedding touching my body was thrown off as I tried to compensate for the heat. Then, almost in seconds, I was shivering violently with chills, calling for blankets which the hospital corpsman would pile on top of me. The cycle of ague kept repeating itself, over and over and over and over, accompanied by headaches that can only be described by imagining spikes being driven into your head. The mind begins to hallucinate from the high fever and the body is wracked again and again by fever and chills. And there's not a helluva lot the doctor or corpsmen can do to alleviate it.

When the siege ended, I was left in an extremely weakened state, so feeble I could hardly get my muscles to move, and with a skin pallor even the Atabrine yellow could not hide. The malaria had been accompanied by dengue fever, which intensified the attack, causing diarrhea and excruciating pain in the body's joints. Worse yet, this would not be my last bout with malaria.

When I was returned to duty, I took up my old station on the Command circuit. Since we were now a shore-based radio station, but with no plans for it to become permanent, we were assigned new call letters: *Z6G* was the tactical identification for RADIO KOLI POINT. The "tactical" designation meant the call letters were for use only in the South Pacific Theater of Operations.

The new speed key I'd ordered from the States months back finally caught up with me, and I was ready to put it into operation after a couple of modifications. I replaced the copper contacts with silver ones, cut from a half dollar, and I added suction cups to the bottom to keep it from "walking" across the desk top as I was sending. I loved that little Vibroplex "Blue Racer". It was as fast as greased lightning and smooth as silk. I tried it out right away, calling NXZ in Noumea to clear Operational Priority traffic. Great! Frank Condron was on the other end—old home week. The volume of traffic on the circuit increased dramatically. I would often spend eight straight hours on watch, clearing both Urgent ("O") and Operational Priority ("OP") dispatches to Admiral Halsey (ComSoPac), take four hours off, and "hit the wind" again. It was no secret we were tooling up for another campaign.

Communications in the South Pacific were often erratic due to some very strange atmospheric effects. Complete blackouts could come any old time. One night, I was trying to reach a Destroyer Squadron Commander just off Koli Point. He was almost close enough to throw rocks at. But the "black" had settled in, and I couldn't raise a peep out of him. After numerous unanswered calls, another signal came up on the frequency, requesting identification. It was, of all places, Radio Adak, *Alaska!*

I asked Adak to clear traffic for me to NPM, Honolulu, for relay to the destroyer via FOX. But the operator was leery, suspecting a Jap trick. Both my call letters and authentication code were exclusive to the South Pacific and Adak couldn't verify them. It was only after I asked him in plain language that he reluctantly agreed to relay; but he wasn't in contact with NPM, Honolulu, only NPG, San Francisco. So the DesRon Commander finally got the message—which went to Alaska to San Francisco to Honolulu to the Solomons, covering maybe 20,000 miles just to get about five miles!

It was not only heavy static and periodic communications blackouts that hindered operations. Our friendly neighborhood Jap operators got into the act, too. They'd come up on our frequencies, interrupting with extraneous transmissions or just plain old-fashioned jamming. They had pretty good electronic gear. In fact, we had a few pieces of captured Jap equipment in use, ourselves. Since the enemy's bases were to the north or northwest of Guadalcanal, his operators rarely could put out a strong enough signal to interdict traffic going from Koli Point to Noumea.

It was when I was trying to copy NXZ's signal from Noumea that the jamming and interruptions caused problems. The Nips would search all frequencies. When they found us transmitting on one, they'd set up shop and do all they could to harass us. Often the Jap would break in and ask for an "IMI", the international code request for a repeat. Unless we caught it, we'd begin sending the message all over again. But that didn't work too often. Enemy transmitters had a different electronic tone from ours, and it was relatively easy to distinguish friend from foe.

When we were not overly busy, Condron and I would play games with the Japs, putting them on and even talking with them directly. All we encountered must have been quite fluent in American English, for they always seemed to understand us perfectly. Probably, so we surmised at the time, all had degrees in communications from USC or UCLA! Anyhow, Frank and I had ways to confound them. We'd use our own "secret" language we'd honed in January, using International Morse liberally salted with Continental Morse, all sent in "banana boat swing". It would drive the Japs nuts trying to figure out what we were saying—don't think they ever broke our code!

Another ploy was to use split frequencies. I'd send on one circuit but monitor NXZ on another. Frank could hear me through the jamming that was more distant than my signal, and apparently the Japs never got wise to my use of the secondary frequency for traffic coming back to me. The only problem I faced then was the inability to monitor my own sending. I had to operate that Blue Racer strictly by "feel" without hearing myself. Any radio operator will tell you that ain't easy. Yet, Frank and I managed to clear traffic steadily for up to eight hours at a time, averaging around 50 words per minute.

The long watches weren't conducive to getting much in the way of sleep. The situation was compounded by the reluctance of old Tojo and his buddies in Tokyo to give up on keeping Guadalcanal in the center of the conflict for many months after withdrawing their ground troops. The U.S. had declared the 'Canal "secure" on 15 February—but nobody ever bothered to tell the slant-eyes! Almost nightly, they had bombers overhead, sending us scrambling for foxholes and bunkers. Only those who've experienced months of "foxhole time" can relate to the kind of strain that puts on a person.

The air raids, mostly by high-level Betty bombers out of the Japs' base at Rabaul some 300 miles northwest of Cactus, usually would make Henderson Field and the storage areas around Lunga Point their primary objective. But as their bombing runs carried them southeasterly along the coast, the next targets were Carney Field and environs. That was *us*. There were also some attacks which skipped the Henderson area, and we'd become Number One on their Hit Parade.

It became, in a strange way, routine. When Condition Red sounded, we'd secure the Radio Shack and head for cover but stand outside the foxhole to watch as searchlight batteries around the Lunga-Henderson area swept the skies to spot incoming Jap planes. As soon as the anti-aircraft batteries began firing shells high into the sky, we'd creep a little closer to our holes, knowing it would be but minutes before those damn' Mitsubishi Bettys would be over our heads. They covered the intervening eight miles in a short time.

As bombs began falling southeast of Henderson, we'd hit the dirt, huddling beneath our palm log roofs in holes maybe four feet deep. The roof wouldn't withstand a near miss or direct hit, but it did shield us from falling shrapnel and "daisy cutters". Not only were we in danger from the hostiles' bombs, we were also vulnerable to the fall-out from our own AA fire. Everything that goes up must come down, and those 90mm shells bursting overhead showered fragments back to earth—at the *same* velocity they went up!

The Marines of the 11th Defense Battalion manning the AA battery next door to us were sometimes frustrated when the Japs would break off a raid and not come far enough for them to get a shot at the intruders. So those idiot jarheads would go out in the daytime and gather up dried kunai grass, old tree limbs, worn-out tires and anything else that would burn. Then they'd pour used crankcase oil over the pyre to make it more flammable and set it afire when a raid came in.

The Nips would get curious, flying over to investigate the blaze. The Marines, yelling like a crowd at a Joe Louis championship fight, would open fire. They were usually successful, too, in scoring hits on the enemy raiders. But it didn't do a helluva lot for my morale. Those bombers could lay some of their eggs *before* they got hit. I went over to have a little heart-to-heart talk with the 11th's gyrenes about luring bombers close enough to drop one on *me*. They cheerfully ignored my pleas, and just painted another "flaming asshole" Jap flag on the gun mount.

In between sending flights of bombers in, the Japs deployed "snoopers" to test our defenses, their approach resulting in Condition Red. And then there was always "Washing Machine Charlie" (sometimes called "Bed-Check Charlie" or "Piss-Call Charlie"). Charlie always came over

JAPANESE MITSUBISHI "BETTY"
Land-based heavy bomber
(Guadalcanal Campaign Veterans - Ted Blahnik)

by himself. The trademark sound of his Mitsubishi engine was accomplished by deliberate mistuning. His purpose was strictly to harass us by keeping us awake most of the night. Charlie was partial to two-o'clock-in-the-morning flights, which sent every one on the island to the foxholes, where we'd languish until Condition Green was sounded. Just to keep us off guard, he sometimes would be followed by full-blown enemy air raids.

I've tried myriads of times to verbalize the experience of sitting in a foxhole during bombing raids, but with little success. It sure was different from an air attack at sea. Even if you're not manning a gun aboard ship, you're still at your battle station, feeling as if you're doing your duty as part of the team. On land, all that can be done is to sit in a gawddam hole in the dirt while successions of bomber formations pound the hell out of everything in sight—and that's something else again.

As the raids came in, we could hear and feel the explosions getting closer and closer as the enemy bombardiers "walked" their eggs down the flight path. When they'd hit on Carney Field we'd scrunch our bodies up tighter, waiting for that errant one to drop near or even on us. The margin of error was small, and we were cognizant that the Japs' bomb sights were less sophisticated and nowhere near as accurate as the U.S. Norden bomb sight.

In that foxhole a wide range of emotions is triggered. The paramount one is Fear of the Unknown. There is no way to see what's going on without substantial risk, and there's no way to fight back. The blackness of the hole is punctuated periodically as the enemy drops flares, as bombs burst within sight, and as the muzzles of the 90-millimeters flash with fire. When the 11th's batteries were blasting with earsplitting cracks, we knew the Jap planes were directly overhead. We could only sit there and *TAKE IT!* On those terrible nights when wave after wave of bombers would come in, the silent plea would go out: "Lord, make 'em stop! For just five minutes—*make 'em stop!*"

It was not so much the fear of dying, but of not knowing if, when, or how; of being badly mangled by a near miss, and still living; of cracking up, of going over the edge, of losing control. Feeling trapped and helpless gave "frustration" a whole new meaning. And each of these emotions intensified as the bombers came closer and closer. All this was mixed with anger. Anger at being there in the first place; anger at the Japs for putting us through this kind of Hell; anger at being helpless to retaliate or do something—*anything!*

Eventually, a kind of fatalism set in as an alternative. Personally, I had, I concluded, long since "used up most of my numbers." I convinced myself I had only so many chances to survive this War. The more times I escaped peril with a whole skin, the lower my odds of making it to the end. Thus, I figured, it was just a matter of time before the numbers ran out completely. My one prayer was: "Lord, make it quick." I did not want to be maimed or to suffer.

There was little conversation in foxholes. Each man was consumed by his own thoughts and fears. Occasionally, there would be a remark about a "close one", or on the Marines' AA fire, or regarding a momentary lull. We didn't hold post-mortems on the raids, either. Just went back to our duties, exhausted from the emotional battering.

February of 1943 saw a significant build-up in American and Allied air power in the South and Southwest Pacific Theaters, which made it more and more difficult for the Jap Navy to reinforce their troops. Much of what was going on we would only learn later. On 3 and 4 March in the Battle of the Bismarck Sea, Allied bombers blasted a Jap convoy carrying some 7,000 troops to reinforce their positions on New Guinea, sinking seven of eight transports and four of eight screening destroyers. In the Solomons our increased air power around Guadalcanal made it difficult for the Tokyo Express to reinforce the New Georgia Islands. At night our Navy was able to bombard Munda and Vila airfields on New Georgia and Kolombangara respectively, a cruiser/destroyer force under Admiral A. Stanton "Tip" Merrill sinking two Jap destroyers the night of 5/6 March. In the future, the Japs would try to reinforce their positions primarily via barges.

In early March, staff officers from Admiral Halsey's South Pacific and General MacArthur's Southwest Pacific Commands flew to Pearl Harbor to work out command relationships. The Central and Western Solomons were in the General's Southwest Pacific domain, and the Army refused the Navy's proposal that upcoming operations here be transferred to the Admiral's South Pacific sphere. Eventually accepted was MacArthur's proposal (code-named ELKTON after the Maryland town of speedy marriages where my father and mother were married!) giving him overall strategic command and Halsey direct command of operations in the Solomons under his general directives, both ultimately dependent on the ships and planes of the Pacific Fleet under the command of Admiral Nimitz. As it turned out, MacArthur gave Halsey a free hand as long as he recognized the General was in charge; and the two titans' mutual respect developed into a lasting friendship, Halsey having succumbed to the charm and charisma of the "self-advertising Son of a Bitch"!

It was 15 March, 1943, when we lost some of our proud identity. A reorganization of U.S. Naval Forces put all ships of the Navy into numbered Fleets. The distinctive (and perhaps glamorous) "SoPac" would be removed from our name. No longer "ComAmphibFor*SoPac*", Admiral Turner was now "ComPhibFor*ThirdFlt*" (Commander Amphibious Forces, Third Fleet). Gone, too, was his well-known and cherished designation as Commander Task Force 62, changed to "ComTaskFor 32". We were now in the Third Fleet. But Kelly Turner still tended to cling to the *SoPac* title, and I never changed it on my return mailing address. With it, my family had some idea where I was located.

These changes led me to believe that the non-combatants back home in the Navy Department had so little else to do they just played numbers games with the deployed forces, and sat around making up new acronyms just to confuse everybody. They had to have something to do toward winning the War, so they just sat around juggling numbers and letters, titles and acronyms.

Early in March, there were many various and sundry "comings and goings" around the Operations tent, and a new word worked its way into our lexicon: Operation TOENAILS. It was the code name for our next campaign, the invasion of the New Georgias beginning with Rendova and New Georgia Island itself. By the end of the month, the go-ahead was given to begin preparations for troop assembly, ship assignments, communications, etc. Second in command to Admiral Turner, in charge of all landing craft, was my old Captain on the NORTH CAROLINA, now Admiral George H. Fort.

Our increased activity wasn't lost on the Japs, who began an intensive air offensive with major attacks on Guadalcanal on April 1st and 7th. They continued their air strikes: 16 April, a gasoline dump and supply depot hit; 17 April, two more raids; 18 April, eight separate raids, the first hitting an ammo dump that burned and exploded throughout the night; 19 April, an early morning strike. We were getting more protection, though, including a squadron of Australian/New Zealander A-20s. They mounted 20mm cannon in the bomb bays, flew above the Nip bombers, and shot them down from above. The hostiles never knew what hit 'em.

Unknown to us at the time, these air raids were planned and directed by top Jap Admiral Yamamoto, who himself was the victim of our planes on April 18th. It seems our intelligence had decrypted a message giving details of the Admiral's inspection and morale-building tour of airfields in the Western Solomons. On orders from Washington to "get Yamamoto", Admiral Halsey ordered Air Solomons Commander Admiral Marc A. Mitscher to send long-range Army P-38 Lightnings to shoot down the Jap Commander in Chief's plane over the southern tip of Bougainville, on the anniversary of the Admirals' carrier raid on Tokyo!

The Japanese viewed the loss of Yamamoto as a major defeat, given the Admiral's ability and popularity in Japan, but our Commanders did not know they'd got their man for sure 'til announced by Tokyo on 21 May. While Admiral Turner exulted in the event, Halsey was not overjoyed: "Hold on, Kelly! What's so good about it? I'd hoped to lead that bastard up Pennsylvania Avenue. . . . "

On 17 May, we got our orders from Admiral Halsey. "ComSoPac" issued the directive: "Forces of the South Pacific Area will seize and occupy simultaneously positions in the southern part of the NEW GEORGIA Group preparatory to a full scale offensive against MUNDA-VILA and later [Bougainville]."

Maybe it was coincidence, but that night Condition Red sounded at 1900, continuing in effect until 2330 with several flights of bombers coming in and laying their eggs. A similar strike came on May 18th and, on the 19th, three separate raids between 2000 and 2345. Between 15 May and 16 June there were, in all, 21 air strikes against targets on the 'Canal. Like I said—somebody oughta tell the Japs Cactus has been "secure" since 15 February!

D-day for Operation TOENAILS was originally set for 15 June, which got everybody in a tizzy trying to get ready by that date. Then, Admiral Turner added a couple of weeks to preparation time and 30 June, 1943, became the actual target date. For a while, it looked as if Kelly Turner would miss this one. As previously mentioned, he spent over a week on the hospital ship SOLACE (AH-5) with both malaria and dengue fever. But he recovered sufficiently just in time for the invasion.

The Admiral was realistic but optimistic, commenting prophetically before Operation TOENAILS: "Some people think Munda's not going to be tough. I think it's a very tough nut to crack. I know we can do it." His biographer, Vice Admiral George C. Dyer, entitles his chapter on the operation: "Tough Toenails Paring".

On 11 June, the McCAWLEY and other transports of the invasion force arrived at Cactus. Until now, although I didn't know it at the time, all my service and medical records had remained on the ship. Thus there are no entries covering the time I was on temporary duty on the island.

Now my records and accounts were being transferred to Commanding Officer, Naval Base, Lunga, to be in the custody of the 4th Naval Construction (Special) Battalion—for, as my personnel file states, " . . . duty on Staff Allowance ComAmphibForSoPac."

For the some four months I'd been at Koli, my service records are, for all intents and purposes, blank.

And now, I would be going on temporary duty—*AGAIN!*

16

THE STRANGE FATE OF THE WACKY MAC

I had been pestering Commander Welker and Mr. Frost to send me back to sea. "I", I proclaimed, "am a blue water sailor, and I want off this stinking rock."

On 10 June, 1943, my pleas were answered. Commander Welker stopped in the Radio Shack to say the McCAWLEY was due in on the 11th, and to ask if I wanted to go back aboard on temporary duty. I jumped at the chance.

"There's a catch, though, Hutch", he added. "You'd remain aboard for the invasion up at Rendova."

"That, to me, Commander, is the lesser of two evils", I answered. I packed a few toilet articles in a ditty bag, bummed a ride to Lunga Point, and took a Higgins boat out to the MAC. I didn't need to take clothing. I'd left some personal effects aboard in my locker, including dungarees, shirts, and skivvies.

It was good to feel a deck under my feet, again, and shortly after I crossed the Quarterdeck, the MAC got underway. Loaded with troops who'd make the landings, we steered a course for Vila Harbor at Efate in the New Hebrides. For the next couple of weeks, the MAC would be rehearsing the off-loading of personnel and equipment and exercising her boat crews for the initial phase of Operation TOENAILS—the invasion of Rendova Island in the New Georgia chain, part of the Solomons. I would supervise communications preparations and, hopefully, get a little rear area rest. It would be a welcome change to be off the 'Canal.

The crew of the old transport was still as "gung ho" as ever and the drills went off without a hitch. Several of the radiomen were taking a break one afternoon. We were sitting around, having a bull session, up on what had been the sun deck when the MAC was a passenger liner. Suddenly, the entire ship seemed to fall completely silent. We sat looking at each other, sharing an eerie feeling. Finally, one of the ship's company radiomen verbalized the premonition we all were sensing.

"This", he said in a near whisper, "is the MAC's last invasion."

For a few moments we just sat and stared at each other. Then, in ones and twos, we dispersed. We knew it to be true.

A few days before departing Efate I came down with the worst malaria attack I'd experienced to date. My fever was over 104° when I checked in to Sick Bay, shaking with the ague so violently I could barely keep the thermometer in my mouth. I wasn't perspiring. I was *sweating* like a quarter horse that had run eight furlongs at flank speed. No sooner would the pharmacist's mate smother me with a stack of blankets, when I complained of freezing to death, than I'd be throwing them off because I was burning up with the fever. The cycle kept repeating itself as my temperature continued to climb. Relief came only when I lost consciousness. Both the Medical Officer and the pharmacist's mate told me afterward they thought I'd never make it.

But I was on my feet again by the time the MAC got underway from Vila Harbor. Weak and wobbly on my pins, I was back in the Radio Shack as we entered Sealark Channel on 29 June and lay to off Lunga Point to take aboard Admiral Turner, senior Navy and Army officers, their staffs, and some casuals. Kelly Turner had left most of his Staff at Camp Crocodile; and if memory serves me correctly, I was the only Flag radioman to go along on Operation TOENAILS.

No sooner had the late arrivals cleared the Quarterdeck, when we got underway for Rendova. The invasion would be the first against an enemy-held island since the 7 August, 1942, landings at Guadalcanal and Tulagi. (There were no Japs on the Russells when we took them, you'll remember.) We had an impressive force to challenge the enemy in the Central Solomons. Backed by four carriers, five battleships, two cruiser divisions, and some 34 destroyers—none of which we ever saw because they were too far out to sea—the Amphibians of Admiral Turner's Task Group 31.1 were ready.

In the assault force were the infamous "Unholy Four" of Transport Division 12: the McCAWLEY (ComTaskForce 31), PRESIDENT JACKSON (APA-18), PRESIDENT ADAMS (APA-19), and PRESIDENT HAYES (APA-20). Then there were the cargo ships ALGORAB (AKA-8) and LIBRA (AKA-12). The screening destroyers were the RALPH TALBOT (DD-390), BUCHANAN (DD-484), McCALLA (DD-488), and FARENHOLT (DD-491). The anti-submarine unit had the GWIN (DD-433), RADFORD (DD-446), JENKINS (DD-447), and WOODWORTH (DD-460). Plus, there were some sixty smaller landing craft and auxiliaries.

We were under radio silence and the tactical circuit which I was guarding would only be used for CTF 31 outgoing traffic after our troops landed. I had been in the Radio Shack most of the time since coming on the midwatch about 2345, 28 June—running strictly on "nerves", cigarettes, and strong java. There was no use trying to sleep. I was too jittery. As we proceeded toward our destination through the night of 29 and 30 June, Admiral Turner logged the weather conditions in his War Diary: "Weather enroute to Rendova—low ceilings, moderate showers, poor visibility in showers, surface wind SE, force four, shifting and gusty in showers, choppy seas."

The transports and tin cans moved into Renard Sound, entrance to Rendova Harbor. It was 0640, 30 June, 1943, when the debarkation of troops began as the MAC hove to in "Transport Area". Our first boat hit East Beach at 0656 and "was smartly back alongside to pick up logistic support at 0709." This had all taken place in heavy rain, but we still had all our assault troops ashore within thirty minutes after the first wave hit the beach. The four APAs put some 6,300 men ashore in little more than a half-hour, a record time. The McCAWLEY landed 1,100 troops, 604 tons of equipment, and the senior Army and Navy commanders and staffs. Since Rendova was lightly defended by only a handful of Japs, resistance was minimal. The big fight would come with the cross-channel strike towards the Munda airstrip where several thousand of the enemy were well-entrenched.

Still, it wasn't exactly a cake walk. At 0708, shore batteries opened up on four of our destroyers—BUCHANAN, FARENHOLT, GWIN, and JENKINS—just westward of Transport Area. The BUCHANAN returned the compliment, firing some 223 5-inch rounds to silence the enemy batteries. The Japs could score only near misses that came within 50 yards of the DD-484, but they were luckier with the GWIN. She took a 4.7-inch round from a Jap battery on Kundu Kundu Island, knocking out her after engine room, but she survived only to be sunk two weeks later by a Long Lance torpedo in the surface Battle of Kolombangara. The hostiles did us a favor by firing on the tin cans. They revealed their positions when they could have waited and taken the transports under fire.

A Jap snooper plane was picked up on radar at 0856. Assuming he might be the advance guard of a heavier attack, we interrupted unloading and got underway. When no attack materialized, we went back to business after about an hour. In the meantime, we got a report that three men had been killed on the GWIN, and that the BUCHANAN had silenced a one-gun hostile battery on Baanga Point. During the day, the gutsy DD-484 would offer herself up as a target for more shore batteries,

APPROACH TO RENDOVA
Marines and Army troops prepare for amphibious landing as McCAWLEY
steams toward Rendova.
(U.S. Navy Photo - National Archives)

then return fire when coming under attack. In all, she wiped out seven of the enemy batteries.

Around 1100, destroyer radar picked up an enemy flight of 27 bombers with fighter escort on the way in. Underway again, we maneuvered into defensive formation, circling the wagons *à la* our pioneer ancestors under Indian attack. But our air cover was superb. The new F4U Corsair fighters went after the raiders with a vengeance; and although the air battle was plainly visible to us in Transport Area, not one Jap plane got close. Relieved off my circuit for a spell, I was on deck outside the Radio Shack. In the center of the island was the cone-shaped Mount Rendova. As I watched, one of our Corsairs chased a Nip Zero around and around the peak, just below the summit. Finally the F4U pilot had enough of that foolishness. He went up and over the top of the mountain, intercepting the Zero from above. "Scratch one meatball!"

There were other dogfights all over the sky and, despite a concerted attempt by some 100 enemy aircraft, the ships in Transport Area were untouched. Aboard the MAC, we were beginning to feel the premonition at Efate had been a delusion. By 1500 all the transports and cargo vessels had completed their unloading and began to form up to head back to Guadalcanal. The MAC took her position as fleet guide of our Task Group as we moved out of Rendova into Blanche Channel. All seemed to go smoothly until the Fighter Director Team on the JENKINS picked up a flight of bogies, sounded the alarm, and called for more air support to counter what turned out to be bandits. The JENKINS would later record that, with respect to the raiders, our "fighters made interception a little too late."

Some 23 Mitsubishi twin-engine Betty bombers, torpedoes slung in their open bomb bays, closed for the attack, coming in fast and low. Every ship in our force opened fire and began emergency turns to avoid the onslaught. One plane was knocked down just 150 yards off our bow. Captain Rodgers swung the MAC in a 90° turn to starboard as another Betty made a run at us. I was standing on the port side just outside the Radio Shack as the Jap bore in from the port quarter. It was stupid of me to be exposed like that, but then there aren't many spaces to hide on a thin-skinned old transport.

As the enemy torpedo plane came under fire from our batteries, I could see the tracers were falling behind the attacker and began screaming at our gunners: *"Lead him! Lead him!! Lead the son of a bitch!!!"*

It was too late. Lieutenant C.M. Wuhrman, the MAC's Gunnery Officer, estimated in his Action Report that about fifteen torpedo planes were attacking the McCAWLEY from the port side. "The 3-inch .50s opened up with a 4-second barrage. Local battery officers took over

DEBARKATION FOR INVASION

Landing craft head for the invasion beaches, 30 June, 1943, Rendova, New Georgia Group, Central Solomons. Photo taken just two hours prior to air attack fatal to the McCAWLEY.

(U.S. Navy Photo - National Archives)

control of the 3-inch battery from then on. The 20mm and .50-cal. batteries opened up when the planes came within their effective range. A torpedo was sighted on the port quarter on a collision course (about 300 yds. away when reported). It was immediately reported to the Bridge."

As the Skipper got the word the torpedo was heading toward us on a collision course, he ordered the rudder put hard a-starboard and the starboard engine backed full. The maneuver was a futile one. The fish hit right in the MAC's after engine room, just forward of Number Four Hold, track angle about 190°. The MAC took a violent list to port, throwing me against the inboard bulkhead. When she righted herself, I was catapulted toward the outboard handrail, hitting the top one so hard it knocked the breath out of me. I didn't take the luxury of being scared. I was infuriated, cussing the Japs with every profane description of their ancestry in my vocabulary. I think I even made up some as I condemned their souls to everlasting Hell.

When the torpedo hit (the time was 1557) the MAC lost all power and went dead in the water. She was still swinging right, with her rudder jammed hard over. There was yelling from the men above me as they sighted two more torpedoes passing close aboard down our starboard side. Around us a wall of fire continued. Every ship in the force blasted away as the torpedo plane attack continued. Then all gunfire ceased. Captain Rodgers, in his Action Report, noted: "the attack ended with all [23] enemy planes shot down by AA fire of Task Force 31.1, McCAWLEY claiming four planes." One of those four was the S.O.B. that threw that fish into our MAC.

From the angle of attack and concentration of planes pouncing on the McCAWLEY, it was obvious the Japs were after Admiral Turner and his Flagship. According to Mike Gydos manning one of the 20mm guns, as soon as the torpedo hit, the Admiral came running out on the deck yelling "Where the hell is everybody?" Whereupon Machinist Mate 2nd Class Gydos yelled back: "Get the hell under cover—I don't matter but they'll need *you!*"

My first thought was of casualties. Certainly the after engine room would have dead and wounded. "Those poor bastards", I thought. I would later learn that fifteen of my shipmates were killed, thirteen enlisted men and two officers. Seven others were wounded. "God DAMN it!" I said, through gritted teeth.

Yeoman 2nd Class Jim Germain "Frenchy" Maurais, the logroom yeoman, was on his way into the engine spaces with the Chief Engineer, Commander John Krebb, when the fish slammed into the ship. Frenchy had come down from his "Transport Area" battle station when we got underway to exit the area.

"I was a couple of steps behind Commander Krebb as we were scooting down the ladder to the main engines control station when she hit." So Frenchy wrote to me. "What saved us was that we were both holding on to the handrails as we were running down the steps of the ladder. The steps flew out from under us and we were left hanging on to the handrails. I remember thrashing around as the water was rising and somebody hollering that they were throwing a line down for anybody there to grab a-hold of. What with the burning oil and the acrid smoke in the total darkness, I don't know how I managed to find the line and grab it but I did. The next thing I knew I was in sick bay and stayed there until I was told we were abandoning ship."

"My helmet, not being buckled, had been blown off and my hair burned off; a part of a front tooth was gone and my face was bloody from pieces of shrapnel which turned out to be slivers of paint which musta come off the bulkheads. My dungarees had come apart at the seams. In a word, I looked a real mess. As soon as I got to sick bay, one of the doctors who began to examine me told a chancre [syphilis sore] mechanic [pharmacist's mate] to stick a mirror to my face. It was coal black, apparently from the soot and dirt flying around the engine room. But all my wounds were superficial and I managed to get my ass off onto the TALBOT on my own."

Only nine other men escaped the engine room. Frenchy was taken first to Guadalcanal, then to a mobile hospital in Noumea. After a two-week rest, he was assigned to another transport, the JOHN PENN (APA-23), along with seven other McCAWLEY survivors.

The smoke of battle had not yet cleared when damage control parties raced into the stricken spaces. The First Lieutenant and the Chief Carpenter's Mate were the first on the scene in the engine room. According to Captain Rodgers's "War Damage" report, the engine room spaces and Number Four Hold were flooded. Sea water was up over the main engines, about ten feet below the main deck level. Shoring of the bulkheads between Number Four and Five Holds, and the forward engine room bulkhead, got underway. At the same time, preparations were being made for the MAC to be taken under tow.

About thirty minutes after the torpedo struck, Commander Welker hurried into the Radio Shack.

"We're shifting the Flag to the FARENHOLT", he said to me. "Bear a hand with all the code books and lay forward to the well deck."

"Aye, aye, Sir!"

It took but seconds to collect the books and put my precious Blue

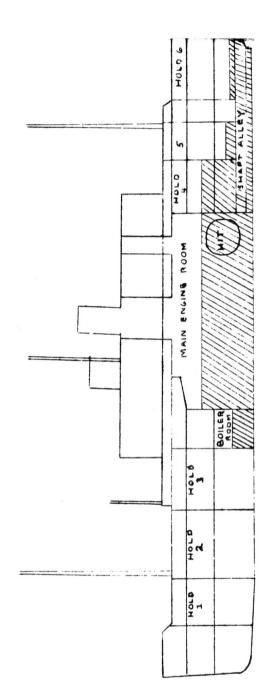

U.S.S. McCAWLEY   APA 4

SHADED SECTIONS INDICATE EXTENT OF FLOODING

HOLD 1 · HOLD 2 · HOLD 3 · BOILER ROOM · MAIN ENGINE ROOM · HIT · HOLD 4 · 5 · HOLD 6 · SHAFT ALLEY

TORPEDO HIT ON McCAWLEY

Diagram from Captain Rogers' Action Report of the damage and flooding following the torpedoing by a
Japanese "Betty" bomber—30 June, 1943.

(National Archives)

Racer speed key into its carrying case. I'd have no time to swing by my locker to pick up personal effects or clothing. With both arms loaded, I stumbled along the canted deck and down the ladders to the well deck. The Higgins boat with Admiral Turner and others of his Staff was already alongside. I was the last one to get there. A cargo net was slung over the side, but I couldn't negotiate it with all the stuff I was toting. So . . . I just took aim at the bottom of the boat and dropped the code books, missing the Admiral by only a couple of feet. He glowered at me, then shook his head and smiled. I hit the cargo net, sliding most of the way down into the bouncing boat. No sooner had my feet hit the deck, when the cox'n slammed the throttle wide open and we headed for the FARENHOLT, hove to a couple of hundred yards away.

As we embarked in the DD-491, I paused to look back at the stricken McCAWLEY. She was now being taken in tow by the LIBRA. After assessing the situation, Admiral Turner ordered the ship to be abandoned, and the RALPH TALBOT moved into position to remove the survivors. Only a salvage party was to remain aboard. It was obvious at this juncture that the MAC most probably would not survive. It's a deeply moving experience to know your ship is lost. The MAC was already settling further by the stern and the list was more pronounced. I raised my hand to my brow in a quick salute to that old rust bucket, then hurriedly got about the business at hand, setting up Flag communications on the FARENHOLT. I would not see the Wacky MAC again. There was a painful lump in my throat.

Landsmen may never fathom a sailor's attachment to his ship. To the uninitiated, she's just a bunch of steel in which to get from one place to another over the sea. But a ship is much more than that to a seafaring man. Each ship has an identifiable air about her. An aura. A feeling. A definite personality. Sailors see no contradiction in referring to a vessel as "she". A ship is a living, breathing, individual. During World War II when destroyers were being stamped out like Christmas cookies, all from the same set of blueprints and were mirror images of each other, each one took on different qualities and traits. I've said you could tie up six FLETCHER-class destroyers (later in the War I would serve on one) side by side alongside a tender, blindfold me, and let me walk from one Quarterdeck to the next, and I could tell you the *instant* I stepped aboard *my own* ship.

Not only is a ship a home where men become closer than blood relatives, but she's the sum of all the men who have ever trod her decks. She is the shield, the protector, of her people. She embodies all the experiences, dangers, storms, good times and bad, of her crews. Ships have reputations of being good or bad vessels in which to ship out. They are characterized as "taut" ships, "happy" ships, "gutsy" ships, or just about any other human distinguishing feature. When one is lost, it is a death in the family, the loss of a parent or close relative. With her go all the attributes that built up aboard her during her existence. And if men of her crew go down with her, she becomes their everlasting sepulcher. She holds forever the spirits of all who ever served aboard her, the quick and the dead. As long as any ship on which I served exists, a part of me shall always be aboard her, and each vessel on which I served will forever be a part of me.

I had barely gotten into the FARENHOLT's closet-size Radio Shack when Commander Welker came in. "Hutch, see if you can contact the PT-boats. They've got orders to attack and sink all shipping around Rendova after the sun sets. The MAC and whatever ships are with her won't make it out before then. Tell Kelly to stay completely clear of her position."

I knew the Op Plans for TOENAILS included orders to Motor Torpedo Boat Squadron 9 (MTBRon 9) under Lieutenant Commander Robert Bolling Kelly to go after any shipping around Rendova after dark, the assumption being all our own ships would be far out of the area by then. Any vessels in the Blanche Channel/Blackett Strait sector would be presumed to be Japanese trying to reinforce their Rendova garrison.

"That shouldn't be too hard", I thought. I asked the FARENHOLT's radioman of the watch for an operating position. Then, after checking the Op Plan communications section to verify the frequencies Kelly should be guarding, I got the tin can's radioman to fire up a transmitter. I began calling on the primary tactical frequency. I called. And I called. And I called. No response. Switched to the voice frequencies. No luck there either. Commander Welker kept sticking his head in the Shack, wanting to know if I'd been successful in raising "the Peter Tares". I had to tell him: "Negative!" I'd been using tactical call letters and authenticators and shifting to alternate frequencies, but even Kelly's base didn't answer.

"What the hell is going on here?" I rhetorically asked the FARENHOLT's Radioman 1st. "That S.O.B. should be coming right back to me. He can't be more than a few miles away, and we've got enough power to reach Honolulu. There's no atmospheric problem. We've been in contact with everybody we've needed to work with all day."

The sun was already sinking below the yardarm. Now I was getting desperate. The next time Commander Welker came in, I got his permission to switch to plain language. I broadcast a "blind" dispatch on the primary frequency, instructing the PTs to avoid Blanche Channel and contact with any ships in the area. Still no Kelly. Finally, it seemed too late. Still I kept an ear glued on the circuit for any transmissions. There were none. At last I pushed the cans off my ears to my temples. A striker handed me a cup of mud and I lit a cigarette, the first since early afternoon. The FARENHOLT was speeding southward towards the 'Canal, pitching easily on the long, low swells. A rain shower was washing the DD-491's decks. I had been awake, now, nearly 72 hours, and this was the first moment I'd had time to relax.

My thoughts turned first to the McCAWLEY and the sudden turn of events after the exhilaration of successfully landing our troops and equipment. The ship's company radioman on the FOX skeds next to me got a break as NPM (Honolulu) paused in its transmissions. He'd already copied several messages addressed "Action" to CTF 31. They'd been decoded and delivered to Admiral Turner, but I'd had no opportunity to snoop around and find out what they said. I wouldn't know anything until the next morning.

The FOX operator interrupted my thoughts. "Tough day", he observed.

"Yeah", I replied, "but at least we got the little yellow bastard that threw that fish into us."

"We got some of 'em, too." The FARENHOLT had done her part, knocking down three Jap planes in the attack, as well as wiping out some of the Nip shore batteries.

The DD-491's Shack had good joe, and as I sipped it from the handleless mug, I wondered why I'd not felt fear when that gawddam Betty drew a bead on us and launched the torpedo. All I could recall was the anger and frustration. In retrospect, I kicked myself hard for standing there on the deck, completely exposed, yelling like a high school cheerleader to our gunners. A leftward swing of only a few feet in the Jap pilot's course, and any one of several things could have put me on the casualty list: the Jap's strafing machineguns, the fish hitting farther forward nearer my position, shrapnel from the explosion . . . .Yeah, lad, you *were* d-u-m-b DUMB! In a reaction delayed by more than two hours, NOW I got scared and started to get the sweats and shakes. I was consoled only by the thought: "Maybe that angel . . . ."

Back aboard the McCAWLEY, the situation had gone from worse to appalling. Although Rear Admiral Theodore S. "Teddy" Wilkinson was aboard as Officer in Tactical Command of the salvage group, it was the Skipper Captain "Speed" Rodgers who filed the Action Report. At 1640, Admiral Turner had ordered the RALPH TALBOT alongside the MAC to remove all personnel except the salvage crew. The LIBRA had taken the crippled ship in tow and was trying to swing her to the right, the maneuver hampered by the MAC's jammed-over rudder. The LIBRA was "in irons" (dead in the water) when the Japs tried to finish off the Wacky MAC right then and there.

Twelve to fifteen Aichi 99 Val dive bombers came screaming down, attempting the *coup de grace*. The attack was a surprise. The enemy planes had not been picked up on radar because of the number of friendly aircraft on all bearings. The Jap dive bombers were within a thousand feet before the McCALLA and the RALPH TALBOT opened fire with their secondary batteries. Each accounted for at least one of the attackers. The MAC's Main Battery gun crews had been among those already removed from the ship, and the nine 20-millimeter and .50-caliber machineguns were manned by the salvage crew. One dive bomber was shot down by Marine Corps Captain Bill Hawkins who was on one of the .50s, manning the weapon in the face of heavy strafing. The Nips lost at least three planes, and all their bombs missed their targets. The sad little group of ships then moved out at five knots, with the LIBRA towing the MAC and the two tin cans screening.

The repair party finally succeeded in getting the McCAWLEY's rudder "amidships" (i.e. straight). All transverse bulkheads had been shored up, but flooding continued in Number Four and Number Five Holds. By 1850, the draft aft was 38 feet, and she continued to settle by the stern. Admiral Wilkinson had no choice. He called the McCALLA alongside and ordered all hands to abandon ship. The Admiral, Captain Rodgers, fourteen officers and 82 enlisted men went over the side to the destroyer. The operation was concluded in ten minutes. At 1930, 30 June, my McCAWLEY became a ghost ship—a derelict.

During the debarkation, the fleet tug PAWNEE (ATF-74) arrived to relieve the LIBRA as towing vessel. What happened after that was one of the more bizarre incidents of the long Solomons Campaign.

The PAWNEE's assignment was to take the MAC back to Tulagi where, hopefully, she could be repaired enough to get her to a drydock in the rear area. Considering the damage at this stage, the odds against saving her were formidable. Her loss, militarily, would not be a major one. But the MAC was a floating symbol of the darkest days of the Cactus-Ringbolt Campaign, and even the mention of her nickname conjured up the grit and courage that marked the determination to win at Guadalcanal. To her crew and the Flag personnel who had boasted "no Jap S.O.B. will ever get the Wacky MAC", her loss would be like a stake through the heart.

Three minutes after the last of the salvage party scrambled aboard the McCALLA, the PAWNEE eased along the port quarter of the LIBRA to relieve her of the towing job. The tug's Skipper, Captain Flave J. George, noted the position as "midway between the northern tip of

Rendova and Mbalumbalu Island in Blanche Channel." "Due to the lack of moon, plus low hanging rain clouds, visibility was extremely limited." They were deep in enemy waters.

The deck hands on the LIBRA secured a 5/8ths inch wire messenger to the heavy tow line in order to pass it across the stern to the PAWNEE. The AKA, understandably, was in a hurry to get the hell out of there. There had been earlier reports of at least one hostile submarine in the area. To expedite the transfer of the towing cable, the men on the LIBRA cut it loose from her bitts with an acetylene torch, much to the consternation of the PAWNEE's crew. The glare from the torch could give away their position to any snooping Japs.

Once away from the MAC, the LIBRA and the RALPH TALBOT—the latter with 20 officers, 270 men (20 wounded), and a great deal of gear from the McCAWLEY, plus her own ship's company—did what came naturally. They "hauled ass" out of Blanche Channel. Lieutenant (jg) Bob Mills was Officer of the Deck on the swiftly retiring RALPH TALBOT. One of the Bridge radio speakers had been set up on an aircraft frequency during the day, and about this time he noted voice activity on the circuit again. Retired Rear Admiral Robert G. Mills wrote to me about that night.

"A Squadron Commander [on the radio circuit] was directing his 'Little Boys' here and there. Since we had listened to our aircraft on this frequency all day, I assumed these were some of [ours]. I checked radar, the director and the lookouts—no contacts. Then the chatter became more excited; they had two contacts, one small and one large. We were one small [destroyer] and one large [cargo ship]; so I pressed radar and the director watch again and again. Absolutely no contacts. Then the radio relayed what sounded like an attack. I reported all to the Captain, assuring him we had checked and rechecked and were sure we had no contacts; so he went back to sleep. The next day we learned what happened."

Unfortunately, neither the PAWNEE nor the McCALLA had a receiver up on that aircraft frequency. The fleet tug was still striving to get her lines over to the McCAWLEY. But when the deck hands heaved in on the wire messenger, it gave way and snapped, severed by the LIBRA's screw or some other sharp projection. A working party got ready to board the MAC to secure the towing cable as the PAWNEE maneuvered to lay her port quarter alongside the derelict transport's bow.

"TORPEDOES OFF THE STARBOARD BOW!"

As the cry went up from PAWNEE sailors topside, Captain George signaled "full astern!" to his diesels, backing her down just enough and just in time. A torpedo crossed her stern with but a scant five feet to spare. Within seconds two more torpedoes (some say four) smashed into the port side of the McCAWLEY with a thundering blast that tore her apart. A secondary explosion, probably a magazine, sent steel and water high into the black night. Captain George's Action Report says: "The bow of the McCAWLEY rose some 75 feet then slid under almost vertically." The MAC was gone in less than thirty seconds. The PAWNEE's Skipper recorded the time as 2028.

While the tug was attempting to pass her lines to the MAC, the McCALLA had been ordered by Admiral Wilkinson to prepare her torpedoes to sink the derelict transport if the settling of that vessel warranted. As the destroyer moved to about 300 yards off the MAC's starboard beam, a lookout spotted a flare about two miles to the northeast. An all-around radar search disclosed no planes or other objects. The McCALLA was equipped with the older model SC radar which could become "land-bound" close to islands, giving off false signals so that surface vessels or objects could not be identified easily.

Almost simultaneous to the torpedoes hitting the MAC, two more fish were heading for the McCALLA. With flank speed and full left rudder, she avoided one which passed ahead of her by only five yards. The second cleared her stern by some fifty yards. Topside officers and enlisted men reported a third torpedo passing directly under the ship just forward of amidships. To avoid colliding with the PAWNEE, Captain Knoertzer turned the DD-488 with a full right rudder and steadied on a course parallel to the torpedo tracks to present as small a target as possible to the attackers.

The McCALLA's Skipper was unable to fix the source of the torpedoes that hit the McCAWLEY and the ones he so skillfully avoided. His Action Report does, however, mention possibilities. His sonar had been searching for some ten minutes prior to the attack without contact, virtually ruling out a submarine. Since four or five torpedoes arrived in the target area almost simultaneously, he speculated there was at least a possibility that motor torpedo boats, using the spotted flare as a firing signal, had fired a salvo, then proceeded west where they were later spotted by the McCALLA. Those boats *did not respond to a blinker light challenge*, so Captain Knoertzer thought they may have been from an enemy base at Munda Point. On the other hand, Admiral Wilkinson, aware of the orders to Kelly's MTBRon 9, believed the boats sighted to be friendly, but did not (in his reports) connect them with the attack.

The first torpedo which skimmed by the PAWNEE's bow was not the only one that came close to striking her. Just after the McCAWLEY took the fatal hits, another zipped past the tug's bow. Then a third drilled toward her spotted with the warning from the deck: "Torpedo off the starboard quarter!" With the tug going "all ahead full!", the fish barely missed her stern. The PAWNEE's crew also believed two more torpedoes hit their ship but failed to detonate; several men swore they heard them bump the hull. The PAWNEE's story is described in full in *We Will Stand By You* (1990) by radioman crewmember and former battleship sailor Theodore C. "Ted" Mason.

In the some four to five minutes it took for all of the action to take place, there was little time to judge the source of the torpedo attack. The PAWNEE's Action Report mentions sighting what was believed to be the conning tower of a submarine breaking the surface about 700 yards away, but this could have been the wake of a PT-boat. At any rate, the PAWNEE's Action Report is entitled: "U.S.S. McCAWLEY APA4, Sinking of by Enemy Submarine Action. . . . "

Still protecting the PAWNEE and seeking to find the source of the torpedo attack, Admiral Wilkinson first had the tug signaled to proceed to sea at maximum speed. Then he directed the McCALLA to reverse course and attack the submarine. As Wilkinson wrote in his official report to Admiral Turner: "Since we had . . . reports of a Japanese submarine . . . [in Blanche Channel], I concluded that the torpedoing was done by a submarine. . . . A number of boats, apparently PT boats, were sighted well ahead and, to avoid fouling them, although *not suspecting* any of them had fired the torpedoes, I abandoned further search for the submarine. . . . *I have, of course, since learned that PT-boats made the attack.*"

All I heard aboard the FARENHOLT was Commander Welker's terse announcement that the MAC had been sunk by a sub. As we debarked at Koli Point, I was already pushing past 80 hours without sleep, but was so keyed up I couldn't wait to get to Camp Crocodile to learn any details of the ship's loss. I was in for a shock. Crawling out of the jeep which brought me back, I started across the compound, only to be hailed by one of our Coding Officers who was carrying a handful of decoded messages to Admiral Turner's quarters.

"Here, Hutch", he said, "take a look at this."

The message was from Commander MTBRon 9 and described his PT-boat torpedo attack on "a Jap convoy of a large transport, a cruiser, a large destroyer and a small transport or destroyer." The transport, the dispatch continued, was unloading troops to reinforce their garrison. The PT-boats launched their torpedoes, sinking both the transport and the cruiser. Claiming near misses on the other ships, the Squadron Commander, Lieutenant Commander Robert B. Kelly, then reported moving in to strafe the transport's survivors in the water while the undamaged ships escaped at high speed! The position report was *exactly*

July 1, 1943

From: The Commanding Officer.
To :   The Commander Task Force 31.

Subject: U.S.S. Mc CAWLEY APA4, sinking of by enemy
              submarine action and events pertaining thereto.

Reference: (a) Commander-in-Chiefs Serial No. 3899 of
               October 19, 1943.

At 1943 love, June 30, 1943, the PAWNEE went along the port quarter of the U.S.S. LIBRA AKA12, to take over the towing of the U.S.S. MC CAWLEY in accordance with Commander Task Force 31 dispatch #0630 of June 30. The position was midway between the northern tip of Rendova Island and Mbalumbalu Island, in Blanche Channel, New Georgia Islands. Due to the lack of moon, plus low hanging rain clouds, visibility was extremely limited. The U.S.S. MC CALLA DD488 was present as screening vessel.

2.   The U.S.S. LIBRA secured a 5/8" wire messenger to the tow line, and passed it to the PAWNEE. The LIBRA then cut the tow line loose from her bitts with an acetylene torch, pulled into the clear and continued on her course. However, when the PAWNEE heaved in on the messenger it was discovered that it had been severed either by the LIBRA screw or by some sharp projection on her stern.

3.   PAWNEE then reversed her heading and approached the MC CAWLEY so as to lay her port quarter alongside the MC CAWLEY'S port bow. A working party prepared to board the MC CAWLEY to heave up and secure the PAWNEE'S tow wire to the MC CAWLEY'S bow.

4.   At 2024, when approximately 100 feet from the MC CAWLEY, a torpedo track was observed heading for the PAWNEE'S starboard bow. With full astern the PAWNEE gathered sufficient sternway to avoid the torpedo by about five feet. A few seconds thereafter two torpedoes struck the MC CAWLEY almost simultaneously, the first on her port quarter, the second just forward of the bridge, the latter hit causing a further explosion probably due to the ignition of a magazine.

5.   A fourth torpedo missed the PAWNEE'S bow by a matter of feet and full ahead with full left rudder checked her sternway sufficiently to cause the fifth and last observed torpedo to pass close astern. At about this time it is believed the conning tower of the submarine was seen to break water at a distance estimated to have been about 700 yards.

6.   The bow of the MC CAWLEY rose some 75 feet in the air and then slid under almost vertically at 2028. The MC CALLA, which had been on the far side of the MC CAWLEY at the time of the attack, circled around the PAWNEE and headed in the direction of the submarine, ordering the PAWNEE to procede to sea at maximum speed. PAWNEE complied.

F. J. GEORGE.

PAWNEE CAPTAIN'S ACTION REPORT
On the sinking of the McCAWLEY
(U.S. Navy Historical Center)

the latitude and longitude of the McCAWLEY's when she went down, and the time was 2028! Kelly and his damned PT-boats had *sunk the MAC*, and here he was claiming an heroic victory over a superior enemy force!!

Robert Bolling Kelly was one of the early heroes of World War II. As Executive Officer and second in command of our Motor Torpedo Boat Squadron in the Philippines, he and Squadron Commander John D. Bulkeley were credited with all sorts of damage to Japanese shipping, including sinking at least one cruiser. It was they who brought General Douglas MacArthur out from Corregidor to Australia, allowing him to escape Jap capture. Their exploits were chronicled in a book *They Were Expendable* (1942) almost immediately followed by a fictionalized Hollywood version in a movie with the same title. Robert Montgomery played the lead; and, ironically, the part of Kelly (with a different name) was played by John Wayne. The picture did much to glamorize the PT-boats and further their image as little guys beating up on the big, bad enemy. It made for pretty good propaganda.

When I finished reading the report, I exploded.

"That no good sonuvabitch!" I fumed.

The Coding Officer said: "Here", handing me the rest of the morning's traffic, "you can have the *honor* of taking it to the Admiral!" The inflection on the word "honor" was loaded with sarcasm.

Admiral Turner looked tired as he began reading. Then he broke into a short laugh that was more sardonic than humorous.

"Any reply, Admiral?"

"Yes", he said, "tell Kelly four words: *That was the MAC*."

I caught up with the Coding Officer, delivered the Admiral's instructions, and headed straight for the sack. I'd sleep ten straight hours, but not peacefully. My dreams were full of disturbing images. In one I was standing stark naked on a deck while enemy planes buzzed around like flies, bombs and torpedoes exploding and the ship beneath my feet bucking like a bronco.

The next day, when the guard mail came in it contained Kelly's Action Report entitled "Loss of the USS McCAWLEY—Report of Patrol in Support of Landings at Rendova, New Georgia." It was dated 1 July, 1943. The written report was a patent attempt to protect and cover his posterior; it contained some obvious variations from his radio report, as well as from the facts as reported by Admiral Wilkinson, the McCALLA, and the PAWNEE. Kelly was in PT-153, leading five other motor torpedo boats. At 2014, so his report goes, his radar "detected a very large target, distance 800 yards, surrounded by eight smaller targets, apparently landing craft." [There were only *four* targets, and no landing craft in the area!] "Targets appeared to be a large destroyer [probably the McCALLA], a 7,000-10,000 ton transport [clearly the McCAWLEY], and a small destroyer or transport [probably the PAWNEE]. . . . "

The PT-153 fired four torpedoes and Kelly ordered the other boats to press home the attack. His report says all four fish hit the transport. But the PAWNEE reported only two. He reports the torpedoes caused a large internal explosion which precluded "any possibility of her having remained afloat more than a very short period." The PT-118, according to Kelly, reported it fired two torpedoes at a small transport or destroyer (the PAWNEE?) and observed two direct hits! As the 118 retired, "her target appeared to be sinking by the stern." Obviously no such thing happened. Another boat, the PT-158, fired two fish at a large destroyer (the McCALLA?) but it maneuvered radically and no hits were observed "although one torpedo appeared to have passed under her."

The PT-158 then fired her last two fish in an overtaking shot at a retiring destroyer at a distance of 1,000 yards and reported they straddled the target. PT-160 reported it fired a single fish, at what she believed was a small transport, but missed. Then she chased a destroyer at high speed; but when the tin can reversed its course, the 160 recognized it as *the silhouette of a friendly ship*"! PT-159 and PT-162 reported sighting a destroyer, the 159 firing two torpedoes, both missing. The 162 did not fire because she was *"uncertain as to the target's identity"*!

Kelly admitted in his report: "No communications between forces ashore and the boats." And he commented further: "Due to the strange behavior of the vessels attacked as reported by various boat captains, this command has reason to believe that *the attack must have been delivered against our own forces.* However Commander General Aperient, Commander, Naval Base, Dowser, and Commander Attack Group, Amphibious Forces assured this command that it had to have been the enemy. All friendly forces had departed the afternoon before and were well clear of the area by the time of the attack. At no time during the torpedo attack were the PTs fired on or challenged. To date confirmation has not been obtained as to what ships were sunk, *although it is rumored that they were friendly.*"

Lieutenant Commander Kelly was already perceived as being an "Admiral's striker", i.e. an ambitious officer set on making a reputation for himself to get on an early track toward Flag status. But this whole incident "lost him a lot of numbers", and his apparent attempt to absolve himself of any responsibility was quite transparent. First, his Action Report was considerably toned down from his radio dispatch of the previous day, but he still included the claim that his boats had sunk

TWO ships! Second, the Action Report *must* have been written *after* he received confirmation it was the McCAWLEY that was sunk; otherwise, how would he have known to put the MAC's name on the cover of the report? Third, he claimed there were no challenges from the attacked ships. Yet, the McCALLA *did* challenge the PT-boats by blinker signal after the first fish were fired, but received no response. This was confirmed in both Admiral Wilkinson's and the McCALLA's reports. Fourth, Kelly's final line still referred to *"ships* sunk" (plural) and then added a strange line: " . . . *although it is rumored they were friendly."* What rumors? Where did they come from? Naval officers don't write Action Reports based on scuttlebutt. To quote Sergeant Joe Friday, "just the facts, ma'am, just the facts!"

But by far the most grievous part of this action, above and beyond sinking the MAC, was the danger to which nearly 500 men and two ships were exposed. There were some 300 ship's company on the McCALLA, plus nearly 100 survivors off the McCAWLEY, and the PAWNEE carried a crew of about 100. Certainly the McCAWLEY was a derelict ship, and her sinking would have been no further loss since she probably would not have lasted the night anyway. But the original and follow-up torpedo attacks on the destroyer and the tug came too damned close to causing a bona fide disaster.

The strange fate of the Wacky MAC is recounted in Vice Admiral George C. Dyer's two-volume biography of Kelly Turner, *The Amphibians Came to Conquer.* As Dyer put it: "Fortunately for the United States Navy, the motor torpedo boats . . . were poor shots."

Lieutenant Commander Kelly already had a reputation in the Navy as a "glory-hunter"; and many of his PT-boat skippers, like "members of the Harvard Yacht Club out on a spree", were following right in his wake. I detest glory-hunters. They get enlisted men killed.

You can bet Admiral Wilkinson, one of the targets of Kelly's torpedoes, wasn't very happy about it. And, of course, Kelly Turner wasn't turning handsprings, either. I'm not aware of any personal reprimand to the MTB Squadron Commander from his superiors; but Admiral Turner issued an order that effectively pulled the teeth of the Motor Torpedo Boat Squadrons by placing them under *direct* control of the Flag and assigning a liaison officer with the Staff to deal with them. No longer would the glory hunters roam at will, firing their torpedoes indiscriminately hither and yon at all and sundry. From then on, they'd hardly be able to warm up their engines without a special dispensation from the Boss Crocodile. And Robert Bolling Kelly's ambition to get that Admiral's star was relegated to the backwaters.

The beloved and legendary "Wacky MAC of the SoPac" rests today in some 340 fathoms at the bottom of Blanche Channel, midway between the tip of Rendova and Mbalumbalu Island in the Central Solomons' New Georgia chain. She may have been an old rust bucket, but she was our old rust bucket. And no other vessel in the Fleet did more with what she had than the U.S.S. McCAWLEY (APA-4)! In the end, the MAC's crew were right. No Jap S.O.B. would *sink* the Wacky MAC—it would take an American S.O.B., an Annapolis glory hunter no less, to accomplish that.

At the conclusion of his Action Report on the sinking of his command, Captain Robert H. "Speed" Rodgers wryly recommended there should be: "Full realization that attack transports are *combat* ships and should be so classified."

In my service record is this entry: "Participation in the occupation of RENDOVA ISLAND (NEW GEORGIA) while serving with Commander Task Force 31 aboard the U.S.S. McCAWLEY and on board when the McCAWLEY was lost as a result of an enemy torpedo plane attack June 30, 1943. R.K. Turner."

There were some collateral losses to the MAC's sinking. Many of Admiral Turner's (ComAmphibForSoPac) files from the Cactus-Ringbolt Operation (many of much historical value) had been stored aboard, as were personnel files and service records. Many of her logs and other records for the month of June likewise went down with her. Personally, all the gear stored in my locker was lost. Some uniforms, and such memorabilia as my Shellback and Golden Dragon certificates, all irreplaceable, were casualties, as was the medical report of my bout with malaria.

A couple of other postscripts: Officers of the Staff told me Admiral Turner never mentioned the McCAWLEY in their presence after the ship's sinking. Frenchy Maurais' recollection of Turner's commitment to the ship sheds some light on this:

"I first ran into Rear Admiral Richmond Kelly Turner", Frenchy wrote to me, "when he read his orders aboard ship in Wellington, New Zealand, in May or June of 1942. A fair rendering of his remarks were to the effect that:

" 'This is my Flagship and I'm going to ride her to Tokyo or until she's sunk.' "

17

THE SPIT KIT NAVY

It was SOP (Standard Operating Procedure) to wait 30 days after the date a ship was lost before releasing the news of the sinking. This allowed time to notify the families of casualties and survivors. In the case of the McCAWLEY, however, there was a SNAFU (situation normal all fouled up).

My family religiously listened each night to radio commentator Gabriel Heatter, and on the evening after the MAC went down (30 June, 1943) his lead story was: "The U.S.S. McCAWLEY, one of our troop transports, has been torpedoed and sunk during the invasion of Rendova Island in the South Pacific." My kid brother George remembers the newscast and the reaction to it. Needless to say there was panic at home.

Back in the Delaware Valley, my dad, sister, and grandmother contacted the Navy in Philadelphia, trying to get some information on my fate. My mother, in San Diego, virtually set up residence at 11th Naval District Headquarters. My name was neither on the list of survivors nor in the casualty count. All the Navy had was a roster of ship's company, and that did not include any members of Admiral Turner's Staff. Thus, for lack of any substantive information on my whereabouts, the Navy listed me in the only other category it had: *Missing In Action!* Obviously that only made things worse at home.

Back on the 'Canal, I was unaware of all this and, due to the press of daily duties, didn't get around to my usual monthly letter until a couple of weeks later. It was just a breezy note without any details included because of censorship, but it did let everyone in the States know I was O.K. By the time the letter got home, I'd been listed as MIA for a month.

Activity in the Camp Crocodile Radio Shack rose to a feverish pace. We were clearing large amounts of traffic to and from the ground forces in the New Georgias; as well as all the traffic with our seaborne units, with our coastwatchers, and with Admiral Halsey.

Little had changed at the Admiral's Camp in the three weeks since I'd left to go back aboard the McCAWLEY. On the nights of 5, 8, and 10

July, Jap bombers were overhead, raiding again, each time spending over thirty minutes dropping their "eggs" on targets from Henderson Field to Koli Point. On the night of the 11th, we got it long and heavy. In three successive raids between 2000 and 0315, the Bettys plastered Carney Field, this time by-passing Henderson. During the second Condition Red, I almost ended up on the casualty list. As petty officer of the watch, it was my job to secure the Radio Shack whenever a raid was imminent. When the sirens went off, all the other radiomen scampered to the bomb shelters while I cut the power and insured the lights were out. This night, though, the sirens were a little late in sounding the alarm.

As I stepped out on the small front porch of the Quonset hut, I heard the unmistakable screech of a dive bomber. Too far from any foxhole to take cover, I was caught in the open and could hear the "whistle" of a loosed bomb overhead. The only refuge was a small pile of palm logs a few yards away. I dove behind them, flattening my body as close to the damp earth as possible, getting dirt up my nose. None too soon. The Jap had dropped a "daisy cutter" anti-personnel bomb. As it exploded, I could hear the shrapnel zinging inches above my head and chewing into the palm logs. The Marine AA battery next door finally got the Jap's range as he tried for altitude and brought him down. I lay quivering on the ground. When I finally arose, I rubbed my hand along the top palm log. The bark was all shaven off by the shards of steel from that "daisy cutter", the log as smooth as if planed down by a carpenter. Had I been on my feet I would have been cut in two. My guardian angel must've been close by that night.

There was a single raid on July 12th, but multiple raids on the 16th and 17th when fuel dumps, a food supply warehouse, and other targets were destroyed. I spent most of both nights in a foxhole. Would the night raids never end?

Meanwhile, as the news filtered back to us, the War around the New Georgias was not going well for the Good Guys. On the night of 4/5 July, one of our coastwatchers sighted a ten-destroyer enemy squadron heading "down the Slot" into that expanse of water between the islands of Kolombangara and New Georgia formally known as Kula Gulf. This "Tokyo Express", under Admiral Akiyama, was attempting to reinforce the Nips' ground forces under General Sasaki. Cruiser Division 9 (CruDiv 9), the HONOLULU (CL-48), ST. LOUIS (CL-49), and HELENA (CL-50), with screening destroyers, was our first line of defense.

I hurried a message out from Admiral Turner to Admiral Walden L. Ainsworth to intercept the hostiles, cutting the orders myself.

The Battle of Kula Gulf was joined. The Japs launched their torpedo attack as our ships' guns opened fire at about 10,000 yards, our first salvos sinking a destroyer—the NIIZUIKI. The Jap flagship went down with almost all hands, including the Captain and Admiral Akiyama. Continuing American gunfire forced the remaining hostile ships, some slightly damaged, to retreat, but not before three of their Long Lance torpedoes tore into the HELENA, breaking her back. When the casualty report came in, it listed 198 men of her crew dead and 38 missing. Eventually some 740, after a long ordeal for many, were heroically rescued from the cruel sea and jungle.

One of the cruiser's survivors was a coxswain named Ted Blahnik. Many years later Ted would become President of the Guadalcanal Campaign Veterans association. When I told him I felt guilty about sending the HELENA up the Slot that night, getting her sunk, he replied: "Well, you sent the best ship you had for the job."

The next day, a report came in that a second enemy destroyer had run aground and was polished off by Air Solomons planes. But the Japs had successfully landed 1,600 fresh troops. Ashore, Operation TOE-NAILS was running into a plethora of problems; and the entire plan to secure the airfield at Munda Point, on the southwestern tip of New Georgia, according to schedule was in dire straits. The Army was dragging its feet. The timetable called for a combined assault on Munda Airfield on 8 July, but it had to be abandoned.

Major General John H. Hester, commanding the Army's 43rd Division, which had been landed on the southwest coast of New Georgia from Rendova, had not gotten his forces to their jump-off positions in time. While he'd lost only 90 men to enemy gunfire at that point, the 43rd (according to the Army's own *History*) had over a 1,000 men out of action in the first three days: "An especially large number of casualties was caused not by wounds or infectious diseases but by mental disturbance. Between fifty and a hundred men were leaving the line every day with troubles which were diagnosed as 'war neuroses'. . . . "

Hester's communications were in such shambles that an inquiry from Admiral Turner as to the whereabouts of Marine Colonel Harry Liversedge, commanding the Northern Landing Group, went unanswered for a full day, and when the reply came, it said: "No contact with Liversedge." Major General Oscar W. Griswold, XIV Corps Commander and Hester's superior, after a personal inspection of the combat area, concluded: "Things are going badly. Forty-third Division about to fold up." Griswold relieved Hester of his command and took over the reins himself.

Colonel Harry "The Horse" Liversedge was having problems of his own, but not due to wavering troops. The Northern Landing Force's mission was to "close the back door to Munda" and prevent the Japs from reinforcing their troops via barges from the neighboring island of Kolombangara. With 2,600 Marines of the 1st and 4th Raider Battalions (the 1st Marine Raider Regiment) and the Army's 3rd Battalion, 148th Infantry, Liversedge landed at Rice Anchorage, the early morning of 5 July, with the intention to seize Enogai Inlet and then take the Jap garrison at Bairoko Harbor, "port of entry" for enemy reinforcements. It took five days for Liversedge's Landing Group to move from Rice Anchorage and to capture Enogai Inlet. The Japs' Kure 6th Naval Landing Force and 4th Company, 13th Infantry, contested every step of the way.

The Marines' advance was hindered by an almost impenetrable jungle, heavy rains and swollen streams, lack of communications and supply problems. The loss of radio communications due to atmospherics necessitated stringing telephone wire and using the Raiders' Navajo Indian "code talkers". If the Japs somehow tapped into the lines, they wouldn't be able to understand the Navajo speaking in their own native tongue. The Indians were used to facilitate necessary communications among our forces. Pretty clever, we native Americans! Supplies were brought up by native bearers, just like in the old Tarzan movies. Effective movements were complicated by maps and charts which were both inadequate and incorrect; the jungle made aerial photographs impossible. Despite the obstacles, Liversedge secured Enogai, counting over 350 enemy killed. Marine losses were 54 dead and 91 wounded.

It's roughly about 3,000 yards from Enogai Inlet to Bairoko Harbor. But it would take the Northern Landing Group until 24 August to dig the Japs out, and I would have a small part in that operation.

On the night of 12/13 July, the U.S. Navy took another beating in Kula Gulf. The second Battle of Kula Gulf, similar to the first engagement, was eventually dubbed the Battle of Kolombangara, for the big island to the west known to the Solomon Islanders as "King of the Waters". Details of the battle would be learned later. On his fifteenth combat mission up the Slot, Admiral "Pug" Ainsworth's force of three cruisers (HONOLULU, ST. LOUIS, and H.M.N.Z.S. LEANDER, a Royal New Zealand Navy ship replacing the sunken HELENA) and ten destroyers ran into Admiral Izaki's force of the light cruiser JINTSU, five destroyers, and four destroyer-transports.

Though the Japs had no radar, their radar detection devices located our ships before our radar found them. Once again, our ships closed range within 10,000 yards and opened fire on the biggest blip on our radar screens. Our gunners quickly devastated the Jap cruiser, which went down with all hands including the Admiral and his flag. But the U.S. force was unknowingly within range of Jap Long Lance torpedoes, one of them slamming into the New Zealand cruiser LEANDER and knocking her out of action virtually for the rest of the War.

With the Jap destroyers on the run, Admiral Ainsworth pursued the "bastards" up the Slot to effect a rout. But the wily Nips hid in a rain squall, swiftly reloaded their torpedo tubes, doubled back and fired some 30 torpedoes at our ships, sinking a destroyer and knocking our remaining cruisers out for many months. The crippled cruisers were the HONOLULU and the ST. LOUIS. The destroyer sunk was the GWIN, which not only had survived the hit at Rendova two weeks before but was the only tin can to survive the battleship action concluding the Naval Battle of Guadalcanal exactly eight months earlier. The Jap destroyers got away scot free (though three of them would be sunk by our planes within two weeks) and their destroyer-transports delivered 1,200 troops to Kolombangara. At the time, our Commanders sincerely thought we had won both night battles in Kula Gulf, claiming to have sunk several Nip ships. The Japs made even more extravagant claims. Each side consoled themselves with "imaginary damage inflicted on the enemy" (Morison).

According to U.S. Navy historian Morison, who was with Admiral Ainsworth at Kolombangara, upon hindsight the Japanese were still superior in night fighting. But their victories added up to a defeat—since they could not afford their losses in ships, planes, and pilots. On the American side, we were still incredibly and inexplicably ignorant of the range and speed of the Jap torpedoes, stubbornly refusing to be taught by the enemy. "Perhaps it is inherent in American thinking to assume that our own gadgets and machinery, from plumbing to atomic bombs, must be the world's best. A dangerous way of thinking, indeed."

Meanwhile, back at Camp Crocodile, some of us were indulging in one of the few diversions we had—blackjack. As we played, we lamented the loss of Admiral Kelly Turner on 15 July. He was moving on to command the newly formed Central Pacific Amphibious Force, and was relieved by Admiral "Teddy" Wilkinson who'd been "in training" under Turner for some months. Kelly Turner was "my Admiral" and I was sorry to see him go. He was one hell of an officer who treated me very well. The true amphibious genius of the Pacific War, it was he, not General MacArthur nor several other claimants to the idea, who developed the famed "island hopping" strategy that considerably shortened the War.

Vice Admiral George C. Dyer, in his two-volume history of Kelly Turner's wartime career *The Amphibians Came to Conquer*, clears up the controversy. In a dispatch from Admiral Halsey (ComSoPac's 11042 of July, 1943) to Turner, Halsey used the term "by-passing"—the first time it appears in any messages or written communication of any kind. The Bull asked Turner for comment on the tactic which would "leapfrog" over major Jap bases and "leave them dying on the vine." It was Turner who then devised and executed the strategy that was followed in planning the future campaigns in the Pacific. I thought highly of my Admiral. He not only was one of the finest officers under whom I served—Admiral Richmond Kelly Turner was "good people".

The card players' conversation took a different tack when I couldn't get a cigarette lit. Inadvertently, I'd left the top off the cigarette can earlier; and, in a short time, the humidity had made the smokes so damp you couldn't have lit 'em with a blowtorch. "There goes a whole damn' 50 cents worth of Luckies", I lamented.

"You won't have to worry about that when we get our new Command ship", one of the players (whose nickname "Buckshot" was of obscure origin) remarked. Immediately, we all began to speculate about the newly designed all-communications Command vessels that had been promised for future amphib operations. We wondered when *ours* would get to us. I was voicing my usual complaint about the stinking 'Canal, coupled with my fervent wish to get back to sea—somehow or other.

Jack Frost had wandered over and had been listening to us for a few minutes. Then he turned to me.

"If you're so all that damned anxious for sea duty, Hutch, I can arrange it", he said.

I looked at him. He hadn't just come by to watch sailors playing cards. The grin on his face was akin to that of a fisherman when a bass takes the bait. I had a feeling I was about to be hooked.

"Mr. Frost", I said with a shake of my head, "you've got me volunteering for temporary duty again, haven't you?" It was more a statement than a question. I already knew his answer.

"Not unless one of these other people want to go."

My good old shipmates suddenly got *very* interested in the cards on the blanket. I sighed.

"Me and my big mouth", I said. "Where to this time, Sir?"

"You're to report to the Captain aboard the APc-38 tomorrow morning."

"What, pray tell", I asked sardonically, "is an APc? Sounds like something you take for a headache."

"It's one of those little coastal transports. You know, little green vessels." I vaguely remembered seeing one or two. They were new in the area.

"She's going up the Slot to Enogai Inlet. The Raiders need food and supplies. They've taken casualties, and they'll have to be evacuated. Get your gear together. Commander Welker will have your orders ready shortly."

"Aye, aye, Sir."

On 27 July, I reported aboard the U.S.S. APc-38, Lieutenant (junior grade) Thomas L. Ray, USNR, commanding.

An APc (Auxiliary Coastal Transport) was an all-wooden vessel designed for inter-island movement of small numbers of troops and cargo, particularly in the narrow and shallow confines of bays and inlets where deeper-draft ships could not maneuver. Drawing only nine feet of water, the APc-38 was 103 feet long with a 21-foot beam; she was powered by a 500-horsepower diesel engine, propelling a single screw. She had a forward hold with a capacity to carry about 40 tons of cargo or 60 troops; a single boom was rigged, capable of hoisting loads up to 2,500 pounds.

The ship's original armament consisted of a "main battery" of four 20-millimeter Oerlikon machineguns, but two .50-caliber machineguns were later added after arriving in the forward area. On the after bulkhead of the Bridge were two Thompson .45-caliber subma-chineguns. The top speed of these vessels was about ten or eleven knots. In the South Pacific, all were painted in solid dark green camouflage so they'd be hard to detect against a jungle background. Because of their shallow draft, they often would pull in close enough to shore to be hidden by overhanging vegetation.

APc's were what the Navy calls *"Spit Kits"* (floating ashtrays!)—the all-encompassing descriptive term for commissioned smaller craft, usu-ally non-combatant, such as yard tugs, rescue vessels, landing and patrol craft, and various other auxiliaries. PT-boats were often included, particularly when the reference was meant to be derogatory. The APc-38 carried a complement of three officers and 22 enlisted men, including one radioman. Since the upcoming mission would require round-the-clock guarding of a tactical frequency (3000 kilocycles), I was aboard to share the duty. We would stand "watch and watch", i.e. back-to-back watches.

To care for the Marine casualties on our return from Enogai Inlet, a Medical Officer, Lieutenant J.D. Johnson, two pharmacist's mates, and a hospital corpsman were aboard for temporary duty. The additional personnel made for overcrowding on the tiny vessel. The hold was loaded with seven drums of diesel fuel, several bags of mail, and 10,000 "B" rations. Eight Marines came aboard, on their way to join the 4th Raiders. And we would later pick up two native pilots to guide us through the reefs and shallows.

U.S.S. APc 38

(U.S. Navy Photo - National Archives)

Our voyage northward from Lunga Point would take us two days, timed to arrive at Enogai Inlet under cover of darkness. On the second day, we lay over at Segi Point for a few hours to avoid arriving too early. Our anchorage was near the end of a coral-surfaced airstrip, and I was surprised to see Army P-40 fighter planes operating from the field—those models General Claire Chennault's "Flying Tigers" had flown and made famous in China.

Prior to getting underway from Segi, our two Melanesian pilots came aboard. The natives sat on the port side of the deck house just abaft the Bridge. I offered them cigarettes from my pack of Luckies, but the first one refused. The other took five smokes, put all of them in his mouth at once, and lit them, puffing away like all the stacks of a Pittsburgh steel mill. In my best pidjin, I asked the first native why he didn't smoke, while his mate seemed to enjoy it so much. Drawing himself up to his full five feet one and sticking out his chest, the "boy" looked derisively at his companion.

"Him fella b'long Catholic. Me fella b'long *Protestant!*"

The Baptist missionaries had done their job well on this Solomon Islander. But Christianity, like everything else in this remote part of the world, eventually became altered to suit the ways of the inhabitants. The missionaries were the South Pacific version of the old circuit riders of America's pioneer days. They'd come to a village, hold a great revival, and report back to their churches that they'd converted all the natives. Then they'd move on to the next island. Almost before they were out of sight, the converts would begin to backslide and/or adapt what they liked to their own mores.

Sooner or later, another missionary of another denomination would show up, convert them all over again—to Catholicism, Methodism, or whatever the faith of the missionary. To the islanders, this had all the aspects of a game; and, to them, it was great entertainment. The one element of these evangelistic visits the natives dearly loved was the singing of hymns. They would joyfully mix Baptist, Methodist, Catholic, and other denominational songs, without discrimination, into their own culture, which was only one generation removed from ritual headhunting. They were pretty good singers, too.

The pause at Segi Point gave me an chance to size up my shipmates. The APc's, newly arrived from the States, were manned by crews that were as green as gourds. It was the first time at sea for the majority, and their training had been short. Most were fresh out of boot camp or trade schools where they'd had only abbreviated, howbeit intense, schooling. The demands of the War dictated getting as many bodies as possible out into the Fleet in the least time possible. I thought of the phrase seasoned old salts use to put upstart short-timers in their place: "I've passed more lighthouses than you have telephone poles."

In this case I could have truthfully said it to most, if not all, of the APc-38's crew. Having seen the war movies and newsreels, they'd envisioned themselves steaming into war on a battleship, carrier, cruiser, or destroyer with all guns blazing. Yet, here they were on an orange crate with a cracker box on top—a glorified fishing boat that didn't even have a name, just a number—plying up and down unfamiliar seas to deliver unglamorous cargo, mail, and passengers to strange places with unpronounceable names. They'd been rushed into this War with little preparation for the travails they'd encounter. To their credit, in the true All-American way, they came through it remarkably well; attaining maturity and confidence, coping with the stress, anxieties, and fears that accompany both the anticipation of and the actuality of combat. They were Spit Kit sailors.

As for me, it was another case of "what the hell am I doing here?" Everybody else is going up the Slot in cruisers and destroyers, but me—I gotta go up this damn' place in an almost defenseless, highly vulnerable little craft. What if we run head on into the Tokyo Express? Heaven help us! I didn't *have* to be here. Mr. Frost would have sent someone else If I'd begged off. Whatever motivated me to volunteer was buried deep inside; at 21 years old, I had neither the knowledge nor experience to practice introspection. If anything, I attributed it to wanderlust; and to just wanting to get off the beach at Guadalcanal—that steaming, stinking island.

But maybe Joseph Conrad was right when he wrote that the sea has ever been "the accomplice of human restlessness." Perhaps there is something to Longfellow's lines:

> My soul is full of longing for the secret of the sea. . . .
> Only those who brave its dangers comprehend its mystery.

On New Georgia's Dragon's Peninsula, the back door to Munda, Colonel Liversedge had begun an assault against the Jap positions around Bairoko Harbor on 20 July, 1943. He jumped off with a force consisting of the 1st and 4th Raider Battalions moving along the Enogai-Bairoko Trail; and with the Army's 3rd Battalion, 148th Infantry, attacking from the east. Except for a few 81-millimeter mortars with the Army units, he had no artillery nor heavy mortars. Close air support was impossible in the heavy jungle, and a requested air strike on Bairoko got lost in poor communications and botched red tape. Colonel Delbert Schultz's 3rd Battalion, 148th Infantry, was involved in a fight to the southeast and out of communication with Liversedge.

The operation seemed doomed from the start, and after two days of heavy fighting the Marine and Army battalions were forced to withdraw back to Enogai to reorganize. Although the opposing forces were roughly equal in size, the enemy was well-dug-in and had both heavy artillery and heavy mortars. Casualties were rising at a high rate among the Marine units. They had advanced to within 500 yards of Bairoko Harbor; but without sufficient heavy weapons to counter the fire of the Jap's 90-millimeter mortars, and without reserves to move forward, the attack stalled.

As the Northern Landing Group began its preparations for another attempt to wrest the strategic harbor from the enemy, the APc-38, in company with the APc-25, was on its way with supplies and medical assistance. We got underway from Segi Point on 28 July and headed northwestward. The sea was choppy as the Skipper steered a course through Njai Passage, and the ship began to pitch heavily. Our native pilots kept giving directions as we weaved among the reefs and shoals. At two or three points, the water was so shallow we scraped our keel on the bottom as the APc fell off into troughs. By 1630, we'd arrived at Mongo Entrance to Kula Gulf.

We cleared Mongo at 1817 as darkness fell, and began to look for our PT-boats off Visu Visu Point. The MTBs were supposed to be our escort, but they failed to put in an appearance. At 1935, we heard a plane overhead in the darkness and killed our engine. The Jap aircraft, probably a float Zero from the seaplane base at Rekata Bay on Santa Isabel Island, suddenly came out of the black of night less than 400 feet above the water and passed close abeam our starboard side but apparently did not see us. Within minutes, a heavy rain squall concealed us and the danger passed. The tactic of stopping our engine was a riverboat gamble. In the highly phosphorescent waters, any movement produced an easily visible tell-tale wake. By killing our power, the wake disappeared. But that left us dead in the water—in irons, as an old sailor would say. If spotted and attacked, we couldn't get way up fast enough to maneuver, making us a stationary target. So, as they say in Brooklyn, "yer pays yer money and yer takes yer cherce."

Without the PT-boat escort, we proceeded toward Rice Anchorage where a Higgins boat was to guide us in to Enogai Inlet. It, too, didn't show. At that moment, a Jap plane of unknown type flew over us and dropped a pair of 100-pound bombs at Rice Anchorage as we passed close to shore. Without guidance, we missed the entrance to Enogai and continued farther along the coast. Suddenly, Captain Ray ordered a "hard to port" and, with a quick U-turn, the APc swung completely around, retracing our course. We had come in close—*too* close—to

CAPTURED JAPANESE "FLOAT ZERO"
The type that operated over Kula Gulf, 1943.
(U.S. Navy Photo - Real War Photos)

Banoko Island, a Jap stronghold. "Kee-rist!" I exclaimed as I watched the island fade away astern. "We almost landed right in the Japs' laps!"

Captain Ray was furious. In unfamiliar waters, with few defined landmarks and those obscured by darkness and frequent rain squalls, we had relied on the PT-boat escort to get us safely to our destination. Without them, we'd almost come to a disastrous fate. The Skipper's opinion of those MTBs was well-peppered with profanity. Easing back along the shore, we located the entrance to Enogai Inlet. Almost simultaneously, the Marines spotted us and signaled by light. A Higgins boat approached and guided us close to the boat pool where working parties came aboard, discharging our cargo in less than an hour. As soon as the forward hold was cleared, some twenty casualties were brought aboard, and treatment of them by Dr. Johnson and his pharmacist's mates began immediately.

While unloading was going on, I stood on the wing of the Bridge with a Thompson gun cradled in my arm, keeping an anxious eye to seaward across the Gulf toward Kolombangara. We knew the Japs were reinforcing their troops on New Georgia, transporting them in *daihatsu*—armed landing barges that carried much more fire power than we had. Bairoko Harbor, preferred debarkation point for enemy troops, was a scant 3,000 yards from our position. Two nights earlier, our PTs had a running skirmish with the *daihatsu*, and tonight there were flares and tracers all over the Gulf, near Kolombangara in particular. Tracers were stitching the black sky with orange threads less than five miles to our west. The tracers were flying horizontally, indicating the scrap was between surface units.

Around midnight, we could hear and see a great deal of activity only a few miles away, including flares dropped by float Zeros and weapons fire, but we weren't close enough to determine the identity of the combatants. Captain Ray said he thought the PT-boats were probably skirmishing with landing barges, again. The scrap, whatever it was, continued as we completed taking the Marines' casualties aboard and made preparations for getting underway. Then some of the fight spilled over to our area. We were just off Rice Anchorage when a Jap plane came out of nowhere, clearing our mast top so closely we could see his exhaust flames. We thought he was after us; but if so, he missed by about a hundred yards, dropping two 100-pound bombs near the Marine positions on the beach. He was in and out before we could bring our guns to bear. We spotted another plane heading toward us, but by that time the batteries on shore opened up and he took off back across the Gulf.

Arriving in the comparatively safe area at Mongo Entrance at 0730, the Skipper told me to inform "ComTaskForce 61" of our status. I cranked up a transmitter and reported directly to Admiral Wilkinson at Koli that we'd successfully completed our mission and were proceeding as ordered to Tulagi. Then, for the first time in over thirteen hours, my body relaxed and the hair on the back of my neck no longer stood up. It had been a long siege of tension, watchfulness, and anxiety.

In a War in which much of the action was at night, the sight of flares was one of the most frightening of experiences, and we'd seen a lot of them. When a target, real or suspected, was spotted by the Japs, the illumination by flares was followed by bombs and/or gunfire. Of all my memories of the War, there are none more vivid than the sight of flares overhead and the apprehension that followed. Only the sound of air raid sirens rivals it in bringing that rush of fear and pounding of heart.

We stopped briefly at Segi Point before going on leisurely toward Tulagi. The APc-25 detoured to the Russells to pick up guard mail and regular mail for both ships, then caught up with us as we steamed into Purvis Bay.

The mention of "Tulagi" and the Bay always brings two stories to mind. The first, surely apocryphal, is one of many accounts of how General Douglas MacArthur got his demeaning nickname. It was said he came to Florida Island on an inspection tour. Fully aware of frequent Jap air raids, his first words on stepping on the dock were: "Where's the nearest foxhole?"

A nearby Mud Marine was supposed to have replied: "Dig your own dugout, Doug!"

But the name "Dugout Doug" most assuredly was hung on MacArthur by his own men when he holed up in Fortress Corregidor in the Philippines and came out only once to visit the fighting front on Bataan during the entire campaign. As they—"the battling bastards of Bataan . . . no mama, no papa, no Uncle Sam"—used to sing to the tune of the Battle Hymn of the Republic:

> Dugout Doug MacArthur lies a-shakin' on the Rock
> Safe from all the bombers and from any sudden shock.

In any event, one of the most famous Generals in American history will always be known to the Navy and Marines of the Pacific, and to some of his own Army personnel as well, as "Dugout Doug". As previously intimated, MacArthur was known in the Navy by worse appellations, such as that "self-advertising Son of a Bitch".

The other story is fully substantiated. In fact, I saw the sign, myself. Overlooking Tulagi's harbor was a big billboard, put there at the order of South Pacific Theater Commander Admiral William F. "Bull" Halsey himself. It succinctly denoted our purpose as South Pacific combat men. In huge letters, the sign read:

ADMIRAL HALSEY says "*Kill japs, kill japs. KILL MORE JAPS*"!
You will help kill the yellow bastards if YOU DO YOUR JOB WELL

The following comment on Halsey's sign by U.S. Navy historian and liberal Harvard Professor Morison, is noteworthy: "This may shock you, reader; but it is exactly how we felt. We were fighting no civilized, knightly war. We cheered when the Japs were dying. We were back to primitive days of Indian fighting on the American frontier; no holds barred and no quarter. The Japs wanted it that way, thought they could thus terrify an 'effete democracy'; and that is what they got, with all the additional horrors of war that modern science can produce."

After debarkation of the Marine casualties, we remained in Tulagi Harbor. One day we were filling our diesel tanks at the refueling dock, when an ensign walked out on the pier and shouted up to Captain Ray.

"Did you see anything of a damaged PT-boat or sight any men in the water up the Slot?" The Skipper shook his head and asked what had happened.

"Well, one of our boats was run down in the Blackett Strait and cut in half by a Jap destroyer. The boat's missing and so is the crew. They've got the whole damn' Navy looking for 'em. The C.O. is some ambassador's son by the name of Canaday, Canady, Kennedy or some such Irish name."

We left the fuel dock and moved over to a small cove to berth. From 7 August until the 13th, we and the APc-25 lay in the cove, conducting routine upkeep and repairs and taking on fresh water, provisions,and ammo. It was a welcome respite. We took baths by swimming in the Bay, always with an armed shark watch on top of the deck house. And we had time to get our laundry done as well as "shoot the bull".

Almost all of our bull sessions were dominated by what we considered the incredible, the unbelievable: that a swift, highly maneuverable PT-boat could have been run down and rammed by a big, slower Nip destroyer. The only way that could have happened, we concluded, was that the boat was either broken down, or that the crew of the MTB *had* to have been goofing off. Turns out we were right on the second count. Between snatches of information we picked up from other vessels while berthed, and what I learned later when I returned to Camp Crocodile, the whole incident was very strange. I would not know until many years later that it would become part of the nation's history—howbeit with some significant, and *intentional*, omissions and distortions.

Fifteen torpedo boats, divided into four sections, went in to interdict

ADMIRAL HALSEY'S SIGN IN TULAGI HARBOR
(Courtesy Ted Blahnik, Guadalcanal Campaign Veterans)

a four-destroyer enemy force from getting through Blackett Strait and delivering reinforcements to Jap positions. Each MTB was armed with four torpedoes, a smaller model than those our destroyers carried. In an implausible scenario, most of our boats fired their full complement of fish, maybe fifty in all, in runs on the Jap tin cans and didn't hit a damned thing! Granted our torpedoes weren't the greatest, but this was ridiculous and could only be attributed to poor marksmanship. One of the Peter Tares, commanded by Lieutenant (jg) John F. Kennedy, didn't even make a torpedo run. When a Jap tin can illuminated his PT-109 with a searchlight, Kennedy turned and ran for safety. The destroyers got through and unloaded their troops and cargo.

In the wee small hours of the morning, the night of 1/2 August, as part of a three-boat picket line set up to warn of any return of the hostiles, the PT-109 was sitting out in the Strait. As we had surmised at the first reports we got, the crew of the MTB was into serious goofing off. At least four men were "crapped out", either in their sacks or on deck; the radioman wasn't monitoring the tactical circuit or, as one report said, had it turned off (which, after the McCAWLEY's sinking, didn't surprise me at all); and only one of the boat's three engines was on line, a serious breach of squadron standing orders. The C.O. was lounging on the Bridge, engaged in a bull session with one of the crew.

The Skipper of one of the other picket-line PTs reported excellent visibility, up to 1,800 or more yards. He spotted the phosphorescent bow wave of a destroyer heading straight for the PT-109 and immediately radioed a warning. With no radioman listening to the circuit, the alarm went unheeded. Too late, someone on Kennedy's boat spotted the on-rushing tin can. Time was too short and the one engine on line was not enough to power the boat out of the way to safety. The Jap ship (later identified as the AMAGIRI) slashed into the PT-109's plywood hull, cutting it completely in half. Two of the crew were killed instantly.

By the time I got back to the Admiral's Camp, the saga of the PT-109 was over. From his mountain hideout, a coastwatcher named Evans had spotted the wreckage of the PT-boat's hull and sent out his native scouts in canoes to look for any survivors. Six days after the MTB had gone down, Kennedy and the other survivors were rescued. Around Camp Crocodile where PT-boat people were not, understandably, held in high regard anyhow, the spectacle of a Peter Tare being run down by a Jap destroyer had become one big joke. Lieutenant (jg) Kennedy, the PT-109's irresponsible Skipper, was the laughingstock of the South Pacific.

How did it happen that the PT-109 permitted the Jap destroyer to catch it unawares? As a matter of fact, that eminent expert on PT-boats Robert Bolling Kelly himself once said—long before the Kennedy tragi-comedy of errors: "Looked like a Jap destroyer. Now an MTB in good condition can outrun any warship afloat." According to William Breuer's *Devil Boats: The PT War Against Japan* (1987), when his rescuer Lieutenant William F. Liebenow in the PT-157 put the question to Jack Kennedy, the Skipper of the PT-109 replied: "Lieb, *to tell you the truth, I don't know.*"

It's what happened afterward that galls every good sailor who knows the full story. Ambassador Joe Kennedy, who'd made his fortunes illegally running Scotch whiskey into the U.S. from Canada during Prohibition, and who had used his millions to buy both "respect" and his way into influence in the Democratic Party, was bound and determined to make his son a hero. He even tried to get Jack the Congressional Medal of Honor or, failing that, at least the Navy Cross. But apparently on this score the upper Navy or government echelons were not intimi-dated by old Joe Kennedy's money or political clout. They weren't buying the planted news stories that made the younger Kennedy a big hero by juggling the facts.

However, the old man did manage to save his son's skin. Had JFK been any other PT-boat Skipper, he certainly would have faced a board of inquiry and the possibility of a court-martial with a charge of criminal negligence. At the very least, he would have gotten a severe reprimand for gross incompetence. But here the old man's clout apparently worked. None of those actions were brought. Kennedy did end up with a Navy and Marine Corps Medal and a Purple Heart—the former for saving the lives of three crewmen whom he'd put in jeopardy in the first place, and the latter for a bad back he'd had even before entering the service.

The deliberately distorted story, repeated so many times, it became "fact" was a major political plus when JFK ran for office, and it got wide play during his presidential campaign. The movie *PT-109*, with script apparently approved by old Joe Kennedy, furthered the myth of his son's "heroism". Omitted are the facts that twice in one night the erstwhile Skipper of the PT-109 was tried and found wanting.

As always seemed to happen when officers screwed up, enlisted men paid the price. This time, two were dead.

18
FAREWELL TO IRON BOTTOM BAY

On 13 August, 1943, orders arrived for me via the guard mail boat from Camp Crocodile. I first thought I was headed back ashore, but I was to report to the U.S.S. APc-25, J.D. Cartano, Lieutenant, USNR, Commanding. Gathering up my gear, I walked across the pier to the spit kit just as Captain Cartano was opening orders for the APc's next mission.

Three days earlier, Marine Colonel Harry "The Horse" Liversedge had begun the second assault on Bairoko Harbor. Now, with reinforcements, the Northern Landing Group consisted of the Marines' 1st and 4th Raider Battalions and the Army's 1st Battalion, 27th Infantry, and the 3rd Battalion, 148th Infantry, plus air defense from Battery K, 11th Marine Defense Battalion. Aided by native scouts, the Colonel's Group attacked down the Enogai-Bairoko Trail.

The battle for Bairoko was underway as the APc-25 proceeded to Lunga Point anchorage to rendezvous with two landing craft, the LCT-325 and LCT-327. Our cargo was sorely needed medical supplies and mail. The LCTs carried equipment, supplies, and Marine replacements. The APc-25 was to lead the little convoy back to Enogai and, upon delivery of our cargo, evacuate casualties.

While waiting for the LCTs to join us, we lay about a half mile off Guadalcanal in the Transport Area. Everyone aboard was on alert. The night before, we had watched from Tulagi as our night fighters shot down a pair of Jap bombers over Henderson Field. This night, for several minutes, we'd been observing anti-aircraft fire over the Russell Islands to the northwest. At 2015, our radio crackled "CONDITION RED" and we immediately went to General Quarters. Two Betty bombers were speared in the searchlights over Henderson, dropping both bombs and flares.

At 2114, with the arrival of the LCTs, we got underway to carry out our sailing orders and began circling while the two landing craft maneuvered into convoy formation. Then, things got hot in our bailiwick. Seaward stationed destroyers opened up on low-flying aircraft, splash-

277

U.S.S. APc 25

(U.S. Navy Photo - National Archives)

ing one that burst into flames and cartwheeled into the water. The tin cans, joined now by other ships in the anchorage, continued fire.

We could hear the sounds of aircraft engines. But it was one of those deep dark, moonless nights off Lunga Point and our lookouts couldn't spot any of the planes. Then, the APc-38, several hundred yards from us, reported a torpedo plane (with its running lights on!) passing directly over her and launching its fish. Albert Allen, a signalman aboard the U.S.S. FULLER (APA-7), wrote in a 1986 letter to me that his ship was in the anchorage that night and he was on the Signal Bridge. He said the FULLER's 20-millimeters on the Bridge opened fire, aiming seaward. The anchor watch yelled to the Bridge that a torpedo was passing just ahead of the ship's stem.

Directly in the path of the torpedo was the U.S.S. JOHN PENN (APA-23). In seconds, the ship exploded with a tremendous blast as the fish rammed into her starboard quarter at Number Three Hold. Allen surmised she may have had ammunition in that space. I recall a survivor saying he thought aviation gasoline was in the hold. Whatever was stored there produced a blinding orange flash, lifting the stern of the JOHN PENN high out of the water. Both Allen and I recall seeing her mast go whirling through the air, like a huge helicopter rotor, amid all the other debris blown skyward.

Captain Cartano, about as gutsy as any officer under whom I served, signaled "emergency full speed ahead!" Leaving our little convoy behind us, the APc-25 was alongside the JOHN PENN in less than three minutes—the first vessel of any kind to arrive—taking a position near the transport's stern aport, where a large number of crewmen were already in the water. Ignoring the burning oil, the Skipper took our little wooden-hulled spit kit right up and into the flames and kept her there, even though the oil continued to spread around us.

Getting in that close was dangerous, not only because of the burning oil, but we couldn't know if more explosions were imminent, whether we might be caught in the undertow if or when the transport went down, nor whether there were more Jap planes around that would sight us silhouetted against the flames. But that did not deter J.D. Cartano. All he saw were many men in the sea, struggling away from their sinking ship and fighting to stay afloat. He maneuvered the spit kit in so close the flaming oil was singeing all the paint off our bow.

The crew of the APc-25 immediately went to the rescue of the JOHN PENN survivors. Four of them, led by Lieutenant (jg) Burdick, not waiting for the ship to heave to, dived into the water. Other crewman hastily launched suitable gear over the side—a rubber dinghy, two ten-man life rafts, and the wherry (a small rowboat).

THE FIERY DEATH OF THE U.S.S. JOHN PENN

Remarkable photo, taken at the moment the torpedo hit and exploded ammunition aboard the ship. Picture shot by a U.S. Navy photographer from the Lunga Point Boat Pool.

(National Archives)

I ran down from the Bridge area to the after well where the freeboard was only about three feet. Men were already reaching up to the gunwales, and I spread on my stomach over the stern to pull them aboard. Others of the crew were assisting men to safety. Forward, cargo nets were lowered over the side for those able to climb aboard unassisted. But we had to lower stretchers for those severely injured and/or burned.

Lieutenant Johnson, the Medical Officer, set up an emergency center, and with the three pharmacist's mates began treating casualties. Gashes, cuts, and burns were bandaged, and sedatives administered to those in pain and in shock. Many were in bad shape. Some were semi-conscious, talking incoherently; others were shock victims, some with concussions; and, worst of all, there were those severely burned.

I had no way of knowing that night that eight men from the McCAWLEY were now part of the JOHN PENN's crew, and I had to wait until 1991 to find this out by way of a letter from Frenchy Maurais.

"Soon after I went aboard", Frenchy relates, "the Skipper, Captain Harry W. Need, as convoy commander, took [the JOHN PENN] and three AKA's to Guadal. It was strictly a personnel and cargo operation. The PENN was loaded with 1,500 tons (I do remember the figure) of ammo, as they were stockpiling and preparing for another push in the island-hopping strategy. If I remember correctly the run from Noumea to Guadalcanal at the time was so secure we didn't even bother with escorts. I'll always be grateful for the fact that 'rank hath its privileges.' The Commodore ordered [our] ship unloaded first, including the ammo, while the others lay out and waited their turn."

"At dusk on the 13th, their mission accomplished, the cargo handling parties began to disembark for shore. Shortly thereafter, we went to GQ [General Quarters] not quite, but somewhat lackadaisically, thinking it was the nocturnal visit from Maytag [i.e. Washing Machine] Charlie coming over to give us greetings and harass the troops ashore, and going to battle stations was more or less S.O.P. [standard operating procedure]. Maytag Charlie devoted his energies to the beach, entertaining the troops. He generally didn't bother shipping."

Frenchy continued: "My battle station was on the Bridge as a phone talker. I remember someone shouting 'Here they come!' and seeing two planes flying low coming in on our starboard side. That's when the shit hit the fan. I saw a flash from the after deck house and the burst of flames from it. My thought was that one plane had crashed into the ship at main deck level and had ignited the gasoline carried on deck as fuel for landing boats. Later I learned that the ship's magazines had exploded and blew up the after part of the ship."

Japs Use New Air Trick, Sink Large U.S. Transport

Nipponese Fliers Make Feint From One Side While Torpedo Plane Attacks on Other.

By Lief Erikkon

GUADALCANAL. — (Delayed) The large Navy transport USS John Penn was torpedoed and sunk in a smartly executed new style Japanese torpedo plane attack on supply ships off Guadalcanal.

Hit squarely amidships, the transport in a few minutes was flaming from bow to stern and sank in a short time but flaming oil on the water lighted the area while loading boats sped out from the beach to pick up survivors.

Luckily, the unloading of troops and cargo from the ship — former American own Export Lines Excambion — had been completed in the afternoon. Casualties among the crew were reported light.

On Allied headquarters communique last Friday announced the loss of the John Penn.

This was the way the enemy executed the attack:

There were one or more high altitude bombers first came in over Guadalcanal from the west or inshore side. Searchlights, antiaircraft and night fighters all concentrated on them.

With attention of defenses diverted a torpedo plane swooped in low over the channel. It was not detected until it was making its run on the transport in bright moonlight.

Antiaircraft guns opened fire but did not hit the plane before it dropped its tin fish. Men aboard ships in the harbor reported seeing a plane go down in flames near it. However, observers were unable to determine whether this was the plane which attacked the transport.

One of the high altitude bombers which served as decoys was shot down by a night fighter.

During the height of the antiaircraft fire from the beach and an flight of Liberator bombers returning from a dusk raid on Kahili flew in and drew a heavy barrage from our own guns before it was recognized as an American bomber.

damaged but made a safe landing. Other planes in the bomber flight had to circle about for some time while the bomber field runways lighted by damaged by bombs dropped from the high level enemy bombers, was repaired.

La dernière escale du "John, Penn"

Cette remarquable photographie a été prise alors que brûlait le transport de la marine américaine "John Penn". Les flammes du navire illuminent la nuit au large de la plage Lunga, à Guadalcanal, et d'autres navires également mouillés à cet endroit. Le "Penn" a éclaté en flammes après avoir été atteint d'une torpille lancée d'un avion. Les soldats qui se trouvaient à bord du "Penn" en étaient débarqués avant l'attaque de même que le navire avait été déchargé de sa cargaison.

My old home, the U.S.S. JOHN FENN (APA23), Sunk Lunga Point, on (Friday) August 13, 1943 Guadalcanal, B.S.I, at 2137.
Sailed in her from July 12, 1943 to August 13, 1943. - from Frenchy Maurais.

"Somebody yelled at me to contact Battle II which was in the after deck house and manned by the Exec, but there was no reply; I couldn't raise the engine room either. I further remember the ship being engulfed in flames and the Captain being told by the Chief Master-at-Arms, who had somehow managed to reach the Bridge, that he should order all hands to abandon ship. And the Captain did just that."

The letter from Frenchy went on: "The Bridge was a shambles and the ship had taken a list to starboard. I didn't know where the hell to jump as the water around the ship was engulfed in flames. It seems that I ran over to the fore part of the ship and spotted a life raft with a young ensign, who I didn't recognize, and a sailor already in it. They were paddling on the same side of the raft, going around in circles and heading back toward the burning surfaces of the water."

"I decided to get the hell off [the raft] and dove back in the water. I swam a ways out and saw the silhouette of a small ship [the APc-25]. Somebody grabbed ahold of me and hauled me aboard. I heard someone holler 'he looks like he's in shock.' Apparently they gave me a shot a'something 'cause the next thing I knew I was on the beach. A corpsman was telling me the JOHN PENN had given 'em all a beautiful sight of fireworks as she blew up. [A couple of days later] I was taken aboard the HUNTER LIGGET to Noumea, then to Treasure Island [and] 30 days leave."

Frenchy added that casualties aboard the JOHN PENN must have been heavy—between a third and half of her crew lost. Of the eight ex-McCAWLEY enlisted men who reported aboard "a Yeoman 2nd Class named Sandell and myself were the only survivors." The survivor concluded: "About this time I started to get the feeling the law of averages was starting to catch up with me." Frenchy had survived the sinkings of two ships in the short time span of just six weeks. To me he said: "I for one am grateful for your APc-25 being in the neighborhood. . . . "

Our spit kit had swung around so her stern was closer to the doomed transport. In the light of the burning oil I spotted a raised arm in the water, waving back and forth. Pulling off my shoes, I went over the side, swimming toward the arm. As I grabbed it, skin, muscle, and flesh all came off in my hand. The unfortunate sailor had been virtually roasted alive—burnt to a crisp—by the explosion that blew him into the water.

I was horrified and almost got sick to my stomach, but I heard splashing and a voice weakly calling nearby. Another man was struggling in the water. Grasping his shirt collar, I towed him to the side of the APc where he was lifted aboard by willing hands. I stayed alongside the ship for a few more minutes, aiding others to a cargo net, then hoisted myself back on board.

In the meantime, nearly every boat and landing craft from the Lunga Boat Pool and from the FULLER and other ships had converged on the JOHN PENN. We transferred those who were able to move to Higgins boats and other craft so they could be rushed ashore for hospital treatment. Finally, Dr. Johnson cleared all the survivors, and at least six boatloads of them were taken to the beach. Captain Cartano and the doctor estimated, conservatively, we had rescued 35 to 40 men. The situation was too confused to keep an accurate count.

The torpedoed transport had been mortally wounded. While we had pressure on our fire mains, there was no possibility we could have fought fire effectively or postponed the inevitable. The blazes had spread quickly and she soon was settling by the stern. At 2155, 13 August, 1943, the U.S.S. JOHN PENN (APA-23) passed beneath the waters of Iron Bottom Bay—the last U.S. Naval vessel to be sunk by enemy action at Guadalcanal.

The JOHN PENN was the 24th Allied ship to be lost in that infamous triangle bounded by Savo Island, Florida Island, and Guadalcanal. Of these, 23 were American, one was Australian. On the Japanese side, the remains of 24 of their ships, too, were scattered across the floor of Iron Bottom Bay.

All reports agreed that the plane which torpedoed the JOHN PENN was shot down; but as far as I can determine, no ship took credit. One report, unconfirmed, gave the kill to one of our night fighters.

Captain Eaton of the FULLER took courageous action. After dispatching his landing craft to aid rescue efforts, he got his ship underway and steamed slowly back and forth to seaward of the stricken transport with all guns manned, covering the APA-23 as she flamed and finally sank. Al Allen said there was "a lot of nervous grousing that all we were doing was silhouetting the FULLER, making ourselves a fine target for the next planes or subs to come along." However, he went on: "But there was a kind of sneaking pride, too—it was a brave thing to do with a thin-skinned transport."

To write *finis* to the long, violent, and bloody saga of Iron Bottom Bay: The JOHN PENN was sunk *one year and six days after the initial invasion of Guadalcanal and Tulagi!*

The APc-25 rounded up our LCTs, moved into convoy formation, and set our course for the Slot; taking our usual route via the Russells, Segi Point, Mongo Entrance, and Visu Visu Point. After changing my wet dungarees, I relieved Tom Burke, the ship's company radioman who'd also gone over the side. I got a funny look from him when I observed it was a relief that we were now leaving the "secure non-combat area" for the "forward area danger zone". He punctuated the look with a dour "hmmph!"

Without taking credit for himself, Captain Cartano concluded his official Action Report on the JOHN PENN's loss by praising his crew:

"The rescue work was carried out by the crew without regard for their own safety. They ignored the danger of burning from spreading oil fire, of exploding magazines or suction from the sinking ship. They kept at their work until their job was done. The work of the men, led by Lt.(jg) Burdick, who dived over the side without waiting for life boats or rafts was especially meritorious. If heroism consists of disregarding one's personal safety in saving the lives of others, the work of the crew was heroic."

Lieutenant Johnson, who had worked diligently to treat the casualties, seconded the Skipper's remarks about the crew. Two other officers aboard as passengers—Lieutenant (jg) R.S. Lundberg, on his way to Naval Base, Segi, and Lieutenant F.H. Robinson, Commander Naval Base, Viru—concurred. The latter recommended a commendation for the Captain "for the cool headed manner in which he maneuvered his ship at the scene of the tragedy and directed the rescue work." Captain Cartano was awarded the Navy and Marine Corps Medal, as were three others of the crew.

In 1986, I sent for and received a copy of my service records from the U.S. Military's Records Center in St. Louis. While leafing through them, I found an entry I had no idea was there. It had been entered 1 January, 1945, while I was aboard the U.S.S. IRWIN. It had taken a year and a half for the good old Navy to locate me and forward it to my current ship. When it did arrive, no one even bothered mentioning it to me. It was dated 18 August, 1943, and was from Commanding Officer, U.S.S. APc-25. It read:

Citation for *Outstanding Service*

"For reasons set forth in [Report of Action and Rescue Work, 15 August, 1943, of C.O. USS APc-25 to ComInCh—Torpedoing of U.S.S. JOHN PENN] You are hereby given this recognition for the outstanding service performed by you on the evening of 13 August, 1943. You certainly deserve at least this much for having materially assisted in saving the lives of so many men. [signed] J.D. CARTANO, Commanding."

As we resumed our original mission, progress toward Enogai Inlet was slow. The LCTs could only make around six knots an hour. The first leg of the 235-mile journey was uneventful. Then, about 2140 on 15 August, some two miles past Lever Harbor, we heard planes off the port

```
                        U.S.S. APc 25
                      c/o Fleet Post Office
                      San Francisco, Calif.


                                            August 18,1943



From:         Commanding Officer, U.S.S. APc 25
   To:      -  Hutchinson,J.A.,RM2c,USN, 243 86 51

Subject:      Citation for Outstanding Service

Reference:    (a) Report of action and rescue work, 15 August
                  1943 of C.O. USS APc 25 to CominCh.

Enclosure:    (a) Same Report


        1.        For the reasons set forth in Reference (a) you
are given this recognition for the outstanding service performed
by you on the evening of 13 August 1943. You certainly deserve
at least this much for having materially assisted in saving the
lives of many men.
```

J.D. CARTANO, Commanding

CERTIFIED TO BE A TRUE COPY
R. J. SHULTZ, II, LCDR, USN

**"Citation for Outstanding Service" awarded author by Commanding
Officer of the U.S.S. APc 25, received 1 1/2 years after the action.**
(Author's Service Records)

bow. It was too dark to see them, but it was just the first evidence of almost constant air activity that would continue all night long. Jap float Zeros from Rekata Bay were patrolling Kula Gulf, dropping flares and looking for targets of opportunity.

At 2235, we spotted a float Zero over Vila on Kolombangara; at 2310, another over Rice Anchorage; and at 2330, two flares lit up the sea about 1,500 yards from us two points off the starboard bow. The Nips were getting closer and closer. Now they were almost in our hip pockets. About a half hour past Visu Visu Point and a mile and a half abeam of Wilson Harbor, a single enemy plane dropped a 500-pound bomb no more than 300 yards off our port bow. On the wing of the Bridge I felt only the concussion. No shrapnel got to us.

Screened to seaward by PT-boats, which for once had gotten the word they were supposed to protect us, we entered Enogai Inlet at 0220. As we and the LCTs commenced unloading, three enemy planes swooped in from over the Gulf, the first making a strafing run on the PTs before heading toward the LCTs. At 500 yards, the landing craft opened fire. The first Jap dropped a bomb that missed, then made straight for us. I was on the port wing of the Bridge and reached in to grab one of the Thompson submachineguns.

The other two float Zeros joined in the attack. Three of our four 20-millimeter machineguns could be brought to bear, along with the two .50-caliber guns. All five opened fire as the planes pressed their assault, both strafing and loosing their bombs. I counted twelve explosions from the latter. These slant-eyes weren't kidding! They were after blood. On one of the passes, a crew member of the LCT-325 caught a shell fragment in the right knee and his left leg was broken near the thigh. Another man took a superficial shrapnel wound. Our only casualties of the fight.

The APc-25's weapons spewed round after round at the Zero making the direct dive on us. As he got closer, I opened up with the Thompson, but with no tracer bullets I couldn't see where the rounds were going. I was just hoping I hit *something!* Besides, I told myself, at least I'm fighting back. The plane went directly over our heads and there was a burst of flame from it as the gunners kept up a steady drumming of fire. He disappeared on a downward path toward the jungle-covered island, and the crew let out a cheer. They *knew* we'd gotten that @#$%&%$@ Jap! The two other attackers retreated out over the inky waters of Kula Gulf.

The following morning, Father Paul Redmond, chaplain of the Marines' 4th Raiders, found the Zero, crashed in the jungle where its course over us would have taken it. One scratched meatball, confirmed by a priest! Can't get much better than that.

For once, I gave grudging credit to the Peter Tares. My old "friend" Robert Bolling Kelly and his MTBs had helped us to avoid sinking or serious casualties, diverting some of the Jap attack from us and dropping smoke bombs to distract the hostile pilots' attention from their targets. Captain Cartano would commend them in his Action Report.

With the excitement over, the crew completed unloading with the help of a shore working party. Leaving the LCTs to discharge their cargo the next morning, we steamed south to Lever Harbor to spend a few hours in a relatively safe anchorage. Departing the harbor at 0240, 16 August, we could hear sounds of small arms fire from the direction of Bairoko Harbor, less than two miles away, as the Marines continued their attempt to neutralize the enemy's port of entry for reinforcements. Clearing the mouth of Enogai Inlet, we watched with intense interest heavy AA fire bursting over Rendova and the Munda area. Searchlights sweeping the skies, caught a bomber in the beams, and one of the defense batteries knocked it down.

Our night was not without tension. We could hear more sorties by enemy aircraft nearer us. As we entered Lever Harbor at 0435, flares were dropping from the sky. At 0455, a Jap bomber flew in at low altitude about 1,800 yards off our beam. It was not in our range, and the gunners were ordered not to fire unless we were directly under attack. We didn't want to disclose our presence or position, if we could help it. As the sun rose, we anchored in Lever Harbor near Kelly's MTB base, then returned to Enogai later in the evening to take on 77 Marine casualties and to escort the LCTs back to the Russells.

On 19 August, I was released from temporary duty on the APc-25 and returned to Koli Point, only to end up in Sick Bay with, of all things, "cat fever", the same malady that put me in the hospital during boot camp at Newport. This attack, however was much milder, and I was out in two days. But the time on the binnacle list gave me an opportunity to catch up on what had been happening around the rest of my world.

The fall of Munda on 5 August did not mean the end of naval action up the Slot. On the night of 6/7 August, there was surface action in the waters between the islands of Kolombangara and Vella Lavella, which became known as the Battle of Vella Gulf.

Criticized for the performance of their ships and torpedoes, destroyermen simply wanted a chance to show what they could do. Up to this point, destroyers had been used primarily to screen cruisers in the fights to stop the Tokyo Express. Finally, Commander Frederick Moosbrugger, an excellent destroyerman, got Admiral Teddy Wilkinson, Admiral Kelly Turner's replacement if you remember, to try a new tactic: Let the tin cans operate independently of cruisers. They got the green light when no cruisers were available and coastwatchers spotted a Jap force of four destroyers, with some 900 troops aboard, trying to bring reinforcements to the enemy garrison on New Georgia.

To meet the Tokyo Express, Wilkinson commanded Moosbrugger to enter Vella Gulf from the south via Gizo Strait, but gave him complete freedom of action in dealing with the Jap force. After the customary S-turn salute to the dead in Iron Bottom Bay upon leaving Tulagi and an uneventful passage south of the Russells and Rendova, the Commander with six tin cans—the DUNLAP, CRAVEN, MAURY, STACK, LANG, and STERETT—steamed through Gizo into Vella Gulf, reaching a position about halfway between Boko Point on Vella LaVella and Vanga Point on Kolombangara. His radar picked up four blips at about 20,000 yards.

In a quick 90-degree turn to starboard, Moosbrugger brought his destroyers' torpedo tubes to bear, launching 24 fish at about 4,000 yards toward the Jap destroyers, which without radar were caught completely by surprise. Three of the enemy ships (HAGIKAZE, ARASHI, and KAWAKAZE) exploded with such force that PT-boat sailors thirty miles away thought the volcano on Kolombangara had blown its top. The fourth Jap destroyer SHIGURE beat a quick retreat while our tin cans finished off the burning ships with their 5-inch .38s. Virtually the whole Jap force was wiped out without our cans receiving a scratch.

The tin can sailors not only posted a very neat victory in our column, but vindicated Commander Moosbrugger's conviction that DDs, operating independently, could be very effective. The Commander became a hero. Before this War was over, I would serve under his command.

I had thought my spit kit duty was over, but no sooner was I discharged from Sick Bay when I was ordered back to the APc-25. We were to take supplies into Enogai Inlet and evacuate wounded. The battle for Bairoko Harbor was in its last days, but there still were casualties. Underway on 24 August, the APc-25 had an uneventful trip northward. When we pulled in at Enogai, we learned the Marine and Army forces had secured Bairoko on the 24th, and the enemy had evacuated its positions in the area. With some 50 wounded men aboard, we began our return journey. Two days later, Colonel Liversedge and his battered 1st Marine Raider Regiment would board APDs (old World War I destroyers converted to high-speed troop transports) of Transport Division 22 and follow us back to Guadalcanal.

One of those people we had aboard was not a Marine but a native scout whom one of the Marines characterized as Colonel Liversedge's "gun-bearer". He was on a stretcher, suffering from malaria and, as the Medical Officer put it, a multitude of other tropical maladies. When the

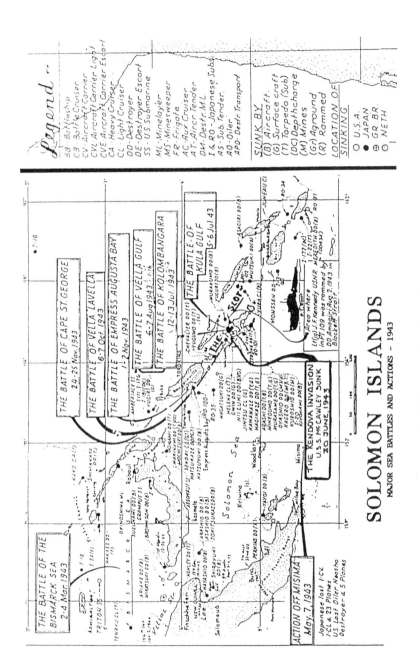

SOLOMON ISLANDS
MAJOR SEA BATTLES AND ACTIONS – 1943

(Courtesy Sgt/Maj. Lester Bamford, USMC, Ret.)

pharmacist's mate took his temperature, it went all the way to the top of the thermometer—106°! No one, the doctor said, should still be living with a temperature that high. When the pharmacist's mates tried to roll the Melanesian over, his skin peeled off in the docs' hands like hide off a scalded hog.

The doctor shook his head and said: "Well, one thing. That fever has killed all the syphilis in him!"

The stench of the native was overwhelming. It permeated the whole ship, and one of the crew wondered if the Japs could smell it and locate us by it. Unbelievably, the native survived until we got him back to Tulagi, but died shortly after. The pharmacist's mate thought the man's temperature had gone higher than the top scale on the thermometer and maybe got up to 110°. "Anyhow", he said, "you can bet it just fried his brain."

The Melanesian scout was not the only malaria victim aboard. I came down with another case of it, either a recurrence or a new bout. I could never tell the difference. Feeling the symptoms, I went to Lieutenant (jg) John Baker (Medical Corps), who was our Medical Officer on that trip.

"If you'll go along with it", the doctor said, "I'll try something we've been working on at the Malaria Experimental Lab in Noumea. It'll either cure you or kill you."

I didn't know whether he was serious about that last part, but once you've had malaria, you'll take any chance to avoid or diminish an attack.

"Doctor, I've had it before and I don't care which", I told him.

"All right. Go lay down on your bunk and I'll be there shortly."

When he came into the berthing deck he had a handful of pills and a cup of water. He told me the tablets contained 36 grains of quinine. I took them all at once. Within minutes, my head took off like all the fireworks in the world. It was a Chinese New Year and the Fourth of July all rolled into one. Brilliant lights flashed and whirled in my brain, and they roared like a flight of Corsairs in a power dive.

I didn't come to until well into the next day. But when I tried to move, I couldn't. My hand was on the side of the bunk, and when I tried to command it to move, it wouldn't obey. I was so weak the muscles just wouldn't react to my brain. At the moment, I wasn't alarmed—I still was not yet completely conscious.

Later, one of the crew noticed my eyes were open and called Dr. Baker. With soup from the galley, he got some nourishment down me, and in a while I was walking around. The quinine didn't cure me—I'd get malaria again—but it certainly cut down on the effects.

Convalescing on deck, I struck up a conversation with one of the 4th Raiders. He had taken hand grenade fragments in his legs during the final push on Bairoko, but he had been with the 1st Marine Raider Regiment from the beginning.

"I'll bet every gawddam Jap on the island had a Nambu", he complained. "They just cut us to pieces."

A Nambu is a .25-caliber automatic weapon, similar to a Thompson submachinegun. The Marines were too lightly armed for the task they had been given; and the Japs, in fixed positions defended by heavy automatic weapons, mortars, and heavy artillery, punished the gyrenes severely. The Americans suffered 51 killed, over 200 wounded; the 4th Raiders took the worst of it, 29 dead, 127 wounded, in the attack on Bairoko.

Raiders were offensive units, trained to strike quickly, then get out. Once they'd taken Enogai, they should have been relieved by regular infantry supported by artillery. Instead, they were forced into a meat grinder that sadly depleted their numbers, and had Colonel Liversedge cussing the Army command for not relieving his Regiment after the initial strike at Enogai.

Even an ordinary seaman could see that U.S. strategy and tactics in the Pacific had to change. As James J. Fahey serving on the cruiser MONTPELIER observed in his clandestine but later bestselling *Pacific War Diary*: "The fighting on Munda was rugged . . . .If we try to take island by island, it will take years to beat the Japs . . . ."

On 2 September, 1943, I concluded my service in the Spit Kit Navy, departed the brave little APc-25, and returned to Camp Crocodile.

As the mopping up on New Georgia was being concluded, there was a stinging assessment of the ground action in the TOENAILS Operation. It came from ComInCh (Admiral King):

"At the termination of Japanese resistance in Munda, there were seven regimental combat teams, totaling more than 30,000 troops in our assault forces. No information differing from our initial estimate of 4 to 5,000 [enemy] troops on Munda, to which reinforcements were believed to have been added for a time, has been received. However, of the Japanese on Munda only 1,671 are known to be dead and 28 captured. The overwhelming superiority of our forces in numbers and equipment had to be applied for 12 days despite air bombing and naval bombardment support before a force not more than one-seventh its size had been overcome. If we are going to require such overwhelming superiority at every point where we attack the Japanese, it is time for radical change in the estimate of forces that will be required to defeat the Japanese now in the Southwest and Central Pacific."

On getting the gist of the assessment from one of the junior officers on Admiral Wilkinson's Staff, I had but one thought:

"At that rate, we won't get to Tokyo by 1958—let alone *by '48!*"

19

THE LONG VOYAGE HOME

I had only been back at my regular duties in the Camp Crocodile Radio Shack eleven days when I headed to Sick Bay once more.

My weight was down some 50 pounds from the 170 I'd carried when I enlisted in 1941. The cat fever attack three weeks earlier had not helped any either. This time I wasn't going to get by so easily; it was the old bugaboo of malaria, diagnosed as the most virulent strain, acute malignant Tertian.

My fever soared and the ague wracked my body violently. As had the attack on the McCAWLEY, it ranged from boiling hot one minute to freezing cold the next. This was at least as severe as the bout on the MAC, aggravated by dengue fever along with it. My joints were aching like mad, and the diarrhea made it all even worse.

I was on the binnacle list five days when Lieutenant D.C. Mead, who treated me, apparently reported my condition to the Senior Staff Medical Officer, Commander R.E. Fielding, who stopped by my cot as I began to recover.

"Lad, I think we'd better get you out of here", he said. "You've had more than your share of these tropical diseases—and frankly, you're not in the greatest physical shape. I'll try to get you back to the States, but right now there's a freeze on transfers with the Bougainville operation coming up."

He paused for a moment. "I'll see what I can do, though." Then he left. Sometime later he returned, waking me from sleep.

"The only way out for you is to volunteer for hazardous duty", he said, and chuckled at the irony.

"Just what are they calling 'hazardous duty' these days, Commander?"

"Aside from flight duty, it's submarines. I see by your medical records you took a physical for sub duty some time ago."

"Yes, Sir, Dr. Lounsberry on the MAC told me I'd passed the preliminary."

"Well, we're going to have to come up with a way around a little obstacle. You wouldn't pass a sub physical now because of the malaria you've had. So I'll let that preliminary exam stand and get a letter to transfer you back to Mare Island. At least you'll be in the States with an opportunity to finagle your way into some better duty."

On 17 October, 1943, I was transferred to Commander Service Squadron Pacific (ComServRonPac) for further transfer to Commanding Officer, Submarine Force, Administrative, Mare Island, California. Authority: letter from Admiral Wilkinson (ComThirdAmphibFor) dated 17 October. I suspect Dr. Fielding also did a little arm-twisting on T.W. Zimmerman, the Staff Personnel Officer. I got priority transportation approved and caught a SCATS DC-3 out of Henderson Field for Tontouta Air Base, Noumea.

Within three days I was standing on the Pan American Airways dock, ready to board one of the fabled Pan Am "Clippers"—the huge four-engine flying boats that regularly spanned the Pacific in peacetime. I was hoping this flight would be a little less exciting that my first two. The Clipper was loaded to the overhead with sacks of mail. I pushed them around to make a comfortable nest and settled back for the first leg of the flight—destination Suva, Fiji. As the big engines of the Clipper settled into a steady drone, I dozed off for a while. When I awoke and looked out the port, all that was below was the broad bosom of the South Pacific. With nothing else to do, I thought back over the seventeen months since I'd left the Mainland.

I wondered how history would treat the Solomon Islands Campaign. That "Guadalcanal" would take its place among the major battles in American military annals, of that I was sure. It certainly would be among the longest and bloodiest. Most accounts, today, inaccurately conclude with the final evacuation of Japanese troops and the announcement that the island was "secure" on 15 February, 1943. Yet, the 'Canal was still a battle zone. Officially, the "Consolidation of the Southern Solomons" was not completed until 20 June, 1943, ten days before the New Georgias Operation. For me, however, "Guadalcanal" was not over until the air raid that culminated in the sinking of the JOHN PENN—one year and six days after the original invasion of 7 August, '42.

Images began to flash across my mind. Some were so vivid and realistic they caused rushes of troubling emotions. Others had already faded into the gray of the half-forgotten. Hundreds of men, some who'd been close shipmates and some whom I'd known only for moments, populated the stage. Already, however, many of their faces and names were becoming difficult to recall. The realities of those months were now beginning to become illusory, the people and places beclouded in my

Name _HOLIDAY, Jon Antony_ ~~HUTCHINSON, John Anthony~~ 9
(Name in Full. Surname to the Left)

243 86 51 _____ Rate ___ RM1c(T)
(Service No.)

Date Reported Aboard: ___ 7 May 1941

U.S.S. NORTH CAROLINA
(Present Ship or Station)

R/S, NEW YORK, N.YL
(Ship or Station Received From)

Authorized to wear the following area
Campaign Medals:
1. American Defense Service Medal.
2. American Area Campaign Medal.
3. Asiatic-Pacific Area Medal.
Authorized to wear one bronze star for each
of the following engagements, to be worn on
the Asiatic-Pacific Area Campaign Medal:
1. Guadalcanal-Tulagi Occupation –
August 7-9, 1942.
2. Eastern Solomons, August 23-25, 1942.
3. Defense & Capture of Guadalcanal,
August 10 to February, 1943.

E.J. McMILLAN,
By direction.

Name _HOLIDAY, Jon. Antony_ ~~HUTCHINSON, John Anthony~~ 9
(Name in Full. Surname to the Left)

243 86 51 _____ Rate ___ RM2c USN
(Service No.)

4TH NAVAL U. B. SPECIAL(For duty on
June 11, 1943
Staff Allowance ComAmphibForSoPac)
(Present Ship or Station)

U. S. S. McCAWLEY (FLAG)
(Ship or Station Received From)

Participated in the occupation
of WENDOVA ISLAND(NEW GEORGIA)
while serving with Commander Task
Force 31 aboard the U.S.S.
McCawley and on board when McCawley
was lost as a result of an enemy
torpedo plane attack, June 30, 1943

R, K. TURNER
HAMILTON HAINS
By direction

Name _HOLIDAY, Jon Antony_ ~~HUTCHINSON, John Anthony~~ 9
(Name in Full. Surname to the Left)

243 86 51 _____ Rate ___ RM1c(T) USN
(Service No.)

Date Reported Aboard: ___ 14 February 1944

U.S.S. IRWIN (DD794)
(Present Ship or Station)

US RS, San Francisco, California.
(Ship or Station Received From)

8 October 1945
Participated in the following:

Capture and Defense of Guadalcanal –
10 August 1942 to 8 February 1943.
Rennel Island – 29 to 30 January 1943.
Consolidation of Southern Solomons –
8 February 1943 to 20 June 1943.
New Georgia Group Operation – 20 June
1943 to 31 August 1943.

- -

C. H. Bakley
C. H. BAKLEY,
Lieutenant (DS) USNR,
Executive Officer.

- -

Changed home address to:

777 Adair Avenue, Atlanta, Ga.

Records corrected accordingly.

- -

Date Transferred _____ C. H. Bakley
Lieutenant, U.S.N.R.
To _____ ~~Executive Officer~~

Signature and Rank of Commanding Officer

Date Received Aboard:_____

(New Ship or Station)

(Last Ship or Station)

Signature and Rank of Officer Authorized to Sign

ORIGINAL
FOR SERVICE RECORD

(Author's Service Record)

mind. It was as if a mental healing process were taking place—the brain's way of shielding me from the disquietudes I felt and the horrors I witnessed. It would be almost fifty years before I would be able to resurrect many of those men and scenes, calling upon them to reappear from the shadowy wings of hazy memory and once again come to Stage Center.

Like Scarlett O'Hara, I decided to think about that tomorrow and concentrated on the future. Fairly certain I wouldn't qualify for submarine school, I thought I would, at the least, have a long time in the States. Perhaps, I hoped, I'd get a new ship under construction and enjoy some rest and relaxation while she was being fitted out before joining the Fleet. Little did I know, then, standing orders called for immediate return to my former command should I be rejected for sub duty. So I just blithely went on daydreaming about my first stateside meal—sirloin steak smothered in onions.

Nighttime flying for civilian aircraft in the Pacific was forbidden, so when we landed at Suva we'd stay until the next morning. The Clipper tied up at the dock, and the crew and I walked toward shore. At the end of the pier was a palm-thatched building serving some eatables and also specializing in Fiji rum. I had no plans to overimbibe, or even get a buzz on, but did condescend to have a few drinks before ordering food. *That* was a mistake. By the time I'd consumed three tall glasses of a barkeep's recommendation, I was drunk as a hooty owl. And it had gone down so smoothly, too. That stuff would turn your toenails purple. *Wow*! I don't know who got me back aboard the Clipper, but whoever did must have had to pour me through the hatch. I didn't wake up until the next day when we were most of the way to Christmas Island, the second stop on the way to Pearl.

The final leg into Oahu was shorter than the others and we landed in mid-afternoon. The Clipper's crew then inaugurated me into an "exclusive" club. I became a "Short Snorter". That is, I gave each of them a one-dollar bill; and they, in turn, each signed another, with the Captain noting on it I had completed a trans-Pacific flight from Noumea to Pearl. He dated the bill. I figured it was a racket of the fly-boys to pick up extra bucks, but still it was one more memento of the times. To the "Short Snorter" bill, I also taped other evidences of my odyssey, paper money from Fiji and a one-dollar "invasion" bill from Hawaii. I reported in to the Navy (ComServRonPac) only to be told I didn't have any more priority travel, and would have to wait until I was assigned surface transportation to San Francisco.

I finally got a berth on a "Kaiser Koffin", one of those mass-produced cargo/troop carrying vessels reputed to be so flimsily built they'd break apart in a storm. The conditions aboard were abominable and the Merchant Marine Skipper was a Captain Bligh. He insisted passengers remain below decks about 90 percent of the time. There was insufficient ventilation in the holds, and seasick soldiers didn't make the situation any better. To get out of that situation, I went up to the galley and volunteered as a mess cook. This kept me out of the hold most of the day and insured I wouldn't have to stand in line for hours to get chow. Only two meals were served each day, and the food, like the ship, was pretty bad. The whole trip was one of the most miserable I ever took.

The only bright spot came when we finally sailed under the Golden Gate Bridge. It had taken me 22 days to get from Koli Point to San Francisco. It had been seventeen months and two days since I'd shipped out of the States on the NORTH CAROLINA, and nearly two and a half years since I'd been home. But I was beholding the Golden Gate, rather than the Pearly Gate, and it was only 1943!

On 8 November, I reported to the Submarine Base (ComSubPacAdmin) at Mare Island and was told I'd get my physical the next day. In the meantime, I'd eat at the Base mess and get liberty for the evening. Instead of steak and onions, I ate a most unusual meal. Submarine chow is the best in the Fleet and I could order just about anything I wanted. When I went into the mess I surprisingly realized it wasn't steak I wanted. There were two items I craved more. A Cook 3rd Class obliged. He gave me a full head of lettuce and steered me to a gallon pitcher of real honest-to-God cow's milk. I was starved for anything green and leafy, and there's no describing how great that milk tasted. The Greek gods on Olympus with their ambrosias and nectars never experienced anything so wonderful. I went back for seconds on *both* milk and lettuce!

I got into my dress blues for 1600 liberty and was shocked. I'd lost so much weight the only thing holding up my trousers was my hip bones. Two safety pins from my sewing kit solved the problem, and I joined a couple of others for the ferry ride from Mare Island over to the town of Vallejo.

Sailors have their own shorthand when putting names to liberty ports. San Francisco, much to the dismay of its inhabitants, was abbreviated to "Frisco"; San Diego was, irreverently, "Dago"; Vallejo (vah-LAY-hoh) we called "Valley Joe".

Navy old-timers will tell you "Valley Joe" was the toughest liberty port in the world, outranking such legendary and exotic spots as Calcutta's Black Hole and Egypt's Port Said. Here you could get your throat cut for a nickel and get four cents change. The chief contribution to that reputation was the extra pay submarine sailors received. "Qual-Sub" (qualified for submarine duty) got them their base pay plus 50 percent. And that was enough incentive to draw an overabundance of hookers, grifters, and con men to any town.

The streets of Vallejo were a sight to see in 1943. From the ferry landing at the foot of Georgia Street (the main drag) there was a solid wall on both sides of the thoroughfare of gin mills, popcorn stands, movie houses, and by-the-hour hotels. I was told (you *know* I would never try it!) there was a standing bet that no one could start at the landing, go up the starboard side of Georgia Street for two blocks, drinking one drink in every bar, cross over to the port side, repeating the process, and make it back to the landing on both feet. There were *that* many bars! Nor could you go more than six feet without being propositioned by a lady of the evening.

Considering I had a physical coming up in the morning, I spent only about an hour in one of the least sleazy of the gin mills, had a couple of drinks, and returned to the Sub Base. I did not want to make good the old saying: "We sailors get money like horses, and spend it like asses."

When I walked into the Yard Dispensary at 0900, I was ushered into the office of Lieutenant Commander S. P. Erlich, Medical Corps. He was sitting on the front edge of his desk with my medical records in his hand.

"I'm not even going to bother giving you the physical, lad", he told me. "The malaria in your record is enough to disqualify you right off the bat. I will say one thing: your Medical Officer on the Admiral's Staff pulled a fast one to get you back to the States and, from what I see, he had every reason to get you out of the islands."

"So what happens now, Doctor?"

"I have no choice but to send you to the Receiving Station at Treasure Island with orders to transfer you back to the Amphibs (ComThirdAmphibFor)."

My heart sank. No way did I want back to the Crocodile Navy. The Amphibs and their damn' islands were not for me.

"Look", he advised, "when you get to T.I. [Treasure Island], pull whatever strings you can find to get reassignment. It's been done before. In the meantime, I'll get you out of here right now so you'll at least have overnight liberty before you have to report in."

I hurried into my dress blues and caught a Navy shuttle bus to San Francisco, finding a small hotel a couple of blocks off Market Street. What a pleasure! A room all to myself without 25 or 50 other guys around, and a real honest to goodness bed with innersprings and everything. I took off my shoes and socks and just luxuriated in walking on the thick-pile rug. Then I shaved and took a shower. The water felt so good I filled the tub and just relaxed in it until it got cold. Surely God had this in mind when he inspired man to invent modern plumbing, I thought, and there's no doubt there are facilities like that Up There, too.

I found a restaurant that looked as if it might have a good steak, but had to wait at the bar for a table. Sipping bourbon and water, I looked around. Next to me were four or five "slick arm" Chief Petty Officers with rating specialties I'd never seen before. A "slick arm" Chief was one who did not yet have four years in the service and consequently his left arm was bare of hash marks. I'd never seen *that* before, either. In *my* Navy, it took at least four years to make Chief—if then.

I struck up a conversation with these guys, discovering they'd *entered* the Service as C.P.O.'s with *no* prior military experience. One of them had an "A" on his "crow" (the eagle on the rating badge).

"What the hell is that?" I asked him.

"Athletic Specialist. I instruct people in calisthenics, organize sports teams and events. Stuff like that." He'd been a second-string football player at some cow college.

As it turned out, *none* of these guys had ever been to sea, and had permanent stateside shore duty. It didn't help any to discover later there were teletype operators who were inducted into the Navy as Chief Radiomen with no sea duty, who knew no code, and who wouldn't know a speed key from a whaleboat. What a racket! And the Navy's sending me back out at the first opportunity?! What a CROCK! Lousy damned way to run a Navy!

I didn't let it spoil my dinner. Finally, I got my steak and onions with all the trimmings, topped off with a banana split and REAL ice cream, not the chalky tasting gedunks made with powdered milk. I then sat back and enjoyed a snifter of Courvoisier. "God's in his Heaven and all's right with the world", I concluded. I'd worry about going back to the Amphibs tomorrow.

The restaurant and bar were overflowing with servicemen, mostly Navy; and females were not only scarce, but each one there was surrounded by three or four men. It was no place to look for unattached women. Besides, I hoped I'd get more liberty before leaving Frisco, so I went back to the hotel, drew another bath, stayed in it until the water cooled, than sank into that elegant bed.

The first person I ran into on checking in at Treasure Island was a Yeoman 1st whom I'd casually known on the NORTH CAROLINA. Turned out he was one of the "Assignment Yeomen", charged with sending men to the right places. He took one look at my orders and sighed.

"You know we're supposed to send you back to your previous command?"

"Yeah, but there oughta be something you could do about it. I haven't had any leave and . . . the last thing I want to do is go back to some stinking island! How do I get out of that?"

"Well, you could volunteer for hazardous duty."

I looked at him. Two clichés popped into mind. This was "playing like a broken record." And it also sounded like "out of the frying pan and into the fire."

"What kind of hazardous duty?"

"Destroyers."

"Tin cans! You mean they're giving extra pay to destroyer sailors, now? It's about time!"

"Well, not exactly. We don't get many volunteers for cans, and the shipyards are turning out new ones so fast we can't find qualified petty officers to man 'em. So when we get some one like you, we give you the option. In your case, tin cans or transports. It's more a matter of priority than a hazardous duty situation."

"You mean tin cans ain't hazardous? You forget I just got back from the forward area. I *know* what kinda duty that is. Anyhow, what about leave? It's been a long time since I've been home."

"Volunteer for destroyers and I can put through a change in orders. Once that's approved by ComServPac, you can request leave. After that, you'll probably be assigned to new construction."

"Hey", I exclaimed with some glee, "sounds like I'll get some time in the States!" I was thinking of the time it takes to get a new ship ready for sea. Optimistically, I was looking forward to six months "in the good ol' U.S. *and* A."

The yeoman immediately dashed those hopes.

"Hutch, you'll probably get 30 days' leave, return here, and be shipped out on a new can within a month or six weeks. They're finishing destroyers up and moving them out so fast the paint on 'em isn't even dry before they join the Fleet."

He seemed genuinely saddened he was "turning my hat around" only to send me right back to combat area so quickly. It's an old sailor's maxim: "Growl you may, but go you must!" Also: "A man that won't growl is just no man at all!"

"Destroyer sailors are berthed in 'N' Barracks, so take your seabag over and pick out a bunk. Then come back and pick up your liberty card", he instructed.

As soon as my gear was squared away, I headed for the nearest telephone. I had waited until I knew more about my future before calling home. The family was ecstatic. I'd let them know in a few days when I'd head back on leave.

I switched into dress blues, picked up the liberty card, and caught the bridge train to San Francisco. My, how that town had changed! When the NORTH CAROLINA had put into port in June of '42, "Baghdad by the Bay" had not yet begun to feel the full effects of wartime activity. Now, the streets were crawling with service people, and the area surrounding the Bay was alive with defense plants and military installations of every variety and description.

I had seen but few women in the service until now. In my absence from the States, WAVES, WACS, WAAFS, SPARS, and "BAMS" had been activated and their numbers substantially increased. "BAMS" was not the official acronym for females in the Marine Corps. The Corps preferred to call them simply Women Marines. But both jarheads and sailors quickly came up with BAMS, i.e. Broad-Assed Marines. It sure seemed strange having to salute women officers.

The first place I headed for was Fisherman's Wharf, seeking one of my favorite dishes, clam chowder. Hadn't had any since leaving Casco Bay. That part of the waterfront was once infamous throughout the world when it was called the Barbary Coast, a wild and woolly area where men were Shanghaied to sea, where opium dens flourished and murder was commonplace. The Navy had cleaned it up with the simple expedient of arraying warships in the Bay and threatening to blow it off the map. Now the seafood restaurants and spaghetti palaces were a-jam with people. The piers were in full use, not an empty berth anywhere, and the broad Bay with Alcatraz in its center was streaked with the wakes of ships of every size from battleships to yard craft.

It was here I experienced my first encounter with the "new" Navy—a Permanent Shore Patrol! In the "old days" shore patrolmen came from the ships in port and, as seagoing men, their primary objective was to keep sailors out of trouble.

Now the Navy, in all its wisdom, decided that order could best be kept in large cities by having the same men handle the job all the time. They didn't want to take experienced sailors off ships; so they used, in most cases, ex-cops. Most of those in San Francisco were from the Los Angeles Police Department. Instead of trying to keep sailors *out* of trouble, they seemed intent on finding any reason to throw a good seagoing man *in* the brig. Even the slightest infraction of Naval District standing orders, or even a mild argument among shipmates, could get unsuspecting John Gobs a trip to SP headquarters and charges filed. Rather than get an inebriated sailor back to his ship without harm to anyone, these ex-cops would toss him in the brig and notify his Commanding Officer.

I had just walked out of the Grotto on the wharf when two of these popinjays, overly impressed with their law-keeping assignment, stopped me for being out of uniform. While eating, I'd unbuttoned my jumper sleeves and turned the cuffs up. The SPs treated the infraction as if it were a major crime. After about ten minutes of lecturing and badgering, some of it obviously intended to anger me and get me further in Dutch, the bastards let me go with a "warning".

People who'd looked down their noses at sailors in peacetime were now falling all over themselves to entertain us. Movie stars and society types all at once discovered servicemen; and USO clubs with "nice, clean entertainment" sprang up like weeds. Well, they might be all right for the green kids fresh from mama's lap, but for us grizzled veterans of sea battles and beachheads, we preferred places that hadn't thrown us out in peacetime. And we weren't "sailor *boys*"—we were *MEN!*

It seemed everywhere I went there was a lot of hype about the Red Cross and the USO "helping our boys". Hell, I never saw anyone connected with either outfit west of Honolulu. Neither was the Pacific War covered well by the news media. I saw only three correspondents (one an Australian) during the entire War from 1942 to 1945.

There was one particular Red Cross poster that incensed every combat man. It showed a wounded man lying on the ground, getting blood intravenously. The plasma bottle, marked with a red cross, hung from an M-1 rifle, and you could see the arm of a corpsman or medic with the red cross brassard on it. The cutline read "Your Red Cross Is There", erroneously giving the impression that the American Red Cross was at the battle fronts. It was a blatant misuse of the international battlefield insignia worn by combat corpsmen and medics to give the impression the Red Cross went onto battlefields. It infuriated us.

Most Navy men hated the Red Cross, anyhow, given their often arrogant personnel and misspent money. When it came to charitable offerings, we gave to the Salvation Army, instead. Their lassies some-times would come into bars to solicit donations. They'd leave with their tambourines filled to overflowing with gifts from the sailors.

It was very frustrating for those returning from the Pacific to follow news of the War in papers and on radio. Even on the West Coast, the emphasis was on the War in Europe and European Operations. We attributed that to the fact that ours was mostly a conflict at sea, and concluded few correspondents had the guts to ship out on a combat vessel. The War with Japan was still the forgotten War.

There had already been a couple of books published about the Pacific War, one of which was Richard Tregaskis' *Guadalcanal Diary*. Unaware of either the book or the movie made from it, I went to see the show after spotting the title on the Base theater marquee at Treasure

Island. Seated in the same row with me were four Marines, all wearing the distinctive shoulder patch of the 1st Marine Division. The movie was pretty accurate but toned down or eliminated much of the blood and guts. Yet, the five of us did a lot of fidgeting, and when the movie got to scenes showing Marines in a foxhole during nightlong bombing and bombardment—that was it.

I started to tremble and my breath was coming in short gasps. It was Koli Point all over again. I headed for the exit, with those four gyrenes trailing in my wake. In the lobby, one looked at me and queried: "the 'Canal?"

"Yep."

"Let's go get some java", one of the Marines offered.

We talked of girls, our home towns, football games. . . . But not one of us spoke of the movie, the Solomons, or the War. I would eventually go to see that movie seven times before I could sit past the bombing part. It became a test of will.

A Chief Yeoman at Treasure Island looked over my service records.

"You haven't had any leave in two and a half years?"

I did a quick mental calculation and nodded.

"Why weren't you sent back to the States after the McCAWLEY was sunk? You rated immediate survivor's leave."

"I was on an Admiral's Staff."

"Well, you'll get leave now. But 30 days is the maximum. I'll have your papers ready tomorrow morning. When you get back, report in to the office in the destroyer barracks. You'll probably get a ship right away."

I called home to tell my folks I'd probably be there in about five or six days. Air travel was difficult to come by and it would take that long by train. For the most part it was a miserable trip. There were no Pullman cars available, and most of the day coaches were relics of a bygone era when passenger cars were made of wood. They'd been pressed into service to meet wartime needs. The heating system often didn't work in "this old rolling stock", and the seats were designed to be as comfortable as the rack in a medieval dungeon. It wasn't hard to visualize the conductor with a black hood over his face and a double-bitted axe in his hand!

Still it was good to be back in the good ol' U.S. of A. America the Beautiful!

O beautiful for spacious skies, for amber waves of grain,
For purple mountain majesties above the fruited plain . . . .
O beautiful for heroes proved in liberating strife,

Who more than self their country loved, and mercy more than life! . . .
America! America! God shed His grace on thee,
And crown thy good with brotherhood from sea to shining sea!

The only bright spot in the whole trip was the stop at the small community of North Platte, Nebraska. We had about a 30-minute layover, and the women of that town were some of the great heroines of the War. They'd used up their own ration stamps and used every subterfuge to get food supplies to make that 30 minutes forever memorable in the heart of every serviceman to pass their way. The interior of the station house was one long mess deck. Table after table was stacked high with sandwiches, cakes, doughnuts, cookies, boiled eggs, lunchmeats, and other fantastic edibles. Steaming urns of coffee and pitchers of fresh sweet milk abounded.

As we piled off the train and entered the station, we were greeted with all the exuberance and affection that would have been accorded these women's own sons and brothers returning from war. These unselfish and wonderful Midwesterners poured forth cheer and love with smiles and greetings I never saw before nor since. Once we'd each been served enough chow to feed the crew of a battleship, the women urged more on us in paper bags so we'd have enough to last the rest of the trip. May God forever bless the women of North Platte, Nebraska—not so much for the food but for their love, spirit, and patriotism.

God bless America, land that I love,
Stand beside her and guide her thru the night with a light from above.
From the mountains to the prairies to the oceans white with foam—
God bless America, my home sweet home!

Finally, the train reached Philadelphia, where I caught another for Wilmington, Delaware, just a ferry's ride across the Delaware River from home in Upper Penns Neck Township near Penns Grove, Salem County, New Jersey.

My arrival at the farm on Georgetown Road was a saddened homecoming. My Uncle Bert whom I loved so much was seriously ill due to a heart attack. The prognosis was not good and the doctor was not encouraging. Even my return could do nothing to improve his condition although his spirits did pick up when I walked in.

The family was determined to make my time at home as pleasant as possible under the circumstances. My grandmother, whose first response to anyone coming to her house was to head for the kitchen to fix something to eat, asked what I'd like to have for dinner.

"Gran, I'd like a steak. We didn't get any in the Solomons, and the first I had was when I got back to the States."

She grew furious. "You mean the government's rationing beef here at home, telling us it's going to you boys overseas and you're not getting any!?"

"Maybe they're sending it to Europe, but it's as scarce as hen's teeth in the South Pacific", I answered.

She grabbed her purse and coat and called to my dad. "Come on, John, we're goin' to see Meyer!"

Meyer Broski was the butcher Gran had been buying meats from for over ten years. When he expanded to open a grocery store, I drove delivery truck for him for a while. Gran stormed into the store with all guns firing. Meyer finally got her calmed down enough to learn the cause of her anger.

"I want the best steaks you have", she told him.

"Well, how many ration stamps . . . ?" Meyer began.

"Damn the ration stamps, Meyer! My grandson's home and he's goin' to have steak."

Meyer decided discretion was the better part of valor and delivered.

I spent as much time with Uncle Bert as I could, but the family urged me to get out of the house, so I went hunting old friends. Most of the guys were gone, either in the military or in defense plants, and I could only find a couple of girls I knew. From them I learned my friends were pretty much scattered all over the world. Tony Checchia, whom I'd run around with for four years in high school, was in the Army Air Corps, a tail-gunner on a B-24 in Europe. Tommy McDonough, another high school classmate, was in the Marine Detachment on the SOUTH DA-KOTA. Neither would survive the War.

Of some, I could get no information. There would be no reunions this time home. I had one date with Alice Miller, a girl I knew from Salem and had gone out with several times before I entered the service. Our time was spent mostly talking about old times and of those who were not present. We parted in a blue mood. The War had certainly broken up that old gang of mine.

The end finally came for Uncle Bert, and we buried him in the family's cemetery plot. Shortly after the funeral, my first cousin Marge, who'd come up from Atlanta, suggested it might be better for me if I returned home with her. She argued that staying in Jersey would be extremely depressing for me and, in the limited time I had, I should at least have the opportunity to enjoy some of my leave. Reluctantly, I agreed, and unknowingly caused some hurt feelings among the family. My sister Betty really never forgave Marge for spiriting me away.

Marge was married to T.K. Wrigley who had two daughters, Dottie and Jane, by a previous marriage. I later suspected Marge had an ulterior motive in bringing me to Atlanta. She was playing matchmaker and hoped Dottie and I would find a great deal in common. If that were so, her plan backfired.

One of the first places we went was a restaurant featuring lunchtime entertainment. We had just finished ordering lunch when a beautiful dark-haired girl stepped to the microphone and, backed by a small combo, began singing George and Ira Gershwin's tender love ballad "Embraceable You". I was enthralled! All that loveliness, and a tremendously talented singer as well. When she finished the set, she came over to our table and Marge introduced us. *This* was *Jane!*

I can't say I fell in love immediately, but certainly I was enchanted by this slim, well-built, Irish girl with a wonderful outgoing personality. She would have dinner with us that evening, she said, and I could hardly contain my joy at the prospect.

From dinner that evening until I boarded the train back to the West Coast, Jane and I were together constantly. She was doing a radio show on station WSB, and also working with Conductor Albert Coleman and the Atlanta Pops, but these weren't taking up a great deal of Jane's time. I borrowed T.K.'s '40 Ford coupe. Mindful of gas rationing, we spent much of the time parked in secluded spots.

Not all was pleasant during my Atlanta stay. I kept having disturbing nightmares, like those on the flight from the Solomons, that would wake me in the middle of the night. Not wanting to go back to sleep lest they recur, I'd get up and walk the streets.

My time with Jane was all too short, but we both were positive we were in love with each other. We promised to write regularly and to plan for my next leave, whenever that might be.

It was a long, lonely, and tedious train ride back to Treasure Island, mitigated only by the memories of my time with Jane.

20

THE PERFECT FIGHTING SHIP

Back at Treasure Island a few days before Christmas, I settled down in the "N" Barracks to await assignment to a destroyer. That's where I first met Floyd Joseph Fitch, Junior, Signalman 2nd Class, USN. Fitch was from a mining family in Montana and had been in the Navy since 1939. Being Regular seagoing Navy, he and I would become best buddies.

Junior was married to a feisty little woman whom everyone called "Butch", and she was staying at a boarding house in Oakland. On our first liberty together, I went with Fitch to meet Butch and, incidentally, get some good home cookin'. Butch and I hit if off well right from the first, insuring the Fitches and I would have some pleasant times together. The daughter of the proprietress of the boarding house was around my age, so the four of us would go out together, mostly to the movies. The camaraderie among us cemented the friendship with Junior and he became my closest shipmate.

On 10 January, 1944, I was assigned to the U.S.S. IRWIN (DD-794) pre-commissioning detail and immediately went back into intensive training. The next day I began classes at the T.I. Radio Materiel School for a refresher course in electronics. The two-week schooling was just over when I came down with, of all things, a case of measles. Hardly had I gotten rid of the last red dot, when I went from Sick Bay to the Advanced Firefighting School at Mare Island.

Fire at sea is the most feared of all calamities that can afflict a ship, and the Navy insured that every vessel had among its crew men who were well-trained to cope with blazes big and small. Fire drills and damage control exercises were a constant part of shipboard routine.

The two-week course was one that had been compressed from a thirty-day school. Starting early in the morning, we kept at the drills all day. The most realistic of these were in the fire tower, a steel and concrete structure built to simulate various spaces aboard ship. In one of the most intensive (and dangerous) exercises, several inches of fuel oil were flooded into concrete troughs over which were fitted steel gratings to emulate conditions in a vessel's engine spaces. The oil was then set afire and the students had to go in to put it out.

A recent development in the firefighters' arsenal was the "fog nozzle". Firemen had long known that pouring water on an oil fire from a standard nozzle only served to spread the flames and make the situation worse. With the fog nozzle at the end of a long, slightly bent, slender metal pipe, water was forced into the fogger at high pressure. The nozzle was punctured with a myriad of tiny holes, causing the water to turn into a fine mist. This mist became so thick it robbed the fire of the oxygen that kept it burning and, in effect, smothered the flames.

Unluckily, I was chosen as the nozzle man on the first four-man crew to go into the simulated engine room. The burning oil threw flames several feet high above the metal grates. There was a stiff breeze off San Francisco Bay, causing an updraft in the fire tower. This not only made the flames higher, but affected the fog, dissipating the mist. The heat and flames were intense and my clothing was getting hot. One of the hose handlers behind me panicked and bolted for the exit. The instructor took his place behind me and calmly said: "Take it on in."

As I moved forward, inch by inch, the fogger began to do its job and, in a few minutes, the fire was out. The only protective clothing we'd worn were heavy gloves and mine were badly scorched. My eyebrows and some of my hair were singed as were parts of my dungarees and shirt. We'd had a few very tense minutes, and I'd been on the verge of bailing out, too. The instructor treated it all as routine and called for the next four-man crew.

Not all of the course was actual firefighting. We also learned cleaning and maintaining of equipment and hoses; operation and care of handy-billies (small gasoline-powered pumps); use of damage control tools and equipment; how to determine if there was fire on the other side of a bulkhead; and other facets of firefighting and damage control likely to be encountered aboard a ship set ablaze by accident or enemy action.

The day after completing the course, the men in the IRWIN Detail departed for the Bethlehem Steel Shipbuilding Yard at San Pedro. We would join others of the pre-commissioning crew and prepare for the ceremonies that officially transferred the ship to the Navy and made her a part of the Pacific Fleet.

As I walked down the dock at Beth Steel and got my first glimpse of the IRWIN, I fell in love! If I could have, I would have thrown my arms around her and kissed her. After those months in the Solomons on a beat-up old transport, ashore on a stinking island, and bouncing around on a pair of spit kits—she was, to me, a combat sailor's dream come true. That beautiful, beautiful ship, so sleek and trim, perfectly proportioned, shipshape in Bristol fashion. As they used to say about good-looking girls in Brooklyn: *"What a built!"*

But like the Dragon Lady in Milt Caniff's "Terry and the Pirates" comic strip, she was not only gorgeous—she was deadly. This was a *combat* vessel, a man-o'-war of the Fleet, built to fight. There was no doubt as to her mission. She epitomized the very warship Captain John Paul Jones had in mind when he said: "I wish to have no Connection with any Ship that does not sail fast, for I intend to go *in harm's way.*" The Father of the American Navy would have been right at home on the Bridge of the U.S.S. IRWIN.

The IRWIN was a 2,100-ton FLETCHER-class destroyer of the later models typically called "low bridge" FLETCHERS. Classes of ships are routinely named after the prototype vessel—in this case for the DD-445, commissioned 30 June, 1942.

"The Classic American destroyer of World War II"!

"The most efficient fighting vessel ever built"!

"The perfect fighting destroyer"!

These are but some of the quotes from naval architects and longtime destroyer officers describing the FLETCHERS. In all, 175 of these "Greyhounds of the Fleet" would be commissioned between June, 1942, and October, 1944. Their combination of flush-decked hull and two prominent rake-capped stacks went to create what was to be the standard profile of war-built U.S. destroyers. For the definitive work on these ships, see Alan Raven's *Fletcher-Class Destroyers* (1986).

What made the IRWIN and her sister ships so awesome was the tremendous amount of armament and firepower they had for vessels so small. The Main Battery consisted of five 5-inch, .38-caliber single rifles in enclosed mounts. Two were mounted forward of the bridge superstructure (Mounts 51 and 52). The "After Three" (Mounts 53, 54, and 55) were at the after end of the deck housing. Mounts 51 and 55 were on the main deck, the others atop the deck house. They were dual-purpose, designed to be used against both surface and aerial targets.

Supplementing the Main Battery, primarily for anti-aircraft protection, we mounted five twin Bofors 40-millimeter rapid-fire weapons, two on either side of the Bridge at the 0-1 level, two amidships on elevated platforms on each side of Number Two Stack, and one atop the deck house aft between 5-inch Mounts 53 and 54. For closer-in AA protection, seven 20-millimeter single Oerlikon rapid-fire cannons were installed—three in a "tub" on the fantail forward of the depth charge racks, and two on each side of the main deck amidships.

In combat situations, we knew by listening to the fire of our weapons how close attacking aircraft were. They were at extended range when

DD 794
BROADSIDE VIEW (18 KNOTS)
COMPLETION
OUTER HARBOR
SAN PEDRO

U.S.S. IRWIN (DD-794)
Port side Identification Photo
(Naval Historical Center)

only the 5-inch guns were in action. They were getting closer when the 40s opened up. It was when the 20s started chattering that we knew the hostiles were too damned close for comfort. We were in range of their weapons. It's the First Law of Combat: "When the enemy is in range—so are YOU."

Our major offensive weapons against enemy warships were our two quintuple 21-inch torpedo tube mounts. Tube One was between the stacks. Tube Two was just abaft Number Two Stack. Added to our offensive/defensive shore bombardment, surface, and anti-aircraft capabilities was our third offensive system—anti-submarine warfare. Two depth charge racks were mounted on the stern, with the 600-pound "ash cans" released over the target by gravity. Six depth charge projectors (K-guns) with 300-pound charges were installed, three on each side of the main deck on the port and starboard quarters. Integrated with these systems were our radar detection gear for air and surface ranging and firing, and the sonar gear for underwater search and detection of submarines. These were the ship's eyes and ears, critical to our combat efficiency.

Destroyers are built for speed. It is both an offensive and defensive capability. To carry out one of our most important missions—that of protecting aircraft carriers, battleships, and cruisers—we needed to be both faster and more maneuverable to keep us between attackers, both surface and air, and our bigger charges. In offensive action, our speed would get us in and out faster, making us a more difficult target for the enemy. To produce that speed, we had a "split" power plant, i.e. two separate engine and fire rooms. The four Babcock & Wilcox boilers delivered 60,000 horsepower to each of the two shafts driving the twin screws or propellers. The war steaming speed was a rated 38 knots, about 45 miles per hour. But on the IRWIN's sea trials, with the superheaters cut in, the black gang, our engineering department, swore we reached 47 knots. Our cruising range was 5,790 nautical miles at 15 knots, 3,090 miles at 25 knots.

Long and lean, the IRWIN's length at the water line was 369 feet. Overall, at main deck level, she measured 376 feet, 6 inches. At the beam (widest part of the hull amidships) she was only 39 feet, 8 inches; tapering to the pointed bow forward, and to about 25 feet across the sternmost part of her fantail. Her draft, from water line to keel, was but 13 feet, 9 inches. From water line to the tip of the radar atop the mast, it was roughly 90 feet. As designed, the flush deck sloped from the 20-foot-high prow to less than nine feet above the water line at the screw guards. The distance between water line and main deck is called "freeboard". As extra gear is added over and above the original plans, it drives the freeboard down. In heavy weather, less freeboard means more seas washing over the decks. Thus wet footing on the main deck was an almost standard condition when the ship was underway.

Destroyers are universally known throughout the Fleet as "tin cans" or simply "cans". The designation is hardly a misnomer, nor without some basis in fact. With all our *armament* (weaponry), we had only token *armor*. The protective armored steel plating on the NORTH CAROLINA reached *sixteen inches*. On the IRWIN, we were accorded only *one-half to three-quarter-inch* ballistic plating for only the Pilot House (Bridge), 5-inch Gun Director, and the decks and sides that protected the machinery spaces. This thin armor was designed to protect from strafing and fragmentation, but would hardly do much more than stop a .50-caliber machinegun bullet.

John C. Reilly, Jr., in his book *United States Navy Destroyers in World War II*, makes the point all destroyer sailors lived and died with: "For the rest of its survival the destroyer had to depend on the combination of speed and agility; firepower; good design and sturdy construction; determined crews carrying out effective damage control doctrine; and in so many cases, what can only be described as the *hand of God*."

The Navy's Bureau of Ships, in post-War studies, concluded: "Despite their comparative vulnerability, numerous cases of war damage have demonstrated that destroyers are rugged vessels and will absorb and survive an astonishing amount of punishment. This is particularly true of the 2100- and 2200-ton classes. Furthermore, it is possible to greatly augment their inherent ability to survive extensive damage by prompt and effective damage control measures. In any consideration of the survival powers of the modern destroyer, the *personnel factor* must be recognized. The ship as built has proved its ruggedness but many vessels survived unprecedented damage largely due to the high degree of training and the *heroic determination of the crews*."

At the same time, some Navy Department statistician was giving our morale a tremendous boost by computing that the life of a destroyer in combat was but *seven and a half minutes!*

Into the spaces aboard not given over to armament, magazines, machinery, offices, working areas, essential storage, and fuel bunkers were crammed 325 officers and men. The crew's berthing spaces were exceedingly cramped, with as many bunks and lockers as it was possible to install. With the bunks down in sleeping position, it was difficult for two men to pass each other in the narrow passageways. There were but 16 inches between the sacks—so, if a man were sleeping on his side, his shoulders would rub on the bottom of the mattress in the bunk above him.

The Navy had learned the hard way that berthing a crew by division could be disastrous. If, for instance, all the radiomen were assigned to the same compartment as had been the peacetime practice, a single hit in that area could wipe out all the men in that specialty and leave the ship without communicators. On the IRWIN, the men of different divisions were split up and scattered so no individual ratings would be concentrated in one space. Fitch and I drew Compartment 205, the most sternward of the berthing decks. We staked out two bunks in the same tier on the port side in the aftermost section.

Our compartment had 64 bunks in a space less than 35 feet long by 25 feet wide. Most of the other berthing areas were even smaller. There was no room aboard ship given over to recreation, relaxation, or off-duty activities. Even the mess deck doubled as a berthing space. Aside from necessary chairs used in working spaces, there were no places at all just to sit down, except on the deck. And that was cold, hard steel. Compared to carrier, battlewagon, and cruiser duty—destroyermen lived a very Spartan existence.

Junior and I stowed our gear in our lockers, made up our bunks, then headed forward, he to the Signal Bridge and I to Radio Central to check out our primary work areas. The Radio Shack was on the Communications Deck, usually referred to as the "0-1 level". It was the first deck above the main deck in the superstructure. The next level up was the Bridge, the rear portion of which was Fitch's Signal Bridge.

Radio Central took up less than 200 square feet to the port side of the centerline of the ship. Into the largest area, nine by twelve feet, were crowded two operating positions with receivers, typewriters, chairs, and two large transmitters. Forward of that space was another operating position, accessible through an open transverse hatchway, in an area five by five feet. The ECM (coding) room, two feet six inches by five feet, was forward of that. There were no ports. Ventilation was by forced-air blowers. At sea, there'd be a minimum of three men on watch at all times.

It was a cozy little place, to say the most! The first thing I did was to check to see what radio call letters had been assigned to the IRWIN. We were identified as *NTMR*. The working conditions of radiomen were not envied by other sailors. As Seaman James J. Fahey wrote, with reference to such on his cruiser the MONTPELIER, in his *Pacific War Diary*: "Working in the radio shack continuously would not suit me as it is confined to a limited space and is very hot."

On Saint Valentine's Day, 14 February, 1944, the U.S.S. IRWIN (DD-794) was placed in commission by Captain S.F. Hein, USN, Commandant, Naval Operating Base, Terminal Island, California. Commander Daniel Byrd Miller, USN, Naval Academy Class of 1926, assumed command. Lieutenant John Dale Pye Hodapp, Jr., USN, Annapolis Class of 1939, was the Executive Officer. Ship's company, the original complement of 19 officers and 302 enlisted men, mustered at quarters for the ceremony through which the ship officially was accepted by the Navy and assigned to the Pacific Fleet.

The IRWIN was named for a hero of the Spanish-American War. Noble Edward Irwin was in command of the BALTIMORE in the Battle of Manila Bay in the Philippines in 1898. He was the only American officer wounded in the conflict. During World War I, he was awarded the Navy Cross for meritorious service as Director of Naval Aviation and was one of the pioneers in that field. Following the War, he commanded the U.S.S. OKLAHOMA, then went on to become Commander Destroyer Squadrons, Scouting Fleet. From 1927 until 1931, he was Chief of the U.S. Naval Mission in Brazil. Rear Admiral Irwin became Commandant of the 15th Naval District in 1931 and retired in 1933. He died 10 August, 1937.

The members of the commissioning crew of a vessel are referred to as "plankowners", and the designation is a subject of great pride among sailors. It signifies that each man "owns" a part of the ship forevermore.

The plankowners of the IRWIN were fortunate, indeed, to have a man we would come to regard as *The Best Destroyer Skipper in the Fleet* on the Bridge. The Commanding Officer of a ship is referred to, formally, as the Captain; but among the crew is also known as the C.O., the Old Man, or simply the Skipper. To us, our Old Man was universally, respectfully, and lovingly called "Cap'n Danny". Not to his face of course. Personally we always addressed him as "Captain".

When I was first assigned to the pre-commissioning detail at Treasure Island, I asked who would command the ship. Told it was Commander Daniel B. Miller, I breathed a sigh of relief. He was well-known in the Fleet as a top-notch destroyer Skipper. At Pearl Harbor on December 7th, he'd been the C.O. of the ALLEN (DD-66), the only "broken-deck four-piper" destroyer still in active service. The old vessel, attached to the Hawaiian Sea Frontier, was of pre-World War I vintage. It was Captain Miller who got her underway and out of the harbor to safety, and who reputedly shot down the first attacking Japanese plane.

Although assigned to the aircraft carrier SARATOGA on graduating from Annapolis, the Captain had spent the majority of his career in tin cans. He served on the BLAKELEY (DD-150) and the RATHBURN (DD-113) as well as the ALLEN. After Pearl Harbor, he commissioned and took command of the new BRISTOL-class McKENZIE (DD-614) in November, 1942. Assigned to the Atlantic Fleet, he took her to the

COMMANDER DANIEL BYRD MILLER, USN (USNA 1926)
First Commanding Officer of U.S.S. IRWIN (DD–794) - 1944
(Courtesy Mrs. Daniel [Dorothy] Miller)

Mediterranean for the Sicily invasion and other Med operations. In May, 1943, while enroute to Casablanca, the McKENZIE depth-charged and sank the German submarine U-182.

When he took command of the IRWIN, Captain Miller was the senior Commander in the Navy, and now was senior destroyer Commanding Officer in the Fleet. Lieutenant Hodapp, who retired as a Commander, confirmed to me recently that Miller had foregone promotions and plush assignments to remain in destroyers, the service he loved so dearly. It was Cap'n Danny who made the IRWIN a unique command. Not only was she a FLETCHER—"the perfect fighting destroyer"—but she became "*the* PERFECT destroyer" in which to serve as the crew came to love the Skipper like a father, an affection for him which continues to this day.

The IRWIN would operate as a unit of Destroyer Division 109 in company with the U.S.S. CALLAGHAN (DD-792), CASSIN YOUNG (DD-793), and PRESTON (DD-795). DesDiv 110—composed of the LAWS (DD-558), LONGSHAW (DD-559), MORRISON (DD-560), and PRICHETT (DD-561)—together with DesDiv 109 formed Destroyer Squadron 55, with the Flag of Commander DesRon 55 on (an officer would say *in*, an enlisted man *on*) the PORTERFIELD (DD-682). They were all FLETCHERS.

Hardly had our commission pennant been two-blocked at the masthead, when the order came over the intercom system to change from dress blues to the uniform of the day, dungarees, and begin preparations to ready the ship for pre-shakedown exercises. The rush was on to get us fully combat-ready to join the Fleet as soon as possible.

The task of whipping the IRWIN's crew into a fighting unit would be a formidable one. Most were green hands. Of the 302 enlisted men, only 83 were Regular Navy, and only 66 of us had been in the service prior to Pearl Harbor. While this small cadre were mostly senior petty officers with combat experience, the vast majority of our crew were new to the service and to the sea. And that included many of our junior officers. Few had ever heard any weapon bigger than a .22 fired. For many of them, this would be their first time away from home. Now, only time, training, and the crucible of combat would tell whether they'd make good tin can sailors. Our lives depended on it.

The Communications Division included quartermasters, signalmen, sonarmen, radarmen, and radiomen. We mustered the Radio Gang on the Comm Deck, the Radio Shack being too small to accommodate us all. Our Chief Radioman was Wilfred Henry Leger, a veteran of some 18 years service. Vincent Krakow (RM1c), Albert Brantly Block (RM2c), John A. Hutchinson (RM2c), John Dekle (RM3c), Frank Guy

COMMISSIONING THE U.S.S. IRWIN
Captain Daniel Miller, at the podium, accepts command of the new
destroyer as she is officially turned over to the Navy and placed in
formal commission. Dignitaries from the Naval Operating Base, Terminal
Island, California attend.
(Official U.S. Navy Photo)

Riddle (RM3c), Fred Hartman (RM3c), and James Smith (RM3c) were the petty officers. Our seaman strikers—Mansell Giffen, Dawson Newton Bressie, Ken Wasson, and Harold Fitzwater—rounded out the plankowner radio people of "C Division". Smith would be transferred for medical reasons during the first week, and Krakow would go to another command when we reached Pearl Harbor.

Chief Leger was a frail, slightly-built man who for health reasons should have been on shore duty. While a top-notch radioman himself, the Chief recognized the ability of his subordinates, leaving most of the day-to-day tasks to his three senior petty officers. He spent most of his time, either in the Chief's Quarters or on the Comm Deck, shooting the bull. Radioman 2nd Class Al Block was an ebullient Texan from McAllen, down in Big Bend country. He always pronounced his home town's name "MACK-Allen". Block was built like his name, stocky and muscular, and he was one of the best radiomen I ever knew.

A quiet, thin Floridian with a dry wit, John Dekle was one of the best-liked of our Gang. He was a very competent operator, going about his duties in a professional way. Another Southerner, Frank Riddle, was a happy-go-lucky North Carolinian, and one of the few Regular Navy men who'd enlisted after the War started. The other 3rd Class, Fred Hartman from Los Angeles, was pretty much of a loner and sort of a surly person who didn't mix much with the rest of the Gang. Our strikers were all filled with the exuberance of youth and the excitement of going to sea for the first time. They were a pretty good bunch of kids and had a lot to learn. In time, they'd do their duty well.

The Communications Officer was Lieutenant Lou Dean, USNR, who bothered us little. A very nice man, he was the oldest officer aboard, excluding Captain Miller.

Radiomen lived a little bit different life from the rest of the crew. Standard shipboard watches were four hours long, with two "dog watches" from 1600 to 1800 and 1800 to 2000. Only radiomen stood watches six hours long: from 2400 to morning mess, morning mess to noon, noon to evening mess, and from chow to 2400. The midwatch (midnight to AM chow) rated "night rations", sandwich makin's from the galley, and they were allowed to sleep in after getting off watch until 1100. We had our own coffee mess, and "the smoking lamp was lit" in the Shack at all times except when refueling or loading ammunition. Qualified watchstanders, that is, those who could stand a circuit watch and copy FOX schedules, were permitted liberty in port at 1300 instead of waiting until 1600 as did most of the crew. All this was standard procedure for radiomen throughout the Fleet.

"Set the Special Sea Detail! All hands make preparations for getting underway!"

The orders crackled over the ship's loudspeakers, and there was a rush of excitement and anticipation as we began our initial sea trials. For the first two weeks, we operated out of San Pedro as necessary—with full power runs, degaussing trials (neutralizing the magnetic field around a ship), structural firing of the Main Battery, anchoring drills, measured mile runs, and other exercises necessary to train a combat crew and check out the ship's performance. Captain Miller was delighted with the crew's progress and noted in the War Diary: "Officers and crew working well with their new ship and forming a war machine."

On 3 March, 1944, we proceeded to San Diego to begin our full-blown shakedown at sea. We were also getting acquainted with our shipmates, principally the other ratings in the C Division—signalmen, quartermasters, radarmen, and sonarmen. We all had duties in and around the Bridge area, and it was necessary we all work well together when we put to sea.

The next month was a hectic one for the IRWIN's crew. We were at sea nearly every day and many nights, testing and training in every conceivable facet of shiphandling, maneuvers, and combat operations. We began with radio direction finder calibration, proceeded to sonar exercises, torpedo run simulation, spotting practice for the Main Battery, night firing, radar calibration, anti-aircraft firing at towed target sleeves, high-speed runs, various simulated attack and defense maneuvers, as well as internal and damage control drills.

We operated both independently and in concert with other vessels. Among these were the LAKE (DE-301), STOCKHAM (DD-683), CASSIN (DD-372), and BOWERS (DE-637), as well as the now repaired and modernized veteran of Pearl Harbor, the CALIFORNIA (BB-44). It was good to see the old "Prune Barge" back in operation. For two days, Captain Frederick Moosbrugger, the hero of Vella Gulf and now of the Training Command, was aboard to act as Officer in Tactical Command (O.T.C.) of our training unit.

In the Radio Shack, we conducted training of the 3rd Class Radiomen and the strikers in call letter authentication and recognition, daily authenticator usage, and Fleet organization in the comparatively new Task Force, Task Group, and Task Unit designations; also in the tuning, operation, and maintenance of receivers, transmitters, and other gear, as well as in daily routine. All were constantly drilled in copying code to keep their proficiency at peak levels.

We got our first taste of what it would be like in the Shack during combat. When 5-inch Mount 52 and/or the twin 40-millimeter AA guns, forward of and on either side of the Shack, were firing, it caused no end of problems for us. While the receivers were mounted on shock absorbers, they still would shake, rattle, and roll from the recoil and muzzle blasts of the weapons, requiring operators to retune them constantly in order to keep 'em on frequency. The din, of course, made it difficult to hear incoming radio signals, and only intense concentration made copying code possible.

One of the first priorities after commissioning was acquisition of a division coffee pot. Each of us chipped in a buck or so and we bought a six-cup percolator. To keep it steady in heavy seas, I salvaged one of the metal cases in which 5-inch shells were stored. Cutting it to size, with a slit for the pot's handle, I bolted it to the top of a junction box affixed to the after bulkhead. As I admired my handiwork, my mind flashed back to Jackson and the JUNEAU. There was a rush of melancholy. I'd forego any Silver Certificates of the Golden Joe Pot on the IRWIN. You think of such things and bleed a little.

We didn't get too many liberties in "Dago". I tried to locate my mother, but was unaware she'd moved to San Ysidro and wasn't listed in any San Diego phone directories. She and Dad had separated (and later divorced) when I was about eleven or twelve, and she'd gone West. Finally, I resolved to call my sister Betty, to see if she knew Mom's address, but we shoved off before I got the chance. I would not see my mother again.

It was on returning from liberty one morning that I witnessed Navy ingenuity at its best. The head (toilets/washroom/showers) was, like everything else aboard, limited in space. The toilets were stainless steel troughs with "form-fitting" seats across them. Flushing was constant as salt water flowed from a pipe at one end and exited the other. Early this day, the head was overcrowded with the duty section readying for the watch and all the returning liberty parties. The occasion for Navy ingenuity?

The seats over the troughs were fully populated, and the guys were taking their own sweet time, some even reading newspapers. A line began to form and not a few men were getting impatient. Finally, one of them (who *had* to go, *now!*) took matters into his own hands. Wadding up a big ball of toilet paper, he struck a match to it and dropped it in the trough where the water flowed in. As it floated down the stream beneath the seats, it caused consternation as bare bottom after bare bottom got scorched. Sailors were popping up off the seats like Jack coming out of his Box! To everyone but the victims, it was hilarious.

On 6 April, after operating with several transports in simulated amphibious landings off San Clemente Island, we were detached to proceed to San Francisco. On the way, we steamed into Monterey Bay for a torpedo firing exercise, and to act as a target for simulated attacks by Navy aircraft. At the end of the day, we sailed under the Golden Gate Bridge for the first time and moored at the pier in the Bethlehem Shipyard at Hunter's Point.

For the next 18 days, we were underway at times for compass and radio direction finder calibration and other routine tests. While moored, we underwent post-shakedown overhaul, but there was little for the shipyard to do. The IRWIN had stood up well in her trials. Captain Miller gave us liberty at every opportunity, knowing it might be a long time before we'd get any more. Most of my liberties were spent with Fitch and Butch, but I did pull a few solo. The ship made the front page of the San Francisco *Examiner* with a photo of one of our junior officers, Ensign N.S. "Red" Irwin, and a contingent of the crew shown marching to a blood bank to make donations. As a result, the ship got a large, extra supply of plasma to take with us. It would come in very handy, as events would show.

The morale on the IRWIN was higher than I'd seen in any command since Captain Badger was Skipper of the NORTH CAROLINA. And the credit had to go to Cap'n Danny. Enlisted men who'd seen combat were very adept at making swift assessments of the competency of officers. Our lives depended on it. The "old hands" aboard rated Captain Miller as a 4.0 commanding officer, and let the green crewmen know they were serving under an unusually able and qualified leader. But it was more than that. The Old Man created an atmosphere in which there was little of the pettiness and harassment of the crew by officers that plagued many ships. It was evident that the Skipper had respect and affection for his enlisted men. He treated the crew with fairness and, through our Executive Officer, Lieutenant Hodapp, put the word out he would brook no bullying of his crew. Yet, he was firm and business-like in training us to be a fighting crew—working us long, hard hours to achieve perfection in combat readiness.

The Captain did let it be known that he expected us to behave as professional seagoing men. At the same time, he laid down the law with great emphasis when it came to profanity in the form of blasphemies and obscenities. At a ship's muster, he ticked off a list of words and phrases which he said he would not abide on his ship. And he backed up his determination to cleanse our language of cursing by the simple expedient of promising an immediate Deck Court-Martial for any man he heard uttering the forbidden swear words. Of course, that didn't completely eliminate "cussing" on the ship, but none was ever heard around the Bridge where the Old Man was most of the time.

The Skipper set the tone of his command early on when, like Captain Badger on the NORTH CAROLINA, he quietly let both officers and enlisted men know he wanted his crew to look smart and wear their uniforms with pride. Abe Fernandes, one of our 3rd Class Gunners Mates, witnessed the incident.

It was at one of our first liberty calls when the Exec, Lieutenant Hodapp, started to lift the liberty card of one of the crew for wearing tailor-made dress blues instead of regs. The Old Man happened to come down to the Quarterdeck about that time and interceded. He told the sailor to stand in front of him, then to turn all the way around. After looking him over, the Captain said: "Mr. Hodapp, this boy looks very nice to me. Give him back his liberty card." To the crewman he smiled and said: "Go on, son, have a good time." The IRWIN was going to be a "happy ship"!

All professional sailors hold exceptional shiphandling in the highest regard, and it was here that Cap'n Danny won our hearts and souls. We had observed his ability to maneuver and put the ship through its paces during shakedown, but there was one incident that solidified our confidence in him.

We had been at sea on a day's exercises and returned to San Francisco Bay with instructions to moor at a pier below Coit Tower. There were two other tin cans with us and we would be the last to tie up. Anticipating an early liberty call, many of us—including the Skipper—were already in dress blues as we stood off the pier waiting for the other destroyers to moor. Now the tides, eddies, and currents in the Bay are notoriously unpredictable and difficult in which to maneuver. The other cans were having one devil of a time getting alongside the pier, being pushed one way or the other by the Bay's currents. As they made one false landing after another, Danny Miller was fuming. He was anxious to get ashore, as were we in the crew.

Finally, after what seemed like an eternity, the other cans got themselves moored. Then our Old Man swung the IRWIN in a wide loop out toward Alcatraz, pointed the bow toward the pier, and rang up turns for speed. The DD-794 headed straight for her assigned berth, churning up a substantial wake in the Bay's waters. Longshoremen looked up to see this destroyer bearing down on them—making knots which, if unchecked, would put the ship somewhere several blocks up on Nob Hill. The "dock-wallopers" bailed out, heading for safety. As our bow came even with the end of the pier, still moving swiftly, the Skipper signaled the engine room "full astern!"—backing her down with all her power.

When Cap'n Danny backed her down full, the sleek tin can responded by coming almost to a stop, then eased alongside the pier only a few feet from the fenders. The deck apes heaved over the lines, doubling them up in record time. With a wisp of a smile of satisfaction, Captain Miller looked around at us on the Bridge and gave the order: "Let's go ashore!" The crew let out a cheer. We thumbed our noses at the wide-eyed crews of the other two tin cans and headed for the gangway. Captain Daniel Byrd Miller was *our* kind of Skipper.

We got two new additions to our Radio Gang during the stay in San Francisco. On 19 April, Don Karl, a tow-headed Seaman 1st and radio school graduate—home town Kalamazoo, Michigan—came aboard from Treasure Island Receiving Station. Two days later, George Mootz, a gangly kid from Iowa, reported from the Naval Receiving Station at Shoemaker.

On 16 April, 1944, with only a little over two months preparation and training, the IRWIN slipped her mooring from Buoy "A" in San Francisco Bay with orders from Commander Western Sea Frontier to proceed at 18 knots for Pearl Harbor, Territory of Hawaii.

I wrote one last uncensored letter to Jane. I was going back to sea, and back to War.

U.S.S. NORTH CAROLINA (BB-55)
Reproduced by special permission of artist Carl G. Evers and the United States Naval Institute

GUADALCANAL CAMPAIGN VETERANS patch

ESCORT TO DANGER
The U.S.S. NORTH CAROLINA and U.S.S. ENTERPRISE under Japanese air
attack—Battle of Eastern Solomons—24 August, 1942
Reproduced by special permission of artist William J. Reynolds

THE SINKING OF THE U.S.S. McCAWLEY
Hit by torpedoes, the "WACKY MAC" explodes as the tug PAWNEE and destroyer McCALLA dodge other "tin fish." Blanche Channel, Rendova, 30 June, 1943. Original painting by Richard De Rosset

The Author—November, 1944

Another pilot rescued by the U.S.S. IRWIN (DD-794), June, 1944
Original painting by Shipmate Bill Needles

21

THE TIN CAN NAVY

Man is a land animal. The great oceans covering two-thirds of the planet are alien to him. Of the great masses of humanity peopling the continents, only an infinitesimal proportion will venture far from their shores. Those who do seemingly respond to some irresistible, perhaps primeval, instinct that overcomes the fear their brethren have of the deep.

It is incomprehensible to most landsmen that one of their own species would willingly choose an environment so foreign and inhospitable. Every tale of the sea is of hardship, privation, danger and death in both war *and* peace. From time immemorial, when vessels reportedly would sail over the edge of the earth, when great monsters would attack, to Coleridge's *Ancient Mariner,* to the mysteries of the Bermuda Triangle—the sea has been a place filled with the foreboding and the forbidden.

Yet somewhere in the souls of the few who become deep water sailors is an innate compulsion to abandon the land and, once enticed, fall under the spell of the sea, seduced by this temptress they come to love with great passion. She offers adventure, challenge, a passport to exotic lands and strange peoples; magnificent and incomparable beauty in her ever changing vistas of color in waves, water, sun, moon, and sky. Her children, the porpoise and flying fish, cavort in a ship's bow wave and wake, and the zephyrs that blow between the Tropics of Cancer and Capricorn caress the brow and cheek in unmatched tenderness.

But the sea is a fickle mistress. Those zephyrs can become brutal, blasting, overwhelming tempests as they move into other climes where they spawn typhoons and hurricanes. Under her deceiving surface lurk the hazards of reef, rock, and shoal; as well as the great predators like the shark, awaiting prey with rows of knife-like teeth. Her winds and waves can smash even large vessels to bits, capsizing them or tossing them like matchsticks against stony promontories. Thus the love of her is well-tempered with respect for her power.

The men who man the vessels plying the oceans of the world will tell you that, while they would never wish for a storm, there is no experience comparable to fighting, and surviving, the hurricanes of the Atlantic and the typhoons of the Pacific. To come through without loss of ship or man, is to be able to claim great victory. And these men will also tell you that the most exhilarating emotion of all comes when their ship casts off the constraints of the land, gets underway, and stands out to the open sea. Once again, we shed the shackles and environmental limitations of the landbound and sail into our own. We are *FREE!*

> You know we're outward bound,
> *Hurrah, we're outward bound!*

Poets of the past have captured in words, to some degree, the sailor's emotional exhilaration upon leaving the land and putting to sea. In the words of B.W. Proctor:

> I'm on the sea! I'm on the sea!
> I am where I would ever be . . . .
> The sea! The sea! The open sea!
> The blue, the fresh, the ever *free!*

Perhaps *Lord Byron* captured it best:

> O'er the glad waters of the dark-blue sea,
> Our thoughts as boundless, and our souls as *free,*
> Far as the breezes can bear, the billows foam,
> Survey our empire, and behold our *home!*

With three years in the service and the long, tough, Guadalcanal Campaign behind me, I might now be considered a battle-hardened old salt. At least the kids in the Radio Gang thought so. "Newt" Bressie, the eighteen year old striker from Kansas, started calling me "Pappy". To him I was an old man—at 22! As for being an "old salt", the term would take on a whole new meaning to me in the Destroyer Navy.

On larger vessels like the NORTH CAROLINA, and even on the McCAWLEY, the sea was not an intimate part of the crew's everyday life. With a main deck perhaps 35 feet above the water line, a broad beam and heavy tonnage, larger ships plowed through the ocean with a gentle motion, except in foul weather. The decks were relatively stable platforms, and men topside seldom felt more than a wisp of salt spray.

On the IRWIN, however, the sea was a constant influence on every facet of our existence, and we had to learn to live with it. Duty on a tin can is about as close to perpetual motion as you can get. Long, lean, and low, often steaming at high speeds, a destroyer is a great deal more susceptible to the vicissitudes of wind and wave than the "heavies" with which she operates. She will "pitch" (i.e. with bow and stern dipping alternately), "roll" (rock from side to side), and sometimes "yaw" (slide sideways off course). Often a destroyer is doing all three simultaneously!

A synonym for "pitch" is "buck, like a horse". As a rodeo hand compensates for the violent gyrations of a bronc, we too learned to anticipate the motions of the ship to maintain our equilibrium. We walked with a peculiar gait, swaying from side to side and/or leaning forward and aft, all the while keeping our feet far apart, and either bracing our legs or bending our knees in concert with the ship's movements. It's about as close to ballet as a sailor ever gets. But years of pounding those steel decks obviously caused damage to feet and legs. As far as I know, though, the Navy never has addressed the problem.

Ashore, it was easy to spot a tin can sailor. He was the only John Gob you'd see walking with that strange step conditioned by long periods of navigating the undulating and uncertain decks of his ship. The unmistakable gait is universally known in the Navy as "the destroyer roll".

> There's a roll and a pitch, a heave and a pitch,
> To the nautical gait they take;
> For they're used to the cant of the quarterdeck's slant
> As the white-toothed combers break . . . .

> They hear of the sound of the seas that pound
> On the half-inch plates of steel;
> And they close their eyes to the lullabies
> Of the creaking sides and keel.

Battleship, carrier, and cruiser sailors had mixed reactions to destroyer duty. While they admired our sleek, fast vessels and envied our relaxed, more informal "dungaree Navy"—few would trade places with us once they'd witnessed a tin can in action, particularly in storms.

> They don't get much of the drill and such
> That the battleship sailors do;
> For they sail the seas in dungarees—
> A grey destroyer's crew . . . .

> They're a lusty crowd that's vastly proud
> Of the slim grey craft they drive;
> Of the roaring flues and the humming screws
> Which make her a thing alive!

We took sort of a perverse pride in perpetuating the reputation of ruggedness in tin can service. When asked how we stood the pounding sea and everlasting bouncing around, we shrugged it off by saying: "we don't consider it rough until we're taking green water over the top of the SG radar" (at the top of the mast). Or: "it's not rough until she rolls so far on her beam ends she dips water in the stacks and puts the fires out in the boilers." We also claimed destroyers were so unstable "they even rolled when tied up alongside the dock." Exaggerations? Yeah . . . but not by much!

In the Tin Can Navy even ordinary steaming in relatively calm seas could be hard riding. At standard fleet speeds of 18 to 25 knots, just crossing the wake of a bigger ship would send torrents of water crashing across the foc'sle (upper deck in front of the foremast; from *forecastle*, the foremost of two castlelike structures on a medieval warship). The sea would slam against the forward 5-inch mounts and smash into the superstructure. The ship would shudder from stem to sternpost, shake herself like a wet puppy, and steam on.

When sea action or course changes put us broadside to or athwart waves and wakes, the inclinometer would register rolls up to 40° or more. In storms, we'd roll as much or more as 50°. These were times when we'd hold our breaths, say short prayers, and just hope she'd come back on an even keel. There are recorded instances of destroyers rolling as severely as 70° and still surviving the sea to make it back to port.

To the raging and relentless winds and seas, the reactions of sailors vary. In Lord Byron's words:

> Strange sounds of wailings, blasphemy, devotion
> Clamoured in chorus to the roaring ocean.

It is fitting that the Book of Common Prayer, after prescribing longer prayers to be used in ships in stormy seas, proposes short prayers in tempests at sea: "O Lord, who stillest the raging of the sea, hear, hear us, and save us, that we perish not. . . . Lord, have mercy upon us. . . . Christ, have mercy upon us. . . . O Lord, hear us. . . . O Christ, hear us. . . ."

The Anglican poet George Herbert, quoting an old proverb, wrote in the 17th century: "He that will learn to pray, let him go to sea." For those who survive "the merciless rage of the sea", the Prayer Book prescribes thanksgiving:

"The sea roared: and the stormy wind lifted up the waves thereof. We were carried up as it were to heaven, and then down again into the deep: our soul melted within us, because of trouble. Then cried we unto thee, O Lord: and thou didst deliver us out of our distress. . . . We, thy poor creatures, whom thou hast made and preserved, holding our souls in life, and now rescuing us *out of the jaws of death*, humbly present ourselves again before thy Divine Majesty, to offer a sacrifice of praise and thanksgiving, for that thou heardest us when we called in our trouble, and didst not cast out our prayer, which we made before thee in our great distress: even when we gave all for lost, our ship, our goods, our lives, then didst thou mercifully look upon us, and wonderfully command a deliverance. . . . "

But some are not so delivered. That tin cans are exceedingly vulnerable to violent storms, was brought home during a Pacific typhoon off the Philippines in December, 1944. Three destroyers—the FLETCHER-class SPENCE (DD-512) and the FARRAGUT-class HULL (DD-350) and MONAGHAN (DD-354)—capsized and sank. The only survivors were: 23 from the SPENCE, 62 from the HULL, and just six from the MONAGHAN. Lost were 790 men, drowned in the violent waters of the Pacific, entombed in tin cans at the bottom of the Philippine Deep.

The state of mind of sailors in these rampaging and overwhelming tempests is depicted by John Donne in *The Storme:*

> Compar'd to these stormes, death is but a qualme,
> Hell somewhat lightsome, and the 'Bermuda calme . . . .
>
> Some coffin'd in their cabins lye, 'equally
> Griev'd that they are not dead, and yet must dye . . . .

The first test for the IRWIN's green hands came early. We'd hardly cleared the Golden Gate when we ran into foul weather. It was not a bad blow, but it lasted the better part of two days. The seas, combined with the long ground swells indigenous to that part of the Northern California coastline, gave the ship her baptism in the "second war" she'd be fighting, the one against the minions of King Neptune and his unpredictable watery domain. The ship weathered the wind and water well despite the onslaught of high seas and heavy gusts that pummeled her, pouring walls of foamy brine across her weather decks each time the eyes of the ship plunged violently downward. A quartering sea was pushing us off course to the south, causing her to roll heavily as well.

In the Radio Shack, we secured for heavy weather by stowing or lashing down all loose gear. We fastened the manila lines from the desks to the pad-eyes on the chairs to keep the latter from overturning or sliding across the deck. Frank Riddle was the 3rd Class and Ken Wasson the striker on my watch. The sea had hardly begun to rev up when the green hands succumbed to "ye olde *mal de mer*"! They got as sick as dogs. Both begged me to relieve them off the circuits, but I made them sit there and take it. It might seem cruel, but the young'uns had to understand the safety of the ship relied on all hands doing their duty at all times, even in the face of the most violent storms or fiercest enemy action. It's what we got paid for.

I wasn't completely heartless. Between the two operating positions I placed one of our metal wastebaskets, commonly called a "shit can", so Frank and Ken would have something convenient in which to throw up. They'd copy and heave, heave and copy, all the while turning white and wishing they were dead. I suspected they wished me the same.

It wasn't until our midwatch the second day out that the novices had their sea legs and were back to normal. The storm had moderated, and the two stopped cussing me. But there should be no stigma to getting seasick when first leaving port, storm or no. It was not unusual, even for old hands. The change in diet, imbibing too many distilled spirits before shoving off, or just getting the inner ear to become used to motion was enough to upset the delicate balance of one's innards. Except in cases of chronic seasickness, sailors usually gain their sea legs after a few days of shipboard routine and ride out severe storms with little trouble.

Neither Al Block nor I succumbed to the motion illness, and we teased the others unmercifully about their inability to withstand what we termed a "minor blow", asking them rhetorically what the hell they'd do in a "real storm". That didn't do a helluva lot for our popularity. Lord Byron's lines on a "minor blow" are apropos:

> Increased at night until it blew a gale;
> And though 'twas not much to a naval mind,
> Some landsmen would have looked a little pale,
> *For sailors are in fact a different kind.*

It's standard on destroyers to serve only sandwiches for chow during heavy weather (for those who feel like eating) so the crew was ravenously hungry when the sea subsided, eagerly awaiting the call to "chow down". But I beat the system. Bill Sharp, the Ship's Cook 3rd Class and former NORTH CAROLINA shipmate, slipped extra and early rations to me. It's nice to have good buddies, especially someone in the galley.

At 0600 on 1 May, 1944, we made landfall on the island of Molokai, and hardly had time to enjoy the beautiful Hawaiian sunrise before we were in training exercises. On our way to Pearl Harbor we commenced anti-aircraft drills; firing 101 Main Battery rounds, plus 975 forty millimeter and 1,589 twenty millimeter rounds. In the process, we knocked down all six target sleeves towed by aircraft. The Skipper noted: "Guns and men working excellently."

Mooring at a buoy in the East Loch at Pearl, we reported to

Commander Destroyers Pacific (ComDesPac). Shortly thereafter, the Flag Personnel Officer came aboard to ask our Exec, Mr. Hodapp, how many replacements the ship needed to replace those who'd missed ship or gone AWOL (absent without leave).

"None", the Exec told him.

The F.P.O. was surprised and unbelieving. "There's *never* been a ship through here that did not require replacements. J.D., you're lying to me."

Mr. Hodapp grinned. "I'll muster the crew and let you count them if you want. But we do not have a man missing. In fact, we're two *over* complement!"

The Personnel Officer still wasn't convinced and kept pressing the point that every ship coming from the States had men missing.

"I can't understand how the IRWIN would be the exception", he said.

"What you don't understand", replied the Exec, "is that our Commanding Officer is Daniel B. Miller, and this crew likes and respects him so much they wouldn't embarrass him by going AWOL."

The Flag Personnel Officer just shook his head. "Well, J.D., it's a first. I've never heard the likes of it. Now all I've got to do is convince the Admiral."

Hodapp accompanied the F.P.O back to the Quarterdeck, swaggering a little with pride, then watched the astounded officer climb into the whaleboat, still shaking his head.

Once in Hawaiian waters, we would begin a long, concentrated training schedule that would continue until 25 May. Also, our time in Pearl would see several personnel changes, some of them in the Radio Gang.

Al Block was promoted to Radioman 1st. Bressie and Wasson both made Seaman Ace. Vic Krakow and Mansell Giffen were transferred. (The latter, after attending radio school, later returned to the ship.) In their places we got Robert Terrell, a 3rd Class, and Joe John Alice, a Seaman 2nd school graduate. Terrell was a big fat guy whose stomach always hung out over his belt, had a myriad of excuses for not working or copying code, and spent most of his time griping about the Navy. Joe Alice, on the other hand, was a good-natured, hardworking kid from Spokane. We were now at full complement in the Gang. Terrell and Hartman caused some friction. But, by and large, the Radio Shack ran efficiently with a minimum of problems. We were about as ready for the upcoming campaign as we could get.

The day after we arrived at Pearl we were ordered to dock at the Submarine Base. There, for some unstated reason, the ten torpedoes we carried in our tubes from the States were replaced with fish from the

Torpedo Shop. Unknown to us at the time, switching torpedoes would become an integral part of the IRWIN's saga, remembered by every member of the crew.

Pearl Harbor and Honolulu had changed considerably in the preceding months. There were damn' near enough servicemen on Oahu to sink it. There were so many sailors and Marines crowding the streets you couldn't stir 'em with a stick. I tried, but couldn't get in P.Y. Chong's restaurant. It was jam-packed with people. The whole island was a beehive of activity, with ships coming and going, repair shops at the Navy Yard operating at full bore, and enough planes flitting around to turn the sky dark.

About the only thing that hadn't changed was the Primo Beer. It was still as "green" as ever—brewed in the morning, lagered all of fifteen minutes, and sold in the afternoon. Junior Fitch and I made a few liberties, but nothing special. Just some civilian-type chow and a few drinks. I thought to myself: "Maybe I *am* getting old!" We had little opportunity to enjoy the island paradise. From May Day 'til the 29th, we were in port only eleven days, three of those at the very end of our stay.

The War in the Pacific had not taken an hiatus while I was lolling around back in the States. We bluejackets tried to keep up with news of the War as best we could, keeping our ears open and questioning those returning from the forward areas.

The "island hopping" strategy, which would have taken ten plus years to get to Tokyo, was replaced by our "leapfrogging" strategy, by which we would "by-pass" Jap island strongholds, leaving them to "die on the vine". In the South Pacific, the frustrating and sanguinary Central Solomons Campaign was brought to a successful conclusion by leapfrogging Kolombangara, landing on Vella Lavella, and laying hold of the island by early October of 1943. In the destroyer Battle of Vella Lavella (night of 6/7 October) Japanese Admiral Ijuin gave our tin cans a beating. But, as at Kula Gulf and Kolombangara, our confidence in final strategic victory surmounted the tactical victory of the Japs.

In the Western Solomons, we took the Treasury Islands in October; and my old boss Admiral Teddy Wilkinson put troops ashore, with a view to building an airfield at Cape Torokina on the west coast of Bougainville on 1 November. In the early morning of 2 November, Admiral A. Stanton "Tip" Merrill's Task Force 39 beat off Admiral Omori's superior force attempting to break up the invasion, not to mention over 100 Jap planes at daybreak, without losing a ship in the complicated cruiser/destroyer Battle of Empress Augusta Bay.

When top Jap Admiral Mineichi Koga, fallen Admiral Yamamoto's successor, sent a large cruiser force south to Rabaul from Truk, the big Jap base in the Eastern Carolines, to disrupt the invasion of Bougainville, Admiral Bull Halsey, bereft of heavy surface ships due to the U.S. Navy's big push in the Central Pacific, countered with two new carrier groups: one under Rear Admiral Frederick C. Sherman, formed around the old SARATOGA and the new light carrier PRINCETON; the other under Rear Admiral Alfred E. Montgomery, which included the new ESSEX, BUNKER HILL, and light carrier INDEPENDENCE. American patriotism, symbolized by our carriers with names reminiscent of the American Revolution, was on a roll. On 5 and 11 November, the carrier forces raided Rabaul and the Nip Navy in the vicinity, downing many planes and damaging many ships, chasing the Jap cruisers back to Truk.

On 25 November, Thanksgiving Day, U.S. Marines repulsed the Jap Army on Bougainville, where the Marines and Army defended the Torokina Perimeter for the first four months of 1944 against a superior Jap force eventually reduced by starvation and desertion. The same Thanksgiving Day, Captain Arleigh "31 Knot" Burke and his Destroyer Squadron 23 (DesRon 23, the "Little Beaver Squadron") enhanced their reputations by sinking, with both torpedoes and gunfire without a hit in return, three Jap destroyers off New Ireland's Cape St. George. Captain Burke reminded Admiral Halsey it was Thanksgiving Day and attributed the victory to the Almighty:

"If this battle brings out no other points, it should clearly demonstrate that fortune of war is a fickle wench and that results hang by a narrow thread. There are many things which would have prevented this battle from being fought, and the Squadron Commander would much prefer to say that these matters were foreseen and steps taken to insure doing the proper thing. But they were not foreseen . . . .The Squadron was so spontaneously grateful . . . that Thanksgiving services were held upon its return to port. The Squadron is proud of its accomplishments, but it is also humbly aware that these accomplishments were made possible by a Force beyond its control."

In the Southwest Pacific, by the end of 1943 Allied Forces under General Douglas MacArthur and Army Air Force General George C. Kenney had defeated the Japanese on Eastern (Papua) New Guinea. The Seventh Fleet under Admiral Thomas C. Kinkaid virtually controlled the Bismarck Sea, as well as the Vitiaz and Dampier Straits, having landed the 1st Marine Division on Cape Gloucester on the western tip of New Britain between Christmas and New Year's.

During the first four months of 1944, the big Jap base at Rabaul on the eastern end of the island, was continuously bombed by Air Solomons

Command. At the same time, to the east of Rabaul, Nissan in the Green Islands was occupied by New Zealanders; to the north, Emirau Island north of New Ireland, by U.S. Marines; to the west, Los Negros and Manus in the Admiralty Islands, by the U.S. Army's 1st Calvary Division. The ring around Rabaul, the Jap's invincible bastion in the Bismarck Archipelago, was complete. Isolated Fortress Rabaul would remain in Jap hands until their final surrender. But the Bismarcks Barrier, to the Philippines and thus to MacArthur's route to Tokyo, was finally broken.

Meanwhile, top American Admirals King and Nimitz had directed the U.S. Navy to open up an alternate route to Japan via the vast Central Pacific, sparsely interspersed with small island groups and coral atolls known as Micronesia. Nimitz' more direct route to Tokyo involved a series of amphibious operations across far-flung Micronesia in order to control the Gilbert, Marshall, Caroline, and Mariana Archipelagos. Handpicked by Nimitz to lead these operations were: Midway hero Admiral Raymond A. Spruance commanding the Fifth Fleet, an armada of more than 200 ships including several new aircraft carriers; and, of course, my old boss Admiral R. Kelly Turner commanding the Fifth Amphibious Force.

The big push in the Central Pacific began in November 1943, some 1,500 miles east of the Bismarck Archipelago, with the taking of Tarawa and Makin Atolls in the Gilbert Islands, near the junction of the Equator and the International Date Line, by the Fifth Amphibious Corps of Marine General Holland M. "Howlin' Mad" Smith fighting against fierce and fanatical Japanese resistance. By February 1944, after heavy bombing raids by Admiral Marc A. Mitscher's Fast Carrier Force, we had taken Kwajalein (the world's largest coral atoll) and Eniwetok ("Land between West and East") of strategic importance in the Marshall Islands. Our Fast Carrier forces also bombed Truk Lagoon, the biggest Jap bastion in the Central Pacific, out of strategic significance, so that we would not have to invade any of the Eastern Carolines and could concentrate next on the Marianas.

On yard liberty I sought out men who'd been in the Gilberts and Marshalls Campaigns, curious for information, especially as to why the 2nd Marine Division had gotten clobbered so badly in the invasion of Betio Island at Tarawa, fighting for an area less than half the size of New York's Central Park. It was a story of one big SNAFU.

The first assault wave of nearly 100 LVTs (light armored amphibious tractors under poetic and heroic Colonel David M. Shoupe, later Commandant of the Marine Corps) had to make a ten-mile trip from their transports to the lagoon where landings were to be made on Red

Beaches One, Two, and Three. The lagoon was shallow, with reefs and sandbars, studded with anti-assault obstacles. It was navigable only at *full flood tide* even by very shallow-draft craft. But H-hour was twice postponed for "unaccountable reasons". By the time the amtracs got to the point of departure, the tide was in ebb at least a full hour.

The amtracs got hung up on both the man-made and natural obstacles. Ninety of the 93 LVTs were knocked out by Jap shore batteries (still operative due to the Navy's overestimating the effects of naval and aerial bombardment) and the surviving Marines had to take to the water. Wading 400 to 500 yards through the shallows, the Marines were cut down by withering Jap barrages from artillery, mortar, machinegun, and rifle emplacements. Being wounded could mean death by drowning. Perhaps 1,500 men were killed or wounded in the initial assault, with some 1,000 not even reaching the beach. But the landings continued, and by nightfall 5,000 men were ashore.

Some of the men I talked with had another version of the time delays. They said whoever designated H-hour had forgotten Tarawa is west of the 180th meridian in another time zone, thus making the assault an hour late and the critical tide that much farther into ebb. That I've never been able to confirm. But if ever the analogy of "shooting fish in a bucket" were apropos, the Tarawa invasion was it. Still, it was perhaps the Marine Corps' finest hour, a worthy successor to "the Halls of Montezeuma and the Shores of Tripoli", not to mention Guadalcanal. And future invasions would benefit from Tarawa's many mistakes.

As the IRWIN began another phase of intensive combat training off the Hawaiian Islands, I snooped around and learned the next big strike would be at the Marianas, a group of Central Pacific islands due east of the Philippines, well over a 1,000 miles away across the Philippine Sea. Operation FORAGER would assault Saipan, biggest of the chain, then take Tinian and Guam. My old Admiral, Boss Crocodile Richmond Kelly "Terrible" Turner, would be in command of the Amphibs.

Admiral Turner's message to all hands when the Fifth Fleet began the push across the Central Pacific at Makin and Tarawa (he was not known as a religious man) applied to us:

"Units attached to this force are honored in having been selected to strike another hard blow against the enemy. . . . The close cooperation between all arms and services, the spirit of loyalty to each other and the determination to succeed displayed by veteran and untried personnel alike, gives me complete confidence that we will never stop until we have achieved success. I lift my spirit with this unified team of Army, Navy and Marines whether attached to ships, aircraft or ground units, and I say to you that I know God will bless you and give you the strength to win a glorious victory."

Captain Miller was putting us through our paces with exercises and drills during May to make sure we were combat ready—honing skills in shore bombardment, anti-aircraft defense, anti-submarine warfare, day and night firing, and maneuvers with other ships. The shore bombardment practice was at targets on Kahoolawe Island, and we practiced firing all phases. The Skipper noted proudly in the War Diary that the IRWIN "qualified at first try." The next time back at Kahoolawe, we again practiced all phases of shore bombardment: e.g. exercises in direct and indirect neutralization of troops and gun emplacements, exercises in reverse slope firing, as well as exercises in night bombardment. Again the word came back from the shore observation party: *The best firing we've ever seen.*

Early in the maneuvers, we operated with Cruiser Division 14—the new VINCENNES (CL-64), INDIANAPOLIS (CA-35), MIAMI (CL-89), and new HOUSTON (CL-81)—then shifted over to working with a pair of escort aircraft carriers, also known as "jeep carriers" or "baby flat-tops". We'd act as screen for the FANSHAW BAY (CVE-70) and MIDWAY (CVE-63) to gain experience in flight operations. On 19 May, one of the MIDWAY's TBFs (torpedo planes) crashed while landing. As "plane guard" destroyer, we moved in and picked up all three airmen from the water. The plane was lost.

In strictly destroyer drills such as repelling simulated torpedo boat attacks, torpedo operations, shore bombardment, AA practice, etc., we were in company with the PORTERFIELD, CALLAGHAN, CASSIN YOUNG, LONGSHAW, LAWS, MORRISON, and ROSS. All but the ROSS (DD-563) were from our own squadron (DesRon 55).

On 15 May, while we were still in training, Carrier Support Task Group One was formed, designated TG 52.14, under Rear Admiral G.F. Bogan. The IRWIN would be in Unit One with the FANSHAW BAY, MIDWAY, CASSIN YOUNG, and ROSS. Unit Two, under Captain O.A. Weller, was comprised of the WHITE PLAINS (CVE-66) and KALINAN BAY (CVE-68), screened by the PORTERFIELD, CALLAGHAN, and LONGSHAW. Commander Task Force 52 was Admiral Kelly Turner, and Commander Fifth Fleet was Admiral Ray Spruance. In Operation FORAGER, we were under Turner's Amphibious Command as support vessels to the landing forces.

Destroyers are the "Mud Marines" of the Fleet, getting all the jobs no one else can or wants to do, and very little credit. The duties are many and varied. Tin can sailors are quick to remind battleship, aircraft carrier, and cruiser sailors that the Navy wouldn't put *any* of those big ships in the water without destroyers to protect them: protect them against air, surface, and submarine attack, and to act as radar pickets to provide early warning of incoming air raids. At the same time, our missions included shore bombardment of enemy defenses during amphibious landings, and gunfire support of troops on land. We would act as fighter direction units, deploying Combat Air Patrols against impending air attack; and we were called upon to use electronic countermeasures (jamming) against radio-supported enemy aircraft.

But that wasn't all. We steamed "plane guard", following in the wake of aircraft carriers during flight operations to rescue pilots and crews of planes that were shot-up or crashed for one reason or another. Destroyers delivered mail at sea throughout the Task Force. We transferred personnel from one ship to another via breeches buoy—canvas pants attached to pulleys to transfer men by lines at sea. Tin Cans were sent out to investigate any suspicious sightings or radar contacts. We exploded floating mines, protected Underwater Demolition Teams (UDTs), rescued men washed over the side from bigger ships, rescued survivors of ships damaged or sunk, and fought fire when other vessels were in need of such assistance. That we tin can sailors took great pride in our versatility, and in our role as the little guys taking care of the giants, goes without saying.

After all, it was part and parcel of the Destroyerman's Creed: "We believe a big-ship man would have trouble filling our shoes. We like to think we would have no trouble filling his . . . . When things are getting too rough for anyone else, they're getting just right for us."

As we lay at anchor in Pearl in the final three days before shoving off for the Marianas, Captain Miller indicated he was highly pleased with the way the crew had evolved into a cohesive fighting command. Our performance during the May training maneuvers, he said, had been exemplary. Men and equipment had not only come through with flying colors, but every department could take credit for its part in our 4.0 execution of duty and responsibility. The Skipper had assured eventual success of his command when he hand-picked four key officers: Lieutenant Tom Knight as Gun Boss; and as Assistant Gunner Officer, Lieutenant (jg) Tom Apple. Lieutenant Hays "Jumbo" Clark was the Engineering Officer; and Lieutenant Lou Dean, Communications Officer. Dean's two assistants were Ensigns Bob Cunningham and Tom Bushey, who did most of the decoding work.

But there were also other officers of considerable experience. Ensign Russ Lanoue, our Navigator, was a "Mustang", rising to commissioned rank from Chief Quartermaster by virtue of experience and superior qualifications. A combat veteran, he was aboard the MADDOX

(DD-622) when she was dive-bombed and sunk by German aircraft during the Sicily invasion, and he was wounded in the attack. He had a reputation as one of the top Navigators in the Fleet. The other Mustang aboard was the Assistant Engineering Officer, Ensign Robert A. "Pappy" Berning, the nickname coming from his prematurely gray hair. A veteran of the Battle of Midway, he was aboard the HAMMANN when she was torpedoed and sunk while trying to protect the damaged and doomed carrier YORKTOWN.

Our Executive Officer, Lieutenant John Dale Pye Hodapp, Jr., was also a veteran destroyerman, having served on the FARRAGUT (DD-334) at Pearl Harbor, and as First Lieutenant on the ABNER READ (DD-526) when she struck a mine during the Aleutians Campaign. Somewhat unlike the Captain in personality, the Exec was lively and energetic, pursuing his duties with a great deal of gusto. As second in command, he was responsible for all personnel, shipboard routine, and discipline. Like the Old Man, the Exec didn't believe in heavy-handed nit-picking and petty enforcement of minor rules. But he followed the Captain's lead in insisting on discipline where it counted.

Now a retired Commander, J.D.P. Hodapp used to supply renowned author C.S. Forester with technical advice for his sea stories and naval novels. Since renewing acquaintances with him in 1982, "J.D." and I have become good friends.

Head honcho of the Deck Force was First Lieutenant J.A. "Long John" McCord; his number two was Lieutenant (jg) John "Jiggs" Thorsen. Lieutenant (jg) George Merrill was our Supply Officer, and Ensign Gene Stout the Torpedo Officer. Assistant Engineering Officer was Ensign F.X. "Frank" Cannaday. The other ensigns, Justin "Duke" Holte, N.S. "Red" Irwin, and A.P. "Vic" Levicki, were assigned to the "O" or Gunnery Division. Our Medical Officer, Lieutenant (jg) James H. Fagan, protocol not withstanding, was "Doc" to everyone, including enlisted men. The closest I can come to describing him is to refer you to the movie *MR. ROBERTS* and the character played by William Powell. That was our "Doc" all over.

Officers and crew had now been together three and a half months. The evolution of the IRWIN's personnel from a bunch of strangers of various qualifications, backgrounds, and experience (or lack thereof) into an able, effective, fighting unit now combat ready, was remarkable. We had unqualified confidence in Captain Miller who, in my experience, was the most capable Skipper under whom I sailed. Our training record spoke for itself and was further tribute to the Captain's ability. The IRWIN was prepared for whatever trials were in our future.

I put letters in the mail to Jane, "the girl I left behind" in Atlanta, and wondered how long it would be until there'd be another opportunity to get mail off the ship.

The forces for Operation FORAGER were forming for the invasion of the Mariana Islands. First target: Saipan.

22

OPERATION FORAGER

On 29 May, 1944, in accordance with secret orders from Commander Fifth Fleet, Admiral Raymond A. Spruance, Task Unit 52.14.1 sortied from Pearl Harbor at 0700.

With the Flag of Commander Task Unit, Rear Admiral Gerald F. Bogan, on the jeep carrier FANSHAW BAY, the force consisted further of the baby flat-top MIDWAY, plus destroyer escorts ROSS, CASSIN YOUNG, and IRWIN. We set our course southwesterly; first destination, Eniwetok Atoll in the Marshall Islands.

The carriers we were screening, designated "CVEs", were built on merchant vessel hulls and designed primarily for transporting aircraft and for anti-submarine warfare. But here in the Pacific, their planes would see duty supporting our ground troops in the landing forces, as well as supplying the Combat Air Patrol over Fleet units. These escort carriers, known as "jeeps" or "jeep carriers" or "baby flat-tops", were too slow to keep up with the big ESSEX-class fleet carriers, had flight decks that were much smaller, and carried fewer planes.

The pilots in the jeep carrier air groups were generally not as skillful as those on the bigger flat-tops, and had a reputation for often losing planes in routine air operations. On the second day out of Pearl, a fighter crashed on take-off from the FANSHAW BAY. The IRWIN, steaming plane guard in the carrier's wake, swiftly moved in to recover the pilot. He was unhurt, but the plane sank immediately. We transferred him back to the CVE via breeches buoy at 2000.

Rescuing men from the sea was a fairly routine operation, but did pose some hazards. We had to slow to less than ten knots, maneuver close enough to the victim to toss him a life ring attached to a line, then haul him alongside to a cargo net slung over the side. If he were injured, at least one sailor would have to climb down the net to assist him aboard. In rough or choppy seas, either or both men could be washed away. And in submarine waters, the ship, almost dead in the sea, was an easy target for a Long Lance torpedo.

The rescued men were always grateful to us for picking them up, sometimes even kissing the deck. But often their jubilance over surviving a dunk in the drink gave way to dismay as soon as the ship returned to cruising speed and began to pitch and roll when back in the carrier's wake. Unused to such motion, they'd get violently seasick. With an arm wrapped around a main deck lifeline stanchion, with head in the scuppers, and heaving up every last vestige of food from their stomachs—they didn't care whether they lived or died—but preferred the latter.

Being the old meany that I am, I did—once or twice—pull a dastardly trick on the poor devils. I'd ask Bill Sharp in the galley to give me one of the pork chops left over from chow, go over to the pilot, tap him on the shoulder, and when he looked up, take a big bite out of the greasy chop. "How're ya doin', Lieutenant?" I'd ask. One glance at me chomping away and he'd groan, try to cuss, and get a mouthful of salt water as the ship heeled over, taking a sea in the scuppers.

Needless to say, those pilots and airmen we picked up were always happy to be returned to their own ship; but without exception, wondering why in the hell any sane man would ever ship out on a tin can.

Throughout our voyage to the Marshalls, the Task Unit conducted training exercises in "flight ops", AA firing practice, star shell illumination and other drills. On 5 June we crossed the 180th Meridian—the International Date Line—and the new kids aboard became "Golden Dragons". As we commenced entry into the Eniwetok anchorage, an F4F Grumann fighter from the FANSHAW BAY crashed and, again, it was the IRWIN to the rescue. Pilot saved. Plane lost.

Eniwetok is only 11° north of the Equator, and steaming once more in tropical waters brought on a certain amount of *déjà vu*. As in the Coral Sea and around the Solomons, flying fish raced along with us just inches above the calm seas. Dolphins (we called them porpoise) romped in our bow wave as if challenging us to a drag race. Our wake sparkled with blue-white phosphorus; the daytime sky was a clear azure; and the stars at night were bigger and brighter than any deep in the heart of Texas. It was a pleasant sensation to feel again the soft trade winds wisping across my cheeks.

The Navigator's chart storage was next to the Radio Shack, and I'd gotten a good look, over the shoulder of Chief Quartermaster John McEuen, at the charts of the Marianas and their bigger islands of Saipan, Tinian, and Guam. This would be the IRWIN's first operation, and as the probability of going back into combat grew certain, I began to get that "old feeling" again. I'd convinced myself you only get so many chances in this life; and, when those are used up, the odds of survival get infinitesimal. Bressie, Wasson, and I were leaning over the Comm

Deck railing shooting the bull, and both wanted to know what combat is like.

"It's different for everybody I'd guess", I told them. "But you'll probably get an initial rush of what probably is fear or intense apprehension. Then you'll be so damn' busy reacting to your training and doing what you're supposed to do that you won't feel much. For most of us, it's only when the shooting is all over that you *really* get scared."

"How do you feel, Hutch, about going back into the War zone?" Bressie wanted to know.

"The odds, Newt, look pretty damn' slim that I'll make it through this War", I told him. "I figure I used up most or all of my numbers in the Solomons, and I'm just living on borrowed time. But, hell, you never know what can or will happen, so you just take it as it comes."

"If something should happen to you, Hutch, how'd you want it to be?" Ken asked.

Images came flashing across my mind: the legless Marine sergeant we took aboard the McCAWLEY, the burned-to-a-crisp sailor off the JOHN PENN, the bodies of my shipmates being removed from the torpedo hole in the NORTH CAROLINA, the men blown over the side of the ENTERPRISE.

"I'd want it *quick*," I replied. "No suffering, no body parts blown away, no charred flesh, no long hours in the ocean. And I don't want to be below decks waiting for the water to reach the overhead."

I paused for a moment.

"You know, I want to see it coming, too. After making it this far, I'd like to get a look at the son of a bitch that gets me."

Bressie and Wasson shook their heads. They couldn't understand that part.

The antipathy to being trapped below decks, where I might look up and see a torpedo's warhead coming through the bulkhead, influenced me to become a "topside sailor". The closer we got to the forward area, the more I stayed out of Compartment 205 and up on deck. I took to sleeping on a blanket on the weather deck, usually on the 0-1 level, visiting the compartment only when I needed to get gear or a change of clothes out of my locker. Then I got a hammock from the sail locker to swing under the overhang of the Bridge's port wing. In foul weather, I'd spread the blanket behind the transmitter in the Radio Shack. The only time I'd be in my bunk was during very heavy weather or a typhoon. No Jap subs or aircraft would be operating then.

Even with my uneasiness and nervousness about the future's uncertainties, I surprisingly found myself eager to return to combat area. There was a strange exhilaration, difficult to verbalize, in being aboard a fleet destroyer of the United States Navy steaming toward the certitude of conflict with the enemy.

It was almost as if I'd developed an addiction to the hazardous life of a combat sailor; combined with a continuing hatred toward the Japs who had yet to be paid back for Pearl Harbor, and who were responsible for the deaths of good American sailors in Iron Bottom Bay, the Eastern Solomons, and the rest of the battle sites where our men had perished. But there was more to it than that.

Every time I heard of a battle or campaign of which I was not a part, I experienced two strong emotions. First there was the feeling of guilt for not being there to help. And secondly, I found I *wanted* to be there in the thick of it. The guilt I can understand. The other part I can't. But as FORAGER approached, I was once more on the job for which I'd been trained, and with a well-defined mission. In a sense, I was back in my natural habitat in which I felt most at home—on a combat vessel at sea, sailing "in harm's way."

In this connection, one is reminded of the comment of the most monumental figure in American military history, namely the legendary Lee, as he looked down longingly on the Union troops amassed on the battlefield at Fredericksburg, which field included my great-grandfather, and observed: "It is well that war is so terrible; else, we should become too fond of it."

On 9 June, with ammunition replenished, fuel bunkers topped off, and food lockers stuffed to capacity, the IRWIN was poised and ready for Operation FORAGER.

Two days later, on 11 June, 1944, on orders from Admiral Turner (ComFifthPhibFor), Task Group 52.14 sortied from Eniwetok. Shortly after getting underway, the PORTERFIELD reported her sonar gear inoperable, so the IRWIN shifted to Station One in the cruising disposition, the "point" for the six-mile-wide circular formation. In our wake steamed the FANSHAW BAY (Task Group Flagship), MIDWAY, WHITE PLAINS, KALINAN BAY, CASSIN YOUNG, CALLAGHAN, and LONGSHAW. The jeep carriers conducted routine flight ops, keeping a CAP over us throughout the daylight hours.

The United States Pacific Fleet was now an imposing fighting force with new ships and aircraft of every type and description turned out on America's 24-hour-a-day, seven-day-a-week assembly lines. The Task Forces arrayed for Operation FORAGER were a far cry from the straggly little expedition that had approached Guadalcanal just two years earlier. What we would have given then, in those dark days, for just a dozen or so of these new vessels and a few squadrons of these aircraft.

Command in the Fleet was now completely reorganized. There

would be two teams: one under Admiral Halsey, commanding the Third Fleet; the other under Admiral Spruance, heading up the Fifth Fleet. Thus, while one team was fighting in an operation, the other would plan and train for the next objective, speeding up the time between campaigns. But as far as we bluejackets were concerned, there was one big negative. Only the *commands* changed. The *ships* and the *men* in the Fifth Fleet were the same ones that were in the Third Fleet! As CinCPac Admiral Nimitz explained it: "The team remains the same, but the drivers change." For us that meant no relief between operations. We'd just go from one combat operation to the next.

Softening up the Marianas had begun as early as February when planes of Admiral Marc A. Mitscher's Fast Carriers made a bombing strike, and fleet submarines began operating against surface targets in the area. Now the Big Show was about to begin. Saipan was our first objective; the invasion would be made with 127,570 troops, about 85,000 of them Marines, backed by some 535 combat ships and auxiliaries, all under the direction of Admiral Kelly Turner as Commander Task Force 52. This was the Admiral's fifth major amphibious operation, having learned more about amphibious warfare than anyone in history.

Kelly Turner was a tough customer and a master of details who had earned the respect of the Marine Corps, often critical of the Navy on which the Marines were utterly dependent. As one Marine officer who served on Turner's Staff as well as that of General Holland M. Smith, put it: "Admiral Turner had an almost unbelievable capacity for work. He drove himself without mercy, and he expected and demanded the same of those around him." Or in the words of "Howlin' Mad" Smith himself, who often tangled with Turner, the superior who got him his command: "Kelly Turner is aggressive, a mass of energy and a relentless task master. The punctilious exterior hides a terrific determination. He can be plain ornery. He wasn't called 'Terrible Turner' without reason."

"Terrible" Turner was not only a master of tactical details, but also a capable and confident strategist. After all, the United States followed his master plan ("Pacific Ocean Campaign Plan") to win the Pacific War. To illustrate the Admiral's martial savvy: McCAWLEY Navigator Len Kenny tells how a sleepless Turner used to go over his charts at night expounding on how to beat the Japs. As early as 1942 during the Guadalcanal Campaign, the Admiral remarked: "We know who's gonna win this War! Where will the next one be?" Whereupon he circled the Korean Peninsula!

The number of men in the assault force may seem excessive in view of the number of Japanese defenders under General Saito—estimated to be some 31,500. But an amphibious attack on a well-dug-in foe, sheltered in caves, pill boxes, and underground revetments, takes an overwhelming number of troops to establish and hold a beachhead, then have sufficient forces to forge inland against a well-trained, well-armed, and fanatical enemy. It was anticipated the Japs would put up a spirited defense. Even though their numbers were small compared to ours, they had the advantage of fighting on their own ground for an island they considered part of the Japanese homeland.

Saipan, Tinian, and Rota had been in Japanese hands since the end of World War I, when they were given mandate over the Marianas, except for Guam. That island had been an American protectorate until captured by the hostiles in the early days of the War. Two thirds of the population of Saipan were Japanese nationals. The rest were Chamorros, the original inhabitants. We would later learn the Jap plan would call for defending the island with all available forces, holding out until Admiral Ozawa and the Japanese Mobile Fleet could arrive to launch an all-out air-sea attack and destroy the American armada.

The Navy was responsible not only to put troops ashore, to support the invasion with naval and aerial bombardment, to defend our forces against attack from sea and air, but also to keep all our forces supplied. This was no simple matter. As Navy Commander in Chief Admiral King put it at the time: "This war has been variously termed a war of production and a war of machines. Whatever else it is, so far as the United States is concerned, it is a war of logistics. . . . The profound effect of logistics problems on our strategic decision are not likely to have full significance to those who did not have to traverse the tremendous distances in the Pacific."

Operation FORAGER was the most extensive amphibious operation attempted up to that time in terms of supply problems, with the nearest U.S. base 1,000 miles away at the Eniwetok anchorage, and Pearl Harbor 3,500 miles away, not to mention that the Marianas were 6,000 miles from the West Coast of the United States. Nevertheless, we were counting on a swift and decisive victory so we could go on to take Tinian, Rota, and finally Guam. But as the poet of my Scots ancestors, Bobby Burns, put it: "the best laid plans of mice and men oft do go astray." Nothing would work out the way either side figured.

There was one strange occurrence in the 13 June pre-invasion bombardment of the Saipan defenses. Seven of our brand new "super battleships" were detached from the Fast Carrier Force and, under the command of Admiral W.A. "Ching" Lee, began to fire at shore installations on the island. But their gun crews were inexperienced in the type of shore bombardment needed and did little damage. So, the next day, some of the old "Pearl Harbor survivors", repaired, refurbished, and modernized, were brought in. The MARYLAND, PENNSYLVANIA, TENNESSEE, and CALIFORNIA, along with NEW MEXICO, MISSISSIPPI, COLORADO, and IDAHO had to show 'em how it's supposed to be done!

Task Group 52.14 took up position some 70 miles east of Saipan. Our mission was to protect the jeep carriers as they provided air cover over the invasion beaches, and launched air strikes as called for by the Marines against targets in the landing areas as well as inland.

Now, all my senses, honed in the Solomons, were operating at full bore, and the old habits kicked in automatically.

When stepping onto the weather deck, I instinctively surveyed the skies a few degrees above the horizon where incoming aircraft most likely to have escaped our radar could be spotted; I checked the relative positions of the ships in the force to see if anything were out of the ordinary; and I located the Flagship which I'd regularly check to see if her flag hoists signaled "Desig Dog Seven Nine Four"—a sure sign we on the DD-794 were about to get an assignment other than our screening duties. And I was intuitively aware of course and speed changes and wind and sea conditions. I'd instinctively look around the ship to see if all was normal, then finally sweep the sky overhead, primarily to locate our CAP.

It was just at sunrise, 0542, 15 June, 1944, when we received the word that Kelly Turner had signaled Task Force 52 to "Land the Landing Force!" On the attack transports of the amphibious units, chaplains offered final prayers, and bos'n's pipes shrilled through loudspeakers, followed by the fateful order: "AWAY ALL BOATS!" The assault on Saipan was underway. Planes from the baby flat-tops were in the air, streaking toward the beaches to provide cover and striking force for the landings, and flight operations continued throughout the day.

We got intermittent reports from the beachheads where the 2nd and 4th Marine Divisions were having a tough time. By nightfall, some 20,000 Marines were ashore; but they were pinned down by withering Jap fire from heavily bunkered and protected positions the battleships' shore bombardments had failed to take out. Casualties already had reached the 2,000 mark. During the night, the Japs staged a vicious counter-attack; but, with the battlefield well-lit by starshells from destroyers and the arrival of five Sherman tanks, the gyrenes held on.

Out at sea, we were having our problems with the enemy, too. Tokyo Rose was telling us via the air waves she knew all the secrets of Operation FORAGER, saying we all soon would find a watery grave. At 2208, the IRWIN's sonar pinged off a submarine—an "excellent sonar contact" bearing 015 and less than 2,000 yards out, easy range for the Nips' vaunted Long Lance torpedoes.

Whipping the ship on a direct course toward the contact, Captain Miller closed for the attack. As I looked astern, I could see the "ash cans" hit the sea in a full pattern. The depth charges exploded with great geysers of water over the target area. When the sea subsided, we re-established the contact, and rolled more depth charges off the fantail, while the K-guns lofted their charges to port and starboard in the classic anti-submarine barrage. Seven 600-pound and six 300-pound charges were dropped in the attack.

As we maneuvered for a third run over the sub, our master gyro compass went on the blink, causing us to cease operations. We scoured the area for nearly two hours, but in the black night and rather choppy seas we could not confirm the kill. However, post-War Japanese documents show that one of their submarines was lost in that immediate area, with its last radio contact with Tokyo only a short time prior to the attack we made on our sonar contact. Although we didn't know it at the time, it looks as if the IRWIN got at least a "probable". In any event, there were no more threats from hostile subs that night.

The submarine incident had been preceded by a small attack by Jap land-based aircraft. At 1807, eight bogies showed up on our radar at 57 miles out. Interceptors were deployed, scoring five kills. But one Kate slipped through the fighter screen and came in almost head on to our bow at an angle of just one degree. It was a lousy angle and we could only bring the forward mounts to bear on the bandit. The Kate launched a torpedo at the carriers, but our gunfire had made him veer off course before launching, throwing the torpedo off course. Weaving at a low altitude through the formation, he finally was set upon by our CAP fighters who brought him down just four miles from us.

The second day of the campaign passed without incident for us. The carriers continued flight ops, their planes flying sorties over the island. Word from the landing forces still reported heavy Jap resistance and continuous artillery bombardment of the Marines' positions. Just before dark, the Army's 27th Division, until then held in reserve, was landed. Early in the morning, the Japs launched a furious counter-attack on the Army front with infantry and some 44 tanks, but were beaten back after a bloody four-hour battle. By daylight, the beachhead was secured, and the business of fighting our way inland got underway.

On 17 June, we rendezvoused with the oiler NESHANIC for fuel, returning to the Task Group around noon while the other DDs retired "for a drink". Around 1800, blips began to pop up in profusion on our radar screens at a range of 45 miles. Within minutes, CIC (Combat

Information Center) had four separate raids of an estimated 70 planes approaching from "all angles"!

When the General Alarm sounded, I was in the berthing compartment, having just come off watch and hoping to catch a quick shower, shave, and change of clothes. It was one of the rare times I was below decks. Slamming my locker door and grabbing a shirt off my bunk, I broke for the ladder to the main deck at flank speed.

Just as I passed the starboard side of Mount 54, the 5-inch battery opened up. The ship was heeling to starboard in an emergency port turn, and the combination of the muzzle blast and the canted deck sent me tumbling "ass over tin cups" (to use an expression of my grandfather).

A Jap Kate that had been diving in on the starboard bow was now directly abeam as the ship swung to bring all Main Battery mounts to bear on the hostile. The torpedo bomber was only about fifteen feet above the white caps, boring straight toward me with machine guns spitting fire and bullets. At amidships, I dove under Mount 43 behind some cases, instinctively covering my head with my arms and closing my eyes. Above me the 40-millimeter crew was blasting away at the Jap with everything they had.

I heard a jubilant shout from the gun tub above me and looked up just in time to see the Kate flame out into the sea with a huge splash. Scratch one meatball! The IRWIN had posted her first aircraft kill, hitting the Kate with shells from both our 5-inch and 40mm guns which blasted it to hell and gone. Fitch would later tell me the attacker was picked up on the scopes about 30 miles out, but that it was lost on the radar because one of our planes was on its tail, confusing the electronic gear. The F6F fighter broke off at about 3,000 yards when our gunners sighted the Kate by naked eye and opened fire.

When I started to get up from the deck, I took quick note of the labeling on the cases that were providing me with "protection": "40MM AMMUNITION" it read. Some safe haven!

I got the hell out of there fast as the attack continued all around us. When I reached the Comm Deck, I spun the wheel on the hatch, but not before I saw smoke coming from the FANSHAW BAY where it shouldn't be. She'd been hit, but I didn't take the time to investigate further. Breathless and undoubtedly a little white, I stumbled into the Radio Shack. Al Block greeted me with an "it's about time you got here—you're missing all the fun!"

I relieved the watch on the NPM FOX skeds as our ordnance department put up barrages on new targets—high-level Bettys. The Jap bombers were part of the flight attacking on our protective quadrant of the Task Force. I'd later learn there were six Kates and 18 Bettys in the

A VAL DIVE BOMBER AIMS AT THE KITKUN BAY
Hit by anti-aircraft fire from the IRWIN during a 70-plane enemy air raid off
Saipan, a Japanese pilot tries in vain to crash into the "jeep" carrier, 18
June, 1944.
(U.S. Navy Photo - Real War Photos)

enemy contingent directly attacking us and the FANSHAW BAY. At the moment, however, I was absorbed in trying to copy FOX while 40-millimeter Mount 42, just a few feet forward of the operating position, was firing again. The paper-thin bulkhead between us didn't provide much sound insulation. The recoil and muzzle blasts had my receiver jiggling on its shock absorbers like Jello atop a jackhammer. The vibration caused the receiver to drift continually off frequency, so I had to keep retuning it with one hand while typing with the other.

The air-sea battle ebbed and flowed. From inside the Shack we could only tell when enemy planes were in range by which and how many of our guns were firing. According to the Skipper's Action Report, we were shooting at three aircraft, then one, then four as the mêlée continued.

Some twenty minutes after the first Kate had made the direct run on us, a second came in, flying about 75 feet off the water, descending to about 25 feet as it got within 500 yards, ready to launch its torpedo. I knew we had to be under direct attack. Eight to ten of our weapons were putting up one helluva racket as they came to bear on the Jap. When the firing subsided, there were victorious shouts from the gun crews, and I knew we'd gotten the son of a bitch. Scratch one more "flaming asshole"! The gunners had splashed him on the fourth salvo.

Finally, after fifty minutes under attack, our guns fell silent. The raids moved out, and the carriers turned into the wind to recover their birds. By now the sun had set, and the pilots were making landings in the dark on those postage stamps the baby flat-tops called flight decks. Four planes were lost, but fortunately their crews were rescued. Later I would learn that two Wildcat fighters, trying to return to the WHITE PLAINS in the fading twilight, were the recipients of "friendly fire" from our own ships and planes. Neither was shot down, but one was so shot up its landing destroyed six planes; some were knocked into the sea, others had to be jettisoned.

It was time to take care of our cripple. Along with the PORTERFIELD and CASSIN YOUNG, we joined on the FANSHAW BAY to screen her until morning when Admiral Bogan would transfer his Flag to the WHITE PLAINS and send the wounded carrier back to Eniwetok for repairs. The bomb she took exploded in her hangar deck, and eleven sailors would fight the Japs no more.

Captain Miller wrote in the War Diary: "Rest of day uneventful."

The "green" youngsters in the Radio Gang were chattering like a tree full of magpies when they sense a cat in the neighborhood. Their nervousness was evident in their voices, several notes higher than usual, but they were euphoric over the victory and elated at surviving. You couldn't blame them for their high spirits.

One of the strikers had made a fresh pot of joe. I poured a cup and took it out on the Comm Deck where I sat with my back to the port bulkhead. The ship felt alive with, it seemed, the entire crew talking at once, each describing his part in the battle. Morale was skyrocket high, with a lot of backslapping going on. But the clamor soon subsided. There was work to be done and there were watches to be stood. It had been a strenuous day, both physically and emotionally, for all hands.

Fitch came down from the Signal Bridge with his own cup of java. Assuming I'd been in the Radio Shack the entire time, he filled me in on the events as seen from the Bridge. And I told him of my race up the starboard side. Then, we both fell silent, lost in our own thoughts.

I had run the same gamut of emotions I'd experienced every other time I'd been under fire, and my nerves were still on pins and needles. I mentally thanked the Good Lord for the loan of that guardian angel. I'd made it through one more scrape in one piece. Maybe there is something to Charles Dibdin's piece *Poor Jack:*

> For they say there's a Providence sits up aloft
> To keep watch for the life of poor Jack. . . . .
> There's a sweet little cherub that sits up aloft
> To keep watch for the life of poor Jack . . . !

Our Chief Gunner's Mate, John "Boom Boom" Kopach, came up the ladder with a notebook in his hand to report to the Skipper on the amount of ammunition we'd expended. He stopped long enough to tell Junior and me we'd fired 152 rounds of Main Battery, 543 rounds of 40-millimeter and 620 rounds of 20mm. He was, and had every right to be, proud of his Gunnery Department. They'd performed well for the first time out.

Releasing the FANSHAW BAY to the care of the ZANE (DD-337) and the PALMER (DMS-5) we reported to Commander Task Force 52 and immediately got a new assignment from Admiral Turner. With our carrier out of action, we could now be spared to screen a retirement group of transports, and for the next couple of days it was routine steaming.

The "retirement group" of transports was constantly changing as a force, with units proceeding into Transport Area off the Saipan beaches to unload, and other ships returning. To keep up a perimeter defense around them turned out to be a herculean task.

At one time all the ships were so concentrated in one small area, it took us several hours of hard maneuvering, working like a shepherd's sheepdog, to get them all straightened out.

Destroyers do a little of everything.

23

THE MARIANAS TURKEY SHOOT

Meanwhile, we later learned, Admiral Spruance was getting reports from our submarine scouts, that a Japanese carrier force was moving up from Tawi Tawi off the north coast of Borneo, via the San Bernardino Strait in the Philippines, to challenge us in the Marianas.

For well over a year or more, the Combined Fleet of the Imperial Japanese Navy had refused to appear in force to challenge Allied advances in the South and Central Pacific. This was due to fuel shortages, to the new and ever increasing U.S. superiority in ships and planes, and above all to the fact that the Nip Navy had lost almost all their aircraft and well-trained aviators. But now with new planes and pilots, howbeit poorly trained, the Japs were looking for a big fight.

According to details learned later, Nip Navy Commander in Chief Admiral Soemu Toyoda, having replaced the supercautious Admiral Koga killed in an airplane accident, issued plans for Operation A-Go, a scheme to lure the U.S. Fifth Fleet close to the range of Jap land-based aircraft in the Western Carolines, where hopefully there would be a decisive battle. But when it became clear on 15 June that we were invading the Marianas, Admiral Ozawa's First Mobile Fleet, with all of Japan's carriers and 90 percent of their naval strength, steamed northeast from the Sulu Sea to attack Ray Spruance's Fifth Fleet in the Philippine Sea.

As the anticipated naval battle drew near, Admiral Toyoda sent out the same message as Admiral Heihechiro Togo before Japan's spectacular annihilation of the Russian fleet in the Battle of Tsushima in 1905: "The fate of the Empire rests on this one battle."

In the weeks and days leading up to the impending battle, U.S. submarines became ever more efficient in sinking Japanese ships and in spotting Jap ship movements to the benefit of our Commanders. Our submarines were to play a crucial role in the Battle of the Philippine Sea. On the other side, Jap I-boats failed miserably before and during the Marianas Campaign, not sinking or damaging a single U.S. ship nor providing information on our fleet movements.

352

At the same time, some seventeen submarines were sunk by our anti-sub hunter-killer forces in the Pacific, beefed up due to victory over the German U-boat in the Atlantic in late 1943. For instance, destroyer escort ENGLAND sank six Jap subs in twelve days in May of 1944. In Washington Admiral King was glad there would always be an ENGLAND in the United States Navy! How did they do it? According to the Skipper: "Personnel and equipment worked with the smoothness of well-oiled clockwork. As a result of our efforts, Recording Angel working overtime checking in Nip submariners joining Honorable Ancestors."

The First Mobile Fleet under Admiral Ozawa, who had succeeded Admiral Nagumo as the Japs' top carrier Admiral, now steaming through the Philippine Sea consisted of nine carriers, five battleships, 13 cruisers, 28 destroyers, and some 475 planes. But their inexperienced pilots had only two to six months' training, whereas our carrier pilots had at least two years' training plus months of combat experience. Arrayed against the Jap force was Task Force 58 with fifteen carriers, seven battleships, 21 cruisers, 69 destroyers, and some 960 aircraft.

In tactical command of TF 58 was our top carrier Admiral, Marc A. Mitscher, wiry and wizened under his long-visored lobsterman's cap, whose compassionate consideration for his men made him one of the most loved C.O.'s in the history of the U.S. Navy. One newsman dubbed Mitscher "Admiral of the Ocean Air". In overall command, making all the big decisions, was Fifth Fleet Commander Admiral Raymond A. Spruance. "Modest by nature, he had a prejudice against publicity in any form. . . . Power of decision and coolness in action were perhaps Spruance's leading characteristics. . . . He envied no man, regarded no one as rival . . . and went ahead in his quiet way winning victories for his country" (Morison).

Contrary to the advice of his subordinates, Admiral Spruance was minded not to go after the Japanese force; but, in one of the great ironies of naval history, to wait for the enemy to attack, just as Japanese Admiral Togo had waited for the Russian fleet in the Tsushima Strait in 1905!

The Jap naval threat prompted some immediate changes in U.S. Fleet deployment. Some of the destroyers and cruisers supporting the ground forces on Saipan were pulled off their shore bombardment stations to reinforce the ships screening the Fast Carriers. The transports ceased unloading operations and sortied with the retirement group some 70 to 100 miles east of the Marianas.

The U.S. Marine and Army forces on Saipan would have to get along without much naval support until our carrier planes dealt with the Nip Navy. Our ground units' progress was slow, agonizing, and bloody as it was. Losing naval fire support wasn't going to make it any easier. The Japs wanted to take the pressure off their troops on the island. The 70-plane attack on the IRWIN's jeep carrier Task Group on 17 June was but a prelim scrap to the Main Event coming up.

On 19 June, 1944, the Battle of the Philippine Sea, perhaps better known as "The Great Marianas Turkey Shoot", broke out in the seas and skies to the west of the island chain. But the first air action that beautiful morning was not between aircraft of the two main carrier forces. It was a furious fight involving land-based enemy planes, flying from airfields on Guam, and American carrier fighters deployed to keep them from going after Task Force 58. Not one Jap plane got through.

Then Admiral Ozawa launched his first air assault on Admiral Mitscher's carriers about 0830 on the 19th. Some 70 Jill torpedo bombers, Zeros carrying bombs, and Zero fighter escorts were in the first strike to be picked up on the U.S. Fleet's radar. The attackers arrived about 1000. Against them went some 140 F6F Grumman Hellcats and F4U Corsairs. In the ensuing mêlée, 42 Jap planes were splashed by our CAP and our ships' AA fire. Not one Jap got through to our carriers. The SOUTH DAKOTA took a direct bomb hit, but the damage was not severe enough to take her out of action. In the air battle, the U.S. lost only four pilots.

Raid number two came about an hour later when some 80 Jap Jill and Judy bombers and torpedo planes, escorted by 40 some Zekes, arrived. Our ships took several near misses, but no hits. At the same time, our Hellcats and Corsairs went after 'em and, together with our AA fire, cut 'em to ribbons. Some 90 Nip aircraft were blasted from the skies, their wreckage scattered for miles in the wake of Task Force 58. According to one picket destroyer Commander: "The battleships, cruisers, and destroyers put up a tremendous barrage which, together with the burning planes all around the horizon, created a most awesome spectacle."

In the meantime, our submarines had penetrated the screen of the Jap task force and were attacking Ozawa's flat-tops. The SHOKAKU, which had been in on the Pearl Harbor attack, was sunk by a spread of fish from the CAVALLA, whose Skipper got in so close "there was the Rising Sun, big as hell!"

But the ALBACORE got the blue ribbon, torpedoing the Jap fleet's flagship TAIHO, the Nips' newest and biggest carrier. She went down so quickly that over 75 percent of her crew perished with her, though Admiral Ozawa and his staff escaped. This resulted from a single torpedo hit, which somehow spread deadly fumes through the ship, that when accidentally ignited caused an explosion blowing the carrier apart.

However, we didn't know the big Jap carrier had actually gone down 'til many months later.

Raid number three, consisting of about 47 aircraft, missed our carriers, 40 returning to the Jap flat-tops. The bigger part of raid number four, made up of some 82 planes, also missed their targets, most trying to land on Guam. But our fighters, flying Combat Air Patrol between Rota and Guam, pounced on them, and wings with "flaming assholes" on 'em went plunging into the drink. The few that escaped tried to land on an airfield bombed all day long by our carrier planes. As a captured Jap diary put it: "When evening came our carrier bombers returned, but the airfield had been destroyed by the enemy and they . . . had to crash. . . . I was unable to watch dry-eyed. The tragedy of war was never so real."

For over eight hours, the air battles had raged above the Philippine Sea, with our ships coming in for their share of the action. This was the greatest single air-sea battle of the War. The Imperial Japanese Navy lost about 340 planes and two carriers; the United States Navy, some 30 planes and no ships, one battleship being slightly damaged. It was an overwhelming victory for the Good Guys. For Navy pilots it was, as one of them dubbed the action, truly a "turkey shoot".

According to U.S. Navy historian Samuel Eliot Morison, the skill and courage of our young aviators made it "a glorious and wonderful battle . . . one of the high points in the history of the American spirit." According to Arleigh "31 Knot" Burke, the Jap air coordinator, whose radio orders to enemy planes were immediately intercepted and translated, gave us specific information as to when and where their strikes were coming. When "Coordinator Joe" signed off and headed for home, an eager officer wanted to shoot him down. But Admiral Mitscher refused: "No indeed! . . . He did us too much good!"

But the Battle of the Philippine Sea was not yet over. The next day, June 20th, Admiral Spruance was minded to go after the Jap carriers. The hunter became the hunted. But Admiral Mitscher could not find them until late in the day when he sent his attack aircraft against Ozawa's remaining flat-tops with a "Give 'em hell, boys", even though our planes would have to be recovered after dark. They sank the HIYO and badly damaged the ZUIKAKU, the only Jap carrier still afloat of those involved in the Pearl Harbor attack.

Our weary pilots, minus twenty or so lost in combat, wended their way back to their floating nests in the pitch-black night. In a daring gamble to save as many as possible, Admiral Mitscher ordered every ship in Task Force 58 to illuminate the skies with their searchlights to guide home the wayward birds. Fortunately, no enemy submarines were close enough to take advantage and launch an attack. As the planes came home, many short on fuel, about 80 were lost, either in flight deck crashes or through emergency ditching. Busy destroyers rescued the majority of the downed crews, but over twenty airmen were lost. "Fortunately rescue work by our destroyers was very efficient" (Morison).

The Battle of the Philippine Sea was over. The Japs lost their three largest carriers, a fourth being badly damaged, and almost all their planes and pilots. They would not mount another significant carrier force during the remainder of the War. America's air and sea might now prevailed in the Western Pacific. Admiral Spruance had not destroyed the Japanese fleet, but he had clipped their wings and protected the invasion of the Marianas.

The next day, June 21st, in our shepherd's role the IRWIN and other tin cans rounded up the transports and headed back to Saipan, where the news from the island was not at all encouraging. The danger of attack by Japanese fleet units and aircraft was now gone. But fierce resistance by General Saito's Army, fighting from well-bunkered and concealed positions, plus strategic concentrations of artillery and mortars, was making life miserable for the American forces, and had slowed our advance to a crawl. Casualties were running high in the 2nd and 4th MarDivs. To give 'em some help, Admiral Turner (CTF 52) released the IRWIN from screening assignments and sent us in to take station off Garapan village in order to supply fire support and counter Jap artillery.

An hour after midnight on the 22nd, our radar made contact on enemy planes, range 25 miles and closing, and we went to General Quarters. The flight came in toward our station but veered off to other targets before reaching us. Then, at 0230, our "ground-pounders" found themselves under heavy artillery fire and yelled to us for help. We took the Jap batteries under fire and, in 30 minutes, wiped 'em out.

But then our master gyro gave us trouble for the umpteenth time, oscillating all over the place. We didn't get it back into commission until 0700. In that four-hour span our capability to deliver accurate fire and to navigate was severely limited. What made the gyro loss even more hazardous was our position. In those pre-dawn hours we stayed on station but it was close inshore, barely yards off the reef spreading out from Tanapag Harbor. A slight miscalculation and we'd have been hung up in the shallows, easy pickin's for enemy counter-fire.

Operational again, we were ordered around to the eastern coast of Saipan off Magicienne Bay to relieve the CALIFORNIA as fire support ship. The Marine Fire Support Officer on the beach put us to work with no preliminaries, calling for 5-inch salvos on several targets. At one point, some 100 Jap soldiers were exposed in a ravine while they were changing positions. The F.S.O. gave us the coordinates, asking for a white phosphorus barrage. We cut loose with the Main Battery, blanketing the target area, killing all of the enemy and setting fire to the brush the Japs had used for concealment. Later, we twice moved in to within yards of the beach to spray visible Nip troop concentrations with our 40-millimeters, getting a grateful "Well done!" from the Mud Marines.

At 1730, we proceeded to station off Tinian to illuminate and intercept any attempts by the enemy to shift troops from one island to the other. Throughout the night we kept the passage lit up with star shells while firing harassing salvos into hostile positions around Tinian town.

In the morning, it was back to Magicienne Bay to check in with our shore bombardment control party who kept us busy all day firing at various targets. The War Diary quotes the F.S.O. as saying "the results were good."

Then it was back to the Saipan-Tinian Channel and another night of illumination. We were far enough away not to be bothered by an air raid on the Transport Area anchorage during the early morning hours.

This routine was beginning to get awfully tiresome. It seemed we were always firing at something—all day, all night. The sleep we got was only in brief naps, if at all.

Back on Saipan's east coast on June 24th, the IRWIN began bombarding the beach again at 0630. I was out on deck when, at 0900, there was a big explosion and a geyser of water erupted close aboard our port beam.

"Some son of a bitch is shooting at us!" I yelled to nobody in particular.

About that time, another round whistled over us and detonated several yards to starboard, close enough to rattle pots and pans in the galley. Everybody topside scurried for cover. A Jap shore battery had us bracketed and was zeroing in on the range. Our screws churned up the sea astern as the Old Man applied the engine power necessary to get us out of the enemy's range while Lieutenant Knight, sitting atop the Main Battery Director, tried to get a fix on the hostile artillery.

Most of the enemy shore batteries were well-concealed, usually in caves. Generally, they were 6-inch naval guns, mounted on railroad tracks, and used hard-to-detect smokeless powder. The Japs would run the gun out on the tracks, fire a salvo and run it back into the cave before it could be spotted. Unless the target (in this case us) was lucky enough to catch the muzzle blast, the guns were almost impossible to locate.

The Jap battery fired five salvos at us before we were clear of the area; but none came any closer, thanks to Cap'n Danny's quick reaction and the IRWIN's speed. We never did locate the cave. So from a new position, we set up to fire at other designated targets intermittently throughout the day.

Then, it was all-night illumination for the forces ashore. An air raid at 2100 had us manning battle stations as bombs and flares dropped over the Transport Area, but we were several miles away and no Jap aircraft got close enough for us to shoot.

The all-day, all-night fire missions were beginning to take a toll on the crew. We were expending from 215 to 270 rounds of 5-inch ammunition every 24 hours, not to count the 40-millimeter firing, and this wasn't very conducive to getting much sleep. About the time I'd settle down for a short nap, we'd get another fire mission. During the nightly illuminations, the *least* we'd fire was one gun every several minutes from dusk 'til dawn.

Finally, we got a little break. Instead of illumination duty, we retired to sea with the LOUISVILLE, plus other cruisers and destroyers, for a night. Wouldn't you know it? I had the cotton-pickin' midwatch. No sleep, again.

A beach party had sighted several mines afloat in a small cove on Saipan's west coast. It was uncertain whether they were tethered or floating free. Either way, they posed a navigational hazard. With no minesweepers immediately available, the IRWIN was dispatched to detonate them. Moving in and laying to nearly dead in the water, we had riflemen shooting at the detonators on the mines, but even direct hits failed to explode them. Two 20-millimeters were ordered to make a try. That worked, but the first mine blew up with such a blast it showered water and mud all over the decks. That was *too* damn' close! So we backed off and switched to the longer-range 40s. That was better and we took out all the mines visible to us.

During the firing, our bow was pointed directly toward the beach where the terrain rose from the water to a low hill. Suddenly, an enemy tank came over the crest and, apparently not seeing us, crunched down the slope toward our position. Mount 51 was unlimbered and, with a single round, knocked the Jap tank into the middle of next week. A few minutes later, a second tank appeared and it, too, must not have spotted the destroyer only a few hundred yards away. As it started toward the beach, Mount 51 put a round right in its fuel tank and it went up like a rocket. Scratch two Jap tanks!

We were using up ammo, fuel, and food stores at a pretty good clip, having had no opportunity to replenish our supplies until we went alongside the oiler THUBAN. The seas were running high, and the fueling situation was, as the War Diary has it, "very bad". The oiler couldn't pump very much into our bunkers and we pulled away still some 30,000 gallons short of a full supply. As we moved out, CTF 52 ordered us to hurry back to Tanapag Harbor in order to supply more fire support, i.e. illumination and interdiction bombardment of enemy troops. The Japs mounted another air attack, but the night was as black as the inside of your peacoat pocket. With visibility limited, we saw no damage caused to any of our ships.

June 27th and 28th were carbon copies of our other missions. Both nights we went to General Quarters as hostile planes came over the Transport Area, but we saw only one plane go down in flames. As a fire support vessel, we continued our assignments even during air raids unless directly attacked. Support of the Marines was our priority. Other ships were designated for anti-aircraft cover.

We had just come off an all-night bombardment/illumination mission off Point Bluff when we got new orders. We were returning to duty screening the baby flat-tops.

In the one week that the IRWIN had "come off the bench" to help the other ships of the shore bombardment group, we'd pumped some 870 rounds of Main Battery shells into enemy bunkers, artillery emplacements, troop concentrations—and we'd foiled at least one Banzai counter-attack. Our 40-millimeter fire was effective in close-aboard strafing of Jap troops; and our star shell efficiency over nighttime battlegrounds, and in interdicting enemy transfer of troops from one location to another, had been most effective. Estimates from our shore parties gave us credit for killing at least 1,200 to 1,400 Japanese troops.

The accuracy of our gunnery in call-fire situations was so exact that enemy night attacks were foiled with shelling as close as just tens of meters from our own Marines without casualties among friendly forces. But it was not just the IRWIN which got kudos for her offshore support of the Marines and GIs on the beach. Rear Admiral Harry W. Hill, a long-time naval gunnery expert, said of the Saipan operation:

"There can remain little doubt that naval gunfire is the most feared and most effective of all weapons which the Japanese confronted in resisting a landing and assault. Without exception, prisoners of war have stated that naval gunfire prevented their movement by day or night and was the *most deciding factor* in accomplishing their defeat."

Jap commanders, prisoners, and diarists were one on the subject: "If there just were no naval gunfire, we feel with determination that we could fight it out with [the] enemy. . . . The greatest single factor in the

American success [was] naval gunfire. . . . I have at last come to the place where I will die. . . . Naval gunfire . . . too terrible for words."

There was another factor that required us to be accurate. We couldn't waste ammunition. Ammo replacement was of constant concern from Day Two, and we were limited in the amount of shells we could expend for troop support, keeping 60 rounds of "AA common" per gun per ship in reserve for surface and air action.

The slow progress in taking Saipan was attributed to another cause. Vice Admiral Turner wrote: "We simply didn't have enough troops here, and the reason . . . was that we didn't have enough ships to bring them in." The shortage of ships was understandable. The 6 June D-Day invasion of mainland Europe had first call on transports and cargo vessels. Later I would wonder if the same operation was a cause of our ammunition shortages.

We got a hearty salute and a reluctant farewell from our last forward fire support observers as we proceeded away from the beaches, headed for a refueling rendezvous with the QUANTICO (AO-49), and prepared to rejoin Task Group 52.14. Alongside the oiler we bummed fresh flour and dried provisions. Our food supplies were at a low ebb.

Then at 1200, 29 June, we received ComDesRon 55 and some of his Staff aboard. The IRWIN would be "SquadDog" (Squadron Flagship) while the PORTERFIELD retired to Eniwetok for repairs to her sonar gear. Captain C.R. Todd, the Squadron Commander, commanded the screen for the CVEs—with the IRWIN, CALLAGHAN, MORRISON, LONGSHAW, LAWS, ROSS, and a new 2,100-ton can, the BENHAM (DD-796), joining. She was the namesake of the DD-397, sunk at Guadalcanal.

In the Radio Shack, the guys were talking about getting some rest, a respite from the days and nights of fire support duty. There'd been precious little time even to keep up with such mundane activities as laundry, showers, and most of all—sleep. But this night, there'd be no rest for the weary.

At 2010, the MIDWAY reported a torpedo streaking past her bow on "course three-double-oh". We were under attack by Japanese submarines and to General Quarters we went. Five minutes later, the CALLAGHAN sighted another wake; and at 2044, while on "course three-five-five", a fish passed our starboard beam less than one hundred feet away. Sonar picked up both torpedo and screw noises, confirming more than one undersea boat in the area, and the CALLAGHAN was ordered astern of the formation to hunt them down. After a diligent search, she didn't make contact. The subs had fled.

I was happy to be in the Radio Shack, above where any torpedo might strike, but I was fully aware that a direct hit by a Long Lance torpedo would blow the ship completely out of the water. Once it appeared the danger had passed, I did breathe a little easier; and when I got off watch at 2400, I stayed on the Comm Deck, sleeping under the port wing of the Bridge.

June had been a busy month and ended as our Task Group moved to a station between the islands of Rota and Aguipan. There was an air alert the night of June 30th, but the attack was on Saipan and no enemy planes came closer than fifteen miles.

The "quick and decisive victory" hoped for in the operations plans did not come as easily nor as quickly as hoped. The Jap defenders of Saipan put up one devil of a fight. On the Fourth of July, the Marines celebrated by finally taking the towns of Garapan and Tanapag.

Then, unknown to us, but later related by eyewitness enemy prisoners of war, Admiral Nagumo, Commander Central Pacific Area and the man who had commanded the carrier force in the attack on Pearl Harbor, ordered a full-scale counter-attack against our forces on the night of 6/7 July. Then he and General Saito, convinced Saipan was lost to Japan, committed suicide with their staffs.

Unaware their commanders were dead, the Jap troops fought with great ferocity, breaking out of their perimeter and pouring through a gap in the lines of the Army's 27th Division in what would become known as "The Great Banzai Charge". The Army units were overrun; and only the guns of a Marine artillery battery, who cut their fuses to explode at only 75 yards, stemmed the tide. After several hours of close fighting, all the attackers were killed. The Japs lost over 4,300 men in that last desperate effort. We lost 406 men killed.

Two days later, the Marines hoisted our Colors over the island's airstrip; and by 1625 on the afternoon of 9 July, 1944, organized resistance ceased, and Saipan was pronounced "secured". Admiral Turner sent us all a congratulatory dispatch: "To our brave troops who have captured Saipan, the naval forces who have striven to assist them, I make a bow of respect."

Casualties in the ground operations on Saipan were high: 15,053, of whom 11,481 were wounded, according to Admiral Turner's figures. Our troops took over 700 Nip prisoners, interred over 25,000 enemy dead, and interned over 9,000 Jap civilians. The battle for Saipan was costly for both sides. But our capturing the Marianas was necessary to secure air bases from which our long-range B-29 bombers could reach Japan, and the Japs were determined to prevent this eventuality.

In a bizarre, almost unbelievable, postscript to the fighting, hundreds of Japanese civilians, following orders from Admiral Nagumo and led to believe the Americans would torture and mutilate them, committed suicide by various means including throwing themselves off cliffs at the northern end of the island. Both adults and children. Many were women, some carrying babies in their arms.

Jap propaganda thus caused the unnecessary deaths of their own innocents. For days after the carnage, bodies could be seen floating in the tides off Marpi Point. The sharks had a feast.

On 9 July, Task Group 52.14 was ordered back to Eniwetok. But the Marianas Campaign was not yet completed. We would have more to do.

The scene in the seas off Saipan is depicted by Seaman James J. Fahey on the MONTPELIER: "Today [13 July] the water was full of dead Jap bodies, you could see them floating by, men, women, and children. . . . The water is full of them . . . the fish will eat good. . . . The Japs are still [16 July] floating around, there must be thousands of Japs in the waters near Saipan. The ships just run over them. You can't miss them all, the water is full of dead Japs. Church services were held topside and as you looked over the side of the ship you could see the Jap bodies in the water. . . . " (*Pacific War Diary*)!

At Eniwetok anchorage we nested with the CASSIN YOUNG, beginning routine maintenance and needed repairs to the ship, and we held a couple of good field days to clean work spaces and berthing compartments neglected during our combat operations. Although at rest, we were kept on twelve-hour sailing notice.

I had always had a consuming interest in the Far East, particularly China; and I finally found someone who could tell me, firsthand, about that ancient country. He was a Seaman 1st gunner's mate striker on Mount 53 named Doon Ying Lee.

Lee had graduated from Peking University and had fled China one step ahead of the Jap invading armies. After finding his way to the States and settling in Washington, D.C., he met and married an Irish girl. The pictures of their baby daughter, which Lee would whip out and display at the slightest provocation, were of one of the most beautiful children I'd ever seen. But then Eurasians are known for their striking beauty.

During those infrequent times when we could just sit and talk, as during our respite at Eniwetok, Lee and I would sit leaning against the gun mount as he spoke long and lovingly about his homeland and the way China used to be. He expounded on its history: the old War Lords, the "Foreign Devils", the Boxer Rebellion, the demise of Sun Yat Sen's attempt to establish a Republic, Chiang Kai-Shek and the rise of Mao Tse Tung's Communists.

I had difficulty putting it all into perspective. Finally, frustrated, I asked him why the Chinese didn't set up a government like ours in the United States.

"How old is the U.S?" he asked.

"Oh, about a hundred and sixty years."

"Well", he said with a grin, "when you get to be *five thousand* years old, come see me!"

My first lesson in Oriental philosophy.

The IRWIN's fuel tanks were full, we'd replenished our ammunition supplies, and we'd finally got enough chow aboard to last a while. It was time to go to sea again.

On 19 July, an augmented Task Group 52.14 got underway for the Marianas. In addition to the WHITE PLAINS and MIDWAY, we were now screening the GAMBIER BAY (CVE-73), KITKUN BAY (CVE-71), and NEHENTA BAY (CVE-74). The baby flat-tops were to provide air cover for the cross-channel invasion of Tinian by the 2nd and 4th Marine Divisions which had just taken Saipan.

Tinian saw the introduction of a new weapon in our arsenal. During one of the IRWIN's shore bombardment missions, I watched as an Army Air Corps Thunderbolt swooped in low, dropping what I first thought was a bomb. But when the missile hit, a great sheet of flame engulfed an entire hillside where the enemy was dug-in. It was the first use of napalm—jellied gasoline—in combat in World War II.

The Tinian landings were made on July 24th; and it took only until August 1st to "secure" the island, despite fanatic resistance by the 9,000-man Jap garrison. Of these, over 5,500 were killed; but the fate of the others remains a mystery.

As on Guadalcanal, the Japs did not get the message the island was "secure". In the next three months, the Marines lost 38 killed, including the son of U.S. Senator Leverett Saltonstall, and 125 wounded—to Jap stragglers.

Marine and Navy casualties were reportedly 389 dead and 1,816 wounded. Some of the Navy losses came when 6-inch Nip shore batteries, like the one that opened up on the IRWIN at Saipan, hit and damaged the NORMAN SCOTT (DD-690) and the old battleship COLORADO (BB-45). Out at sea, our Task Group went unmolested by the enemy.

When air support by the CVEs was no longer needed at Tinian, we were ordered to Guam where, for three days, the jeep carriers' planes flew air cover for that invasion. We were liberating the loyal islanders in response to their plea sung in Jap concentration camps:

Oh Uncle Saum, Oh Uncle Saum,
Won't you please come back to Guam!

Then, as we were ordered back to Saipan, I copied a long message addressed "ACTION" to Destroyer Squadron 55.

We were getting new orders.

24

THE IRWIN MAKES THE VARSITY

We hoisted anchor at Saipan on 5 August, 1944, and got underway to rendezvous the next morning with Task Group 58.4. With us were the BIRMINGHAM (CL-62), the PORTERFIELD, and the CALLAGHAN. Now DesRon 55 would be operating with the Big Boys—the Glamour Fleet—the Fast Carrier Task Force whose primary mission was to take the fight to the enemy.

Our Task Group Commander was Rear Admiral Frederick C. "Teddy" Sherman, and his Chief of Staff was Captain Arleigh "31 Knot" Burke of destroyer fame in the Solomons. Pretty prestigious company with which to steam! The Group's Flagship was the ESSEX (CV-9), the first of the new class of fast flat-tops. Two light carriers, the LANGLEY (CVL-27) and the BELLEAU WOOD (CVL-24), would add to our air punch. In the beginning, the carriers would be screened by the BIRMINGHAM and another light cruiser, the SAN DIEGO (CL-53), and by three more DesRon 55 cans—CASSIN YOUNG, MORRISON, and LAWS.

We began training for the next operation immediately, first topping off our fuel bunkers. For a week, the TG conducted flight ops and AA firing at towed sleeves, repulsed simulated air attacks, and practiced maneuvering and screening techniques unique to operating with the bigger and faster ships. The only dark moment came when an ESSEX pilot crashed off our bow. The CALLAGHAN, just astern of us, recovered the pilot's body.

Then we got two weeks' rest, in port at Eniwetok, undergoing routine maintenance and upkeep, and getting availability alongside the destroyer tender MARKAB (AD-21) for repairs beyond our own ship's capabilities. And there was liberty—if you can call going ashore on a coral atoll for two bottles of warm beer "liberty".

There weren't any tourist attractions on the island, except for the remnants and debris left from the battle for this low-lying strip of land. Besides, I'd had my fill of islands in the Solomons, so I passed up the liberty call. Managing to snag surreptitiously a couple of bottles of beer when no one was looking, I put them in a bucket and doused them with a shot of CO-2 from the Radio Shack fire extinguisher. That made 'em icy cold.

Ensconced on the port side of the Comm Deck out of traffic, the bottles hidden under a skivvie shirt brought along for the purpose, I poured the cool suds into my coffee mug and langorously enjoyed a quiet afternoon, gazing out on the ships swinging around their hooks in the anchorage. The balmy trade winds whispered gently through the signal halyards in the rigging above, dispersed some of the tropical heat rising from the steel decks, and blew snippets of salt spray off tiny sun-struck wave tops into miniature rainbows.

From my dungarees pocket I pulled four letters from Jane that had come in the morning's mail call. Each envelope had a lipstick lip print on it and the letters S.W.A.K.—sealed with a kiss! A faint whiff of her perfume was still on the paper, and as I read and reread them I put the War thousands of miles away. Only the clamor of the returning liberty party was noise enough to interrupt my reverie and remind me I had the next watch. I hurried to beat the rest of the crew to the evening mess line.

That night, I slept in my bunk for the first time since the Saipan invasion. But nightmares disturbed me, and Junior Fitch had to poke me to wake me up to stop moaning. The War was never so far away that letters from home could erase it for any length of time. Despite the afternoon's quiet reprieve from reality, I didn't completely relax. The vigilance mechanisms and memories of past experiences were still there.

It was during this respite that Cap'n Danny bruised his own dictum to refrain from foul or vulgar language—to make a point. After he'd indicated earlier he'd not strictly enforce uniform regulations, there was not a word said to crewmen who, in the oppressive tropic heat, wore shirts with sleeves cut off at the shoulders or rolled up to the biceps, shirts completely unbuttoned, or no shirts at all. Some wore only skivvie shirts. Some had dungarees made into cut-offs and, in the case of some of the older men like me, had tailor-made dungarees. I even had a pair of *white moccasins* I wore quite often. Hats were worn at the individual's discretion. At sea, we looked about as "military" as a Chinese junk.

I set this scene because it was about this time that we had a visit from our Destroyer Squadron Commander Captain C.R. Todd (ComDes-Ron 55). He'd come aboard to visit the Skipper, an old friend, and to make an informal inspection. The "Squad Dog" and the Old Man toured the ship and had gotten back by the Number Three Mount where Abe Fernandes was wiping up some spilled oil. It was he and a couple of others who overheard the conversation between the two officers and spread the word throughout the ship.

Captain Todd looked around at the topside sailors in their various states and stages of dress and undress, then turned to our Skipper and said: "Dan, you have got to have a bunch of the scroungiest looking sailors in the entire United States Navy!"

Cap'n Danny got that characteristic little half-smile on his face. "Yes, I know, Todd, but they are a *bunch of fightin' sons o' bitches!*"

None of us were to hear the Skipper use such language again, but his "fightin' sons o' bitches" wouldn't have traded his remark for the Congressional Medal of Honor.

I must add that we became a lot more "regulation" as we neared combat areas. It was not a matter of orders from above. But the old-timers, the senior petty officers, impressed on their juniors the importance of wearing a full set of dungarees with shirts buttoned up, sleeves rolled down, and helmets and lifejackets on at topside battle stations. A few eye-witness descriptions of men burned by muzzle flashes, explosions, or oil fires, or wounded by shrapnel and flying metal, graphically made the point.

Admiral Halsey now relieved Admiral Spruance as Commander of the Fleet, redesignated the Third Fleet, on 26 August. The Fast Carrier Task Force changed from TF 58 to TF 38, but was still under Admiral Mitscher until a suitable replacement could be trained. Mitscher's Flagship was the new carrier LEXINGTON (CV-16). Halsey's would be the new 45,000-ton battleship NEW JERSEY (BB-62).

At 0810, 29 August, with all operations orders aboard for the upcoming campaign, the IRWIN weighed anchor to sortie with Task Group 38.3 destroyers, forming a patrol lane outside the Eniwetok channel entrance to screen the heavy ships as they proceeded to sea. Our first mission was pre-invasion air strikes on targets in the Western Carolines. We set a west-by-south course, conducting further drills and AA gunnery practice as we steamed.

Bill Blevins, a deck force Seaman 1st, turned into Sick Bay, complaining of lower abdominal pains. "Doc" Fagan quickly diagnosed the problem as acute appendicitis and told the Skipper an emergency operation was called for. The Old Man informed the LEX and asked permission to fall out of formation, reduce speed and sail a straight course while the operation was performed.

With the Captain holding the ship as steady as possible and slowing to ten knots, Doc got his patient on the Officer's Wardroom mess table. There, with battle lanterns for extra light held by Bill Needles and others, the good doctor went to work. He knew he must proceed as swiftly as possible. Alone, steaming a straight course, at slow speed, the IRWIN was highly vulnerable to submarine and/or air attack. In just an hour and forty minutes, the operation was successfully completed. The Skipper bent on the knots and we tore up the Pacific to rejoin Task Force 38. Everybody in the crew was slapping Doc Fagan on the back—he'd come through in the pinch.

Our southwesterly course took us across the Equator at 155° 28" East longitude, and all the "Pollywogs" aboard became "Shellbacks" as they were inducted into the Mysteries of the Deep on 1 September. Since the Task Group had retired this far south for a refueling rendezvous, we were out of range of enemy planes. Thus the Skipper gave his permission to hold the ancient rite of the sea. The origin of the ceremony is lost somewhere in the mists of time, but it had begun aboard sailing vessels. The probability is that it all started just to give all hands a break from the boredom of long voyages. Since windjammers frequently became becalmed in these nether latitudes, the crews had little to occupy their time.

Gunner's Mate 1st Class Bill Smith organized the ceremony and served as *Neptunus Rex* (King Neptune). He appointed me to be the Devil in what was laughingly hailed as a masterpiece of type-casting! While Smitty would preside, it was I who was to sit by the Judge who handed out "sentences" to the Pollywogs, and amused or abused them as each would plead his case in hopes of escaping the initiation into the Mysteries of the Deep.

The old-timers rigged up the gear for the induction of the initiates. After "sentencing" by the Judge, each would have to crawl through a canvas chute rigged on the port side near the depth charges. In the chute was garbage and all sorts of smelly stuff. The Pollywog would start into the chute and then be boosted along the way by streams of water from a fire hose. At the end, he'd be washed down with another sea water stream. Next on the agenda was a haircut by the Royal Barber, who used rotten eggs for shampoo and wielded scissors and clippers with abandon. The Pollywog's head ended up looking like that of a modern-day punk rocker.

Next the initiate came to the Royal Doctor. An operating table was set up aft of Mount 55, with a pool of water at the end. The canvas pool was covered with a tarp so the Pollywog couldn't see it. The Royal Doctor's table was covered with waste meat, catsup to simulate blood, and other gory debris. The Doctor, sinisterly waving a carpenter's saw in one hand and the biggest carving knife the galley boasted in the other, prepared to "operate" on whatever he found wrong with the Pollywog.

U.S.S. IRWIN (DD794)

Initiation Procedure

The evening before initiation, Polly-wogs be given all night watches to keep them out of mischief.

The charges will be read to them after entering port if time permits Charges will be read by the Judge with Court assistance.

Extra tasks for the evening before, can be made up by any shellback. Such as singing, speeches, look outs etc.

DEVIL- HUTCHINSON, R.M.2c. Sits by Judge to amuse Pollywogs when he tries to plead his case.

Pollywog officers serve morning mess to shell backs, who go through line first, having to rig gear.

Rig canvas chute on Port side by depth charges, filled with garbage etc, using a hose to start pollywog through, and no beating while in chute Royal Police stationed on the route to keep the men moving. Police stationed at after end with spray nozzle.

Barber chair rigged on Port side of Gun #5. Barber will use no grease or graphite. There are a few rotten eggs in ice box, for shampoo if man needs one.

Rig operating table directly aft of Gun # 5 beside the pool. Have canvas draped over edge of table so P.W. can't see pool. The table will be decorated with waste-meat and Catsup for effect. When royal Doctor finds trouble and applies knife man film falls into pool.

The Baby will be with the Royal Family. Having baby placed directly in front of Gun #1 so the P.W.'s won't see him. The babies' stomach and after end covered with mustard. The baby lies with stomach up when kissed. Pollywog is blindfolded for kissing baby.. When P.W. is through kissing baby, the baby rolls over on stomach and man's blindfold taken off Leaving a slight doubt in mind.

After P.W. goes through initiation he will be sent up on Gun # 4 deck to watch and not allowed to go forward and put out dope. Pollywogs clean up ship

As he was about to make an incision, the Doctor's assistants lifted the table, unceremoniously dumping the poor victim into the pool.

Finally, the Shellback's initiation involved a bit of skull-duggery and baleful deception. One of our more portly shipmates, whose name I'll forego mentioning to spare embarrassment, represented the Royal Family's Royal Baby. Positioned forward of Mount 51 so the Pollywogs could not observe the action, the Baby's stomach and after end were covered with mustard. The initiate was blindfolded and instructed to kiss the Baby's stomach. When he was through with the kissing, the Baby rolled over on his stomach, elevating his posterior toward the Pollywog. At that moment, the Pollywog's blindfold was whipped off, leaving the initiate with, as Smitty put it, "a slight doubt in mind"!

After each Pollywog went through all these humiliations, he was allowed to watch his successors, but not to give them any dope as to what was coming. Once all had been inducted into the exclusive fraternity, the newly-initiated ones suffered one more indignity. They were detailed to clean up the mess, making everything shipshape, and storing all the gear. A good time was had by all. A treasured memento of all Shellbacks is the official wallet card attesting to survival of the initiation and Crossing the Equator.

After refueling the next day, we were joined by Cruiser Division 13 and Destroyer Division 100 to beef up our screen against possible enemy air attacks. The IRWIN raced ahead of the force to take up the radar picket station twelve miles in the van. On 6 September, we shoved off on a high-speed run toward the Palau Island group in the Western Carolines. Our planes flew strikes against ground targets on the 7th and 8th, then we headed due west at 25 knots for Mindanao in the Southern Philippines. When the carriers turned into the wind, the Western Pacific was in one of its most placid, quiet moods. There was no wind at all of which to speak, certainly not enough to provide lift under the wings of planes taking off. So . . . we had to produce our own.

Fleet speed was rung up to 30 knots, and we cut in our superheaters with all boilers on the line to maintain station. Our little can dug in her heels with characteristic exuberance, bow high, stern low, throwing a "rooster tail" (water hurled up by the screws) high in the air and speeding across the seas like a thoroughbred in the home stretch under the whip. With "a bone in 'er teeth" (appearance of the bow wave at top speed) and a broad, white, boiling wake, it was an inspiring sight for any sailor. Maneuvering in formation with the other cans of DesRon 55, all driving through the Philippine Sea at 30 plus knots, it was the stuff newsreel shots and recruiting posters were made of.

Task Force 38, with nine fleet carriers, eight light carriers, six battleships, fourteen cruisers, and sixty destroyers, raided across the Western Pacific at will, reminiscent of the forays of my Viking ancestors, or of the corsairs of the Caribbean in the days of Blackbeard. Our fighters and bombers stung the enemy like angry hornets all the way from the Carolines north to Okinawa Gunto and westward across the South China Sea to Formosa. Bull Halsey led us across the Visayan Sea west of Leyte, in range of ten Jap airfields, whence 2,400 sorties were flown against the hostiles, destroying over 200 of their aircraft in two raids. Only one challenge came to the Task Force. On 13 September, a single Kate bomber sneaked through, dropping a bomb which fell harmlessly astern of the ESSEX. The lucky Jap got away.

On September 15th, the 1st Marine Division (the good old First!) hit the beaches at Peleliu. It would not be an easy campaign for the most famous division of the War. For over two months, the gyrenes battled before the island was secured. The 13,000-man Jap garrison fought almost to the last man. Only some 300 survivors were taken as prisoners of war. The Marines suffered nearly 10,500 casualties; of which some 1,950 were killed in a battle many feel shouldn't have been fought. Peleliu was taken to be used as an advance base for the Philippines invasion, but its airfield and other facilities were never brought into play in that campaign.

Steaming with Task Force 38 followed, for many weeks, a routine that had one day running into the next. But it was a tough routine for destroyermen. While the heavies maintained a steady fleet speed and seldom made radical course changes, we would be cutting back and forth across the 15 to 20 mile radius of the cruising disposition at clips far faster than the "standard cruising" speed. The wakes of the bigger ships, and often choppy seas, would have us bouncing and pounding, pitching and rolling.

A typical day for us would have the IRWIN coming off radar picket duty some 12 to 15 miles ahead of the main body, head for refueling from an oiler, battleship, or carrier, from which we'd pick up both guard and regular mail. Then, in between flight operations aboard the flat-tops, we'd speed around to each ship in our command, delivering mail, transferring personnel from one ship to another, and often breaking from that duty to hurry into our regular screening station at the threat of attack by Jap shore-based aircraft. With that out of the way, a flag hoist from the ESSEX would signal "Desig Dog Seven Nine Four", and we'd take position a few hundred yards in the wake of one of the carriers, steaming plane guard.

We delivered so damn' much mail that Bill Needles, our artist in residence, painted a banner to hang over the side of the Bridge every

MAIL CALL
Transferring a bag of mail to a carrier in choppy seas off Formosa. The bag is the white object just over the water even with Number Two stack, lower right.
(U.S. Navy Photo - National Archives)

time we got the mail runs. It depicted a sailor with a sack over his shoulder, full of letters, and the legend proclaimed us "FPO 794"—FPO standing for "Fleet Post Office". The only benefit derived from being the Task Group's postman was a small ration of ice cream we occasionally received. We had no facility to make it ourselves, but all the bigger ships had gedunk stands. Out of the goodness of their hearts, they'd usually send us over enough for each man aboard to have a scoop.

Transfer of anything between ships at sea is a difficult operation, even when the ships slow to ten or eleven knots and the weather and sea are calm. Yet, the IRWIN never lost a man, never injured one, never dropped a sack of mail nor a carton of gedunks.

We'd come alongside the larger vessel, plowing through its wake, heave over a messenger line, either by hand or by a line gun, to which a hawser was bent on (i.e. a heavy line or rope tied on). At the same time, the deck hands would rig a breeches buoy for the transfer of people, mail bags, sometimes food, or other supplies. Both ships had to maintain an even speed and course, although it was the responsibility of the tin can to keep its position alongside with the proper intervals. In rough weather, this took considerable seamanship and shiphandling skill to avoid careening into the side of the heavy, or severing the lines between the vessels. The men of our deck force were in constant danger of being swept over the side by seas breaking over the bow; and passengers in the breeches buoy were at jeopardy should the lines slacken and dip them in the water, or snap if the ships pulled apart.

During most of the IRWIN's duty with the Fast Carriers, we saw little of the enemy. After the Marianas Turkey Shoot, the Japs could mount little in the way of a seaborne offense, and most of the land-based planes which ventured toward us were destroyed by our CAP. The offensive punch of Task Force 38 was in its air arm, and our pilots took a terrible toll among hostile land-based aircraft; they also plastered shore installations and shipping in strikes against Luzon, Leyte, Mindanao, Formosa, and Okinawa.

After 27 days of roaming the Western Pacific and the China Seas like the sea raiders of old, striking like lightning at a reeling foe, we retired to Kossol Passage in the Palaus for a breather on October 1st. But while the bigger ships enjoyed a rest at anchor, the IRWIN was out patrolling the harbor entrance against the possibility of sub or air attack during the day. Then at night, all ships got underway for retirement to sea where we could maneuver and therefore were much less vulnerable to any Jap excursion against us.

During operations we had been refueling almost every 24 hours. As the Exec Lieutenant Hodapp recalls: "We burned fuel damn fast in those days. Also, one never knew when we would be dashing off, out of range of our tankers. So, the order of the day was to keep the cans topped off whenever possible."

Now, we filled our bunkers to the brim off the NIORRARA, managed to get some provisions aboard, and got underway once again, leaving Palau for Ulithi in the Western Carolines. That island had been occupied unopposed and would become the main base for our operations for the rest of the War. It has a superb, large harbor that can accommodate over 600 ships at one time. But our arrival on October 2nd would be anything but routine.

Steady rain, high winds, and low visibility delayed the heavies' entry into the harbor as the IRWIN took up patrol in Mugai Channel. When we entered, we had to use radar to locate our berth as the weather grew more threatening. The engine room was put on one-hour notice in case a storm necessitated a speedy departure. At 2235, we were forced to shift to a secondary anchorage as the heavy rains, increasingly strong winds, and mounting swells caused us to yaw 80 degrees, endangering nearby vessels. The engines went on 15-minute notice, as we got orders from Admiral Halsey to be ready for an emergency sortie. A Pacific typhoon was making its presence felt.

At 0254 on October 3rd, we shifted berths for the third time. Our anchor had been dragging as the ship was buffeted by increasing winds. In the Radio Shack, I had lashed down everything movable, and Frank Riddle and Don Karl had secured the heavy weather lines on their chairs. We were rolling in the swells better than 30° and we could hear the winds whistling like massed bos'n's pipes across the weather decks. By now, they'd reached above gale force to 80 knots in gusts, and Admiral Halsey ordered a sortie at dawn. By 0817, all ships of Task Group 38.3 were clear of the harbor, had formed into cruising disposition, and were heading southward.

The murky seas were gargantuan, powered by blasts of wind now over 100 knots (120 miles an hour). Our little vessel was taking a pounding as her head plowed down into the huge waves and tons of salt water roared over the Bridge, decks and deck housing. It was like being under Niagara Falls in a rowboat. When she'd come up, the bow would lift high out of the water and she'd roll 40° to 45°, showing all her bottom 'twixt wind and water. As she slid downward again, her screws would clear the sea and spin like eggbeaters in the air. Each time she'd go over on her beam ends, Riddle, Karl, and I would just look at each other—saying silent prayers that she'd pull herself back upright, all the while hanging on for dear life.

Our fleet course to the south was taking us out of the worst of the

TYPHOON ON THE WAY
Fighting high seas and rising winds as the Pacific storm begins to make
its presence felt.
(U.S. Navy Photo - U.S. Navy Historical Center)

storm, and the winds and seas began to abate. By 0700 on October 4th, Admiral Halsey ordered us to reverse our heading and return to Ulithi. We dropped anchor at about 1200, but kept the engine room on four-hour notice. The next day we refueled from the CIMARRON, then returned to our anchorage for routine maintenance and upkeep. One is reminded of Halsey's comment: "No one who has not been through a typhoon can conceive its fury."

Just after morning mess on 6 October, we went alongside the SOUTH DAKOTA. The battleship was acting as a relay vessel for stores and provisions from the cargo ship ALDEBARON. The IRWIN was the inboard can, next to the BB-57, with three other destroyers nesting outboard of us. As the supplies came aboard, we'd take those allotted to us; *but* we also exacted a little tribute in the way of provisions destined for the outboard cans, secreting them in various parts of the ship. Since this was an all-hands evolution, each of our divisions was confiscating goodies for itself. Even with this filching going on, we loaded 35 (official) tons of fresh, frozen, and dry chow in 50 minutes. We'd eat well for a while for a change.

At 1632 the same day, Task Group 38.3 moved out Mugai Channel as we screened the heavies, formed in cruising disposition, and set a course for Okinawa Jima. The IRWIN hurried to the fore of the formation to take up radar and anti-submarine picket duty. It was back to Fast Carrier operations, once again.

On October 8th, just as we finished refueling from the SABINA, a plane off the light carrier PRINCETON (CVL-23) crashed about 4,000 yards from us. As the closest destroyer, we went to the scene, but we couldn't get there in time to rescue the crew. After searching for an hour, we gave up and rejoined the Task Group.

With all boilers on the line and our superheaters cut in, we began a 25-knot-per-hour approach to Okinawa. At 0535 on 9 October, the carriers swung into the wind to launch the first of many air strikes that day against targets on the island. Jap land-based aircraft followed the attackers back toward the Task Force, but our ever vigilant Combat Air Patrol intercepted them, and no ships came under enemy assault. The IRWIN had the mail duty again during the day.

The following morning we refueled from the WASHINGTON and were just clearing her side when another PRINCETON plane hit the drink. This time we got our man, plucking him from the water neatly on the move. We then received several passengers from a CVE in the fueling group and spent the rest of the afternoon delivering 'em to the ships to which they were consigned. Hardly had we dropped off the last man when we cranked back up to 25 knots, took our screening station, and headed with the Task Group for Formosa and the East China Sea. All that running around was at a pace much faster than the Task Force's standard speed, and all the extra work involved in refueling and transferring mail, etc., kept us from getting bored—that's for sure.

Operations in the Radio Shack were routine during this campaign. As a petty officer of the watch, my job was supervisorial. I double-checked all incoming traffic from the FOX skeds; looking for messages either addressed to us or, because of the addressees, perhaps of interest to the Skipper. We rotated men around the watch sections so the 3rd Class and the striker on each watch changed regularly. Promotions, too, made it necessary to give men different assignments. Bressie and Wasson had both made Radioman 3rd, John Dekle got his 2nd Class stripe in July, and Fred Hartman was out of the Gang after being given a Summary Court-Martial and reduced in rate to Seaman 1st. Claude Uzzell (from ComDesRon 55) was aboard on temporary duty.

Ken Wasson and Joe Alice were on my watch during most of this time, sharing the FOX sked duty. I'd only take over during times atmospheric interference made the signal from NPM (Honolulu) difficult to copy. For the most part, though, I often had time to go out on the Comm Deck to watch what was going on around the Task Force. Any dispatches pertinent to the IRWIN, or to Fleet or Task Group operations had to be decoded, and I'd send Alice to get Mr. Dean or the duty Coding Officer to come to the Shack for that purpose. Within our Task Group, however, most intership communications were via TBS (ultra high-frequency radio), by flashing light, or by flag hoist.

Al Block and I shared the copying of "Radio Press News". This was a commercial plain English broadcast of mostly Associated Press news which every ship copied. It was our only way to find out what was happening in the rest of the world, and sometimes the only word we got of what *WE* were doing! In the afternoon, I'd pick up a handful of stencils and head for Emergency Radio. Located on the port side of the main deck inside the midships passageway, this shack was tiny, about five by six feet, with one operating position and the emergency transmitter. Here I'd tune in commercial station "Mackay Radio" from the States, broadcasting at 36 words per minute.

Because the space was so small, I usually left the door open and some shipmates would squeeze in to read the news over my shoulder. With a mug of joe and a cigarette, I'd copy about four single-spaced pages of the latest news from home. The process served to keep up my copying skills, and I'd test myself by "laying behind" the transmission as much as a whole paragraph. When I'd make a typo, I'd whip out the correction fluid, remedy the error, then catch up with the feed.

The radio strikers who'd often watch were impressed when I'd drink coffee, smoke a cigarette, hold a conversation with them, and at the same time copy the 36 wpm broadcasts. That did my ego some good, and I'd take pride in my showboating. When I finished, the stencils would go to the Yeoman's Office, to be run off and copies distributed about the ship, but always first to the Captain. Bill Needles often would decorate the front page with a cartoon, and our Press News looked pretty good, if I say so myself.

Planes from all four groups of Task Force 38 began air operations in and around Formosa (Taiwan), beginning at 0549, 12 October. For the next four days, our guys attacked everything that moved and most of what stood still—airfields, shore installations, shipping and other targets of opportunity. Enemy aircraft came out to challenge us, but no Jap got within shooting range on the 12th or 13th.

On October 14th, the IRWIN went alongside the ALABAMA (BB-60) to refuel, even though hostile "shadowers" (planes) were closing the formation occasionally. After making the battleship's side and connecting the fueling lines, a sudden sea crashed across the foc'sle, carrying our First Lieutenant, "Long John" McCord, over the side into the rough waters. Bill Needles, also in the fueling detail, went over, too, but fortunately clung to a line and was hauled back aboard, somewhat the worse for wear after banging against the hull several times.

Lieutenant McCord, meanwhile, was fast disappearing astern. Captain Miller never hesitated. Immediately releasing all lines and breaking the fueling connections, he ordered a sharp turn to port, increased speed to 25 knots and went after Long John, who was one of the best-liked officers aboard. McCord was wearing a lifejacket, mandatory for the fueling detail; so, unless he were injured, we were fairly sure he'd be recovered. In just 17 minutes we had him back aboard, were back alongside the ALABAMA, and were reconnecting the fueling hoses.

While the oil was pumping, we were getting a lot of badmouthing from the deck of the battlewagon. Diesel fuel had sprayed her slab sides when we broke loose, and her deck apes would have to clean it up. At the same time, the 'BAMA's Skipper was chewing out Cap'n Danny for breaking the lines and soiling his precious gray paint. Besides, we weren't supposed to go after a man overboard, but leave that to some ship to our rear.

Finally, our Old Man got on the TBS, called the ALABAMA's Captain by name, and said: "This is Dan Miller. Now . . . if you don't keep quiet, I'll tell the whole Fleet about the time you . . . ."

The battlewagon's C.O. immediately interrupted. Apparently, our Skipper knew of some peccadillo the Captain of the 'BAMA would just

REFUELING A TIN CAN AT SEA CAN BE HAZARDOUS TO YOUR HEALTH
(U.S. Navy Photo - National Archives)

as soon forget. His voice softened as he said: "Now, Dan, there's no need to bring that up. By the way, would you like some ice cream?"

I was on the Bridge, having gone up to watch the refueling operation and chat with Fitch. The entire Bridge crew was in stitches. Our little tin can had put a mighty battleship in its place!

Our diversion was short-lived. General Quarters sounded in anticipation of a Jap air attack, but our CAP took care of the invaders this time. It was no false alarm later in the afternoon, though, when ten Kates bore in on our side of the formation. Flying low and coming in from the south, the enemy torpedo bombers were immediately taken under fire, first by the RENO.

We joined in, firing barrage after barrage with our 5-inch guns, then the 40s, then the 20s. The curtain of fire forced the Kates off their torpedo runs, but not before the IRWIN's guns scored a direct hit on one Kate. As he fell a-flaming, the Nip pilot pulled his plane toward the RENO and suicide-crashed into the cruiser's fantail. And damned if the RENO didn't take credit for the knockdown! We were given an "assist".

A total of seven hostile planes bit the dust. We might have gotten more, but for the failure of our master gyro and faulty ammunition, experienced for the first time. Out of 81 Mark 32 projectiles (proximity-fused to explode near the target) we fired, all exploded prematurely, the bursts coming at 500 to 1,500 yards from the gun muzzles. Only our Mark 18 AA common rounds got to the targets.

Immediately after the 14 October raid, the flat-tops swung into the wind to recover their birds, and we began retiring to a fueling rendezvous with the KASKASKIA (AO-27). Radar continued to pick up enemy aircraft on the scopes, but none closed. We had gotten fleet mail while alongside the oiler and now delivered it to various units in the Task Group. At 2000, we were separated from TG 38.3 to cover the retirement of two cruisers that had been hit in the battle area off Formosa.

From the beginning of the attacks on Okinawa on 9 October, some 1,400 sorties had been flown against targets in that area, with over 100 hostile planes destroyed at a cost to us of 21 aircraft and nine fliers. In the four days we pounded Formosa with some 2,350 sorties, the Japs lost about 500 planes; and our attacks against shore installations destroyed strategic stores, ammo and fuel dumps, hangars and repair facilities. The Japs countered with over 1,000 sorties against Task Force 38 in a series of raids, the largest to be mounted by the Nips against a carrier force at anytime during the War. But few of their planes got through to the ships. Our air cover frustrated most of the enemy attacks at a cost to us of 76 aircraft.

But on 13 October Betty bombers did score hits on the new heavy cruiser U.S.S. CANBERRA (CA-70) namesake of the Australian cruiser sunk in the Battle of Savo Island in the Solomons. The next day, the new HOUSTON (CL-81) took an aerial torpedo. The two ships survived but were badly damaged. The HOUSTON took a second fish in another attack on the 16th as the crippled pair were trying to limp to safety.

It was then the IRWIN was dispatched to provide protection for the wounded cruisers until they were out of range of enemy aircraft, and until an "old friend" from the Solomons showed up to take the HOUSTON in tow. It was the doughty PAWNEE, the fleet tug which had made the valiant effort to save the McCAWLEY, and whose exploits are chronicled in Ted Mason's book *We Will Stand By You* (1990). As the sad little group, to become known as "CripDiv One" (Crippled Division One) disappeared over the horizon to safety, the IRWIN headed back to Task Group 38.3.

On the way, our lookouts sighted a floating mine, which we took under 40mm fire and exploded. Some fifteen minutes later, another was discovered. Just as we detonated it with a Mark IV 300-pound depth charge from a K-gun, a lone Jap plane came out of nowhere to make a run on us. Our batteries immediately opened fire on the Frances. Again our ammunition failed us, the Mark 32s bursting prematurely. A heavy running sea didn't help much either. But the fire we did put up was too much for the Jap. He put 'er in high gear and disappeared to the west, flying down on the wave tops, not ready to give up his life for the Emperor that day. The Old Man turned on the juice as we hastened to rejoin our Task Group.

Throughout September and October, we had been steaming so hard, so fast, for so long, the bricks were literally falling out of the fire boxes in the boiler rooms. Intensive heat generated under the boilers, and the almost constant use of our superheaters, caused the metal retainers actually to melt, allowing the bricks to crumble. To remedy the situation, the black gang would pull one boiler off the line at a time late at night when there was the least probability of an enemy attack. Bill Needles, who was a welder as well as having other talents, then would repair and replace the metal clips, after installing new bricks for those damaged. It was touchy, because he couldn't wait for the fire boxes to cool completely.

The hard steaming was tough on the men, as well. The gun crews were standing "watch and watch" (four hours on, four off) plus General Quarters, as were most of the rest of the divisions. With few opportunities to reprovision, our chow was getting down to Spam, beans, and rice, again. We had sandwiches for meals more often than we got to eat a "sit down" meal on the mess deck. Coffee and cigarettes almost became our lifeblood. There was something comforting in pausing to sip a hot cup of joe and lighting up a Lucky or a Camel.

There are many of us who swear we would never have made it through the War without our java and our smokes. Yet, we didn't get a chance to indulge in either that much. The smoking lamp was only lit at specified times. No smoking was permitted at General Quarters, when refueling, or when handling ammunition. Most watch stations, particularly in the gunnery department, prohibited smoking, and there was no smoking on the weather decks after dark. Even one who was a heavy coffee drinker like me seldom consumed more than four or five cups a day. But it was those rare moments when we could relax with that a cup o' jamoke and a cigarette that seemed to bring a sense of normalcy back to us in the midst of all the demands of wartime operations.

In mid-October, Admiral Halsey turned his four Fast Carrier Groups of Task Force 38 toward the Philippines to cover the invasion on the beaches of Leyte Island. On 20 October, General Douglas MacArthur finally realized his goal: his promise to the Filipinos, "I shall return", was kept. The Navy took a dim view of Dugout Doug's publicity machine that kept his name prominently in front of the folks back home while the likes of men like Admirals Spruance and Mitscher went completely unheralded.

To us in the Navy, MacArthur was a pompous ass, a glory hunter, and a posturing fool who took credit for himself when others did the job. It had been the Navy and the Marine Corps which fought the major battles to get us back to the Philippines. And the corn-cob-pipe-smoking General couldn't have gotten there "without the help of God and the United States Navy." The only way he could cross the sea was on the deck of a Navy vessel. As the saying went in the Fleet: "Even Dugout Doug can't walk on water—he don't have no Jesus shoes!"

Our Task Group 38.3 was stationed east of Luzon, the northerly force to interdict any attempt by the enemy to send a counter-strike down from the north. We were almost due east of the Polillo Islands at about the same latitude as Manila. From that position, we were set to strike at land targets, as well as any Jap fleet activity in the Sibuyan Sea, in addition to protecting our northern flank.

On the night of the invasion of Leyte, with the knowledge the Philippine Campaign could be a long one, and with uncertainty as to the part the IRWIN would play, I wrote (through censorship) a letter to my sister Betty. In part, I said:

"Since last I wrote, Fitch, my buddy, has received word—IT'S A BOY! I couldn't begin to describe Jane to you and anyhow it would be a biased opinion. I'll just drop in this snapshot. She's much more beautiful than any of the photos, tho'. We're making lots of plans via the mail. If I'm away long enough, we won't have anything to do but get married!

Of course, I can't say what goes on where I am, but after more than two years out here, it's all routine. If the war doesn't last *too* long, I probably won't get home 'til it's over, but if there's another two or three years to go, I *may* make it home, again, before the end. It's still my opinion, tho', this is a LONG war, any way you look at it.

Love,
Your brother, Jack"

The next few days would prove me a lousy prophet.

25

THE DEATH THROES OF THE PRINCETON

For three days, the planes of Task Group 38.3 pounded and punished ground targets on Luzon. Land-based enemy aircraft made persistent efforts in force to attack our ships, but our fighter cover successfully repelled their raids.

By October 23rd, we'd gotten word of sightings of Jap fleet movements toward the U.S. 6th Army's landings on the Leyte beachheads. The major enemy force, steaming up from Singapore, apparently was to join a second group coming down from Formosa. The third bunch of hostile ships had sortied out of Japan's Inland Sea, moved easterly, then started south toward our position. We'd later learn this was a decoy deployment to keep the Fast Carriers occupied in the northern Philippine Sea and away from reinforcing and supporting our fleet units in and around Leyte Gulf.

On October 24, 1944, Task Group 38.3 was fielding the Fleet Carriers LEXINGTON, Flagship of Vice Admiral Mitscher, and the ESSEX, flying the Flag of Rear Admiral Teddy Sherman; the light carriers PRINCETON and LANGLEY; battleships SOUTH DAKOTA and MASSACHUSETTS (BB-59); and four light cruisers: SANTA FE, BIRMINGHAM, MOBILE, and RENO. The destroyer screen was composed of 13 ships: The PORTERFIELD, Flagship of DesRon 55, IRWIN, CASSIN YOUNG, PRESTON, LAWS, LONGSHAW, AND MORRISON, all of Destroyer Squadron 55; and from DesRon 50 were the C.K. BRONSON (DD-668), COTTEN (DD-669), DORTCH (DD-670), GATLING (DD-671), and HEALY (DD-672).

The light carriers were a new breed of ship. In 1941, the hulls of nine light cruisers had been laid down, as ordered by the Bureau of Ships. But the Navy Department saw a more urgent need for carriers in a war where aircraft would become a major offensive weapon. BuShips then ordered the cruisers to be converted. With hulls and power plants built for speed, these hybrids were capable of operating with the fast fleet carriers where speeds of 32 knots or better were required.

Designated "CVL", the light carriers displaced 11,000 tons, and had flight decks 623 feet long and 109 feet wide. With air groups supporting 45 fighters and torpedo bombers, plus regular ship's company, the CVL's crew totaled some 1,600 men. In an unusual feature to have as much flight deck space as possible, the four smoke stacks came out of the center of the ship horizontally, then turned up the starboard side, outboard of the flight deck. On the same side was the "island"—the superstructure which housed the Bridge and other topside facilities. The CVLs weren't very pretty ships, but they sure as hell got the job done.

I had the midwatch the morning of the 24th and was already in the Radio Shack when we went to routine General Quarters a half-hour before sunrise. Funny thing, I thought to myself, of all the hundreds of times I'd gone through this drill, I knew of no time when the enemy struck at sunrise, except at Pearl Harbor. Oh, snooper planes or probes, yeah, but no major assault. Nor was there any at routine sunset GQ either. Yet, the Navy said these were the hours when an attack was most probable. There would be enemy air sorties this morning, but the surface ships would not be involved until long after dawn GQ.

With the Radio Shack manned and ready, I stepped out on the Comm Deck with a fresh mug of java to watch the LEX and ESSEX launch their Combat Air Patrols and their "search, sweep, and destroy" flights. The latter were headed for the Sibuyan Sea, Mindoro Strait, and land-based targets on Luzon.

The sun was just shoving aside the low-lying clouds with fingers of light on the eastern horizon when our fighter cover reported shooting down a pair of snoopers. Then our radar picked up more bogies, this time in force, and the CAP went after them. Several hostiles got within eight or ten miles of the surface units, but they didn't survive tangling with our fighters. None closed within AA range. A half-hour after sunrise, with no bogies within 20 miles showing on the scopes, the Skipper secured us from GQ, but ordered two thirds of the crew to remain at battle stations while one third went to chow. The Old Man was taking no chances of being caught unprepared.

I hated the powdered eggs we had for mess. Today they were more watery than usual. "Must be getting low on chow, again", I concluded. To make up for the eggs, I heavily buttered three slices of bread, baked fresh overnight, and returned topside. There was little use trying to sleep in from the midwatch. At the merest sign of Jap intruders, we'd be back at full battle readiness. There went my hopes for a shave, shower, and change of clothes. Didn't want to be caught naked during an air raid! I was a little edgy, anyhow, with that feeling something was going to happen—none of it good. We'd been on radar picket station all night, and now enemy action appeared more than probable.

"Tallyho! Many, many aircraft!"

Bandits spotted, heading toward us from the north.

The GQ alarm began its clang-clang-clang; and we were fully manned and ready, again. From Admiral Sherman (ComTaskGroup 38.3) came signals for emergency turns and maneuvers to get our wagons in a circle to repel the hostiles, and fleet speed was rung up to 24 knots. A busy Combat Air Patrol intercepted the bandits, and were splashing them all over the place well before the Jap planes could reach the ship formation.

They couldn't get 'em all. At 0837, a single Judy bomber, skirting the outer DD screen, came flying low, and closing us from 9,000 yards, dead on the bow. The forward mounts opened fire as the Old Man swung the ship to port, bringing the other guns to bear. In face of the barrage we put up, the Nip apparently had second thoughts about taking us on directly, did a 180 and opened the range—fast! In the meantime, the fighters were polishing off the rest of the raiders.

With the danger over, at least temporarily, the Task Group turned into the wind for flight ops; both to refuel the CAP fighters, who'd had a busy morning, and to mount more strikes on enemy targets over towards Luzon and the Sibuyan Sea. By 0900, our radar scopes were clear of any bogies; and at 0935, we secured from battle stations, keeping the ship two-thirds manned, while the second shift headed for the chow line.

I had just started down the ladder toward the galley to bum a couple more slices of bread from Sharp when I heard 20-and 40-millimeter fire somewhere in the Task Group. A quick scan of the formation and I spotted tracers arching up from one of the CVLs. They had a vertically climbing Judy bomber bracketed but were not scoring any hits. From the carrier came a dull "hurr-*UMPH!*" The Jap Judy disappeared into the cloud cover.

At two steps at a time, I climbed the ladder to the Signal Bridge where Fitch already had his binoculars trained on the carrier.

"It's the PRINCETON", he advised. "There's smoke coming from her after quarter."

From the TBS speaker in the wheel house came a calm voice:

"Maxwell from Hatchet. I have taken a bomb. Will keep you informed." ("Maxwell" was the voice radio call sign of Admiral Sherman, CTG 38.3. "Hatchet" was the PRINCETON.)

Admiral Sherman then asked the PRINCETON's C.O., Captain

HELP ON THE WAY
The IRWIN approaches the stricken PRINCETON, victim of a 500
pound bomb dropped by a solitary "Judy" torpedo bomber.
Coming from astern to the windward of the carrier, the DD-794 rigs
to fight the raging fires and to rescue survivors, some of whom are
already in the water.
(U.S. Navy Photo - National Archives)

William Bruacker, if he wanted to slow down, and got a "negative". But the situation was more serious than first surmised.

The IRWIN's War Diary states: "PRINCETON held formation speed until 0948 and then commenced dropping astern, position 15° 13' North, 123° 23' East." Then the carrier went dead in the water.

Thus began one helluva damned day.

"Clinker [CASSIN YOUNG], Reliance [IRWIN], Leather [GATLING] and Bayonet [RENO] designated to stay with Hatchet." The rest of Task Group 38.3 steamed on.

The RENO, as senior ship, ordered the IRWIN to go close astern the stricken PRINCETON, then followed with another command:

"Reliance from Bayonet. Go alongside Hatchet for fire and rescue work."

By now, the prevailing winds and seas had turned the light carrier broadside to the elements, and she was wallowing in the choppy waters. Already some of her crew were in the water. One was blown over the side when the bomb hit, and the CASSIN YOUNG took after him. While making the rescue, she came under attack by a Betty bomber. With the help of one of our fighter planes, she knocked it down.

Captain Miller took the IRWIN up the windward side of the PRINCETON, handling the ship gingerly to avoid survivors in the water. As our bow came even with the carrier's, the unpredictable sea heeled us to starboard; the carrier simultaneously rolled to port, and the two ships smashed together with a crash of metal on metal, wrecking portions of our superstructure around the Bridge.

I was nearly thrown off my feet. As I recovered there was one helluva huge explosion from deep in the bowels of the flat-top just abaft midships. A blast of flame, hot metal, and debris sprayed through the IRWIN's upper works, showering pieces of metal down on our decks. It was incredible that not one man topside was injured.

The 550-pound bomb that had pierced the CVL's flight deck just forward of the after elevator had exploded below the hangar deck deep in the PRINCETON's "innards", setting fires and knocking out part of the carrier's firefighting apparatus. Secondary gasoline and ammunition explosions spread the blazes rapidly.

As our deck hands on the foc'sle attempted to get lines over to the carrier, there was another major blast aboard her that rocked both ships. Then a 40-millimeter magazine blew, sending the bursting projectiles whizzing through our superstructure and rigging. Everybody hit the deck. It scared the hell out of me and everyone else around the 0-1 and Bridge levels. No casualties, however. That blast led Captain Miller to order all of our ammunition removed from the starboard side, and men were stationed in the magazines, ready to open the flood cocks should fire break out aboard the IRWIN.

The continuous crashing together of the ships caused us to back down away from the carrier, clearing astern. But Cap'n Danny was tenacious in his determination to aid the stricken flat-top. Back alongside we went, maneuvering carefully. Aboard both ships so many actions were taking place simultaneously it's difficult to place them all in chronological order. Firefighting and rescue work were going on rapidly and continuously.

All our starboard projecting booms and radio antennas had been wiped out during the initial approach to the carrier. That side of the Bridge was in shambles, and there was other extensive damage to the IRWIN. As the Skipper held us bow to bow with the PRINCETON, the ships formed a "V" that was constantly changing its open end aft. The pushing and pulling of the seas caused the distance between the sterns of the vessels to range from a few feet to several yards. Forward, we were at once up under the carrier's flight deck, then rolled apart by the sea, only to be crashed again into the CVL.

There had been PRINCETON men in the water from the time we made our initial approach, and now the crew was abandoning her at all points clear of the fires. The rescue work began. Lieutenant Hodapp's 29-man swimming team plunged into the water to aid burned, injured, and exhausted survivors. Along both the port and starboard sides, cargo nets were lowered as IRWIN crewmen reached out to help PRINCETON men aboard.

Our damage control people and repair parties, along with firefighting personnel, were attempting to bring the carrier's fires under control, rigging hoses to our fire mains and starting up gas-powered handy-billies. The trick was to get the streams of water up over the side of the carrier and down into the hangar deck. The high freeboard of the carrier and the low silhouette of the destroyer made that a difficult task.

Some of our guys muscled a hose up to the searchlight platform on Number One Stack. It was one of the few ways to spray water effectively on the fires. Three incredibly gutsy PRINCETON crewmen, timing their jump perfectly, leaped from the flight deck to our Bridge, grabbed a hose and, when the ships rolled back toward each other, again with perfect timing jumped back to the rolling carrier and pulled the hose aboard the CVL. But with no pressure on her own fire mains, the below-deck fires aboard the PRINCETON steadily gained headway.

Admiral Sherman, advised of the seriousness of the situation that had developed, decided we needed more help and dispatched the BIR-

USS PRINCETON, OCTOBER 24, 1944

BOMB DAMAGE TO THE "PEERLESS P" FLIGHT DECK
(Photo of the damaged, burning PRINCETON)
(Courtesy "The Tiger Rag")

MINGHAM and MORRISON to join the rescue flotilla. Captain Thomas B. Inglis of the cruiser thus became Senior Officer Present Afloat (S.O.P.A.) and took charge of operations. As he did, Captain Miller informed him at 1030: "From this side can't tell if fire is coming under control or not." Cap'n Danny also suggested to Inglis that: "all [ships] stand by to pick up survivors from Hatchet."

The other ships in the rescue unit formed a protective ring around the PRINCETON, with the CASSIN YOUNG and the GATLING stationed astern where they could best pick up survivors who floated away from us. The sea between the IRWIN and the carrier was like a sluiceway. As men hit the rushing water, they were swept aft. Once they cleared our stern, they were in open sea. Then their best hopes for rescue lay in being spotted by the CASSIN YOUNG and GATLING. They were, as Virgil put it in the *Aeneid*, "a few swimming in the vast deep."

Not all the men abandoning ship got their feet wet. Pete Callan (now of Yucca Valley, California) wrote to me of how he made it:

"I was an Aviation Ordnanceman 2/c. I was in an armory on the port side, just opposite the island. We had no water pressure so the fire got quickly out of control. . . . We had hundreds of 100-pound bombs stored aft instead of being in magazines. I guess the idea was that they would be handy if we needed them. Before the first explosion, I moved forward on the flight deck. A series of explosions on the hangar deck blew off most of the flight deck and inflicted numerous casualties."

"By then the IRWIN was on our port side. We were ordered to abandon ship. The men who went off the port side were caught between the PRINCETON and the IRWIN. When the ships smashed together, that was the end of them. The situation was not too good. On the port side everyone I could see in the water was dead. On the starboard side everything was obscured by black smoke. I didn't have a life jacket and went to look for one but had no luck. When I returned I saw that the IRWIN was hung up on our anchor. It took some doing to get her off."

"By this time another ordnanceman and I were the only ones left on the foc'sle. The IRWIN was preparing to pull away. We decided the time to do something had arrived. We jumped from the PRINCETON to the bow of the IRWIN. It was quite a jump. We were both a little battered by the impact but no bones were broken. We wouldn't be alive today except for the crew of the IRWIN and none of us will ever forget that."

Not all reached safety so quickly. Ben Tomczak, in a letter printed in *The Tiger Rag*, the PRINCETON Association newsletter, recalled:

"I was a Seaman First and my GQ station was 20-mm gunner when we got hit. I went overboard and got picked up *almost two hours later* . . . I think by the MORRISON."

THE IRWIN ALONGSIDE THE PRINCETON

Returning after a brief disengagement, the destroyer, despite the ever-present threat of more explosions, snugs close to the carrier, to pour streams of water onto fires while simultaneously rescuing men from the flight deck and from the sea. Photo taken from the CASSIN YOUNG.

(Real War Photos)

Captain Miller was doing a masterful job of shiphandling. Keeping the IRWIN in position alongside the PRINCETON took all the skills of an expert mariner, as well as a lot of guts. Knowing he was putting his own ship and crew in jeopardy, he nevertheless was undeterred in upholding the highest and one of the oldest traditions of the sea—going to the assistance of a vessel in distress.

With the winds and the seas growing worse, the carrier's flight deck smashing into the IRWIN's upper works as the swells threw us harder and harder into the flat-top, and with the responsibility to rescue men and fight fire—the Skipper was faced with one decision after another in rapid-fire order. It called for great courage as well as great seamanship—to do battle with "Dat ole davil, sea" (Eugene O'Neill).

During much of the operation, I was observing the events from the 0-1 level, having no specific duty station in rescue and firefighting situations. Now, as our weather decks were filling with PRINCETON survivors, many atop the deck house, I made my way aft to see if there was any way I could help.

A kid who didn't look over fifteen years old, his clothes still dripping water and bandages on his burnt arms, looked up at me.

"Hey, Mac, you got a smoke?"

I lit a Lucky for him, and asked how he was doing.

"I'll feel a hell of a lot better when we haul ass outa here", he replied.

By the time I reached Number Three Mount (Mount 53, first of the After Three) I'd given away all the cigarettes in the pack I had. So I went down to my locker in Compartment 205 for a fresh deck. As I returned to the fantail, I saw several men, who apparently had jumped from the after part of the PRINCETON, struggling in the water. In their fight to keep from being washed astern into open sea they were losing the battle to make it to the IRWIN's side.

I stepped over to the lifelines. The cargo nets a few yards forward were jammed with survivors trying to get aboard and with men trying to help them. It was not a conscious move on my part. It was just an automatic response. It was the JOHN PENN all over again. I shed my shoes and hit the water.

The first man I reached was a bluejacket who was completely exhausted. He had no life jacket so his head was low in the water, and he was swallowing a lot of it. When I got him in tow, I looked at the cargo nets. Still jammed. So I pulled him over to the screw guard which protrudes out from the stern about four feet above the water line. I had to wait until the ship heeled to starboard and the guard dipped downward enough to get the sailor up so he'd hang over it. From above, hands reached down and pulled him to the main deck.

The second man wore the single gold bar of an ensign and the wings of a pilot. This time, as I got close to the screw guard, I felt the tug of an eddy from the screws turning over. I had to hold the ensign off until the screws stopped, so both of us wouldn't be sucked under the ship's counter and be chewed up by the propellers.

I went back for three or four, maybe five more PRINCETON men before I could take the chilly waters and the physical demands no longer. As a couple of my shipmates hoisted the last one aboard, I dragged myself over the screw guard and climbed to the fantail.

I never knew the names of any of the men I assisted until 1990 when I got a letter from Charlie Donovan, an Aviation Machinist's Mate 1st Class of Chalfont, Pennsylvania. Through the PRINCETON Association, we were put in touch. He said he was completely "out of gas" in the water and could make no headway toward the IRWIN. Without my help, he said, he never would have made it. Then he apologized. "Climbed aboard and forgot to say thank you. The Dumb Irish. Now I want to thank you for saving me."

As I headed below, a call came over the speaker system. "Will the photographer please lay up to the Bridge."

At the time, that boggled my mind. "What in the hell are they worrying about pictures for at a time like this?" Now, I'm glad some photos were made and wish there'd been more.

There was a torpedoman—I think it was Jim Platt—standing watch over the depth charges as I passed by the racks. He'd already set them on "safe" just in case our crashing into the carrier shook them loose. At the same time I noticed a sentry with a rifle. "Shark watch", I thought, but attached no significance to it at the time. It was standard procedure with men in the water. I went below to my locker.

After changing into dry dungarees I turned to see one of the survivors sitting on the deck against the after bulkhead. His eyes had that glaze—a "fifty-fathom stare". His clothes were singed by fire, torn and ripped in places, and still soaking wet. I pulled a clean skivvie shirt and a spare pair of dungarees from my locker and handed them to him. The act seemed to break him out of his hazy state, bringing a faint smile to his face. "Thanks . . . shipmate", he said softly.

I looked disgustedly at the wet pack of Luckies from the shirt I'd taken off. "A whole dime shot to hell!" I complained. Tossing them in the trash, I got another pack and headed topside.

As I reached the deck and began picking my way through the crowd of survivors sitting or lying on nearly every inch of space, another heavy explosion rocked the PRINCETON, throwing "much debris on this vessel but did not start any fires" (War Diary). But it did make everybody think this was *the END!* We all "ducked and covered" (hitting the deck and covering our heads with our arms) as the hot metal rained down. Nobody hurt, though, and the IRWIN was still afloat.

The wind was picking up again, gusting above 25 knots. That carried the PRINCETON downwind faster and made Captain Miller's task of remaining alongside that much more difficult. As the flat-top moved away, he had to use our engine power judiciously to stay close. At the same time, the carrier began to roll and wallow a great deal more, and each time the two ships careened together the damage to us grew more extensive.

The continuous colliding was taking a major toll. A partial list of damages now included loss of the starboard Torpedo Director, a 40-millimeter Director, the pelorus (ship's compass), both starboard 40mm mounts, and structural damage to the superstructure. The Main Battery Director was off its track, as were both forward 5-inch gun mounts. There was so much damage to the Bridge that the Skipper ordered all electrical, radar, and radio circuits cut out to prevent the possibility of electrical fires. Some small blazes did erupt but were quickly brought in hand by the damage control parties. With power to the Bridge off, the delicate task of controlling the ship's direction was shifted to Steering Aft, with communication by non-electrical sound-powered telephones and the steering telegraph.

When I returned to the Comm Deck, some of the guys were staring at the side of the PRINCETON. We watched with bated breath as a speck of flame appeared about halfway down the hull of the carrier and began to burn an arc in the gray metal. It was an acetylene torch being used to cut an escape hole by men trapped in a below-deck compartment.

As the cut grew longer, I was silently cheering the men on, hoping whoever was in that space could get a hole cut fast enough and big enough to get out. But the cut was less than half completed when another internal explosion boomed from within the carrier. In horrified fascination, we saw the flame go out, never to reappear. With great dismay, and with a mental image of what those last few seconds were like for those poor devils, I turned sadly away.

Somewhere during this time, our little force came under attack by land-based enemy aircraft. The RENO, charged with protecting us, was the only ship with clear bearings on the oncoming Jap bombers. She opened fire, splashing two of the bandits, while our fighter cover from the ESSEX got four more.

Rescue work continued. Large numbers of the PRINCETON's crew were congregated on her bow. Some were sliding down two or three lines that hung from her catwalk. Others attempted to time their jumps with

SHARK WATCH
A CASSIN YOUNG officer, with an '03 Springfield rifle, scans the waves
for the menacing dorsal fins of sharks, well-known to be numerous in
these waters.
(Real War Photos)

the rolling of the ships so they'd land on the IRWIN's narrow and cluttered foc'sle. It was a small and moving target as our bow pitched heavily and the ships rolled back and forth. Some of them made it. Others missed, splashing in the water, only to be crushed between the clashing steel hulls. Then there were those who waited until the ships swung apart and went directly into the water, swimming aft to avoid being sandwiched between the hulls.

Around our Sick Bay, Doctor Fagan, along with Chief Pharmacist's Mate Walt Davis and the two 1st Class, Al Murray and Bob Hutcheson, were inundated with casualties. Getting help from surviving PRINCETON medical personnel, they were treating the wounded, the burned, the shock victims, setting broken bones and bandaging assorted cuts and bruises among the hundreds of survivors now aboard.

Out on deck, some of the men pulled from the water needed artificial respiration, and our crew members were administering it to them. It was an almost overwhelming task. Some had survived injury aboard the carrier only to break bones jumping from the flight deck to our foc'sle. Many could thank the foresight of the IRWIN crew when we got extra plasma aboard in San Francisco by donating blood to the blood bank.

Every survivor had a tale to tell. One told me he was in the water, looked up and saw our shark guard with a rifle, and his only thought was: "Oh, my God! I just escaped a burning ship. Now they're gonna shoot me!"

At the mention of the shark watch, I recalled the sentry on the fantail. I'd not even thought of sharks when I went over the side, but several of the PRINCETON men (and later our own crewmen) told me that sharks were there in the waters around the ships. One survivor was certain a man near him who disappeared suddenly beneath the waves was a shark victim.

Another danger, that of being sucked under by the eddies generated by the IRWIN's screws, apparently cost the lives of some. Both ship's company and carrier crewmen told me of "several" who'd been swept under the IRWIN's counter when, to maneuver closer to the CVL, our engines turned over. They said those men never resurfaced.

There was still optimism the PRINCETON could be saved. At 1040, Captain Miller called the BIRMINGHAM:

"Papoose from Reliance. If you can put another DD alongside can control fire in Hatchet." The CASSIN YOUNG was ordered to assist. At 1050, we relayed a message to the BIRMINGHAM, that the PRINCETON requested the RENO move in to fight fire. The BIRMINGHAM instructed us to remain where we were and ordered the others to rescue survivors.

Two things now were becoming apparent. The IRWIN was no longer able to fight fire effectively, and we were near capacity in caring for more survivors. Too, any further sustained stay alongside the PRINCE-TON would simply bring additional damage to the ship with little to show for it.

After some time and consideration, Cap'n Danny reluctantly backed down from alongside the carrier. We'd held that position for over an hour and fifteen minutes—a long, long, *long* hour and fifteen minutes. As we maneuvered away, the CASSIN YOUNG cautioned: "Reliance. Lot of men in the water all around you. Be careful."

Those of our swimming team still over the side were brought back aboard. They'd done an outstanding job under harrowing circumstances, rescuing among them some 120 PRINCETON men: some who were wounded, some who were poor swimmers, some who simply feared the water, and all too exhausted to help themselves. (After the war began, swimming requirements were relaxed in boot camps.) On the rescue team was one of the Radio Gang—George Mootz.

The Skipper eased the ship away from the carrier, clearing the overhang of the catwalk, flight deck, and forward gun nest. As we widened the gulf between the two ships, more men leaped into the waters and we maneuvered to rescue them, lowering one of the whale-boats to assist, but still continued bringing others up the cargo nets.

The IRWIN, battered and beat, packed with PRINCETON survivors, had done all she could do, and more, to aid the burning and ravaged flat-top.

We'd still have more work to do, however, and the day would conclude with both bizarre and tragic events.

26

THE BOOMERANG TORPEDOES

The saga of the sea wore on. As late as high noon, Captain Bruacker was still confident he could save his ship.

At 1201, the PRINCETON's Skipper called on all the destroyers to make ready to transfer his hull and engineering personnel back aboard the carrier. At the same time, the BIRMINGHAM took the IRWIN's place alongside the carrier, got lines over, and began to bring her fire hoses to bear.

As Officer in Tactical Command, Captain Inglis then deployed the ships in the small group to specific tasks. He instructed the RENO to cover us against air and/or submarine attack. In this, the cruiser got assistance when the ESSEX sent a fighter group up over us, advising the planes would be available until 1315. The IRWIN was placed in charge of continuing to rescue any men in the water. The CASSIN YOUNG, GATLING, and MORRISON were to assist and to continue to screen the force.

But the MORRISON, which had gone alongside the carrier's starboard (leeward) side, was having troubles. In attempting to get close enough to fight fire and to help men trying to abandon ship, she had fallen victim to the rolling carrier, and to winds and swells that drove the flat-top right down on top of her. The MORRISON was literally a captive of the vessel she was aiding, her superstructure jammed up under and between the PRINCETON's stacks and wedged up underneath the flight deck.

As the flat-top and the tin can banged against each other the destroyer's mast was carried away. To add insult to injury, first a tractor used to move planes around the flight deck rolled off the carrier and on to the DD's Bridge. Following the tractor, a jeep likewise came hurtling down, carrying away the entire port wing of the Bridge. Luckily warning shouts prevented casualties, but the MORRISON was still stuck in the stacks of the carrier and would need assistance to clear.

On the IRWIN, we were solving one problem, only to have another crop up. The electrician's mates cut the circuits back in to our Bridge, and steering control was again in the pilot house. But some fifteen minutes later, we lost power to the port engine, severely reducing our ability to maneuver and lowering potential speed to about ten or twelve knots. Debris, a great deal of it frayed hemp line (and some said body parts), had been sucked up into the main circulator and had plugged the condenser scoop.

We started to resume screening since we could see no more survivors in the water. But about that time, an air alert came over the TBS radio:

"KODAK [Task Group 38.3] from MAXWELL [Commander Task Group 38.3]. Many bogies zero three five degrees and closing!"

Fortunately, the ESSEX fighter cover intercepted the raid and kept any hostile planes from reaching us. With her decks crawling with men and many of her guns unable to operate, the IRWIN was not in the greatest condition at the moment to take on a full-scale air assault.

"Reliance [IRWIN] from Hiawatha [MORRISON]. Are you going to give us a line and help us out from under the overhang?"

Captain Miller replied: "Hiawatha from Reliance. I am not there now but will proceed. We have only one engine."

We rounded the PRINCETON's bow, coming in toward the MORRISON's bow and heaving a messenger line to which a wire rope towing cable was bent on. As we backed down in an effort to pull the trapped destroyer free, the cable snapped, whipping across our foc'sle. Thank God, it didn't hit anyone; it would have decapitated any in its way. Heavy swells threw us into the other two ships, making it necessary for us to clear. It was very difficult trying to maneuver with just one engine.

The sea—always the sea—caught us as we came around, scraping our port side against the starboard side of the BIRMINGHAM—destroying our port motor whaleboat, ripping off the port anchor and causing other damage to the superstructure. We tried again to aid the MORRISON, but smoke spewing from the fires aboard the burning carrier almost blinded us. Whether our initial tug with the wire rope on the MORRISON's bow helped or not, she finally got loose from under the flat-top's uptakes (stacks).

In the meantime, we got a partial return of power to the port engine as the snipes in the black gang jury-rigged a solution. The engine could now make 130 turns which might get us up to 20 knots. But the main circulator was still out of commission.

At 1407, four hours after we'd first gone alongside her, the PRINCETON reported fires aboard were segregated in the after section of the ship and seemed under control. The BIRMINGHAM was still alongside the carrier, pumping water from her hoses into the hull. The RENO was

TO HELP THE MORRISON
The IRWIN disengages from the PRINCETON, rounds her bow, and proceeds to lend a hand to the MORRISON, trapped under the carrier's uptakes.
(U.S. Navy Photo - National Archives)

on her assigned anti-aircraft/anti-submarine station while the four destroyers formed a circular screen 3,000 yards from the CVL, steaming clockwise at twelve knots, all the while keeping a weather eye out for any survivors we might have missed.

I was beginning to feel some relaxation of tension, since we were now away from the flat-top and the situation seemed well in hand. Aside from the three incursions by Jap aircraft that had been driven off, we had only had one other possible threat from the enemy. An hour earlier, while we were trying to help the MORRISON, the CASSIN YOUNG had picked up a submarine contact which it pursued for twenty minutes or so before her sonar no longer got any echoes.

On the IRWIN, we were trying to adjust to having the equivalent of two extra destroyer crews aboard. Many PRINCETON survivors were below in the berthing spaces. Those in various stages of injury, or who were ill from swallowing too much salt water, were given bunks; but the majority were on the weather decks, from abaft the Bridge to the fantail on both the main deck and atop the deck house. In the galley, the ship's cooks were trying to figure out how they were going to feed all these folks. None had eaten since breakfast, some not since the night before.

Junior Fitch leaned over the port flag bag and signaled me there was a fresh pot of jamoke on the Signal Bridge. As I joined him, the TBS came alive with a request from the BIRMINGHAM:

"All ships report number of Hatchet [PRINCETON] personnel aboard."

"Papoose [BIRMINGHAM] from Reliance [IRWIN]. Reliance has 500." (This was strictly an estimate. We'd not had time to muster the PRINCETON men aboard.)

" . . . from Leather [GATLING]. I have between 175 and 200."

" . . . from Clinker [CASSIN YOUNG]. I have approximately 100."

" . . . from Bayonet [RENO]. I have 5 on board."

The MORRISON's TBS radio was out. She reported by visual signal.

"Reliance [IRWIN] from Papoose [BIRMINGHAM]. Do you know of any men or groups of men in the water?"

" . . . Reliance. Negative."

Suddenly, CTG 38.3 (Admiral Sherman) was on the horn, warning of bogies heading for us. The Japs seemed determined to finish off the PRINCETON and probably us along with her. The IRWIN was extremely vulnerable—with only the After Three of the Main Battery available, and those in "local"; with no radar or Main Battery Director to detect targets, plus range and train the guns; and with two 40mm mounts and our 20s unable to fire.

CRASHED BY THE BIRMINGHAM
The cruiser scrapes down side of the IRWIN as both ships maneuver
around the PRINCETON. The destroyer has much of its port side
damaged, and considerable topside gear, including the motor whaleboat,
is carried away. Note the crowded conditions on the IRWIN's decks.
Photo taken from the bridge of the BIRMINGHAM.
(U.S. Navy Photo - National Archives)

To get more firepower into the act, the BIRMINGHAM backed down from the PRINCETON, clearing so she could bring her guns to bear on any aerial targets. The ESSEX and the LEXINGTON had new flights of CAP fighters up, and they splashed one bandit about 18 miles from us. Another got closer. The RENO opened up on it at about 8,000 yards, continuing to fire until the Jap intruder beat it out of there.

The weather, which had moderated a little for a while, now was turning nasty, again. That was good news and bad news. It would hamper enemy air intrusions, but it also made efforts to save the PRINCETON more difficult. Admiral Sherman then wanted to know if the carrier had any headway (self-propelling engine power) to which the BIRMINGHAM replied:

"We are putting crew back aboard to see if they can get headway."

The BIRMINGHAM then requested the RENO to prepare to tow the stricken carrier. But the AA cruiser had no towing gear. It had been demolished on 16 October when the plane the IRWIN shot down suicide-crashed into her fantail.

The increasing swells affected the BIRMINGHAM's efforts to return to a position close aboard the PRINCETON. It took her three tries to make it, coming in on the port quarter. As the deck crew began getting lines across to the salvage crew still on the carrier, the fires below must have gotten to those 100-pound bombs Pete Callan wrote about.

Without warning, the entire rear quarter of the PRINCETON was torn asunder by one gigantic blast—spewing debris, shrapnel, metal shards, parts of decks and bulkheads in every direction.

From 3,000 yards away I felt the shock waves as they rolled across the open water. The entire after section of the flight deck was lifted skyward, flipped forward upside down and slammed down on the forward deck area, shattering it apart and sending huge portions into the sea.

Around me, PRINCETON survivors and IRWIN sailors were stunned at the magnitude of the explosion and at the huge column of smoke that rose so quickly above the hapless vessel. If ever the Biblical reference to "hellfire and brimstone" had an earthly counterpart, this was it. The eruption looked all the world like a volcano blowing its top.

Shocked disbelief gave way to expressions of horror and tears of grief. "Oh, my God!" . . . "Those poor bastards!" Each man in his own way was voicing his anguish. Among the carrier's men, some sobbed unabashedly.

That the BIRMINGHAM had also been severely stricken came in a terse TBS message: "Bayonet [RENO] from Papoose [Birmingham]. Take command. We have many casualties on Papoose. Take command!"

From the RENO came a "Roger." Passing of command of the rescue unit could mean only one of two things. Either Captain Inglis was badly wounded, or the BIRMINGHAM's Skipper was dead. (He was, we later heard, seriously wounded).

Other ominous messages followed:

"Bayonet from Papoose. Try to contact the [SANTA FE] and tell him we need our other doctor as soon as possible."

" . . . from Bayonet. Do you wish one of our doctors?"

" . . . from Papoose. Affirmative. Would like you to send over some corpsmen."

It was the next transmission that sent a chill through me.

" . . . from Papoose. We have about 100 to 150 killed and about the same number wounded."

A casualty count that high meant a great number of the cruiser's crew had been topside and the explosion had ripped across her decks, taking everyone and everything with it. The final casualty lists and the descriptions we later got of the disaster could only tell a part of the story of the destruction.

Over half the crew of the BIRMINGHAM was in exposed positions as the cruiser went alongside the PRINCETON. Not only were there working parties on the foc'sle and weather decks, but dozens more had taken vantage points elsewhere to watch the operation. When the bombs exploded—setting off other ammunition and inflammables and sending a searing rush of super-heated air across the cruiser's decks—the carnage caused was almost too terrible to contemplate.

BIRMINGHAM crewmen I talked with after we got back to the States described a gruesome scene. Bodies and body parts were strewn across the decks. Blood ran an inch deep in the scuppers. The moans of wounded and dying men filled the air. Men in shock, many with serious wounds, walked aimlessly about. Gun crews had been roasted to death in their mounts.

Stories of the Civil War told by my great-grandfather, passed down to me, described the ghastly effects of cannonades of grapeshot on massed infantry. It was too grisly to comprehend, yet that's the way it was on the BIRMINGHAM. The hail of fragments of the PRINCETON, some of ash can size, that blasted across the cruiser's decks, mowed men down like a huge scythe in a wheat field.

When the figures were eventually totaled, there were 241 dead and 421 wounded. That was an appalling *fifty-three percent* of the cruiser's 1,243-man complement! It was a terrible toll.

When all hell broke loose (the time was 1503) there were only about

50 men still left aboard the PRINCETON. Some 25 were in the vicinity of the bomb storage and perished instantly.

Of the remainder who abandoned ship, every one suffered injuries, including the Navigator, Lieutenant Commander Vic Moitoret. Unbeknownst to either of us, his path had crossed mine before. He was on the HORNET in September of 1942 when the WASP, O'BRIEN, and NORTH CAROLINA were torpedoed in the Coral Sea. Then he later survived the HORNET's sinking in the Battle of Santa Cruz in October of 1942.

Captain Bruacker, although wounded, still wanted to try to save his ship. But when the reports of the damages to the carrier and the cruiser were relayed to Admiral Sherman by the RENO, and thence to Admiral Mitscher, the order came back:

"Sink the PRINCETON." Time: 1706.

"Reliance [IRWIN] from Bayonet [RENO]. Torpedo and destroy Hatchet [PRINCETON]. Over."

" . . . Reliance. Roger. Out."

" . . . Bayonet. Torpedo and use gunfire if necessary."

" . . . Reliance. Wilco."

"Reliance from Bayonet. Expedite. Over."

" . . . Reliance. Roger. Out."

Captain Miller, now with the sad and emotional task of destroying a proud ship with which we now had the strongest of ties, maneuvered the IRWIN to within 2,500 yards of the derelict flat-top. Ensign Gene Stout, our Torpedo Officer, and Chief Torpedoman Duane Ashmead, readied the tubes.

At 1718, the first fish from Tube One shot out over the starboard side and splashed into the sea, headed for the PRINCETON.

I was about 15 or 20 yards away and wondered what the hell was wrong when the torpedo tube mount began whipping as it was fired. The track of the fish, however, looked normal. It ran hot, straight, and true for about 1,500 yards, then unaccountably veered to port. It struck the carrier near the bow, exploded, but did little damage.

"Fire Two!" Like the first, the torpedo stayed on course about the same distance before it too changed course, going to the right and passing the CVL's stern. The fish went on out into empty waters without exploding.

"Fire Three!" Again, hot, straight, and normal. Then the torpedo began an erratic course, turning 180 degrees, and zeroing in on the IRWIN like a homing pigeon, coming directly at us!

I leaped from the Comm Deck ladder over to the top of the deck house and scrambled up to the searchlight platform on Number One

Stack. If that damned torpedo hit, at least I had a chance of being blown free. I was sweating bullets!

On the Bridge, the Skipper called up every turn the snipes could squeeze out of our battered power plant. As he noted in the War Diary in masterful understatement: "Increased speed to avoid erratic torpedo."

"Gawddamn!" I said aloud. "Here I survived twice being hit by enemy fish, and now I'm gonna get killed by one of our own!"

The torpedo began broaching like a porpoise playing in a bow wave, then passed astern and disappeared.

"Fire Four!" It ran normal, then like one of its predecessors swung left, passing the PRINCETON's bow. So did the fifth fish.

Cap'n Danny was frustrated, so he ordered our Main Battery After Three 5-inch guns to open up. They were firing in local control, and after 27 rounds poured into the PRINCETON, we succeeded only in setting afire planes still left on the forward flight deck. The Skipper decided to try a torpedo one more time.

"Fire Six!" Hot, straight, true . . . for about 1,500 yards. Then this gawddamn fish did what Number Three had done. It looped around and headed directly for us! This was getting to be too much for me. I had a feeling every @#!$%&%! torpedo in every tube in the whole blasted Pacific—Japanese AND American—had a personal vendetta against me and was intent on blowing me out of the water, one way or another.

As the Skipper poured on the coal and maneuvered to avoid the rogue torpedo, it broached and started chasing us right up our wake! But with one last plunge, the fish disappeared. The Old Man, again with typical restraint, wrote in the War Diary that we were "forced to clear the area." I admire his reserve, but what he did was two-block the engine room telegraph and get our rear ends out of there!

I was shaking like an aspen leaf in a gale. Where did these boomerang torpedoes come from, anyhow? I looked down at the tubes below me and saw no preparations to fire again. That made me feel a little better but I was still scared as hell. Down on the decks where the PRINCETON rescued were crowded together like sardines in a can, there came a great, audible sigh of relief. Our guys were breathing easier, too.

"Reliance [IRWIN] from Bayonet [RENO]. Bayonet will fire broadside of torpedoes. Stand clear when she comes in. Over."

The RENO, bless her, was taking over. She fired a spread that went right to the target, hitting in the forward area of the PRINCETON amid magazines and gasoline storage. A massive explosion rent the air as 80,000 gallons of aviation fuel and thousands of rounds of ammo went up.

Within less than a minute the valiant PRINCETON—"The Peerless P"—was gone to her final resting place—80 miles east of the Polillos, 15° 12′ North, 123° 36′ East. There she would sink to the bottom of the Philippine Deep, three miles down. The time was 1750. The date, 24 October, 1944.

The ups and the downs, the gamut of emotions that had marked the day, left me completely rung out. But I had the duty coming up. Swinging by the galley, I conned Sharp into giving me a couple of lunchmeat sandwiches, my first food since early morning, and made my way to the Radio Shack to relieve the watch.

At the 0-1 level, Bressie had good news. "Hey, Hutch, there's a fresh pot o' joe in the Shack."

"I thank you, Newt, and I'll see you get to heaven for being so thoughty."

I took my accustomed place in the five-by-five foot forward section of Radio One, after checking to see if the call signs of the IRWIN and other commands were encoded and posted above the FOX sked position where Frank Riddle was pounding away at the mill.

"Frank, we need to copy everything, tonight, so if atmospherics get bad, give me a holler. There may be a lot of traffic concerning us and the Old Man'll want to see it all. Maybe we'll get our orders to a Navy Yard, and instructions on what to do with the PRINCETON guys."

Frank nodded and kept on copying. I didn't have much to worry about with him. He was steady as a rock on the circuit. But Wasson put a log in the number two typewriter, tuning the receiver to NPM, and began copying back-up. I went back to my sandwiches and java.

It'd be sometime before all the action reports and statistics were available on the events of the day. When they were compiled, they'd be appalling. As Marsha Clark and Captain Thomas Bradshaw wrote in their book *Carrier Down*—the PRINCETON's story—there were nearly a thousand casualties that day. The carrier lost 114 killed or drowned, and 190 wounded.

To that, add the BIRMINGHAM's 241 dead and 412 wounded, and you have a total of 957—more lives lost and more men wounded than in the Battle of Midway. Midway would go down in history as one of the most important battles of the War. Our "Part of a Battle" (the title of C.S. Forester's article in the *Saturday Evening Post* on the sinking of the PRINCETON) would get, at most, a couple of lines in histories of the War—but probably not even a footnote in American history books.

When all the PRINCETON noses on the IRWIN were counted, the tally came to 646! In the hour and fifteen minutes we'd spent rescuing them, we had pulled an average of *over eight men* out of the water *every minute*. And, of all the wounded Doc Fagan and his pharmacist's mates treated, they lost but one patient.

Finishing the sandwiches, I took what was left of the java in my cup out on the weather deck. The ships of the rescue unit had now formed up with the BIRMINGHAM in the center as guide, and the RENO advised Admirals Mitscher and Sherman: "Duty completed. Am rejoining." She and the CASSIN YOUNG went back to Task Group 38.3. Darkness was now falling over the Philippine Sea.

After assessing the RENO's report of damages to the IRWIN, MORRISON, and BIRMINGHAM, Admiral Mitscher designated the three of us and the GATLING —which had some 200 PRINCETON survivors aboard and was the only one of our little group to be fully operational—as Task Unit 38.3.6 and detached us to proceed to Ulithi. As we set a course for the Western Carolines, we got a message by way of a farewell from Admiral "Bull" Halsey: "You and your group have done a fine job today. I am proud to ride with TG 38.3."

We proceeded at 21 knots, about all the speed the snipes could squeeze from the IRWIN's limping power plant. The clogged circulator in the port engine, and a bent starboard propeller shaft, slowed us down.

To say the ship was crowded, would be to severely understate the reality. We had over 970 men aboard a vessel designed to accommodate only 325 in its meager living spaces. Obviously, most of our passengers had to remain topside on the weather decks. But we were heading southeast, and that October of 1944 was fairly mild in the climes we sailed.

Both below decks and topside, sentries had to be posted to keep men from moving about in order to maintain order and minimize the risk of capsizing due to our inherently low center of gravity. PRINCETON men had to stay put, except when permitted to go to the head, and then only a few at a time. Food and medicine were dispensed by passing them hand to hand.

Feeding the rescued and the crew was a monumental task, and we were scraping the bottoms of our food lockers. Fresh water, too, was a problem, and the order went out it was to be used only for drinking. No showers, no shaving, no laundry. We would all go a week without a bath or change of clothing.

I got off the evening watch when relieved at midnight, got my hammock and slung it in the usual place—port side of the Comm Deck. Joe Alice was looking for some place to spread a blanket. His bunk was given over to an injured PRINCETON survivor, as was mine, and there was little space anyplace else.

"Wish I'd thought of something like that", he said, pointing to my hammock.

"That's the advantage of having served in the Olde Nyvy, lad", I teased. I reached up and grabbed a transverse beam in the overhead and started swinging into the sack. "I've been awake nearly 26 hours and, as my grandpop used to say, I'm all tuckered out. Do me a favor, Joe John, don't wake me up until I make Chief."

I finished the swing and was dead to the world almost before my derrière hit the center of the hammock mattress. In the poet's words:

Rocked in the cradle of the deep
I lay me down in peace to sleep . . . .

Almost half a century later, our Engineering Officer, then Lieutenant Hays "Jumbo" Clark, told me the tale of that first night that neither I nor other crewmen knew at the time. It's a story that even now brings chills of fear, the drama of what was nearly a major catastrophe that could have wiped us all out.

According to Mr. Clark, the IRWIN's badly beat-up superstructure meant we had no operable communications systems due to power outages. We could still copy the FOX skeds but not send any messages. Our radar antenna was down. As for our propulsion system, we were hampered by a cracked condenser intake which rendered our main starboard engine virtually inoperable.

"I was in the after engine room with the engineering crew", Mr. Clark said, "trying to make the after condenser operable so we could use the main engine, and to effect repairs on the cracked condenser. We were fearful the crack might open and cause major flooding in the engine room. Then General Quarters sounded. At that time my assigned battle station was in Combat Information Center (CIC), but I was unable to get through the passageways to my station because they were crammed with men standing and sitting everywhere."

"Jumbo" Clark would learn from Captain Miller that our Task Unit was getting visual recognition challenges for identification from unknown ships in the area. We were not able to answer for our Task Group because all our communications, including signal lights and TBS radio, were again without power. Code books on the Bridge, containing the proper responses, had been mislaid somehow in all the confusion while alongside the PRINCETON, and it took much hustling around to find a way to answer the challenges from the unknown vessels.

Years later, Mr. Clark learned that our tardiness in answering those challenges almost got the IRWIN, MORRISON, AND BIRMINGHAM blown out of the water! (The GATLING was screening far to starboard and apparently knew nothing of the incident.) Hays Clark got his information firsthand. Long after the War, he met and became friends with Rear Admiral Richard Tuggle who, on that fateful night, was senior Captain in command of three cruisers en route to the Philippines. When the cruisers' radar picked up "a large bogey contact", they went to General Quarters, each tracking the "contact" with their twelve 6-inch main battery rifles. Attempting to establish identification via the various recognition options available, the cruisers got no response.

"Now," our old Engineering Officer continued, "put yourself in Captain Tuggle's position. A professional line officer of the Navy, he was tracking three targets of unknown origin within the battle zone. Should he open fire . . . or not? The unknown vessels were not acting belligerently, even though they did not respond to the challenges. He had to consider that if he fired on them and they were American, it probably would have been one of the biggest naval fiascos of World War II. On the other hand, if the bogeys turned out to be Japanese and he did not attack, he risked having his own command come under fire. It would have been a severe blow to the Navy and to Captain Tuggle's career."

Now two of the three cruisers were brand new, never having fired their weapons in combat. With itchy trigger fingers, their Skippers wanted first crack at the enemy and kept requesting time and again: "Permission to fire, Sir!" Captain Tuggle's Staff agreed with the requests, but the Task Group Commander had a feeling something was not quite right here. The scenario of Japanese ships in that area not maneuvering in a menacing way, did not add up. Finally and most fortunately, visual recognition was established before a shot was fired, and each Task Group continued on to its destination.

According to Jumbo Clark, we aboard the IRWIN can thank the Good Lord that Tuggle had the wit, courage, training, intuition, and background to make the tough decision that turned out to be the correct one. Had he decided to attack, we all would have been blown to Kingdom Come with a horrible loss of life. The crews of the three ships plus the survivors of the PRINCETON disaster, over 2,500 men in all, would not have stood a Chinaman's chance in hell. "All of us", Jumbo said, "can be thankful to Admiral Tuggle for his experience and judgment that night."

Considering what happened that night, all that happened to the IRWIN before and after this "incident", including clearing the PRINCE-TON just before she blew up, and all that we would encounter later—some old crewmembers would say "The Fighting I" was just "a lucky ship". But it had to be more than that. I'm far more inclined to second Jumbo Clark's assessment: "The IRWIN was truly a blessed vessel!"

Throughout the night, the BIRMINGHAM continued the grim task of identifying her dead and burying them in the sea. Many of those wounded did not survive. The rituals of committing the bodies of these sailors to the deep and their souls to God would continue until shortly after noon on October 25th.

In the meantime, the doctors and pharmacist's mates on all four ships were working around the clock treating the wounded and trying to save as many lives as possible. They won some, lost some. At 0700 we transferred extra plasma to the cruiser.

Somewhere between the Philippines and Ulithi was a refueling group, the fleet oiler PLATTE and escorts. At 0730 we sighted a friendly plane we figured was flying Anti-Sub Patrol for the tanker. Seeing it made us feel a little safer, believing we were now in friendly territory. At 1000, we buried, with full military honors, the one PRINCETON man who'd died aboard the IRWIN.

Then the unbelievable happened, shattering any delusions we had of being out of danger. At 1140 our lookouts sighted a lone twin-engine bomber, a Jap Frances, coming at us from a due north bearing, range seven miles!

With the two 40-millimeter mounts and the two forward 5-inch mounts out of commission, with our Main Battery Director off the track, and with no power to any of the other mounts—we were in poor shape to withstand any air attack. The After Three and the remaining 40s and 20s would have to be pointed and trained the "old fashioned way"—by hand, with sighting and ranging by opticals, rather than radar. For any determined attacker, we were as close to being a sitting duck as you could get. Orders were shouted to the PRINCETON people to hit the deck and stay clear of the batteries as they were being trained.

As the Frances closed to within 6,000 yards, our weapons opened fire while the Skipper maneuvered in emergency turns. The Jap circled astern of our formation, decided not to make a run at us, and headed westerly. Many of our bursts were close, and some of the PRINCETON men, as well as some of our crew, claimed the plane was shot down. I didn't see it splash, and the War Diary makes no claim. We fired 38 rounds of 5-inch, 288 rounds of 40mm, and 400 rounds of 20mm. If nothing else, we put up enough lead to discourage the pilot of the Frances.

Among the crew and passengers, still trying to cope with the events of the previous day, it was an extremely anxious and frightening several minutes, and no one breathed much easier even after the danger had passed.

At 1214, the BIRMINGHAM signaled she had completed all burials at sea. We had been flying our Colors at half staff, in memoriam and in respect, since the ceremonies began. Now, we two-blocked the Stars and Stripes to the top of the flagstaff.

I looked around our battered little Task Unit at the mastless MORRISON, the ravaged BIRMINGHAM, and our own battered and mangled IRWIN. When we escorted the HOUSTON and CANBERRA out of Formosan waters to be towed by the PAWNEE, they'd nicknamed their flotilla "CripDiv One". That being the case, I figured we could at least lay claim to the title of "CripDiv Two".

We made our rendezvous with the PLATTE (AO-24), commenced refueling, and also took on 10,000 gallons of sorely needed fresh water. We'd still get no showers, though, until we off-loaded our passengers. The oiler also gave us our mail, and we made various transfers of personnel and materials within the Task Unit. Among other things, we got an SG radar transmitter from the MORRISON to replace the one we lost. Now we had our "eyes" back.

That afternoon, I set up to copy the "Radio Press News" in Emergency Radio. One of the top stories was a communiqué from General MacArthur's headquarters on Leyte. As I copied it, I hit the overhead.

"That no-good son of a bitch!" I yelled aloud. "That gawddam publicity-hunting bastard! He's pre-empted the Navy, again!"

MacArthur had announced the loss of the PRINCETON! Now the families of nearly 1,600 men would go through the pain and uncertainty of wondering whether their sons, husbands, or brothers were dead or alive. There would be no 30-day waiting for next of kin to be notified, nor for survivors to write or call home.

The General had done it once before when a destroyer in the Southwest Pacific was sunk. And, that time, he vaingloriously claimed it was "a ship of MY navy!" The Navy howled, protesting all the way to the White House. Now, once more, MacArthur was playing "oneupmanship" with the Navy, and the PRINCETON men and their families were the victims.

When word reached the survivors on our decks, there was hell to pay. They were absolutely livid. I could empathize with them, having gone through the premature release of the McCAWLEY's loss. But this was something different.

MacArthur acted *deliberately*, and it was not his prerogative to announce Navy losses. The PRINCETON was not under his command. The glory-hunting General's ancestry came into serious question, and men who may never have cussed before invented a whole new vocabulary to vent their spleen at the perpetrator of this unconscionable act: MacArthur was a God-damned *ARMY* officer!

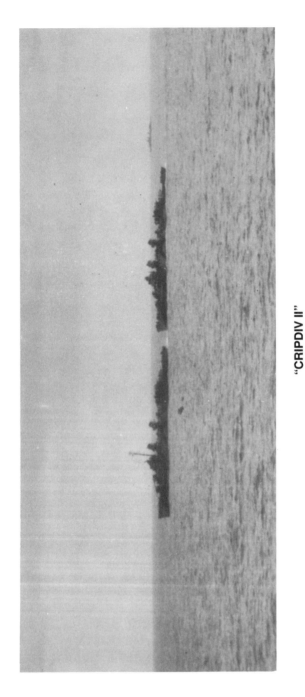

"CRIPDIV II"

The damaged IRWIN, followed by the mastless MORRISON, heads for Ulithi after refueling from the oiler PLATTE. In the background is the GATLING.

(U.S. Navy Photo - National Archives)

On October 27th, we entered Mugai Channel and proceeded to anchor in Ulithi Harbor. After refueling, we discharged all but 75 of our passengers. Them we'd transport to Pearl Harbor. The wounded went to a hospital ship, and the others were to get further orders.

Receiving two days availability alongside the Destroyer Tender MARKAB, we had some emergency repairs made. Divers were sent down to clear the main circulator and condenser scoop, restoring full power to the port engine. But the divers also discovered a large chip in the port screw.

On the 30th, with sailing orders from Commander Service Squadron Ten, we got underway with the BIRMINGHAM and MORRISON for Pearl, bidding "So long and Godspeed" to our compatriot, the GATLING. She was heading back to Task Force 38.

It had been only six days since "Desig Dog Seven Nine Four" had sent us to the aid of the helpless and burning PRINCETON, yet it seemed almost eons ago.

And one little guardian angel I knew, had sure put in a lot of overtime.

HOLIDAY, Jon Antony 9

Name HUTCHINSON, John Anthony

(Name in full, surname to the left.)

No. 243-86-51 Rate RM2c {A. A.
                                {P. A.

Date reported 14 Feb 1944

Ship
or   U. S. S. IRWIN (DD-794)

Station
From   US RS SAN FRANCISCO, CALIF.

Participated in fast carrier Task
Force operations against the enemy
during the months of September and
October, 1944.

                    J.D.P. HODAPP, Jr,
                 Lieutenant Commander, USN
                    Executive Officer.
✻✻✻✻✻✻✻✻✻✻✻✻✻✻✻✻✻✻✻✻✻✻✻✻✻✻✻✻✻✻✻✻✻

1 November 1944: Cited by Commanding
Officer at Meritorious Mast. Cited
for "Meritorious performance of duty
during fire-fighting and rescue operations incident to the bombing and
sinking of the USS PRINCETON(CVL23).
This man conducted himself at all
times in the best traditions of the
service".

                    J.D.P. HODAPP, Jr,
                 Lieutenant Commander, USN
                    Executive Officer.
✻✻✻✻✻✻✻✻✻✻✻✻✻✻✻✻✻✻✻✻✻✻✻✻✻✻✻✻✻✻✻✻✻✻✻

Date transferred

To

_____
Signature and rank of Commanding Officer.

Date received

Ship
or
Station
From

_____
Signature and rank of Commanding Officer. 4—6111

THE SECRETARY OF THE NAVY

WASHINGTON

        The Secretary of the Navy takes pleasure in presenting the
NAVY UNIT COMMENDATION to

                        USS IRWIN (DD 794)

for service as set forth in the following

CITATION:

        For exceptionally meritorious service during salvage
operations after USS PRINCETON had been critically damaged
by enemy Japanese action in the Battle off Samar, Republic
of the Philippines on 24 October 1944. Undeterred by foul
weather, fires raging on the flight and hangar decks of
the stricken carrier, and a series of violent internal
explosions, USS IRWIN (DD 794) gallantly went alongside.
Operating in a choppy sea as the wind steadily rose and
rain reduced visibility, USS IRWIN rigged her hoses and,
despite dense black smoke and the constant danger of falling debris, succeeded in directing them on fires in the
forward part of the hangar deck. Later, when a terrific
explosion blew off the major portion of USS PRINCETON's
stern, USS IRWIN immediately dispatched boats and stood by
at close quarters to assist in the rescue of survivors,
recovering 646 men from the sea and from the decks of USS
PRINCETON before this carrier was ordered to be sunk. By
their high standards of loyalty, professionalism, and
self-sacrificing devotion to duty, the officers and
enlisted personnel of USS IRWIN (DD 794) reflected great
credit upon themselves and upheld the highest traditions
of the United States Naval Service.

                        /s/   JAMES FORRESTAL

                        Secretary of the Navy

NAVY UNIT COMMENDATION
Presented by the Secretary of the Navy to the USS IRWIN (DD-794).
Note: This copy was not received by author until 1988 and only after
considerable correspondence with the Navy Department.

In reply address not the signer of this
letter, but Bureau of Naval Personnel,
Navy Department, Washington 25, D. C.

Refer to No. Pers-10

NAVY DEPARTMENT
BUREAU OF NAVAL PERSONNEL
WASHINGTON 25, D. C.

-7 MAR 1947

To: Mr. John Anthony Hutchinson, Ex-RM1, 243 86 51, USN   lmk
2596 Acorn Ave., N.E.
Atlanta, Georgia

Subject: Navy Unit Commendation awarded to U.S.S. Irwin (DD-794).

1. The Secretary of the Navy has awarded the Navy Unit Commendation to the
U.S.S. Irwin for extremely meritorious service during Salvage Operations
after the U.S.S. Princeton had been critically damaged by enemy Japanese
action in the Battle off Samar, 24 October 1944.

2. By virtue of your service in the IRWIN on 24 October 1944, you are hereby
authorized to wear as part of your uniform a Navy Unit Commendation ribbon,
one of which is transmitted herewith.

3. This authorization has been made a part of your official record in the
Bureau of Naval Personnel.

By direction of Chief of Naval Personnel;

⁄ JOE W. FLOYD
Lieut. Comdr., U. S. N.
FINISHED FILE

Assistant to Director,
Medals and Awards.

Encl:
1. NUC Ribbon.

CERTIFIED TO BE A TRUE COPY

R. J. SHULTZ, II, LCDR, USN

OFFICIAL NOTIFICATION OF THE NUC AWARD
Note that it took the Navy until March, 1947, two years and five months
after the PRINCETON was lost to notify officially the author of the award.

27

STATESIDE ONCE AGAIN—BUT BRIEFLY

There was unbounded jubilation at the Skipper's announcement we'd be going back to San Francisco's Hunter's Point for repairs. On the Navy's list of Favorite Liberty Ports, Frisco was an overwhelming Number One. We had worried we would get no farther than Pearl, but now it was "Stateside, here we come!" And with it, the Old Man let us know, would be leave.

"Hey, Hutch, you going back to Atlanta to marry that gal?" Fitch wanted to know.

"If I get enough time and she still wants me", I grinned in a way that would put the fabled Cheshire cat to shame. We were sitting on the flag bag, drinking Signal Bridge java and reveling in the good news.

"And you'll get to see your son for the first time", I added.

"Yeah. Up to now, all I got are these pictures from Butch."

There had been letters from Jane in the mail sacks we'd picked up from the PLATTE. I got a note off to her quickly enough to catch the next plane to the States. Unfortunately, censorship regulations didn't allow me even to hint I might be heading home.

As we sortied from Ulithi on 31 October, 1944, there was a noticeable relaxation of the tension we'd been under for so long. The crew, after standing "watch and watch" most of the time, now swung gratefully into the standard three-section watch routine (four hours on, eight off). The extra time was spent on field days to clean up the ship and to make complete surveys of her damage. Although we'd had some emergency repairs alongside the tender, including a temporary starboard wing to the Bridge, putting the IRWIN back into mint condition would require major restorations to our topside, gunnery, fire control, and internal communications. Damage assessments were being forwarded to Hunter's Point Naval Shipyard so the Yard could get a head start on plans for reparations even before we arrived.

The crew was getting ready, too. Dress blues were being scrubbed, shoes shined to a high gloss, and lines were forming for haircuts. And, for the first time in months, we had the opportunity to engage in the bluejacket's favorite pastime: shooting the bull. In this we were joined by some of our 75 PRINCETON passengers.

Still grateful and somewhat amazed at their escapes from the carrier, the men of "the Peerless P" joined in the discussion of the question: "What if the fatal explosion that so devastated the BIRMING-HAM had happened while *we* were alongside?" With more than double the number of men topside on the much more fragile destroyer, there was little doubt the casualty lists would have been much longer and with many more fatalities. Few thought the tin can would have survived at all. If she had, she'd have been wrecked beyond salvage. Among us, we knew there were few who would not now be dead. We had been rescued, for whatever reason, "out of the jaws of death."

When the subject turned to the boomerang torpedoes, the talk got a little lighter. The phenomenon now was being treated in the time-honored way of combat men who'd had close calls and survived. We began to make jokes about being the only ship in the United States Navy to have its own fish come back to chase her. Someone wondered if the torpedoes bore a "Made in Australia" label, handcrafted by the Aborigines. But, underneath, we knew it was no laughing matter.

There was some political talk, what with the Presidential campaign going on at home. The Republican Governor of New York, Thomas E. Dewey, was challenging President Roosevelt's quest for a fourth term. Not many aboard were interested, most being too young to vote. Some of the younger guys could hardly even remember when we'd had a Chief Executive other than FDR. They were solidly for him.

Among older hands, particularly the Regulars, there wasn't much enthusiasm for, and much criticism of, the President. We'd grown up during the depths of the Depression and watched him float numerous schemes, most of them socialistic and some even unconstitutional, in a ten-year effort to revive the economy. None had worked. Only the War and the demand for weapons from "the Arsenal of Democracy" had put America back to work. But the sharpest attacks on him concerned the debacle of 7 December, 1941. FDR, as one-time Assistant Secretary of the Navy, made a big deal of proclaiming himself "the Navy's friend". Yet, if he had not "let Pearl Harbor happen", we felt he was, at the very least, responsible for the tragedy in underestimating the Japanese threat. After all, he was the Commander in Chief, and "he had the watch."

"Boom Boom" Kopach was Roosevelt's most vocal critic. Like a few of us aboard, he'd been in the Solomons. The Chief Gunner's Mate added another blot on the FDR escutcheon by pointing out how undermanned, undergunned, and undersupplied we were in those early days, while the President was bowing to Britain's Churchill and funneling heavy assistance to the European Theater, including Communist Russia, leaving us in the South Pacific so little with which to fight. But Roosevelt won the election.

We arrived in Pearl on 10 November and immediately debarked the PRINCETON survivors. There was a lot of backslapping and handshaking as they went over the side. In different ways, they all voiced the same sentiments: "I'll never forget you guys and the IRWIN. She's one lucky ship with one hell of a tough crew."

We had barely moored at Berth K-1 when a whole passel of gold braid came aboard, including four officers of Flag rank. They were, I was to learn, from the Bureau of Ordnance, Torpedo Shop, and Naval Intelligence. They met with Captain Miller and our Torpedo Officer, Ensign Gene Stout. The latter recalled to me that he and Cap'n Danny "caught hell" over the performance (or lack thereof) of our torpedoes during the PRINCETON episode. He said the brass were taking the position that nothing could be wrong with the fish, and any difficulties were of the IRWIN's making.

Gene told the investigators: "All routine for the upkeep of a fully ready torpedo had been carried out to the fullest extent. No attempt had been made to overhaul any section of the torpedoes by shipboard personnel." He added: "The ship was subjected to severe punishment by the surging of the vessels and explosions. Much damage was inflicted to the starboard side. Internal damage to the torpedoes had not been determined before firing. It is entirely possible there were sticky steering engines or restrictions in the lines to the steering engines."

But the big brass persisted in trying to put the onus on our C.O. and our Torpedo Officer, even to the extent of putting out an ALNAV (Communication to All the Navy) strictly forbidding any modifications or tinkering with torpedoes by shipboard personal, and implying that such was the cause of the erratic performance of the IRWIN's torpedoes. Captain Miller was furious at the inferences that there had been negligence or deliberate tampering with the IRWIN's fish. There was, he declared, absolutely no conclusive proof the ship was at fault. Everything about the torpedoes as they were prepared for firing was visibly OK; and the torpedomen had followed standard procedure in setting the spindles controlling speed, depth, and course.

After we reached San Francisco, the Skipper and Gene Stout were to go to a meeting, but the Captain told the Torpedo Officer to remain aboard. He said there was "no need to put you through all this." And he told the ensign he had "evidence" the cause of the erratic behavior of the torpedoes was not the responsibility of anyone on the ship. Captain Miller must have been sure of himself because he told Mr. Stout: "I'm going to demand a full apology." What that evidence was, the Torpedo Officer never learned, but some six months later he got word he was "vindicated" in the incident. He later received a "letter of assurance" after the War, while in his Naval Reserve unit, absolving him of any blame. That, however, is not the end of the boomerang torpedoes story. More would come to light, and I'll relate the details later in these chronicles.

On 11 November, we lost our 1st Class Radioman at Pearl. Albert Brantley Block was transferred to Commander Destroyers Pacific (Com-DesPac) for eventual assignment to the CALLAGHAN. I'd miss ol' Block. We'd had a good cruise together. With no other "First" aboard, I'd assume his duties. At 1323, after Al left the ship, we got underway for San Francisco. Now designated Task Group 15.1, "CripDiv Two" cleared the anti-sub nets, rounded Diamond Head, set course 048° True, and proceeded at 17 knots.

Everyone aboard was in high spirits, and it was routine steaming for two days until we got a dispatch that brought us suddenly back to reality. A baby flat-top "hunter-killer" anti-submarine group stationed along the sea lanes between Hawaii and the West Coast had just sunk a Japanese sub not more than ten miles off our course. Immediately, our lookouts put less emphasis on watching for surface shipping and tuna boats and began to scan the seas carefully for periscopes and torpedo tracks. With all the news reports of combat coming from the far off Western Pacific, the American people didn't realize the enemy was still operating within shouting distance of our shores as late as 1945.

The rest of our voyage was without incident and we passed under the Golden Gate Bridge on November 17th. Once more, as a year before, I was privileged to behold the Golden Gate before '48! Proceeding to Mare Island, we unloaded all our ammunition and explosives preparatory to entering the Navy Yard. At the ammo depot, the BIRMINGHAM was moored astern of us, and I went over to get a firsthand look at the damage to her, as well as to talk to some of her crew for eyewitness accounts of the blast which had decimated her ship's company. The stories were gruesome, the damage more widespread than I'd anticipated.

By evening, we were moored dockside at Hunter's Point. Leave and liberty were being granted while yard birds swarmed aboard to begin restoring the IRWIN to her former self. I made a beeline to the nearest phone to call Jane in Atlanta. At the sound of my voice, she let out a war whoop that could be heard all the way to Stone Mountain. I told her I'd be getting fourteen days' leave and would be on my way as soon as air transportation could be arranged. Much of the rest of our conversation was taken up with wedding plans. When we finally said our goodbyes and she ended with "Jack, I love you"—I was in an advanced state of euphoria.

I was getting ready to go on liberty with Fitch the next afternoon when one of the guys in the compartment yelled over to me.

"When you get ashore, Hutch, you better go buy some campaign ribbons."

"How come?"

"Oh, the damned Shore Patrol stopped me last night. They said the Commandant had put out a directive that everybody had to wear their fruit salad. Otherwise, they'd be put on report. And you'd better salute all officers on the beach, too. The Navy's gettin' chickenshit, again."

"If they want me to wear ribbons, they'll issue 'em", I told him.

"They told me that's no excuse."

It might have been perverse thinking, but many of the sailors who'd seen a lot of combat wouldn't wear any ribbons. In the first place, they reasoned, they knew what they'd done and didn't need a colored piece of cloth to advertise it. Secondly, the Navy was supposed to issue us any such awards, and since it hadn't, we shouldn't have to spend our own money on 'em. And third, the honor of the ribbons, which represented medals, was cheapened by "Feather Merchants" who'd never been near salt water, sporting more ribbons than a Swiss Admiral—ribbons they'd never earned.

Not wanting to risk being on report and missing my leave, I walked into a uniform shop. The clerk asked me what ribbons I wanted. I told him: "Hell, I don't even know which ones I'm supposed to have." We checked a chart, and I got five, one of which I found out later I didn't rate. After I put 'em on, I had a fourth reason for not wearing them. The ribbons were mounted on metal bars and worn above the left breast pocket. I'm lefthanded, and every time I reached for a beer, the damn' bar jabbed me in the shoulder. I got bruises.

Returning from liberty, I stopped at a little shack near the Navy Yard entrance that sold cigarettes, candy, hot dogs, etc. The radio in the place was blaring out the top hit of the day: The Mills Brothers' "Paper Doll". As I poured sugar into a cup of coffee, I heard a familiar voice. It was Boom Boom, so I joined him on the way back to the ship. The Chief Gunner's Mate had an odd and unique way of talking. He had a voice quality that suited his nickname, and he spoke out of the side of his mouth in a manner not unlike that of a boxer who's taken one too many left hooks to the chops. I asked him what kind of liberty he'd had.

He chuckled and said he'd seen our Chief Pharmacist's Mate Walt Davis with a girl. The way he put it was:

"And-a there-a wuz that Chief Chancre Mechanic a-steamin' a-down a-Market-a Stah-REET with a chippie on-a his-a arm, and-a she-a had a stah-HERN on 'er like a la-HIGHT-a cah-ROOO-zer!"

Decades later, I met Doc's wife for the first time at a ship's reunion. I diplomatically asked if they had been married at that time, since I didn't want to get Doc in any trouble. They assured me they were, so I asked Sherli, imitating Boom Boom as closely as I could, if she were that "chippie with a stern on her like a light cruiser" steaming down Market Street with Doc. She broke into gales of laughter, then turned her back to me and said: "See? I've got proof!"

Flying across country in the War years could be a real test of endurance and patience. There were no non-stop flights, and there were six stopovers and three plane changes between San Francisco and Atlanta. The first leg was from Frisco to Burbank, with a five-hour wait for the next plane to Phoenix, Dallas, and so on. I almost didn't make it past Burbank.

I had just gotten off the plane from SanFran and was walking down a corridor when I heard a shout.

"HEY IRWIN!"

Turning, I saw three Navy pilots bearing down on me. They were PRINCETON fliers I'd pulled out of the water, and the first thing they wanted to do was buy me a drink. Five hours and I don't know how many drinks later, they poured me on the Phoenix-bound plane. That binge ranked right up there with any of the more memorable of previous drinking bouts. We'd had a glorious time and the pilots were unstinting in showing their appreciation. But the doozy of a hangover lingered through most of the way to Georgia. Thanks to understanding steward-esses, black coffee and aspirin, I luckily became navigable by the time I reached my destination. It took the better part of two days to make the flight and I really needed all that time to recover from the largess of those fly-boys of "the Peerless P".

Jane and I were immediately caught up in a whirlwind of activities in preparation for the wedding. The ceremony was held at her mother's home in Garden Hills and, in keeping with wartime austerity, was relatively simple. We spent a few days making the rounds visiting relatives and attending parties before heading for the West Coast. We were deliriously happy and ever so much in love. We had a couple of days to ourselves before I reported back to the ship. Then we took a

Author's Cousin Marge Wrigley, Grandmother Margaret Hutchinson, Jane Wrigley, and her father, T.K. Wrigley.

room at the place Fitch and Butch were staying so Jane would have company while I was at the Navy Yard. During most of the time I had free gangway, and we spent wonderful evenings touring the city, dining at the Top o' the Mark or on Fisherman's Wharf and seeing the sights.

While I'd been on leave, the crew was moved off the ship to quarters in Quonset huts in the Navy Yard. With all the welding, riveting, and repair work going on 'round the clock, we were just in the way of the yard birds. On the first night back from Atlanta, I had the most terrifying moments of my service in the United States Navy. Here I was, safely back in the States, thousands of miles from Jap ships, planes, and submarines. I was secure in the knowledge there was no danger, that this was a haven where nothing could happen to me. I was enjoying a beautiful honeymoon with my bride and the War was eons away. All my conditioned defenses were on hiatus, pushed deep into my subconscious. After all, I was in the sanctuary of "home".

It was just at dusk as I stepped out on the Quonset hut porch, ready for liberty in my dress blues. Fitch would soon join me, so I relaxed with a cigarette, enjoying the evening air. Throughout the Navy Yard, nighttime illumination was provided by vapor lights mounted on high poles, and there was one near our hut. At that moment, the automatic timer switched on those lights. They first flickered with a yellowish glow, then flashed to full brilliance. The sequence and colors were almost identical to those of a flare or star shell, so often the first warning from the enemy of impending danger. My automatic reflexes kicked in and all I could think of was *"FLARE!!"* I panicked.

My mind was telling me it really wasn't an enemy attack, not a flare at all but just a plain old electric light. But my nervous system, so well conditioned during the long years in the forward areas, completely took over. I let out one unintelligible yell, hit the dirt in front of the hut, and frantically began digging a foxhole with my bare hands right then and there. Three shipmates, astounded by my actions, grabbed me but couldn't stop me from clawing at the earth until help came. The clamor got the attention of one of our pharmacist's mates who had his first-aid bag in the hut. With about four or five men holding me down, the Doc stuck a needle in my arm to sedate me. It didn't completely knock me out but did serve to slowly bring me back to rationality.

I had been absolutely overwhelmed and completely consumed by terror. Never before, nor since, had I so totally lost control. In combat area, it would have been just another flare, calling for extra vigilance. But here in this safe stateside haven, my defenses were down and I was unprepared for the unexpected. Reaction without reason was automatic. Should I live to be a hundred, I shall never forget the blinding, uncontrollable dread I felt that night.

Fitch called Jane to say we'd be a little late; then helped me settle down, clean up my blues, and get the blood and dirt off my hands. Doc put some iodine on the cuts and scratches, and Junior and I finally headed for the Navy Yard gate. I didn't tell Jane what happened, explaining away the cut and bruised hands by saying I'd been splicing wire rope. I don't hold much truck with psychiatrists or psychologists, but I've since wondered how one would analyze *that* incident.

From Radio Press News, some decoded dispatches, and scuttlebutt during our short stay in Pearl, we picked up bits and pieces of the naval actions occurring while the IRWIN was preoccupied with the PRINCETON. In the States we finally got a rough account of what would become collectively known as "The Battles of Leyte Gulf". During less than 72 hours on 23, 24, and 25 October, 1944, there were four separate engagements: the Battle of the Sibuyan Sea, the Battle of Surigao Strait, the Battle off Samar, and the Battle off Cape Engaño.

The Imperial Japanese Navy, with their Combined Fleet divided into four separate forces, reacted to the October 20th landings of the

U.S. Army's XXIV Corps at Tacloban and Dulag on Leyte, as soon as they got the word *where* the amphibious operations were taking place, according to the Sho-Go (Victory) Plan of IJN Commander in Chief Admiral Toyoda. From Japan's Inland, Sea Admiral Ozawa's Northern Force of a fleet carrier, three light carriers, two battleships, three light cruisers, and eight destroyers sallied forth to a position in the Philippine Sea off the northeast coast of Luzon. His mission was to decoy Admiral Halsey's Task Force 38 away from supplying aerial protection over the Leyte beachheads.

Also from the north came, via Formosa and the South China Sea, the Jap Fifth Fleet with three heavy cruisers, two light cruisers, and about ten destroyers under Admiral Shima. He was supposed to join with Admiral Nishimura's Southern Force of two battleships, one heavy cruiser, and seven destroyers. This would be the southern arm of a pincer movement sailing through the Sulu Sea, then between Negros and Mindanao into Surigao Strait, heading straight for Leyte Gulf.

Then there was the Jap Second Fleet, the Center Force under Admiral Kurita which, like Admiral Nishimura's, was approaching from anchorages near Singapore, with a stop at Brunei on Borneo for fuel. This was the largest Jap force centered around the two biggest battleships in the world, the giant YAMATO and MUSASHI, and including three older battlewagons, ten heavy cruisers, two light cruisers, and twelve destroyers. They would cruise past Palawan through Mindoro Strait, strike through the Subuyan Sea past Panay, then slip through the San Bernardino Strait between Luzon and Samar to drive south into Leyte Gulf, forming the northern arm of the pincer movement.

The invasion was beginning its third day and Lieutenant General Walter Krueger's Sixth Army was rapidly widening its control of the beachhead areas. Transports, cargo ships, and landing craft hurried their debarking, anxious to get out of the confines of Leyte Gulf before the Imperial Japanese Navy showed up. The curtain was about to rise on the four great sea Battles of Leyte Gulf, comprising the most extensive naval conflict in history.

The warm-up featured a pair of daring U.S. submarines, the team of DACE and DARTER. Patrolling the Palawan Passage on October 23rd, the subs sighted Admiral Kurita's Center Force. The DARTER fired her bow torpedoes at the Admiral's flagship, the heavy cruiser ATAGO; then cut down on another cruiser, the TAKAO, with her stern tubes. Both went dead in the water, and the Admiral's flagship later sank. The DACE loosed a spread of fish at a third cruiser, the MAYA, which exploded with such violence nothing was left but an oil slick. In the poorly chartered waters, the DARTER then ran aground on Bonbay Shoal, and was abandoned after the DACE rescued her crew.

The two spunky subs had done their job, not only in taking out the cruisers but in flashing the size of Kurita's force and its course to Admiral Halsey's Third Fleet, i.e. Task Force 38, other U.S. Navy forces in the Philippines being now in Admiral Thomas C. Kinkaid's Seventh Fleet involved in the Leyte invasion. The stage was now set for Act I—the Battle of the Sibuyan Sea.

Halsey's Task Force 38 was dispersed along a broad front. Task Group 38.1 had retired eastward toward Ulithi to refuel, TG 38.2 was off San Bernardino Strait, TG 38.4 was off southern Samar, and our TG 38.3 had the northernmost station, due east of the Polillo Islands. The dawn attacks aimed at us on 24 October by some 200 land-based planes from the former U.S. Air Bases at Clark and Nichols Fields, kept our air cover too busy to launch a strike against Kurita's ships, but our early dawn search planes were out looking for him. Only 70 Jap aircraft were left to retreat after our CAP finished off the land-based assault, but that one Judy got through to drop its deadly 550-pound bomb on the PRINCETON.

While the IRWIN was vainly trying to save the PRINCETON, carrier planes of Task Force 38 went after the Japs' Center Force in the Sibuyan Sea with a vengeance, flying 259 sorties and sinking the super battleship MUSASHI, inflicting heavy casualties as they poured 19 torpedoes into her and polished her off with 17 bomb hits. They took the heavy cruiser MYOKO out of action as well as damaging several other ships. The air assaults slowed down Kurita and caused him to reverse course, thus throwing off his timetable for rendezvous with Nishimura's and Shima's Southern Force, which he hoped to join after they came through Surigao Strait. By sundown on October 24th, the Battle of the Sibuyan Sea was over, the PRINCETON gone, and the IRWIN on her way for repairs.

Now I get a chance to correct history and stick a needle in the desk jockeys in the Pentagon. The IRWIN's Navy Unit Commendation (along with some other accounts) describes the PRINCETON's loss as part of the Battle off Samar. Task Group 38.3, on 24 October, was due east of the Polillo Islands off *Luzon, 200 miles north of Samar!* The Battle off Samar involved the escort carriers which ran into Kurita's Center Force on *25* October, some *twenty hours after* the PRINCETON went down. So whoever wrote up the citation that went with our NUC had us in the *wrong position*, on the *wrong day*, in the *wrong battle!* As the old Navy saying goes: "There's always *somebody* who doesn't get the word."

Act II opened with TF 38 search planes sighting both fleets of the

Japs' Southern Force around noon on the 24th. Admiral Kinkaid, Commander of the U.S. Seventh Fleet off Leyte to provide surface protection for the invasion, correctly judged the enemy would make a nighttime thrust toward Leyte Gulf through the Surigao Strait. He got his scouts out, deploying 39 motor torpedo boats in groups of three across the eastern end of the Mindanao Sea to report as soon as the hostiles showed up.

Next, Rear Admiral Jesse B. Oldendorf would form a Battle Line with his bombardment and fire support ships, including six "old" battleships, to go head-to-head with the Jap intruders. Four heavy cruisers and a destroyer division would screen the battlewagons. Two other tin can divisions would deploy down the alley, with another division in reserve. All the players were on stage for the Battle of Surigao Strait. Right after 2400, the PT-boats made contact with the Jap battleships. After alerting Admiral Oldendorf, they made a torpedo run, missed every enemy ship, and got shot up by an enemy destroyer. All across the line, PT-boat sections attacked with their fish and, as had happened in Kula Gulf in 1943, missed with every one of them.

As usual, it was up to the destroyers to get the job done. At 0300, five tin cans of Destroyer Squadron 54 launched torpedo attacks, hitting the battleship FUSO and taking out three destroyers as well. As the five U.S. destroyers retired untouched, three more cans of DesRon 24 hit the enemy from the other side, finishing off a destroyer and getting another torpedo into the battleship. As Admiral Nishimura steamed doggedly on, he had only the battleship YAMASHIRO, heavy cruiser MOGAMI, and destroyer SHIGURE left. Facing an overwhelmingly superior force, he was steaming into a trap set by Admiral Oldendorf licking his chops with the adage: "Never give a sucker a chance!"

In a classic naval maneuver—that of "crossing the T "—the WEST VIRGINIA, TENNESSEE, CALIFORNIA, MARYLAND, MISSISSIPPI, and PENNSYLVANIA went out to do battle. Our battleships managed to catch the Jap force steaming in single file through the narrow strait and cross in front of it at right angles so as to be able to bring all their big guns to bear while the Japs could only fire their forward guns. The first three U.S. battlewagons did most of the shooting, but the others joined in as well. Only the PENNSYLVANIA never got off a round. With our cruisers and destroyers adding their part to the fray, short work was made of the YAMASHIRO. The MOGAMI was damaged and later sunk by carrier planes. Only the SHIGURE, although hit, survived to retreat to safety. The Battle of Surigao Strait was all over in some seventeen minutes. The old surviving Pearl Harbor battlewagons had got some measure of revenge.

Admiral Shima's Fifth Fleet, which never linked up with the now drowned Admiral Nishimura, having gone down with his flagship, now put in an appearance and came under fire. Shima had his cruisers launch their torpedoes at American targets. No hits, and he was facing overwhelming odds. So he decided he'd better get his derrière out of there. With two heavy cruisers and four destroyers, he made it back to Brunei on North Borneo.

Act III—the Battle off Samar—was one of the strangest in naval history, pitting a heavy-ship surface force of battleships and cruisers against escort carriers, destroyers, and destroyer escorts. No naval tactician had ever dreamed of such a confrontation, so the script was written as the battle raged.

Admiral Kurita's Center Force, with its nose bloodied but not bowed, had been in retreat in the Sibuyan Sea, a fact passed on to Admiral Halsey by his scout planes. The "Bull", apprised as well of Admiral Ozawa's Northern Force steaming southward to the north and east of the Philippines, decided now was the time for all good ships to go after Ozawa's carriers. What Halsey didn't know, was that Ozawa was a decoy to pull Task Force 38 away from Leyte, and he fell for the ruse.

Meanwhile, Kurita, undaunted by the casualties inflicted by TF 38 air attacks on the 24th, suddenly and undetected reversed his course and headed through the San Bernardino Strait and down the Samar coast straight for the Transport Area in Leyte Gulf. The only Americans in his way were Rear Admiral T.L. Sprague's Task Group 77.4, composed of three units now famous for their radio call signs—Taffy 1, Taffy 2, and Taffy 3—and they were dispersed over a thirty to fifty mile area. Taffy 3, under Rear Admiral C.A.F. Sprague, with six escort carriers, three FLETCHER-class destroyers, and three destroyer escorts, was closest to San Bernardino Strait when Kurita charged through. Contact was made at 0645 on the 25th, and by 0658, the Jap battleships were in range of Taffy 3, opening up on the carriers with their heavy guns while still hull down on the horizon. The jeep carriers, with flank speed of only 17 1/2 knots, launched their aircraft while the tin cans raised smoke screens around them. A rain squall helped, and Taffy 3 retreated south.

The Taffy 3 destroyers made a gallant if futile effort to protect the baby flat-tops, turning to make torpedo runs on the Jap battlewagons. The JOHNSTON (DD-557) launched her fish, as did the HOEL (DD-553), forcing the Nips to maneuver radically to avoid hits. Both destroyers went down with guns blazing as heavy shells pounded them to pieces. But they had slowed down the enemy attack. Soon after, the S.B. ROBERTS (DE-413) suffered the same fate as the DDs. The Japs pressed on, sinking the GAMBIER BAY and severely damaging the FANSHAW BAY and KALINAN BAY. Now, in a battle that was already two hours old, coordinated attacks by fighters and dive bombers from the other jeep carriers in Taffy 2 and 3, began to riddle Kurita's force, sinking three of his heavy cruisers. A fourth had already been damaged by the JOHNSTON's torpedoes. At 0911, Kurita called it a day and, with his tail between his legs, withdrew back through San Bernardino Strait to safety.

It was during this battle that the Japanese *kamikaze* planes put in their first appearance of the Pacific War. The suicide corps of pilots first dived on the jeep carrier SANTEE (CVE-29), setting fires, but she survived. The escort carriers SUWANEE (CVE-27), KITKUN BAY, and KALINAN BAY all weathered *kamikaze* crashes. But the jeep carrier ST. LO (CVE-53) was not so lucky, going down after a suicider caused a huge explosion aboard. The U.S. Navy had not seen the last of the suiciders.

Act IV, the closing scenes in the Battles of Leyte Gulf, took place 300 miles away off the northern tip of Luzon east of Cape Engaño. The search planes of Admiral Halsey's Task Force 38 finally sighted Ozawa's Northern Force. It was 17 ships and 29 planes (most of the Jap carrier planes had been expended in futile attacks on our Task Group 38.3 the day before) against a U.S. force of 64 ships and 787 planes! Japanese industry simply was not capable of producing planes and ships to compete with the American Armada in the Pacific produced by the Arsenal of Democracy.

With Admiral Mitscher as Officer in Tactical Command of the three Task Groups, the first air strike against Ozawa reached the enemy around 0800 on 25 October. In the next three hours, TF 38 planes sank all four Jap aircraft carriers including the ZUIKAKU, the only surviving Jap carrier involved in the attack on Pearl Harbor. They also inflicted heavy casualties on many of the other enemy ships. All in all, the once proud and powerful Japanese Combined Fleet was in complete shambles and would never again pose a threat in the Pacific War. Except for a few scattered skirmishes, the vaunted Imperial Japanese Navy was out of business for good.

According to U.S. Navy and Harvard historian Samuel Eliot Morison, the Battles of Leyte Gulf should be "an imperishable part of our national heritage." But today, who remembers these eminent events of our naval history? What percentage of the American people, particularly of our young people, know or care anything about the illustrious battles of the War in the Pacific?

Back in the States, it was December, 1944, and most of the IRWIN's

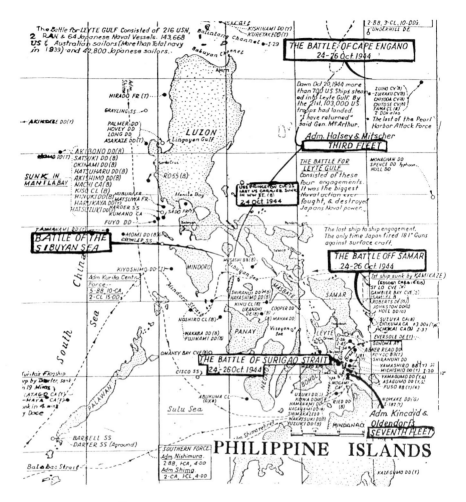

The Battle for LEYTE GULF Consisted of 216 USN, 2 RAN & 64 Japanese Naval Vessels. 143,668 US & Australian sailors (More than Total navy in 1939) and 42,800 Japanese sailors.

2-BB, 3-CL, 10-DD's
UNDERHILL DE

KISHINAMI DD (T)
KURETAKE DD (T)
I-29

Balintang Channel

Babuyan Channel

Aparri

THE BATTLE OF CAPE ENGANO
24-26 Oct. 1944

Dawn Oct 20, 1944 more than 700 US Ships steamed into Leyte Gulf. By the 21st, 103,000 US troops had landed.
"I have returned" said Gen. McArthur.

ZUIHO CV (2)
ZUIKAKU CV (B)
CHIYODA CV (B)
CHITOSE CV (B)
TAMA CL (B)
2 DD's also
The last of the Pearl Harbor Attack Force

Adm. Halsey & Mitscher
THIRD FLEET

HIRADO FR (T)
GRAYLING SS
AKINOSUKE DD (T)
PALMER DD
HOVEY DD
LONG DD
ASAKAZE DD (T)

LUZON
Lingayen Gulf

Santa Cruz

MONAGHAN DD
SPENCE DD Typhoon
HULL DD

THE BATTLE FOR LEYTE GULF
Consisted of these four engagements. It was the biggest Naval action ever fought, & destroyed Japans Naval power.

AKONO DD (T)
AKEBONO DD (B)
SATSUKI DD (B)
OKINAMI DD (B)
HATSUHARU DD (B)
AKISHIMO DD (B)
NACHI CA (B)
KISO CL (B)
HINUKI DD (B)
HARUKAYA DD (T)
HATSUZUKI DD (T)
FUYO DD

SUNK IN MANILA BAY

RO 55 (B)

HUBURAER
MATSUYA FR
HARDER SS
KUMANO CA
SADO FRY

Manila Bay

USS PRINCETON CVE-23 LAST US CARRIER SUNK IN WW II. (B)
24 Oct. 1944

The last ship to ship engagement. The only time Japan fired 18 I" Guns against surface craft.

TAMANAMI DD (T)

BATTLE OF THE SIBUYAN SEA

MOMI DD (B)
CROWLER SS

Panay

South China Sea

KIYOSHIMO DD (T)

MINDORO

Adm. Kurita Centr. Force--
5-BB, 10-CA
2-CL 15-DD's

Mindoro

MUSASHI BB (B)

Sibuyan Sea

MASBATE

THE BATTLE OFF SAMAR
24-26 Oct. 1944

1st ship sunk by KAMIKAZE)
(ESCORT CARRIERS)
ST LO CVE (B)
GAMBIER BAY CVE (3)
(SAMUEL B.
ROBERTS DE (B)
JOHNSTON DD (B)
HOEL DD (B)

SAMAR

SHIRANUI DD (B)
HAYASHIMO DD (B)
KINU CL (B)
URANAMI DE (B)
COOPER DD
MAHAN DD

SUTUYA CA (B)
CHIKUMA CA #3 DD's (T)
CHOKAI CA (B) I-37

NOSHIRO CL (B)

Visayan Sea

LEYTE

EVERSOLE DE (T)

SONOMA AT
ABNER READ DD
(KONJC B3 (T))
SHIRANUHI DD
YAMASHIRO BB (T) 31
MICHISHIO DD (T) I-20
YAMAGUMO DD (T,6)
ASAGUMO DD (T,6)
FUSO BB (T)(4)

WAKABA DD (B)
FUJINAMI DD (B)

PANAY

OMANEY BAY CVE (B)

THE BATTLE OF SURIGAO STRAIT
24-26 Oct. 1944

CISCO SS

NEGROS

BOHOL

MOGAMI

NOWAKE DD (G)

Adm. Kincaid & Oldendorf
SEVENTH FLEET

Kurita's Flagship up by Darter, sank in 19 Minutes.
ATAGO CA (T)
MAYA CA (B)
unk in 4 min
y Doce

PALAWAN

ABUKUMA CL (GXB)

Sulu Sea

KONWA DD (B)
HAMANAMI DD
NAGANAMI DD (B)
SHIMAKAZE DD
WAKATSUKI DD (B)
YUZUKI DD (B)

RIED DD (B)

MINDANAO

BARBELL SS
DARTER SS (Aground)

SOUTHERN FORCE
Adm. Nishimura.
2-BB, 4-CA, 4-DD
Adm. Shima
2-CA, 1-CL, 4-DD

Jim Shima retired

PHILIPPINE ISLANDS

KAZEGUMO DD (T)

Balabac Strait

crew were back in San Francisco from their leaves. So it was time to throw a ship's party. It was held at the Palace, up on Nob Hill. Captain and Mrs. (Dorothy) Miller were the hosts, and in time-honored Navy tradition, left early so their presence wouldn't inhibit the revelry. There was a pretty good dance band, and everyone had a great time. There were no undue disturbances, howbeit some boisterousness and some guys were not too steady on their pins. None of that, however, was violent nor overly raucous. Just youthful exuberance, and the knowledge we'd soon be shipping out again. But someone called the Shore Patrol and, as crewmen exited the Palace, the SPs rounded them up, packing them into paddy wagons. Those who left by side or rear doors escaped the dragnet.

The next morning, as senior Communications Division petty officer aboard, I joined in making the Morning Reports. Every division reported a number of men absent, and the Captain wanted to know where his crew was. When we told him they were in the Shore Patrol brig on the beach, he became highly incensed and told the 1st Class petty officers to draw side arms from the armory. With us in tow, the Skipper climbed into a station wagon and headed for Shore Patrol Headquarters with a Navy bus in our wake.

The Old Man strode into the office of the SP Lieutenant Commander (a former Los Angeles police lieutenant, we later were told). Gunner's Mate 1st Class Bill "Smitty" Smith and I took up station in the doorway.

"I understand", Captain Miller said to the Shore Patrol Officer, "you have some of my crew in your brig."

"What ship is that, Commander?"

"The IRWIN", snapped the Skipper.

"Oh, yes. The bunch that was raising so much hell up on Nob Hill last night."

"I've come to get them", the C.O. said firmly.

The SP Officer tapped his desk with a pencil and with condescension in his voice replied he wasn't going to let them go until he got instructions from the Naval District Commandant on their disposition.

Captain Miller's voice got a steely edge to it. "Those men are *my* crew. Any discipline is up to me. Now release them!"

The SP Officer started to object when Cap'n Danny put the clincher on.

"You, Mister, are a short-time Reserve in this man's Navy. Maybe you don't understand that, as a ship's Commanding Officer and an Annapolis man, I could have you reduced to Apprentice Seaman and assigned to *my ship* by *tomorrow morning!*"

I don't know if Cap'n Danny could have done *that*, but I wouldn't have argued with him. Smitty and I made a show of pulling our .45s and throwing the safeties off. The Shore Patrol officer turned a little ashen. In a minute or so, Smitty and I had the cell block keys and were releasing our guys, getting 'em on the bus. As we left, the Cap'n was warning the shaken Lieutenant Commander.

"And advise your Shore Patrol to keep their hands off my crew!" No more trouble for us from the SPs after that. All we had to do was mention "IRWIN" to 'em.

The IRWIN had been in Hunter's Point a couple of days short of two months when she was pronounced completely repaired, fit and ready for sea. On 15 January, 1945, we restocked our magazines at the Mare Island Ammunition Depot. Then, for the next five days, we conducted full power runs, degaussing exercises, sound gear and compass calibrations, and structural firing of our weapons off the coast, returning to port each evening. Time was running short. We'd soon be rejoining the Fleet.

Several changes in the Radio Gang took place while the ship was being repaired. After two years in rate, I was promoted to Radioman 1st Class (RM1c) with a base pay of $84 a month. With the additional 20 percent sea pay, I was now making $100 a month (rounded off). Keeping only what money I needed for incidentals at sea, I made out an allotment to Jane, and had her named beneficiary (in place of my kid brother George) on my National Service Life Insurance policy. She'd get $10,000 if I didn't make it back.

Joe Alice and Don Karl both got their 3rd Class stripes. Two new men—Les Frisch, a Radioman 2nd, and Chester Karsten, a Seaman 2nd striker—reported aboard. Another striker Chester Duflo, like Karsten a Seaman Deuce, would be added when we got to Pearl. Chief Leger, Frank Riddle, and Robert Terrell rounded out the petty officer complement. The remaining strikers were Mansell Giffen, Gordon Gregerson, Frank Hansen, and George Mootz. The Radio Gang was ready to go back to the War.

We had quite a few new hands aboard who would have to be trained on our way back to the Western Pacific, and we really missed our shipmates who had been transferred. But the old IRWIN spirit was still intact. We were particularly proud of our new symbol of "accomplishment". Bill Needles had painted an insignia on the Torpedo Director depicting a triumphant bluejacket brandishing a boomerang while riding a bucking torpedo. Not only had we rescued 646 PRINCETON crewmen, but we'd survived an attack by our own torpedoes!

On 22 January we had our last liberty. Jane and I spent it quietly, making a last trip to the Top o' the Mark to hold hands and look out over

San Francisco Bay and the city where we'd spent the beginning of our marriage in a pretty romantic way. We had known each other only a couple of weeks before deciding to get married, and we'd had less than two months together before we'd be separated by the War. Those days had been the most marvelous ones of my life; and leaving Jane behind was most, most difficult. Nor would it be easy for her, not knowing whether I'd ever return. She would stay with Butch for a short while, then return to Atlanta to live with her sister Dottie.

The old sailors used to sing:

> See there she stands and waves her hands upon the quay,
> And every day when I'm away she'll watch for me,
> And whisper low when tempests blow for *Jack* at sea. . . .
> *The sailor's wife the sailor's star shall be . . . !*

As the crew straggled back to the ship from our final liberty, one grand brouhaha broke out on the dock. A certain Boatswain's Mate 2nd named Jack Bové, one of the real characters in the crew, showed up roaring drunk. He'd taken literally the line from "Anchors Aweigh": "It's our last night ashore, drink to the foam. . . . " As Jack later wrote in his diary, he was in "a great state of intoxication and full of violent fight"!

When Bové balked at going aboard, the Officer of the Deck ordered some of the deck hands to corral him. But this Jack was one of the strongest, toughest, meanest men in ship's company. Several of Bové's buddies tried to bring him in, but he managed to escape all their ploys, swinging wildly at anybody within target range and exerting superhuman strength to break out of the holds of all hands. All this was attended by loud shouting as the spectators began to take sides. Some were urging Jack on; others, including the O.D., were yelling encouragement to his would-be captors.

Just when his pursuers thought their quarry cornered against a railing on the pier, Jack jumped over the rail and, after fighting off his rescuers for several minutes, "had to be pulled from the cold waters" of San Francisco Bay. Finally, by sheer force of numbers, the bos'n's mate was pinned to the ground, lashed down to a Stokes stretcher, and hauled aboard to sleep it off. It was two days before Jack's head would be clear enough to write in his diary: "Gradually recuperating from the effects of last wild orgy ashore in San Francisco. Continuing rough seas make recovery slow. Summoned to Mast [disciplinary hearing] in front of Captain. Severe admonishment and grim warning were result. Consider myself fortunate."

Jack Bové was lucky. A Skipper less compassionate than Captain Miller would have thrown the book at him, a Deck Court-Martial being the least he could expect. However, the Old Man—somewhat amused by the episode and realizing that it just might have been the bos'n's mate's last night ashore (we were going back to war)—went easy on Jack. But an IRWIN legend was born. Bové must have had one HELLUVA liberty—one for the *Guiness Book of Records*.

By 1802 on 23 January, we were underway from Hunter's Point. The Special Sea Detail cast off the lines. The Captain eased the IRWIN out into the stream and headed for the channel to pass beneath the Golden Gate. I'd made it back twice, now, since I first heard that little rhyme in the Solomons.

But this was only 1945, not 1948, and where we were going there was still the probability I'd see the Pearly Gate before then.

28

IWO, TOKYO AND THE TYPHOON

After an uneventful passage, marked with training drills and exercises, the IRWIN arrived in Pearl Harbor, mooring at Buoy D-2 in the Middle Loch. It was 29 January, 1945. I had been in the Navy exactly four years, rated a hash mark and, thanks to "Jughead" O'Neill's boot camp advice, the Navy Good Conduct Medal.

For the next five days, we were conducting more training and tests at sea, operating at various times with the PITTSBURGH (CA-72), VICKSBURG (CL-84), HUTCHINS (DD-476), and ZELLARS (DD-777), returning to port each evening. Again, ComDesPac's Fleet Personnel Officer came aboard, inquiring how many replacements we needed. Lieutenant Hodapp once more told him "none." The F.P.O. was flabbergasted. Not only had the IRWIN broken the record once, we'd done it TWICE. It was unheard of, but this time the Exec got no argument.

The Personnel Officer did, however, marvel at the devotion of the IRWIN's crew to our own Cap'n Danny. The Exec told me, years later, that Captain Miller did not have to come back to sea with us this second time. He could have had a cushy shore job but refused the assignment. He just couldn't give up the IRWIN, his crew, and his beloved destroyers. And people wondered why his men held him in such high esteem.

On 4 February, Admiral Walden L. Ainsworth, Commander Destroyers Pacific, came aboard to award Navy and Marine Corp Medals to the 29 members of the swimming team for their actions in saving men off the PRINCETON. But when the Admiral spotted our boomerang torpedo insignia, he hit the overhead! Bill Needles was ordered to paint it over IMMEDIATELY if not sooner. We were crestfallen. It was our badge of honor. The crew, at the time, was unaware of all the controversy surrounding the incident, and didn't understand what the big deal was.

February 4th was also my birthday. I was 23. The next day, in company with the VICKSBURG, we shoved off for Eniwetok, where we refueled and immediately left for Saipan in the Marianas. Arriving on the IRWIN's "birthday", 14 February, Valentine's Day, we reported to Commander Task Force 51—my old boss, Admiral Kelly Turner in the

EL DORADO (AGC-11)—and were assigned to Task Force 51's destroyer screen.

There was a little flurry as we proceeded to our screening station. An air alert sounded but no planes came near. Seemed like old times. Saipan's Tanapag Harbor was crammed with attack transports and landing craft. It all spelled "invasion". Ken Richmond, a Quartermaster 1st, was pulling charts from the storage locker, and I ambled over to see which ones. The legend on them read "Volcano Islands—Iwo Jima". I soon learned we'd be escorting the invasion force in to the beach.

When I went back in the Radio Shack, Don Karl wanted to know where we were going this time.

"I want you to know, Don, me boy, that you work for a most considerate Navy. They got us all repaired and fixed up just in time for the next invasion. Now what other Navy would do that for us?"

"Where to, this time, Hutch?"

"A rock out in the middle of nowhere called Iwo Jima in the Bonin Islands. We'll chaperone a bunch of transports stuffed with Marines and screen 'em while they make the beachheads." I paused. "We're back in the War, lad."

Task Force 51 commenced to sortie out of Saipan at 1600, 16 February. The invasion force of some 495 ships, maybe eight times the number when we invaded Guadalcanal, was transporting some 70,650 Marines, under Generals Holland Smith and Harry Schmidt, toward the tiny island. The IRWIN took her screening position with Task Group 51.12, riding shotgun to the attack transports of the Amphibians. The passage was routine; and we made radar contact on Iwo Jima at 0412, 19 February. At 0503, we formed the anti-submarine screen to protect the APAs and AKAs in the outer Transport Area, then two hours later began patrolling on a three-and-a-half-mile station at 15 knots.

Ironically, the invasion of Iwo Jima was known as Operation DE-TACHMENT! The pre-landing bombardment of the Japanese positions on the island was ferocious, sending clouds of smoke and volcanic dust high over Iwo. Round after round after round of high explosives from the bombardment group, including both the old and some new battle-ships, constituted the heaviest shelling to precede an invasion any time in World War II.

Iwo Jima was a natural fortress which the Japs had honeycombed with interconnecting caves, revetments, and fortifications. Unlike the invasions in the Central Pacific, there would be no element of surprise at Iwo. It would be one tough nut to crack. The Marines were facing perhaps 20,000 defenders under Jap General Kuribayashi. The Japs' attitude was epitomized by a comment in a captured diary: "We must live on, right or wrong, and keep striking until we have . . . wiped the Anglo-Saxons from the face of the earth."

D-day minus one was a Sunday, and Marines received from a Chaplain the famous prayer of Sir Jacob Astley before the Battle of Edgehill in 1642:

> O Lord! Thou knowest how busy I must be this day:
> If I forget Thee, do not Thou forget me.

At 0645, 19 February, Kelly Turner commanded "Land the Landing Force!" And throughout the Transport Area went the familiar order "Away All Boats!" The first landing craft hit the beach at 0900, but almost immediately the Marines of the first wave were pinned down by hostile enfilade fire. That is, the Japs had the target area in range, indeed every inch of the island sighted in for their artillery and mortars. The fire support vessels offshore increased their bombardment in an effort to clear out those Nip gun positions, but to little avail. The enemy was dug in too deeply.

The IRWIN's patrol lane terminated at its southwesterly extreme almost under the lip of now legendary Mount Suribachi. As we reached that point, a cruiser's spotting plane requested "call-fire" on gun emplacements and blockhouses at the foot of the huge dormant volcano. We opened up with our 5-inch Main Battery, but the smoke and dust was so thick we could observe no results. I had borrowed a pair of binoculars from Fitch and was scanning Iwo, watching what I could see of the landings through the heavy layers of volcanic dust and gunpowder smoke.

The monolith of Mount Suribachi towered over the island. Below it the Marines were pinned down on a "terrace" which rose sharply from the high-water mark. The soft volcanic ash made it almost impossible to move on foot or get tracked vehicles up over the terrain. From their well-bunkered positions, the Japs were laying down a fierce and murderous mortar and artillery barrage. Casualties mounted by the minute, running to over thirty percent among the landing force. I could see small craft returning to the transports laden with wounded men. As a one-time Amphibian, it was almost too much for me to take.

I could only exclaim: "Oh, those *poor bastards!*"

The IRWIN continued to shell targets intermittently as directed by the spotter plane. It was getting close to noon, and one third of our crew was lining up on the port side just abaft the superstructure break, ready to go below for chow. About that time we got return fire from somewhere on the dead volcano. Three or four rounds exploded close aboard and the chow line guys hit the deck as one. But the Japs made no hits. We changed position—fast. At 1150, we were relieved on station by the

ROOKS (DD-804). Then came the signal from Admiral Turner: "Desig Dog Seven Nine Four. You are hereby detached. Proceed in accordance with previous orders. God speed." We were rejoining the Fast Carriers of Task Force 58.

As at Saipan, the Iwo invasion was under Admiral Spruance, Admiral Halsey's Third Fleet having become Spruance's Fifth Fleet after our invasions in the Philippines. Task Force 38 was TF 58, again under Admiral Mitscher. Admiral Turner commanded the Amphibs of TF 51. During the invasion Radio Tokyo broadcast the following concerning "the Alligator": "He is the man who can be termed a devil man, being responsible for the killing of countless numbers of our own younger and elder brothers on the various islands throughout the central Pacific area. Turner's career in war against our own men began with the operations on the island of Guadalcanal. . . . The true nature of an alligator is that once he bites into something he will not let go. Turner's nature is also like this. . . . "

We would not be around to see the historic planting of our Colors atop storied Suribachi (code name "Hotrocks"). But there was a Solomon Islands connection to that ceremony. The Marines who took the Stars and Stripes up the sides of that mountain were from the 28th Regiment, 5th Marines, commanded by Harry "the Horse" Liversedge, late of Enogai Inlet and Bairoko Harbor. We gave the Suribachi end of the island a wide berth and swung on a northerly course, bending on 20 knots to make a refueling rendezvous. Some of the off-watch Radio Gang had gathered on the Comm Deck with me, and as we looked back at Iwo Jima growing smaller in the distance I was glad we were departing.

"Let's get out of this God-forsaken place, chop chop", I remarked.

One of the new strikers looked at me quizzically: "Chop chop?"

"Yeah. Old China talk. Means 'get your fanny in gear', 'move it', 'expedite'. There are lot of good Mud Marines dying on those damned beachheads, this morning, and a helluva lot more'll never get off that rock. Since we can't do much to help 'em, I'd just as soon not stay around to watch it."

I was already shaken by what little bit we'd witnessed. Frustration at not being able to help, and compassion for those gyrenes under devastating fire, welled up within me. You just can't watch something like what those Marines were going through, even from a distance, without feeling strong, compelling emotions. As later at Okinawa, the enemy wanted to make Iwo so costly we'd think twice before invading the Home Islands of Japan.

Iwo was not really "secured" until the end of March, and the Army continued to mop up 'til June. When the final casualty count would come

in, it would list nearly 20,000 wounded Navy and Marine Corps personnel and almost 7,000 Marines dead at Iwo Jima. The infantry regiments
of the 4th and 5th Marine Divisions had a monstrous *seventy-five percent*
battle casualties! According to General "Howlin' Mad" Smith: "Iwo Jima
was the most savage and the most costly battle in the history of the
Marine Corps."

The IRWIN steamed independently through the night, making
contact with our fueling group at 0500 on 20 February. We topped off
our bunkers and rejoined Task Group 58.3 at 0928. The make-up of TG
58.3 had changed some. Admiral Sherman was still in the ESSEX, but
Admiral Mitscher had now switched his ComTaskFor 58 Flag to the
BUNKER HILL (CV-17). The battlewagons NEW JERSEY and SOUTH
DAKOTA along with DesDiv 109 and DesRon 62 rounded out the force.
The next day we were joined by the battle-cruiser ALASKA (CB-1), the
light cruiser FLINT (CL-97), and the rest of DesRon 55, less the
MORRISON. We were on station to supply carrier air support to the Iwo
operation.

Late in the afternoon, land-based enemy aircraft from the Northern
Bonin Islands were picked up on radar, and we circled the wagons to
repel them, at the same time cutting in our smoke generators to obscure
the Task Group from the Jap pilots. Those generators, oil fired, caused
some anxious moments. They erupted with huge blasts of flame at
various times, giving the false impression of explosions aboard the tin
cans in the force.

The enemy planes came in dropping "window"—showers of small
pieces of aluminum foil. It caused our radar to show hundreds of blips
on the scopes and was intended to keep the operators from being able
to detect which were foil and which were enemy targets. At about 1955,
we got a good solution on our scope on an intruder, range 8,000 yards,
and opened fire with the Main Battery. We couldn't eyeball him due to
the smoke screen, but he disappeared off the radar screen after we'd
fired only six rounds. Some 25 minutes later, we picked up another bogie,
firing nine rounds with the same result. Score two "probables" for the
IRWIN's gunners.

On 21 February, as if an omen of things to come, Jap *kamikaze*
aircraft crashed into two escort carriers off Iwo, the LUNGA POINT
(CVE-94) and the BISMARCK SEA (CVE-95), slightly damaging the
former but sinking the latter. At the same time, several suicide planes
crashed into the venerable carrier SARATOGA, knocking out old SARA
for three months. Lost were 42 planes, 123 men killed and missing, 192
wounded.

On February 23rd, Admiral Spruance in the INDIANAPOLIS

"EASY RIDING?"
The IRWIN approaches the port side of the BUNKER HILL in a "calm
sea" to deliver mail. Just an example of a destroyer's routine perpetual
motion.
(U.S. Navy Photos - Real War Photos)

joined us, bringing with him three cruisers—the WILKES BARRE (CL-103), PASADENA (CL-65), and the (new) ASTORIA (CL-90). Then, after refueling, the IRWIN hung out our "FPO 794" banner on the wing of the Bridge, and took off at 25 knots to deliver mail to Commander Task Group 58.4 in the (new) YORKTOWN (CV-10), to CTG 58.5 in the good ol' ENTERPRISE, as well as to CTG 58.2 in the (new) LEXINGTON and CTG 58.1 in the (new) HORNET (CV-12). After transferring two officer passengers for delivery to the new 45,000-ton battleship MIS-SOURI (BB-63), which had just now joined the Fleet, and to the BILOXI, we made the rounds of the destroyer screen, dropping off orders for the Fast Carriers' next mission.

After all that running around, we took our regular station in cruising disposition as Admiral Spruance set a fleet course of 015° True—Destination TOKYO!

The weather began to get bothersome during the night and, by 0700 the next morning, there was a pretty good sea running. Squalls brought strong wind gusts and intermittent heavy rains. We were approaching the NEW JERSEY from astern, to top off our fuel tanks for the run to Tokyo, when she signaled "Man Overboard!"

A sailor had been caught topside when the wagon took a sea over her bow which washed him into the water. Our lookouts sighted him and the Skipper maneuvered to pick him up. It was both a tricky and a dangerous operation. At exceptionally slow speed, the IRWIN was wallowing in and out of deep troughs, rolling to excess. Bill Needles, secured by a line held by shipmates, went down the side of the ship and grabbed the hapless sailor. As the rescuee was hoisted aboard, the ship canted heavily to starboard, banging Bill into the hull. But both men were finally safe, and only a little bit worse for wear. It'd taken only ten minutes to effect the rescue.

We then pulled alongside the NEW JERSEY, big new 45,000-ton sister ship of the MISSOURI, and commenced refueling, but the seas were too rough to attempt transferring the sailor back aboard. He'd have to stay on the IRWIN until the weather calmed. Had we not been directly in the battleship's wake, the sailor would have been lost at sea, since we were under strict orders not to stop to rescue those washed over the side. He was at once both a lucky, lucky man *and* a most unfortunate one. He'd hardly been aboard ten minutes before he became violently seasick, and he stayed that way most of the time he was aboard.

If not for us on the IRWIN, the NEW JERSEY sailor would have fulfilled the destiny of the wretched subject of William Cowper's poem

The 45,000-ton NEW JERSEY buries her bow deep into the sea as water
cascades over Number One Turret. The carrier ESSEX is in the
background.
(U.S. Navy Photos—Real War Photos)

The Castaway, who was "washed headlong from on board":

> Of friends, of hope, of all bereft,
> His floating home for ever left.

Our northerly course on 24 February sent us head on into the prevailing winds and seas, and the weather was worsening. The Chinese have a word for it—*tai fung.* English translation—*typhoon.* The huge waves crashing directly into the eyes of the ship, boiling up over 5-inch Mounts 51 and 52, were hammering the ship like a blacksmith beating a horseshoe on an anvil. Admiral Sherman ordered fleet speed reduced from 20 to 18 knots, hoping the destroyers in his force would ride easier.

The younger lads that had come aboard at Hunter's Point were predictably having a tough time. Like the battleship sailor, they were victims of *mal de mer.* Now, the guys who'd been teased by Block and me our first time out had a chance to do the same thing to these green hands. The wind-driven seas crunching into our foc'sle suddenly carried away all the life line stanchions from the bow back to the Bridge structure, tearing holes in the deck through which salt water poured. We backed our speed off to 16 knots on signal from the Flagship, and a repair party went to work plugging the holes.

Admiral Spruance was still intent on making a carrier plane strike on the Japanese homeland and, with all boilers on the line, Task Force 58 made its final approach run towards Tokyo. Even at reduced speed, though, the tin cans were taking one helluva beating. But at 0700 on 25 February, the seas and the winds abated, the carriers turned into the wind, and the first strikes were launched toward the Japanese capital. Flight ops continued throughout the morning, despite the persistent low cloud ceiling. On the IRWIN, we got no direct reports of the raids' results. But even if the bombings did little physical harm, it must have shocked both the citizenry and the Japanese General Staff to see *carrier* planes over Tokyo!

The respite from the foul weather was only temporary. By noon, Admiral Spruance decided we'd better retire from the area, head west-by-southwest and see if the climate was any friendlier for a strike on Nagoya. By 1700, we were making 22 knots and passing through the eye of the typhoon. The seas calmed and the winds subsided.

As we made the passage between Tori Shima and Sumisu Shima, the second half of the typhoon hit us with a vengeance. By 0200 on 26 February, the giant storm was pounding the hell out of us, even more severely than had the initial half. Huge combers, descending on us with the roar of a dozen rogue freight trains and often higher than our masthead when we fell into troughs between them, would crash down

It is the destroyers which take the worst pummeling in typhoons. An ESSEX photographer captures us as we plough into a gigantic wave all the way up to the bridge and the ship almost disappears in a deep trough.

(U.S. Navy Photos - Real War Photos)

upon the ship, burying it in tons of frothing foam and solid water. The next instant, our gallant little vessel would be atop a crest, her screws out of the water, churning open air fruitlessly. She'd yaw, sliding sideways down a mountain sea, rolling almost to her beam ends. Any man aboard not hanging on securely or well-braced would be thrown against the steel bulkheads or an almost vertical deck.

Only those who had essential watches were at their stations. The rest of the crew remained below decks, most of them lashing themselves in their bunks to prevent being buffeted about by the violence of an angry sea. I was in the Radio Shack most of the time. To attempt to reach my bunk, I'd have to travel three quarters the length of the ship on the weather decks and risk being washed over the side. As long as we were on a course heading directly into the winds and the seas, I could go out the aft-facing hatch by the Radio Shack and be in the lee of the superstructure on the 0-1 level. I made a couple of such ventures just to witness and experience for myself how awesome this tempest was. I wanted to see, too, if it might be possible to get back aft to my compartment, but one look and I gave up that idea. I wanted to get out of the tiny confines of the Shack, which seemed to get smaller and smaller as the turbulence continued unabated.

At each onslaught, the ship would tremor, shudder, shiver and shake, straining to keep herself in one piece. It was a time when you hoped the beads run by the Bethlehem Steel welders in San Pedro would hold just once more. Time after time, the tin can took blow after blow from the seas which engulfed her forward, then poured a-roar aft down her decks; boiling over the superstructure, deck house and gun mounts, and exiting in a cascade across the fantail and out through the depth charge racks. One such sea carried away one of our 300-pound depth charges. Fortunately, it was set on "safe" and did not detonate.

The untamed force of storms, thought by the ancient Romans to be the writhings of King Neptune, god of the deep, angry at mere mortals, is a fearful phenomenon that can bring nought but respect for the powers of nature. Nothing man can contrive can come close to equaling the forces unleashed when nature goes on a rampage. Or as Christian poet Dante Gabriel Rossetti put it: "The sea hath no King but God alone."

As I watched the rain, blown horizontally by the 130-knot-per-hour winds, pelt the metal of Number One Stack, making sounds like buckshot hitting a trash can, I thought: "No man can call himself a bluewater sailor until he's experienced the likes of this!"

According to the ancient Greek poet Homer in the *Iliad* (as translated by Alexander Pope):

TYPHOON!
Even the "heavy" ships take a beating in the high winds and
mountainous seas of a Pacific typhoon. The light carrier LANGLEY rolls
hard to starboard as she's buffeted by the 100-plus knot winds. The
NEW JERSEY is in the background.
(U.S. Navy Photos—Real War Photos)

Pale, trembling, tired, the sailors freeze with fears;
And instant death on every wave appears.

The vivid experience of sailors tempest-tossed by violent seas is well expressed in Psalm 107:

"They that go down to the sea in ships, that do business in great waters; These see the works of the Lord, and his wonders in the deep. For he commandeth, and raiseth the stormy wind, which lifteth up the waves thereof. They mount up to the heaven, they go down again to the depths: their soul is melted because of trouble. They reel to and fro, and stagger like a drunken man, and are at their wit's end. Then they cry unto the Lord in their trouble. . . . "

There's a feeling of utter helplessness when your ship is being battered by violent storms. It's not unlike, to some degree, being in a foxhole during a bombing raid. There's not a damned thing you can do about it but wish for it to be over. Failing that, you just want it to let up for a few minutes to give you a respite. And there's the ever present and gripping fear that comes with being in imminent danger of perishing.

No wonder sailors acknowledge the Almighty, and the Book of Common Prayer prescribes the following in view of "the alleged sins of seafaring men":

"O most powerful and glorious Lord God, at whose command the winds blow, and lift up the waves of the sea, and who stillest the rage thereof; We, thy creatures, but miserable sinners, do in this our great distress cry unto thee for help: *Save, Lord, or else we perish.* We confess, when we have been safe, and seen all things quiet about us, we have forgotten thee our God, and refused to hearken to the still voice of thy word, and to obey thy commandments: but now we see how terrible thou art in all thy works of wonder, the great God to be feared above all. . . . *Help, Lord, and save us* for thy mercy's sake in Jesus Christ, thy Son, our Lord. *Amen.*"

By 1000 on February 26th, Admiral Spruance gave into reality. There could be no flight operations in such weather, and the toll on men and ships was heavy. There was scuttlebutt, later, that the Task Force had lost at least one man a day during the operation, washed over the side into the seas. The destroyers in the force had taken a terrible beating. Fortunately, none met the fate of the SPENCE, HULL, and MONAGHAN—all capsized and sunk during the typhoon off the Philippines just two months earlier.

American Admirals were criticized for taking our Task Forces into such heavy weather. But they replied that they would avoid such storms if they had halfway decent weather forecasts. The Admirals had a point.

Our meteorologists in the Pacific weren't known for the accuracy of their predictions.

The foray to the Japanese Home Islands would be known as "The Second Carrier Raid on Tokyo". The first, of course, had been Jimmy Doolittle's 16-plane B-25 assault off the old HORNET in April of 1942. Now the enemy knew that the U.S. Navy was back with full-force deployment, and should have realized the Rising Sun's days were numbered. But it would take more than that to bring the implacable and fanatical foe to his knees.

Army Air Corps B-29 Superfortresses were already bombing Japan from their bases in the Marianas. The eventual capture of Iwo Jima would give us airstrips close enough to Japan for fighter planes to escort the big bombers, and Iwo would also serve as an emergency airfield for damaged planes returning from their raids. A Marine wounded on Iwo said: "I hope to God that we don't have to go on any more of those screwy islands!" A B-29 bomber pilot, who made five emergency landings on the halfway haven between Japan and the Marianas, said: "Whenever I land on this island, I thank God and the men who fought for it."

For the three days that we'd been fighting the *tai fung*—which was worse, we concluded, than battling Jap air raids—those of us in the crew that felt like eating had only sandwiches, and then only during a couple of times the seas abated enough to allow the cooks to make them and get them to the watch stations. The Radio Gang watches had only been able to make java by the half pot; a full pot would have sloshed mud all over the Shack. By the afternoon of the 26th, we were running out of the last vestiges of the storm, bending on 23 knots, and getting a Combat Air Patrol aloft over the Task Force. It was time to chow down with a *real* meal.

The off-watch radiomen informally gathered on the Comm Deck, sniffing with anticipation the cooking odors coming up from the galley. Some of the newer and a couple of the older hands were still a little green around the gills and shaken by the ordeal of the typhoon. Those who'd never experienced a storm at sea were overwhelmed by the violence of it all. As "there are no atheists in foxholes", so there are none, either, when *Neptunus Rex*, alias Mother Nature, unleashes the full fury of winds, rains, and seas.

It was either Karsten or Duflo who wanted to know how close the IRWIN had come to floundering or capsizing.

"A moot question, lad", I ventured. "A couple or more degrees when she rolled the most might have done it. Or just the incessant pounding of the sea could have broken her up if the welds that hold her together gave way. But one thing you can count on. We had the best man in command to get us through it. Cap'n Danny was anticipating every sea, every wind direction change, and every movement of the ship. Under the circumstances, we couldn't have had a better shiphandler to keep 'er in the best positions to avoid disaster. Now I'm hungry. Let's go to chow."

Steaming was back to normal by the morning of 27 February and fleet speed was a brisk 23 knots. We hung out our "FPO 794" sign again, as the Task Group headed for a noon rendezvous with an oiler, delivering mail and photographs to various flat-tops. We went alongside the NEW JERSEY, rigged a breeches buoy between the two vessels, and prepared to return their rescued swab jockey back aboard. As we made the approach, I stood chatting with the battleship sailor. Being on a destroyer, he complained, was like living in a cement mixer.

"I don't know how you guys ride these gawddamned cans day in and day out, month in and month out. Even now, in a calm sea, we're bucking and rolling. When I get back to the JERSEY, I'll tell 'em what it's like to be in the *REAL* Navy!"

"Well", I told him, "you caught us at a bad time. It's not all that bad. But . . . if you'd like to join our *real* Navy, I think it could be arranged."

"Not on your @%#$&@!# tin type, Mac! You couldn't keep me on here with a ball and chain. I'm going back to that wagon where, for all practical purposes, I've got shore duty!"

Perhaps the thought was going through his mind, well put into words by Ralph Waldo Emerson: "The wonder is always new that any sane man can be a sailor."

He climbed into the breeches buoy, gave a big smile, a wave, and shouted to everybody on deck "Thanks for saving my life!" I had a feeling he'd not soon forget the DD-794. The NEW JERSEY's Skipper sent us over some ice cream and thanked Captain Miller over the TBS for taking good care of his crewman. Men along the battleship's life lines waved at us in a salute as we pulled away.

After fueling from the NEOSHO (AO-23), we scurried around the Task Force for the next three and a half hours, delivering more mail. At 1900 on the 27th, the Flagship set a westerly course, speed 19 knots, and we commenced an approach to Okinawa Gunto for air strikes. No rest for the weary. Reaching the Okinawa area, the carriers began launching their squadrons at daylight on 1 March. The forays continued throughout the day, with little opposition from Jap defenders, and we got reports the raid results were "good to excellent". All birds returned safely from their raiding sweeps by 1930.

The next morning, "Desig Dog Seven Nine Four" flew from the Signal Bridge of the ESSEX once more. DesDiv 109 was getting special orders. With the CASSIN YOUNG, CALLAGHAN, and PRESTON, the IRWIN was detached to go look for the crew of a downed B-29 on life rafts somewhere near the small island of Parece Vela. Jap-held, the island was near the flight path of the Superfortresses flying out of Saipan and Tinian to raid Japan. It was on a line between the Marianas and the Ryukyu Islands (e.g. Okinowa) and had strategic importance. The enemy had a radar-detection and radio station there, to give the Home Islands advance warnings of B-29 raids.

In column formation at 25 knots, we made our approach to Parece Vela. At 1100, the morning of March 2nd, the four cans formed a scouting line at intervals of 10,000 yards to search for the air crew's rafts, combing the area until about 1530. An air-sea rescue plane from Saipan aided in the search; and the PRESTON and CALLAGHAN finally located the downed crew, whom the PRESTON picked up. There was an urgency to the operation caused by fears the Japs might send out boats to take the survivors prisoner.

It was 2000 in the evening before we got into position to bombard Parece Vela. The column slowed to ten knots to give our gunnery departments the steadiest platforms from which to fire. The first section, CALLAGHAN and PRESTON, took the right hand targets; the IRWIN and CASSIN YOUNG, those to the left. Our radar singled out the buildings, towers and antennas to be destroyed as we moved in to less than 7,700 yards. On a signal from our Division Commander (ComDesDiv 109) on the CALLAGHAN, all four ships opened fire, continuing the bombardment for some twenty minutes. The IRWIN pumped 150 rounds of 5-inch shells into the complex, destroying all the targets in our sector and setting huge fires that still burned as we departed the area. By 2200, we were speeding away from Parece Vela at 25 knots to rejoin Task Group 58.3. Mission accomplished.

During the operation, we had some equipment failures. The train receiver indicator on Number One 5-inch Mount (51) went out of commission, caused by extensive shipping of water during the typhoon. And the master gyro went "blooey" on us again, oscillating from 10° West of meridian to 25° East.

We no sooner got back to our outfit when we got another assignment as Task Force 58 was being reformed and a new Task Force 59 was temporarily organized. The IRWIN and Destroyer Division 109 joined with Battleship Divisions 7 and 8 for training operations, with the Command (CTF 59) in the SOUTH DAKOTA. For the next three days, we conducted simulated surface battle conditions, including torpedo runs by the DDs and anti-aircraft dispositions during simulated attacks by planes from TF 58. Along with the CALLAGHAN and PRESTON, we operated with BatDiv 8. The exercises were completed by the afternoon of 5 March, and we entered Ulithi's harbor, proceeding to an ammo ship for replenishment and to an oiler for fuel. We were about to get some rest and a chance to do upkeep maintenance.

For the next two weeks, we got a well-earned break, which included the opportunity to send recreation parties ashore on the atoll. There were some departures however from the normal at-anchor routine. On March 7th, ComDesRon 55, in the person of Captain A.E. Jarrell, came aboard to present Captain Daniel B. Miller with the Silver Star Medal from Commander Second Carrier Task Force in recognition of his actions during the PRINCETON rescue and firefighting operation.

Once again, I decided to forego the beach parties, preferring instead to catch up on the "rest" part of "R & R". A couple of times I snagged two bottles of beer and repeated the drill I'd followed before, dousing them with CO-2, pouring the suds in my coffee cup, and parking in solitude on the port side of the 0-1 level. It was then that I read and reread the stack of letters from Jane that had built up while we were bouncing around up Tokyo way.

The NORTH CAROLINA was in port with us, and I bummed a ride on the guard mail whaleboat one day to see if any of my old shipmates were still aboard. Jimmy MacPherson and Phil Phillips came running up to the Quarterdeck when word was passed for them, and we spent the whole afternoon reminiscing about the good old times in Brooklyn. A day or so later, Phil and Mac came over to the IRWIN and I gave them "the Cook's tour". They couldn't get over how small the ship was, how cramped the Radio Shack and how crowded the quarters. Mac said he thought he'd get claustrophobia if he had to serve on a tin can. Phil said he preferred battlewagon duty and wanted no part of destroyers. This would be the last time I'd see Mac. We lost all track of him after 1945; and it would be 46 years before Phil and I would meet again.

The IRWIN spent a day and a half alongside the YOSEMITE for tender upkeep and repair, and then three days 45 miles out on radar picket station. Then we went alongside the ammo ship NITRO to load to capacity. There was another operation in the offing, and we had ammunition stored in every nook and cranny of the ship. A whole batch of operations orders came aboard, and activity around the Ulithi anchorage increased as ships filled their storage spaces with food and their magazines with ammunition. It was obvious to even the greenest hands that "something" was in the wind. That "something" was "Operation ICEBERG". When the quartermasters broke out the charts for the Ryukyu Islands, my guess that our next objective would be Okinawa Jima was confirmed.

Mr. Dean, the Communications Officer, took Chief Leger and me aside to brief us on the upcoming operation. We got all the communications plans and frequency assignments which (I was not too happy to see) included circuits used in communicating with shore parties, i.e. forward fire observers. That meant laying to, close in to the beaches, for shore bombardment. And there were communications setups to be utilized for radar picket duty, Combat Air Patrol fighter direction, and other nice little things that put gray hairs in one's head.

I was told to make out two watch lists: one for three-section watches, and another for "watch on watch". The latter I greeted with some misgivings. Mr. Dean was anticipating long, long hours on duty for the whole Gang. I also made reassignments in General Quarters stations to put the best men in Radio Central and in Emergency Radio during GQ. Chief Leger, of course, did not stand watches; and as leading and senior petty officer, I would handle all day to day operations. As of 20 March, 1945, we had, in addition to Leger and me, two 2nd Class Radiomen, Frisch and Riddle; three 3rd Class, Karl, Alice, and Terrell; and our Seaman 1st strikers Mootz, Hanson, Gregerson, Fitzwater, and Duflo, as well as Seaman 2nd Karsten.

For the ship as a whole, however, we were shorthanded. Our operating allowance called for 309 enlisted men. We had only 297. Through transfers and attrition, many of the men who'd left us were experienced senior petty officers, and nearly all replacements were green hands. And we were two officers short of complement. Why, I wondered, were we deploying for a major combat mission without a full crew? It was understandable in the early days of the War. But by 1945, there were *over three million men* in Navy blue.

The IRWIN and DesRon 55 were assigned to Task Force 54, the Gunfire Support and Covering Force, under the command of Rear Admiral Morton L. Deyo, which was built around nine of the old battleships, screened by cruisers and destroyers. Overall command for the amphibious operation was under Admiral Turner, still in the EL DORADO; who, as Commander of the Joint Expeditionary Force, flew the Flag of Commander Task Force 51 (ComTaskFor 51).

At 0630, 21 March, 1945, we sortied from Ulithi and headed north. Operation ICEBERG was underway.

29
ORDEAL AT OKINAWA

I was just coming down from the Signal Bridge, where Fitch and I had been drinking java and speculating about the upcoming campaign, when Lieutenant Hodapp stopped me.

"Hutch", said the Exec, "since you're now 1st Class and the leading petty officer in your gang, how'd you like to move into Chief's Quarters? There's room up there now that we've lost some C.P.O.'s to transfers."

The Chief's Quarters were in the bow of the ship and it was a little rougher riding up there. But the mattresses on the bunks were about three or four inches thick, the joe pot was always on, and there were rations in the refrigerator at all times. I gratefully accepted the invitation. "R.H.I.P.", I grinned to myself.

Don Karl was petty officer of the watch, with Joe Alice on FOX. Karl had just sent Hansen, his striker, down for water to make a fresh pot of coffee, and I was at the forward position, using the mill to type a letter to Jane.

"What do you think about this invasion, Hutch?" Karl wanted to know.

"Remember that week or so when we were shore bombarding at Saipan? Well, that's what a Gunfire Support and Covering Force does. But this'un'll be a lot tougher. Okinawa is the Japs' front porch and they'd like nothing better than to slam the door on us. I don't see how they can with their Navy all but non-existent and no carriers. They'll still have air capability, though. There are strips on Kyushu, Shikoku, and in the Nansei Shoto Islands, all well within range of Okinawa. They'll put up just as much or more of a fight on land as they did at Iwo and Saipan."

Karl looked at my face. It must have reflected my real thoughts about the upcoming operation.

"What about us, Hutch? Think we'll be in much of it?"

"You know how it is, Don. The battlewagons and cruisers sit miles out, throwing their shells thousands of yards, while the tin cans will be in close, a few hundred yards off the beach, riding the white caps and getting shot at. As usual, we'll end up getting all the dirty little jobs no one else wants to do. That makes us easy targets."

"You're worried about this one." It was a statement, not a question.

"Yeah. I been out here too long. The damned odds keep getting shorter and shorter. But then, I worried about 'em all."

Hansen came in with the joe pot full of water, and I went back to the letter to Jane, trying to think of positive, happy things to write. I also wondered if guardian angels had jurisdiction in the East China Sea.

By the time I'd finished the letter and took it down to have it cleared by an officer-censor, Hansen's java was done perking. I poured a cup and went out on the Comm Deck where some of the off-duty guys were watching the ships in the Task Force.

"What are some of those battleships, Hutch?" Mootz asked.

"Their silhouettes have changed some since I first saw them in ship identification drills in boot camp. They've been modernized since the Pearl Harbor survivors among them got repaired, but I think I know most of them. There's the 'WeeVee', the WEST VIRGINIA; the MARY-LAND, the TENNESSEE, the 'Prune Barge', that's the CALIFORNIA; the MISSISSIPPI, IDAHO, TEXAS, and COLORADO. That's the NEW MEXICO over there off the starboard bow."

Bressie wanted to know how many ships were in the invasion force.

"Damned if I know, Newt", I answered. "We've got nine battleships here, and I haven't counted the cruisers. But there's the INDIANAPO-LIS, flying Admiral Spruance's Com Fifth Fleet Flag. Then we've got the BIRMINGHAM, BILOXI, PORTLAND, LOUISVILLE, and TUS-CALOOSA that I can see just standing here, and there are 22 tin cans in this Task Force alone. West of us are all the Fast Carriers in TF 58 and their screens—plus the transports, AKAs, LSTs, minesweeps, aux-iliaries, and submarines out there someplace."

"Now", I continued, "if you want to know about the landing forces, I only know for sure that the 1st and 6th Marine Divisions will hit the beach, and I think the 2nd MarDiv is in reserve. I did pick up that four Army Divisions are going in—the 7th and 96th, I think, plus a couple more. Seven full divisions would be somewhere around 175,000 men."

They would comprise the Tenth Army commanded by U.S. Army Lieutenant General Simon Bolivar Buckner, Jr.—former Commandant at West Point, son of the Confederate Commander of the same rank and name, fighting for the government his famous father fought so well against more than 80 years before! (One is reminded of the similar parallel of "Light Horse Harry" Lee and his son R.E. Lee, having served as military leaders in the Revolutionary and Civil Wars over 80 years apart.) The Tenth Army would face an estimated 77,000 enemy troops (actually over 100,000, perhaps 110,000) comprising the Jap 32nd Army under General Ushijima. Neither Commander would survive the ordeal at Okinawa.

My experience with the Amphibs was coming in handy in trying to figure out what was going on. I knew, however, ICEBERG was a much more complicated and far-reaching operation than I could grasp, particularly with the limited information I'd been able to scrounge. British observers called it "the most audacious and complex enterprise yet undertaken by the American amphibious forces."

"I guess we're ready", I told the guys. "Boom Boom says we loaded 2,450 rounds of Main Battery ammo, including star shells and white phosphorus, 12,000 rounds of 40-millimeter, and 42,000 rounds of 20-millimeter. He says we couldn't load a single shell more, even if it was only a .22. But, he says, that Number One 5-inch Mount is still a problem. The tender couldn't fix it, so it'll only fire in local control."

The logistics of Operation ICEBERG involved supply lines of over 4,000 miles from Pearl Harbor and 6,200 miles from San Francisco. Apart from some critical ammunition shortages (more of this later) the Navy took pretty good care of us. For example, during one five-week period at Okinawa, the Navy delivered 24,117,599 letters to ships and shore units.

Okinawa Gunto is a group of islands in the Ryuku chain clustered around the main island, Okinawa Jima. The island of Okinawa is about 300 miles south-by-southwest of the lower tip of Kyushu, the southernmost Japanese Home Island. It's about 67 miles long and from two to eighteen miles wide. The terrain ranges from sandy beaches to rugged low mountains, the tallest of which rises to some 1,650 feet. And one more major fact about Okinawa and the Ryuku (pronounced ree-OO-k'yoo) Islands that would figure into our operation: the rainfall totals from 50 to 120 inches a year—much of it arriving in the form of typhoons, of which there can be as many as *forty-five a year!*

The Ryuku island chain stretches almost 800 miles between Japan and Formosa (Taiwan). The Chinese had invaded Okinawa as far back as the 5th century. The island had been under nominal Japanese control since 1609 and was annexed to Japan in 1879. In 1945 Okinawa was grossly underdeveloped and overpopulated. The inhabitants were of ancient Ainu aboriginal descent, Chinese ancestry, and of course Japanese. Okinawans were mostly a mixture of Ainu and Chinese. Historically they were pacifists, Napoleon being flabbergasted when told by British Captain Basil Hall in 1816 that they had no arms. Also ironic, in view of the events of 1945, they were not enthusiastic supporters of their Jap overlords.

On course 327°, force speed 15 knots, Task Force 54, with the IRWIN and PRESTON 12 miles in the van as radar pickets, steamed toward Okinawa Gunto, conducting drills and exercises as we went. It was 21 March, 1945.

At 0750, the (new) O'BRIEN (DD-725) relieved the PRESTON; and at 1009, we were relieved by the CALLAGHAN. During the afternoon, there was a briefing on shore bombardment, including "reverse slope" firing. At sunrise on the 23rd, the IRWIN took "the point" again as radar picket vessel, refueled later from the WEST VIRGINIA, and then delivered mail. At 1900, the HEYWARD L. EDWARDS (DD-663) got a sonar contact and launched a depth-charge attack on an enemy submarine. She and the PRESTON then reattacked, but the Task Force steamed on and we didn't hear if they got the sub. At 0300 on the 24th, the BRYANT (DD-665) got an echo on her sound gear and followed it aft of the formation, staying with it until daylight to keep the Japs' heads down at least. And I was back to sleeping topside, again.

At 0500, 25 March, we made radar contact with Okinawa, distance 31 miles, and began operating south of a small island group called Kerama Retto, some 15 miles from the main island. Operation ICEBERG was warming up. A landing force was sent in to secure Kerama Retto so its harbor could be used as a "rear area" during the campaign. Admiral Turner's plan was that we should have an anchorage, or home away from home, in the operation. This idea was strongly opposed, but the plan was pushed by the hard-driving, sweating, swearing "Kelly"—whose brain could conceive more new ideas and retain more details than any other Flag officer in the Navy (Morison).

The comparatively shallow waters around Okinawa and nearby smaller islands allowed the Japs to sow a plethora of minefields. The minesweepers had moved in early, but the task of clearing all the underwater explosives would take weeks. The first objective was to sweep channels and mark them with buoys. We and the PRESTON got the ticklish job of leading a column of transports through one of these channels in the early morning hours of the 26th; then we were detached to screen Mine Sweeping Unit Two near Ie Shima, a small island off Okinawa's northwest coast.

But tragedy struck one of our destroyers which, unaccountably, steamed through an unswept area on her way to a shore bombardment station. The HALLIGAN (DD-584) was blasted out of the water with such force that she sank almost immediately, taking with her almost half her crew, including the Captain and all her officers but two. Only 176 men survived. The FLETCHER-class DD was the first tin can lost in Operation ICEBERG, meeting her end at 1835, 26 March. She would not be the last.

At 0336 on the morning of the 27th, while in night retirement, the ST. LOUIS (CL-49) alerted us to an enemy plane closing the IRWIN from astern, sneaking in only 80 feet above the surface. The twin-engine Frances crossed our quarter, but our bearing on the target was fouled by the positions of other ships. As the Nip opened out from the formation, he zipped by the PORTERFIELD, clipping the can's SG radar off the top of her mast. The close call cost the DD-682 one wounded man and sent her to the rear area for repairs. She thus became the first unit of DesRon 55 to become a casualty at Okinawa. But there would be more.

We came under air attack again at 0617 when enemy planes struck at us from nearly every point on the compass. We took three under fire, all of which were splashed by ships' fire. We had two in our sights and got "assists" on 'em both as we joined other cans in screening the old battlewagons and repelling the raid. As we lay some six to ten miles off the mouth of the Bisha Gawa River, screening the wagons as they bombarded, we got word the KIMBERLY (DD-521) had been hit by a *kamikaze* off Kerama Retto the preceding morning, losing four killed and 57 wounded. Then, in rapid succession, came news the MURRAY (DD-576) and the new O'BRIEN had taken hits in separate assaults. The MURRAY was torpedoed by a Val, losing one man killed and four wounded. The O'BRIEN took a *kamikaze* on her port side, amidships, which killed 50 of her crewmen and wounded 76. Both ships survived.

KAMIKAZE! The very mention of the word can bring chills of fear to the destroyermen of Okinawa—even today!

The expression has its roots deep in Japanese history. In the 13th century, 1281 to be exact, Chinese Emperor Kublai Khan sent an armada to conquer Japan, but the Chinese fleet was destroyed by a typhoon. The Japs attributed their good fortune to heaven who'd sent "the Divine Wind" or *Kamikaze* to save them. In this War the name was given to a new tactic the enemy conjured up in an effort to save their homeland from an overseas foe once again. A corps of airmen was formed with but one mission—destroy American ships by crashing explosive-laden aircraft into them. *Kamikaze* aircraft were, in essence, guided missiles—missiles steered and aimed by the humans who flew them in suicidal attacks.

There was more than just aircraft in the overall plan. The Japs had developed a short-range rocket they called an "*oka*"; and it, too, was piloted by a human. Transported to the attack area in the belly of a bomber, the *oka* (which we Americans called a "*baka* bomb", *baka* being the Japanese word for "idiot") was launched and aimed by an airman who'd never survive. And Japanese suicide missions in the Okinawa Campaign were not limited to air attacks. The hostiles had suicide boats, suicide midget submarines, suicide swimmers, and suicide troops who would chain themselves to machineguns and artillery pieces so retreat was impossible.

The IRWIN was with Fire Support Unit Four, screening the heavies, as minesweepers scurried between us and the beach to clear the area of mines so we could move in closer for our fire support mission. I was in the Shack when I heard a terrific explosion and rushed out to see what had happened. Less than 5,000 yards from us, one of the sweepers had hit a floating mine and other minesweeps were rushing to her aid. One of our signalmen identified the stricken ship as the SKYLARK (AM-63). She was burning fiercely and within 30 minutes sank beneath the surface. We got no casualty report, but her losses must have been heavy if the size of the explosion were any gauge.

During the night of March 28th and early morning hours of the 29th, our Fire Support Unit of 26 ships retired to sea, but were constantly harassed by enemy aircraft. The IRWIN was on radar picket duty 12 miles from the formation when a bogie came within three miles but opened out as soon as we took him under fire. At 2331, the CASSIN YOUNG made a depth charge attack on a submarine contact. Results unknown. At 0400, another bogie came near enough to take under fire and was splashed by barrages from us and another DD. Give the DD-794 another "assist".

At 0628, we rejoined the Fire Support Unit, then took our station 2,500 yards directly west of the Bisha Gawa River in support of the Underwater Demolition Teams. We laid down barrages of neutralization fire just 300 yards above the low-water mark to keep the Japs from picking off the "frogmen". The UDTs were dropped from their boats to clear the beach approaches of obstacles in preparation for the upcoming amphibious landings. All was completed by 1735, and we took our patrol station three miles west of Point Zampa Misaki.

I came off watch at midnight and was asleep in my topside hammock when I was awakened by the feeling of the ship under me increasing speed rapidly and changing course sharply. I had just hit the deck when the GQ alarm went *BONG-BONG-BONG-BONG!* "Another damn' kamikaze raid", I concluded.

Scrambling to my feet and rounding the corner of the superstructure, I sighted spurts of automatic weapons fire coming from almost abeam on the starboard side; then came the bigger flash of a naval gun.

"Lock and load!" I yelled to guys who'd also been sleeping on deck. "We're under attack! That's *surface* fire!"

The After Three blasted a salvo toward the enemy craft. Then fire came at us from off the starboard bow. "Gawddam! There's more'n one of the bastards!" I yelled to the guys around the Comm Deck.

Our radar had picked up three blips out there in the darkness, interpreted as being of gunboat or patrol craft size. That meant they mounted heavy machineguns similar to our .50-calibers and one or more weapons comparable in caliber to the 3-inch .50s we had on the McCAWLEY. The Skipper had the helmsman spinning the wheel in a deadly game of roulette as he maneuvered us both to keep the gunboats from getting our range and to present as small a target as possible. At the same time, he was swinging the IRWIN to bring all our batteries to bear on the bastards. The hostile craft had spread out so the three of them could come at us from different angles, and they were pressing home their attack. It was the lone lawman against a passel of renegades.

Now all our 5-inch guns joined in, along with the 40-millimeters. One salvo made a direct hit on the first of the gunboats, setting it afire, the blaze continuing for some twenty minutes before its hull sank below the surface. The other two Jap boats continued maneuvering and kept up their fire, but now from longer range. Their automatic weapons bursts were falling short. Some of their 3-inch shells exploded close aboard but caused us neither damage nor casualties.

It was an eerie and frightening feeling, being fired at by an enemy who I knew was there but whom I couldn't see, and the only evidence of his presence were the salvos with which he was trying to kill us. When those muzzle flashes flared, I had no idea where they'd land, how close they might come, or whether they'd hit us. I stood there as I had on the deck of the MAC when the Betty dropped its torpedo. It's strange how hypnotizing something like that can be. But then, when it was over, I *really* got the shakes.

Finally, one of our salvos blasted a second gunboat with a direct hit that must have exploded in its magazines. For a great ball of fire blew high into the sky, and the target completely disappeared from the radar screen in an instant. We'd been playing on a big chessboard with these three yahoos for nearly an hour and a half, our Skipper outmaneuvering them at every turn. Now they'd been checkmated, the third craft taking off through a minefield through which we could not safely follow. The powers that be in the Task Force gave us credit for the sinking of the first gunboat, but only a "probable" for the second. The Old Man and the crew didn't think much of that. If we didn't blow it to Kingdom Come, where did it go?

Anyhow, as far as I've been able to determine, the IRWIN's duel with those three Japanese gunboats was *the final surface to surface naval action of World War II!* Unfortunately, historians have not taken note, and *"the Fighting I"* may never get the place in U.S. Naval lore she earned in the early morning hours of 29 March, 1945.

On orders from the screen commander, we retired to Kerama Retto for logistics, but heavy swells in the anchorage threw us against the LST-277 when we tried to load ammo. We finally gave up, rejoining the Fire Support Unit off the Hagushi beaches for night retirement, without replenishing our ammunition supplies.

D-day minus one (31 March) the BARTON (DD-722) laid down a depth-charge pattern on a submarine contact at 0115. The formation moved to clear. At 0706, we spotted several bomb splashes dead on the bow, but saw no planes. A few minutes later, Admiral Spruance's Flag-ship the heavy cruiser INDIANAPOLIS took a bomb hit. No report to us of damage or casualties, but she did remain operational.

At 0710, we were again ordered to Kerama Retto for logistics and fuel. On the way, we sighted a two-mast Jap lugger (sailing vessel) about four miles out of the harbor. Sank same. Again, we had numerous problems trying to get fuel and ammo due to a heavy running sea. Finally got ammunition but could only pump 15,000 gallons of fuel before ComDesRon 55 ordered us back on patrol. At 1900, while on Patrol Station P-10 off Zampa Misaki Point, we received orders to commence bombardment of Yontan Airfield with interdicting fire at uneven intervals, to expend about 40 rounds an hour to keep the Japs from making any use of the airstrip. In a few hours, the invasion would begin.

Lieutenant Hodapp told me years later that Captain Miller, after considering what our missions in ICEBERG would be, decided it would be best for the safety of the ship and all hands if either the Old Man or the Exec were on the Bridge at all times. They were, in effect, standing "watch and watch". Thus it was, in the early morning hours of 1 April, that Lieutenant Hodapp had the deck and the C.O. was in his sea cabin, just abaft the Bridge. At 0105, we made radar contact with LST groups approaching the assault beaches from the northwest, sortieing for the landings. At 0152, we drove off an attack by a low-flying twin-engine bomber with our after 40mm battery. At 0202, another bogie came within five miles, but turned tail and ran when we opened fire.

Then all was quiet for the next three hours and the Skipper was getting some needed sleep. Battle stations were two-thirds manned which, by now, was routine. I hadn't even bothered to rig my hammock, just spreading a blanket on the Comm Deck. I'd just managed to doze off when automatic weapons fire began bursting all around us. At first I thought we were under attack again. But it was those LSTs who were shooting at an aircraft and weren't too particular which way their guns were aimed. At that moment, Lieutenant Hodapp ordered our batteries into action to fire at a low-flying bomber coming directly at us from dead on the bow. The plane appeared so quickly the Exec hadn't time to sound General Quarters, and the Captain came barreling out of his sea cabin, wondering what in the world was going on.

Our gunners already had the Betty bomber in their sights, pouring round after round into it, scoring several direct hits. The Jap pilot, his craft already doomed, tried to make a sharp bank away from our barrage, but one wing dipped into the water. Splash one Betty! Forty millimeter mounts one (41) and two (42) on either side of the Bridge continued to strafe the fuselage of the plane—still afloat—until, in the darkness, we lost sight of it. Some 35 minutes later, the lookouts sighted a flashing white light in the vicinity of the plane's crash sight and saw several men in the water. We stayed clear until daylight, then moved in to try to pick up any of the bomber's survivors.

Just about the whole crew was topside, watching, as the Skipper maneuvered toward the Jap crewmen. When we approached, they thrashed at the water, swimming away, refusing to be rescued. We got close to one, and the deck hands hooked the flier with a line and grapnel, hauling him aboard. The wet and obviously terrified Jap was manacled to one of the brackets that held emergency four-by-four shoring stored next to Number One Stack just above the galley.

A sentry, armed with a rifle, was posted for two reasons: one, to prevent the prisoner from committing suicide; and two, to keep any crewman from slitting his throat if the opportunity presented itself. In our crew were several survivors off ships sunk earlier in the War, and not a few knew what Japanese soldiers had done to American Marines they'd captured. Without a guard over the prisoner, there was no doubt someone would have had no compunctions about wielding a well-honed blade across the Jap's esophagus.

We had little time to ponder the fate of our captive. Cap'n Danny swung the IRWIN around, heading her toward our "Love Day" (Landing Day), pre-H-hour bombardment station off Black Beach Six, the northernmost of the landing targets. At 0800, H-hour minus 30 minutes, we commenced neutralization fire in our assigned sector, taking out Jap machinegun nests and small troop concentrations, trying to wipe out as many enemy as possible before the Marines had to hit the beach.

At 0830 on April 1, 1945, the first wave of 6th Division Marines, under the protective fire of the IRWIN and the other ships of the Fire Support Unit, stormed ashore at Okinawa Jima. The day was both Easter Sunday and April Fool's Day—a rare occurrence on the calendar.

Throughout Holy Week our ships had pounded the hell out of the landing beaches.

Nearly every type of ship and craft in the Navy's arsenal, some 1,213 in all, was in the assault force: battleships, cruisers, destroyers, destroyer escorts, minesweepers, transports, cargo ships, APDs, LSTs, LCIs, DUKWs, LCSs, LVTs, LCMs. You name it, we had 'em, EXCEPT for one type of craft—Motor Torpedo Boats. The PTs were conspicuously absent. I figured the reason they weren't there—confirmed in Admiral Dyer's history *The Amphibians Came to Conquer*—it was Admiral Turner, himself, who blackballed 'em. According to Dyer, Kelly Turner, and many other officers who had witnessed PT-boat performances in the Solomons, knew the Peter Tares were "anywhere from somewhat to vastly overrated by the public and the press." Turner ruled they not enter the Okinawa area until D-day plus four—if at all. He had no use for them. My old boss was exacting a measure of revenge for the sinking of the McCAWLEY. At least that's the way I saw it.

The Okinawa landings were made under some difficulty due to the weather. Visibility was not the greatest due to low clouds and mist, and the smoke from our ships' guns bombarding the beaches caused further navigational problems. But by 1600, approximately 50,000 troops had been landed against only token resistance from the enemy. This was a pleasant surprise due to what Admiral Spruance called "the unpredictable Jap". In his Pacific War memoir, William Manchester, who was there, called it "the greatest April Fool's Day joke of all time".

Our neutralization fire had been effective, and it was apparent the Japs had other defensive plans in mind that did not include a massive fight at the beaches. As the landing forces formed up, the Marines turned to the left and struck northward up the island. From where they landed, their objective was to secure the northern two thirds of Okinawa. The Army divisions swung southward toward the town of Shuri and what would become known as the "Shuri Barrier".

We stood by in support in case the Marines needed us until 1700, then proceeded to a position some 3,000 yards off the Bisha Gawa River mouth to supply night fire support and to screen the ships in Transport Area. At 1907, enemy planes in force struck from landward, three of them heading toward us. With other ships, we raised a curtain of fire, splashing all three. Give the IRWIN three more in the "assists" column. But another plane had enough control to kamikaze into the WEST VIRGINIA 3,000 yards from us. The damage to her, however, was not enough to put the tough old "WeeVee" out of operation.

As L-day came to a close, we hooked up with a shore party for "call-fire" (they called on us to bombard targets they spotted). This time, the Marines had run into Jap resistance around a warehouse district, where counter-attack was probable during the night. Just to keep the hostiles' heads down, the Marines requested harassment fire of four-gun salvos every 15 minutes in grid #8494Q. Intermittently through the night, numerous enemy planes closed our position. None came within range. But it kept us on alert through the dark hours, and there was no sleep for anyone.

Shortly before noon on April 2nd, we were relieved and spent the rest of the day at Kerama Retto, loading ammunition and refueling. Our Jap P.O.W. was handed over to the Harbor Master for transfer to Army Intelligence. Then we went back again to our screening of the battleships and cruisers. Several bogies approached during the night, just to keep us awake. "Washing Machine Charlie" must have gotten a transfer out of the Solomons.

Out on Radar Picket Station One (RP 1) another DesRon 55 destroyer was having a helluva lot tougher night than we. The PRICHETT was posted about 60 miles north of Point Bolo, her mission to provide early warning of air (kamikaze) attacks and to direct a Combat Air Patrol of night fighters to intercept incoming bandits. At 0100, she went to General Quarters when radar picked up bogies. The first incoming bomber she splashed, but the second dropped a 500-pound bomb that near-missed close enough to blow a section of the DD-561's fantail off, starting fires and seriously flooding her after compartments. For four hours, she continued to beat off another 16 attackers before being relieved and limping to Kerama Retto. In one huge piece of luck, the PRICHETT suffered no casualties.

The Japanese people received news of the invasion of their front porch on 2 April, and April 3rd was Emperor Jimmu Day, commemorating the Emperor who 2,500 years earlier inaugurated the Rising Sun's expansion with the conquest of Yamato. At the same time the giant battleship of the same name was being readied to steam to Okinawa for battle! Japan's military leaders, who had initiated the War in continuation of this historic policy, knew the game was up; but still had to prolong the hostilities for four more bloody months, at the cost of hundreds of thousands of lives, in order to "save face".

As dawn broke on the 3rd, the IRWIN got our fire support assignment from Admiral John L. Hall (ComTaskFor 55) and we took up a position off Point Zampa Misaki. Our spotting party on the beach was Number 833, with whom we'd work often in coming days. Both the ship and the shore unit had charts of Okinawa which were divided in squares—maps gridded like a waffle. Each grid had a number. The shore party would ask us to fire a spotting round in a certain grid and, when we'd complied, would give us instructions on how to adjust our fire to zero in on the targets the Marines wanted us to take out. It was a routine we'd follow hundreds of times during Operation ICEBERG.

This day, a small town in grids #8378H and #8377I was providing cover for Jap troops contesting the advancing Marines. Old Number 833 called for destructive fire on the buildings, and we let loose with white phosphorus (WP) shells, setting the whole town on fire. We then shifted from WP to AA common ammunition and destroyed several machinegun nests inhibiting the gyrenes' advance. Number 833 didn't stop to take a body count; but told us we'd accounted for many, *many* Japs, and said we'd "done good".

Just because we'd done so well, we got a couple of hours off and then got an all-night mission, Number 833 calling the shots. We were to keep four target grids illuminated with star shells in case the enemy decided to counter-attack. When mortar shells began raining down on the Marines, they yelled for help and it was the IRWIN to the rescue. We shifted to AA common ammunition to destroy the mortar emplacements, throwing in effective fire on rifle pits just for good measure. We kept firing for the Marines as an air raid developed, leaving the kamikazes to our night fighters, who shot down at least one of the Japs. The "jarheads" were very appreciative.

We didn't get a chance to go over to Kerama Retto for ammo, replenishing from the LST-615 at Hagushi anchorage; but we did screen the IDAHO, NEW MEXICO, PORTLAND, and TUSCALOOSA while they made the trip. When we returned to Hagushi, we were ordered over to the eastern side of the island to screen minesweepers off Tsugin Jima, a small island at the mouth of Nakagusuku Wan, the large bay on Okinawa's southeast corner. Relieved at 1800, 5 April, we began screening a pair of APDs, the old World War I high-speed destroyers converted to troop transports. The SCRIBNER and the KINZER, along with LCS(L) Unit One and LCI-988, were landing a Fleet Marine Force battalion for reconnaissance and to clear Tsugin Jima of any enemy installations. We maintained station about three miles off the Bay all night and into the afternoon of 6 April.

April 6th, 1945, is a day every tin can sailor at Okinawa will remember 'til the day he dies. The day before, we'd received warnings of imminent heavy air attacks, but the Jap had shown no more aggressiveness than we'd already experienced. Still our gun crews didn't stray too far from their battle stations, and we remained either two-thirds manned or at General Quarters, Condition Easy. That meant we were fully manned but not in imminent danger of attack. But on 6 April Japan's Admiral Toyoda launched Operation Ten-Go, sending some 700 aircraft, of which 355 were kamikazes, against us. It was the destroyers that took the brunt of the attack, suffering the heaviest losses in both ships and men. The Japs had declared open season on destroyermen, and Tokyo Rose predicted not a one of us would survive.

The IRWIN and CALLAGHAN were screening the MARYLAND, heading for night retirement east of Kerama Retto where we were least likely to be set upon by kamikazes. At 1611 on the 6th, our lookouts sighted two Vals attacking a destroyer escort—the WITTER (DE-636). I was just coming forward on top of the deck house when the Skipper put the ship into high gear and turned sharply to port just as our 5-inch battery opened up to starboard. The old empty knot in the stomach, weakness in the knees, and no breath in the lungs came on with a rush. I looked to see our AA shells right on one of the Japs about 9,000 yards out. Two more rounds tore into the hostile, sending him a-flaming.

But that damned slant-eyed son of a bitch was bent on taking somebody with him and that somebody was the WITTER. Crossing over the DE about 1,000 feet as we continued to throw lead into him, he made an almost vertical dive into the ship, exploding against her starboard side amidships. The IRWIN had scratched another "flaming asshole", but the swap was hardly an even one. The WITTER, badly damaged, was later scrapped. Six of her men were killed, and six wounded. Val number two was knocked down by fire from the CALLAGHAN and MARYLAND. The mauled WITTER, limped toward Kerama Retto, fighting fires aboard as she went. To those of us who watched her and so many other ships take casualties, it was always a time of great sadness, and for thanks as well—"for there, but for the Grace of God, go we."

As usual, however, there were more pressing concerns. Bogies were still on the radar, and we had the MARYLAND to protect. We hurried eastward, hoping we'd be out of kamikaze territory. Suicide missions were now an integral part of Jap strategy and tactics. As one Jap apologist put it, land-based suicide planes were necessary since "it was no longer possible to challenge the enemy in an ordinary naval engagement."

At about the same time we were taking out the Val, two destroyers out on Radar Picket Station One, 120 miles to the north of us, were catching unrelenting hell. The BUSH (DD-529) and the COLHOUN (DD-801) were under vicious, constant assault by wave after wave of the *Kamikaze*. When they came in like that, the flights were called *kikusui* (Japanese for "floating chrysanthemums"). In all, there were ten *kikusui* at Okinawa between 6 May and 22 June.

The BUSH got it first. She'd been fighting kamikazes off and on all

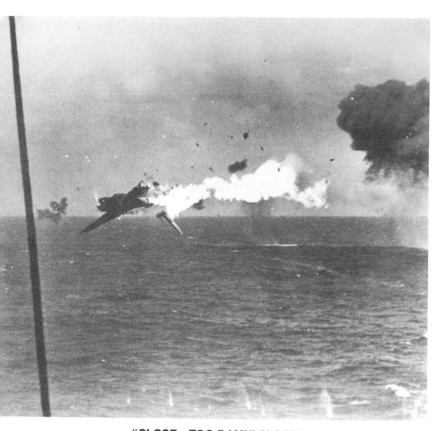

"CLOSE—TOO DAMN' CLOSE"
Anti-aircraft fire takes out one of dozens of kamikazes (kikusui) in an attack on the Task Force, splashing another "meatball" (the identifying red circle [ball] on Japanese aircraft) before it can crash into the ship.

(U.S. Navy Photo - National Archives)

day. Her luck ran out about 1600 when a lone suicide plane, coming right in on the white caps, slammed between her stacks. The bomb the Jap was carrying then exploded in the forward engine room, and fires raged all the way from the Bridge to the after end of the deck house. For a while, damage control efforts kept the can afloat. Rushing to help her was the COLHOUN, moving over from her own picket station.

But the Japs weren't letting up and, at 1700, another flight of 15 "floating chrysanthemums" roared against the two destroyers. One of them hit the COLHOUN amidships, and she went up in flames. Both crews battled valiantly to save their vessels, but to no avail. At 1830, the BUSH broke up and sank, taking with her the bodies of 94 good destroyermen, among them seven officers including the Destroyer Squadron Commander. Of her survivors, 42 were wounded. The COLHOUN held out longer; but by 2300 she was abandoned, leaving behind 35 men dead. The CASSIN YOUNG, arriving too late to assist, sank her with gunfire. Between the BUSH and COLHOUN, they'd accounted for a least eight of the attacking Jap aircraft. There were just too damn' many slant-eyes to get them all.

It wasn't just the picket station tin cans that became victims of Operation Ten-Go. The gunfire and support ships were getting it, too. The EMMONS (DD-457) was hit by five kamikazes and went down, losing 64 dead and 71 wounded. The NEWCOMB (DD-586) was hit by three kamikazes; the LEUTZE (DD-481), coming to her aid, took a hostile plane in the fantail. The HOWORTH (DD-592), HYMAN (DD-732), RODMAN (DD-456), MORRIS (DD-417), MULLANEY (DD-528), HAYNESWORTH, (DD-700), FIEBERLING (DE-640), and the DEFENSE, a minesweeper—all were victims of Operation Ten-Go. So were the LST-447 and two cargo vessels, the HOBBS VICTORY and LOGAN VICTORY. The LEUTZE, MORRIS, NEWCOMB, and WITTER all were so heavily damaged they had to be scuttled. Repairs to the MULLANEY, RODMAN, and DEFENSE were not completed before War's end.

The casualty report for 6 April, 1945, listed 367 destroyer sailors killed in action and 408 wounded. It's a day that should be remembered by the United States Navy, one Americans should never forget.

Jap losses were staggering as well. All 355 kamikaze planes went down, and some 340 conventional bombers and other aircraft were destroyed.

And April had hardly begun.

30

THE CRUELEST MONTH

On the morning of 7 April, 1945, the IRWIN and TWIGGS (DD-591) were screening the TUSCALOOSA in Fire Support Area Three off Nagagusuku Wan. At 1300, we received urgent orders to join Task Force 54 off Hagushi on the other side of Okinawa. We proceeded, joined by the SAN FRANCISCO and CALLAGHAN.

I wondered what was up and why we'd broken off a fire support mission so fast. I was in the passageway outside the Radio Shack and chart storage, when the Navigator came down from the Bridge.

"What's going on, Mr. Lanoue?" I asked.

He hesitated, then said: "Confidential, so keep it under your hat for now. The YAMATO and a Jap task force has cleared the Bungo Straits and is loose in the China Sea. We're going after her."

The YAMATO! I searched my mind for what I knew about the massive Japanese battleship. Fully loaded, she displaced nearly 73,000 tons, making her the largest ship in the world. Packing nine 18.1-inch rifles in her main battery, she also mounted some 150 anti-aircraft weapons, including 6.1-inch mounts. She was reputed to be equipped with radar, and had a rated speed of 27.5 knots. Against any surface units we had, the YAMATO outgunned them by a wide margin.

"Remember, Hutchinson, keep it quiet."

"Aye, aye, Sir."

I must have looked a little disturbed when I stepped back into the Shack. Frisch asked, "What's the matter, Hutch?"

"Must've been that sandwich I had about an hour ago", I answered.

I poured a cup of joe and went out on deck to mull over the startling word from Mr. Lanoue. By that time, we'd reported in to Admiral Deyo (ComTaskFor 54) and were awaiting orders. In the next few hours one of the strangest stories of World War II would unfold. In its aftermath, I would eventually get enough dope to piece together the chain of events. In the meantime, I was exceedingly apprehensive, foreseeing the IRWIN going up against the YAMATO in a David and Goliath confrontation.

The big Jap battleship had gotten underway from Tokuyama on the

Inland Sea with a light cruiser, the YAHAGI, and eight destroyers. As she made her way past Bungo Suido (Bungo Strait) reconnaissance submarines, the THREADFIN and HACKLEBACK, reported her movements to Admiral Spruance. Rounding Van Dieman Strait, the YAMATO task force, under command of Vice Admiral Ito, turned almost due west, attempting to disguise her true course. She was spotted on that leg by a search plane from the ESSEX. Thus began the "ultimate kamikaze mission".

The YAMATO had only enough fuel for a one-way trip to Okinawa, only five days' rations for her crew; but her magazines were crammed to the limit with over 1,000 rounds of ammunition for her main battery, alone. Here was a suicide mission to end all suicide missions. She hoped to get to Okinawa, destroy our shipping in concert with kamikaze air attacks and, it was thought, beach herself to become a stationary fortress from which her heavy guns would supply superior artillery support for General Ushijima's ground forces. A desperate plan on the part of the Japs.

Admiral Mitscher's Task Force 58 was given the go-ahead by Admiral Spruance to "take them". But what if YAMATO's force did make it through and/or bad weather prohibited flight operations and the carriers could not launch an air attack? The always shrewd battle tactician Spruance had a back-up plan. And the IRWIN was part of it. At 1610, 7 April, we approached our disposition with six old battlewagons of BatDiv 3 (NEW MEXICO, COLORADO, and MARYLAND) and BatDiv 4 (TENNESSEE, WEST VIRGINIA, and IDAHO) at the center of the Battle Line. The light forces, destroyers and cruisers, were disposed 70 degrees right and left of the axis at 4,000 to 5,000 yards. Our station was Section One with the LAFFEY, PORTERFIELD, PRESTON, and BARTON (ComDesRon 60). The IRWIN took the point as lead destroyer on the right flank as we maneuvered until 1845, and then settled down for night cruising in approach disposition on course 270° to intercept the YAMATO.

I looked out at those older battlewagons, each and every one of them definitely inferior in speed, fire power, and main battery range to the Jap battleship. Knowing our mission, I pictured them not as great dreadnoughts going into battle, but six very reluctant dragons going out to meet a modern well-armed bully. The YAMATO's main battery outranged the rifles on our ships by more than 8,000 yards. She was faster, more maneuverable; and she could sit out of our range, picking off BatDivs 3 and 4 one ship at a time. Contemplating a head-to-head engagement and assuming our tactics would be classic battle line operations, I really got scared. Maybe it was because, in this instance,

I had plenty of time to think of the probabilities. If Admiral Deyo was planning a standard attack on the YAMATO, the destroyers would be going in first, making torpedo runs on the hostiles. Since the IRWIN was first in the screen formation, we'd obviously be leading the pack.

"Oh! My God!" I thought. "If that Jap opens up on us with those 18-inchers, there'll be nothing left of us but a grease spot! Even her 6.1-inch secondary battery outranges our 5-inch! Plus that, there's at least one cruiser and a bunch of destroyers we'd have to worry about. They'll be after us, too." I was sweating bullets, again. Perspiration stood out on my brow.

Suddenly, I was brought out of my thoughts with a jolt; 40-millimeter and 5-inch guns were throwing up a barrage almost directly astern of us. Tracers were arching into the dusk as two kamikazes dived toward the last battleship in the line. We were too far away to take them under fire. But our "tail-end Charlie" in the formation, the MARYLAND, got one of the suiciders before the second crashed into her Number Three Turret with a terrific explosion and blast that lit up the skies.

Unknown to me at the time, my old NORTH CAROLINA shipmate, Red Campbell, was aboard the MARYLAND. Red told me later the carnage was terrible; the explosive charge carried by the kamikaze blasted through the heavy armor atop the turret, killing men inside; 20-millimeter gunners and crewmen topside were blasted into pieces. It was, he said, an awful sight. He hadn't realized how much damage one enemy plane could cause. The blast blew a hole in the 15-inch armored steel turret top, and fires broke out. There were 53 casualties: ten men confirmed dead, six missing and presumed killed, and 37 wounded. The missing were blown over the side and, despite search efforts by destroyers, were never recovered. In notes taken at the time, Red says: "It [the kamikaze] circled our formation. As it completed orbiting, it started a suicide dive on us. We put up a terrific barrage but he came through it and hit our #3 turret. Men and guns were blown to bits."

More bogies were still being picked up on radar, so the destroyer screen assumed an anti-aircraft disposition as Task Force 54 steamed on, the IRWIN still in the lead position in the formation. At 2000, we received word the YAMATO and her escorts had been destroyed by carrier aircraft of Task Force 58. What we didn't know until the next day, was that had all taken place *before* Task Force 54 sortied to go after the Jap battleship. Be that as it may, there was one tin can sailor who breathed great sighs of relief, and figured guardian angels are pretty good at keeping watch, no matter what nor where.

The YAMATO, the reports said, had been a tough target to take out, even for the experienced fliers of TF 58. She had no air cover to protect

U.S.S. MARYLAND KAMIKAZED
The venerable old battleship is crashed by a suicider which blasted into
Number Three Turret. Sixteen men killed, 37 wounded.
(U.S. Navy Photo - Real War Photos)

her when the first of our planes launched the initial strike about 1230. In all, somewhere between 280 and 300 of our fighters, bombers, and torpedo planes would make runs on her in wave after wave. Her AA batteries just couldn't cope with such concentrated attacks. Besides, her gunners, having spent so much inactive time in port, weren't the most accurate. Torpedoes pierced her armored hull; bombs took out her guns, one by one, until her weather decks, superstructure, and batteries were torn to shreds. For almost two hours, she battled to survive until, in the end, torpedo damage overwhelmed her watertight integrity. At 1423, with the Rising Sun imperial battle flag still flying, she rolled over and plunged beneath the sea that would be the everlasting resting place for almost all the 2,767 men who manned her. Only 269 Jap sailors survived the sinking of the super battleship.

The Task Force 58 attackers didn't spare the YAMATO's escorts, either. The light cruiser YAHAGI went down under twelve bomb and seven torpedo hits. All eight destroyers came under the blistering strikes. Only four survived to make it back to Sasebo, their home port, and they were badly damaged. The last gasp war sortie of the Imperial Japanese Navy, once conceited in its control of the seas in all the Western Pacific, ended in disaster, while American losses were only twelve airmen and ten aircraft. As American naval historian Morison commented, when the biggest battleship ever built went down, five centuries of naval warfare went with her.

While we were out after the YAMATO, the kamikazes were still taking a toll among the tin cans around Okinawa Gunto. For instance, on April 7th, the BENNETT (DD-473) was badly damaged; losing three dead, 18 wounded. The same day, the DE-184, the WESSON, was hit; eight dead, 25 wounded. But both cans made it back to Kerama Retto.

Ashore, the Okinawa Campaign during the first week had been moving according to plan. In fact, the Marines were ahead of schedule. They'd taken abandoned Yontan Airfield (with bombardment support from the IRWIN) before noon on the first day, and Army troopers captured the Kadena airstrip shortly thereafter. By April 3rd, the Army lines stretched all the way from the west to the east coasts; the same day, 6th Division Marines were seven days early in occupying the Ishikawa Isthmus. I took special interest in the 6th MarDiv. The core of the Division (commanded at Okinawa by Major General Lemuel C. Shepherd, Jr.) were the 1st, 2nd, 3rd, and 4th Raider Battalion veterans of the Solomons Campaign. Some of the shore spotting parties with which the IRWIN worked on gunfire support missions were gyrenes from those battalions. It was like old home week.

We resumed shore bombardment missions on April 9th, getting

kudos from our shore party for our accuracy in taking out enemy artillery batteries and splattering Japs all over the place. A "Red Alert" sounded at 1900, and we joined with ships in the force to repel the kamikaze attack. During the night we got word that the GREGORY (DD-802) got it during a suicide plane attack on the 8th. Three more tin cans would become casualties on this date. The STERETT (DD-407), veteran of Guadalcanal, was kamikazed by two Vals; the HOPPING (DE-155) took a hit from a shore battery; and the CHARLES J. BADGER (DD-657) was the target of a high-speed suicide boat that came roaring out of the pre-dawn darkness to drop a depth charge right next to her hull. The underwater explosion ruptured the can's thin skin and caused so much damage the ship was out of action for the rest of the War. It happened so quickly not a shot was fired at the Jap. But no one was hurt.

For the next two days and nights, it was what would become an exhausting routine. Load ammunition all day; fire at artillery, machinegun, and rifle pit emplacements all night. April 12th brought a change in the grind. We'd begun our fire support missions at 1245 on the 11th and were still at it at 1153 the next day. At 1300, we closed the BISCAYNE to pick up mail, when we received emergency orders to rejoin Task Force 54. A major enemy air assault was on the way. We took Station Eight in the screen around the battleships and cruisers in anti-aircraft disposition. AT 1450, the suiciders struck the northern sector of TF 54, away from us. Several were shot down, but two made direct hits. One crashed the ZELLARS, killing 29 men, wounding 37, and putting her out of the War for the duration. The other dived into our Flagship the TENNESSEE—25 men dead, 104 wounded (33 horribly burned)—apparently trying to get Task Force C.O. Admiral Deyo and his guest aboard, U.S. Navy historian Morison.

The kamikazes kept the pressure on. AT 1547, a Jill, flying at only fifty feet above the white caps, came at us directly on the starboard beam. One of our 5-inch projectiles made a direct hit; but the Jap, flaming, kept coming at us! I was sure he'd crash the ship. Our 40s were pouring rounds into him. The Captain cranked up flank speed (to 320 revolutions in just one minute) to avoid being hit by the Jill. That worked, and the suicider went in the water, just yards away and only seconds from hitting us. The IRWIN had another Jap flag to paint on the scoreboard. Bogies continued to be on our radar the rest of the night. Two came in at us and we opened fire at seven miles as flares were dropping all over the Task Force. Apparently it was a torpedo attack. Too dark to see, but none hit a target. We felt several explosions which we took to be fish exploding at the end of their runs. The bandits opened out rapidly.

We had escaped a kamikaze hit. But not so lucky were other DDs and DEs, including our sister ship the CASSIN YOUNG which, along with the PURDY (DD-734), manned Radar Picket Station One, 51 miles due north of Point Bolo. If you remember, the Japs called their mass suicide attacks "*kikusui*" ("floating chrysanthemums"). The CASSIN YOUNG fought off several waves of *kikusui* until, finally, one Val, strafing as it came in, hit the foremast. Its bomb exploded about 40 feet above the Bridge superstructure, debris and shrapnel spraying every which way, causing damage and casualties. Knocked out was the radar, making her useless on a picket station. She headed for Kerama Retto (and later to Ulithi) for repairs—counting one man dead, 59 injured. The PURDY, left behind on her own, then became a victim a few hours later. Crashed by a kamikaze, she lost 13 dead and 27 wounded, and was severely damaged.

The new MANNERT L. ABELE (DD-733) had the dubious honor of being the first ship sunk by a "*baka* bomb". On Radar Picket Station Three, she was first hit by a pair of suiciders. Then, released from the belly of a bomber, in came the *oka*. Guided by its pilot, it went straight into the forward engine room, detonating with an unholy blast. The ABELE went down in just three minutes, taking with her 79 men. Of the survivors, 35 were wounded.

On April 12th, 236 tin can sailors died; 284 more were wounded. The next day (12 April in the U.S.A.) we lost our Commander in Chief. President Franklin Delano Roosevelt died at the Winter White House in Warm Springs, Georgia, of a cerebral hemorrhage. When the Armed Services issued the daily casualty list, his name was at the top. The word spread throughout the ship in a matter of minutes and was met with great sadness. Although I was no supporter of FDR, disagreed with most of his domestic policies, and held him at least partly to blame for Pearl Harbor, I still felt a sense of loss. He had been President of the United States over half of my life.

As I twirled a stencil into the Emergency Radio mill to copy the press news that afternoon, more than the usual number of curious shipmates gathered around the door in the midships passageway. They were eager for details of the President's death and how it was being received back home. It was the longest story I ever remember copying from Mackay Radio, filled with tales of grief expressed by nearly every U.S. Government official and the leaders of our Allies. All America was saddened and the mood of the sailors beside me was somber. Many had tears in their eyes.

When the name "Harry S Truman" appeared in the text, I began wondering what changes the Vice President, now President, might make to affect the conduct of the War. Truman was, I knew, a "political pro", product of the infamous Pendergast Machine in Kansas City. A former haberdashery salesman who had served as a Captain of Artillery in the First World War, he had struck me as a strutting peacock with no class. But the *President* Truman would, in a matter of less than four months, take an action that would save my life. In the meantime, we had a War to fight, and the IRWIN was underway to a pre-invasion bombardment for another amphibious landing.

On 13 April, we went up to Ie Shima (where famed war correspondent Ernie Pyle was killed by machinegun fire a few days later) with other vessels to support a recon mission by our Underwater Demolition Teams, and to do a little softening-up bombardment against Jap fortifications. Low on ammunition, we returned to Transport Area off Hagushi and reloaded our magazines from an LST, then joined the retirement group for the night. Chief Leger put in one of his appearances on the Comm Deck and we talked about the beating the tin cans were taking in this campaign. Already three DesRon 55 destroyers had felt the hot breath of the "Divine Wind". Would we be next?

Bogies on the radar during the night and early morning watch disturbed any rest, and I was fully awake as we returned to Ie Shima. The frogmen were going back in to destroy the underwater obstacles they'd reconnoitered the previous day, all in preparation for a landing by the Army's 77th Division. The IRWIN took up station on the south coast of the small island some 2,500 yards due south of Ie Shima Peak, and began troop neutralization and destructive shore bombardment. The UDT teams hit the beach at 0900; and when they came under fire, we countered by destroying two pill boxes and spraying the landscape with 40-millimeter fire. We expended 286 rounds of 5-inch and 334 rounds by the 40s. At 1100, we pulled back to screen the TEXAS (BB-35) and the BIRMINGHAM while they pounded the enemy with heavier caliber salvos.

At 1730, the Task Force formed to sea for night retirement. It was then we heard the SIGSBEE (DD-502), commanded by G.P. Chung-Hoon, had taken a kamikaze in the fantail, putting her out of action—four men killed, 74 injured.

The Ides of April opened with us in Kerama Retto, refueling from the oiler MONONGAHELA; and loading ammo from the LST-735, an all-day, all-hands evolution. No fire missions that night. We were hitting Ie Shima the next morning. At 0630 on the 16th, we were on station, and commenced neutralization fire on Japanese troops at 0725 to clear the beaches and surrounding areas, firing at pre-arranged targets. The first wave of 77th Division GIs hit the beach at 0800 on the nose. We'd been getting numerous reports of enemy aircraft in the vicinity, but our radar was partially landlocked and we had no contacts. At 0947, our lookouts sighted a plane seven miles out, heading directly toward us at about 150 knots.

I had been watching the shore bombardment from the Comm Deck, but was unaware of the approaching bandit until Cap'n Danny began evasive maneuvers and the Main Battery opened fire. I jumped about three feet straight up at the first salvo, then sighted the kamikaze, which by now had machinegun fire spitting from its weapons. Several of our 5-inch bursts hit right on target at about 3,200 yards. Chalk up another meatball for the IRWIN. The Kate went down in flames, ending its attempt to suicide into us. I was beginning to get the feeling guardian angels *did* work in the East China Sea. I let out the air I'd been holding in my lungs since the first salvo as an involuntary shiver raised goose bumps all over me.

For the first time, there was no big celebration by the crew as had always happened before when we shot down one of the enemy's planes. There were a few shouts; but as we returned to our more mundane task of fire support, the men were quiet. I looked at my shipmates. Their faces were tired and drawn. Shoulders slumped down. Eyes were a bit dull. The fire-support missions, constant danger of air attack, frequent General Quarters, steady steaming, long watches, plus still carrying out normal shipboard duties—it all was wearing them down, bit by bit.

At 1600, the heavy ships departed, leaving the IRWIN and HALL, along with some landing craft, to remain in support of the troops. We got call-fire requests and spent most of the night illuminating target areas with star shells. It was when the BILOXI joined us the next morning that we learned 16 April had been another one of those days for the destroyers of Okinawa.

The PRINGLE (DD-477), attacked by three suicide planes, fought off two; but the third, loaded with a thousand pounds of explosives, careened into her just abaft Number One Stack, breaking her back. She went down in five minutes, losing 65 men. Among the survivors, 110 were wounded. The BRYANT, LAFFEY, HARDING (DD-625), HOBSON (DD-464), and BOWERS (DE-639) were all kamikaze victims, all except the HOBSON with heavy casualties. The HARDING was scuttled. The others survived, but were not repaired until the fighting was over. To add to the carnage, the INTREPID (CV-11), out with Task Force 58, took a kamikaze. The ESSEX-class carrier was badly damaged. There were some 204 destroyermen killed and 289 wounded on 16 April, 1945.

My dear Admiral:

As I see our American Flag flying on the pinnacle fortress on Ie Shima, I take great pleasure in passing on to you and to members of your command this 77th Infantry Division GI remark as a commendation:

"General that Navy fire was great and the air bombing sure gave the Jap bastards hell. It was a grand feeling to land and strike the Jap rats with that support."

I can add nothing better to the statement of the tough guy who advances under your support.

Sincerly,

A. D. BRUCE
Major General, U.S. Army
Commanding

- -

1st Endorsement on   COMMANDER AMPHIBIOUS GROUP FOUR
CG, 77th Inf. Div. ltr   UNITED STATES PACIFIC LEET
dated 21 April 1945

                                              22 April 1945

To :   All Hands, Fire Support Ships and Support Craft, IE SHIMA
          Attack Group.

Subject: Commendation - Forwarding of.

    1.   I take pleasure in passing this commendation on to the gunfire support ships and aircraft which made the "GI" of the 77th Infantry Division feel so grand.

                         L. F. REIFSNIDER,
                         Rear Admiral, USN,
                    Commander IE SHIMA Attack Group

Distribution:
    ComCruDiv 13   ISHERWOOD
    TEXAS   ROOKS
    WEST VIRGINIA   BILOXI
    TUSCALOOSA   LONGSHAW
    BERMINGHAM   LAWS
    MOBILE   LITTLE
    PORTLAND
    PORTERFIELD
    HALL
    IRWIN
    PRESTON
    TWIGGS
    H.L. EDWARDS

We got word there was a Jap task force north of us and formed up to intercept. We were the lead destroyer on the port flank with the LAWS, LONGSHAW, PRESTON, and HALL in our wake. With us were the BIRMINGHAM and ST. LOUIS. ComTaskForce 54 (Admiral Deyo) was in the TENNESSEE, leading the Battle Line of the WEST VIR-GINIA and NEW MEXICO. We operated for the night about ten miles north of Ie Shima, but the enemy force never materialized. It was a false alarm, although we had bogies on our scopes all night.

At 0600 on the 17th, we were released by CTF 54 and proceeded to Kerama Retto for fuel and ammo replenishment. The IRWIN picked up mail from the TENNESSEE, then relieved the LAWS on a fire support station three miles east of Hedo Saki on Okinawa. Rounding the north-ern tip of the island, we suddenly lost all communications. Every radio circuit, except the NPM FOX skeds, developed excessive interference. We never did find out what caused *that.* Now we'd also developed an engineering problem. The guardian bonnet valves were leaking exces-sively and getting worse—probably caused by gunfire vibration while we were laying to on fire support missions. We anchored off Hagushi to effect the repairs.

On April 21st, it was back to shore bombardment again, this time in Fire Support Sector Five; where we conducted harassment fire, with spot by the SAN FRANCISCO's OS2U Kingfisher recon plane. For three solid days (21–23 April), we threw shells into enemy targets almost without a pause, utilizing both aircraft spotting and shore party direc-tion. The forward observers of the shore parties reported "heavy casu-alties" among the enemy troops in the IRWIN's target areas, and we got a "well done" from 'em. Meanwhile, enemy planes were almost con-stantly in our area, but none came near enough to take under fire. Less fortunate was the ISHERWOOD (DD-520) struck by a kamikaze with losses of 43 men killed, 41 wounded, while she was on anti-submarine patrol.

Late on the afternoon of the 23rd, we rejoined Task Force 54 as part of the screen. At 0300 the next morning, the new BARTON reported a sonar contact and we went to investigate. We picked up a submarine, including screw noises, on our underwater "ears"—range 1,400 yards—but for an hour and 45 minutes, kept losing, then regaining the contact. When we finally got pings at only 300 yards, we closed and lay down an eleven charge, medium deep, pattern. The depth charges ex-ploded with huge geysers of water astern. Not long after, a heavy oil slick spread across the surface. Following our report, ComDesRon 55 credited us with sinking a midget sub, one of the suicide variety.

At 0705 on the 24th, we left TF 54 for logistics at Kerama Retto. On the way, we got the word the IRWIN was being reassigned to radar picket duty. The Task Force was running low on tin cans. As Admiral Ainsworth, Commander Destroyers Pacific Fleet, once observed (in his Introduction to Theodore Roscoe, *United States Destroyer Operations in World War II*): "When at grips with the enemy on the sea, under the sea, or in the air, no Task Force Commander ever had enough destroyers."

When we went alongside the MOUNT McKINLEY (AGC-7) to pick up a fighter-director team of two officers and three enlisted men, we also said "Farewell and Godspeed" to Lieutenant John Dale Pye Hodapp, Jr., our Executive Officer. He was being transferred off the IRWIN to eventual command of the HALL. He and Captain Miller had been a good team under which to serve, and his loss as a combat-experienced officer would certainly be felt. The Skipper moved Lieutenant "Jumbo" Clark up from his Chief Engineer post to replace Mr. Hodapp as Exec. Mr. Clark was one of those four officers the Old Man had personally selected to serve with him on the ship.

As the IRWIN was refueled, provisioned, and received more anti-aircraft ammunition in place of shore bombardment ammo, there wasn't a man aboard who didn't feel apprehension at our new assignment. The crew was pretty nervous about the mission and it showed in the faces of us all.

At 2330, 26 April, the IRWIN arrived on Radar Picket Station Fourteen, 72 miles north-northwest of Point Bolo—the RP station closest to the Japanese home island of Kyushu, and the outpost most likely to be the first target of incoming *kikusui* raids. It's where the PRINGLE went down in just five minutes after being hit by kamikazes. She'd lost 65 men only ten days earlier. Relieving the WICKES, we joined the BACHE (DD-470), LSM-196, LCS-62, and LCS-64 on patrol, steaming in column and changing course every half hour. The landing craft had come to be called "the Pallbearers", since their primary purpose was to rescue the survivors of the picket-duty destroyers sunk by the kamikazes. *That* will do a lot for your morale!

It didn't take long for a Nip to put in an appearance. AT 0315 on the 27th a bogey was on the radar scope at 27 miles. When the bandit got within 8,000 yards, we opened fire with the Main Battery. The first two rounds were very close, and the Jap immediately reversed his course, ducking our fire as he rapidly retreated. He maybe was just a scout, checking us out. No more Japs came in, much to our relief. The weather was kicking up with a "number four sea" running, winds gusting at 25 to 30 knots, and the ceiling down under 5,000 feet. It was not good flying weather; and maybe it was worse over Kyushu, keeping the kamikazes grounded. Nevertheless, our Combat Air Patrol, with two fighter divisions and two picket planes, were up over us all day. So we felt a little more secure.

Then, an unforeseen danger cropped up. At about 1500 in the afternoon, our Main Battery Director went completely out of service. Apparently the cable which transmitted data from the Director to the gun mounts failed, leaving us with no automatic radar control of the 5-inch Main Battery. This was one helluva time for *that* to happen. It was fingernail-biting time. The fire controlmen worked feverishly to make repairs, finally managing a jury-rig, but it held for only short periods. In the event of an attack, we were in serious jeopardy.

The weather moderated by midnight and, at 0035 the next morning, two bogies were picked up on our search radar, orbiting 16 miles away and slowly closing. Shortly, three more popped up on the scope. At every battle station, the men took deep breaths and cinched up their courage a couple more notches. When the bombers got within 6,000 yards, we opened fire with the Main Battery in local control. By using the search radar to get range, altitude, speed, and course, then relaying the data to the gun mounts by sound-powered telephone circuits, the gunners could get an approximate solution on the targets. The fire was effective. The enemy planes skirted wide of us, across the stern, heading south toward Okinawa, dropping "window" (aluminum foil to confuse our radar) as they went. We notified the Transport Area of incoming bandits.

At 0330, two more formations appeared on the SC radar screen: one coming in on course 175°, range 12 miles; the other, on course 158° at 9 miles. We split the Main Battery; the Forward Two taking one contact, the After Three the other. Our bursts lit up the sky, already brightened by a brilliant full "bombers' moon". All but one of the hostiles changed course and opened out the range. That one took a hit from our After Three, a proximity fuse round that burst close aboard him. Clearly visible in the night sky, the Betty opened to the northwest, flames spewing from his fuselage. The way he was burning and losing altitude, he'd never make it home to Kyushu. But we lost him visually, then off the radar, before he splashed. Score him a "probable" for some damned good IRWIN gun crews.

We had notified the command (ComScreen) of our inoperative Director. At 0600, the ROBERT H. SMITH (DM-23), a SUMNER-class DD converted to a minelayer, relieved us on station, and we scurried back to the Hagushi anchorage to see if we could repair our recalcitrant Main Battery Director. While at anchor, I heard a commotion on deck and looked out the Comm Deck hatch to see an officer, his back to me, coming aboard from the whaleboat with his baggage. I shrugged, paid little attention, and went back in the Shack. We got pretty busy during the night. The Japs mounted an air attack on Yontan Airfield and other targets, and numerous bandits were in the area until sunrise. We and other ships laid down an effective smoke screen. We weren't under direct assault, but the raids kept us on alert.

The next morning, the buzzer on the Radio Shack's sound-powered phone sounded, and I picked it up.

"Radio, aye."

"Hey, Hutch, this is Boz." Ernest Bosworth was our Chief Yeoman.

"Yeah, Boz. Watchya got?"

"Didn't you tell me one time about a PT-boat officer named Kelly?"

"Yep. He's the sonuvabitch that sank the McCAWLEY."

"Well, he came aboard yesterday afternoon to take over command from Captain Miller."

I was stunned! Utterly speechless!!

"Hutch, you there?"

"Say that again, Boz. Slowly."

"I repeat: Commander Robert Bolling Kelly is going to be our next Skipper." Boz's Southern Louisiana accent wasn't so thick I couldn't understand *that* message.

"Oh, Kee-rist Almighty! God help us all! All we need in this campaign is a glory hunter, and a gawddamn PT-boat man at that!"

"Well", said Boz, "live it up while you can. He takes over in five days."

What the hell can the Navy be thinking of? Right in the middle of the toughest destroyer campaign of the War, they pull the best damn' tin can Skipper in the world out of action and turn his command over to some S.O.B. like Kelly! Unthinkable! Why didn't they just leave Hodapp with us? The *only* destroyer experience Kelly had was 28 months as an engineering officer on the old four-piper EDSALL before the War. For the past year, he hadn't even been to sea. He was living it up in Miami as officer in charge of PT-boat shakedowns. What kind of qualifications does he have for destroyer command? In *combat?!*

All these things were raging through my mind while my heart sank down around my shoetops. There was no doubt the IRWIN—*my* IRWIN—was going to be changed into God knows what. The word was now passing through the ship that we were going to lose our much loved, greatly respected Danny Miller. Of all that happened to the DD-794, the day of his departure was the saddest in her history. The crew was in shock.

It wasn't long before shipmates who became aware I'd known of Kelly before came seeking information about him. They got the full story of the sinking of the McCAWLEY. Their concern was instantly reflected in their faces. First, it didn't make sense to relieve Cap'n Danny. Second, they could have at least sent us an experienced *combat destroyerman* to command our beloved IRWIN.

Late that afternoon, I was leaning on the Comm Deck rail when Kelly came down from the Bridge.

"Good evening, Commander", I said.

"Hello, Sailor. What are your duties aboard the ship?" he asked.

"I'm Hutchinson, Radioman 1st, Sir." I paused. . . ."It's been some time since our paths crossed, Commander."

Kelly peered at me. "I don't think I recall you. You weren't in PT-boats?"

"No, Sir, I was on Admiral Turner's Staff on the McCAWLEY at Rendova."

The Commander was visibly taken aback. He obviously had not expected anyone from his past to show up on the IRWIN. But he recovered quickly.

"I see", he said. "It's good to have a man of your experience in this command. Carry on." And he disappeared down the ladder to the wardroom.

In the year following that exchange during which I served under Captain Kelly, I don't think he said more than a hundred more words to me after that.

While repairs were being attempted on the Main Battery Director, I had a chance to catch up on events elsewhere in this bitter campaign. At sea, the ammunition ship CANADA VICTORY, hit in an air attack, exploded spectacularly and went down. A dynamite-laden suicide boat crashed into the hull of the HUTCHINS, causing such damage she'd later be scuttled. The RATHBURNE, an APD (formerly DD-113), was kamikazed and put out of action. Fortunately, neither DD-type took casualties. But the kamikazed RALPH TALBOT had five killed and nine wounded. The suiciders even crashed the hospital ship COMFORT, fully lit up according to the Geneva Convention, amidships in the surgery—killing several wounded and all those operating on them. The Geneva Convention meant nothing to the Japs.

Ashore, the Marines had completely secured the northern two thirds of Okinawa. But it had been Japanese strategy from the outset to hole up behind fortifications, in caves and in tunnels in the southern third of the island, to let U.S. forces beat themselves to death against a well-dug-in and fanatical enemy. And it was working for them, so far. In a month of constant fighting along the Naha-Shuri Line, much of it hand-to-hand, the Army's 37th and 96th Divisions, having made little progress and taken heavy casualties, were exhausted. But Okinawa was needed as a supply and military base for the upcoming invasion of Japan.

Lieutenant General Simon Bolivar Buckner, Jr., Commander of the U.S. Tenth Army and later killed in action on Okinawa, relieved the exhausted troops, bringing in the 1st and 6th MarDivs to anchor the eastern end of the line, with the Army's 7th and 77th Divisions on the west flank. By 1 May, General Buckner was poised to renew the assault against General Ushijima's crack 32nd Army; which, at the campaign's start could have comprised as many as 110,000 troops. Dominating the landscape in the center of all this modern warfare was Shuri Castle—an ancient, medieval-style, stone bastion incongruously out of place in this 20th century conflict.

The IRWIN spent the next few days at Hagushi, with one trip to Kerama Retto for logistics. With the Director still unrepaired, we transferred to the BACHE the fighter-director gear and people we'd taken on board a few days before. Although we got no fire support missions while the land action was still in stalemate, and it was relatively quiet, nevertheless there were Jap air sorties every night. Still, for the first time in five weeks, we relaxed a bit. From the last week in March to the first day of May, we'd been on the go continuously on mission after mission, grabbing chow on the run and sleep when we could.

For the moment our guns were silent, but we knew it was only temporary until the next push against the Shuri Line began. We were keenly aware of the beating our Gunfire Support and Covering Force had taken. The destroyermen and their ships which were lost were on our minds, and we fully understood our own fate was still in the hands of God.

This campaign, so difficult to this point, was far from over. And, although I wouldn't get the notice for several days, I had a deep, deep personal loss. My mother died in San Diego on April 30th.

T.S. Eliot, in his poem *The Waste Land*, opined that "April is the cruelest month." For the destroyermen of Okinawa, that had proven to be *the* masterpiece of understatement.

The title of the section of Eliot's poem from which that quote is taken is "Burial of the Dead". Nothing could be more apropos.

31
ICEBERG—HOT AS HELL!

If April were the cruelest month, May and June were just as grueling.

At 1300, 3 May, the formal change of command took place while the IRWIN lay at anchor off the Hagushi beaches. It was a bizarre ceremony. The C.O.-to-be ordered the crew into full uniform, undress blues, and we assembled on the foc'sle.

After the passing of the command from Captain Miller to Captain Kelly, the new Skipper stood at a lectern he'd had built for the purpose and launched into a long speech. None of the crew could remember a word he said. We were all scanning and scouring the skies for kamikazes. Here we were in combat area and he had us massed topside, vulnerable as hell if enemy planes attacked. Cap'n Danny, standing near, was obviously as disapproving and uncomfortable as we, from the look on his face.

When the ceremony concluded, we paid our respects to our Captain Miller as he was piped over the side. Bob Martin, cox'n of the motor whaleboat summed up the crew's emotions. It was, he said, a black day. And not only did Kelly have us in blues for the ceremony, he wanted us to wear 'em as uniform of the day! There wasn't a tin can in the Pacific Fleet on which, at sea, anything other than dungarees was uniform. We went alongside the BUTLER (DD-636) shortly after the ceremony to transfer ammunition, and her crew was laughing like hell at us. Maybe their Skipper talked Kelly out of requiring blues. Anyhow, in a few hours, word was passed to change to dungarees. The whole drill was a humiliating one for us.

To underscore our trepidation and anxiety over being massed topside, the Hagushi anchorage was only 43 miles, about three minutes by air, from Radar Picket Station Five, where only five hours later the suiciders swarmed two of our destroyers. Several kamikazes slammed ablaze into the LITTLE (DD-803) and the new AARON WARD (DM-34). The LITTLE went down with 30 men. Among her survivors, 79 were wounded. The AARON WARD, so badly damaged she'd never be repaired, counted 45 men dead, 49 injured. Kamikazes also crashed two landing craft "pallbearers" trying to assist the tin cans, sinking one and severely damaging the other. The same day, the suiciders also struck the MACOMB (DD-458), killing seven and wounding 14. But she survived.

Our new Captain got a taste of what Okinawa was like the next day. On our way to Kerama Retto for supplies and ammo, we had to stand off because the anchorage was under air attack. There were bandits all over the place. An Oscar dive bomber crossed our bow, but the smoke screen was so heavy we lost him in seconds. Six minutes later we took a Val under fire, range 4,000 yards off the port bow. Between us and another can, we splashed him. Give the IRWIN another "assist" on a meatball. Maybe now our new Skipper would realize this wasn't the peacetime Navy out here, and the uniform was a working/fighting one—dungarees.

Our vulnerability was brought home to us all, that memorable 4th of May. Our own DesRon 55 compatriot for months, our buddy during the loss of the PRINCETON, the MORRISON, with men aboard we knew well, went down. On Radar Picket Station One with the INGRAHAM (DD-694), our old friend beat off suicide runs by Zekes and Vals, one after another, until there were just too many of them.

A Zero got through the MORRISON's furious barrages and smashed with a violent explosion just between Number One Stack and the Bridge, right into the Comm Deck. Out went all her electrical systems, and with fighting capability thus severely diminished the DD-560 was an easy target for two old twin-float biplanes that catapulted into her in succession. Internal explosions wracked her repeatedly and, within minutes, she plunged stern first below the waters of the East China Sea. Some 84 percent of her crew were casualties: 159 men perished, and 102 were wounded and/or burned. The gallant MORRISON was gone.

Out on the same Radar Picket Station One, the INGRAHAM did not escape either. Under attack by the same suiciding *kikusui*, she was damaged badly enough to be out of the War—losing 14 men killed, 37 wounded. The suiciders were also after the "pallbearers", i.e. the landing craft out on the radar picket stations to pick up survivors, sinking one out with the INGRAHAM with a loss of 13 missing and 23 wounded.

The loss of the MORRISON was not the only "close to home" tragedy that day. The unfortunate cruiser BIRMINGHAM—with whom the IRWIN also had close ties and now Admiral Deyo's CTF Flagship since the suiciders had struck the TENNESSEE—was hit by a kamikaze that exploded in the Sick Bay, adding 51 dead and 81 wounded to her long list of casualties in the Pacific War. She had to go to Guam for repairs but lived to keep on fighting.

THE AARON WARD IN KERAMA RETTO'S "GRAVEYARD OF SHIPS"
Savaged by kamikaze attack, the destroyer-minesweeper is low in water,
her topsides all but wiped out. She would later be scuttled (sunk) by our
own forces. 45 men were killed and 49 wounded.

(U.S. Navy Photo - Navy Historical Center)

Two more tin cans got it on May 4th as well. The LUCE (DD-522), out on Radar Picket Station Twelve, lost nearly half her crew, 149 men, when she went down after two kamikazes smashed into her starboard side amidships and into her port quarter; 94 of the survivors were on the wounded list, only 92 of a crew of 335 escaping unhurt. In the same attack the suiciders also sank a "pallbearer" (LSM-190)—13 killed or missing, 18 wounded. Almost simultaneously, out on RP 14, the SHEA (DM-30) lost 27 of her crew killed and 91 injured, to a *baka* bomb (man-directed missile) after shooting down the parent plane, while surviving a suicide attack that put her out of the fighting. Elsewhere that day, several other cans survived near misses. Total radar picket station losses on 4 May amounted to two destroyers, two landing craft "pallbearers", and 370 officers and men, not to mention several ships damaged.

If this kept up, there wouldn't be a destroyer or a destroyerman left at Okinawa. Tokyo Rose's prediction that no tin can sailor would live through the campaign seemed to be coming true. We were catching H-E-L-L—HELL! But it wasn't all one-sided. We were giving the Japs a taste of our own brand of the devil's own fire.

How concerned was the Navy? On hearing the news of 4 May at Pearl Harbor, Admiral Nimitz asked his Chief of Staff Admiral Forrest P. Sherman whether the suiciders would soon lay off the picket station destroyers for bigger game. Sherman thought not. Nimitz then remarked: "Anyway, we can build destroyers faster than they can build planes."

This seemingly callous remark is not lost on the destroyermen who took the brunt of the kamikaze attacks in Operation ICEBERG. Apparently the Commander in Chief of the Pacific Fleet was more concerned with the hardware of war than with the real people manning the tin cans targeted by the hostiles. Nimitz was a "desk Admiral", who had never commanded a ship or task force in combat. You can't replace flesh and blood with steel—his comment still rankles us.

As U.S. Navy historian Morison, who reported Nimitz' comment as a firsthand witness, put it: "Few missiles or weapons have ever spread such flaming terror, such torturing burns, such searing death, as did the kamikaze in his self-destroying onslaughts on the radar picket and other ships. And naval history has few parallels to the sustained courage, resourcefulness and fighting spirit that the crews of these vessels displayed day after day after day in the battle for Okinawa."

Or to hear the destroyerman in charge of tin cans at Okinawa, Captain Frederick Moosbrugger: "The performance of the personnel of the screening and radar picket ships. . . was superb throughout the

Okinawa Campaign. Acts of heroism and unselfishness, fighting spirit, coolness under fire, unswerving determination, endurance, and qualities of leadership and loyalty exceeded all previous conceptions of standards set for the United States Navy. . . . Never in the annals of our glorious naval history have naval forces done so much with so little against such odds for so long a period. Radar picket duty in this operation might well be a symbol of supreme achievement in our naval traditions."

Or to hear Morison again: "Although your historian himself has been under kamikaze attack, and witnessed the hideous forms of death and torture inflicted by that weapon, words fail him to do justice to the sailors on the radar picket stations. We need a poet to do it. . . . Men on radar picket station, to survive, not only had to strike down the flaming terror of the kamikaze, roaring out of the blue like the thunderbolts that Zeus hurled at bad actors in days of old; they were under constant strain and unusual discomfort. . . . For days and even nights on end, the crew had to stand general quarters, and the ship kept 'buttoned up'. Men had to keep in condition for the instant reaction and split-second timing necessary to riddle a plane bent on a crashing death. Sleep became the rarest commodity and choicest luxury, like water to a shipwrecked mariner."

In a masterpiece of understatement, Admiral Turner remarked: "The suiciders hurt the Navy badly at Okinawa." Nevertheless, my old Admiral was grateful that the kamikaze pilots went after the picket station destroyers, and that the tin cans thus screened his amphibious ships and transports from the suiciders' onslaughts. "By their steadfast courage and magnificent performance of duty in a nerve wracking job under morale shattering conditions, the crews of ships and craft in the Radar Picket Stations emblazoned a glorious new chapter in naval tradition."

What in the world went through the minds of the suiciders? Two former naval officers of the Kamikaze Corps tried to answer this question in a remarkable book entitled *The Divine Wind: Japan's Kamikaze Force in World War II* (1958). But as Vice Admiral C.R. Brown remarks in his Foreword, the Western mind vainly seeks the key to the enigma. "No one has yet successfully explained to the Western mind this Japanese phenomenon of self-immolation, and perhaps it is not given to the Westerner to understand it."

The suiciders were doubtless brave men ready and resigned to die for their ancient country in the true samurai spirit of *Bushido*, the will to suppress and sacrifice the ephemeral individual for the sake of the eternal ideal of Imperial Japan. This was the testimony of their leaders, whose outlook was remarkably akin to that of Adolf Hitler, their ally in the Western world. They operated on the assumption that Japan would *never surrender.*

Admiral Onishi, founder of the Kamikaze Corps, looked upon his young pilots descending from the skies as part of nature's cycle of life and death, as falling cherry blossoms, his philosophy being summed up in the motto he gave the Corps:

> In blossom today, then scattered;
> Life is so like a delicate flower.
> How can one expect the fragrance
> to last forever?

Perhaps the Jap Admiral was prophetic beyond his ken when he once remarked to an aide: "A man's value can never be determined at his death. In my case there will probably not be anyone, even in a hundred years, to justify what I have done."

The dying testimonies of the suiciders are all tragic, tragically human. For example: "I am a human being and hope to be neither saint nor scoundrel, hero nor fool—just a human being. As one who has spent his life in wistful longing and searching, I die resignedly in the hope that my life will serve as a 'human document'. . . . The world in which I lived was too full of discord. As a community of rational human beings it should be better composed. Lacking a single great conductor, everyone lets loose with his own sound, creating dissonance where there should be melody and harmony."

The 4 May *kikusui* coincided with General Ushijima's all-out ground offensive of the same day. But we beat them back, and the Marines and GIs were launching their second attempt to breach the Shuri Barricade. The fighting was fierce, furious, bloody, and unspeakably violent. The Japs were making them pay for every inch of Okinawan mud, fanatically resisting and giving no quarter. The "jarheads" and "doughfeet" needed every bit of help we could give 'em with our gunnery. Our fire support missions seemed unending. . . . We just went from one to another. As an Army historian noted: "Naval gunfire was employed longer and in greater quantites in the battle of Okinawa than in any other in history."

On 5 May, we relieved the PRESTON off the city of Naha; sending volley after volley into enemy troops, caves, pill boxes, artillery emplacements, and machinegun nests as our shore party spotter pinpointed target after target for us. All day, all night, and until 1800 the next day, the beach spotting team kept calling for fire, ofttimes within less than

50 yards of its own position. During the night, we kept the grid area daylight bright with star shells, illuminating even more enemy strong points to take under fire. As the Army historian continued: "Naval gunfire. . . supported the ground troops and complemented the artillery from the day of the landing until action moved to the extreme southern tip of the island, where the combat area was so restricted that there was a danger of shelling American troops."

Our accurate gunners, we were informed by the shore party, opened a gap in the Jap lines and our troops were gaining some ground. Our night mission on 6 May had us illuminating and providing harassing salvos from three and a half miles off Itoman until 0645. The Captain then sent two gunnery officers ashore to assess the results of our bombardment. They came back with laudatory reports from the shore commands. Our right-on-the-target shelling had killed scores upon scores of the enemy; and had taken out strongholds protecting artillery, as well as mortars and machineguns.

Low on ammunition, we retired to Kerama Retto on May 8th, but had difficulty getting some of the types and amounts of ammo we needed. We were begging, literally begging, for proximity-fuse anti-aircraft shells. With these, we didn't have to make a direct hit on a kamikaze, just come close. We could not understand, this late in the War, why there should be any ammo shortages at all.

During the night of 9 May, after all-day bombardment missions, we were called for intense illumination and supporting fire when the Japs counter-attacked elements of the 1st Marine Division (at Okinawa under Major General Pedro A. del Valle) in our sector. With one 5-inch gun steadily lobbing star shells over the front lines, the rest of the Main Battery was blasting away in the grids where the hostiles were swarming. At times, our shore party was calling for volleys on Jap Banzai charges within bare yards of their own position; and we were obliging with salvo after salvo in pinpoint accuracy, otherwise our shells would be falling on our own people. When we ran out of star shells, the NEW MEXICO relieved us of illumination duties; and we took over her direct fire as well as continuing with our own, keeping up blistering barrages until dawn when the Jap Banzai boys, badly beaten and their ranks decimated, retreated from the field.

We had been so concerned with our own operations we hardly had time to acknowledge the announcement that Nazi Germany had surrendered and the European War was over. Given our not being able to get all the ammo we wanted, our only reaction was summed up in Chief Gunner's Mate "Boom Boom" Kopach's acid comment: "*Now* maybe we'll get some gawddam help out here!"

If we needed any reminder of the hazards of our duties, we got them each time we steamed into Kerama Retto for replenishment. Ship after ship—the LEUTZE, HUTCHINS, RATHBURNE, AARON WARD, and so many other victims of the fury of the Divine Wind—were there awaiting final disposition. The most severely damaged would be scuttled, i.e. towed to sea and sunk. Now they were a graveyard, their once sleek, seagoing configurations blasted into grotesque metal deformity by the kamikazes. Once proud fighting vessels. Now useless hulks in which young Americans who had worn Navy blue went to their deaths; or were wounded, maimed, burned and scarred, carrying souvenirs of Operation ICEBERG. As we passed the silent, damaged hulks each time—on our way to the oilers, ammo lighters, and supply vessels—a silence would come over the IRWIN. There but for the Grace of God. . . .

On 9 May, kamikazes from Kyushu, attacking as common at twilight, added more ships to Kerama Retto's junk pile. Out on anti-sub patrol, in the same onslaught the veteran destroyer escorts ENGLAND (DE-635) and OBERRENDER (DE-344) were damaged beyond repair, to be eventually scuttled. Between them they lost 43 men killed, 80 wounded. The ENGLAND, you'll remember, was the proud ship that had sunk six Jap subs in twelve days a year before.

On 11 May, the HUGH W. HADLEY (DD-774) and EVANS (DD-552) joined the junk yard, hit by kamikazes out on Radar Picket Station Fifteen. The two destroyers came under a morning attack of over fifty suiciders. The EVANS got it first, hit by four kamikazes and parts of four others, losing 30 killed and 29 wounded. Attacked by ten planes at once, the HADLEY received four hits including one by a *baka* bomb, but a valiant crew saved the ship, suffering 28 killed and 67 wounded. Her wounded Captain survived to write:

"No captain of a man of war had a crew who fought more valiantly against such overwhelming odds. Who can measure the degree of courage of men who stand up to their guns in the face of diving planes that destroy them? Who can measure the loyalty of a crew who risked death to save the ship from sinking when all seemed lost? I desire to record that the history of our Navy was enhanced on 11 May 1945. I am proud to record that I know of no record of a destroyer's crew fighting for one hour and thirty-five minutes against overwhelming aircraft attacks and destroying twenty-three planes. My crew accomplished their mission and displayed outstanding fighting abilities. . . . Destroyer men are good men and my officers and crew were good destroyer men."

The same day, out with Task Force 58, Admiral Mitscher's CTF 58

Flagship the BUNKER HILL, with which the IRWIN had steamed so many miles, was clobbered by hostiles suiciding into her; 396 of her crew perished, including 14 of the Admiral's Staff, while 264 more were wounded, and she was out of the fighting. Admiral Mitscher moved his Flag to the ENTERPRISE, where it lasted all of four days.

Back with the tin cans, the BACHE, our picket station companion earlier, lost 41 dead and 32 wounded, when the *kikusui* finally caught up with her on 13 May. But she, too, survived.

The next day, 14 May, the venerable aircraft carrier ENTERPRISE, the most decorated and most famous fighting ship of the War, fought her last battle, losing 13 killed and 68 wounded to the Divine Wind. A single hit by a plane and its bomb blew parts of her forward aircraft elevator some 400 feet into the air. She survived, but no more battle stars for the Big E. She already had *twenty*! The veteran of so many battles—Midway, Eastern Solomons, Santa Cruz, Gilberts and Marshalls, Marianas and Philippine Sea, Philippines and Leyte Gulf, Iwo Jima and Okinawa—would come to the end of the line at Okinawa. It *was hot as hell* in Operation ICEBERG, and it wasn't going to get any cooler.

The IRWIN made the rounds in Kerama Retto, getting ammo for our almost bare magazines from the FOMALHAUT, full fuel bunkers from the WHIPPET, and provisions for our food lockers and cold storage from the BRIDGE and ANTARES. Among the chow coming aboard were 25 canned hams, which somehow just disappeared into thin air. Ensign Merrill, the Supply Officer, didn't have time to inventory them that afternoon; and that night, there was the tantalizing aroma of ham frying on hot plates all over the ship. Since the Radio Gang always got night rations anyhow, none of our guys had pilfered a ham, but just about every other gang on the ship had. The signalmen, who benefited often from our night rations, shared theirs with us.

The next morning, Mr. Merrill discovered the discrepancy. If it had been maybe two or three hams, he could have covered it up. Twenty-five? Nope. To protect himself, he had to report it to Captain Kelly. When he did, the Old Man hit the overhead, calling all officers to an "emergency" meeting in the wardroom.

Ensign Frank Cannaday, one of the engineering officers, later told me what went on. Kelly said he wanted *every one* of those hams returned. They were to be brought to the Comm Deck that night under cover of darkness. No one would be watching, and there'd be no punishment if all the hams showed up by morning. The only problem with that was—most of the hams had already been eaten or partially so. During the evening watch, I kept peeking out the hatch to see if any hams were there. By morning, some five or six were on the deck.

Kelly was infuriated. He would not allow a crew to defy him like this! He ordered all division officers to search all their spaces with a fine-tooth comb. Frank said he went down into the engine room, calling out in a loud voice: "I hope I don't find any hams down here." As he searched, he knew the snipes in the black gang were taking hams from where he hadn't searched and were bringing them around behind him to be stashed in nooks and crannies he'd already passed. Frank was in a touchy position. He'd enjoyed a couple of ham sandwiches, himself, the night before.

It must also be recorded here that the atmosphere in the wardroom between Kelly and the rest of the officers was already strained. As Torpedo Officer Gene Stout put it: "There was a lot of tension in Officers' Country." They didn't like Kelly to begin with, and they were afraid to do much of anything for fear the Old Man would come down on them hard. Nor did any of the department heads want to finger any group of enlisted men, especially those in his own division. The search turned up not one ham.

The Captain then played what he figured was his trump card. There would be no coffee or night rations for any one—neither crew *nor officers*—until all 25 hams were returned. When that came down, both officers and crew went completely sour on the Old Man. Days went by and resentment grew. The wardroom atmosphere was so thick you could cut it with a knife. On deck, grumbling by the crew was constant, and little effort was made to hide their feelings. Captain Kelly's stock was at its nadir. To cut off coffee from sailors, for *any* reason, was looked upon as tantamount to taking mother's milk from a baby. But the Captain was adamant. No hams—no java.

Finally, it was good old Doc Fagan who came to the rescue and resolved what could have been a major crisis. He went to the Old Man to report that he had been treating an outbreak of minor injuries among the crew—cuts, bruises, abrasions, smashed fingers, sprained ankles and wrists. In his medical opinion, he told Kelly, these accidents were the result of crew members not being as sharp as they should be, and that turning off the joe pots was the root cause. Doc predicted more accidents would happen, and that a serious one probably would take place, reflecting unfavorably on the ship and certainly on her Commanding Officer.

Captain Kelly, faced with the probability of having to explain a major mishap to a crewman or crewmen to his superiors, relented. Within minutes after he rescinded his order, joe pots were happily perking away in every space aboard. But a mention of Kelly's name to any man aboard—at the time, or even today—will get you the same response: *"That Son of a Bitch!"*

Years later, when Herman Wouk's novel *The Caine Mutiny* was made into a motion picture, the incident of the stolen strawberries was to me, as that well-known and profound philosopher Yogi Berra would have put it, *"déjà vu* all over again"! And my shipmates of the IRWIN all saw it as a replay of "the canned hams episode", even likening Kelly to Captain Queeg. Those I've laughed with about the incident have wondered whether Mr. Wouk might not have had a spy aboard the IRWIN and just substituted strawberries for hams in his story. Nah, he wouldn't have done that.

From what I gathered about the wardroom situation, the Captain's demeanor deepened the gulf between him and his officers. They felt Kelly was heavy-handed and dictatorial in his relations with them. Further, they and the crew lacked confidence in the Skipper's shiphandling. One assessment of the Old Man: "He wants the crew under peacetime battleship regulations while he's trying to handle a tin can like a PT-boat." As for the crew, the Captain must have known the depth of their resentment—he never walked the weather decks at night.

In fairness to Robert Bolling Kelly, his was not an enviable position. He had taken over from an enormously popular Captain. The Navy could have sent us "Bull" Halsey or "31 Knot" Burke, and *they* would have had to establish their bona fides, before the crew of the IRWIN would have accepted either as a proper replacement for Danny Miller. Kelly's style of command, his attitude toward his officers and men, was 180 degrees from Miller's, which only tended to exacerbate the situation. Yet Kelly, in his official reports, repeatedly praised his men for their performance of duty under fire. But apparently he rarely, if ever, complimented anyone directly. He was not the easiest man to understand.

Given the Navy's heavy losses at sea to the suiciders, Admiral Turner was putting pressure on General Buckner to speed up the land campaign against the stubborn Japs. The Tenth Army's May offensive began on 11 May, and the ensuing ten days witnessed the bloodiest fighting of the bitter Okinawa campaign. According to Marine sergeant William Manchester: "There was so much death around that life seemed almost indecent."

As on Guadalcanal, and other islands, the fighting was nip and tuck. Ironically, the most poignant comment on this offensive came via Japanese propaganda from Tokyo, obviously written by some Nip who at one time had lived in the States:

"Sugar Loaf Hill. . . Chocolate Drop. . . Strawberry Hill. Gee, these places sound wonderful! You can just see the candy houses with the white picket fences around them and the candy canes hanging from the trees, their red and white stripes glistening in the sun. But the only thing red about these places is the blood of Americans, Yes, sir, these are the names of hills in southern Okinawa where the fighting's so close that you can get down to bayonets and sometimes your bare fists. . . . I guess it's natural to idealize the worst places with pretty names to make them seem less awful. Why, Sugar Loaf has changed hands so often it looks like Dante's Inferno. Yes, sir, Sugar Loaf Hill. . . Chocolate Drop. . . Strawberry Hill. They sound good, don't they? Only those who've been there know what they're really like."

As pointed out in J.H. and W.M. Belote's *Typhoon of Steel: The Battle for Okinawa* (1970), the Marines and Army might not have been able to advance at all apart from the constant fire support of the Navy offshore. By the end of the Okinawa Campaign, our gunfire support ships had fired 23,210 16-inch and 14-inch shells and 31,550 8-inch shells, plus over 45,000 6-inch and 475,000 5-inch projectiles. The destroyers, with the continuous firing of their 5-inch guns, had the worst of it.

"Nightfall brought little relief to the destroyers. Unlike the battle-ships and cruisers which retired seaward, destroyers had to remain off either coast firing star shells containing bright parachute flares to expose Japanese infiltrators. Although the sailors could (and did) learn to sleep soundly through the ear-rending crack of the 5-inch .38-caliber guns, the constant strain of the bombardment and screening work, and the punishing all-hands task of taking on ammunition and supplies every third or fourth day from LST supply ships at the Keramas, gradually wore down the destroyer men. Merely being at sea was tiring on a constantly rolling destroyer; one could seldom walk a straight line down a deck. There were always watches to stand, little maintenance tasks to do. The prospect of the sudden appearance of a kamikaze added mental to physical strain."

May 18th was another dark day for DesRon 55. After four days and nights of steady bombardment, the LONGSHAW, on a fire support mission south of Naha, made a navigational error that stranded her, crunching her bow up on Ose Reef. For over three and a half hours, her Skipper, Lieutenant Commander C.W. Becker, led frantic efforts to free her. To lift her bow clear of the reef, all movable material forward was shifted aft. That meant opening the forward ammunition magazines to hoist the shells to the deck and tote them to the stern.

At the same time, the Captain of the LONGSHAW tried to back her down with full power, her screws churning the brownish shallow waters into something akin to a giant milkshake. A rescue call went out to the fleet tug ARIKARA. She rigged towing cables through the stern chocks,

THE DEATH OF THE LONGSHAW

In this remarkable photo, the damage inflicted by Japanese shore batteries is extensive and the ship is settling in the sea. Men are seen helping wounded shipmates. The body of one man can be seen hanging from #1 stack. Seventy-nine men, including the Commanding Officer, were killed, and 95 others were wounded. The LONGSHAW was finally destroyed by our own gunfire. *(U.S. Navy Photo - Navy Historical Center)* and put her powerful engines in high gear. Straining with all her might, the tug could not budge the hapless and helpless destroyer.

The plight of the DD-559 had not gone unnoticed by the Japs ashore. By 1100, they had 6-inch naval guns in place and opened up with salvo after salvo, ripping the destroyer to ribbons, causing casualties and setting fires. Ammunition exploding, fires out of control, and under murderous barrages from the enemy, the LONGSHAW was doomed. Finally, a direct hit into the open number two magazine wracked her, and Captain Becker ordered "Abandon Ship!" Seriously wounded, he himself didn't make it; and he was last seen on the main deck with fires blazing around him, futilely waving a .45 automatic at the Japs. Only nine of the ship's 22 officers survived; 66 enlisted men were lost, and 95 of those who made it to safety were wounded, several dying of their wounds.

Cause of the grounding wasn't established. But the LONGSHAW, like the IRWIN, had been on fire support duty since the 26th of March. Officers and crew were as exhausted as we. Someone, perhaps with attention dulled, committed a fatal error. The LONGSHAW was the ninth of the original 22 cans of the Gunfire Support and Covering Force to go down, picked off one by one. DesRon 55 was taking a helluva licking. On the IRWIN we could but sorrowfully shake our heads and hope we'd avoid a similar fate. We knew it could happen to us.

All that week (15–21 May) it was business as usual. Alternating between the Hagushi anchorage on Okinawa's west coast and Nagagusuku Wan on the east, we ground out days and nights of the old "routine" (which was anything *but* routine) as we shelled the hell out of everything our shore parties targeted. Our only respites came when we ran out of ammo and had to replenish our magazines.

The shore parties with whom we worked told us we were the most accurate gunship in the bombardment group. Our tally of destroyed targets continued to mount: gun emplacements, artillery pieces, even a town destroyed; enemy machinegun nests wiped out, troop concentrations and counter-attacks broken up with heavy casualties, and caves collapsed on their Jap inhabitants. We took out a mortar battery, that was lobbing shells over the top of a hill into Marine foxholes, by using reverse slope firing. And we kept the Japs' heads down at night with both star shell illumination and harassing fire.

On 21 May, after an all-night mission, we were proceeding independently en route to Hagushi when a Red Alert sent us to the battle stations we already had two-thirds manned. At 1914, we made visual contact with four enemy Tony kamikazes. As I watched, one was in the act of suiciding close aboard an LCI landing craft. Another made a run on us, and we opened fire while simultaneously taking evasive action. The Tony flew down our port side at about 300 feet altitude, then circled to the starboard bow. The remaining two Japs had swung around our stern and headed out of range of the after batteries. But the one intent on taking us out changed course to come in about four points off the port bow. Our 5-inch and 40-millimeter gunners threw up a hail of hot steel, scoring hit after hit. At 4,000 yards, still coming on a collision course, the Tony virtually disintegrated as it flamed out into the water. Scratch one more kamikaze meatball.

One of the other planes in the flight turned around to approach, and we took it under fire at 6,000 yards. That Jap decided he'd better not try us, and reversed course, opening the range to the northeast. Apparently he was not yet ready to die for Emperor Hirohito.

As I wiped the sweat off my brow and shook off the chills with a feeling of relief, we headed for an all-night mission two and a half miles off Okaha Island. All night long, we fired illumination star shells for close-in support of LCIs—which, with us, were assigned anti-suicide boat and swimmer patrol.

While our primary missions were fire support, the IRWIN occasionally drew "flycatcher" duty. Because five ships, including two destroyers, had been damaged by suicide boats, patrols of usually one destroyer and several landing craft were regularly assigned to counter them. These operations were generally effective, made more so by bombardment of the caves and other suicider hiding places. Yet, no ship on station close ashore could afford to relax vigilance. Both the high-speed boats, loaded with heavy explosives, and the suicide swimmers, who would slip aboard unsuspecting vessels or place explosives next to hulls, were a constant threat. Whenever the IRWIN was at anchor or laying to, we regularly posted a "suicide watch", usually with two men on the foc'sle, two amidships, and two on the fantail, all armed with rifles, to thwart any attempts by swimmers and to watch for the boats.

Ed Carroll, who'd just made Sonarman 3rd Class on 1 April, was one of those who stood those suicide watches. We'd been getting reports all along of sentries aboard other ships being killed by Jap swimmers who would either climb up the anchor cables or over the screw guards, knife one or two men, then dive back into the water. Ed had the 2400 to 0400 watch one night toward the end of May when the IRWIN and three other destroyers were anchored at the extreme western end of Nagagusuku Wan. We were closest to the beach, while the other cans were to our port.

Ed reported in to the Officer of the Deck as he took the watch, only to be told the suiciders had sneaked aboard each of the other destroyers earlier, killing the bow sentry on one, the bow sentry and the O.D. on another, and the fantail sentry on a third. The latter tin can was only about 150 yards from the IRWIN. Ed suggested that sound-powered phone talkers be added to the sentries for quick communication among those on watch; he also drew a Thompson submachinegun from the ship's armory. The O.D. instructed the watch to call him first to get permission to fire at any suspected target.

After two uneventful hours, Ed was on the mess deck, getting coffee for the sentries, when his messenger ran in to tell him he was needed on the bow immediately. The sentry thought he'd spotted a swimmer!

"The sentry pointed toward the water", Ed wrote to me, "and it looked like a man treading easily through the water. You could see small waves of water separate from the black object in the bay. I told the talker to contact the O.D. and get permission to open fire at a suspected suicide swimmer. We received permission immediately."

"The sentry fired several rounds and. . . no signs they hit the target. I told the talker to fire, too. After several more rounds were fired, there were still no signs the target had been hit. I took my Thompson gun and also began to fire. After several rounds, the shear pin snapped off and the Thompson wouldn't stop firing. I laid it on its side and kept criss-crossing the target until the magazine was empty. When it was over, we found no sign of the swimmer. We reported this to the O.D. and resumed normal watch."

Ed turned in to his bunk at the end of the watch. At 0630, Ed said, he was awakened by a messenger and told to report to the Executive Officer. The sentry and the sound-powered phone talker were already there when he arrived. Our new Exec Mr. Bakley had each repeat the orders of a sentry, then reached down by his desk and pulled out a beat-up anchor marking buoy. The bottom of it was intact, but the top of it was nothing but splinters. "We had been shooting at our own anchor buoy!" Ed said. "The Exec then congratulated us on our vigilance and said *if* it had been a suicide swimmer, we'd have blown the hell out of him!"

"But as a reminder to be more cautious the next time, Mr. Bakley said we'd have to pay for the ammo we used", Ed concluded, "and it cost me two dollars and fifty cents!"

Life aboard the IRWIN settled into an habitual, wearisome, yet hazardous grind—oversimplified by someone's statement that "we loaded ammunition all day and fired it all night." More often, we were on constant bombardment missions for three days and three nights; then replenished ammo, fuel, and provisions during one day before returning to station that night to fire some more.

There was hardly a time our War Diary didn't record "numerous enemy aircraft in the area during the night." They were there from dusk 'til dawn. Sleep we got in short takes, usually at or near our battle stations. Our own gunfire through the nights, General Quarters for a Red Alert as enemy aircraft closed, or close proximity to the beach—all kept us from grabbing more than a few winks at any one time.

Food was something we got irregularly whenever we could. I can recall only a handful of times we got a real, honest-to-goodness, sit-down meal at the tables on the mess deck. Coffee, cigarettes, lunchmeat or cheese sandwiches, and occasionally hot soup became our regimen.

Although we were dog-tired and our nerves constantly on edge, there was still no lack of vigilance lest a suicide swimmer, suicide boat, or kamikaze plane slip in under our guard. My combat senses, sharpened now by years in the forward areas, never let me down.

Neither did the long combat duty dull my reactions to immediate danger, and my adrenalin raced just as fast when a kamikaze attacked as it had the first time in combat at the Battle of Eastern Solomons, to be followed by the same reactions I'd had then.

As each incident of peril passed without tragedy striking, I knew a guardian angel, even though overworked and probably as exhausted as everyone else, was still on the job. How long he could keep it up, I had no idea.

The atmosphere aboard had, of course, changed considerably. The new green hands had become able and competent destroyermen. The old sea dogs continued to be "Navy", but the horseplay and joshing that normally goes on among such men was missing.

Little laughter was heard. Few jokes were told. No long "sea stories" were related.

It was all strictly business, a deadly business, and a matter of survival.

32

JUST ROUTINE DESTROYER DUTY

From time immemorial men at war have had to worry not only about serving and surviving in combat, but also about what's going on with their loved ones back home. It was no different in the ordeal that was Okinawa.

Although our mail service was pretty good, letters from Jane came less frequently, were shorter and less personal. Then I got a six-page one. She wrote that she had an opportunity to advance her singing career by moving to New York; and, despite objections from her parents and advice from friends, she was determined to go. She spent most of the letter justifying her position. I got that sinking feeling, but answered with a supporting letter. Yet, I couldn't shake off the premonition that this spelled future trouble for our marriage. It was almost like getting a "Dear John" letter.

The weather around Okinawa during the last week of May turned wet, with haze and limited visibility. As my grandpop would have said, it was "raining pitchforks and hammer handles."

On the beach, the Marines and GIs were up to their rear ends in sticky, gooey mud. They'd taken Sugar Loaf Hill, overlooking the western approaches to Shuri Castle. The 1st MarDiv and the Army's 77th Division assaulted the defenses around the Castle. But the Jap defenders repulsed every attack until, finally, with massive shore bombardment support from us and the other ships of the Gunfire and Support Group, our guys broke through the outer ring. Then came those rains and the advance slogged to a halt in the sloppy slick mud of Okinawa. With the fighting stalemated, General Ushijima pulled his forces back from the Shuri Barrier to set up a new defense line farther south. Shuri Castle fell to the Marines on 29 May, 1945, but the Japs had gotten away to fight some more.

For several days, as the saying went, the most important General on the island was "General Mud"!

Early on the morning of 25 May, despite less than favorable flying weather, the hostiles launched another big air assault against us. We were on special anti-aircraft screen station within the confines of Nagagusuku Wan while, at the same time, supporting the Marines with illumination and harassing fire. As we were shifting positions, we lost our port anchor and chain when somehow the stops failed to keep the chain from running out the hawse pipe. We anchored in Berth B-45 with just the starboard hook and were still there at 0820. I was just coming on deck from the Chiefs' Quarters when our batteries opened fire. I ran toward the ladder to the Radio Shack and finally sighted the target. A Tony, off our starboard bow, was circling over the Kuba Saki area about 8,000 yards away. As our salvos hit him, sending him down in flames, he made an unsuccessful attempt to suicide into a transport. Paint another meatball on the Bridge splinter shield.

We hurriedly got underway to take up our anti-aircraft screening station as I watched heavy AA fire over the transports off Kuba Saki. About that time, our 5-inch and 40-millimeter guns commenced fire off the port beam. I swung around to see a Kate at about 5,000 yards, altitude about 350 feet, in a low glide right at us, passing over the fleet tug TAIWAKONI (ATF-114). The Kate was already afire, hit by us and probably by rounds from the tug and the PRESTON. It crashed just clear of the PRESTON off Kutaka Shima. Chalk up another "assist" for the IRWIN.

The gun crews had just begun to figure it was time to stand easy after the radar showed no nearby blips when the lookouts sighted a pair of Betty bombers, low on the water at about 7,000 yards, escaping our radar, bearing 200 degrees, speed 180 knots. The gunners blasted away, some rounds starting a fire in the one Betty's bomb bay. It crashed into the sea with a big *BAH-ROOOM*, apparently from extra explosives it was carrying. One less "flaming asshole" to worry about. The second Betty took off for parts unknown.

Released from special anti-aircraft screening at noon, we went back to Berth B-45 and anchored to resume fire support. Shifting berths often, we supplied call-fire, directed by both a shore party and a cruiser's Kingfisher float plane until 0913 the next morning. However, the War Diary, after detailing our bombardment schedule, which included illumination and harassing fire all night long, notes "it was a quiet night"!

We had been scheduled to be relieved at Okinawa on 5 May to return to Ulithi for availability alongside a destroyer tender. We were long past due for major repairs and preventive upkeep. But the demands for fire support and anti-aircraft defense, along with our heavy losses in destroyers to the waves of kamikazes, led ComDesRon 55 to rescind the order. Now, we would finally get a chance to get the sorely needed work done on engine room repair and solve the problems of our Main Battery

Director. But it'd be no "rear area" for the IRWIN. The tender HAMUL (AD-20) had come to Nagagusuku Wan, and we'd stay right here at Okinawa, mooring in a nest on her port side. We spent the first night under heavy smoke screen cover as bogies orbited the area.

The IRWIN had been operating at Okinawa, the most grueling combat and campaign in naval history, with serious deficiencies both in combat readiness and in personnel.

Most of the time, our Main Battery Director was of little use due to a faulty G.S.L. cable, a condition which had lasted two and a half months. It failed when we were on Radar Picket Station, which took us off RP duty. That may have been a blessing, considering the ships lost out there. But it also put us in jeopardy when attacked by kamikazes during our AA defense and shore bombardment missions. Without the Director, our Main Battery was firing in local control. And our Number One 5-inch Mount had been out of operation, in both local and automatic, during the entire Okinawa operation. Although the mount fired over 2,000 rounds in shore bombardment in manual control, its use to us in air attack situations was limited, reducing our air defense capability perhaps fifteen to twenty percent. Under the circumstances, our gun crews were nothing less than outstanding, accounting for at least five planes knocked down and several probables and assists.

Chief Yeoman Boz Bosworth showed me Captain Kelly's report on our personnel situation. I'd been somewhat aware of the loss through transfers of officers and crewmen. But the report, as of 28 May, raised a lot of questions as to what the hell the Navy was doing to keep us fully manned. The answer: not much, not anything!

Our rated complement was 16 officers and 309 enlisted men. We began Operation ICEBERG with 17 officers and 297 bluejackets. After 69 days, we were down to 13 officers and 294 men. The Navy's Bureau of Personnel had transferred four of the key officers—Commanding Officer, Executive Officer, First Lieutenant, and Gunfire Liaison Officer—while supplying replacement only for the C.O. Then, the Engineering Officer, Mr. Clark, who was made Executive Officer, was hospitalized on 27 May. Captain Kelly was forced to report the ship "not ready for sea". We had no qualified Exec aboard! It wasn't until then that we got Lieutenant Newton Bakley as our new Exec. But we were still undermanned, and most of the people transferred were key combat-experienced veterans whom we could ill afford to lose.

How could BuPers and/or Task Force Commanders keep sending a destroyer into combat, day after day, without a full crew? When we finally left the tender, we were still *fifteen people short*—three officers and twelve bluejackets. On a tin can, *EVERY* man counts.

I went over to the HAMUL to requisition radio tubes and other spare parts, and to catch up on the latest news and scuttlebutt. In the Radio Shack, a Radioman 1st gave me the latest dope on ship casualties. ICEBERG was *still* hot as hell. In the eight days from 20 May to 28 May, *thirteen* destroyers and destroyer types had been kamikaze victims. The DREXLER (DD-741), BARRY (DD-248), and BATES (DE-68) had all gone to Davy Jones' Locker—with combined losses of 179 men killed, 116 wounded. Damaged beyond repair were the CHASE (DE-158), THATCHER (DD-514), BUTLER (DD-636), ROPER (DD-147), and FORREST (DD-461). Their combined casualty lists totaled 40 dead, 126 wounded. Damaged and out of action for the rest of the War were the STORMES (DD-780), O'NEILL (DE-188), and BRAINE (DD-630). Only the lightly damaged LOY (DE-160) returned to the fighting. On these ships, a total of 90 men lost their lives, and 100 were injured. Tin can sailors were still taking very heavy casualties.

I was standing in line at the HAMUL's gedunk stand, waiting for the rare treat of an ice cream sundae, when a Chief Torpedoman tapped me on the shoulder.

"Were you on the IRWIN when her fish came back and chased her?" he asked.

I nodded.

"Is it true those fish were sabotaged?"

"Where'd you hear that, Chief?"

"I just came out from Pearl and that's the scuttlebutt going around."

I was non-plussed. "First I heard of anything like that", I told him. "The official explanation says they were damaged by the ship's banging against the PRINCETON."

"Well, maybe so, but I was told by an old shipmate at the Torp Shop that Naval Intelligence found out they'd been tampered with."

"How was that done and who did it?" I wanted to know.

"Don't have any idea. It's all supposed to be very hush-hush."

"It's hard to believe", I ventured, "and scuttlebutt is still scuttle-butt."

I stepped up to get my gedunk. When I turned around, the Chief was gone. Shrugging my shoulders, I chalked it up to a glitch in the Navy's grapevine.

"No-o-o", I said to myself, "that couldn't be."

It was around that time that I was sitting in our Chiefs' Quarters, having a cup of joe, when I heard Duane Ashmead, our own Chief Torpedoman, say something about "Mr. Stout says we were cleared of any blame when the fish boomeranged." But I didn't consider that pertinent at the time. That, I thought, ended the incident of the errant fish. Years later, Ensign Stout told me that Captain Kelly had called him up to his stateroom to inform him that Captain Miller, Torpedo Officer Stout, and the IRWIN had been "completely exonerated" of any responsibility for the torpedoes' malfunctioning. But Kelly went no further than that. Mr. Stout still believes Kelly knew more than he was telling his Torpedo Officer, that there were details the Skipper was not revealing.

On 1 June, Captain Kelly, the C.O. of the HAMUL, and Captain A.E. Jarrell (ComDesRon 55) held a meeting, deciding to extend our tender availability until all repairs would be completed. In addition to the Main Battery Director and Number One Mount, more time was needed to work on leaking boilers and a defective number one generator. While the stay alongside the tender was without incident, we were under smoke screen every night as bogies showed up on the radar screen. And we kept sentries posted against suicide swimmers. We weren't *that* far from the War.

Out at sea, our Fleet fought a titanic typhoon on 4 June. We were again the Third Fleet, and our carrier forces now Task Force 38, since Admirals Halsey and McCain had replaced Admirals Spruance and Mitscher on 27 May. Several ships suffered severe damage, though none were sunk, and this time the destroyers rode out the typhoon well. TF 38 lost 76 planes and six sailors killed or washed overboard. A Navy Court of Inquiry later recommended reassigning Admiral Halsey, but he survived the inquest since he was a popular hero and Washington did not want to boost enemy morale by relieving him of his command.

On 8 June, we went back to work. Reporting to ComDesRon 55 as "ready for sea" (less Number One Mount), we joined with the LAWS, PUTNAM (DD-757), ROOKS, and HEYWOOD L. EDWARDS off the south coast of Okinawa, spaced 1,000 yards apart, and began blasting away at Jap strongpoints on the beach, continuing harassment and illumination fire all night. At 0530 on the 9th, our shore party called for us to move in as close as we could to "neutralize" a concentration of enemy troops. We hit 'em with 200 rounds of 5-inch in 30 minutes; and, according to our observers, wiped out a whole bunch of Jap troops, for which we got a "well done". Then we spent the rest of the day sporadically bombarding whatever targets were called for by the forward spotting observer and/or the spotting plane.

The enemy tried to play games with us on a couple of occasions. We got instructions via radio, in good old American English—doubtless spoken by Japs brought up in the U.S.A. whose loyalty remained with Japan—to depart the fire support area, saying our services were no longer required. On checking with our own shore party, it turned out to be a bogus message. In another instance, we were directed, on the spotter's frequency, to fire into a certain grid. Our troops were moving fast, and we knew the grid called for was behind our own lines. A check with our spotter revealed no such instructions had been given.

Wrapping up the day mission—during which we destroyed several buildings concealing Jap troops, closed up caves, and took out a strong-point enemy pill box—we began the night by joining with the ROOKS, CALLAGHAN, LAWS, and GUEST (DD-472) on stations 1,000 yards apart with a repeat of the previous night's assignment. We were also on call to provide illumination for landing craft on "flycatcher" duty.

We got word that on June 10th, the WILLIAM D. PORTER (DD-579), while out on RP 15, was sunk by a kamikaze exploding close aboard. No men killed, but 61 were wounded. Earlier, two destroyer-minelayers, the J. WILLIAM DITTER (DM-31) and HARRY F. BAUER (DM-26), had been damaged. Ten dead, 27 wounded on the former, but no casualties on the latter. At 0340 on the 11th, we got a typhoon warning and joined the heavy ships as a screen off Okinawa's southwest coast. The storm was passing well to the west of us. But, although it brought more heavy rains, winds, and some high seas, the storm did not prevent us from being back at our fire support station by 1911 that evening. The next four days and nights were carbon copies of our previous fire support missions. Just "routine destroyer duty"!

After refueling, reprovisioning, and replenishing our ammo supply, the IRWIN was back on station southwest of Okinawa at 2000 on 16 June to resume shore bombardment. I had folded up a blanket and was sitting on it on the 0-1 level, secure in the knowledge there'd be little sleep again this night, when I heard the sound of an aircraft engine. Since no General Alarm sounded, I figured it was one of our night fighters. Within minutes, however, there was one violent explosion northwest of us that lit up the sea and cloudy sky with a huge orange fireball. Our guns went silent as Captain Kelly turned the IRWIN toward the scene where now flames were leaping from a destroyer and spreading to the waters around her. From her relative position to us, I knew it was the TWIGGS (DD-591), which had joined our bombardment group just that day.

On orders from ComTaskGroup 32.11, we were close by the stricken ship in minutes, lowering our boats and making ready rescue operations. The TWIGGS was burning fiercely, and in the light of the flames I could see her entire bow was blown away. She'd taken a torpedo right in her number two magazine. The after part of her was afire, as well. The kamikaze, later identified as a Jill torpedo plane, had first launched his fish into the destroyer, then suicided into her. Other ships and landing craft converged on the TWIGGS. The task now was rescuing survivors since the tin can was mortally wounded. Our boats picked up some 25 men, many of them wounded and/or badly burned. Many of those lost, that night, were victims of the oil burning on the surface of the sea. Within a half hour, the fires in the after section had reached number three, four, and five magazines. With one more tremendous explosion, the TWIGGS vanished beneath the waters.

The IRWIN continued to help in the search for survivors. Captain Kelly took a huge risk in ordering our 36-inch searchlights on to sweep the seas as small craft scudded around, finding one man here and one there. With those big lights spearing the darkness, we were visible for miles to any kamikaze or shore battery that might want to take a crack at us. Again, the IRWIN was lucky. Not so the men of the TWIGGS. Over forty percent of her crew, 126 sailors including the Captain, went down with her; and 34 of the survivors were injured. Only three of her officers made it, and all of them were wounded. Finally, the Task Group Commander ordered the search for survivors to cease. We hoisted our boats aboard, returned to our station, and resumed illumination and harassing fire on the Japs.

In conversation with our Chief Gunner's Mate about the incident years later, Boom Boom said he, too, had heard the plane and sighted it trying to make a run on *us*. But the Jap was coming in too high to torpedo the IRWIN. He passed over us, apparently spotted the TWIGGS, changed course a bit, and then launched his torpedo. Thus were we spared her fate. Once more, the enemy had come after us, and missed.

Proud of the IRWIN's record in rescue operations—in saving downed pilots, the PRINCETON's crewmen, the sailor washed off the NEW JERSEY, even a Jap flier, and now the men of the TWIGGS—the crew was flabbergasted and mad as hell the next morning. After dawn, the Skipper looked down from the starboard wing of the Bridge to see that his gig (the Captain's whaleboat) was splashed with oil, its canvas canopy smudged and dirty, and blood on the cushions. He called the boat crew to the Bridge and just raised pure hell with them for letting his gig get so messed up! How could he, on the one hand, have the guts to turn on searchlights, risking attack to save men's lives, then have the unmitigated gall to complain about his gig getting soiled saving those lives?! Strange man, our Captain Kelly.

On each fire-support mission, now, our stations were moving steadily farther to the southern end of Okinawa Jima, evidence the Japs' 32nd Army was being relentlessly driven back and back until they'd be jammed against the water's edge. Word from our Marine shore party told of furious fighting in which the hostiles were resisting to the very last man and were determined to take as many Americans with them as they could. The Nips were fighting to the death; and many, when they saw all was lost, committed suicide, often by pulling the pin on a hand grenade held against their bellies. Others went to certain death in desperate charges against dug-in GIs or Marines. But few surrendered. In the whole campaign, our forces had taken less than 500 prisoners of war.

As defeat was now inevitable, General Ushijima, refusing to capitulate, committed *hari-kari*, himself. The approximately 110,000-man enemy force had all but been annihilated in the three-month struggle for Okinawa—the battle Winston Churchill characterized as the most bitter of the War. To quote Churchill's message to President Truman: "The strength of willpower, devotion and technical resources applied by the United States to this task, joined with the death struggle of the enemy, . . . places this battle among the most intense and famous of military history."

We were back alongside the HAMUL trying to get Mount 51 fully repaired—finally, once and for all—when, on 21 June, 1945, the official announcement came:

"OKINAWA SECURED BY U.S. FORCES."

Unfortunately, as at Guadalcanal, nobody bothered to tell the Japs. That very night a Jap Hamp flew over us and suicided close aboard an unidentified cargo vessel off Goruma Shima. Kamikazes hit the HALLORAN (DE-305), killing three and wounding 34. The CURTIS, a seaplane tender was heavily damaged, losing 41 men—13 killed, with 28 wounded. And the LSM-59 was sunk; however, all but two of her crew were saved, though eight survivors were injured. The next day the LSM-213 and LST-534 were damaged. The Japs were giving the landing craft "pallbearers" no rest.

American losses at Okinawa were heavy. On the ground, the Tenth Army suffered some 7,375 killed or missing in action, including its Commanding Officer. There were roughly 31,800 wounded and over 26,000 non-battle casualties, in all about 35 percent of the troops engaged. At sea, the U.S. Navy lost over 4,900 men killed or missing; some 4,825 were wounded. *The Navy lost some 600 more men killed than the Army, and about 2,000 more than the Marines!* Thirty ships and craft were sunk, and 368 damaged. At Okinawa we lost more men and ships by far than in any other naval campaign in our history.

The Japanese and Okinawans suffered much more. After the War, the Japs estimated roughly 75,000 dead among those having fought in their 32nd Army, not to mention their losses at sea and in the air.

Possibly 80,000 Okinawans died in the campaign, an estimated 20,000 conscripts and 60,000 civilians.

The IRWIN had been in combat 89 straight days, from March 25th to June 21st. During that period, we were never out of range of the dreaded kamikazes. The announcement that Okinawa was "secure" did not mean that we were out of the peril of combat, only that there would be a respite from gunfire support missions. We barely acknowledged the cessation of fighting ashore. There were still air attacks probable, and the suiciders could still reach us.

As in the past, we'd just gone from one operation to the next with, at most, a couple of weeks at ease. The next one was code-named Operation OLYMPIC, the invasion of Kyushu; to be followed by Operation CORONET, the assault on Honshu. We were poised to participate in the invasion to end all invasions—the amphibious landings on the Japanese Home Islands! It would be an operation that would make the Normandy invasion look like child's play at a Sunday school picnic.

There was now a noticeable decrease in enemy air activity. The Japs had apparently given up on the large-scale *kikusui* raids to conserve, we were to learn, the planes of the Kamikaze Corps for use against the invasion fleets of Operation OLYMPIC. The Japs fully expected an assault on their shores in the near future. Still, we did not relax our vigilance around Okinawa. We kept up regular patrols, and all Radar Picket Stations remained fully manned.

As the troops ashore continued the dirty and dangerous task of digging out the last Jap survivors from their holes, Task Force 38 under Admiral Halsey kept up pressure on the enemy with a series of carrier raids along the eastern coasts of Japan, while Army Air Corps B-29s and other types of bombers plastered Tokyo and other cities. The fire-bombing of the Jap capital city was particularly devastating. Hardly a building in the huge metropolitan area was left untouched.

Meanwhile, an enormous build-up of troops and supplies continued on Okinawa in preparation for the Kyushu landings. After seemingly innumerable island invasions, "the Alligator" had advanced to the invasion of the Home Islands of the Empire of Japan itself. Admiral Kelly Turner's plans called for an initial assault force of over 787,000 men—*four times* as many as had invaded Normandy. The IRWIN's job, now, was to conduct anti-aircraft and anti-submarine patrols in order to protect Okinawa until kick-off time for Operation OLYMPIC.

On 1 July, the ships of our Task Group were designated a part of Task Force 99. As we had since the securing of Okinawa, we manned Radar Picket Station Fifteen Able and RP 9A, occasionally picking up enemy snooper planes. Twice we got sonar contacts on enemy submarines, but they slipped away before we could get a good fix on them. In the meantime, it was a welcome relief no longer to be kept awake by the constant blasts of our own gunfire. Even Captain Kelly had eased up on us. Some of the tension had gone out of our lives, now, and the Skipper was not so insistent on enforcing some of the petty rules he'd laid down.

We were on anti-submarine patrol (ASP) on 17 July in company with the RICHARD P. LEARY and DYSON (DD-572) when we were ordered to investigate a possible contact. As we approached the area, one of our ASP aircraft made a run over a target and dropped a load of depth charges. We sped to the spot, only to find that his "submarine" was a hapless whale—now bloodied, badly mangled by the depth charges, and most assuredly dead. Just in case, we cruised the area, only to sight several other large whales. Returning to the dead one, the Skipper eased the IRWIN up to within a few feet of it at very slow speed. Nearly every bluejacket in the crew crowded the life lines for a look. It *was* a sad sight. But in defense of the pilot of the ASP plane, better safe than sorry.

The next day typhoon warnings went up, and we screened several transports in retiring to the east. The storm was a big one, but we were just on the eastern edge of it, where winds barely reached gale force and seas were just moderately rough. The tempest was all over by the next morning; and we returned to Nagagusuku Wan, now renamed Buckner Bay in honor of the Army General who'd led the land forces during the late campaign. He'd been killed during the last few hours of the fighting.

All had been relatively quiet during July around Okinawa—too quiet. Enemy air activity was minimal and our Fleet units were assuming the kamikaze threat was over until we invaded Kyushu. But, beginning on 29 July, just after midnight, the dreaded suiciders struck in one final episode. And four DesRon 55 destroyers were right in the middle of it.

The crew of the CALLAGHAN was ecstatic. They had their orders to go home. The DD-792 was on Radar Picket Station Nine Able, a station the IRWIN was rotated to man on a regular basis since Okinawa was secured. As soon as the CALLAGHAN was relieved by the LAWS that night, the tin can would head for the States for yard availability and overhaul. The LAWS was on her way to take over on RP 9A, 225° True, 60 miles from Zampa Misaki (Point Bolo), and was scheduled to arrive shortly. With the CALLAGHAN were the CASSIN YOUNG and PRICHETT. The CASSIN YOUNG's Action Report described the weather conditions: "The moon was high and bright, visibility very good, sea calm . . . *perfect suicide weather!*"

At 0031, a single bogey blipped on the radar scopes and all three ships sounded the General Alarm. Then more blips. At 0034, the CALLAGHAN and PRICHETT opened fire at a slow-flying old twin-float biplane at 8,000 yards. At 0041, the suicider, maneuvering to avoid the 5-inch barrages, crashed into the CALLAGHAN's number three ammunition upper handling room which exploded with a thunderous blast. The after end of her deck house just disappeared and the after compartments began to flood. The Skipper, Captain C.M. Bertholf, ordered all hands except the damage control party to abandon ship. For another hour, the salvage crew tried to save their tin can; but at 0334, the Captain ordered the remaining crewmen over the side, and before long the CALLAGHAN's bow rose high above the sea to disappear beneath the waves, taking with her 46 bluejackets and one officer. Of the survivors, 73 were wounded.

The PRICHETT and CASSIN YOUNG had been slowly circling the stricken vessel, struggling to rescue as many survivors as possible. Then, at 0150, another kamikaze came blowing in, making its run on the PRICHETT. It was knocked down, but crashed only six feet from the can's side, killing two of her men.

When the LAWS arrived, she found no ship afloat to relieve as she took over the Radar Picket Station. The PRICHETT and CASSIN YOUNG had returned to Buckner Bay; transferring the CALLAGHAN's survivors to a transport, the CRESCENT CITY. The CASSIN YOUNG then took up a position off the Bay's entrance at Patrol Station King Three. In the early morning of 30 July, 1945, she came under attack by two kamikazes. She shot down the first; but the second bore in to crash into her superstructure, setting fires, wiping out radio and radar equipment. The crew worked valiantly to save her; and they did, though 22 men perished in the assault and 45 were wounded. The CASSIN YOUNG was the last of the many U.S. Navy ships to be victimized by combat in World War II.

Thus, the last three ships to be kamikazed at Okinawa were our sister vessels of Destroyer Squadron 55. Even Squadron Commander Captain A.E. Jarrell, aboard the CALLAGHAN when she was hit, was not spared the experience of surviving a sinking by the suiciders. He had to "abandon ship", escaping in an LCS "pallbearer". Out of the Squadron's nine destroyers, only three escaped unscathed from the ordeal that was Okinawa. In one of the strange coincidences of the War, the last two kamikaze victims were destroyers named for officers killed aboard the cruiser SAN FRANCISCO in the 1942 Naval Battle of Guadalcanal—Rear Admiral Daniel J. Callaghan and Captain Cassin Young.

The CALLAGHAN may have been the last U.S. Navy ship sunk in

World War II. At almost the same moment the suicider slammed into the DD-792, the heavy cruiser INDIANAPOLIS, returning to the Philippines without escort after delivering the triggering device for the first atomic bomb to Tinian, was torpedoed by a Jap submarine (I-58). It was one of the worst and most senseless tragedies of the War. Of the 1,199-man crew, some 800 survived to abandon ship. But no word got to anyone she'd gone down. Finally, 84 hours after the torpedoing, a plane accidentally sighted the men in the water. By then, nearly 500 had fallen victims to wounds, exhaustion, the sharks, and the cruel sea. Only 316 sailors survived the sinking of the INDIANAPOLIS. After the War, the sub's C.O. Hashimoto was summoned to Washington to testify at the court-martial trial of Captain Charles Butler McVay III, whose father had once commanded the U.S. Navy's Asiatic Fleet.

When I heard the CALLAGHAN was sunk, my first thought was of our old shipmate Al Block. There was no way, at the time, to find out whether he'd survived. But just before the CRESCENT CITY was to get underway, who should come bouncing into the IRWIN's Radio Shack but Albert Brantley Block, himself. We were extremely happy to see him, and glad he'd survived the sinking. His ship had been only minutes away from getting out of the War all in one piece. The Gang all gathered 'round to congratulate him on being safe, commiserating with him on the loss of his ship. But we secretly envied him, too. He was heading for the States, right now! He had only a few minutes before the CRESCENT CITY shoved off.

Operation ICEBERG was a nightmare for tin can sailors. It was the longest sustained action of the War in which we were constantly operating in a combat situation—day in, day out. The cold statistics tell only a smidgen of the story. Of the roughly 4,900 sailors killed or missing in the bloody Okinawa Campaign, over 2,100 went down with destroyers. Thus a lopsided *FORTY-THREE PERCENT* plus of all sailors lost at Okinawa were destroyermen. Almost 45 percent of those wounded were on tin cans. Of the 30 ships of all types sunk, 12 were DDs, and 118 destroyers and destroyer types were among the damaged, many of them so badly mangled they were scuttled, accounting for some 44 percent of the 368 ships damaged at Okinawa.

What is not reflected in the numbers is the stress and strain visited upon the men who experienced these ordeals. Captain Jarrell, in his DesRon 55 Action Report on the Capture of Okinawa Gunto, states: "Personnel performance has never been better, within my knowledge. Naturally, there were a few cases of combat fatigue. There was one suicide." (The suicide was not on the IRWIN.) He does not point out, however, that there was no one on any of the destroyers able to diagnose "combat fatigue". The Medical Officers were just that. None I know of were schooled in psychiatry or psychology. A post-War study commissioned by the Defense Department concluded that, after *28 days* in combat *98 percent* of any unit would develop "war psychoses". The destroyermen of the Gunfire Support and Covering Force at Okinawa were in combat *over three times* that long!

Like every other man on the IRWIN, I was completely exhausted, weary down to the very marrow of my bones, with nerves stretched as taut as fiddle strings. There had been little respite from the almost incessant firing of our guns, from the knot in the stomach that came automatically when bogies were on the radar scopes, from the necessity to be constantly alert for enemy action.

After we finally ceased the bombardment missions, I was shaving one day when I took a real look at my face in the mirror. My skin was sallow, my cheeks were hollow, and my eyes looked like two burnt holes in a blanket. After dressing, I went up to Sick Bay and asked Dr. Fagan if I could weigh myself. I topped out at just under 125 pounds. It would take me until 1953 before I got back to the 170-pound weight I'd carried on enlistment in 1941.

There was little doubt that nearly every man aboard the IRWIN experienced at least some symptoms of combat fatigue. You only had to look at them to see their weariness. Yet, the only way a man would be classified as having "war neuroses" was for him to go berserk, or be incapable of carrying out his duties. The men of the IRWIN endured the tedium of her missions, and only three were transferred for hospitalization. A remarkable accomplishment for a crew whose official Battle History said of her performance at Okinawa:

"Of the many ships whose blasting of enemy shore positions raised the curtain on the Okinawa Campaign, the IRWIN was one of *less than a half-dozen* that stayed continually on the scene, week after week, month after month, until final victory was achieved. The IRWIN saw hundreds of ships come and go, saw some of her sister ships damaged and returned to rear areas for repairs. And when those ships once more returned, the IRWIN was still there, slugging the Jap with everything she had."

The Battle History continues: "The *kamikaze* technique had been developed and destroyers became the special targets of the suicide pilots. The IRWIN saw and knocked down her share of these. Her guns blasted torpedo boats that slipped out of hiding places along the shore to attack our forces under cover of darkness. She searched out and destroyed suicide boats in their camouflaged shelters. She hurled thousands of rounds of ammunition into enemy troops, gun emplacements and pill boxes on Okinawa and Ie Shima."

There was scuttlebutt DesRon 55 had been recommended for the Presidential Unit Citation. Of the twelve destroyers sunk at Okinawa, three—the MORRISON, LONGSHAW, and CALLAGHAN—were from the Squadron. Three others of the six remaining—the PORTERFIELD, PRICHETT, and CASSIN YOUNG—were damaged. That's some 66 percent casualties! Only the IRWIN, PRESTON, and LAWS survived intact—which, under the circumstances, had to fall in the "miracle" category. As for Squadron personnel, 315 men were killed, and 352 were wounded—more than enough men to man two destroyers. No other Squadron took such a beating. Yet the Citation was never awarded. We figured there were two reasons: one, there are no Admirals on tin cans; and two, we now had an *Army* man in the White House.

The ships of DesRon 55 did well in Navy Unit Commendations. Of the some 500 destroyers in service during the War, only 30 received the NUC from the Secretary of the Navy. Of those 30, *four* were DesRon 55 cans: IRWIN, MORRISON, PRICHETT, and CASSIN YOUNG. Pretty good percentage, but the other five should have been commended, too.

For the IRWIN's long, tortuous, duty at Okinawa, the crew earned just the battle star on their Asiatic-Pacific Campaign Medals awarded all ships that participated in the Campaign—whether they were there one day, or the entire 128 days from pre-invasion bombardment through the last kamikaze attack; whether they saw action, or just came and went.

Ironically, Captain Kelly was awarded a Bronze Star for "heroic achievement as Commanding Officer of USS IRWIN in action against enemy forces. . . . " The citation went on: "With his ship relentlessly attacked by hostile suicide planes and boats in waters that were infested with mines and submarines, Commander Kelly furnished fire support for our troops over long periods of time. . . . " Hell, Kelly didn't even come aboard until six weeks into the campaign, and he inherited Captain Miller's well-trained, battle-hardened crew that *got* him the medal. Kelly never thanked us either, as Cap'n Danny did for helping him win his Legion of Merit.

Upon leaving the IRWIN, our beloved Skipper Danny Miller was promoted to the rank of Captain. After serving in the 6th Naval District Command, Daniel B. Miller served on other stations and commanded other ships, including the PRESIDENT JACKSON. Returning once more to the 6th Naval District, he was promoted to Rear Admiral upon retirement in 1957. Admiral Miller died in 1968.

After decommissioning the IRWIN, Commander Robert B. Kelly

taught engineering at the U.S. Naval Academy, later commanding other ships and eventually a Destroyer Division. But he never made Admiral, retiring with the rank of Captain in 1961. When Captain Kelly died in 1989, in a bit of irony his obituary in the *Los Angeles Times* never mentioned his having commanded the IRWIN!

That the IRWIN was extremely lucky in surviving Operation ICE-BERG, is indicated in the statistics of the Campaign. Destroyers *alone* suffered more men killed, and nearly three times the number of wounded, as there were among *all* Navy units at Pearl Harbor on December 7th, 1941. Tin can sailors at Okinawa suffered about 44 percent of the casualties—some 2,100 killed and 2,065 wounded—incurred by the Fleet as a whole. There were more destroyers sunk than any other ship type; but in addition to the 12 listed in most of the reports, generally omitted are the 17 *more* so badly damaged they had to be scuttled, bringing the complete tally to *29* destroyers sunk. In no other campaign in World War II did one ship type take such a clobbering.

Although the IRWIN's successes at sea against kamikaze aircraft, patrol gunboats, and other targets are well-documented in the War Diary, there's no record I've found to indicate her massive contribution in support of the Marine and Army ground forces on Okinawa itself. I have found some lists of targets, but they are fragmentary and often incomplete. The only yardstick we have for a rough estimate are the reports we got back from the shore party on Saipan where, in just one fire mission, we were credited with wiping 1,200 to 1,400 enemy troops.

In hundreds of fire support assignments at Saipan, Tinian, Parece Vela, Ie Shima, and Okinawa, we pounded enemy ground units with thousands of shells—firing 12,750 rounds of Main Battery ammunition at Okinawa, *alone*. In stopping banzai charges and neutralizing troop concentrations; in bombarding buildings, airfields, fortifications, pill boxes, machinegun nests, suicide boat caves and hideouts, communications and radar installations (not counting the crews of two tanks and the air crews of planes we shot down)—the toll taken by the IRWIN among enemy ground forces had to be several thousands killed and wounded. Those 12,750 rounds fired at Okinawa, in 89 days in action against the enemy, computes out to firing *one round every ten minutes, twenty-four hours a day, for THREE MONTHS!*

In his book *Great Campaigns of World War II*, Hanson W. Baldwin wrote of Okinawa as the greatest air-sea battle in history. "In retrospect, the battle for Okinawa can be described only in the grim superlatives of war. In size, scope, and ferocity it dwarfed the Battle of Britain. . . . Okinawa was an epic of human endurance and courage." With respect

THE DOOMED U.S.S. PRINCETON EXPLODES

U.S.S. IRWIN showered with debris as the destroyer fights fire and rescues 646 survivors. 24 October, 1944, 2nd Battle of the Philippines

THE BURNING PRINCETON
Fires rage through the bombed light carrier as seen from the destroyer IRWIN. Photo from motion picture film from Cdr. J.D.P. Hodapp, USN (Ret)

USS IRWIN-DD-794

The U.S.S. IRWIN "BOOMERANG TORPEDO" INSIGNIA
Designed and painted by Shipmate Bill Needles

SCRATCH ONE MEATBALL
U.S.S. IRWIN downs a Japanese Val torpedo bomber as Kamikazes attack the destroyer, U.S.S. MARYLAND and one crashes into the WITTER (DE-636). Okinawa Jima, 6 April, 1945
Original painting by Richard DeRosset

BNS SANTA CATARINA (Brazilian Navy) nee U.S.S. IRWIN—1988

The Author with President-to-be Ronald Reagan—1979.

O GRAYBACK SS.

From April to late June 1945 there were 10 kikusui-attacks against Okinawa, consisting of 1465 Kamikaze planes and 1351 others, Sinking 21 Ships & damaging 66.

TOKYO 845 MI.

○ ---- MANNERT L ABELE DD (B) ·

WM. D. PORTER DD (B) ----○
  ○ OBERRENDER DE (B)

Northern tip reached 19 Apr
HEDO MISAKI

LITTLE DD (B)

Ernie Pyle † IE SHIMA

● I-56

CHINA 500 MI.

77ᵀᴴ Div. 16 Apr
10ᵀᴴ Army Lands 1 Apr

ZAMPA MISAKI (POINT BOLO)

BARRY APD
DICKERSON APD

● I-44 (G)

MORRISON DD
BUSH DD
BATES APD
TROUTSS

LUCE DD (B)

KADENA AIRFIELD

SWORDFISH SS

HAGUSHI BEACHES

○ TRIGGER SS

SHURI CASTLE
NAGAGSUKU WAN (BUCKNER BAY)

TSUKEN SIMA

PRINGLE DD
LONGSHAW DD ○ COLHOUN DD

NAHA

EMMONS DMS
THORNTON AVD

ITOMAN

○ KETE SS ○ HALLIGAN DD
(M)
○ GRAYBACK

FORMOSA 400 MI.

0 5 10 15

CALLAGHAN DD (B)

○ SWALLOW AM

OKINAWA

Secured 21 June 1945
○ U.S. NAVY SHIPS SUNK BY ENEMY ACTION
● JAPANESE SUBMARINES SUNK

○ TWIGGS DD (B)

DURING THIS OPERATION THERE WERE
ALSO 57 DD's & DE's DAMAGED BY KAMIKAZE AIRCRAFT
17 DD'S SO BADLY DAMAGED THEY WERE ORDERED SCUTTLED.

● I-8

(Courtesy Sgt/Maj. Lester Bamford, USMC Ret.)

to the U.S. Navy, the author, military editor of the *New York Times*, observed (italics his):

"*The simple accolade applied to the brave men of the little ships, 'They stuck it out with demonstrated valor', is equally applicable to all those of Okinawa, dead and living, who stood, fought, and endured in the greatest battle of U.S. arms. But to the 'small boys', the 'spitkits', the 'tin cans'—the little ships of the radar picket line—belongs a special glory. They bore the overwhelming share of death and destruction; they were the thin and bloodstained line that stood between the Sons of Heaven and dominion of the East China Sea.*"

The IRWIN's Battle History is more modest: "There was no let-up, no rest period. By day and by night for weeks at a time, the ship fired continuously. Sleep was a wistful dream, like 'home'. The tin can sailors who, when the magazines were empty, lugged ammunition all day, then fired it all night. They weren't heroes, for the work they did was not heroic. It was *routine destroyer duty*, only unique in that it was probably one of the longest and toughest 'routine' jobs on record."

33

THE BOMB, THE VICTORY

Once our ground forces had defeated the Japanese on Okinawa, the need for shore bombardment ended, and the IRWIN's missions turned to anti-aircraft and anti-submarine patrol.

While mass air raids were no longer a threat, the enemy still sent planes over the Okinawa area. Our radar continued to pick them up on a regular basis. And, on three different occasions, we made sonar contacts which appeared to be submarines, but the echoes were distant and lost before we could attack. The assumption was that the enemy was snooping to assess our build-up for Operation OLYMPIC.

I could get no firm confirmation on the part the IRWIN would play in the upcoming operation, but the scuttlebutt emanating from the wardroom indicated we'd again be in the pre-invasion Gunfire Support and Covering Group as lead destroyer in the invasion formation. That didn't do a helluva lot for my morale; nor for any of the rest of the crew, for that matter.

With the resilience of youth, a few good nights' sleep, and a number of full meals under our belts—the physical exhaustion began to wane. The mental fatigue, however, would last much, much, much longer. Having faced the perils of Operation ICEBERG, the demeanor of the men was much more sober than it was prior to the 128 days of combat strain at Okinawa. On the other hand, there was a feeling of confidence in ship and crew that only surviving such an ordeal can bring.

We were still in combat mode, despite the diminished hostile activity. Our anti-aircraft missions had us alternating between Radar Picket Stations Nine Able and Fifteen; and we regularly were on seaward patrols, protecting transport areas and harbor entrances. We were now part of Task Force 99, designated as "Offensive Screen, Garrison Forces, Okinawa Jima". I wasn't sure what that "Offensive" meant, but it sounded ominous to me.

July of 1945 ended in typical Okinawa fashion. We were under another typhoon warning. I told the three new radio strikers—Blaise Buffamante, Gino Piroli, and Del Waddell—that I'd ordered it up just to celebrate their reporting aboard. They'd hardly stowed their gear before we got underway to screen the transports as we put to sea. With the LAWS, PRICHETT, and PRESTON, we herded the big ships southwesterly to avoid the full blast of the storm, but still it gave the new youngsters a taste of rugged weather—high seas, winds in the 55 to 60 knot range. We returned to Buckner Bay on 3 August.

August 6th was a quiet, routine day aboard the IRWIN. We refueled at Hagushi, then switched to a berth in Buckner Bay. Former striker George Mootz, just earning his Radioman 3rd Class (RM3c) "crow" on the 1st, asked me what our next assignment was. When I told him we would be patrolling on Radar Picket Station 9A (RP 9A) the next day, he took great delight in trying to frighten the three new lads by pointing out the CALLAGHAN had been sunk on that station just one week before. I think he succeeded.

There's no notation in the IRWIN's War Diary about the significance of 6 August, 1945. I heard some fragmentary talk from the wardroom about a bomb being dropped on Hiroshima, a city toward the southeast corner of Japan's Honshu Island, but paid scant attention. We'd been bombing Japan for months, now. That evening, though, the lead story I copied from Mackay Radio Press News service was all about the city being hit by an "atomic bomb" dropped by a B-29 Superfortress bomber named the "Enola Gay" flying out of Tinian in the Marianas. It said the bomb had caused "great devastation". Having no yardstick by which to measure the incomparable destruction a nuclear weapon could inflict, we thought it was just another heavy raid to soften up the hostiles in preparation for Operation OLYMPIC. We were more concerned with the possibility of kamikazes coming in on us when we got to RP 9A.

Things began to look more promising when we heard President Truman was calling on the Japs to surrender. But we remained on a war footing, fully aware of the enemy's proclivity for deception and perfidy. When there was no sign from Tokyo leading to capitulation, we thought this atomic bomb thing hadn't been as effective as it had been billed to be, and any expectations we might have had for the end of the War were considerably diminished. As I told the guys hanging around the 0-1 level: "I don't trust the Japs, and I'll only believe they've surrendered when we can sail into Tokyo Bay without getting shot at! Even then, I'd want the Old Man to have us at battle stations with all batteries loaded and trained!"

On 9 August, President Truman ordered a second A-bomb dropped, this one on Nagasaki on the west coast of Kyushu. The same day, the opportunistic Soviet Union declared war on the Japanese Empire. Truman followed up the bombing with another demand for "unconditional surrender" in terms of the Potsdam Declaration, the alternative being "prompt and utter destruction". Scuttlebutt swept through the ships around Okinawa like wildfire. On two successive nights, gunners on merchant ships and some transports stupidly fired 20- and 40-millimeter weapons in the air in premature celebration of the War's end. The idiots could have gotten somebody killed. Navy ships had no bogies on radar, otherwise we'd have figured it was an air raid.

Still no word out of Tokyo.

Apparently, so it came out later, the Japanese people couldn't conceive of their being conquered and were utterly unprepared for a capitulation, believing to the bitter end that they were winning the War. So effective was Tokyo's propaganda, that older Japs on Oahu who couldn't understand English, believed they had won even after War's end, gathering on hearsay to witness their Navy victoriously entering Pearl Harbor (Morison)!

As for the Nip government, we would learn later there was a great debate going on among the members of the Japanese Imperial Conference. The military leaders, headed by Admiral Toyoda, had a laundry list of conditions they wanted the United States to accept. The senior officers tried to get Emperor Hirohito to agree to "one last great battle" to "save face"—the national honor. To his credit, Hirohito put his foot down ("we have to bear the unbearable"); and, on 14 August, Radio Tokyo announced his decision to the World. On 15 August (14 August in the U.S.A.) after a military coup was foiled, the Emperor broadcast the notice of surrender to the Japanese people, following it with official notification to Washington.

The President of the United States immediately declared 15 August "VJ-Day" and issued a proclamation calling for a two-day holiday to celebrate the victory over the Empire of Japan and the end of World War II. On the 16th, a ceasefire order went out from the Imperial Palace to all Japanese naval and military commands. Meanwhile, leading Japanese militarists committed suicide—including, most appropriately, Admiral Onishi, father of the Kamikaze Corps.

The Rising Sun had suddenly set!

At 1300, 15 August, 1945, Admiral Halsey sent the following message, especially appreciated by those of us who had been in the Solomons, to the Fleet:

"Men, . . . the war is ended. . . . You have brought an implacable, treacherous, and barbaric foe to his knees in abject surrender. This is the first time in recorded history of the misbegotten Japanese race that they as a nation have been forced to submit to this humiliation. . . . Your names are writ in golden letters on the pages of history—your fame is *and shall be immortal. . . .* Whether in the early days, when fighting with a very frayed shoestring, or at the finish, when fighting with the mightiest combined fleet the world has ever seen, the results have been the same—victory has crowned your efforts. *The forces of righteousness and decency have triumphed."*

The War was over.

The end came so abruptly it was difficult for us to absorb the ramifications. Aboard the IRWIN there was no big celebration apart from broad smiles, handshakes and backslapping. I had been at war so long I found the concept of "peace at last" almost incomprehensible. Gone from my life in nearly an instant was the purpose for which I'd begun training four and a half years before. I had become so habituated to sailing "in harm's way" nothing else seemed natural. I thought of Saint Paul's statement in 2 Timothy 4:7—"I have fought a good fight, I have finished my course, I have kept the faith." Then I asked myself: "NOW WHAT?"

Captain Kelly decided we should have some sort of special marking of the occasion and ordered the ship's cooks to spare no efforts in preparing a "Victory Dinner". We sat down to a scrumptious meal—best we'd had since leaving the States—of sirloin steak and eggs, pie a la mode, and all the fixin's. The Old Man added a nice tribute to the crew on the menu, decorated with Bill Needles' drawings:

A MISSION COMPLETED

"A good fight and a safe return"—thus was IRWIN christened. Since then IRWIN has fought hard and has fought often. Her battle roll is impressive. And never has she suffered damage by the enemy. To her crew which enabled IRWIN to fulfill her mission—"Well Done!" Robert B. Kelly, Commander, U.S. Navy, Commanding.

The preparations for the formal surrender of the Japanese went forward apace. There's one facet of those preparations that is not well-known and is not in the history books. It concerns Oscar Badger, my old NORTH CAROLINA Skipper. Admiral Badger was flying his Flag from the IOWA as Commander Third Fleet Heavy Ship Strike Force. His Flag Lieutenant was (now retired Commander) Jack Schroeder who was also the Admiral's son-in-law. In answers to inquiries from me, both the Commander and Mrs. Schroeder wrote a long letter in which the days just prior to the Jap surrender were chronicled.

Admiral Halsey asked Badger (presumably via Admiral Nimitz, CinCPac) to be the Naval Force Commander in the initial occupation of Japan. Admiral Badger and his Staff moved over to join Halsey in the NEW JERSEY where plans were drawn up for the formal Japanese surrender. After some days, Badger and his people transferred to the

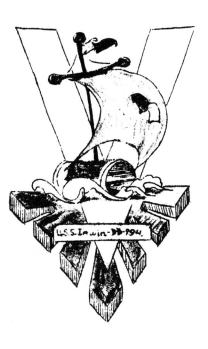

IRWIN's BATTLE ROLL

* * * * *

* Invasion of SAIPAN and TINIAN

* Supported Carrier Strikes
PALAU, PHILIPPINES, FORMOSA, RYUKYUS

* 2nd BATTLE OF PHILIPPINES

* Invasion of IWO JIMA

Supported 2nd Carrier Raid on TOKYO

* Invasion of OKINAWA

Occupation of JAPAN

V_I_C_T_O_R_Y D_I_N_N_E_R

* * * *

EAT, DRINK AND BE MERRY
FOR TOMORROW YOU MAY DIET

- o O o -

Chilled Fruit Juice

Cream of Pea Soup

Sirloin Steak and Fried Eggs
Worchestershire Sauce

French Fried Potatoes - Carrot Sticks
Baked Golden Bantam Corn--Pickled Beets

Peach Pie à la mode

Parkerhouse Rolls - Butter - Jam

Coffee

Mixed Hard Candy - Mixed Nuts

Cigarettes

A MISSION COMPLETED

* * * * *

"A good fight and a safe return"—

thus was IRWIN christened. Since

then IRWIN has fought hard and has

fought often. Her battle roll is

impressive. And never has she suf-

fered damage by the enemy.

To her crew which enabled IRWIN to

fulfill her mission - "Well Done!"

Robert B. Kelly
ROBERT B. KELLY,
Commander, U.S.Navy,
Commanding.

anti-aircraft light cruiser SAN DIEGO (CL-53) and got underway accompanied only by a single minesweeper. As Commander Schroeder wrote, they steamed into Tokyo Bay with "no air cover, no nothing!" And no surrender had yet been announced, either.

"When we anchored for the night [off Yokosuka Naval Base]", the Commander continued, "you can imagine it was a bit tense. The SAN DIEGO wardroom was jammed with our augmented Staff. The Admiral tapped his water glass, stood up, and broke the tension with these words:

'Gentlemen, I have but this to say: if we are alive tomorrow, we'll know we've won the war.'"

Schroeder added: "We landed at Yokosuka the next morning—and the maze of negotiations began—culminating in the much-photographed MISSOURI ceremony. As far as I know, we were the first Navy people ashore. Certainly he [Admiral Badger] was the first Flag Officer."

Navy historian Morison mentions the danger faced by our forces at this critical juncture: "We must . . . point out that even after two atomic bombs had been dropped, the Potsdam Declaration clarified, the guards' insurrection defeated and the Emperor's will made known, it was touch and go whether the Japanese actually would surrender. Hirohito had to send members of the Imperial family to the principal Army commands to ensure compliance. His younger brother Prince Takamatsu was just in time to make the Atsugi airfield available for the first occupation forces on 26 August, and to keep the kamikaze boys grounded. They were boasting that they would crash the MISSOURI when she entered Tokyo Bay."

Oscar Badger's daring exploit didn't surprise me one iota. Such action was, to me, "pure Badger". It's an ironic coincidence that Admiral Oscar C. Badger, whom I esteemed so highly, and Admiral Frank Jack Fletcher, for whom I had so little regard, were both Congressional Medal of Honor winners who each earned the Nation's highest honor on the same day in the same action.

During the 1914 Mexican Revolution under Victoriano Huerta, a U.S. Naval Squadron was sent to Veracruz to protect American lives and investments. When it was learned a German vessel was about to deliver a load of arms to Huerta, a landing force of sailors and Marines was ordered to seize the customs house to prevent the munitions from reaching Huerta's army. On 21 and 22 April, the brigade was "opposed by an enemy they could not see, in the streets of a strange city where every house was an ambush and every church tower a fighting top." Then Ensign Badger was cited for "fighting at the head of his company, and was eminent and conspicuous in his conduct, leading his men with skill and courage." Then Lieutenant Fletcher, in charge of the ESPER-

ANZE, succeeded in getting on board over 350 refugees. "Although the ship was under fire . . . he succeeded in getting all placed in safety." Fletcher was cited for being "eminent and conspicuous in performance of his duties."

On 26 August, 1945, on orders from Port Director, Okinawa, the IRWIN (with Captain Kelly as Commander Task Unit 99.6.10) got underway at 1511, en route to Tokyo Bay, escorting the first merchant ship convoy to Japan. On the 30th, our lookouts sighted an untethered mine. We took it under fire, exploding it. Otherwise the voyage was uneventful. The discovery of the mine, however, affected my attitude and actions. I still didn't trust the Japs; and, although they'd given us charts of their minefields and we'd swept them, I wasn't convinced there were no more mines out there. As we steamed up the channel towards Yokosuka, I watched the scenery go by from the searchlight platform on Number One Stack. In case a mine exploded against our hull, I stood a chance of being blown free.

We dropped our hook in Berth F-24, and I looked out at the U.S. Third Fleet assembled in Tokyo Bay. There was hardly a place to anchor one more ship. If the Japanese people had any doubts about the awesome power we had built up since Pearl Harbor, they sure got a good look at it now. Wordsworth's words come to mind: "With ships the sea was sprinkled far and nigh. . . . "

In my imagination, I had seen a very different entrance into the heart of the Japanese Empire, assuming I survived to make it that far at all. Back in Noumea, when Admiral Halsey said to us sailors "See you in Tokyo!", my mental image was of the Fleet steaming in, *en masse* and in battle formation, with flags and bunting flying, bands playing, gun salutes, and sailors "manning the rail" in a triumphant celebration. But the IRWIN had arrived almost unnoticed; and now it had begun to rain, obscuring the big ships around us in a gray haze. As darkness fell, I went in the Radio Shack, got a fresh cup o' mud, and returned to the 0-1 level, sitting with my back to the lee bulkhead and watching the rain.

"Hell!", I thought, "I've spent nearly four years getting to this damn' place the hard way and this is how it all ends? Hardly seems worth it."

The scene seemed surreal—a grotesque anti-climax, abrupt and aberrant, to years at war. That night, I dreamed I was back on the 'Canal, huddled in a foxhole with Jap bombers overhead. I woke in a cold sweat about 0230, got up and walked the deck 'til dawn.

After morning chow, we got underway to refuel from the NECHES (AO-48), then went alongside the PIEDMONT (AD-17) at Yokosuka Naval Base to transfer one of our guys for medical treatment. Up on the Bridge, Fitch handed me his binocs, saying "Look over there." Focusing

VICTORY AT LAST
The U.S. Fleet in Tokyo Bay
(U.S. Navy Photo - National Archives)

the lens, I pointed the glasses where Junior indicated. Stacked up like cordwood were seemingly hundreds of two-man suicide submarines. So this is what the Japs had in store for us if we'd launched Operation OLYMPIC? I wondered what else they had up their sleeves.

Latter-day critics of the A-bomb attacks on Hiroshima and Nagasaki, who never fought the Japs nor apparently dug deep enough to obtain the facts, have claimed Japan did not have the military capability to resist effectively an invasion. These pundits thus make light of projections that an amphibious assault would have cost U.S. forces a million casualties and the Japanese perhaps twenty million. Naval and military authorities I respect, including Harvard's eminent naval historian Samuel Eliot Morison in his books *The Two-Ocean War* and *Victory in the Pacific*, give the lie to those critics. According to Morison, the certain carnage of the planned invasions of Kyushu and Honshu, if executed, "stagger the imagination".

The OLYMPIC invasion force would have first faced concentrated air attacks by some 10,000 aircraft, over half of them *kamikazes*, dispersed and hidden in caves or camouflaged hangars scattered throughout the Japanese Islands. Some 5,000 of these were "conventional" aircraft, including bombers rigged with manned "*baka* bombs", and likewise secreted. Their primary targets would have been the slow, lightly armed transports loaded down with troops, and the Gunfire Support and Covering Force destroyers. The IRWIN was slated for pre-invasion bombardment, as we were at Okinawa. We would have been among the first to catch the brunt of *kikusui* attacks. In Morison's words: "It simply is not true that Japan had no military capability left . . . ."

The volcano-formed Japanese Islands come almost straight up out of the sea. There are few shore lines where a large amphibious landing can be made, and the Japs had those waters mined and studded with undersea obstacles. The beaches were targeted by artillery and automatic weapons, well-dug-in or concealed in concrete pill boxes interconnected by tunnels. As we'd seen at Saipan, Iwo Jima, and Okinawa, these fortifications were almost impervious to aerial and naval bombardment. Backing up these defenses was a Japanese Army of over one million men—which, as three years of fighting the Japs on Pacific islands had demonstrated, would have fought to the last man. And, had the Emperor ordered his civilian population to fight to the death to defend their homeland, they would have taken a lot of Americans with them, not to mention the possibility of protracted guerrilla warfare.

The Japs had one more threat such resistance might have given them time to get operational—an atomic bomb of their own! Little

'Japan's Secret': building a bomb of their own

L.A. Life, Daily News—August 6, 1985

By Bruce Cook

Daily News Book Editor

Of all the justifications and rationalizations put forward to explain the dropping of the atomic bomb on Hiroshima, the one that most of us haven't heard is the one that may well stand up best to scrutiny in a hundred years' time: It was them or us.

Robert K. Wilcox, a journalist, novelist and screenwriter now living in Studio City, has written a fascinating account of the Japanese atomic bomb project, one that may not have all the answers but poses questions that should keep historians digging for decades.

"Japan's Secret War" (Morrow, $15.95) is the product of five years of determined research and writing. It was done with no cooperation from the Japanese and could certainly not have been written without documents that came into Wilcox's hands through the Freedom of Information Act.

"I had always been a World War II buff, and back in 1980 I came across an article in the New York Times that made reference to a Science magazine story on the Japanese atom bomb. I read the article in question and found that very little was known about it but that there was firm evidence that they were making an effort to develop such a weapon. Well, I was just fascinated. Up to then, the Japanese had been regarded solely as victims. I started digging, and the deeper i got the more interested I got," he said.

"I came up fairly early with two conclusions. First, that yes, the Japanese did have a program of nuclear scientific research right in Japan. It started about 1938 or 1939, and it went on until the end of the war and even after. Second, and more startling, our intelligence after the war began to get reports from North Korea that during the war the Japanese had a big nuclear complex operating there. A top-level intelligence chief said that we must give credence to the fact that they may have made a bomb. Of course, the Russians moved in there at the end of the war and dismantled all the factories — perhaps that one, too."

Talking with Wilcox in the study of his comfortable home as his son splashes in the pool outside, all this seems a little unreal — especially when he adds: "There are fascinating aspects to this story. Los Angeles and San Francisco could have been blown up. The late Derek deSolla Price of Yale, who was the foremost scholar of the history of science — he theorizes that the Japanese could have delivered it by submarine. They had no air capability for it. They were actually looking for the opportunity to use it in a defensive way and were hoping to do it at Saipan.

"After all, to make an atomic bomb is not such a tough situation as far as the physics of it goes. They had the engineering problem of separating uranium into fissionable uranium. And it was aggravated by the fact that they didn't have a lot of uranium to work with. In general, you could say that Germany had the uranium and the Japanese had the knowledge. As a matter of fact, the last submarine to leave the big submarine base at Kiel at the end of the European war was loaded with 2,000 pounds of uranium to be delivered to the Japanese. They also sent along the plans for their jet fighter. But when he heard the news of Germany's surrender, the commander gave up. There's a mystery as to what finally happened to the load of uranium, but it was discovered when the sub surrendered, and that was the first inkling the Americans had that the Japanese were trying to make a bomb."

This knowledge must, of course, have influenced President Truman in his decision to drop the bomb — though no documentation has been uncovered to prove this. Nevertheless, Wilcox did discover that three days after the Japanese surrender an intelligence team was sent into Japan to find out how far the Japanese had gone in their own nuclear research. Although the Japanese denied that any such program existed, they did eventually find out that the main center for homeland nuclear research had been destroyed in a general bombing raid in April 1945. And in November 1945, MacArthur sent forces into the physics laboratories of Japanese universities, and they dismantled and destroyed five cyclotrons that were then still in use.

But when Wilcox started digging in the National Archives and requesting documents under the Freedom of Information Act, he discovered an intelligence summary on North Korea that substantiated suspicions that the Japanese had conducted atomic bomb research there at Hungnam. It was all hush-hush at the time.

But, as Wilcox said, "There were many reports cited from those who had actually worked there, and all reports agree that experiments were conducted. One Japanese code message referring to the Hungnam project said, 'We have tested at (blank), and it came out all right.' During the occupation, we kept digging up new stuff that indicated that they were in the final stages of constructing a bomb. During the Korean War, there was one news report that they had found remnants of a uranium plant in a mountain cave, and a couple of days later there was an official denial of this. It sounded phony."

The overwhelming burden of Wilcox's research was done from official American sources. When he went to Japan to find out what he could of that side of the story, he was stonewalled: "They gave me the cold shoulder and the runaround. I had a month to find out the truth. You don't do that in Japan. You need a year to sip tea and talk. I came away with a lot of information but not the key stuff. I admit there's more to be done in the way of research on this subject, especially in Japan. I just hope my book will spur further inquiry by other writers and historians.

"I wish the book had all the answers, but I feel like I'm just one guy who got onto something really big. I'm not going to be able to punch a hole in this thing all by myself. There'll have to be some others who'll follow my lead."

(Los Angeles Daily News—L.A. Life)

known to Americans is the fact the Japanese had been working on a nuclear weapon since 1938 or 1939 (see *Japan's Secret War* by Robert J. Wilcox). They were even cooperating with Nazi Germany on its development. Whether it could have been completed in time for use against Operation OLYMPIC is a moot point. Had they developed the bomb, the Japs *would have used it*. They have, of course, steadfastly stonewalled any significant investigation of their nuclear development or capability, before or since. However, a German submarine was on its way to Japan with 2,000 pounds of uranium and heavy water when the European War ended. The sub's skipper returned to Kiel without making delivery. It may have been the possibility of completing the A-bomb that led the Jap military leaders to plead with Hirohito to continue the War. But the Emperor feared another A-bombing by the U.S., not knowing we had dropped the only two we had!

What many Americans don't realize is that the fire-bombing of Japanese cities was more destructive than the A-bombs. For instance, according to Japanese authorities, the B-29 raid on Tokyo on the night of 9/10 March, 1945, five months before, produced a million homeless and incinerated some 83,800 of human kind—it was "indescribably horrifying".

President Truman's decisions on Hiroshima and Nagasaki ended the War and Operation OLYMPIC never came to pass. Had we had to invade Japan, millions of lives, both American and Japanese, would have been sacrificed to the god of war and Jap fanaticism. Aware of the IRWIN's mission, there is no doubt in my mind my shipmates and I would have been among them. Along with many others, I wouldn't have seen the Golden Gate in '48 or any other year. Whatever else I may think of him, I have no doubt President Truman saved my life and that of millions more.

On hearing of the horrors of POW camps near Tokyo from escapees, Bull Halsey sent his Staff, including former Minnesota Governor Harold Stassen, on rescue missions. So we would hear later. When one emaciated bluejacket was told who sent the rescue party, he exclaimed: "I knew it! I told these Jap bastards that Admiral Halsey would be here after us!"

Admirals Nimitz and Halsey were disgusted with the Japs for not cleaning up their filthy Yokosuka Naval Base for their conquerors as ordered, as was General MacArthur when his Jap car kept breaking down! But whereas MacArthur and Nimitz "entertained a feeling of compassion toward the fallen foe" (Morison), Halsey did not, and Nimitz had to rescind the Bull's order not to offer the Japanese surrender delegation customary courtesies such as coffee and cigarettes.

The IRWIN wouldn't get to stick around for the historic surrender ceremony aboard the MISSOURI (BB-63) on Sunday morning, September 2nd, 1945. We would not see the Colors that had flown over the Capitol in Washington on December 7th, 1941, nor the 31-star Flag carried by Commodore Matthew C. Perry into Tokyo Bay in 1853. We would not witness the brief and bland proceedings aboard the battleship. "In this firm and stern setting, Japan acknowledged her defeat in a war forced upon her by an ambitious and reckless military clique. The ceremony was conducted in an atmosphere of cold formality; no pageantry, no roll of drums, no handing over of swords or colors, not even a handshake; nothing to recall historic surrenders such as those of Saratoga, Yorktown and Appomattox. Nevertheless, the atmosphere was charged with emotion" (Morison).

We were underway from Sagami Wan, passing within a few hundred yards of the "Big MO" at 1638, 1 September, enroute back to Okinawa.

It was petty politics, so we thought, that put the formal ritual of capitulation on the decks of the MISSOURI. She'd seen action (and not much of that) in only two campaigns—Iwo Jima and Okinawa. But she was named after President Truman's home state. The selection angered the combat sailors of the Fleet who figured there were many vessels a lot more deserving including the battleships NORTH CAROLINA, SOUTH DAKOTA, and WASHINGTON. But it would have been poetic justice if one of the old Pearl Harbor survivors—WEST VIRGINIA, TENNESSEE, CALIFORNIA, MARYLAND, PENNSYLVANIA, or NEVADA—had gotten the assignment. Furthermore, given the predominant role of the Navy and Marine Corps in the Pacific War, the instrument of surrender should have been received by Pacific Fleet Commander, Admiral Chester W. Nimitz, rather than by some Army General.

But it was Nimitz who chose the MISSOURI, probably because it was Halsey's Flagship, possibily out of respect for President Truman, perhaps to be politically correct. Immediately after the ceremony the Admiral broadcast to all ships and stations:

"On board all naval vessels at sea and in port, and at our many island bases in the Pacific, there is rejoicing and thanksgiving. The *long and bitter struggle* . . . is at an end. . . . We . . . pay tribute to those who defended our freedom at the cost of their lives. . . . To them we have a solemn obligation—the obligation to insure that their sacrifice will help to make this a better and safer world in which to live. . . . "

At the same time the unnamed Army General, never at a loss for words and ever eloquent, broadcast to the American people:

"Today the guns are silent. A *great tragedy* has ended. A *great victory*

has been won. The skies no longer rain death—the seas bear only commerce. . . . *The holy mission* has been completed. . . . I speak for for the thousands of silent lips, forever stilled among the jungles and the beaches and in the deep waters of the Pacific. . . . A new era is upon us. Even the lesson of victory itself brings with it profound concern, both for our future security, and the survival of civilization. . . . And so, my fellow countrymen, today I report to you that your sons and daughters have served you well and faithfully."

Interestingly and ironically, Captain Fuchida, who led the Japanese attack on Pearl Harbor and became a Christian after the War, thought it strange that the surrender should be handled by the two Armies. After all, it was Admiral Nimitz, not General MacArthur, who had really beaten the Japanese. "At the time I believed Japan had been beaten by the U.S. Navy, not the U.S. Army. . . . It was the same with Japan—our army never fought much against the U.S. Army. The Pacific war was mostly a naval war."

"Well, the War's over. Let's go home!"

This came from most of the crewmen who were in for the duration only and saw no reason, now, for us to hang around out here in the far reaches of the Pacific. Speculation over demobilization was the Topic of the Day. I still had another year and five months to go on my cruise, so I took little part in the bull sessions. I was still trying to get used to peacetime steaming. Old habits die hard. Each time I came topside, my eyes scanned the horizon for bogies or unidentified surface craft, my

THE IRWIN RADIO GANG - August, 1945
Front row: L-R - Les Frisch, Gordon Gregerson, Don Karl, Joe Alice, Del Waddell; Second row: Frank Riddle, Chief Wilfred Leger, Blaise Buffamante; Third row: Frank Hansen, Mansell Giffen, Gino Piroli, George Mootz, Harold Fitzwater. Chester Karsten, John Hutchinson (in watch cap).

mind kept the relative positions of other ships sorted out, and every course and speed change was immediately noted.

The most difficult aspect of this peace thing was accepting the end of "darken ship" at night. I just could not get used to our masthead and running lights burning, open hatches spewing light out on the decks, or even smoking topside. It made me feel they were beacons calling to any I-boat or kamikaze that wanted us for a target. The impulse to go around closing hatches, turning out lights, and yelling at guys to put out their cigarettes was almost irresistible. My shipmates urged me to calm down, not let the "war nerves" get to me.

We were back in Okinawa by 3 September for availability alongside the destroyer tender CASCADE (AD-16) for repairs to our power plant. Again, I was asked if it were true our torpedoes had been sabotaged. There were references to Naval Intelligence arresting someone in Pearl Harbor's Torp Shop for tampering with fish. There was no way, at the time, to confirm or refute any of this scuttlebutt.

Beginning on 15 September, "Okinawa", which had done its damn'dest to destroy us during the campaign, took one more shot at the IRWIN. Typhoon warnings went up at 2037 while we were nested with other ships alongside the CASCADE in Buckner Bay. We stood by to execute Typhoon Plan "Xray"—to put to sea if the storm got too rough. At 0430 the next morning, as violent winds and torrential rains tore at us, the cable securing the BULLARD (DD-660) to the tender parted, increasing the strain on the IRWIN's forward lines. At 0500, Captain Kelly set the Special Sea Detail to make preparations for getting underway as the tempest increased in intensity.

At 0511, all forward lines on the seaplane tender HALF MOON (AVP-26) snapped with loud cracks like rifle shots. She and the BULLARD began drifting aft, the HALF MOON colliding with the IRWIN's stern, causing minor damage. 0524: The IRWIN's number one line parted, its bitter end whipping across the deck. 0600: Underway and backing down from alongside the CASCADE, the Captain misjudged the distance, and our starboard bow caught a boat boom protruding from the tender, tearing a long gash in the steel hull just abaft the hawse pipe. Now, Kelly had really done it. We were no longer seaworthy and could not put to sea to ride out the storm. The hole would ship more water than we could accommodate. We were now forced to seek anchorage in Buckner Bay where we could not easily maneuver to avoid other vessels.

The area around the CASCADE was already heavily congested, so the Skipper began maneuvering at various courses and speeds to avoid the other ships. It was a ticklish job, weaving among craft both anchored and underway. Some smaller vessels were already adrift without power and were being blown across the waters of the Bay. The winds by now were topping 55 knots an hour and gusting higher. In the confines of the Bay, passage was very restricted and the limited space prevented us from swinging the bow into the wind, making it impossible to anchor. 0633: The seas took us temporarily out of control, lifting the bow high in the air and crashing us down on the fantail of the now derelict destroyer OBERRENDER (ex DE-344) which was without command.

"Good Lord!" I exploded. "This gawddam island couldn't get us with over a hundred thousand Japs. Now it's going after us with a typhoon!"

The collision shook the IRWIN from stem to stern; and, for a moment, I feared we might have another hole in the hull, this one below the water line. Fortunately, a damage control party inspection turned up no serious damage. Clearing the OBERRENDER, the Old Man set out to seek a suitable spot to drop our anchors. Torrents of rain, lashing the ship in great sheets of water driven by gale-force winds now over 75 miles an hour, made it almost impossible to see more than a few yards. The running seas were buffeting and tossing us around like a kayak in a cascade. 0715: We reached Berth L-61, immediately putting both anchors out and keeping all boilers on the line to help ease the strain on the cables.

I struggled to open the hatch leading to the 0-1 level. A gust caught the heavy steel door, whipping it back against the bulkhead. A roll of the ship brought it back and I secured it as I hung on, bracing against the wind. The urge to see for myself how the ship was faring had been too strong to resist. The danger to us came not only from the huge storm itself, but from the other ships in the Bay. They had no more control over holding their positions than we, and many smaller vessels had no control at all. Through the driving rain I could see vague shapes passing scant yards away as the tempest drove them across the Bay. There was an incredible amount of debris tossing on the waters, including structures as big as small houses. Even they posed a danger to us.

We'd only had our hooks out twenty minutes when I could feel them dragging. I heard our engines pulse as we heaved in on the chains and got underway, seeking a more protected haven—if there was such a thing. With the ship's head no longer turned into the wind, I was getting broadsided by the wind and rain and retreated back into the Shack to tell the watch what I'd seen going on. An hour later, the ship reached Berth B-124; fighting the typhoon, now with winds in excess of 90 knots, all the way. We managed to stay put until about 1600. With the ship whipsawed by the typhoon that continued to increase in intensity, the Skipper kept using the engines to ease the strain on our anchor cables to prevent us from being blown up on the beach and stranded.

At 1849, with a crashing noise and a running out of the chain through the hawse pipe, our port anchor parted at the stem and was lost. Heaving in on the remaining anchor, we were underway again, using our engines in an attempt to maintain position and to avoid other ships. 1904: We dropped anchor in Berth B-133, but our single hook and all the power of our engines couldn't hold us steady, and we kept losing ground to the storm, now with wind velocity passing 120 knots an hour. It blew us all the way to Berth B-93. 2030: The Captain, in the War Diary, entered an estimate that the typhoon had reached its peak in intensity, with winds in excess of 130 knots (around 150 miles per hour).

By 2300, the tempest began to abate. But the Great Okinawa Typhoon of 1945 was not yet done with the IRWIN. Riding out such a storm is a tremendous strain on the crew; for there are so many unpredictable factors, all of them bad. Although the ship rolled in excess of 50 degrees at times, we were not in immediate danger of capsizing. But . . . there was always the possibility. A man tossed into the violent waters would stand little chance of survival. Buckner Bay was littered with logs, trees, heavy timbers, and other large objects that would crush a man. Propelled by sea and wind, they were hazardous to the ship as well, easily capable of gouging holes in the thin steel skin of the hull.

At 0130, 17 September, visibility improved only to disclose a large pontoon barge bearing down on us. But a crosswind caught it, and it zipped past only 20 yards off the port beam. 0214: A small boat crossed our bow, distance 50 yards. 0327: An unidentified but out-of-control freighter came within 300 yards of us. 0347: The patrol craft PC-584, blown from port to starboard, grazed our stern. 0400: We reached Berth B-92, having dragged our anchor to that position. Ships, small craft, and debris continued to menace us. But the typhoon was subsiding; and by 1000, our single anchor was holding well enough to cease using engine power to ease the strain. By 1623, 44 hours after the leading edge of the typhoon reached Buckner Bay, the danger was past. We dropped our hook in our assigned Berth L-87, finally riding easy at anchor.

The devastation caused by the huge storm was almost indescribable. As far as we could see, there was destruction everywhere. Around the rim of Buckner Bay, scores of craft of all sorts and sizes had been catapulted onto the beaches. Even big LSTs were stranded several yards up on land. A yard tug was perched atop a pile of debris nearly 100 yards inland. Several ships within our view had suffered damage to their topsides. Masts had been sheared off and superstructures damaged. The surface of the Bay was littered with logs, trees, and the ruins of buildings. Small craft, half sunk, were floating by. Ashore, acres of structures had been leveled. Power poles were down, and vehicles lay in grotesque positions, blown over by the winds. Flooding was island-wide, and seas of mud brought everything to a halt. Word from commands ashore pronounced the island paralyzed. We got no casualty count, but certainly there must have been many deaths and injuries.

For the first time in over two days, the IRWIN's galley could serve up a meal. I was starved enough to have eaten even the New Zealand mutton turned down on the McCAWLEY if the ship's cooks had not turned out a good supper. We hadn't slept, either, fearful of being in our sacks if rammed by another ship or stranded on the beach. Again, the luck of the IRWIN held—no thanks to Captain Kelly, whose shiphandling had punched a hole in our hull. Except for that and a few scratches and dents, we'd survived yet another travail. At least one angel had not gone into retirement at War's end.

On 26 September, our repairs completed and our port anchor replaced by one off the derelict OBERRENDER, the IRWIN sortied clear of Buckner Bay in company with the LUNGA POINT (CVE-94), destination Wakanoura Wan, the big bay on the south coast of Honshu. The jeep carrier conducted flight ops on the way, with the IRWIN in the familiar role of plane guard. Arriving on the 28th, we reported for duty to Commander Task Flotilla One—a unit of Task Group 51.3, which was the Covering Group supporting the Occupation Forces in the Japanese industrial city of Wakayama. The IRWIN was attached to Amphibious Group Eight for courier duty. We'd have to dust off our old "FPO 794" banner, again, to run mail and passengers between Wakayama and Okinawa.

With the cessation of hostilities, there began almost wholesale personnel changes on the ship. New men coming aboard, old hands departing. Among the officers, we lost our Navigator, Lieutenant (jg) Lanoue; the assistant Gun Boss, Lieutenant Tom Apple; and Dr. Fagan, our Medical Officer.

Junior Fitch, who'd shipped over aboard while the War was still on, now left from Japan to return to the States for 30 days' reenlistment leave and 20 days' rehabilitation leave. It would be the last time I'd see him. Fitch's departure was a particularly sad one for me. We'd been buddies since before the IRWIN was even commissioned.

Chief Leger was leaving, too, and I would assume all the duties as senior petty officer of the Radio Gang. This actually changed my duties little since I'd been handling most of the work anyway. There were two other changes in the Gang. Robert Terrell got a Deck Court-Martial, was broken to Seaman 1st, and transferred for hospitalization. He'd been charged with inefficiency in performance of duty and disrespect toward a superior officer. And, on 1 October, Mansell Giffen made Radioman 3rd class.

The first day in Wakayama, I pulled Shore Patrol duty with two other 1st Class petty officers. When the Exec mustered us on the Quarterdeck, he told us to draw side arms from the armory. I demurred.

"Mr. Bakley, I still have a deep distrust of the Japs. If I'm going ashore, I want something with a little more firepower than a .45 . . . like a Thompson gun." He nodded understandingly. I drew a submachinegun and one drum of ammo.

When I stepped out of the whaleboat at the Fleet landing at Wakayama and onto the soil of Japan, it was the first time my feet had stood on solid ground in *eight months!* It took me most of the day to get used to walking on *terra firma*, and I still wasn't at all comfortable with it. If anyone ever strode with a "Destroyer Roll", it was I.

The Shore Patrol Officer assigned us to a small stone bridge that spanned a shallow creek on the road leading in to Wakayama from the countryside. We were to check all who passed that way for weapons and hold for questioning any Japanese who looked suspicious. We were told, however, that Shinto priests were allowed their ceremonial daggers and were to be allowed passage. With but one or two exceptions, we encountered only groups of peasant women who giggled and tittered behind their hands when they saw American sailors. The day went by without incident.

We loaded passengers and U.S. mail on 1 October and shoved off for Okinawa, arriving on the 3rd. The next day: more passengers, more mail, and back to Japan. We got there just as storm warnings went up. Another typhoon was heading in from the East China Sea. We proceeded to our typhoon anchorage, Berth T-66, preparing to ride out the storm in accordance with instructions. This typhoon couldn't hold a candle to the Okinawa blast. Yet, we had to use our main engines to aid in maintaining the ship's position when the full force of the winds hit, and we still dragged our anchor some 800 yards. The center of the typhoon passed about 100 miles to the northwest, and it was over in about 24 hours. Some of the new men aboard got very nervous, never having experienced anything like a typhoon before.

On 15 September (three years to the day after the torpedoing of the WASP and the NORTH CAROLINA in the Coral Sea) Mr. Bakley had me come down to the Yeoman's Office to sign a statement that, as of that date, I had served on Active Duty outside the Continental Limits of the United States four years, one month, and three days; and I acknowledged that the number of "points" I had, by which men were being returned to the States, added up to 61 3/4.

The "point system" was based on how much time a man had in the service, how long he had been overseas, how many battle stars he had earned, etc. The men with the most points were being sent home first. But the points applied only to Reserves and "Duration of the War" men. At the time I signed the statement for my personnel records, men were being returned home if they had *45* points. I had more points than all but a couple of others aboard, and figured I should be shipped back, even though I was Regular Navy. I asked the Exec for permission to see the Captain. Permission granted, I went up to the Old Man's cabin and rapped on the door.

"I realize, Captain, that I'm Regular Navy and the point system doesn't apply to me. But I've been out here a long time. I'm bone-tired and have had only 44 days leave since the War started. I want to go home, and I request a transfer back to the States."

Kelly mused about that for some minutes, then walked over and put his hand on my shoulder.

"Hutchinson, you and I won this War. You and I will stay out here and keep the peace."

That blew it. I completely lost control of my temper, more due to Kelly's self-serving and condescending attitude than to the refusal of my request. Out of sheer frustration, as I turned toward the door, I blurted out:

"*Son of A Bitch!*" And I slammed the door behind me so hard one of the hinges came loose.

When I cooled off and realized what the consequences might be, I got an A-1, first-class, giant-sized case of the worries. If Kelly went true to form, the *least* I could expect was a Deck Court-Martial. For three days, I sweated, waiting for the hammer to fall. When nothing happened, I called down to the Yeoman's Office, knowing if a court-martial were in the works, that's where the specifications would be written up.

Boz Bosworth had been transferred in August for medical reasons, so I talked with Yeoman 2nd Fred Schrum.

"Fred, has the Captain said anything to you about me?"

"He did ask for your personnel records, Hutch. He kept 'em for a day, and when I went up to get them, he told me not to accept any requests from you for transfer. You're staying aboard."

"Anything else?"

"Yeah. He said not to bother bringing him any recommendations for Chief Radioman, either."

I was both greatly relieved and angry at the same time. I'd have time-in-rate to go up for Chief in two and a half months. I was also peeved Kelly didn't tell me face to face. But then, I'd broken one of

Name HOLIDAY, Jon Antony

___3 36 51___ Rate R 1c

Present Ship: U.S.S. IIWIN (DD794)

26 October 1945: In accordance with ALNAV
352-45, this man is eligible for WORLD WAR
TWO VICTORY MEDAL and is authorized to wear
the ribbon.
- - - - - - - - - - - - - - - - - - - CMB - - - -

26 October 1945: Serving with FIFTH FLEET
supporting the occupation of Japan, during
the period 6 September 1945 to 26 October
1945.   CMB

C. N. Bakley
C.N. BAKLEY
Lieutenant, U.S.N.R.
Executive Officer

(Service Record)

Jughead O'Neill's cardinal rules. Depending on how you look at it, I probably was lucky, even if you consider my outburst in the Captain's cabin to be justified.

Since the end of the shooting War, I'd been plagued with flashbacks and terrifying dreams. When we did get a little sleep during the long months in Operation ICEBERG, it was a sleep of exhaustion and I dreamt not at all. Now, it was all apparently catching up with me. Label it "war nerves", "combat fatigue", or any other name—it got to the point where I dreaded hitting the sack.

Some of the nightmares were replays of actual experiences—mostly from the Solomons. But where I'd originally gone through them just being scared, the reruns were marked by feelings of great terror and panic. Other dreams were surreal. One that kept coming back, even into the 1960s, was very strange. I'd be in a jungle, sitting behind an old World War I British Vickers machinegun. All around was a heavy mist. Through it I could see human forms moving. When they were almost identifiable, I'd hit the thumb trips to fire the Vickers. It wouldn't fire and I'd wake up yelling, soaked with sweat, and in sheer terror.

My sleep also was interrupted by leg cramps. I'd been pounding steel decks and braced against the ship's motion so long, that I'd get "charley horses" in my leg muscles. The Medical Officer told me there was no treatment, even though he acknowledged the pain could be excruciating. I really wasn't in the greatest physical shape, anyhow. Now, my weight was down to about 120 pounds, and my waist had shrunk to 27 inches.

We made one more milk run to Okinawa in mid October. Then, on the 22nd, we were ordered to report to Commander Fifth Fleet (Admiral Spruance) for further orders. Hoisting anchor, we shoved off for Tokyo Bay, mooring at Yokosuka to await assignment.

The orders came on 25 October. Depart Japan on the 26th. Destination: Puget Sound Navy Yard, Bremerton, Washington, via Pearl Harbor and San Francisco.

The IRWIN was going home.

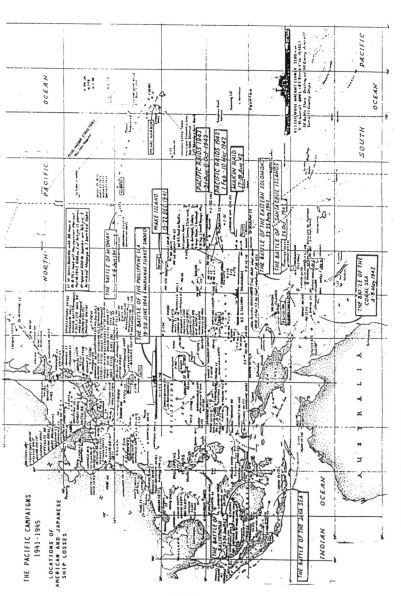

"THE PACIFIC CAMPAIGNS 1942-1945" *(Courtesy Sgt/Maj. Lester Bamford, USMC Ret.)*

U S NAVAL OPERATIONS

H.I.J.M.S. HYUGA 30,000 T. 683'x 94' B.147/45i
16· 5"50s AA. 1360men 5 Aircr. 2 Catapults

PACIFIC OCEAN AREAS
WORLD WAR II

U.S.S. SOUTH DAKOTA 42,000T. 680'x 108' 9 16'50i 16·5"38i
100· 40&20mm AAi 2500 men 4 Aircr (Marianas Turkey

OPPOSING NAVAL STRENGTHS
Dec 1, 1941

	US Navy (Pac & Asiatic)	H.I.Japanese Navy
9 Battleships	10 Battleships
3 Carriers	10 Carriers
13 Heavy Cruisers	18 Heavy Cruisers
11 Light "	17 Light "
80 Destroyers	111 Destroyers
55 Submarines	64 Submarines

PERSONNEL USNAVY

7 DEC 41	31 DEC 42	31 DEC 43	31 DEC 44
337,349	1,259,167	2,381,116	3,727,575

U.S. MARINE CORPS
| 66,043 | 238,423 | 405,163 | 477,637 |

U.S. COAST GUARD
| 25,336 | 141,746 | 171,941 | 169,832 |

SOUTHWEST PACIFIC FORCES

ABDA FLEET	JAPAN
0 Battleships	2 Battleships
0 Carriers	6 Carriers
2 Heavy Cruisers	13 Heavy Cruisers
7 Light	6 Light
23 Destroyers	43 Destroyers
46 Submarines	15 Submarines

ABDA - AMERICAN, BRITISH, DUTCH &
AUSTRALIAN.

GUADALCANAL CAMPAIGN
NAVAL LOSSES

	U S N Incl Australia	H.I.J NAVY
0 Battleships	2 Battleships
2 Carriers	1 Carrier
6 Heavy Cruisers	3 Heavy Cruiser
2 Light "	1 Light "
14 Destroyers	11 Destroyers
0 Submarines	6 Submarines
126,240 Tons	134,839 Tons

BATTLE OF MIDWAY
NAVAL LOSSES

US NAVY	H.I.J NAVY
1 Carrier	4 Carriers
1 Destroyer	1 Heavy Cruiser
150 Aircraft	332 Aircraft
307 Men	3500 Men

Japans first Naval Defeat since 1592.
Also damaged in this engagement
were 1 Japanese Battleship
1 "	Heavy Cruiser
3 "	Destroyers
1 "	Tanker

JAPANESE MERCHANT SHIPS
SUNK 1941 to 1945 Includes
only ships over 500 Tons

Army Aircraft
260 ships 774,680 Tons
Navy Land based Aircraft
130 ships 363,518 Tons
Carrier Aircraft
359 ships 4,329,184 Tons
Submarines
1,150 ships 4,859,634 Tons
Mines
210 ships 397,412 Tons
Surface Craft
16 Ships 77,145 Tons
Casualties
908,402
Unknown
16 ships 31,632
TOTALS
2,259 Ships 8,141,591 Tons

BATTLE OF LEYTE
NAVAL LOSSES

US NAVY	H.I.J NAVY
	3 Battleships
1 Light Carrier	1 Large Carrier
1 Escort "	3 Light Carriers
	6 Heavy Cruisers
2 Destroyers	4 Light Cruisers
2 D.E's	11 Destroyers

BATTLE OFF SAMAR
Battleships vs Baby Flattops
Taffy 1 (us) Ships Crews 283 Dead
Taffy 3 · " 792 ·
All aviators 55
Total 1130 + 913 wounded

IWO JIMA LOSSES
Killed in Action USMC 4554 USN 363
Died of Wounds " 1331 · 70
Missing Presumed dead " 46 · 448
Wounded in Action " 17,272 · 1,917
Combat fatigue · 2643 ?

TARAWA
The lives of 1000 + Marines & Sailors and
over 2000 wounded were sacrificed but
not wasted. Much was learned for
future Amphibious operations.

BATTLE OF THE CORAL SEA
The first battle fought by Naval
planes from ships that had neither
sight nor range of the enemy.
US lost 66 planes 543 men
Japan lost 80 planes 900 men

BATTLE OF THE PHILIPPINE SEA
(Marianas Turkey shoot)

U S NAVY LOST	H.I.J NAVY LOST
	2 Large Carriers
126 Aircraft	1 Light Carrier
(from all causes)	2 Oil Tankers
76 Airmen	424 Aircraft

OPPOSING SHIPS & AIRCRAFT

US NAVY	H.I.J NAVY
7 Large Carriers	5 Large Carriers
8 Light "	4 Light "
7 Battleships	5 Battleships
8 Heavy Cruisers	11 Heavy Cruisers
13 Light "	2 Light Cruisers
67 Destroyers	28 Destroyers
475 Fighters	222 Fighters
232 Dive Bombers	113 Dive Bombers
184 Torp. Bombers	95 Torpedo Bombers
65 Float Planes	43 Float Planes

Japan had Operational 1,644 Land
based Aircraft & 455 Carrier Planes
500 Land based planes on SAIPAN, TINIAN,
GUAM & ROTA in 1st 2 USN Air attacks
JAPAN was Losing 80% in ferrying.

SPECIAL NOTE
Adm Nagumos carrier force, the first 4
months after attacking PEARL HARBOR
operating 1/3 way around the world, had
sunk 5 Battleships, 1 Carrier, 2 Cruisers,
7 Destroyers, damaged other capital
ships, disposed of 200,000 Tons of Aur-
s. Merchantmen and hundreds of aircraft without damage to one of his
striking force.

U.S. NAVY SHIP LOSSES WW II

2 Battleships	3 Seaplane Te
5 Aircraft Carriers	6 9 Motor Torp.
6 Escort Carriers	40 Tank Landg
7 Heavy Cruisers	22 Inf ·
3 Light Cruisers	6 Support ·
71 Destroyers	10 Tugs
11 Destroyer Escorts	6 Tankers
52 Submarines	21 Troop Trans
3 Minelayers	36 Dist Patrol
24 Minesweeps	152 Misc Crai
18 Subchasers	4 Cargo Vessi
12 Gunboats	22 Misc Auxi
15 C G Vessels	

IWO JIMA was invaded Feb 1
by U.S Marines. They used 495 s
including 17 Aircraft carriers
planes, 111,308 troops U.S. Loss
5,812 killed, Japan 20,000 kille

OKINAWA was invaded Apr 1
the last land campaign of the
Troops used 1300 ships. The fi
was terminated after 83 days
the formal suicide of two Jap
generals.
US Losses 12,520 killed 36,631 v
Japan - 110,071 lost 7,400 pris

(Courtesy Sgt/Maj. Lester Bamford, USMC Ret.)

34

HOMEWARD BOUND

"Home" to the Reserves (USNR), men who'd come in the Navy for the "duration of the War", meant returning to their families and to the life they'd left behind.

But to us Regulars (USN), the Navy and the *ship* were home; the crew, our *shipmates,* were family. Like the men who'd be discharged once they had enough points, we Regulars were anxious to return to the States. But to us it meant a chance to *visit* the homefolks, then settle down to "peacetime Navy" routine.

Like other Regulars, I had found a home in the Navy, which functioned as an extended family. As I used to say: "Home is where I hang my hat, and the only hat I own is a white hat!"

As we shoved off for Pearl, in company with the ROOKS, we were in a joyous mood. In the words of the old sailors' song:

> You know we're homeward bound,
> *Hurrah, we're homeward bound!*

When we reached the 180th meridian, the demarcation line between the Eastern and Western Hemispheres, on 31 October, we celebrated crossing the International Dateline with a "Homeward Bound" dinner of roast Long Island turkey and all the trimmings. Refueling at Pearl Harbor on 3 November, we departed for the West Coast the next day.

At 0700, 10 November, 1945, the IRWIN steamed under the Golden Gate Bridge. Every man who didn't have duties elsewhere was topside. I was on the ship's Bridge, back by the port flag bag. Gazing up at the great span guarding the entrance to San Francisco Bay, I had a rush of emotions and thoughts. From the Solomons Campaign onward, the Golden Gate had symbolized a safe return home to the States. I thought of that little rhyme that had viewed the War so pessimistically in August, 1942.

"Old Lady", I said silently to the Golden Gate, "I never expected to see you again. And I certainly never thought, if I did, it would be this soon. I guess the Pearly Gate will have to wait. For the record, 1945 is a helluva lot better year for this than '48!"

Our entrance into San Francisco Bay went completely unnoticed—no welcoming crowds lining the waterfront, no fireboats spraying colored water into the air, no whistles or fog horns sounding from other ships, no gun salutes or sailors manning the rail, no parades with marching bands. We just routinely refueled from a yard oiler, then moored at Pier 54.

When liberty call sounded, I went to a phone to call Jane. She had returned to Atlanta from New York and was back living with her sister. Already knowing the ship would be going to Puget Sound Navy Yard, I wanted her to join me there. She said she was working, could only take a week off, but would fly to Seattle. I then went over to Oakland to the boarding house where Fitch and Butch had stayed to see if the landlady knew where they might be. I'd not heard from Junior since he left the IRWIN in Japan. The landlady had no forwarding address.

By 1450, 13 November, we were underway to the Pacific Northwest, making the passage through the Juan de Fuca Straits into Puget Sound on the 15th. After transferring several men slated for discharge at Elliot Bay, we off-loaded our torpedoes at the Keyport Torp Station and our ammunition at Sinclair Inlet.

On completion, we moored at Pier 3 in the Navy Yard at Bremerton for availability. The ship was to be put in first-class condition and stripped of all extraneous gear, spare parts and supplies, in preparation for "mothballing". The Skipper reported for duty to Commander Nineteenth Fleet, Bremerton Group, Inactive Fleet; thus officially ending my overseas duty after a total of *four years, three months, and three days* outside the Continental Limits of the United States. However, I was still technically on "sea duty" so long as I was ship's company on a commissioned vessel.

Jane and I spent four quiet days together. But there was a distance between us that I couldn't close. After she returned to Atlanta, I knew, inside, we were destined to part eventually.

There were two events I recall most during my stay in the Seattle area. I saw my first ice hockey game and was fascinated by it. The other incident was a little more violent, if only slightly so.

It was between paydays, and I had little money, but still wanted to get off the base for a while. Washington State, at the time, had no bars where liquor or mixed drinks were sold. Outside the Navy Yard Gate, however, was a tavern with a bartender who was quite cooperative once he was satisfied a customer was not the law. He kept a stash of several bottles of bonded stuff under the bar and, upon request, would lace your glass with a goodly shot of bourbon or blended whiskey.

Sailors on liberty from the Yard would usually stop in the tavern for a couple of pops before catching the ferry to Seattle. It was late when I walked in and I was the only customer in the place. When I asked the barkeep to "pour me a good one", he grinned, drew a glass of draft, ducked down behind the bar a moment, then set the glass in front of me. I took a long swig. As I set the glass down, the whole damned place began to pitch and roll like a tin can in a typhoon!

"Wow! Some drink!" I exclaimed.

"Drink, hell!" The bartender yelled as he leaped over the bar and headed for the door. "That's an *EARTHQUAKE!!*"

I was but seconds behind him when he reached the street. The shaker was over in a matter of seconds, but it did do some damage. In the Navy Yard, a dry dock caisson was split, flooding it and damaging a destroyer that was up on blocks. In another dock, a tin can was heeled over, causing damage to her superstructure. It was my very first quake. I would experience other tremors after moving to California in 1969.

While in Puget Sound there were further changes in the Radio Gang. In November, Les Frisch was promoted to Radioman 1st, and was discharged in December. Don Karl made Radioman 2nd, and Gordon Gregerson made Radioman 3rd.

We remained in Bremerton until 21 February, 1946, then got underway for the Destroyer Base in San Diego to complete the moth-balling of the IRWIN. We arrived at the DesBase in late February and began to work toward decommissioning the ship. Both in Seattle and in San Diego, the old pre-War condescending attitude toward sailors surfaced again. One incident during this period in San Diego stands out as typifying post-War attitudes toward those of us who'd served our Country as professional sailors.

There was a seaman named Gleason, off one of the other cans being decommissioned, with whom I occasionally chatted when we'd meet on the dock. One day, he seemed particularly depressed. His wife, he told me, was pregnant; and the nearest government hospital to his home in Arkansas was a hundred miles away in Memphis. "If I could just get her out here", he said, "she'd go to the Naval Hospital. I could be right there with her and we'd be together after the baby's born. But I just don't have the money."

The sailor wondered if the Red Cross might help, but he didn't know how to go about it. The American Red Cross had its own office building right there on the DesBase, supplied rent free by the Navy. Parked around it was a fleet of big new cars and station wagons, courtesy of the taxpayers. It was all pretty fancy. But the Navy felt it was worth it, I guess, to have assistance right there on the base when sailors needed assistance.

I told the kid I'd go with him and present his case. We were ushered into an office replete with plush carpeting, overstuffed chairs, and a desk as big as a battlewagon's fantail. Behind it sat a man in Navy regulation officers' khakis (without the USN insignia). He leaned back in his big swivel chair and, without even asking us to sit down, inquired as to the reason for our visit. I filled him in on the details of Gleason's problem and said the kid needed a loan.

Now anytime a sailor borrowed money from the Red Cross, he made out an allotment; and the money, plus interest, was deducted from his pay. There was no risk involved in repayment. The Red Cross guy listened with a bored expression on his face, tapped his pencil a few times on the polished desk top and, in an imperious tone of voice, replied:

"We've got too damn' many Navy broads and their brats out here now. We don't need any more of 'em!"

I came unhinged. *"YOU BASTARD!"* I yelled, and went right over the top of the desk at that son of a bitch's throat.

The suddenness of the attack terrified the guy. He was as white as a sheet, and with good reason. Gleason said later he *knew* I would have killed the S.O.B., adding "I never saw anybody that mad before in my life!"

The kid had better presence of mind than I. Getting a gorilla's grip around my waist with one arm and prying my fingers from around the Red Cross guy's throat, he dragged me back across the desk, saying "We better get the hell out of here!"

As we headed to the door, I turned to issue warnings: "If you report this, I'll spread the word to every sailor on the base, and one fine morning they'll find you floating face down in the bay. And if I catch you outside the gate, there won't be enough of you left to swab the deck of a dinghy!"

"Come on, kid", I told Gleason, "I'll get you your money." It was almost time for liberty call, so we got into dress blues and went in town. There on Broadway in an old building that had seen better days, we climbed a couple of flights of stairs to a door with "NAVY RELIEF" stenciled on its glass. A gracious lady listened patiently to Gleason's story and asked how much money he'd need.

"'Bout two hundred and fifty dollars."

"Oh", said the lady, "you'll need more that that. We'd better double it."

In a few minutes, the Arkansan had signed an allotment chit and was heading for Western Union to wire the money to his wife. As we parted he shook my hand and thanked me profusely.

"No sweat, kid. The Navy takes care of its own."

I walked over to a gin mill called "The Pirates' Cave" to hoist a brew. I was feeling pretty good about myself. So good, in fact, that when a Salvation Army lassie came in seeking contributions, I dropped a five-dollar bill in her tambourine. "To hell with the Red Cross!" I said to myself.

Transfers and discharges continued to reduce the number of ship's company. As May of 1946 dwindled down to its last few days, there were less than 60 men aboard. Only Del Waddell, Gino Piroli, and I remained in the Radio Gang. And only 17 of the original "plankowners" remained of the 325 officers and enlisted men who'd come aboard at commissioning on 14 February, 1944.

On 31 May, the crew mustered at quarters for the ceremony that would decommission the U.S.S. IRWIN (DD-794) as a Fleet Destroyer of the United States Navy. The rite of passage was brief but emotional, particularly for the plankowners. When the final act of lowering her commission pennant was complete, there were pictures taken and handshakes all around. I tarried as long as I could; then reluctantly heaved my seabag onto my shoulder, and slowly walked down the dock to the PORTERFIELD to which I'd been transferred.

The loss of my home was a traumatic experience. Only those who've gone through such an event can truly understand. I loved that little can with a passion. She was my girl, "my baby"; and she'd taken me through hell and back safely, with no scars. She was a valiant vessel, a gallant ship which did the job, and *much* more, that she had been commissioned to do. And now, not only was *she* lost to me, but so was my *family*, the crew with whom I'd lived and shared a thousand experiences, sailing in hostile waters in harm's way.

I was on the PORTERFIELD only two weeks when orders came through, transferring me to the Staff, Commandant 11th Naval District Headquarters, at the foot of Broadway in San Diego, under the command of Admiral Jesse B. Oldendorf. With the transfer came authorization for "subsistence and quarters". I'd be receiving a money allowance to "live on the beach". The "subs and quarters" added up to $3.50 a day.

Now that I had shore duty, I tried to get Jane to join me in San Diego. But she refused, saying she wanted to remain in Atlanta.

Checking in at ComEleven, I reported to the Communications Officer to learn that I would be on duty eight hours, off twenty-four, and stand the watches in dress blues. He gave me the rest of the day off to find a place to live, advising me to report for duty at 0800 the next day.

DECOMMISSIONING OF THE IRWIN
Captain Robert B. Kelly presents an award to Chief Gunner's Mate John
Kopach during the final ceremonies placing the ship out of commission
and in Fleet Reserve.

I found a boarding house up on 5th Street, across from Balboa Park, run by a remarkable woman, a real frontier character who was the widow of a "wildcatter" in the early days of oil exploration in Texas and Oklahoma. I regret not taking notes on stories she told of her days in the oil fields. Unfortunately, I can't remember her name, either. But I do recall how well she fed her boarders. You'd have thought we were a crew of roustabouts, "spudding in gushers" in Burkburnet!

The duty at ComEleven was easy. We monitored the FOX skeds and guarded it for ships in port; we were responsible for communications among various vessels and shore facilities. But, with the War over, there wasn't a great deal of that going on. It was the off-duty time that finally became such a drag.

The Navy, I assumed, had thought it was doing me a favor by transferring me to shore duty. But, after a couple of weeks, I began to feel like a beached whale. There wasn't a great deal of camaraderie among the men in the Com Eleven Radio Shack, and all of us went different ways on our time off. I began to spend my time wandering through Balboa Park, but was irresistibly drawn to the waterfront.

I missed the sea. I missed a good ship under my feet and the company of a close-knit crew. In John Masefield's famous words on *Sea Fever*:

> I must go down to the seas again, to the lonely sea and the sky,
> And all I ask is a tall ship and a star to steer her by. . . .
> I must go down to the seas again, for the call of the running tide
> Is a wild call and clear call that may not be denied. . . .

Or in the sentiment of A.C. Swinburne's *The Triumph of Time*:

> I will go back to the great sweet mother,
> Mother and lover of men, the sea.
> I will go down to her, I and none other,
> Close with her, kiss her and mix her with me.

I longed for what the poet (Epes Sargent) meant when he wrote:

> A life on the ocean wave, a *home* on the rolling deep,
> Where the scattered waters rave, and the winds their revels keep!

No, it was no favor to take away my "home" and disperse my "family" even though I'd been assigned to what many would call a "dream job". I was lost on the beach; and, walking the quays and piers of San Diego, felt very much *"THE LONE SAILOR."*

In T.S. Eliot's words: "the sea has many voices. . . . "

Shortly after I came on duty one day, a lieutenant came in, asking for me. "I understand you were on the IRWIN when her torpedoes came back at her", he said.

When I acknowledged I was, he asked I never reveal his identity, and went on to tell me I had a right to know why those fish boomeranged because they'd put me and the rest of the crew in jeopardy.

"But if you ever tell who gave you this information, I'll deny it."

"Go ahead, Lieutenant, I can keep a secret", I assured him.

"Those torpedoes", he said, "were sabotaged by a Chief Torpedoman in the Torp Shop in Pearl, paid by Japanese spies on Oahu. When Naval Intelligence got conclusive evidence, he was charged, court-martialed, and hung."

The lieutenant hinted that ours was not the only case of rogue torpedoes, that the IRWIN was one of the lucky ones, that perhaps more information would come out later. He turned on his heels and left.

Because I would be out of touch with the Navy for many years, I'd thought the IRWIN was the *only* ship in the Fleet to have her torpedoes come back and chase her. Then, in research for this book, I found we were not alone. Post-War reports and documents of "circling" or "boomerang" torpedoes give positive proof the erratic behavior of the IRWIN's fish was not unique to her, and that something had gone wrong somewhere.

When decades later I got in touch with Gene Stout, the IRWIN's Torpedo Officer, he said he'd heard the same story about sabotage, and had assumed the notification he'd gotten from the Navy absolving him, Captain Miller, and the IRWIN of any dereliction of duty in the matter was a result of those findings.

Later, I learned the fate of the U.S.S. TANG (SS-306), a fleet submarine lost on the *very same day* the PRINCETON was sunk. I got a copy of the TANG's Action Report filed by her Captain, R.H. O'Kane. Operating on that 24 October, 1944, off the China Coast, the TANG attacked a Jap convoy. In a night surface assault, the TANG's torpedoes sank three transports, two oilers, and a destroyer. With only two fish remaining in her tubes, Captain O'Kane fired the 23rd of his 24 fish at a "cripple" to finish it off.

"When its [the 23rd torpedo's] phosphorescent wake was observed from its point of aim . . . the last [24th] torpedo was fired from Tube Number Four. This torpedo curved sharply to the left, broaching during the first part of its turn and porpoising during the remainder. Emergency speed was called for . . . and a fishtail maneuver partially completed in an attempt to get clear of the torpedo's turning circle. This resulted only in the torpedo striking the stern abreast of the after torpedo room instead of amidships."

Captain O'Kane reported that about thirty men of his crew reached an escape position; but only nine, including himself, survived to be picked up by a Jap destroyer rescuing men from burning and sinking ships. The Americans became prisoners of war. Upon release after cessation of hostilities, the TANG's Skipper wrote his account. O'Kane's report concludes with these remarkable words: "When we realized our clubbings and kickings were administered by the burned, mutilated survivors of our own handiwork, we found we could take it with less prejudice."

Then, as I was concluding this book, I received a copy of *Pull Together*, the newsletter of the Naval Historical Foundation and Naval Historical Center (Fall/Winter 1990). Here Captain Edward L. Beach (USN Ret), the author of the best-selling novel *Run Silent Run Deep* (made into a movie starring Clark Gable) recounts his experience aboard the U.S.S. TRIGGER (SS-237). Operating off the Bungo Straits, the fleet sub fired a wide spread of four torpedoes at a Jap tanker:

"Two to hit. Came left to bring bow tubes to bear. Two hits. Went [down] to 100 feet. Target went over our stern and dropped one depth charge at a range of about 500 yards. About one minute later, there was a violent explosion *absolutely not a depth charge*."

"It is now most likely (I feel it's certain) that one of our torpedoes ran in a circle, and that we were most fortunate to have been submerged and clawing for depth besides," Captain Beach continues. "The torpedo was fitted with a magnetic influence exploder, and when it passed overhead it detonated magnetically, probably fewer than fifty feet above us, and most of its force vented harmlessly upward."

"It remains only to point out", writes Beach, "that two out of the seven submarines we lost in the war, from which survivors later came back, were sunk by their own torpedoes." The Captain estimates "no fewer than eight" submarines were probably sunk by "circling torpedoes". He closes by saying with respect to losing these submarines: "At the very least, *we should never forget that criminal negligence may be the reason*."

With regard to the mystery of the boomerang torpedoes, it is inconceivable to me that all the instances in which all the fish behaved almost exactly the same—running true and straight for about 1,500 yards, then turning toward the ship that launched them—could have been accidental. Nor can I believe the fault could lie with the shipboard torpedomen. The absolution given the IRWIN's torpedomen is proof of that.

The account of sabotage in Pearl Harbor's Torp Shop is probably true, although I have only scuttlebutt that this was in fact the case. This story is given credibility by the fact that not *all* the fish were defective, and the fact that all those that did behave erratically did so in exactly the same pattern.

Out of the thousands of torpedoes fired in the Pacific War, only a very few behaved after the same erratic pattern. Had the failures been more general (i.e. large numbers of torpedoes exhibiting the same characteristics) then the problem could have been a design flaw. But the boomerang torpedoes were so few, and the behavior of those boomeranging so similar, the probability of sabotage (i.e. tampering), or as Captain Beach put it "criminal negligence", seems to be a viable conclusion.

Our torpedoes performed poorly enough as it was, having been of inferior design in the first place, and they were not improved during the War. Why not? An enemy Long Lance torpedo was recovered by us early in the War, yet none of its superior technology was ever incorporated into American weapons systems by the Navy's Bureau of Ordnance. One senior officer told me BuOrd held the hidebound opinion, before and throughout the War, that our torpedoes were the world's best and ignored repeated complaints about their performance during the War. If so, this was as much "criminal negligence" as the apparent sabotage in the Case of the Boomerang Torpedoes.

The IRWIN was indeed fortunate to survive her circling torpedoes. As far as I can determine, she was the only *surface* ship to have her fish come back and chase her.

I had just come on watch one day, when there was a long distance call for me from Atlanta. It was Jane with news we were going to have a baby! And she wanted to come to San Diego. I rushed around, getting Navy housing and sending money to her for an airline ticket. Now, I thought, perhaps we can put our marriage back on a stable footing.

Three weeks after Jane arrived, our daughter Melody Christine was born—and was she beautiful! But after a couple of weeks, Jane wanted to return to Atlanta where her family could help with the baby and, she said, find a place for us to live. Although I would have preferred she stay with me, I agreed. But I'd miss them both, and Chris was the apple of my eye.

In October of 1946, the Chief Yeoman came down from the Admiral's Office to ask if I were planning to "ship over" (i.e. re-enlist). I had been wrestling with that question for some time, and still had not reached a decision, even after Chris was born. I still had four months to go on my cruise and asked the Chief why he needed to know so soon.

"Your status with the Flag is being changed from 'duty on board' to 'temporary duty on board,' he answered. "If you ship over, you'll be reassigned to the U.S. Consulate in Tsingtao."

At the time, the Navy Bureau of Personnel had a directive in force that men reenlisting had the option to remain on the same ship or station for a year, or they could request transfer—without, of course, any guarantee as to whether or where. That's one reason I hadn't made a decision on "reupping".

"Tsingtao!" I exclaimed. "Tsingtao, *China?*"

During most of my Naval career—going back to Ochoa's stories of Asiatic Station duty when we were on the NORTH CAROLINA, and to the long talks about China with Doon Ying Lee on the IRWIN—I had dreamed of going to that fascinating and, to me, mysterious country.

The Chief told me the Navy needed to supply a Radioman 1st to the Diplomatic Service who would be available for four years. I'd leave after the first of the year on a four-year tour of duty, and probably make Chief Radioman quickly. I told him I needed to think about it. "Don't take too long, Hutch. They want a name soon, and you'll want some leave before you go."

Up until then, my options had been: either to reenlist and stay in San Diego for a year on shore duty, which I would've done had Jane and Chris been with me; or reup and request a transfer, and probably go back to sea; or finish out my cruise, become a civilian, and join Jane and Chris in Atlanta. I had been leaning strongly toward the latter since Chris came into the picture. Now the decision would be tougher.

Off duty, I was back to pacing the waterfront, damn near wearing grooves in the walks. I even took the ferry over to Coronado several times to stand and gaze across the broad bosom of the Pacific as if trying to see what China would be like.

What China *was* like, at that moment, was a country torn apart by civil war between Chiang Kai-Shek's Kuomintang and Mao Tse-tung's Communists. Someone told me there'd already been two Marine guards at the Tsingtao Consulate killed by sniper fire. I'd already spent nearly four years in one War, and now would be facing the prospect of going into someone else's conflict *and* another four years overseas.

Still, China exerted a strong pull on me. Finally, I did, with some reluctance, turn down the assignment. Had I known what the future held, my decision might have been different, particularly since I later learned I would have served again under Admiral Oscar Badger, who was in Tsingtao in 1948 and 1949.

On 21 November, 1946, I was transferred back to the Destroyer Base for separation from the service—from the United States Navy!

The final determination to leave my beloved Navy was both agonizing and traumatic. I had come to detest shore duty, which had left me cast adrift like a ship without an anchor. Had I been returned to sea duty after the IRWIN's decommissioning, I might well have stayed until retirement. Now, I had a family to which I felt great obligation, and I knew Jane would never become a "Navy wife". I would join her and Chris in Atlanta and become a civilian.

I had not taken any leave after returning to the States. I wanted to stay with the ship until she was decommissioned. Besides, Captain Kelly was reluctant to let me go because I was senior radioman and the only one with the knowledge and experience to prepare the radio gear and spare parts for mothballing.

Afterwards, since Jane was not with me, I had no compelling reason to take time off; and by not taking leave, I could leave the service before my enlistment was up. At ComEleven, the Yeoman's Office had computed I had received but 58 days leave since enlisting on 29 January, 1941. As of 1 September, 1946, I had a total of 95 days coming to me. Saving it all until the end of my enlistment, I would get paid for all the leave I had coming and get to go home early. In other words, I'd get to leave early and get cash, too.

I went through the routine of signing all the papers, getting my leave documents and separation pay, and a final physical examination. There were no psychological exams or guidance counselors to help in the transition to civilian life. They just paid you off and that was that.

In my dress blues, I walked slowly toward the DesBase Gate and another world. The impulse to turn, go back, and ship over was very strong. It was as if the sea were calling me to come home to her.

When I reached the flagstaff where Old Glory was two-blocked to the masthead, I stopped, looking up at my Colors. I had followed them for hundreds of thousands of nautical miles over half the ocean areas of the world.

At Okinawa, late one afternoon, we were underway from one shore bombardment mission to another. It had been cloudy most of the day, but as I walked down the deck and looked up at the ensign flying from the jackstaff, a ray of light from the setting sun bathed the Flag in gold. She was soiled with gunpowder smoke, she was torn by the winds of the East China Sea, and her trailing edge was tattered.

But her stars and stripes were still identifiable, whipping proudly in the wind. The long, tortuous, campaign had ground me down, and I'd despaired of it ever ending. That moment, seeing the Flag of my nation and my people flying with such glory, I was reminded I was a destroyerman of the United States Navy and I had to stay with the mission until it was successfully completed.

Name HOLIDAY, Jon Antony
~~HUTCHINSON, John A.~~

243 86 51   Rate RM1c(T), USN

Present Ship: U.S.S. IRWIN (DD794)

Statement of Active Duty outside of
Continental United States:

Ship or Station	Yrs	Mos	Days
USS NORTH CAROLINA	01	07	25
USS ARGONNE	00	00	20
USS MC CAWLEY	00	04	20
NavBase Lunga	00	04	27
USS IRWIN	01	07	01
	04	01	03

As of 9/15/45

I acknowledge that total points as of 15
September 1945 in accordance with ALNAV
252-45 is: Sixty-one and three fourths
(61 3/4)

John A. Hutchinson
(Signature)

Certified: _C. N. Bakley_
C. N. BAKLEY, Lieut.,(DE) USNR
Executive Officer

Name HOLIDAY, Jon Antony
~~HUTCHINSON, JOHN A.~~

243 86 51   Rate RM1c(T)

Present Ship: U.S.S. IRWIN (DD794)

Serving outside the continental limits of
the United States on 25 August 1945. C. N. Bakley
for Robert B. Kelly Comdr. USN.

8/26-31/45: Serving on board this vessel
when it escorted the first merchant ship
convoy to Tokyo, Japan and with the U.S.
Occupation Forces in Tokyo Bay from 8/31-
9/1/45.   CNB

25 August 1945: This man is entitled to
wear the following:
AMERICAN AREA CAMPAIGN MEDAL;
ASIATIC-PACIFIC AREA CAMPAIGN MEDAL with
a total of nine (9) bronze stars.
PHILIPPINE LIBERATION RIBBON with one (1)
bronze star.
AMERICAN DEFENSE SERVICE MEDAL with one (1)
bronze star.
GOLD CONDUCT MEDAL   CNB

C. N. Bakley
C. N. BAKLEY
Lieutenant, U.S.N.R.
Executive Officer

Whose broad stripes and bright stars, through the perilous fight,
O'er the ramparts we watched were so gallantly streaming. . . . .
'Tis the Star-spangled Banner—O long may it wave
O'er the land of the free and the home of the brave. . . . .

Other bits and pieces of my tours in the Pacific began to flash through my mind. I wondered how others might view my service. Certainly there were sailors who were in combat areas longer than I; there were men who saw more action than I, who were in more hazardous situations than I; and there were those who committed acts of great heroism and courage, far above anything I ever did.

There were ships that were in more battles, took heavier casualties, and were more severely damaged than those on which I served. I supposed that if the IRWIN's 128 days at Okinawa could be characterized as "routine destroyer duty", then my six years of service in the United States Navy could only be termed "routine bluejacket duty".

I looked up again at the Colors flying on the flagstaff and came to full-brace attention. As I did, the westerly wind—perhaps, I thought, coming all the way from the 180th Meridian—caught the Flag, causing it to wave in great billowing undulation.

I *snapped* my right hand to my brow in salute.
"So long, Uncle."

EPILOGUE: IRISH PENNANTS

"Irish pennants", says the *Bluejacket's Manual*, "are loose ends of rope yarn or lines hanging about the rigging or decks", adding that their appearance is "very unseamanlike".

Far be it from this old sailor to leave these chronicles in any condition but shipshape and in Bristol fashion. To secure this log without some reflection in light of subsequent events, would be tantamount to leaving Irish pennants wafting in the trade winds. It would be *most* unseamanlike.

The first years after doffing Navy blue for the final time were difficult. Jane and I were divorced, and with her went Chris. There were no jobs for which my Navy radio training would qualify me. An accident, in which my left leg was severely burned, landed me in the Veteran's Hospital at Chamblee, Georgia, meaning months of limited physical activity. But there was a plus side to the hospitalization. The Veterans Administration gave me a "vocational rehabilitation test", and I was advised to use my G.I. Bill benefits toward a college education.

Eventually, I returned home in 1947 and repeated my senior year of high school—Penns Grove Regional High School, Carney's Point, New Jersey—from which I had graduated in 1939. Then in 1948 I entered the University of Pennsylvania in Philadelphia to major in journalism, gaining some extra-curricular experience as a reporter for the *Daily Pennsylvanian,* as a radio announcer on WXPN the campus station, and as a stringer for the *Philadelphia Bulletin.* At the time, Penn's journalism department was limited; and after one year, I transferred to the University of Georgia at Athens, where I carried a full academic load and worked a 48-hour week at WGAU Radio, my first commercial broadcasting job. It paid 50¢ an hour, supplementing the G.I. Bill benefits of $72 a month.

In 1950, I was offered a job at WAYS Radio, Charlotte, North Carolina, at $50 a week. I was 28 years old and anxious to get on with a career. Georgia's Journalism Dean John E. Drewry reviewed my transcripts. I had deferred taking some of the prerequisite courses in order to cram in all the broadcasting and journalism courses available. The Dean said the School of Journalism had taught me all it could in my major (I minored in music) and, unless a degree was indispensable to my plans, I should accept WAYS' offer. It was the first big step into the profession I would follow the rest of my life.

In the volatile, high-pressure world of radio broadcasting, I lived a transient existence in order to move up to higher positions and bigger markets. In the 26 years I worked in stations, I lived in Athens, Charlotte (three times), Greensboro, Little Rock (where I also did TV news), Raleigh, Winston-Salem, Roanoke, El Paso, Kansas City, Los Angeles, Spokane, and Seattle. In one 18-year span, I moved ten times!

After I switched to radio syndication in Seattle in 1974, supplying programming to stations, the moves were less frequent. In 1979 we moved to Los Angeles' San Fernando Valley to work with the company syndicating the daily five-minute radio commentaries of Ronald Reagan, who at the time was readying his drive for the Presidency. We had him on over 250 stations across the country, and he later credited the program with being critical to his winning the White House. In 1989 I moved to San Clemente to be close to the sea. I now live, close to the Pacific, in Coos Bay, Oregon.

In 1953, I married Nancy Jane George of Winston-Salem—a great cook, an excellent businesswoman, and a great source of encouragement and help to me. From 1959 through 1963 we worked together in two radio stations we owned with a partner. Our first daughter, Toni, was born in 1964; Dixie, our second, in 1967. But some thirteen months later, Nancy died suddenly and unexpectedly, and I was left to raise the girls myself. Eventually, I remarried. My new wife was Laura Sals Duncan of Los Angeles. Our son, Jonathan, was born in Spokane in 1970. Four years later, Laura and I were divorced.

I "retired" in 1983 after heart surgery, but found inactivity intolerable. With no capital, but with help from a couple of friends, I started my own syndication business, developing and marketing Big Band Swing music programming, for radio stations in this country and abroad under the trademark "Swing Era II". It brings in a few bucks and keeps me off the streets and out of trouble. Besides, it's a labor of love, and I have fun doing it.

And then I lost my head and started writing this book!

As I collected data, memorabilia, and photographs, I began to frame some of the material and put it on the den walls. A friend stopped by one day and after viewing the display, turned to my daughters and said: "You know, your Dad's a real hero!"

I was completely taken aback. To me and all my shipmates, "heroes" were ordinary guys who committed extraordinary acts of courage above and beyond the call of duty. Most of the "heroes" we had known were dead. None of us ever considered ourselves heroes.

My generation, which had grown up during the Depression, was reared to take on responsibility, do our duty to the best of our ability, and expect little in the way of thanks—just the satisfaction of a job well done.

If you were privileged to listen to a group of us talk about the War, you would hear only humorous banter about the funny antics or strange incidents we experienced or witnessed. Seldom, if at all, would you listen to any accounts of heroism or sacrifice. The very mention of such would be greeted with embarrassment. We just did not believe we did anything exceptional. In the face of combat, none of us felt very brave—just scared as hell. Consequently, we take little stock in medals and awards, and most of us are unaware of those to which we are entitled.

When Commander J.P.D. Hodapp and I visited together in 1985, and I was laughingly telling him about the three PRINCETON pilots who got me drunk in Burbank in 1944, the Exec wanted to know if I'd ever received the Navy-Marine Corps Medal for rescuing them. I told him I didn't even know I'd been recommended for one. In that case, he said, he'd send the papers in to get it for me. All the required data, documents, and supporting information were gathered and submitted. The life-saving medal is one of the few to which I would attach any significance.

The Navy acknowledged that, indeed, I qualified for the medal; but an arbitrary cut-off date of 1954 for such claims precluded making the award, unless new data were forthcoming. PRINCETON crewman Charlie Donovan's testimony to my saving his life was sent in as new information. But, to date, the Navy has never sent the medal. Apparently the paper work is still floating around somewhere in the bowels of the Pentagon. But I'd had fair warning. Admiral Arleigh Burke, in a letter on another subject, told me: "Remember, when you're dealing with the Pentagon, you're surrounded by hostile Indians!"

The ship's reunions I've attended—particularly the 50th Anniversary of the NORTH CAROLINA's commissioning and the very *first* gathering of the IRWIN crew in 1991—were unforgettable experiences. The Baby Boomers who witness World War II veterans in the lobbies of the reunion hotels, greeting each other with whoops and bone-crushing handshakes, must wonder about these old sea warriors with silver hair, paunchy midriffs, and faces that appear to be fashioned from well-worn saddle leather. What explains our solidarity and comradery?

Even wives, seeing their husbands greet shipmates not seen in half a century, are perplexed at the emotional outbursts. How could men so long apart suddenly display such obvious and intense affection for one another? As one of the wives put it: "It's amazing. You guys are not just old buddies. You're closer than *brothers!*" No, ma'am we're even closer than that—we're *shipmates!!*

The ties that bind us blue water sailors who shipped out in U.S. Navy combat vessels are thicker than the armor on a battleship's barbette and as shiny and strong as Solingen stainless steel. To sever them would be as difficult as undoing the Gordian Knot while wearing boxing gloves. Welded together by common experience and the crucible of combat—where the survival of all is inexorably linked to the mutual loyalty of each sailor to his shipmates—*you can't get any closer than that!*

It was the memories of the closeness to former shipmates that got me out of the cocoon I'd woven around myself and to attend ships' reunions. Ironically, my closest buddies in the Navy, namely Jimmy McPherson and Junior Fitch, I've not been able to locate even after years of searching.

But at gatherings of all World War II veterans—particularly those who served in the Pacific—there lurks underneath a sadness over what our country has become and the threat that a rejuvenated Japan poses. The most frequent question heard is: "*What the hell did we fight the War for?!*"

When former Marine sergeant William Manchester returned to the Pacific in the late 1970s, to come to grips with the meaning of experiences buried for 35 years, he concluded that the victors in the Pacific War had been outsmarted by the vanquished. He was astounded to see two brand-new destroyers, flying the Rising Sun battle flag (supposedly outlawed) of Imperial Japan, moored in Pearl Harbor. Japanese affluence and influence were everywhere in the Pacific. "In peace Hirohito's subjects have achieved what eluded them in war: dominance of a Greater East Asia Co-Prosperity Sphere."

Pearl Harbor veterans gathering to commemorate the 50th anniversary of December 7th, 1941, reportedly had trouble finding hotels on Oahu not owned by the Japanese. This was confirmed to me by former NORTH CAROLINA shipmate Mario Sivilli. After attending the Guadalcanal Campaign Veterans' 50th anniversary commemoration of the landing, "Frenchy" Maurais commented in a letter to me: "Guadalcanal is now fully Nipponesed; that is, the Japs own the Hilton and just about everything else on the 'Canal. . . . I wonder if all the hell we went through was worth it."

The Japanese we faced in the Pacific were not the stereotypic, kimona-wearing, deep-bowing, cherry blossom tenders of our high school geography books. They were a fierce and ferocious foe, fanatically cruel and inhuman in the extreme. It has long been a source of indignation and frustration to us Pacific War veterans that Americans remain abysmally ignorant of the awful truths of Japanese brutality and barbarity demonstrated by their inhumane treatment of prisoners; their slaughter of innocent, non-combatant men, women, and children; their routine torture methods, their mutilation of their victims. Without much ado, with methods too terrible to mention, the Japs simply slaughtered the peoples of the Pacific Rim by the millions.

While hardly a few days go by without some reference in today's media to the Nazi Holocaust, there is little or no mention of the "Jap Holocaust" in which millions more were slaughtered. Apparently the lives of *Asians* are not worth as much as the lives of Jews or Europeans.

There is an almost endless litany of atrocities committed in the name of the man-god Hirohito: the Rape of Nanking, the Bataan Death March, Santo Tomas prison, etc. The Japanese were not a signatory to the Geneva Convention's rules of warfare. They took few prisoners. Captured Americans, tortured in unmentionable ways, died horrible deaths. Those who lived were forced into slave labor, working until only starvation blessed them with death. Typical was the treatment of 526 American military POWs compelled to work in the Kinkaseki copper mines on Formosa. Only 65 survived. Such statistics tell nothing of the hell these men went through during their years of incarceration. This is not to mention many other cruelties—like enslaving some 200,000 teen-age girls (Korean, Chinese, et al.) to serve the sexual needs of Japanese soldiers as "comfort women".

For a Japanese scholar's frightful account of his country's brutality, see Saburo Ienaga, *The Pacific War, 1931-1945: A Critical Perspective on Japan's Role in World War II* (1978). Here Japan's wartime atrocities are recounted *ad nauseam*. But historian Ienaga has failed in his one-man crusade to make his country's ultra-conservative Ministry of Education at least mention these horrors in school textbooks. The Japanese Government has banned his history textbook. Jap wartime propaganda prevails even long after the War! Having lost in Jap courts, Ienaga appeals to the court of history. But the Japanese people remain, on the whole, ignorant of the history of their conduct in the Pacific War.

Americans are painfully ignorant of the Oriental mind and Far Eastern cultures. As a nation, we tend to feel the Japanese follow the same set of morals, ethics, standards of decency, including respect for human life and dignity. But there is a vast gulf between East and West. Perhaps Rudyard Kipling was right when he wrote " . . . never the twain shall meet."

Over the years, the U.S. Government has seemed more concerned with aiding and abetting, and not offending, the Japanese, than with helping and not offending those who went through hell to deliver the world from the Japanese menace. The ultimate affront and offense to the destroyermen surviving the holocaust of Okinawa came after the War. The United States Government awarded salvage rights to the hulks of the ships sunk by the *kamikazes* in the waters around the island to the Okinawan *Japanese!* Those sunken ships were the graves of American fighting men who gave their lives for their Flag and Country, only to have their last resting place violated by an enemy seeking to profit from the sale of steel from their gallant vessels!

It seems the American people and government are as incredibly naive today, as in 1941, when it comes to the threat posed by the Japanese. Of this we veterans of the Pacific War are convinced. American servicemen who faced and finished the Japanese war machine have watched as our government has permitted the enemy to steal our technology and achieve a measure of economic ascendancy over our Beloved Country. In the 1940s the Japs were well along in the development of atomic weapons. Do they have the capability to produce atomic and hydrogen weapons today? The answer is "apparently so". A 1991 Associated Press News report, that's gone largely unnoticed, claimed Japan "*continues* to import *weapons grade* plutonium"! Our newspapers continue to print articles on Japan's continuing nuclear build-up.

At any rate, it is certain that Americans today are incredibly ignorant of the lessons of World War II, of the War in the Pacific and of what it cost countless of their countrymen to halt the Japanese juggernaut and bring the Sons of Nippon to their knees. When asked, American school children have never heard of Bataan or Corregidor, the Coral Sea or Midway. As for the sanguinary Solomons Campaign, I once asked a school girl if she'd ever heard of *Guadalcanal.* She shook her head: "Isn't that some big ditch they dug somewhere down in Central America?"

President Truman proclaimed a two-day holiday (15–16 August, 1945) to celebrate our Victory over Japan. For some ten years in the 1980s, I tried repeatedly, to no avail, to get the media (TV, radio, newspapers) in the Los Angeles area to take note of VJ-Day on August 15th—the end of the Second World War—to honor those who fought to win the Pacific War. While VE-Day (Victory in Europe, May 8th) is sporadically mentioned, Americans apparently could care less about the Victory over Japan. *It's as if the Pacific War had never happened!*

The Japanese do not forget. In 1992, according to one newspaper account, Emperor Akihito led a ceremony commemorating the end of the Pacific War, in which an estimated 3,100,000 Japanese servicemen and civilians died, attended by more than 5,200 survivors in a martial arts hall near the Imperial Palace.

On Pacific island battlegrounds, Marine veteran Manchester was furious to find elaborate Japanese memorials; whereas American monuments were few and far between, paltry and defaced. Are the Japs prouder of their dead than we? Couldn't the Pentagon spare a few dollars out of its billions for a decent memorial? What about private contributions via the Veterans of Foreign Wars and/or the American Legion?

Our immediate purpose in the conduct of the Pacific campaigns, as Admiral Halsey so succinctly put it, was to: "Kill Japs! Kill Japs! And kill *more* Japs!" It was to avenge Pearl Harbor, drive the enemy from the seas, force him to surrender, and bring about peace.

Wars are fought by young men in their teens and early twenties. Few, if any, thought much past getting the War over and going home. Among these lads there was little philosophizing about loftier aims such as President Roosevelt's four essential human freedoms: Freedom of speech, Freedom of religion (for each to worship God in his own way), Freedom from want, and Freedom from fear—everywhere in the world. If pressed, my shipmates would most probably have said they were fighting to preserve the American way of life—the Flag, our Country, its Constitution and Bill of Rights—along with mom, baseball, and apple pie.

Today, my former shipmates and comrades in arms are appalled at the state of our Nation. We had hoped to leave the United States to our descendants in much better shape. It grieves us that the future of America looks so bleak, and that there is little we can, at this late date, do about it. Those freedoms for which we endured the worst war in history are fast disappearing to be replaced by alien ideologies promulgated in the name of "protecting the rights of minorities".

Our generation, the men of World War II, is itself now a small minority, diminishing in numbers as age takes its toll. What can we do?

> O say, does the Star-spangled Banner yet wave
> O'er the land of the free and the home of the brave . . . ?

Over ninety-five percent of the American Armed Forces in World War II were Caucasian and nominally Christian. We did not fight the War to see our Western heritage and the faith of our fathers come under sustained and unrelenting attack in our own country by those who would replace them with alien ideologies. Our basic freedoms, articulated in the Constitution and the Bill of Rights, are being whittled down inexorably by spurious and outlandish misinterpretations of the "original intent" of the Founding Fathers. Revisionists are rewriting our history to rob our children of our Christian and American heritage.

I find it most ironic to hear people on television, with names I can't pronounce and accents I can't understand, trying to tell *me* the meaning of the Constitution of the United States of America. My knowledge comes not only from that revered document, but from the teaching handed down from my great-great-great grandfathers who fought to bring it into being.

James Madison, the Father of the Constitution and our fourth President, said that our form of government would *"only work for a religious and moral people."* And John Quincy Adams, our sixth President and son of John Adams, our second President and one of the foremost of our Founding Fathers, stated an empirical truth: "The highest glory of the American Revolution was this: It connected in *one indissoluble bond* the *principles of civil government* with the *principles of Christianity."*

But now our beloved country is under siege from within. Organizations with such misappropriated and misleading terminology in their titles as " . . . for the American Way" and "American Civil Liberties . . . " assail those principles of Christianity at every turn, seeking to turn us from a nation of Christian beliefs and ethics into an atheistic state wherein God and Christ can only be mentioned in church. Once that is accomplished, the church is next.

These self-anointed "liberals" have waged a war for "separation of church and state" in complete violation of the First Amendment which guarantees "Congress shall make no law respecting establishment of religion (which it hasn't), OR PROHIBITING THE FREE EXERCISE THEREOF." They have succeeded in removing Christianity from our schools, from our public buildings, and will continue until God's Word is removed from our lives.

We veterans of World War II did not fight to see "diversity" and "multi-culturism", tending to "Balkanize" our Nation into ethnic enclaves of "hyphenated Americans", replace the principles of Christianity and patriotism, the love of God and Country, that made America strong and great. Without James Madison's *"religious and moral people"*, it is small wonder our government is not working and our society is in moral shambles: dishonesty, robbery, brutality, promiscuity, homosexuality, etc. Traditional sins are no longer *sin* but attributed to *society.* This moral irresponsibility is the responsibility of those instrumental in removing from our schools and public life the teachings of Christianity.

Our most revered patriotic songs are hymns. They tell us that there is *an indissoluble bond* between God, God's law, and liberty in our land—between the God of our fathers and the freedoms they sought and fought to plant, preserve, and promulgate. From the Army and Navy *Hymnal* of 1942, hear John Greenleaf Whittier's "Our Fathers' God":

> O make us, thro' the centuries long
> In peace secure in justice strong;
> *Around our gift of freedom draw*
> *The safeguards of Thy righteous law.*

Or Daniel C. Roberts' "God of Our Fathers":

> *Thy love divine hath led us in the past,*
> In this *free* land by *Thee* our lot is cast;
> *Be Thou our ruler,* guardian, guide, and stay,
> *Thy word our law, Thy paths our chosen way.*

Or Katherine Lee Bates' beloved "America the Beautiful":

> O beautiful, for pilgrim feet whose, stern impassioned stress
> A thoroughfare for *freedom* beat across the wilderness!
> *America, America, God mend thine every flaw,*
> *Confirm thy soul in self-control, thy liberty in law.*

Or Samuel F. Smith's "America", which we used to sing in our schools, but no more:

> My country, 'tis of thee, sweet land of *liberty,*
> Of thee I sing;
> Land where my fathers died, land of the pilgrims' pride,
> From every mountain side let *freedom* ring! . . .
> *Our fathers' God, to Thee, Author of liberty,*
> *To Thee we sing;*
> *Long may our land be bright with freedom's holy light;*
> *Protect us by Thy might, great God, our King.*

Lest my perspective on these matters lead to being branded a religious zealot, let me add a disclaimer. I only need to point out that, much to my brother's dismay, I have not attended a regular church service since my youngest daughter was christened in 1969. While I hold strong moral, ethical, and religious beliefs, I am a very private man who usually keeps these tenets within. I feel my relationship with my Maker is just between Him and me.

On January 29th, 1941, I took a solemn oath to protect the United States "against all enemies, foreign and domestic." There are those misguided souls, however, who would deny me and all other citizens the right to protect ourselves, our families, and our property against the lawless domestic enemies on our streets who threaten the "domestic tranquility" our government is constitutionally bound to insure. They would abrogate the Second Amendment, wherein "the right of the people to keep and bear arms shall not be infringed." If the government fails to live up to its obligation to insure domestic tranquility, we must be able to protect our lives and property.

My generation was pretty remarkable, tough and resilient. Before we went off to fight for nearly four years in the Second Great War, we lived through the Great Depression. Without welfare, unemployment checks, or any other government handouts, we survived. Now we see ever increasing numbers feeding at the public trough while hard-working Americans are being taxed beyond all rationality by a rapacious government which has already piled up enough national debt to impoverish our children and grandchildren well into the next century.

It is these problems, and many more—including flag-burning, drug-trafficking, illegal immigration, the rewriting of history (before we participants in the events are even dead!), the escalating crime rate, the precipitous decline in morals, the neglect of personal and national responsibility, the denigration of Western civilization and culture—that so sadden my generation. When we returned following the defeat of Nazi Germany and the capitulation of the Japanese Empire, America was the strongest, proudest, free-est nation in the world's history. We could outfight, outproduce, outinvent, outwork all the rest of the peoples on this earth put together, and we'd just finished proving it.

But some fifteen years later, as we entered the 1960s, the generation to follow ours set into motion a decline in the face of America which has continued unabated to this day. And it shows no signs of stopping. We veterans of World War II did not fight for what America has become, any more than we fought to let Japan buy up some of our more precious institutions, wage economic war on our industries, and insult our people. With our youngest members now in their mid-sixties, our numbers dwindling down to a precious few, we can only ask again, rhetorically: *"What the hell did we fight the War for?"*

The following anonymous lines should be taken seriously by a generation that makes heroes out of the likes of contemporary athletes and show business personalities.

> When a land forgets its legends,
> Sees but falsehoods in the past,
> When a nation views its sires
> In the light of fools and liars—
> 'Tis a sign of its decline,
> And its glories cannot last.
> Branches that but blight their roots
> Yield no sap for lasting fruits.

While our perspectives doubtless differ in some respects, the comments from William Manchester's *Memoir of the Pacific War*, found at the conclusion of this chronicle, though perhaps somewhat overstated, are most perceptive. Along with Robert Louis Stevenson's individual epitaph for this old sailor, Manchester's words could serve as his eulogy, indeed the eulogy of all us old bluejackets who served our Country in the Pacific War: The United States was a different country then. Later the rules would change. *But we just didn't know—we simply didn't know any better.*

As strange as it may seem, while there is a Jewish Holocaust memorial in Washington, there is no national memorial to the men who fought in World War II. Nevertheless, after some 200 years, the United States Navy finally has its own memorial in Washington City. Although authorized by Congress in the days of "wooden ships and iron men", it has taken all this time to reach realization—erected by donations from Navy men, not taxpayers' money. Fitting and proper is the center piece of the Memorial: *"THE LONE SAILOR"*! It's a bronze statue of an *ENLISTED MAN—a BLUEJACKET!*

Thus it's also appropriate that an enlisted man became the top individual contributor to construction. Not an Admiral nor a Captain, but a *bluejacket,* my old IRWIN shipmate, Chief Gunner's Mate John "Boom Boom" Kopach—who according to the special plankowner edition of the Navy Memorial's book *A Living Tradition* (1987), donated over $50,000. Boom Boom told me in 1988 he'd donated some $53,000 up to that time. After retirement, he spent some 24 years in weapons testing with General Dynamics, bringing his total association with naval weaponry to over 47 years, undoubtedly a record. But one of his Navy cruises may have hastened his death. In his last letter to me, the Chief said: "Radiation fallout from the nuclear bomb testing in the Marshall Islands is now giving me skin cancer." He was piped across God's Quarterdeck in 1990.

The Japanese suffered the horrors of the War they began at Pearl Harbor. In his letter Kopach told a poignant story of his post-War experiences while aboard the U.S.S. CABILDO (LSD-16). The ship was in part at Muroran on Hokkaido, Japan's northernmost Home Island. In the center of town is a memorial to 3,800 Japanese sailors and marines lost aboard ships in the Solomons Campaign.

"Every family", Boom Boom wrote, "lost either a husband, son, nephew, father, uncle or close cousin. Dozens of women would come down to the dock where the CABILDO was tied up and, through interpreters, ask the sailors if there were any men aboard who were in the Solomons during the war. They wanted to know if any of these Japanese sailors or marines by chance could have gotten off those sinking, burning Japanese ships and perhaps drifted ashore in life rafts or life jackets and were hiding in the island jungles. I was the only man on the CABILDO who had been in the Solomons, and I just didn't have the heart to tell these women those Japanese warships or troop ships, once hit by heavy naval gunfire were nothing but burning, exploding, blazing blast furnaces."

I don't know if there's anything now in the Navy Memorial to do with the PT-109 and her C.O., John F. Kennedy. When he began to become prominent in politics, and I made the connection between the politician and the PT-109, I couldn't believe Kennedy's partisans had the unmitigated gall to claim he was a *war hero!* Surely, I thought, his political opponents would challenge it with the real story of what happened. When the movie *PT-109* was released and no one raised a doubt about its accuracy my reaction was "Lord help us!" To this old bluejacket, Kennedy proved to be about as competent a Captain of the Ship of State as he was a Skipper of the PT-109.

There are some misconceptions, today, about veterans' benefits available via the Veterans Administration (VA). Under the G.I. Bill, I received $72 a month, plus tuition and books, while attending college, and I bought a house with a VA-guaranteed loan. But, since I did not remain in the service until retirement, I am ineligible for any other benefits. I cannot be admitted to a Veterans' Hospital unless I declare myself practically indigent. Since I wasn't wounded, I have no service-connected disability (apart from a recurrence of malaria) and so don't qualify for hospitalization as a veteran.

It was a good thing I never sustained any wounds. My Navy medical records and "dog tags" both proclaimed my blood type as "O". When I was signing papers after a heart operation in 1983, I noted the surgeon had listed me as Type "A". "But I'm Type O", I told him. "That's what the Navy listed me as having." "Good thing you never got wounded and needed a transfusion", he said. "You most probably would not have survived!" But regardless of blood type, cut me and I still bleed Navy blue!

You didn't get rich in the old Navy. My gross pay for six years, including sea pay, totaled $6,290. (I figured the total on hearing Uncle Sam gave each Jap internee, including those returning to Japan, $20,000!) True, I did get free room and board. But accommodations were not always first-class, and I still had to buy all but my original-issue uniforms.

Yet, I got rich in other ways. I wouldn't go through it all again for a million dollars; but, at the same time, I wouldn't *take* a million dollars for the experience, nor for the comradeship of the men with whom I served. The seagoing fraternity of sailors surviving combat is a unique collection of men—a rare breed—and we may never see the likes of those who served in World War II again.

Yes, we combat veterans of World War II are a unique bunch, "the generation that saved the world." We are by no means heroes or supermen, but as characterized by John Steinbeck: "homesick, weary, funny, violent, common men . . . who lug themselves through as dirty a business as the world has ever seen and do it with humor and dignity and courage."

Sometime back (on October 24th, 1991, anniversary of the sinking of the World War II PRINCETON) I was invited to a go on board the new PRINCETON—an Aegis cruiser, which by the way the old FLETCHER-class destroyers could run rings around. I was taken aback by the new Navy. When I asked for a cup of java, a fresh pot could not be found, and I was told sailors now imbibe Cokes and Dr. Pepper. My response: "How the hell could you ever win a war without coffee?"

There seemed to be little love for the sea and pride in the ship. According to one Chief, these were 9:00 to 5:00 sailors, more interested in what the Navy could do for them (e.g. free schooling) than in what they could do for the Navy. They seemed to know their job specialties, but the spirit of the old Navy's professional sailor simply wasn't there. Despite all the computers and technological superiority, it still takes *men and morale* to run a ship. Morale is still the key to military efficiency.

Hopefully these impressions were not representative. But maybe they are. When recently at the Navy's boot camp in San Diego, I was informed that the whole six weeks are devoted exclusively to preparing recruits to perform in their graduation exercises! There is none of the old traditional training of a seaman—no swimming, shooting, boat-handling, knot-tying, etc.—designed to enable the sailor to survive at sea and in war. Chief Gunner's Mate Jimmy O'Neill would turn over in his grave.

Among all those who wore Navy blue, none are more distinct than the men who rode destroyers, those who strode the decks of tin cans. It is my most fervent hope this book will give the reader a vivid sense of the duty they performed, and of the character of the men who sailed in harm's way on those fragile craft.

After I joined "The Tin Can Sailors", an organization for destroyer-men, I suggested a slogan. It wasn't adopted, but most of my shipmates think it's a good one: *"Old Destroyer Sailors Never Die—They Just Sit On Their Cans!"*

There is one other slogan of a veterans' organization, however, which is much more serious and certainly to the point. It's the reason I subtitled this memoir *"Golden Gate . . . Or Pearly Gate . . . By '48!"* The words on the magazine and the stationery of the Guadalcanal Campaign Veterans read: *"It Is Not The Cost of Belonging—It's The Price You Paid To Be Eligible."*

Recently, my brother asked me what I'd learned from the war experience and what I'd want to pass on to my children. The short answers are: to the first question, *survival*; to the second, *accept responsibility!*

I hadn't given much thought to the question of why I survived the War until my brother posed it. In military conflict, some live and some die. I'm not sure why. Through most of the Pacific campaigns, particularly from the bombings on Guadalcanal onward, I wasn't too confident I'd make it the rest of the way.

Some may find a paradox in the thought I'd "used up all my numbers" on the one hand, *and* the belief one of God's guardian angels was looking after me on the other. Fatalism and Christianity are, theoretically, mutually exclusive, in that God's sovereign will is rational and not fortuitous fate. But, empirically, constant exposure to hazardous situations can produce, in a man's mind, both perspectives.

The Christian perspective is well put by Colonel E.F. Carlson, leader of Carlson's Raiders of Guadalcanal fame: "It is not given to us to know the process by which certain of us are chosen for sacrifice while others remain. We can only rest our faith in the infinite wisdom of God who guides our destinies."

Aside from the spiritual, there are tangible reasons I survived. There is no doubt the Navy prepared me well: instilling and reinforcing discipline, honor and responsibility, a sense of purpose and duty; pride in self, the ship, the crew, the Navy, the Country and its Flag.

The traditions of the Navy gave a sailor in my day a granite-like base on which to build character and the desire and will to "carry on" in each and every circumstance. It is for this reason that I am a firm believer in the value of military training.

Simply put, however, I survived the War because the Good Lord figured He might need me later on.

I can think of no reason for returning safely, other than that it was God's will.

EPITAPH

HOW WE WOULD BE REMEMBERED

How we would be remembered! Originally, this Epitaph was to have consisted, along with the lines from Robert Louis Stevenson's *Requiem*, of several excerpts from former Marine sergeant William Manchester's *Goodbye, Darkness: A Memoir of the Pacific War* (1980). However, though permission was requested to quote the excerpts some sixteen months prior to his response, at the last minute author Manchester refused permission via rather condescending letters from both the author and his literary agent, making it clear in no uncertain terms that the excerpts were not to be quoted in *BLUEJACKET.*

Of all those asked for help in producing this memoir, Manchester is the only one to refuse. Maybe a measure of darkness remains—darkness engendered by post-War success. In any event, whatever his reasons, this old bluejacket would have expected a more liberal and charitable attitude from a former comrade in arms in the Pacific War. What is so astounding about the refusal, is that it seems to vitiate and contradict one of the major thrusts of Manchester's memoir: that is, the comradery, the mutual love, the sacrificial solidarity among combat veterans which is essential for survival; that in combat men fight, less for country or glory or any other abstraction, than for each other, each willing to die to save the life of his comrades in arms. The excerpts from *Goodybye, Darkness,* which every *BLUEJACKET* reader should peruse, are to be found on pages 116, 246, 247, 391, and 393 to 395.

How we would be remembered? Would we be remembered at all? Manchester makes the point that those of us who fought in the Pacific War believed we would be remembered, that future generations of school children would hear of our sacrifices and know the names of our most illustrious battles: Midway, Guadalcanal, Tarawa, Saipan, Leyte Gulf, Iwo Jima, Okinawa. However, we didn't reckon with the tempo of history since the Second World War, which would leave the *War* in a cloud of murky dust and misty haze. It is astonishing that to this day, there is no national memorial to those, living and dead, who fought to win World

War II. With succeeding generations and our school children, *it is as if the Pacific War never happened!* They are abysmally ignorant, knowing nothing to remember. But we would want to be remembered—that's in part the rationale for writing *BLUEJACKET.*

How we would want to be remembered? For example, in terms of the excerpts from Manchester; we would be remembered as the products of a different country and society from what the United States of America has become in the last fifty years. We would be remembered as the products of a far more disciplined society with rather rigid moral and social standards to which everyone was expected to conform given how society chastened and disciplined offenders. Cheating and promiscuity carried consequences. The way of the transgressor was hard. We were taught individual responsibility, that evil is due to character flaws in the individual and not to the shortcomings of society. We were taught to depend on God, to persevere in adversity, and to take care of ourselves and our families, and not to depend on society or government to look after us.

How we would be remembered? We would be remembered as the products of an avowedly religious nation which, with all its sins and shortcomings, professed Christianity, a country and society where prayers and other outward forms of religion were the ideal, where the Protestant work ethic was still very strong, where marriage was supposed to be sacred and families nuclear and extended were still the bulwark of social stability, where men and fathers were to take responsibility and thus be in authority and women and mothers were ladies receiving special deference and respect, where fathers and mothers were to be obeyed and loved by their children, where boys were to fight overseas for their country's values and girls were to support them with letters from home. We would be remembered as tough, resulting form the struggle for survival during the Great Depression and World War II.

How we would be remembered? Speaking personally, we would be remembered as young men who fought for their Flag and that for which it stands, one nation under God with liberty and justice for all; for the United States of America, which was the envy of the nations in spite of all her flaws. We would be remembered as the generation which won *the War* and saved the civilized world from godless tyranny and diabolical atrocity; the most productive generation in American history, bequeathing to our descendants the most powerful and magnanimous, the wealthiest and greatest nation yet to appear on the stage of human history.

Finally, we would be remembered as grateful patriots who remem-

ber our history and our forefathers, as God-fearing men who remember
God's manifold grace shed on America, as sentimental men who remember each Memorial Day and every day those who more than self their
country loved and mercy more than life, as old well-worn warriors who
would ever sing with great affection for "America the Beautiful":

> America, America, God shed His grace on thee,
> And crown they good with brotherhood from sea to shining sea . . . !
> America, America, God mend thine every flaw,
> Confirm they soul in self-control, thy liberty in law . . . !
> America, America, May God thy gold refine,
> Till all success be nobleness, and every gain divine . . . !

That's how we would be remembered!! This old sailor's personal
epitaph follows in the words of Robert Louis Stevenson.

> Under the wide and starry sky
> Dig the grave and let me lie:
> Glad did I live and gladly die. . . .
> This be the verse you 'grave for me:
> *Here he lies where he long'd to be;*
> *Home is the sailor, home from the sea. . . .*
> —Robert Louis Stevenson
> *Requiem*

AFTERWORD BY REV. GEORGE P. HUTCHINSON D.PHIL. (OXON.)

O LORD, my God, you are very great. . . .
How many are your works, O LORD! . . .
There is the sea, vast and spacious. . . .
There the ships go to and fro . . . (Psalm 104)!

It has been a privilege and pleasure to help my esteemed brother prepare for publication his marvelous memoir of World War II in the Pacific. As a kid brother, I was fascinated by these accounts and anecdotes of experiences and episodes far away across the sea. I can still remember the sinking of the McCAWLEY in 1943; and recall riding to the family plot in the cemetery, with my big brother in his Navy blues, for the burial of our great-uncle and friend Gilbert C. Hutchinson, affectionately known as Uncle Bert. After nearly fifty years, these stories have not lost their fascination; they keep me spellbound still. This is a tale crying to be told, both on the personal and on the historical level, a contribution to the history of our family and our country.

As a brother, it goes without saying, I am extremely proud of my brother's military service, of all he went through to preserve our beloved country and the American way of life with all its faults and foibles. I am also exceedingly proud of his memoir; not only of the book itself, but also of the courage necessary to relive all these events and experiences in order to preserve them for posterity, including our family and my four sons (John, Bert, Chet, and Jack). Helping my brother with his book has been a matter of family solidarity and responsibility. Frankly, there is another motivating factor: there is no doubt that our family, both immediate and extended, failed my brother to a significant extent after the War, when the psychological adjustment to an anticlimactic civilian life was doubtless difficult indeed. If we were insensitive and failed to understand then, perhaps we can make up for it and support him now nearly fifty years later.

As an editor, I am particularly pleased with the book's form as well as its content, its style as well as its story. My concern has been to discern the intent and conserve the content of what the author wanted to express while trying to improve the memoir with regard to clarity, orthography, and readability. With respect to content, I have drawn out of the author additional material of interest; as well as added some new material, for instance items adding color to the historical narrative. But often the author has roundly rejected suggested improvements! Prevailing upon an older brother, set in his old sailor's ways, is no simple matter. In all honesty, I am amazed at my brother's ability to write and powers of self-expression. Thus the book is his, not only in concept and content; but also down to style, vocabulary, and phraseology. For example: the sublime description of the Battle of the Eastern Solomons in Chapter 10, and of the seduction of the sea at the beginning of Chapter 21.

As a student and lover of history, I naturally have a vital interest in preserving historical verity for posterity. Of course, not being privy to all the historical sources and records relevant to this story, I cannot personally vouch for the accuracy and authenticity of every last detail. However, I have verified whatever I could. Nor am I responsible for all my brother's opinions historical and otherwise. Nevertheless there is no doubt that he has spent years researching all the records available to him, and that he has reconstructed and recounted historical reality from historical records and personal recollections as best he could. From the nature of the case, ultimately only God fully knows all that really happened—history *as it actually was* (*wie es eigentlich gewesen*), to use an expression of famous German historian Leopold von Ranke.

In the annals of American history, maybe in all military history, perhaps no episode is more amazing and fascinating, with the possible exception of the War Between the States (1861–1865), than that of the Second World War in the Pacific (1941–1945). The Pacific War, between the United States of America (and our Allies) and the Empire of Japan, commenced with one of the most incredible events in human history: Japan's sneak air attack on the U.S. Pacific Fleet anchored at Pearl Harbor! How is one to explain the unbelievable audacity of the Japanese? The answer lies in the fact that the flagship of the carrier strike force steaming toward Pearl Harbor in 1941 flew the very same Rising Sun imperial battle flag flown by the Nipponese Navy that decimated the Russian Fleet at Tsushima in 1905. Having forced the mammoth Russian Empire, spanning two continents, to the peace table, the island Empire of Japan thought it could do the same after Pearl Harbor with the American continental colossus.

The Pearl Harbor venture was brilliantly conceived by Harvard-educated Admiral Isoroku Yamamoto; who personally, and indeed prophetically, considered any attack against the sleeping American giant to be virtual military suicide. Nonetheless, with the Japanese warmongers in the Army bent on war, as a patriot and military professional the island Empire's top Admiral planned the attack attempting to neutralize the United States Navy in one devastating blow. This incredible incident, virtually unbelievable not only before but even after it happened, initiated the most unique and extensive military conflict in the whole of human history heretofore—a bitter, bloody, and relentless war *on*, *above*, and *under* the vast expanse of the Pacific, ironically an ocean supposed by the Spanish explorer Vasco Nuñez de Balboa, when he discovered it in 1513, to be peaceful! Indeed, the *Pacific War* is, formally, a contradiction in terms!!

In the whole Pacific Basin and beyond—from Asia to America, from Australia to Alaska, from California to China, from the Indian Ocean to the North Pacific almost to the Arctic Ocean, from the South Pacific to the South China Sea, from Honshu and Kyushu to Oahu and Honolulu, from Japan's Inland Sea to the Java Sea and the Solomon Sea, from the Dutch East Indies to Dutch Harbor in the Aleutian Islands, from the Coral Sea to Midway in the Central Pacific, from the Panama Canal to Guadalcanal, from Puget Sound to Ironbottom Sound, from the Eastern Solomons to the East China Sea and Okinawa, from the Santa Barbara Channel to the Santa Cruz Islands, from New Zealand to New Guinea, from the Bismarck Sea to the Bering Sea, from Melanesia to Micronesia and the Marianas, from Polynesia to the Philippines and Formosa, from Seattle to Singapore, from San Diego to Sazebo, from Guadalcanal to Tokyo, from San Francisco Bay to Tokyo Bay, from the Golden Gate to the Pearly Gate and doubtless to the Gates of Hell as well—in between these storied places and criss-crossing these stupendous spaces, unrelenting war was waged and violently raged.

Moreover, the War in the Pacific was utterly unique, one for the ages in the annals of human conflict, unprecedented among those epic and tragic martial struggles that have betokened and bedeviled mankind from time immemorial and throughout the sanguinary and melancholy history of this wretched race. Never before had there been such a war. Never before were sea battles decided from the air by air power in the form of airplanes operating off ships known as aircraft carriers as well as from bases on land. Never before was there ever such a colossal conflict over such an immense expanse; involving sea, air, and land forces, with limited communications, but with virtually unlimited space and areas in which to maneuver.

Indeed, given political and especially technological factors, it is highly unlikely that such a war will ever take place again. My brother witnessed events unusual and remarkably unique in human history: from the biggest broadside in naval history from the guns of the NORTH

CAROLINA; to the great sea and air battles of the South and Western Pacific; to the relentless Japanese suicide strategy at Okinawa Jima and in the East China Sea. Are events like these, or anything remotely similar, ever likely to occur again? This is not to mention the fact that the Pacific War is the only conflict in human history to involve nuclear weapons. Will there ever be another? As historian Ronald M. Spector put it: "The War between the United States and Japan was in many ways a unique and unprecedented conflict—the first, and probably the last, to be waged on such a scale and upon such a stage."

Furthermore, the Pacific War is especially fascinating in that its history hinged and turned on a few fateful factors—some seemingly in human hands, others apparently beyond human ingenuity and intelligence—certain, perhaps better uncertain, momentous *what ifs.*

What if at Pearl Harbor the U.S. Navy's aircraft carriers had not been at sea, but had been put out of action like the battleships on battleship row? This contingency boggles the mind in terms of contemplating possible consequences. The United States Navy would have lost control of the entire Pacific, certainly for many crucial months, probably for several critical years; precluding any but dire defensive action and permitting the Japanese to dominate the vast Pacific, turning it into an enormous and endless Nipponese lake, so that the Japs could have established and entrenched themselves in every island archipelago. The Empire of the Rising Sun could have captured the Hawaiian Islands; the Imperial Japanese Navy could have operated with impunity off the West Coast of the United States, except for harassment by land-based aircraft, until new carriers could be constructed and commissioned on the East Coast.

What if the Japanese, quite apart from not finding the American carriers at Pearl Harbor, had fully executed their plan, and carried out the intended third air strike on Oahu, so as to destroy not only U.S. ships and planes but also their bases and petroleum resources as well? What if American cryptographers had not cracked the Japanese naval code before the crucial Battles of the Coral Sea and Midway, so as to give the U.S. Navy the decided advantage of knowing beforehand Jap plans and movements? What if the American carriers had been sunk by superior Japanese forces in the Coral Sea or in the Central Pacific at Midway? What if the quiet and unassuming Admiral on the ENTERPRISE had not planned and guessed aright in that fateful battle, resulting in the decimation in less than ten minutes' time of the main Japanese carrier force that had attacked Pearl Harbor? What if the Japs, instead of spreading themselves too thin, instead of holding back and fighting defensively, from the beginning had put all their superior forces and resources into the Solomons Campaign? What if the Japs had employed suicide tactics extensively early on in the War, for instance in the South and Central Pacific?

What if the Japanese had been given time to develop further their military technology, in some areas superior to ours as it was, for example in the field of electronic ingenuity (e.g. their torpedoes) not to mention an atomic capability? What if Japan had developed nuclear weapons first? Or what if the United States had not developed and dropped the atomic bombs on the Japanese cities of Hiroshima and Nagasaki? What if we would have had to invade the Japanese Home Islands with conventional forces; to have reduced the Japanese people to surrender or suicide mile by mile, village by village, city by city? The ensuing cost in human lives staggers even the darkest imagination. Given the fortitude and fanaticism of that remarkable race, that incredibly clever and capable nation, the Pacific War might not have been over till 1958 let alone 1948!

What almost all Americans did not realize at the time, doubtless due to racial stereotype and prejudice, and few fathom even today, was that the Pacific War was a stupendous struggle, a colossal clash, between two very different but very gifted and capable societies, two proud and presumptuous peoples, two confident and arrogant nations, nations (one old, one new) that had never really known defeat in war. For the United States, the War in the Pacific was a life and death struggle against an enigmatic enemy, a ferocious foe with a long and distinguished patriotic and military tradition that for centuries had never known anything but victory in war. Only recently, with the rise of Japanese economic prowess and power, are average Americans beginning to apprehend what American forces were up against in the Pacific. The Japs were indeed a formidable foe.

Hopefully this memoir of the Pacific War will give many of our countrymen a better and greater appreciation of the struggle that was World War II; and of the many gallant and valiant men that lived and died fighting for the land of the free and the home of the brave against the Japanese juggernaut. With respect to Midway, Guadalcanal, and other early battles of the Pacific War, Winston Churchill's words with reference to the Battle of Britain are perhaps just as appropriate: *Never in the field of human conflict did so many owe so much to so few!* Yet those heroic and courageous men—those lion-hearted and death-defying sailors, soldiers, marines, and airmen—are all but forgotten today. Given Korea, Viet Nam, and the Gulf War—who cares, who "gives a damn," about World War II anymore? But perhaps it could also be said of Americans with reference to World War II what Churchill said of the British: *This was their finest hour!!*

Unfortunately, one of the generic weaknesses of the American national character is a presumptuous disdain and dislike for history. Henry Ford even said *history is bunk!* (Henry Ford is now history. Thus even Henry Ford is bunk!) On the whole, Americans could care less about history. We are incredibly ignorant of our own history let alone that of other nations. For instance, every British schoolboy and school-girl knows the name of the famed Horatio Nelson, the Admiral commanding the British Fleet that decimated the combined French and Spanish Navies at Trafalgar. After all, Nelson is perched atop his victory pillar in London's Trafalgar Square. Whereas hardly one American in ten thousand would know the name of the American Admiral in tactical command at Midway—a naval victory even greater and more momentous than Trafalgar—namely Raymond A. Spruance! Where is his memorial, or any memorial for that matter, to the U.S. Navy's illustrious and hard-fought victory in the Pacific?

Of all the fabulous episodes in the Pacific War, perhaps the two most fascinating are the bitter and bloody struggles for supremacy in the Solomon Islands and at Okinawa Gunto. The Solomons Campaign, consisting of true tales of the South Pacific, was the longest of the War, in that here the Americans generally were up against superior Japanese forces and resources. While at Okinawa American naval and air forces were far superior to the Japanese, the fanatical Jap suicide strategy dragged out the campaign—injecting a novel and foreboding factor into the fray (the Japs had occasionally employed suicide tactics before but sporadically not strategically) namely the certain anticipation that henceforth the War would be fought on this footing to the bitter end.

Like Harry Truman in the first days of his Presidency, the American forces at Okinawa knew nothing of the atom bomb; they anticipated that they would have to face the Japs' suicide strategy from here on out, that henceforth this is the way the War would go all the way to Tokyo. Our men at Guadalcanal also anticipated a rough road to Tokyo. Without a doubt this memoir is a distinctive and significant contribution to the history of these colorful campaigns (the color all too often being blood red) as well as to the history of the War in the Pacific as a whole. This is especially the case, in that this account is uniquely written by an *enlisted man* from an enlisted man's perspective, representing an enlisted man's point of view; rather than by an officer or commander from an officer's perspective, writing with his professional reputation on the line. After fifty years, the enlisted man has nobody's posterior to protect, not even his own.

Interestingly, this memoir also demonstrates the distinction between historical reality and national publicity, the discrepancy between
what really happens in a war and what appears to be the case in the
perception of the people back home as manipulated by the media and
the military. For example, John F. Kennedy permitted his fast PT-boat
to be run down by a slower Japanese destroyer, and should have been
court-martialed or at least reprimanded for negligence. Yet he goes
down in American history as a war hero! How is this possible? The
power of money to manipulate the media? The money-mad media's
tendency to believe and propagate what they want? The mousy military's failure to set the historical facts straight given political factors?
The occupational fears of military officers with their careers on the line?
Doubtless there are many other similar discrepancies between reality
and publicity, image and substance, in the perception of World War II in
American history. Let us never forget the unknown and unheralded
heroes of that War to preserve our way of life, including the freedom of
the media and the military to manipulate the perception of the people.

Who ever heard of John A. "Jack" Hutchinson and countless other
unknown heroes of the Second World War, men who risked their lives
time after time, time and time again as a simple matter of duty, without
ever giving it a second thought, to win the War, save the lives of their
countrymen, and protect their beloved country from tyranny? Upon
finding among our father's papers after his death a list of *seven* occasions
when the old man had escaped death in his younger days by a whisker,
I mentioned this to my half-brother (we have the same father but
different mothers). He responded rather matter-of-factly: "I could come
up with a list of *seventy!*"

Above and beyond the book's contribution to military and in particular naval history, this memoir is replete with events and episodes of
intense human interest. Once having read them, who could ever forget,
for example, Texas beef being beaten behind boot-camp barracks, or the
barroom brawl with British sailors in the American Bar in Norfolk?! Or
the Marines meekly marching into the oily waters of Hampton Roads,
or the drunken sailors spontaneously diving into the icy waters of Casco
Bay after their bottle of booze?! Or the young sailor experiencing combat
for the first time, gripping the splinter shield for dear life, himself
gripped by the panoramic scene from Sky Control atop the NORTH
CAROLINA, at the Battle of the Eastern Solomons?! Or the frightful
plane ride from Noumea to Henderson Field on Guadalcanal with the
whacky DC-3 pilot's firing at the Jap sub with a .45 caliber pistol?!

Or the endless enemy air raids on Guadalcanal, including instinctively gutting the Jap scavenger in the foxhole with a screwdriver picked

up as an afterthought?! Or the frightened survivor of so many air raids exiting the movies in the middle of *GUADALCANAL DIARY*, or digging in the dirt for cover when the evening lights flashed on in San Francisco?! Or the episode with the Captain of the IRWIN and the missing hams, or the titanic struggles with typhoon and kamikaze in the East China Sea?! Or many other scenes, not to mention the psychological odyssey of one lone sailor seduced by the sea, and fascinated by this sad and sanguinary saga of the sea, in which he was predestined to be not only an enchanted participant but also a charmed survivor?! Perhaps these elements and incidents of human interest will contribute the scintillating scenes of one more monumental movie of World War II to commemorate the Pacific War and those who fought it on the fiftith anniversary of its abrupt ending! Lest we forget, lest we forget!!

Hopefully this history will highlight once more the combat veterans of World War II and what they went through. They are indeed a vanishing breed of men all but forgotten today. Having grown up in the Great Depression of the 1930s, they were survivors, unbelievably tough and tenacious, incredibly rugged and resilient, prepared to endure the crucible of war in all its ghastly horrors and terrors physical and psychological. One wonders how many American youths today, spoiled by affluence and welfare, could or would endure if tested by a *real* war. The Gulf War was a piece of cake, a cakewalk compared to World War II. It is a national disgrace that World War II combat veterans are forgotten to the extent that, despite all the handouts provided by our welfare system to all comers, they and their medical needs (unless emergencies or proven to be service related) cannot even be taken care of in veterans hospitals without virtually declaring themselves indigent. Why do combat veterans continue to "get the shaft" while others who never fought for their country are taken care of by the government?

The indifference of our society and government to combat veterans is scandalous and a crying shame. How could the U.S. Government be so insensitive to those whose service proves they love this country the most? Despite numerous attempts throughout the entire War in the Pacific, the Japanese could not sink the aircraft carrier ENTERPRISE. The LEXINGTON, the YORKTOWN, the WASP, the HORNET—all went down—but not the Big E. Still, despite numerous pleas to preserve her, indifferent bureaucrats in Washington could scrap the most celebrated and combat-experienced ship in American naval history. How is it possible for Washington, which can waste money (one of my boys once inadvertently spelled it *Wastington*) on all manner of folly and frivolity, to refuse to preserve the ENTERPRISE—as a perpetual symbol of the most unique war in human history, and an historical memorial to all the valiant combat veterans of the Pacific War? Such shortsightedness seems par for the course for the day-dreamers and night-crawlers in Washington who, reflecting the national character, apparently could care less about history.

To this day, though one exists for veterans of the Viet Nam War, there is no national memorial to those who fought and died in World War II! How is such a scandalous fact to be explained? Perhaps the answer is to be found in William Manchester's observations quoted at the conclusion of this chronicle. For instance, the United States of America is a different country and society now, and our standards and values are rather different from what they were then. Moreover, the pace of post-War history, with its incessant inundation of sensationalism, has trivialized the history of the Second World War and minimized the generation of Americans who fought and won it.

It is extremely difficult for combat veterans of the Pacific War, waged against Japanese hegemony and military tyranny, to witness the decline of American industry and economic ascendancy in the face of Japanese economic superiority and hegemony in so many areas. They ask: "What the hell did we fight the war for? Did we whip the Japs so that they could accomplish economically what they could not politically and militarily?" When our father was dying in 1986, I asked my brother, tongue in cheek, if he would buy a Jap car. The ready reply: "Hell no, it was a goddamn Mitsubishi that sank the McCAWLEY!" He would be utterly aghast at the sight in Atlanta's Fulton County Stadium of the huge stadium screen's flying a giant fluttering Stars and Stripes just above the large letters MITSUBISHI!

Come on, Americans, we can do better than this. We have a distinguished history and have accomplished so much in the past. We should be gratified with our country's past economic and political accomplishments, and that we are the only conquering nation in history with the magnanimity to help defeated foes to economic glory as well as political autonomy. But what has become of energy and ingenuity in our work? Why do we continue to tolerate incompetence in every area and on every level of American society? Psychology and personality are no substitutes for logical rationality and the hard facts of empirical reality. Image is not substance, publicity is not reality, psychology is not rationality. All the American auto companies have to do, is build better vehicles than the Japanese, and once again the world will beat a path to their door.

What about the attitude of Pacific War combat veterans toward the Japanese? Given the content of this chronicle and Japan's post-War economic recovery and subsequent economic ascendancy, it is certainly understandable that my brother and his comrades in arms would resent the Japs to the point of rancor. It should be pointed out that this rancor is not racial since their attitude toward the Chinese and other orientals is rather different. But surely the economic ascendancy of the Japanese is not their fault but ours. We have only ourselves, our own arrogance and incompetence, to blame.

Furthermore, surely some human empathy and sympathy for our Japanese enemy in the Pacific War is in order. To be sure, the Japs were unnecessarily cruel in the War. But they were brought up and trained in the military to be that way. They did not know any better—we did. Moreover, many Japanese military professionals, just like their American counterparts, were simply attempting to do their duty under orders from their Government—but of course the Japanese Government was dominated during the War by bloodthirsty miltarists. Indeed, most Jap combatants were drafted and trying, just as our draftees, to serve their country and survive as best they could—though of course their militaristic culture and training tended to turn them into savages.

At any rate, the Japs certainly put up "one hell of a fight", and there was nothing "yellow" about them. As James J. Fahey put it in his *Pacific War Diary:* "You have to admire their bravery, they are no pushovers." Certainly the Japanese were and are an amazingly gifted and accomplished people and society with much of positive value to teach us. Are we Americans "too damn proud" to learn from the Japs? If so, God help us!

In any event, all combat veterans of the Pacific War should ponder the attitude of one of the central characters of this chronicle, namely Admiral Richmond Kelly "Terrible" Turner who certainly contributed as much to the defeat of the Japs as anyone. Immediately following the surrender ceremony on Sunday morning, 2 September, 1945, Admiral Turner commandeered a car to drive to Tokyo, at considerable personal risk since the U.S. Army's 1st Calvary Division had not yet occupied the Japanese capital, to pay his respects to our fallen foe, bowing according to Nipponese custom at the Shrine of famed Admiral Heihechiro Togo!

In the context of the respect and admiration that naval officers and men of the sea have always had for each other, perhaps Longfellow's lines are apropos:

> The dim, dark sea, so like unto Death,
> That divides and yet unites mankind!

In spite of all the terrible things Japanese propaganda said about him, "Terrible" Turner forgave the Japs and thought we should be friends again. While not a church-going Christian, as his biographer points out, Kelly Turner had one of the great Christian virtues—he could forgive his enemies. While castigating the cruelty of individual Japs, the Admiral admired the Japanese people and corresponded with certain Nipponese naval officers till his death. As Turner said at Togo's Shrine on surrender Sunday: "If we play our cards well, the Japanese will become our best and most worthwhile friends. They have certain fundamental virtues in their character which in time, I hope, will be appreciated by all worthwhile Americans. We should be most careful to respect their . . . traditions, and I hope they will come in time to respect ours."

But do we still respect our own American traditions, let alone those of the Japanese? Doubtless the most striking and significant side of this memoir, to me as a Christian minister, is its religious and spiritual dimension. True, most of the participants, in particular the professional military men, were not practising Christians in the traditional sense, but personally rather profane in language and life-style. At the same time, they still retained a basically Christian and spiritual worldview and outlook on life—the cultural residue and result of their intellectual and spiritual heritage, the legacy of 4,000 years of teaching reflected in the Bible. Even when they were personally profane and did not practise these precepts and principles, they still accepted intellectually the religious foundation and framework of Western Christian culture and civilization.

Today one wonders whether this Christian culture and consensus still prevail in our land. To be sure, Christian sentiment and sensitivity still hold sway in certain quarters, but on the whole hardly dominate our society and public life. It appears that the religion of *pluralism* so-called has replaced 2,000 years of Christian and 400 years of American civilization. Not a relative and circumscribed pluralism within defined ends and bounds; but an absolute and unrestrained pluralism become an end in itself without higher purpose or parameters, which will produce the political tyranny of the politically correct with no traditional reins or restraints. In the nature of the case, endless and listless pluralism amounts to spiritual suicide as well as cultural and social disintegration. In any event, despite all their sins and shortcomings, surely our forefathers did not fight for what America has become, the new America with its new brand of unbridled pluralism run amuck. For sure, the veterans of World War II did not fight for a country intimidated by homosexuals—no way did they fight for a "queer nation"!

As for the state of the nation, if my brother is a representative indication, World War II veterans think the country is "going to hell in a handbasket." They may well be right. Is our country on the right track? Or is America on the *broad way* leading to destruction?

Certainly there are ominous signs of degeneration in our society. From the point of view of Biblical Christianity and Western civilization, doubtless the most frightening for the future are: intellectual subjectivism, the primacy of psychology over rationality; substituting subjectivity for objective facts, subjective for objective standards of truth and right; moral relativism, the decline of classical Christian ethics in every area, especially in traditional family standards and discipline; and political liberalism so-called, not the old classical love of civil liberty but the psychological and political tyranny of so-called democratic liberalism—which eventually will tolerate anything but opposition to its new morality, subtly abridge and then abrogate our traditional liberties, and ruthlessly repress all deviation from its politically correct agenda, all in the name of democracy and freedom.

While by no means agreeing with all my brother's political opinions, I am amazed that the old salt is astute enough to see that divorcing Almighty God from civil government eventually will subvert and suppress not only our civil liberties but also the Churches' freedom to teach Christian doctrine and practise church discipline. Today it is incredible that Christian teachers from the United States are holding seminars for state school teachers in the once atheistic former Soviet Union, in order to teach Christian ethics as foundational to society, while in our own once Christian country the Ten Commandments and the Christian religion are barred from public school classrooms!

At the same time, if history provides any insight into human nature, it is not an uncommon phenomenon for one generation to behold itself as the best, view the recent past as the norm, and see moral degeneration everywhere especially in the deviations of younger generations. However, every human society is exceedingly complex, which makes moral decline and social progress difficult to determine, depending on one's norms and the areas and arenas under consideration. All human societies are mixed bags, progressing in some areas and regressing in others, depending on one's point of view. In many respects and from various perspectives, including that of Biblical Christianity, America in 1780 or 1860 or 1940 was as much in need of improving and reforming as is the case today. Since those dates there has been significant moral and social progress in our land as well as decline. So things may not be as bad or hopeless as they seem.

This is not the place to pontificate on the issues of the day—spiritual, ethical, social, and political—but simply to testify, from a Christian point of view, that the ultimate solution to America's ills are not political and social but spiritual and moral. However pessimistic his view of human depravity, the Christian is optimistic as to what God by sovereign grace can and will do in a fallen world, encouraged by the Scriptures and the revivals and reformations of the past. Nevertheless, past spiritual revivals, from the Protestant Reformation in the 16th century to the Third Great Awakening in the mid 19th, presupposed the foundation of Christian civilization and conviction. But if this basis be bygone, if the great intellectual battles of the past have to be fought all over again—it appears that the Lord and his servants have more work on their hands than heretofore.

As a preacher of the Gospel of the Master's Kingdom, needless to say, I cannot condone the profanity periodically appearing in this old sailor's sea story. Nevertheless, in the interest of historical authenticity, this is certainly the way it was. Indeed, I am most grateful that he has cleaned up the language of the United States Navy (a few blasphemies and no obscenities!) almost beyond recognition! Doubtless this is the case not so much for the sake of his reverend brother as out of respect for his old skipper Danny Miller. In point of fact, the vernacular was infinitely worse, not only in the Navy but also in the community and extended family in which both my brother and I were brought up. The Lord have mercy on us all—our family, our society, our country—*"for the LORD will not hold him guiltless that taketh his name in vain"* (Exodus 20:7).

The Sailors' Confession in the Book of Common Prayer is appropriate for us all:

"Almighty God, Father of our Lord Jesus Christ, Maker of all things, Judge of all men; We acknowledge and bewail our manifold sins and wickedness, Which we, from time to time, most grievously have committed, By thought, word, and deed, Against thy Divine Majesty, Provoking most justly thy wrath and indignation against us. We do earnestly repent, And are heartily sorry for these our misdoings; The remembrance of them is grievous unto us; The burden of them is intolerable. Have mercy upon us, Have mercy upon us, most merciful Father; For thy Son our Lord Jesus Christ's sake, Forgive us all that is past; And grant that we may ever hereafter Serve and please thee In newness of life, To the honour and glory of thy Name; Through Jesus Christ our Lord. Amen."

There are two alleged quotations, picked up in his youth, my brother has been afraid to look up all his life. The one is that Shakespeare somewhere said that the only thing important in language is to be understood! The other is that the Bible says that the sins of seafaring men are forgiven!! Whether the first is spurious, I do not know. But the second, I had to tell him, is not in the Book. Or is it? Certainly not in so many words, and surely forgiveness is not automatic without repentance and faith in the Lord's mercy. But God graciously forgives all sinners, even sailors, who in sincere sorrow for their sin pray and plead his mercy: *"God, be merciful to me a sinner"* (Luke 18:13)! After all, it was the old slavetrading sea captain John Newton who wrote *"Amazing Grace*—how sweet the sound—that saved a wretch like *me"!*

Perhaps this old sailor will consummate his saga of the sea, in his own lone sailor's mind at least, as did the *Ancient Mariner* his tale to the Wedding Guest:

> O sweeter than the marriage-feast,
> 'Tis sweeter far to me,
> To walk together to the kirk
> With a goodly company!
>
> To walk together to the kirk,
> And all together pray,
> While each to his great Father bends,
> Old men, and babes, and loving friends. . . .
>
> Farewell, farewell! but this I tell. . . .
> He prayeth well, who loveth well. . . .
> For the dear God who loveth us,
> He made and loveth all.

In any case, hopefully the reader of this sea story will correspond to the one told the *Ancient Mariner's* tale.

> He went like one that hath been stunned,
> And is of sense forlorn:
> *A sadder and a wiser man,*
> *He rose the morrow morn.*

As an inveterate landlubber, having suffered seasickness and fed fish in the English Channel, I am in awe of the sea and admire those who brave the dangers of the deep. At the same time, since reading Melville's *Moby Dick* in high school (as did my brother), the sea has fascinated me. Moreover, throughout this earthly pilgrimage the parallel between the sailor's life *and* life in general and the Christian life in particular has meant much to me.

As a young boy, I used to sing in church with gusto at the top of my voice (*fortissimo*):

I was sinking deep in sin, far from the peaceful shore,
Very deeply stained within, sinking to rise no more.
But the *Master of the sea* heard my despairing cry,
From the waters lifted me, now safe am I. . . .
Souls in danger look above, Jesus, completely saves;
He will lift you by his love out of the angry waves. . . .
Love lifted me! Love lifted me!
When nothing else could help, *Love lifted me!*

As a young man, facing the future as an undergraduate at Princeton University, I would pray:

Jesus, Savior, pilot me over *life's tempestuous sea*;
Unknown waves before me roll, hiding rocks and treacherous shoal;
Chart and compass come from Thee; Jesus, Savior, pilot me. . . .
Wondrous *Sovereign of the sea*, Jesus, Savior, pilot me . . . !

In the midst of life's many storms and momentous struggles, surely I had long since gone under without that sure and steadfast "anchor of the soul" (Hebrews 6:19).

Though the angry surges roll on *my tempest driven soul,* . . .
I've an anchor safe and sure, that can evermore endure. . . .
Mighty tides around me sweep, perils lurk within the deep. . . .
Through the storm I safely ride, till the turning of the tide. . . .
Troubles almost 'whelm the soul; griefs like billows o'er me roll. . . .
But in Christ I can be bold, *I've an anchor that shall hold.* . . .
And it holds, my anchor holds: Blow your wildest, then, O gale,
On my bark so small and frail: By His grace I shall not fail. . . .

As a Christian minister, many a worship service have I opened with the hymn "Jesus calls us o'er the tumult of our *life's wild restless sea.* . . ." And in many a sermon have I quoted, with life's storms and my brother in mind, the old sailing song: "Sailing, sailing, over the bounding main . . . *many a stormy wind shall blow, ere Jack comes home again!*"

As a believer in the Master of the Sea, I still cherish Tennyson's hope in *Crossing the Bar:*

For tho' from out our bourne of Time and Place
The flood may bear me far,
I hope to see my Pilot face to face
When I have crost the bar.

Finally, there arises from the blood, sweat, toil, tears and fears depicted in this chronicle the question as to its higher meaning, indeed the irrepressible philosophical and theological question as to the meaning of man and human conflict. Why all these extraordinary events? What can we learn from them?

Why did such a savage War rage in the Pacific? Why were men maimed and mangled, blown to bits, roasted in turrets, entombed in ships? Why did so many young men have to die? Why were so many civilians incinerated in cities? Why all this seemingly senseless suffering? Why? Why? Why? Is it all only *a tale told by an idiot, full of sound and fury, signifying nothing?*

This is not the place to try to wrestle in depth with such hard questions. Nevertheless, on the personal level, each one who peruses these pages will have to grapple with them on his own—including the author himself, who has to ask why he survived so many close calls, why and for what purpose he is still alive. From the standpoint of Christianity, the significance of these events must transcend time to be found in eternity. Surely, more was involved in the Pacific War than simply national purpose, preserving one's country and national heritage.

But personally coming to grips with the higher meaning of events is no easy exercise. While remembering the Lord's leading His people in the past (e.g. the Exodus) the Psalmist sounds like the lone sailor at sea as to what is going on in his personal life:

"In the day of trouble I sought the Lord. . . I remembered God, and was troubled . . . and my spirit was overwhelmed. . . I have considered the days of old, the years of ancient times. . . Will the Lord cast off forever? . . . Hath God forgotten to be gracious? . . . And I said, this is my infirmity. . . I will remember the works of the LORD . . . thy wonders of old . . . . I will meditate also . . . Thy way, O God, is in the sanctuary. . . The waters saw thee, O God, . . . the depths also were troubled. . . *Thy way is in the sea*, and thy path in the great waters, and *thy footsteps are not known*" (Psalm 77).

From a Christian perspective, we shall never have in this life all the answers as to the Lord's specific purposes in the Pacific War. But we must know that nothing was in vain, that God's thoughts are higher than our thoughts and his ways than our ways, that our limited understanding is not the measure of all things nor of the purposes of the Almighty. In the words of William Cowper's classic hymn:

> God moves in a mysterious way His wonders to perform;
> He plants His footsteps in the sea, and rides upon the storm . . .
> Blind unbelief is sure to err, and scan His work in vain;
> *God is His own Interpreter, and He will make it plain.*

Much of what happens in the world in general, and in war in particular, is to be laid to the Lord's judging and testing humankind in order to advance his truth. In the American Civil War, both sides recognized the conflict as an indication of God's judgment for sin, individual and social, and despite all the carnage and suffering there was a revival of personal Christian faith in both camps. Was this the case, eighty years later, with World War II?

This traditional Biblical and Christian perspective is well expressed, in very personal terms, in the "Battle Hymn of the Republic":

> Mine eyes have seen the glory of the coming of the Lord;
> He is trampling out the vintage where the grapes of wrath are stored;
> He hath loosed the fateful lightning of *His terrible swift sword.* . . .
> I have seen him in the watchfires of a hundred circling camps; . . .
> I have read His righteous sentence by the dim and flaring lamps. . . .
> He is sifting out the hearts of men before *His judgment seat*;
> O be swift, my soul, to answer Him, be jubilant, my feet. . . .
> In the beauty of the lillies Christ was born across the sea,
> With a glory in his bosom that *transfigures you and me.* . . .
> As He died to make men holy let us die to make men free. . . .
> Glory, glory, hallelujah! Glory, glory, hallelujah!
> *Glory, glory, hallelujah! His truth is marching on.*

When the Pacific War ended, when the Pacific was pacific again, the thanksgiving prescribed in the Prayer Book for victory at sea was in order. But was all the glory of victory ascribed to God alone? Or did we Americans take credit for ourselves and extol our virtues? To what extent did we put feet to our prayers: "we beseech thee, give us grace to improve this great mercy to thy glory, the advancement of thy Gospel, the honour of our country, and, as much as in us lieth, the good of all mankind"?

On the evening of surrender Sunday, we should not forget, Admiral Halsey and other Flag officers assembled on the British Flagship DUKE OF YORK for a sunset service of thanksgiving in accord with our British Christian heritage. The flags of all the Allies were lowered in unison during the final hymn "The Day Thou Gavest, Lord, Is Ended".

> So be it, Lord; thy throne shall never,
> Like earth's proud empires, pass away:
> Thy kingdom stands, and grows for ever,
> Til all thy creatures own thy sway.

On the national level, one thing appears clear from the history of the Pacific War *and* its economic sequel: Regardless of past accomplishments, humiliation awaits proud and presumptuous peoples, conceited and condescending countries, whether the Empire of Japan or the United States of America. *"Pride goeth before destruction and a haughty spirit before a fall"* (Proverbs 16:18)! *"Cease ye from man, whose breath is in his nostrils: for wherein is he to be accounted of?"* (Isaiah 2:22)!

If nothing else, the Pacific War unmasks man's madness if not badness. Man is insane if not inane, bad if not mad; and if not mad, then very bad. If nothing else, the Pacific War discloses the depth of human depravity, if not insanity, mankind run amuck in sin and self-destruction.

> I will sing to the LORD all my life . . . .
> May my meditation be pleasing to him . . . .
> But may sinners vanish from the earth . . . .
> Praise the LORD, O my soul (Psalm 104)!

Reverend George P. Hutchinson, D.Phil.
Presbyterian Church in America
Gainesville, Hall County, Georgia
June 5, 1992, 25th Wedding Anniversary
50th Anniversary, Battle of Midway
(Fought across the International Dateline
June 4-6, 1942)

APPENDICES

MORE IRISH PENNANTS

I

JAPANESE AIRCRAFT CODE NAMES

Japanese Army and Navy fighters and Navy reconnaissance float planes were assigned male names. Navy flying boats and torpedo and dive bombers, as well as Army and Navy reconnaissance planes and high-level bombers, were given female code names.

From time to time, the Navy changed the code names for various Japanese aircraft, as new models were introduced by the enemy. The descriptions of the following combat planes, those mentioned most in this memoir, are from 15 August, 1944 (Technical Air Intelligence Center, Summary #2):

ZEKE: The famed ZERO! There were five different models of these carrier-borne fighter planes. Four were built by Mitsubishi, and one by Nakajima.

KATE: A carrier-borne attack plane and the earliest Jap torpedo bomber, there were three models—one built by Nakajima; one by Mitsubishi; one by Hiro, Aichi, and Nakajima.

VAL: The principal carrier-borne dive bomber early in the War, the VAL was the Aichi 99 with engines by Mitsubishi. There were two models, which were converted to trainers when replaced by the JUDY.

JUDY: Four models were built by Aichi; they were carrier-borne torpedo bombers to replace the VAL. Some were also modified to be launched from catapults. Some were used for reconnaissance.

JILL: Two models were built by Nakajima; they were carrier-borne attack aircraft carrying bombs or torpedoes, the principal torpedo plane in the Japanese arsenal in 1944.

FRANCES: This bomber was a late model (newly coded in 1944) and was followed by a second model converted to night fighting. Built by Yokosuka, Kaigun, and Gijutsushe, it was land-based.

BETTY: There were five models of this land-based Navy bomber built by Mitsubishi. It was the workhorse of the Navy's non-carrier bombers and the principal bomber used in the high-level attacks against U.S. installations on Guadalcanal.

Some BETTY bombers were modified to launch *oka* ("baka") bombs. Others were converted to transports.

Any and all Japanese aircraft, including obsolete planes, were used by *kamikaze* pilots. The best and latest models generally were reserved for *conventional* air attacks and were flown by the better pilots.

The enemy still had some 10,000 aircraft to hurl against us at the time of the surrender. Roughly half of them were conventional, and half kamikaze.

II

THE FATE OF KEY FIGHTING SHIPS

The United States Frigate CONSTELLATION is moored in Baltimore Harbor. She has been restored and is maintained in much the same condition as during my time aboard. Open to the public and a major tourist attraction, she is a vital part of our U.S. Naval heritage and an important link to America's past.

The U.S.S. NORTH CAROLINA remained in the Fleet after the War until she was decommissioned on 27 June, 1947, and mothballed at Bayonne, New Jersey. In 1960, when the Navy announced its intention to scrap the venerable vessel, an organization of North Carolinians was formed to save her for posterity. Over $330,000—including hundreds of thousands of pennies from school children—was raised in contributions from citizens. In 1961, the "Showboat" was towed to North Carolina's Cape Fear River where she was moored across from downtown Wilmington. On 29 April, 1962, the ship was dedicated as a State War Memorial. She attracts hundreds of thousands of visitors annually. Basically the same as when I was aboard, the ship is the permanent site of the annual reunions of the crewmen who served aboard her during World War II.

The U.S.S. APc-25 and the U.S.S. APc-38, the "Spit Kits" on which I served in the Solomons, were sold as military surplus shortly after the conclusion of World War II.

The U.S.S. IRWIN was recommissioned on 26 February, 1951, joining the Sixth Fleet in the Mediterranean. After returning to the United States, she sailed for the Pacific on 1 April, 1953, where she was assigned to the Seventh Fleet carrier operations off the Korean coast. On 18 June the IRWIN, along with her sister ship U.S.S. PRESTON, were part of the blockade of Wonson Harbor, participating in shore bombardment, when an enemy shore battery scored a hit on the main deck, starboard side, wounding five men in Mount 52. After repairs in Japan, the "Fighting I" returned to Korea. On 8 July she came under heavy fire off Songjin from North Korean shore artillery as some 80 rounds of 76-millimeter shells rained around her. One shell hit power cables to the mast, with shrapnel wounding five men on the Bridge, including the Captain Jack Macginnis who suffered serious wounds. The Korean War ended on 27 July, 1953; but the IRWIN remained on active duty until decommissioned on 10 January, 1958.

In May, 1968, the DD-794 was sold to the Brazilian Navy. After substantial renovation, the U.S.S. IRWIN was rechristened the B.N.S. SANTA CATARINA (D-32) and joined Brazil's Second Destroyer Squadron. For the next twenty years, the ship served her new nation with distinction.

In 1987, from correspondence with Rear Admiral Roberto de Oliveira Coimbra, Brazilian Naval Attaché in Washington, I learned my old "home" had participated in many fleet exercises and joint maneuvers with other Navies, and had won awards for excellence in both engineering and gunnery, earning the coveted "White Star" for gunnery as the most efficient ship in her class. She was a member of the task force involved in rescuing the Apollo XIII spacecraft in the South Atlantic in 1970; received the "Blue Ribbon" classification in 1977 for excellence in engineering and crew's performance; took part in the 1975 and 1985 "Dragao" (amphibious) operations, and in the 1983, '84, '85', '86, and '87 "Tropicalex" operations, Brazil's biggest fleet exercises. Through 1987, the SANTA CATARINA had steamed 357,198 nautical miles and was at sea 1,279 days since joining Brazil's Navy. She was still upholding the traditions of our IRWIN!

On 17 May, 1993, I received a letter from Captain Kleber Luciano de Assis of Brazil's Ministry of Naval Affairs with information on the fate of the B.N.S. SANTA CATARINA (D-32). The destroyer was decommissioned on 28 December, 1988, and subsequently used as a gunfire target. She was sunk on 20 March, 1990, after being hit by one Mark 8 torpedo. Time: 2345. Position: 23°, 46' South; 42°, 56', 5" West. This position is, as close as I can figure, almost right on the Tropic of Capricorn, some 500 miles due east of Sao Paulo, within Brazil's Naval Gunfire Practice Range. The U.S.S. IRWIN (DD-794) had made her final cruise.

There are several U.S. Navy ships of World War II vintage on exhibit in America's coastal cities and on the Great Lakes. Two of them deserve mention here:

The U.S.S. CASSIN YOUNG (DD-793), the IRWIN's sister ship, is berthed in Boston Harbor as part of the same exhibit displaying the U.S. Frigate CONSTITUTION ("Old Ironsides"). The destroyer, as seen today, reflects the same Korean War modifications made to the IRWIN.

The *only* FLETCHER-class destroyer preserved in World War II configuration is the U.S.S. KIDD (DD-661) moored in the Mississippi River at Baton Rouge. A Louisiana War Memorial, the ship is almost a mirror-image of the IRWIN as she was during my service aboard. To go aboard the KIDD is like "going home" to me; and to the thousands of FLETCHER-class tin can sailors who visit her each year, often holding their own ship's reunions in Baton Rouge.

If only *one* of the hundreds of U.S. Navy ships, which survived World War II had been preserved for posterity, it should have been the aircraft carrier U.S.S. ENTERPRISE (CV-6). No other vessel even approached her combat record of twenty battle stars. Nor did the planes from any of her sister carriers cause more havoc and destruction to enemy ships, aircraft, and ground installations. No ship in the Fleet was so feared by the Japanese or was such a burr under their saddle. According to wartime Secretary of the Navy James Forrestal, the

"Big E" was "the one ship that most nearly symbolizes the history of the U.S. Navy in World War II."

Yet the ENTERPRISE was not to be so honored. In the 1950s a herculean campaign was mounted to preserve the "Big E", led by Admiral "Bull" Halsey himself and supported by thousands of Pacific War veterans. I heard that nearly half a million dollars, quite a sum in those days, was collected for the project, including my own $50 donation. Nevertheless, the Federal Government consigned the ship to the salvagers' cutting torches. There was scuttlebutt to the effect that political considerations were behind the decision to scrap "the Galloping Ghost of the Oahu Coast". But I still do not know why the valiant and illustrious ENTERPRISE was sent to such an ignominious fate. Nor do I know what happened to the money raised—hopefully it went to a good cause such as Navy Relief.

Since no one has seen fit to erect a national memorial to the veterans who fought and died in World War II, having the "Big E" as a reminder of that conflict would have provided some measure of compensation for this strange and insensitive oversight. How is it possible that the Federal Government, which can squander "scillions" on all sorts of silly schemes, be so indifferent to us combat veterans of the Pacific War and to the historical heritage we represent?

III

COMMENTS ON THE "NEW NAVY"

23 October, 1992

I'm starting this letter tonight, George, because I want to get things down while they are still fresh in my mind. I'll finish it tomorrow night.

The Navy frigate U.S.S. LOCKWOOD (FF-1064) is in port here in Coos Bay and will have "open house" tomorrow. I went down just to see where she was moored so I wouldn't have any problems when I take Dixie and Don (her boyfriend) with me. I walked out on the pier and while looking the ship over struck up a conversation with the Chief Petty Officer who had the deck. After a while, he invited me aboard, took me on a "Cook's Tour" and then to dinner in the Chief's Quarters.

The LOCKWOOD is the smallest of the Navy's escort-type vessels and roughly equivalent to a World War II destroyer as to mission and function. But she still is much larger than the IRWIN: 438 feet long, 46 feet 9 inches at the beam, with a displacement of 4,200 tons compared to the IRWIN's 2,100. Yet the old DD-794 would run rings around her in speed trials. The LOCKWOOD's rated speed is only 27 knots. Along with other weaponry she carries one 5-inch gun forward, an anti-submarine rocket launcher (ASROC), Harpoon missiles, and four Mark 32 torpedo tubes used against both submerged submarines and surface craft. She also carries a helicopter. Ship's complement is 18 officers and 270 enlisted men, 37 fewer than the IRWIN.

In talking with the Chief, I told him about the attitude of the sailors I met on the new Aegis cruiser PRINCETON visited just a year ago tomorrow. He told me my conclusions were correct, that today's crewmen are lazy, lack strong discipline, and are "spoiled". Those who operate the "push-button" weaponry, radar, sonar, and other equipment are so used to doing tasks that are simple, in that computers and other electronic gear do all the work, they approach their duties with a nonchalant attitude that borders on listlessness. He worried that in a combat situation these sailors of 1992 might not meet the test. When I asked him how the U.S.S. STARK got hit when the ship had all the detection gear and weaponry she needed to ward off the missile that struck her, he said he'd just told me the reason. I thought of JFK and his PT-boat. Like Kennedy and his crew, the STARK people were just goofing off.

The love of the sea is missing, as well as pride in the ship and the Navy. I did not see one enlisted man who knew how to shape and wear a white hat properly. Another Chief I talked with told me the term *"shipmate"* is seldom used anymore, and then only by senior petty officers—the "old-timers". What meant so much to us in the "Old Navy", is almost a forgotten relationship as we knew it. They don't even *talk* like sailors, calling the bow "the front of the ship" and the stern "the back". The only positive occurrence was in the Chief's Quarters where they had pretty good coffee. But there were still two soft drink machines aboard!

Even though it is peacetime and there's plenty of time to keep the ship clean, I was disturbed by the condition of her topside paint job and with seeing paper and other debris in the passageways below decks. None of the spit-and-polish of the "Olde Nyvy"! We kept the IRWIN cleaner than that when we were still dusting off kamikazes at Okinawa!

The LOCKWOOD (named for World War II Pacific Fleet Commander of Submarines Vice Admiral Charles A. Lockwood, Jr.) is one of the older frigates and will probably be decommissioned in the near future. Much of her gear is now obsolete compared to the new ships, but that's no excuse to let her look run down. The average civilian wouldn't notice these things. But shoot, the NORTH CAROLINA is in better shape, and she's over *fifty* years old!

I'm concerned about my Navy. With cut-backs coming, that will be even more severe if Clinton wins, it'll be a wonder if the Navy will be combat-ready. To me, all this is inviting another Pearl Harbor. The Chinese have nuclear weapons, are buying up a lot of the old Russian regime's weaponry, and with two billion people could take 250 million casualties (equal to the U.S. population) and never flinch.

We're going back aboard tomorrow afternoon. I'll write more then.

24 October, 1992
48th Anniversary of
the Sinking of the
PRINCETON (CVL-23)

I took Dixie and Don down to the LOCKWOOD, and we were given an hour tour of the ship. Since it was more extensive than the one I got yesterday, I had opportunity to observe the vessel more closely. She's in worse shape than I'd noticed yesterday. Her motor whaleboat in the davits was filthy, the gunwale stripping was damaged and showed evidence it had occurred some time ago, but no attempt had been made to repair it. There was a lot of rust showing here and there, etc.

Only a couple of the sailors who demonstrated her communications and abilities could properly explain the functions. One was a Quartermaster 3rd who not only really knew his job but showed that "extra" attitude that seems so lacking among today's enlisted men. After he explained all the modern navigational aids, including satellite positioning which will give the ship's location within a tolerance of nine meters, I asked him if he ever used a sextant. He said there was no need to do so, but he'd shoot the stars three or four times a week, just to keep his hand in and because he enjoyed doing it the "Old Navy" way. That's more like it! But I think he's a tiny minority.

Dixie and Don were ecstatic about visiting the ship and were most excited after taking the tour. I didn't mention any of the deficiencies to them, not wanting to dampen their enthusiasm. Apparently, the local citizenry was just as curious as were Dixie and Don. I was told there were 769 visitors who took the tour, and a larger number were expected Sunday.

25 October, 1992

I went back down to the LOCKWOOD this morning to see the Supply Officer. Some of the sailors wore baseball caps with their rating badges on them in addition to "U.S.S. LOCKWOOD FF-1064". I wanted to know the source of this headgear, since some of my IRWIN shipmates had also seen similar caps and wanted to know if we could get any.

While I was waiting for the Supply Officer on the Quarterdeck, the Captain came by, dressed in jogging shoes and shorts! He introduced himself, and we chatted for a few minutes. Afterward, an ensign came up and asked me about the IRWIN (I was wearing my IRWIN cap and jacket). He said his dad had served on the BUNKER HILL, and I mentioned we'd steamed with the carrier many times. He seemed genuinely interested in learning more about World War II, and I briefed him on some of my experiences. He was the only one, except some of the Chiefs, who asked me about the Second World War.

All of the officers and men were most cordial and answered my questions about the "New Navy". All in all, my visits with them were very pleasant; and it was somewhat like "old home week" to be back on a deck, again. My conclusions about readiness and the attitude of enlisted men, however, are unchanged.

Your brother,

Jack

P.S. The Captain told the local newspaper: "The sailors of the nineties are far and away the best in the last fifty years." *Ha!*

IV

THE BRASH AND SASSY GENERATION

Among my generation—the survivors of the Great Depression, the Second World War, and some seventy to eighty years on this planet—there is a consensus that the generations of Americans after us lost the ball somewhere along the way.

There is a constant barrage from scientists, researchers, doctors, and others—whom we all lump into about the same class as politicians, psychiatrists, used car salesmen, and other charlatans—whose primary mission seems to be to proclaim that everything good in life is bad for all the citizenry.

Here we are, the elders of the population, who grew up on a diet of meat, gravy, potatoes, real butter, everything fried in lard, and milk with two inches of cream at the top of the milk bottle—who smoked cigarettes, drank our whiskey with a flain, and enjoyed a barroom brawl with great gusto and without rancor. But the kids now tell us, we didn't know what was good for us.

Today the "experts" are saying that all these things are bad for us, that they will bring about all sorts of dire consequences. The steak we enjoy, the coffee, the tobacco, the ice cream, and the little nip at the end of the day, we are told, will send us to an early grave. Well, my generation is not buying it. We're not like today's timid, whining, fearful folks who eat tofu and bean sprouts and drink bottled water. We made it this far and intend to make it a lot farther. Hell, we just might outlive the current generation!

We are pictured as ancients sitting around in rocking chairs and nursing homes, sadly awaiting the arrival of the "Grim Reaper". If you think of us as doing nothing more strenuous than walking to the mail box to pick up our Social Security checks, think again. Until you've seen a bunch of septegenarians jitterbugging to Benny Goodman's "Jersey Bounce" with an élan, energy, and wild abandon that would make Michael Jackson look like a sloth, you just haven't tuned in the right channel!!

The present generation of Americans seems to live in fear of nearly everything. Just about any enjoyable activity or consumable product is hazardous to one's health. Holy Toledo! Even *milk* is bad for you. Another one of those know-it-all scientists concluded that if you followed today's recommended diet and exercised as much as the doctor prescribes, it would add to your lifespan a total of *forty-five days!* I'm gonna give up steak and chocolate ice cream for *that?* They'd be the lousiest forty-four days of my life.

You guys need a transfusion of vigor, confidence, sense of humor, and intestinal fortitude from your grandparents. Sure, none of us will get out of this world alive, but why be so damned miserable while we're here? So, young'uns, break out the Benny Goodman, Tommy Dorsey, Glenn Miller, and Count Basie records! Go out for a big roast beef dinner and eat it in the smoking section. Stop listening to the hysterical rantings of the doomsday prophets, and enjoy life!!

One of the Presidents we had in my lifetime said: *"The only thing we have* to fear is fear itself." We followed his advice to ignore that fear and we outfought and outproduced every other nation in the world. We left you a vibrant country that—filled with pride, patriotism, independence, and individual initiative—was the unchallenged leader on earth and envy of all the nations of the world.

You could do a lot worse than follow in our footsteps! Pick up the ball and run with it!!

ACKNOWLEDGMENTS

THANKING ALL THOSE WHO ASSISTED IN SOME WAY

I owe a considerable debt to the many who contributed so much in terms of documents, personal accounts, and other materials to this memoir. Since the gathering of data spanned nearly ten years, I may miss naming some who supplied pertinent information in my early research. To those, I profusely apologize. To *all* who aided me with their invaluable input, I offer my *sincere gratitude*.

U.S.S. NORTH CAROLINA Contributions:
   U.S.S. NORTH CAROLINA Battleship Commission, Wilmington, NC
   Leo Neumann, who provided data from the ship's War Diary, Deck Logs, and
       Action Reports
   Radio Gang buddies Alan J. Campbell, Albert L. Phillips, Lew Metz, Denzil
       Myers, Charles Paty, Mario Sivilli
   Charles A. "Chuck" Pavlich of the Marine Detachment
   Commander and Mrs. John "Jack" Schroeder, son-in-law and daughter of
       Admiral Oscar C. Badger
   U.S.S. NORTH CAROLINA Reunion Association

U.S.S. McCAWLEY/Guadalcanal and Rendova Contributions:
   Ted Blahnik, Guadalcanal Campaign Veterans *Echoes* Editor (HELENA)
   Bob Duey, 14th SeaBees (Guadalcanal)
   Charles Conter, Rear Gunner, VMSB 234 (Guadalcanal)
   Jim Germain "Frenchy" Maurais (McCAWLEY/JOHN PENN)
   Commander Leonard Kenny, USN (Ret), Navigator (McCAWLEY)
   Mike Gydos (McCAWLEY)
   Ray Adams (McCALLA)
   Rear Admiral Robert Mills, USN (Ret), (RALPH TALBOT)
   Jack Massey Green (FARENHOLT)
   U.S.S. McCAWLEY Reunion Association

U.S.S. IRWIN Contributions:
   Mrs. Dorothy Miller (deceased) widow of Rear Admiral Daniel B. Miller

Mrs. Danielle Miller Farias, daughter of Rear Admiral Miller
Commander J.D.P. Hodapp, Jr., USN (Ret)
Hays "Jumbo" Clark, Engineer Officer
Gene Stout, Torpedo Officer
F.X. "Frank" Cannaday, Assistant Engineering Officer
John "Boom Boom" Kopach, Chief Gunner's Mate, USN (deceased)
Shipmates Bill Needles, Bill Weideman, Jim Platt, Bill Degenhart, Ken
  Belknap, Ed Carroll, Bob Martin, Fred Stafford, Jack Bové, Abe
  Fernandes
Jack Smith, son of Bill "Smitty" Smith
All members of the IRWIN's Radio Gang, who are acknowledged in the text
U.S.S. IRWIN Reunion Association

U.S.S. PRINCETON Contributions:
Captain Vic Moiteret, USN (Ret)
Charles Donovan, Pete Callan, and others whose letters to the *Tiger Rag*
  contributed background material
Marsha L. Clark, co-author of *Carrier Down*
U.S.S. PRINCETON Reunion Association

OTHER CONTRIBUTIONS:
Ed Ward, Executive Secretary, Tin Can Sailors, Inc.
Tim Rizzuto, Curator, U.S.S. KIDD, Louisiana State War Memorial, Baton
  Rouge, LA
Dean C. Allard, B.F. Cavalcante and Staff, Naval Historical Center, Wash-
  ington, DC, who provided voluminous data and information
Staff of The National Archives, Washington, DC, which provided War Dia-
  ries, Action Reports, Deck Logs, Official U.S. Navy Photos and other data
Staff of The United States Naval Institute, Annapolis, MD, which provided
  photos, biographies, and other information
Rear Admiral William Thompson, USN (Ret), The United States Navy
  Memorial Foundation, Washington, DC
Captain Joseph Taussig, USN (Ret), Assistant Secretary of the Navy, The
  Pentagon, Washington, DC
Sergeant Major Lester "Bam" Bamford, USMC (Ret), who provided the
  Battle Charts of the Pacific Theater
Captain Cleo I. Erfe, Naval Attaché, Republic of the Philippines Embassy,
  Washington, DC, who provided medals and awards
Teh-Kang Lee, Services Coordination Division, Republic of China (Taiwan)
  Embassy, Washington, DC, who also provided medals and awards
Rear Admiral Roberto de Oliveira Coimbra, Brazilian Navy, Naval Attaché,
  Brazilian Embassy, Washington, DC, who provided information regarding
  B.N.S. SANTA CATARINA (D-32) née U.S.S. IRWIN
Captain K.L. de Assis, Ministerio da Marinha, Brasilia, Brazil, who also
  provided information regarding B.N.S. SANTA CATARINA

SPECIAL CONTRIBUTIONS:

Special gratitude is due the artists who contributed the outstanding marine paintings of the ships on which I served:

To Richard W. DeRosset for his superb renderings of the sinking of the McCAWLEY, the IRWIN alongside the PRINCETON, and the IRWIN under kamikaze attack at Okinawa—the latter two paintings done exclusively for this book. I can only marvel at his talent in bringing alive those incidents on canvas. His attention to detail and accuracy is phenomenal. He would call me several times while working on these canvases to double-check even the most minor point. Such dedication to detail is rare in this world today.

To William J. Reynolds, painter of the NORTH CAROLINA during the Battle of Eastern Solomons, for permission to reproduce his outstanding work in *BLUEJACKET*. I am the proud owner of one of the limited edition lithographs of this work entitled *Escort to Danger*. For one who has difficulty in drawing a straight line without a ruler, I am constantly amazed at those who can translate action to canvas.

To Carl G. Evers for his beautiful painting of the NORTH CAROLINA at sea, and to the U.S. Naval Institute for permission to use it in this book. The picture is a particular favorite of mine and of my shipmates who served on the "Showboat". A large reproduction of it also hangs on my wall.

To Bill Needles, the IRWIN's "artist-in-residence", whose painting of the rescue of a downed pilot also graces these pages, and whose painting of the "Boomerang Torpedo" insignia is the heart and soul of the IRWIN's crew. Bill did many drawings, often under difficult circumstances, while aboard the DD-794, and he took a scrawly freehand drawing of an idea of mine to produce the IRWIN's 50th Anniversary insignia. His shipmates are indeed proud he is among our number.

A very grateful salute is due all those who encouraged me to write *BLUE-JACKET*, whose moral support kept me at what turned out to be a long and tedious task, one filled with emotions that sometimes got in the way.

Ted Mason was the first to suggest I write for publication, and acted as a cheerleader along the way.

Old friends John and Dorothy Fuller gave tremendous moral support, reading bits and pieces and telling me to keep going.

Two employees of the U.S. Post Office in San Clemente, Rob O'Leary and Lynn Wallin, continued to show interest and encourage me during the time I was writing in California. Rob has even called me in Oregon to check on the book's progress.

Another long-time friend, Ginny Miller Wiprud, likewise was very supportive; as was Foreword author Mitch Paige, once he'd read my first draft.

I must pay tribute to the tolerance of my daughters Toni and Dixie, who put up with me during much of the most difficult part of the project. They were most patient with me, and never once did they complain.

My *extra special thanks and gratitude* go to my sister-in-law, Linda L.

Hutchinson, who spent long, tedious hours over many months entering into the computer all the many additions and corrections my brother and I supplied. It not only was a tiresome task, but required she exhibit the patience of Job. That she did so, is a tribute to her unbounded unselfishness.

If this book enjoys even a modicum of success, much of the credit must go to my brother, Dr. George P. Hutchinson. It was he who devoted many months to editing, proofreading, checking for accuracy, and suggesting changes and additions. His advice and assistance, counsel and encouragement, coupled with an objectivity I could not bring, have been of inestimable value.

As a Presbyterian minister, he doubtless felt somewhat out of place in the rough and profane world of seafaring men. Suffice it to say, he held up well under the ordeal, although somewhat less naive about the secular lives of sailors than when he started!

Words fail me at this point in an effort to express my whole-hearted gratitude for his exceptional dedication to get his older brother's story into print. Perhaps just a simple "Thanks, Brother" will convey my feelings.

BIBLIOGRAPHY

SOURCES AND PUBLICATIONS CONSULTED

In addition to the U.S. Navy Personnel and Medical Records of John A. Hutchinson (USN 243-86-51), the War Diaries, Action Reports, and Deck Logs of the following were consulted:

U.S.S. NORTH CAROLINA (BB-55) U.S.S. McCAWLEY (APA-4)
U.S.S. APc-38 U.S.S. APc-25
U.S.S. IRWIN (DD-794) U.S.S. PRINCETON (CVL-23)
U.S.S. TANG (SS-306) ComDesRon 55 (Okinawa Summary)

I have also used various U.S. Navy Statistical Reports. Unless otherwise indicated, all photos are "Official U.S. Navy" from the following sources: National Archives, Real War Photos, U.S. Naval Institute, U.S. Naval Historical Center. The following periodicals published by Veterans' Organizations and Reunion Associations were consulted:

Guadalcanal Echoes Ted Blahnik, Editor
The Tarheel (NORTH CAROLINA) Mario Sivilli, Editor
The Tiger Rag (PRINCETON) Vic Moiteret, Editor
The Kidd's Company (KIDD) Tim Rizzuto, Editor
The Tin Can Sailor (TCS Inc.) Ed Ward, Executive Secretary

Recommended as portraying some of the action and atmosphere in this memoir, are the following movies and videos:

VICTORY AT SEA *FLYING LEATHERNECKS*
TORA! TORA! TORA! *SANDS OF IWO JIMA*
THEY WERE EXPENDABLE *THE CAINE MUTINY*
MIDWAY *MISTER ROBERTS*
GUADALCANAL DIARY *WINDS OF WAR*
AWAY ALL BOATS! *WAR AND REMEMBRANCE*

The following books (the list is by no means exhaustive) were consulted to some extent in the preparation of this memoir:

Belote, J.H. & W.M., *Typhoon of Steel: The Battle for Okinawa* (1970).

Bennett, I.L. (ed.), *The Hymnal—Army and Navy (1942)*.

Bergamini, D., *Japan's Imperial Conspiracy* (1972).

Bradshaw, T.I. & Clark, M.L., *Carrier Down: The Sinking of the U.S.S. Princeton* (1990).

Breuer, Wm., *Devil Boats: The PT War Against Japan* (1987).

Buenzle, F.J., *Bluejacket* (1939, 1987 repr.).

Dyer, G.C., *The Amphibians Came to Conquer: The Story of Admiral Richmond Kelly Turner* (2 vols., 1969).

Fehrenbach, T.R., *FDR's Undeclared War 1939-1941* (1967).

Frank, R.B., *Guadalcanal* (1990).

Griffith, S.B. II, *The Battle for Guadalcanal* (1963).

Guadalcanal Campaign Veterans Association, *The Guadalcanal Legacy* (1987).

Hamilton, J., *War at Sea 1939-1945* (1986).

Hammell, E., *Guadalcanal: The Carrier Battles* (1987).

Harrod, F.S., *Manning the New Navy: The Development of the Modern Enlisted Force, 1899-1940* (1978).

Hoyt, E.P., *The Glory of the Solomons* (1983).

Ienaga, S., *The Pacific War, 1931-1945: A Critical Perspective on Japan's Role in World War II* (1978).

Inoguchi, R. & Nakajima, T., *The Divine Wind: Japan's Kamikaze Force in World War II* (1958).

Kolb, R., *FDR's Undeclared War in the North Atlantic* (nd).

Manchester, Wm., *Goodbye, Darkness: A Memoir of the Pacific War* (1980).

Mason, T.C., *Battleship Sailor* (1982).

Mason, T.C., *"We Will Stand By You": Serving in the Pawnee, 1942-1945* (1990).

Morison, S.E., *History of United States Naval Operations in World War II* (1947-1962):

        III. *The Rising Sun in the Pacific* (1948).

        IV. *Coral Sea, Midway and Submarine Operations* (1949).

        V. *The Struggle for Guadalcanal* (1948).

        VI. *Breaking the Bismarks Barrier* (1949).

        VII. *Aleutians, Gilberts and Marshalls* (1951).

        VIII. *New Guinea and the Marianas* (1953).

        XII. *Leyte* (1958).

        XIV. *Victory in the Pacific* (1960).

Morison, S.E., *The Two-Ocean War: A Short History of the United States Navy in the Second World War* (1963).

Polenberg, R.P., *War and Society: The United States, 1941-1945* (1972).

Potter, E.G., *Bull Halsey* (1985).

Prange, G.W. et al., *God's Samurai: Lead Pilot at Pearl Harbor* (1990).

Raven, A., *Fletcher-Class Destroyers* (1986).

Reilly, J.C., Jr., *United States Navy Destroyers of World War II* (1983).

Reynolds, C.G., *War in the Pacific* (1990).
Roscoe, T., *United States Destroyer Operations in World War II* (1953).
Spector, R.H., *Eagle Against the Sun: The American War with Japan* (1985).
Steinberg, R. et al., *Island Fighting* (1978).
Stephan, J.J., *Hawaii Under the Rising Sun* (1984).
Tregaskis, R., *Guadalcanal Diary* (1943, 1959).
U.S. Naval Institute, *The Bluejacket's Manual* (10th ed., 1940).
White, W.L., *They Were Expendable* (1942).
Whitley, M.J., *Destroyers of World War II* (1988).
Wilcox, R.K., *Japan's Secret War* (1985).

Note: With respect to quotations from the works of Samuel Eliot Morison mentioned above (in each case in the text Morison is acknowledged as the author) the author of *BLUEJACKET* is grateful for permission to quote this material from the publisher Little, Brown and Company.

INDEX

PEOPLE, PLACES, AND SHIPS

NOTE: The following index is *not* a comprehensive subject index; it is selective, concentrating on people, places, and ships. Nonetheless, the Index gives the prospective reader a fair idea of *BLUEJACKET*'s specific contents (it does not cover the general Table of Contents). The Index does *not* include all the people, places, and ships mentioned in the book; but rather those of particular interest to the story, the author, his editor, and the United States Navy. For example, Japanese and other foreign vessels are not included; nor are Japanese Admirals, except for those commanding the entire Imperial Japanese Navy (e.g. Yamamoto). Also, apart from ships, military units are not mentioned, except for the First Marine Division. Moreover, the Index does not cover the color photos, which are without page numbers. With respect to individuals, though nicknames are sometimes mentioned, no ranks or rates are given, since these were constantly changing. In general, well-known historical figures are included, as well as literary figures quoted in the text. With regard to U.S. Navy ships, hull numbers are given, and sometimes nicknames. It goes without saying, given human error, it is doubtful that every page number is accurate, or that the Index includes every page on which any given item is mentioned, either explicitly or implicitly.